LAW AND THE
INDO-CHINA WAR

LAW AND THE

INDO-CHINA WAR

BY JOHN NORTON MOORE

PRINCETON UNIVERSITY PRESS

PRINCETON, NEW JERSEY   1972

This book has been composed in Linotype Baskerville

Printed in the United States of America
by Princeton University Press
Princeton, New Jersey

TO MY WIFE
Patricia Morris Moore

The principles of the Charter are, by far, greater than the Organization in which they are embodied, and the aims which they are to safeguard are holier than the policies of any single nation or people.

Dag Hammarskjöld

Foreword

THE SECURING AND MAINTENANCE of minimum public order in the sense of the prevention and control of unauthorized violence and other coercion, long recognized as a problem of first priority in all of man's communities, is today commonly perceived as having acquired, because of our contemporary weapons of catastrophic destructiveness, a unique urgency in the larger global community. In this distinguished book Professor Moore brings high craftsmanship and creative imagination to bear upon exploring the potentialities of law in the management of this problem. The conviction that inspires the book is that, despite past failures and the gravity of the contemporary situation, our transnational processes of authoritative and controlling decision can be reconstructed and improved, for the better clarification and implementation of common interest, and hence for movement toward a preferred, more inclusive minimum public order; both the pessimism of the naked power proponents, who minimize the role that expectations about authority play, and can be made to play, in world processes of effective power, and the facile optimism of the utopians, who make a fetish of the potentialities of abstract rules and grand new institutional designs in disregard of the variables that in fact affect control, are rejected. For more relevant exploration of the potentialities in reconstruction and improvement of world constitutive processes of decision, Professor Moore suggests, develops, and applies in detail, largely with reference to the Indo-China War, a comprehensive and systematic, explicitly policy-oriented, framework of inquiry, making a number of distinctive emphases. The most important of these emphases are clarity about observational standpoint; the deliberate and explicit postulation of a comprehensive set of general community policies; both comprehensiveness and selectiveness in focus upon particular problems; and the systematic performance of several different, but interrelated, intellectual tasks, all indispensable both to effective inquiry and to rational decision.

The observational standpoint Professor Moore seeks is that of the scholar, or responsible citizen, who identifies with the whole community of mankind and is concerned with enlightenment about the conditions for clarifying and securing the common interests of all members of that community. The maintenance of this standpoint requires that the observer distinguish himself—insofar as the biases of culture, class, interest, and personality permit—both from the active participants in community process who make claims before processes of authoritative decision and from the decision-makers who respond to such claims. The perspectives and operations of the claimants and decision-makers are but data for the observer, and, if he is to contribute to enlightenment, he must make observations that are confirmable or disconfirmable by other observers similarly situated and motivated. A most important task for the scholarly observer may, further, be that of clarifying for the participants in community process common interests which they themselves have not perceived.

The basic general community policies commonly postulated, as in customary international law and the United Nations Charter, as constituting "minimum public order" Professor Moore recognizes to be complementary in character. The employment of violence and other intense coercion against the human person is fundamentally incompatible with human dignity and, hence, a general community, which aspires toward human dignity values, must seek to minimize the employment of such violence and coercion as instruments of major, and even minor, change in the shaping and sharing of values; arbitrary coercion is destructive of all human dignity values and at least a minimum protection against such coercion must be established if a community is to entertain any hope of an optimum shaping and sharing of values by persuasive processes. Yet in a world arena in which authoritative and effective power is still largely unorganized and decentralized, it cannot be expected that the various lesser communities of mankind can achieve even a minimum security, much less larger human rights, if they are denied appropriate measures in, and capabilities of, self-help. The authoritative prescriptions of customary international law and the United Nations Charter thus, quite rationally, distinguish between impermissible coercion ("acts of aggression," "threats to the peace," "breach of the peace," "intervention," and so on) and permissible coercion ("self-defense," "collective self-defense," "police action," "humanitarian intervention," "reprisals," and so on) and simultaneously demand, in further complementarity, the promotion of human rights, self-determination, and economic development.

For delimiting particular problems in inquiry about general community control of coercion, Professor Moore recommends, in lieu of such traditional categorizations as "aggression," "intervention," "civil war," "domestic jurisdiction," and so on, which make an intermingled and confused reference to both facts and legal consequences, a more comprehensive and selective focus upon facts which raise common policies and are affected by comparable conditioning factors. In pursuit of such a focus he suggests systematic and detailed description (1) of the different processes of coercion, of many varying degrees in intensity, in which the peoples of the world continuously engage each other; (2) of the particular types of claims to authoritative decision which arise from these processes of coercion; and (3) of the principal distinctive features of the world constitutive process of authoritative decision which affect the effectiveness and economy of responses to such claims. Illustrative of the detail with which he works in these descriptions is his six-fold breakdown, with many sub-categorizations of situations in which claims are made about interference in "internal conflict": "non-authority-oriented intervention," "anti-colonial wars," "wars of secession," "indigenous conflict for control of internal authority structures," "external imposition of authority structures," and "cold-war divided nation conflicts."

For the detailed clarification and application in particular instances of alleged coercion of the inescapably complementary general community policies, Professor Moore recommends an objective, systematic, configurative examination of all the potentially significant features of the challenged acts or events in their larger context. Established decision-makers and others, who are asked to evaluate particular instances of alleged coercion, are confronted in the beginning with the manifest, articulated, competing claims of the contending participants about the operative facts (value processes affected and sought to be protected), about the relevant general community prescriptions, and about appropriate decisions and measures in redress of public order. The first task of the decision-maker, as of the scholarly observer, is to cut through these exclusive, competing claims of the participants for ascertaining what is genuinely at stake from larger community perspectives: What are the appropriate evaluations and characterizations of the potential facts, from the standpoint of a disinterested or community observer, and what is the whole range of potentially relevant prescriptions and choices in application?

The features of potential significance to general community policy in challenged acts of coercion and their context are of course in most instances many and complex. Even the most modest suggestion must include the varying characteristics of the participants, and of their allies and affiliates; the distribution of perspectives of attack and defense, expansion and conservation, deliberateness and coincidence, inclusivity and exclusivity, consequentiality and inconsequentiality; the *locus* of events, as within a single community or transcending different communities, and the geographic range of the impacts of events; the timing of events, and their continuity or discontinuity; the differential distribution of the bases of effective power; the variety and characteristics of the different strategies—diplomatic, ideological, economic, and military—employed; and the various outcomes in intensity and magnitude achieved, of the fact, and expectation, of coercion and destruction of values.

When decision-makers and observers are appropriately informed of potential facts and potential policies, other tasks in clarification include observing the successes and failures that have been achieved in the past on comparable problems by invocation and application of varying alternatives in prescriptions and options in decision, estimating the factors that will probably affect the success or failure of possible future decisions, and calculating the relative costs and benefits, in terms of *all* relevant community policies, of the various alternatives in decision. The final task of the decision-maker, in the performance of which no single black letter rule (or other proposed automation) can afford him succor, is that of choosing the alternative that will promote through time the largest net aggregate of common interest.

Insofar as the traditional rules of international law, whether derived from customary behavior or the United Nations Charter, have any utility, it is in aid of decision-makers and others in the performance of these different tasks in clarification and application. It is obvious, as Professor Moore amply demonstrates, that much improved principles of both content and procedure could be devised. Certainly, however, even with present formulations, the systematic, disciplined, contextual examination he recommends is not an expression of arbitrariness; indeed, what he recommends stands at the opposite extreme from all single-factor emphases, all "definitional" exercises, and other fragmented approaches which fix with an illusory rigidity upon a few features of the context.

The past decisions Professor Moore evaluates in his more detailed clarification of general community policies are those proffered by the Indo-China War. Some observers may disagree with his characterizations of the events in this war to which the decisions were response; others may question his choices among the relevant complementary general community prescriptions; and still others, some perhaps for reasons of special interest, may reject his conclusions about the lawfulness or unlawfulness of particular decisions. Systematic, contextual analyses cannot, any more than black letter definitions and rules, eliminate personal responsibility for choice among competing potential facts and policies. Yet it is only by such analyses, with their comprehensive and disciplined evaluations of all the potentially significant features of a decision and its context, that either decision-makers or observers can be assured that particular necessary choices bear any relation to a genuine clarification of common interests in terms of all relevant general community policies. Hence, whatever the ultimate verdict of disinterested consensus about the substantive merits of different appraisals of the Indo-China decisions, Professor Moore's careful documentations and evaluations would appear to establish at least a modest presumption in their favor. Critics of his appraisals who would be persuasive must be equally candid about all the general community policies they serve and bear the burden of the same or equivalent procedures of inquiry.

The quality of the general community's minimum public order decisions Professor Moore finds to be affected by many variables, both predispositional and environmental. One factor of great importance is that of the capabilities of authoritative and controlling decision-makers to achieve identifications with the whole community of mankind and to perceive and clarify the common interests of the members of that community. From the standpoint of a community-wide observer the facts of interdependence, which establish common interests, are expressed in every feature of global interaction:

> the accelerating rate of population growth, along with the pluralization of both functional and territorial groups;
> growing common demands for the greater production and wider sharing of competitive values, both expanding and contracting identifications with territorial and functional groups, and expectations of many varying degrees of realism about the conditions under which values can be secured;
> a tremendous increase in the range and intensities of interaction on a global scale, the relative disappearance of distance, the compression of time, and permanence in the crises of nuclear and other confrontations;
> the depletion and spoilation of resources on a global scale, the universalization of a science-based technology, and the rapid democratization of enlightenment, skill, health, and other values;
> fantastic improvement in the strategies of communication and cooperation, as well as of destruction;
> a tremendous increase, and potentialities for still greater future increase, in the production and distribution of values, as well as for the destruction of values;
> interdependences between the different value processes in the shaping and sharing of all values;
> growing disparities between the rich and the poor in the shaping and sharing of all values; and so on.

The critical question is whether the authoritative and effective decision-makers dispersed about the globe can overcome their parochial identifications, with provincial allegiances to contending ideologies, and achieve a realistic understanding of the conditions which bind them to a common fate for both minimum and optimum order.

The probable future Professor Moore foresees includes both an acceleration in interdependence and new breakthroughs in weapons technology, enhancing the potentialities of both comprehensiveness and intensity in destruction. In such a world the traditional distinction between violence and coercion internal to a particular community and that which transcends it will become even more diaphanous, and the similar distinction between major and minor coercions will, because of the omnipresent threat of escalation and cumulative destruction, be increasingly irrelevant.

The alternatives Professor Moore recommends for the better maintenance of minimum world public order extend, beyond improved principles of content and procedure for the making of judgments about lawfulness or unlawfulness, to a wide range of new institutional structures and procedures. He recognizes that the overriding goal of *minimizing* violence and other coercion, includes, when given detailed empirical reference, various subgoals such as long-term prevention, short-term deterrence, the restoration of order after its breach, the short-term rehabilitation of victims, and long-term reconstruction of communities and individuals. Among the many, diverse recommendations he makes for the better securing of these different sub-goals are strengthened "collective community decision processes for authorizing needed change," the development by the general community of more reliable observation and disclosure capabilities, international reporting of military assistance, an increased role for the General Assembly in making recommendations, strengthened collective procedures for responding to claims of unauthorized coercion, mechanisms for the settlement of "internal conflicts" in earlier stages, techniques for collective recognition, a permanent United Nations emergency relief force, an enhanced role for regional organizations and a clearer specification of the relative responsibilities and competences of such organizations and the United Nations, a thorough revision of the laws of war, and a reconstruction of national constitutive processes for more effective participation in minimum public order decisions. The most difficult, yet inescapable, task is, Professor Moore emphasizes, that of creating in all effective decision-makers the perspectives appropriate to putting these or equivalent measures into controlling practice and, thus, of reducing the reasons why individuals and communities take to violence.

We are all in debt to Professor Moore for a wise, balanced, and mature contribution to enlightenment, documented by reference to some of the most controversial issues of our time, about the conditions of minimum public order in the world of tomorrow.

Myres S. McDougal

LAW AND THE
INDO-CHINA WAR

Introduction

DEVELOPMENT of the law, as well as other areas of human endeavor, seems frequently to result from cataclysmic events. The Great Depression was a significant contributing factor to the legal realist movement which revolutionized the way lawyers think and which transformed law from a brooding omnipresence in the sky to a tool for social engineering grasped firmly by the hand of man. In international law, the tragedy of war has frequently served as such an event. World War I gave impetus to the League of Nations with its procedural checks on resort to war and the Kellogg-Briand Pact with its idealistic renunciation of war as an instrument of national policy. The Spanish Civil War reawakened interest in the control of foreign intervention and the implementation of neutrality. World War II gave rise to the United Nations with its improved system of collective security and its prohibition of force as a modality of major change in international relations. The Indo-China War, which has now lasted longer than any of these wars, has had a similar triggering effect on the development of both international and constitutional law. For all its tragedy, it has served as a catalyst for rapid development in the international law of non-intervention, and in the internal constitutional law concerning the relative power of Congress and the President to commit the nation to war. And in other areas of the law, such as reform of the laws of war and restructuring of the national security process to more systematically take international law into account, it has had a tentative impact likely to accelerate with time. The chapters in this volume were written over the last four years during the course of the Indo-China War and deal with both the specific legal issues presented by the War and the future development of international and constitutional law to take account of the lessons learned from the War. Though legal debate on the Indo-China War has been important in its own right, it is more important that international and constitutional lawyers vigorously follow through after the War to assimilate the lessons learned and to improve the international and domestic legal systems where improvement is needed.

A central point of the worldview forming the intellectual basis for this volume is that the fundamental Charter principle which proscribes unilateral force as a modality of major change in international affairs is a critically important fundament for the assessment of state conduct in the present international system. This principle, embodied in Article 2(4) of the United Nations Charter, is the evolutionary product of four hundred years of international legal development from the "just war" notions of Hugo Grotius and St. Thomas Aquinas, through the nineteenth-century preoccupation with the amelioration of on-going war, to the Kellogg-Briand Pact prohibition of war as an instrument of national policy.

It is frequently tempting to attempt a personal assessment of the justice of the cause of contending belligerents and to assess responsibility accordingly. Such an assessment is particularly tempting in a world beset by contending ideologies and in an intellectual climate, both international and domestic, which increasingly flirts with the use of force to remedy the social and political injustices with which the world abounds. But in addition to the formidable moral and practical difficulties of assessing where "justice" lies (in most complex public order disputes it usually lies partially in each camp), or whether the end justifies the means, a formula which rationalizes the initiation of coercion in the service of a particular ideological vision is a prescription for disaster. Professor Stanley Hoffmann describes the present international system as a revolutionary system tempered principally by the potential for mutual nuclear annihilation.[1] In such a system, the dangers of confrontation, miscalculation, and escalation resulting from aggressive expansion of contending world order systems pose a threat to the very future of man. In a recent reiteration of a statement which is as timely today as when originally made in 1957, Eugene Rabinowitch wrote in the September, 1967, *Bulletin of the Atomic Scientists*:

> The danger of nuclear war makes all revisionism (even if it can be justified by strong historical or ethnic reasons) too

---

1. See Hoffmann, *International Systems and International Law*, in S. HOFFMANN, THE STATE OF WAR, 88 (1965).

dangerous for it to be used as a power-political tool. . . . There is only one firm basis for East-West accommodation. This is the . . . abandonment [by both sides] of all attempts to change . . . [the World] by force, whatever the merits of various revisionist causes may be.[2]

This is emphatically not identical with a guarantee of military support of all existing regimes against all their internal enemies.[3]

It should also be added that this is emphatically not an argument for maintenance of the status quo. There is a critical need for change in the world to improve social and political justice and to maximize human dignity as measured by a range of meaningful economic, political, educational, and health indicators. Needed change must be pursued by cooperative and non-coercive strategies, however, and not through the arrogance of unilateral power. Unilateral resort to force for the purpose of extending national values, whether by the United States in Cuba, North Korea in South Korea, the Soviet Union in Hungary and Czechoslovakia, the Palestinian Liberation Organization in Israel, or North Vietnam in South Vietnam, Laos, and Cambodia, is much too destructive and dangerous in the present revolutionary international system. Moreover, it seems particularly in the interest of the United States, which is the principal non-revolutionary power (and as it becomes less revolutionary increasingly in the interest of the Soviet Union as well), to emphasize long-run interests in world order and the stability of the international milieu rather than yield to pressures to compete with revolutionary powers in kind. Accordingly, adherence to a consistent vision of world order which condemns the unilateral resort to force for extension of national values, but permits the use of force necessary and proportional to the conservation of major national values subjected to armed attack, may well be the best strategy for the United States in the present revolutionary system. Such a strategy should also rely more substantially on those institutions such as the United Nations which are capable of making and implementing

2. Rabinowitch, *What Is Sauce for the Goose Is Sauce for the Gander*, 23 BULLETIN OF THE ATOMIC SCIENTISTS 41, 42, 43 (September, 1967).
3. *Id.* at 42.

collective decisions for change. It is not necessary for the United States either to become the policeman for the world or to neglect vigorous pursuit of social justice throughout the world in order to maintain a clear focus on the importance of a consistent and coherent world order. Such a focus should be a matter of national priority.

One of the difficulties in maintaining a clear focus on a consistent vision of world order is that it is not always obvious what the requirements of world order are in situations of competitive intervention in internal conflict. The diversity of the contexts in which intervention takes place and the enormous difficulty of normative regulation have left national decison-makers with only marginal guidance. Moreover, the generalities of Articles 2(4) and 51 of the United Nations Charter have proved of only limited relevance to the problem of control of intervention. The United Nations Charter, like the League Covenant before it, was in large measure a response to the world order problems which brought it about. As a result, the Charter was aimed principally at controlling World War II style open aggression across international boundaries. Since then, however, the nuclear conditon, among others, has radically altered the international system and substituted limited war, particularly competitive intervention, as the major world order threat. Though the basic Charter principle of non-use of unilateral force for the extension of values is still highly relevant, it needs special adaptation to the major internal conflict problem of the present international system. A major portion of this volume is devoted to this issue of transcendent importance for international law. The way in which this issue is resolved will go far toward determining the future of law as a tool for the management of international conflict.

The constitutional issues presented by the Indo-China conflict are also of enormous significance. The national debate about the powers of Congress and the President, and the role of the Supreme Court in passing on those powers, is likely to shape the constitutional outlines of the national security process for the foreseeable future. It is imperative that the issues in the debate should receive full consideration and that the balance which emerges should be one which has prospective rather than exclusively Indo-China relevance. Past excesses of one branch should not be remedied by future excesses of another. If these caveats are observed, it is likely that the basic good sense and restraint of all three branches, sensitized by the Indo-China debate, will result in a materially strengthened national security process.

John Norton Moore
Charlottesville, Virginia
June 12, 1971

A Postscript on "The Pentagon Papers"

THE chapters in Part III dealing with the specifics of the Indo-China conflict were completed prior to the publication by the *New York Times* of a summary of the classified Pentagon study on American participation in the Vietnam War.[1] The published record of these "Pentagon Papers," however, strikingly confirms the major factual assumptions made relevant to the legal aspects of the conflict. In fact, the degree of congruence suggests that the public record of United States involvement is so nearly complete that further disclosures which will alter the major topography of the record are unlikely. The record of North Vietnamese involvement, on the other hand, is considerably more sketchy and one can only regret lack of access to a comparable North Vietnamese study.

From an international-legal perspective four points seem particularly important in evaluating the significance of the Pentagon papers.

First, the study is not an international-legal analysis but rather is largely an analysis of working papers, policy memoranda, and contingency plans available in Pentagon files relating to the stra-

---

1. A summary of the Pentagon study was published in the *New York Times* beginning on June 13, 1971, interrupted on June 16 pending court action on a temporary restraining order and resumed on July 1 after a favorable Supreme Court ruling. Subsequently, the complete *Times* series was published in a *New York Times* paperback book entitled THE PENTAGON PAPERS (1971). The *Times* series is a condensed summary of the full 47 volume study which is said to comprise approximately 3,000 pages of analysis and 4,000 pages of supporting documents and which at least in part remains classified. The classified study was initiated by Secretary of Defense Robert McNamara and was prepared in the Department of Defense by a team of 36 anonymous researchers. The study is somewhat marred by the limited access of the researchers to sources of information other than Pentagon files.

   The most complete version of the Pentagon study published to date is "The Senator Gravel Edition" published in four volumes by the Beacon Press. According to the Preface it reprints "about 2900 pages of narrative, 1000 pages of appended documents, and a 200-page collection of public statements by government officials . . ." I THE PENTAGON PAPERS: THE DEFENSE DEPARTMENT HISTORY OF UNITED STATES DECISIONMAKING ON VIETNAM xiii (1971).

tegic options pursued by the United States during the course of the War. As such the study is principally useful to the legal scholar as a source of additional factual information about the War and for insight into the role of law in the functioning of the national security process. Unfortunately, the evident lack of sophistication of the authors with respect to the international-legal issues substantially lessens the value of the study. An example is the failure of the authors to systematically relate the levels of United States involvement in the South and North with the levels of North Vietnamese involvement in support of the insurgency in South Vietnam. Similarly, the authors sometimes fail to relate alleged United States breach of the Geneva Accords with prior North Vietnamese assistance to the insurgencies in Laos or South Vietnam in disregard of the Accords.[2] Resulting judgments seem to bypass both the United Nations Charter and the legal effects of forceful North Vietnamese breach of the Accords. Apparently also there was little consideration given to the important history of efforts and lack of efforts to ensure compliance with the laws of war during the conduct of hostilities.[3]

Second, the Pentagon papers confirm that the principal United States objective in the Indo-China War was to assist Vietnam and Laos (and subsequently Cambodia) to defend themselves against North Vietnamese military intervention. It was not to expand United States or South Vietnamese hegemony in Southeast Asia. A cablegram from the United States Mission in Saigon to the Department of State on August 18, 1964, is illustrative:

> Finally we should reach some fundamental understandings with Khanh and his government concerning war aims. We must make clear that we will engage in actions against North Viet Nam only for the purpose of assuring the security and independence of South Viet Nam within the territory assigned by the 1954 agreements; that we will not (rpt not) join in a crusade to unify the north and south; that we will not (rpt not) even seek to overthrow the Hanoi regime provided the latter will cease its efforts to take over the south by subversive warfare. . . .[4]

2. N.Y. TIMES, THE PENTAGON PAPERS 79-83 (1971).
3. *Id.* at XXIV. 4. *Id.* at 349, 350.

And in a "Draft Position Paper on Southeast Asia" of November 29, 1964, circulated to principal top-level officials it was said that

> U.S. objectives in South Vietnam (SVN) are unchanged. They are to:
>
> 1. Get Hanoi and North Vietnam (DRV) support and direction removed from South Vietnam, and, to the extent possible, obtain DRV cooperation in ending Viet Cong (VC) operations in SVN.
>
> 2. Re-establish an independent and secure South Vietnam with appropriate international safeguards, including the freedom to accept U.S. and other external assistance as required.
>
> 3. Maintain the security of other non-Communist nations in Southeast Asia including specifically the maintenance and observance of Geneva Accords of 1962 in Laos. . . .[5]

And in a draft memorandum from Secretary of Defense Robert McNamara to President Johnson on October 14, 1966, McNamara wrote:

> . . .[W]e should seek ways—through words and deeds—to make believable our intention to withdraw our forces once the North Vietnamese aggression against the South stops. In particular, we should avoid any implication that we will stay in South Vietnam with bases or to guarantee any particular outcome to a solely South Vietnamese struggle. . . .[6]

As top secret memoranda these documents provide some of the best possible evidence of United States war aims and cannot be dismissed as propaganda. The objectives which they evidence are a paradigm of lawful collective defense under Article 51 of the United Nations Charter.[7]

5. *Id.* at 373, 374.   6. *Id.* at 542, 549.

7. The Pentagon papers suggest that national decision-makers did not view public statements of "aggression from the North" as mere rhetoric for public consumption. Thus, Secretary of Defense Robert McNamara wrote to President Johnson in a memorandum of October 14, 1966: "The intelligence estimate is that evidence is overwhelming that the North Vietnamese dominate and control the National Front and the Viet Cong. . . ." *Id.* at 542, 549.

Third, the Pentagon papers provide additional evidence of North Vietnamese involvement with the insurgency in South Vietnam supporting the conclusion that United States assistance was lawful counter-intervention to offset prior North Vietnamese intervention in both Laos and South Vietnam. According to the *Times* summary of the study the insurgency in South Vietnam probably began in earnest sometime during 1956-57 at the initiative of Communist cadres left behind at the time of regroupment in 1954. Subsequently, according to the *Times* summary,

> North Vietnam's leaders formally decided in May, 1959, at the 15th meeting of the Lao Dong (Communist) party's Central Committee, to take control of the growing insurgency. Captured Vietcong personnel and documents report that as a result of the decision the Ho Chi Minh Trail of supply lines was prepared, southern cadre members who had been taken North were infiltrated back to the South and the tempo of the war suddenly speeded up.[8]

The insurgency grew upon local discontent with the Diem regime and in its early years drew heavily on sources of supply and manpower within the South. Nevertheless, the Pentagon papers suggest that beginning in 1959 the insurgency was taken in hand and rapidly intensified by Hanoi.[9] The *Times* account also indicates:

> Infiltration from North Vietnam had actually begun as early as 1955, United States intelligence reports show, but only in 1959, did the C.I.A. pick up evidence of large-scale infiltration.
>
> To operate the infiltration trails, a group of montagnard tribesmen from Quangtri and Thuathien Provinces were given special training in North Vietnam in 1958 and 1959.
>
> Early in 1959 also, the C.I.A. reported, Hanoi formed "special border crossing teams" composed of southerners who went to the North in 1954. Their mission was to carry food, drugs and other supplies down the trail network.
>
> And in April, 1959, the C.I.A. learned, the 559th Transportation Group was established directly under the party's

8. *Id.* at 69. 9. *Id.* at 67-78.

Central Committee as a headquarters in charge of infiltration.

Large training centers for infiltrators were reportedly established early in 1960 at Xuanmai and Sontay, near Hanoi. During 1959 and 1960, United States intelligence officials estimated, 26 groups of infiltrators, totaling 4,500 people, made the trip south.[10]

In comparison with this North Vietnamese intervention during 1959 and 1960, the study indicates that the first increase in United States forces in South Vietnam over the 685-man limit purportedly set by the Geneva Accords followed from a decision by President Kennedy on May 11, 1961, to send 400 Special Forces troops and 100 other American military advisers to South Vietnam. On the same day President Kennedy is also said to have ordered the start of a low level campaign of clandestine intelligence gathering activities and light harassment against North Vietnam and against Vietnamese bases and supply lines within Laos.[11] Such actions would seem a proportional response to the escalating North Vietnamese interventions within Laos and South Vietnam which had been underway for well over a year at the time of President Kennedy's response.

The Pentagon papers also indicate that the United States initiated a program of covert military activities against North Vietnam and Vietnamese forces in Laos beginning on February 1, 1964, and designated by the code name Operation Plan 34A.[12] These activities included U-2 overflights of North Vietnam, small-scale commando raids directed against bridges and coastal installations, intelligence-gathering missions, psychological warfare, and air operations over Laos. As with earlier United States "escalations" of the War, the Pentagon papers indicate that these activities were directed against ongoing North Vietnamese intervention in both Laos and South Vietnam. Thus, at the time the 34A operations were initiated, North Vietnamese forces were conducting military operations in Laos in flagrant disregard of the recently signed 1962 Laotian Accords. Similarly, at the time 34A

10. *Id.* at 76-77.
11. *Id.* at 82-83, 119, 123-24, 126, 127.
12. *Id.* at 234-40.

operations were begun in North Vietnam, North Vietnam had been directing the insurgency in South Vietnam and providing assistance to it in men and material for over four years. A comparison of the levels of North Vietnamese and United States actions through time suggest that the 34A operations were a proportional response to what amounted to a continuing armed attack directed against South Vietnam.

Fourth, although the Pentagon papers support the lawfulness of the basic outline of the United States role in the Indo-China War, the papers also provide dramatic evidence that the national security process is poorly structured to take international-legal considerations into account and that the failure to systematically take such perspectives into account has had an adverse impact on American foreign policy. The predominant tone of the papers is one of *Realpolitik* planning heavily influenced by contemporary decision theory. In contrast with this pragmatic sophistication the papers evidence little awareness of the international-legal issues and how they might affect the shaping of goals and the implementation of policy. One of the principal examples of this failure to take an international-legal perspective into account is the designation of the initiation of sustained bombing of North Vietnam as a "sustained reprisal," apparently without consideration of the lawfulness of reprisals under the United Nations Charter or the advisability of instead forthrightly designating the bombing as a defensive response to a continuing North Vietnamese armed attack. The papers also evidence inadequate concern with the possibility of United Nations or International Control Commission initiatives, general unfamiliarity with intervention theory as an aid to clarifying and articulating United States goals in the conflict, and for the most part little normative thinking about permissible and impermissible state conduct. At times, as in the McNaughton memorandum of March 24, 1965,[13] this preoccupation with the national interest approaches a flirtation with callousness.

13. Memorandum from John T. McNaughton, Assistant Secretary of Defense for International Security Affairs, to Secretary of Defense Robert S. McNamara on March 24, 1965, setting out what are termed "U.S. aims" which heavily weight maintenance of the United States reputation as a guarantor and only lightly weight "a better, freer way of life" for the people of South Vietnam, *id.* at 432.

Notably missing from the papers is any discussion such as whether a campaign in the United Nations during 1961 or even 1964 to demonstrate North Vietnamese involvement in South Vietnam and Laos and perhaps a public call for free elections supervised by the United Nations would have reduced North Vietnamese involvement or at least have strengthened the United States position prior to its counter-interventionary response. There is also little discussion of the importance of the laws of war and measures necessary to ensure effective compliance except with respect to an evident concern to minimize civilian casualties in the bombing of the North.[14] It is probable that many of these issues were considered at lower levels within the Pentagon, the State Department, and the National Security Council, or even discussed at top levels and not reported in the study. But it seems evident from the published papers that such perspectives were not adequately taken into account in top level planning. The United States is a nation with a proud tradition of concern for international law. If that concern is to be effectively implemented the international-legal tradition must be more systematically represented in the national security process.

John Norton Moore
Charlottesville, Virginia
December 22, 1971

14. The Joint Chiefs' order to begin bombing of Hanoi's oil facilities on June 22, 1966, indicates the seriousness with which efforts to avoid civilian casualties were pursued in the bombing of the North. The cable from the Joint Chiefs to Admiral Grant Sharp, the Commander in Chief of Pacific Forces, included the following paragraph: "Decision made after SecDef [the Secretary of Defense] and CJCS [the Chairman of the Joint Chiefs of Staff] were assured every feasible step would be taken to minimize civilian casualties would be small [sic]. If you do not believe you can accomplish objective while destroying targets and protecting crews, do not initiate program. Take the following measures; maximum use of most experienced ROLLING THUNDER personnel, detailed briefing of pilots stressing need to avoid civilians, execute only when weather permits visual identification of targets and improved strike accuracy, select best axis of attack to avoid populated areas, maximum use of ECM [electronic counter measures] to hamper SAM and AAA fire control, in order to limit pilot distraction and improve accuracy, maximum use of weapons of high precision delivery consistent with mission objectives, and limit SAM and AAA suppression to sites located outside populated areas." *Id.* at 499, 500.

Acknowledgments

For the most part, progress in the development of international and constitutional law tends to be incremental. As such, it would be impossible to adequately acknowledge the intellectual debts incurred in analysis of a major world order issue. One debt stands out, however, and that is my indebtedness to Myres S. McDougal and Harold D. Lasswell, whose friendship and enormous jurisprudential achievements have fired my enthusiasm for international law and informed my approach to law. I am also indebted to the American Society of International Law, whose commitment to the free exchange of ideas has provided invaluable opportunities for testing, refining, and reinforcing the ideas in this volume. Participation in the work of the ASIL Panel on the Role of International Law in Civil Wars under the chairmanship of Richard A. Falk and Wolfgang Friedmann has been particularly rewarding in my effort to develop a comprehensive theory of the control of foreign intervention in internal conflict. The University of Virginia School of Law has also provided support in a number of meaningful ways: the friendship and encouragement of former Dean Hardy C. Dillard, now a Judge of the International Court of Justice, the opportunity to test new ideas in discussion with colleagues and students, and the financial support of the Law School Foundation during the summers of 1967, 1968, and 1970. I would also like to thank Mr. Stephen Dichter, who assisted with the compilation of the documentary appendices and the bibliography on Indo-China and the legal order, my wife Pat, who assisted with the task of footnote revision, Miss Elizabeth G. Jolley, who prepared the index, and Mr. George Robinson of Princeton University Press, whose editorial assistance was invaluable.

Chapters which appeared earlier have been reprinted with the kind permission of the AMERICAN JOURNAL OF INTERNATIONAL LAW, THE NAVAL WAR COLLEGE REVIEW, THE UNIVERSITY OF VIRGINIA LAW REVIEW, THE VIRGINIA JOURNAL OF INTERNATIONAL LAW, THE YALE LAW JOURNAL Company, Fred B. Rothman & Company, and Princeton University Press. Chapter II, "Prolegomenon to the Jurisprudence of Myres McDougal and Harold Lasswell," was first published in 54 VIRGINIA LAW REVIEW 662 (1968); Chapter III, "Intervention: A Monochromatic Term for a Polychromatic Reality," was first delivered at the Princeton Conference on Intervention and the Developing Countries, November 10-11, 1967, and was published in II FALK (ED.), THE VIETNAM WAR AND INTERNATIONAL LAW 1061 (1970); Chapter IV, "The Control of Foreign Intervention in Internal Conflict," was reprinted from 9 VIRGINIA JOURNAL OF INTERNATIONAL LAW 205 (1969); Chapter V, "The Elephant Misperceived: Intervention and American Foreign Policy," was published in 56 VIRGINIA LAW REVIEW 364 (1970), as a review of Richard Barnet's influential book INTERVENTION AND REVOLUTION: THE UNITED STATES IN THE THIRD WORLD (1968); Chapter VI, "The Role of Regional Arrangements in the Maintenance of World Order," was written for III C. BLACK & R. FALK (EDS.), THE FUTURE OF THE INTERNATIONAL LEGAL ORDER: CONFLICT MANAGEMENT 122 (1971); Chapter VII, "The Lawfulness of Military Assistance to the Republic of Vietnam," was reprinted from 61 AMERICAN JOURNAL OF INTERNATIONAL LAW 1 (1967); Chapter VIII, "International Law and the United States Role in the Vietnam War: A Reply to Professor Falk," was reprinted by permission of the YALE LAW JOURNAL Company and Fred B. Rothman & Company, from 76 YALE LAW JOURNAL 1051-94 (1967); Chapter IX, "Law and Politics in the Vietnamese War: A Response to Professor Friedmann," was reprinted from 61 AMERICAN JOURNAL OF INTERNATIONAL LAW 1039 (1967). Chapter X, "Legal Dimensions of the Decision to Intercede in Cambodia," was reprinted from 65 AMERICAN JOURNAL OF INTERNATIONAL LAW 38 (1971); an earlier version delivered at the American Society of International Law forum on the Cambodian Incursion and International Law: International and Domestic Issues, Washington, D.C., June 16, 1970, was reprinted in a compilation prepared for the Senate Foreign Relations Committee *Documents Relating to the War Power of Congress, The President's Authority as Commander-in-Chief and the War in Indochina, Senate Committee on Foreign Relations,* 91ST CONG., 2D SESS. at 120 (Comm. Print 1970). Chapter XI, "The National Executive and the Use of the Armed Forces Abroad," was delivered as a lecture at the Naval War College on October 11, 1968, and reprinted in 21 NAVAL WAR COLLEGE REVIEW

ACKNOWLEDGMENTS

28 (1969); Chapter XII, "Congress and the Use of the Armed Forces Abroad," was delivered as testimony before the House Subcommittee on National Security Policy and Scientific Developments on June 25, 1970, and published by the House Foreign Affairs Committee in a Committee Print of the Hearings *Congress, The President, and the War Powers, Hearings before the Subcommittee on National Security Policy and Scientific Developments of the Committee on Foreign Affairs of the House of Representatives*, 91st CONG., 2D SESS. at 124 (1970); Chapter XIII, "The Justiciability of Challenges to the Use of Military Forces Abroad," was delivered at a regional meeting of the American Society of International Law on the Constitution and the Use of Military Force Abroad, Charlottesville, Virginia, February 28-March 1, 1969, and was reprinted in 10 VIRGINIA JOURNAL OF INTERNATIONAL LAW 85 (1969). A number of chapters have also been reprinted in Volumes I-III of the American Society of International Law reader on THE VIETNAM WAR AND INTERNATIONAL LAW edited by Richard A. Falk.

Contents

CONTENTS

PART ONE
OBSERVATIONAL STANDPOINT

Introduction

THERE is continuing confusion about the role of law in major world order disputes such as the Indo-China conflict. Popular opinion is skeptical that law is relevant to such issues, and in the last several decades George Kennan, Hans Morgenthau and other highly regarded internationalists have even warned that the legal tradition may be dangerous for objective assessment of the national interest.[1] Chapter I, "The Role of Law in the Management of International Conflict," attempts to demonstrate why this anti-legalist tradition, though expressing some valid insights, is dangerously simplistic.

It would be naive to believe that, in the present revolutionary international system, international law is going to bring world peace. It is equally naive, though not as obvious, to fail to realize that the neglect of international law will adversely affect the shape and stability of the international system. Of the disciplines concerned with international affairs, international law provides the principal focus on long-run world order considerations and the common interest of states in a reciprocally tolerant international milieu. As such it serves both as an important component of the national interest and as an independent normative basis for the appraisal of state conduct. In addition, it may usefully inform policy-makers of a range of options and strategies for the management of international conflict, as well as serving other conflict-management roles.

The outcome of the debate between the legalists and the anti-legalists is of more than merely academic interest. A principal point of the first chapter, which is developed in Chapter IV with reference to the problem of control of intervention, and which is illustrated in Chapter X with reference to the specifics of implementing the Cambodian decision, is that the confusion surrounding the role of law in national security decisions has left us as a nation poorly equipped to take international law systematically

---

1. See HARDY C. DILLARD, SOME ASPECTS OF LAW AND DIPLOMACY (1957), *reprinted* in 91 HAGUE ACADEMY RECUEIL DES COURS 447 (1957); Falk, *Law, Lawyers, and the Conduct of American Foreign Relations*, 78 YALE L.J. 919 (1969).

into account on such decisions. This failure to take international law into account has been, and until remedied will continue to be, costly in the design and implementation of our foreign policy. The point is not that we are a nation of law-breakers—my conclusion on the general outline of the United States participation in the Indo-China War is to the contrary—but that our national security process is tragically ill-equipped to take into account the insights of an important tradition in international affairs.

An international-legal perspective is also important for national security affairs in informing of the constitutional and internal-law aspects of national security decisions. Misinformation about the constitutional structure of the foreign policy process is rampant not only popularly but sometimes in the executive and legislative branches as well. The importance of legal perspectives, international and constitutional, on national security issues suggests a new specialization in law which might be termed "the law of international conflict management." The new specialization would focus on the international and domestic legal aspects of world order disputes and national security issues. Though the unifying focus would be on legal aspects of the control of international conflict, such a specialization should not be narrow. For example, the function of international law in defusing potential international conflict by assisting with programmatic solutions of major global problems would certainly be relevant.

Although law is an important input in the consideration of world order problems and national security decisions, lawyers should avoid the simplistic view that all lawful alternatives are necessarily in the national interest. It is important to ask not only whether a particular national policy is lawful, but also whether it is otherwise in the national interest and whether in light of the cost-benefit expected there are preferable alternatives available.[2]

> 2. As a first stage complexity in evaluating any national policy the following issues should be considered in addition to the legal issues:
>
>   1. Are the goals consistent with the national interest?
>   2. Are the goals realizable in the context in which they are pursued?
>   3. If the goals are realizable are they realizable at a cost-benefit ratio which makes their pursuit in the national interest?

Legal scholars should also avoid the temptation to let their views of the national interest (whether for or against a particular policy) determine conclusions on the legal issues. Unless law is to be merely a rhetorical technique for rationalizing policy choices, it must be rooted in an intellectual integrity of its own. That integrity, of course, requires reference to articulated policy preferences, but such preferences should be rooted in the requirements of the international system rather than the special interests of any one nation.

The jurisprudential underpinnings which consciously or unconsciously shape one's view of law are an important factor in legal judgment, particularly when dealing with the legal aspects of major public-order disputes. Characteristically, such disputes present complex factual and legal issues in which solutions are not obvious. Moreover, the normative systems involved, those of international and constitutional law, tend to be more open—with consequently greater choice available—than many paradigms of domestic law. Judgment thus depends on selection of relevant facts and rules from a confused and much larger pattern. It is particularly important in analyzing public-order issues, then, to inform the analysis with a clearly articulated theory *about* law. Chapter II, "Prolegomenon to the Jurisprudence of Myres McDougal and Harold Lasswell," sets out an introduction to a jurisprudential methodology whose insights have been frequently drawn on throughout this volume and which should be no stranger to most international lawyers. Though to date the principal impact of the McDougal-Lasswell jurisprudence has been felt in

---

4. Are preferable policy alternatives available to achieve the same or similar goals at a more favorable cost-benefit ratio?

For an analysis roughly in these terms of United States participation in the Indo-China conflict see Stanley Hoffmann, *Vietnam and American Foreign Policy*, in II R. FALK (ED.), THE VIETNAM WAR AND INTERNATIONAL LAW 1134 (1969). It should also be pointed out that there is a feedback between the legal and political issues, particularly the legal issues and the question of whether the goals of a particular policy are consistent with the national interest. Since international law is an important part of the long run national interest it is also an important input for goal selection.

international law, it may well be the most important general jurisprudential achievement of the century (the statement is made only after soul-searching provoked by its enormity!). Their system, sometimes imprecisely called "the New Haven approach," blends the ecclectic and original legal realism of Myres S. McDougal, a lawyer and past President of the American Society of International Law, with the behavioral and methodological insights of Harold Lasswell, a political scientist and current President of the American Society of International Law. Whether or not one accepts all of the McDougal-Lasswell approach (I am inclined to agree with the criticism that the emphasis on complementarity of legal rules may sometimes overemphasize the fluidity of law in the manner of the extreme legal realists), many tenets of the system reflect the fundamental jurisprudential premises of post-legal-realist thinking and are indispensable for modern legal analysis. Some of the most important of these premises are that law should be policy-oriented and functional, that is, aimed at the solution of real problems instead of being merely an exercise in internal logic-chopping in an artificial rule system; contextual, that is, explicitly located in its broadest social context and prescribing that legal issues be identified by factual settings presenting common policies and conditioning factors rather than by doctrinal labels; and interdisciplinary, that is, actively related to relevant data in neighboring disciplines. To avoid confusion in intellectual tasks, legal scholars should also clearly separate their description of what the law is (which may include widespread expectations about ought) from their own personal policy recommendations about what the law ought to be, and they should candidly and explicitly identify the reasons for the inevitable rule and fact selections which they make and the policies underlying their personal policy recommendations. These are not prescriptions for muddling or fuzzing the law. Rather, if followed, they provide opportunity for greater depth of understanding and appraisal of the views of others. The common concern that the McDougal-Lasswell system abandons the normative control achieved by an exclusively rule-oriented Kelsenian system both naively misconceives the choices available in a rule-oriented system and overlooks the teachings of the mainstream of jurisprudential development in the twentieth century as to how best to control such discretion.

Despite the importance of jurisprudential underpinnings, it would be a mistake to ascribe all differences of opinion among international lawyers to the underpinnings which they consciously or unconsciously espouse. Professor Richard A. Falk and I differ sharply about legal conclusions concerning the War, even though we both make substantial use of many of the insights of the McDougal-Lasswell approach.[3] The test of a jurisprudence is not whether scholars using it always reach the same result—differences in value inputs and appraisal of consequences of alternative actions are sufficient to account for differences in result—but whether it focuses dialogue on the real issues, promotes intellectual clarification of those issues, and facilitates appraisal of the contending positions. In these qualities the McDougal-Lasswell approach excels.

3. See Falk, *International Law and the United States Role in Viet Nam: A Response to Professor Moore*, 76 YALE L.J. 1095 (1967).

CHAPTER I

The Role of Law in the Management
of International Conflict

A THRESHOLD problem in consideration of the legal aspects of world order issues such as the Indo-China War is the frequently encountered skepticism about the usefulness of an international-legal approach. Sometimes this skepticism is taken to the point of warning of the dangers of legal approaches to international affairs. In an editorial on the occasion of President Nixon's appointment of William Rogers (a lawyer but not an international law specialist) as Secretary of State, *The New York Times* warned:

> Law functions within a structure of shared assumptions; its starting point is the acceptance, by all parties, of the legitimacy of the legal structure and of the values it embodies.
>
> Everyone understands that this shared value commitment and belief in the adjudication of conflict does not exist in more than a fragmentary manner in international society. Nevertheless, the legal habit of mind has sometimes led the United States to discount these difficulties, even to assume for itself and its own policies an international legitimacy which other states were unwilling to concede. Along with this has gone a trust in formal arrangements and alliances which the social and political realities have not at all times justified.[1]

As Richard Falk has pointed out, the intellectual underpinnings of this view were supplied by George Kennan and Hans Morgenthau in "celebrated critiques of American foreign policy made more than a decade ago."[2] More recently, this view has been

1. N.Y. Times, Jan. 6, 1969, at 46, col. 1.
2. Falk, *Law, Lawyers, and the Conduct of American Foreign Relations*, 78, YALE L.J. 919, 924 n.15 (1969). See G. KENNAN, REALITIES OF AMERICAN FOREIGN POLICY (1954); G. KENNAN, AMERICAN DIPLOMACY, 1900-1950 (1952); H. MORGENTHAU, POLITICS AMONG NATIONS (3d ed. 1966); H. MORGENTHAU, IN DEFENSE OF NATIONAL INTEREST (1951).

championed by such highly placed foreign-policy makers as the late Dean Acheson[3] and Henry Kissinger[4] and provided a firmer intellectual foundation by Stanley Hoffmann in critical appraisals of the limitations of international law in an international system which he would characterize as "revolutionary."[5]

Alternatively, the role of international law is sometimes over-estimated out of an excess of idealistic zeal or preoccupation of the American bar with adjudication as a technique of conflict resolution. From time to time there have been suggestions from lawyers that the Indo-China or Arab-Israeli conflicts should be resolved by submission to the International Court of Justice.[6] The slogan of the American Bar Association, "World peace through World law," carries overtones of this same preoccupation with judicial process and deemphasis of the often harsh realities of the international system.

Although it might be difficult to cage and exhibit a pure representative of either camp, the extremes which they represent have largely shaped the way in which international law is taken into account in our foreign policy planning and to a lesser extent in our teaching of international law. Not surprisingly, in view of the intellectual default of the legalists, for the most part the anti-legalists have prevailed. Both camps, however, exhibit a dangerously incomplete model and the victory of the anti-legalists

---

3. See the remarks by Dean Acheson at the 1963 Annual Meeting of the American Society of International Law in *1963 Proceedings of the American Society of International Law* 13, 14 (1963).

4. See Kissinger, *The Viet Nam Negotiations*, 47 FOREIGN AFFAIRS 211, 222-23 (1969).

5. See Hoffmann, "International Law and the Control of Force," in K. DEUTSCH & S. HOFFMANN (EDS.), THE RELEVANCE OF INTERNATIONAL LAW 21 (1968). Hoffmann, "International Systems and International Law," in K. KNORR AND S. VERBA (EDS)., THE INTERNATIONAL SYSTEM (1961), *reprinted* in S. HOFFMANN, THE STATE OF WAR 88 (1965); Hoffmann, *The Study of International Law and the Theory of International Relations*, 1963 PROCEEDINGS OF THE AMERICAN SOCIETY OF INTERNATIONAL LAW 26, *reprinted* in S. HOFFMANN, THE STATE OF WAR 123 (1965); Hoffmann, *Introduction* to SCHEINMAN AND WILKINSON, INTERNATIONAL LAW AND POLITICAL CRISIS xi-xix (1968).

6. See Holton, *Peace in Vietnam Through Due Process: An Unexplored Path*, 54 A.B.A.J. 45 (1968); Bassiouni, *The Middle East In Transition: From War to War, A Proposed Solution*, 4 INT'L LAWYER 379, 387-90 (1970).

has been achieved at a substantial cost in flexibility and effective implementation of United States foreign policy.

One of the difficulties with the debate between the legalists and the anti-legalists has been the diffuseness of the subject, a diffuseness that has frequently contributed to a debate without dialogue. The legalists have focused largely on the similarities in the domestic and international legal systems and the role of law in moderating behavior in the international system, while the anti-legalists have focused on the dissimilarities in the domestic and international legal systems and the role of the international system in limiting the effectiveness of international law. Other issues, such as the role of international law in the national decision process, have gone largely unexplored.

In refining the models of both camps, it will be helpful to focus on the full range of issues in the debate. First, what do we mean when we speak of international law and, as a corollary, what is the scope of our inquiry as to the role of international law? Second, what are the similarities and differences between the domestic and international legal systems, and what is their significance for our inquiry? Third, what is the impact of the international system on the development of international law and the significance of that impact for our inquiry? Fourth, how does international law moderate or otherwise influence other features of the international system of which it is a part? Fifth, what is or should be the role of international law in national security decisions? Sixth, how should the national security process be structured to effectively take an international-legal perspective into account? And lastly, what are the merits of competing approaches to international law, and how would the predominance of one or another approach influence answers to the proper role of international law? In the interest of clarifying an analytic framework useful in integrating the insights of all camps, as well as in revealing the selective emphasis of each, the material which follows will briefly develop each of these principal intellectual issues.

Analytic and Terminological Clarification

Much of the confusion in the debate about the role of international law in war-peace issues has resulted from failure to clarify what is meant by international law. "International law," like "law" in general, is subject to a variety of meanings. The task of the scholar is not to select any one meaning as true or false but to recognize the diversity of meanings and to select those meanings which are the most useful, usefulness being measured by our purpose in asking about "international law." If we say "there is no international law" we may be affirming that there are no rules of international law or that states are never influenced by international law. Used in either of these senses the statement would be patent nonsense, since it is observable that there is a large body of scholarly writing about the rules of international law and that at least some such rules play a greater or lesser role in modifying state behavior. Similarly, the controversy about whether international law is binding is answerable by empirical observation. As H.L.A. Hart has observed: "The proof that 'binding' rules in any society exist, is simply that they are thought of, spoken of, and function as such."[7] Any international lawyer could quickly produce evidence that at least some rules of international law are regarded by the relevant community as binding.

That the statement "there is no international law" is nonsense if used in a literal sense, then, suggests that the meaning of the phrase usually lies elsewhere. It may affirm that there is no international law of war-peace issues as opposed to international law in general, or that enforcement of the rules is weak or nonexistent, that application of the rules is largely left to auto-interpretation by the interested parties, that there is no centralized legislative competence in the international system, or all of these things. When we have narrowed the meaning in this fashion, the issue really becomes, as John Fried has observed, not whether international law exists but the extent to which it is a significant force in managing international conflict.[8] It is not an adequate answer to this question to demonstrate, as some of the legalist writers have, that international law is quite effective in regulating a host of international interactions such as the exchange of diplomatic representatives. If the issue is one of the role and effectiveness of

7. H.L.A. HART, THE CONCEPT OF LAW 226 (1961).
8. See Fried, "How Efficient Is International Law?," in K. DEUTSCH AND S. HOFFMANN, THE RELEVANCE OF INTERNATIONAL LAW 93 (1968).

11

international law in managing international conflict, its role and effectiveness must be judged by those issues (ignoring for the moment the probable feedback effect on conflict prevention from successful regulation of non-conflict issues).

In clarifying this point of the effectiveness of international law in war-peace issues, it is indispensable to refine further what we are talking about when we refer to "international law." Law is most usefully thought of as the conjunction of patterns of authority and patterns of control. Authority refers to expectations that an action is consistent with community beliefs about permissible decisions, decision-makers, and procedures. It is this focus on expectations concerning community-decision processes that separates patterns of authority from international morality. As H.L.A. Hart has pointed out, discussion on the basis of law and morality frequently refer to quite different bodies of knowledge. Law proceeds on the basis of precedent, practice, and appeals to authority, morality on the basis of appeals to conscience.[9] Control refers to the degree to which community practices actually conform to expectations of authority or are sanctioned for deviation. Rather than speculating on the proper mix of authority and control to constitute international law, it is more useful to observe that the international lawyer should be concerned with both international patterns of authority and international patterns of control.

It is important for an adequate understanding of international law to realize that expectations as to the authoritativeness of conduct may play a significant role in encouraging conformance to community expectations or, in the event of violation, precipitating community sanction. For example, perceptions of the authorita-

9. See HART, note 7 *supra*, at 223. Failure to recognize the nature of this distinction between "law" and "morality" is one of the traps into which Dean Acheson fell in his famous remarks at the 1963 Annual Meeting of the American Society of International Law, in which he expressed skepticism about the role of international law in major war-peace crises. According to Acheson: "[T]he quarantine is not a legal issue or an issue of international law as these terms should be understood. Much of what is called international law is a body of ethical distillation, and one must take care not to confuse this distillation with law." 1963 *Proceedings of the American Society of International Law* 13, 14 (1963).

tiveness of the United States Supreme Court (or the International Court of Justice) may be a significant factor in encouraging compliance with Court decisions even when there is only a low expectation of sanction for non-compliance. Conversely, as the authority of the Court declines on a particular issue, non-compliance may rise even though expectations of sanction for non-compliance remain constant or even rise. The widespread non-compliance with the "Bible Reading"[10] decisions is a domestic example of this latter principle.

Similarly, authority and authority deflation may be critical factors in assessing the role and effect of international law on war-peace issues despite a seeming lack of visible sanctions for non-compliance. Because of this feedback effect of authority on control, patterns of control, i.e., patterns of compliance with community expectations as to authority, are a far more meaningful indicator for assessing the impact of international law than the more limited and visible sanctioning process. In turn, of course, patterns of control may influence patterns of authority, either increasing or decreasing authority as decisions are to a greater or lesser extent complied with or ignored. The point is that rather than focusing on the generality "international law," it is much more useful in assessing the role of international law in conflict-management to focus both on patterns of authority and patterns of control. And perhaps more importantly, patterns of compliance are a more useful indicator of the efficacy of law than reliance on the more visible sanctioning process alone. These distinctions are not mere academic or debaters' points. In the relatively decentralized international system, expectations about the authoritativeness of international legal rules may be a substantial factor in encouraging compliance even in the absence of more easily observable sanctions.

For purposes of assessing the role of international law in war-peace issues it also seems more useful to focus on the legal process and an international-legal approach to national security issues rather than narrowly confining law to a set of rules for regulating

10. School Dist. v. Schempp, 374 U.S. 203 (1963). See also the "School Prayer Case" Engel v. Vitale, 370 U.S. 421 (1962).

conduct. Law is most usefully conceived as a process by which authoritative expectations are created, modified, and terminated rather than as a static set of hierarchical norms. Moreover, the international lawyer achieves a different focus from the international relations theorist not only in his concern for normative rules but also in his concern for policy alternatives offered by international organizations and in his general focus on international processes of authority rather than primarily on power relations. As such, to focus only on the normative aspect of the international lawyer's concern is to ignore skills which may be highly useful in the management of international conflict.

For the most part, neither legalists nor anti-legalists have adequately focused on the scope of their inquiry or the most useful meaning of international law in relation to that inquiry. The anti-legalists have been particularly guilty of failing to take account of the effect of widespread expectations of authority and of broader notions of law as process and institutional structure.

The Nature of the International Legal System

The difficulty in empirical study of the role of international law in the management of international conflict has encouraged comparisons with the domestic legal system as an alternative battleground between the legalists and anti-legalists. The anti-legalists have pointed out that the international legal system lacks a high degree of institutionalization, centralized prescriptive competence, centralized applications competence resulting in an auto-interpretation problem by which each actor is largely free to judge his own cause, and centralized sanctioning process, and that the rules of the international system are likely to be at a higher level of generalization and more incomplete than their counterparts in domestic legal systems.[11] Though these differences in the international legal system are real, the legalists have effectively countered with a demonstration that, on the whole, the anti-legalists have exaggerated the differences and that there are plenty of examples in domestic legal systems of the same kinds of

---

11. See, *e.g.*, H. MORGENTHAU, POLITICS AMONG NATIONS 275-311 (3d ed. 1966).

difficulties.[12] The legalists have also urged that the comparisons between international and domestic legal systems, or between the international legal system and private law aspects of domestic legal systems, are misleading. Thus John Fried writes:

> The central point is that *domestic law insofar as it applies to petty everyday affairs cannot suitably be compared with international law*. In its most important aspects, international law regulates the behavior of states, that is, of large collectives; it deals with highly complex matters involving interests of macro-organisms. Hence, it should be compared, not with domestic law pertaining to minor issues, as implied in the statement "If someone steals he ought to be punished"; but with that part of domestic law which deals with analogous matters of great import and regulating the behavior of large collectives, namely, *constitutional law*.[13]

Fried then points out that on this level many of the differences between the international and domestic legal systems disappear or are at least narrowed.[14] In general, this round seems to have been won by the legalists, who have convincingly shown that the formal differences have frequently been exaggerated. Their own zeal to make their case, however, has sometimes resulted in exaggerations of their own as to the similarities between the international and domestic legal orders. For example, H.L.A. Hart rightly criticizes exaggerated similarities equating war and forceful retaliation with the sanctioning process in domestic law and equating peace treaties with the domestic legislative process.[15]

Though both the anti-legalists' attack on and the legalists' defense of the effectiveness of the international legal system have contributed to greater understanding of the system, the essentially impressionistic description of the system and the preoccupation with comparison with domestic legal systems have

12. See, *e.g.*, Fried, note 8 *supra*; HARDY C. DILLARD, SOME ASPECTS OF LAW AND DIPLOMACY (1957), *reprinted* in 91 HAGUE ACADEMY RECUEIL DES COURS 447 (1957).
13. Fried, note 8 *supra*, at 102.
14. Fried, note 8 *supra*, at 102-132.
15. See H.L.A. HART, note 7 *supra*, at 226-27.

sidetracked more thoroughgoing inquiry about the nature of the international legal system and its role in the management of international conflict. In the final analysis, to conclude that the international legal system is or is not like the domestic legal system is considerably less important than thorough description of the international legal system and its role in conflict management. Recently, Professors McDougal, Lasswell, and Reisman have undertaken a comprehensive description of the processes by which international law is made, applied, and terminated. Their systematic description of what they term the international constitutive process of authoritative decision has utilized an intellectual framework developed by McDougal and Lasswell for the description of any legal system. A principal feature of the framework is that any legal system must perform seven authority functions. They are: *intelligence gathering,* or the obtaining of information concerning possible prescriptions; *promotion* of new prescriptions; *prescription,* or what we loosely term legislation; *invocation,* or the provisional application of a prescription; *application* of a prescription to a particular fact situation; *termination* of prescriptions; and continuing *appraisal* of prescriptions. In a two-part article in the *Journal of Legal Education*[16] which is a prelude to a book, the authors systematically describe the performance of the international legal system with respect to each of these functions. The effect is conclusively to demonstrate that there is an effectively functioning international legal system which creates authoritative expectations concerning a range of international issues including war-peace issues. The existence of such a process of authoritative decision coupled with the importance of patterns of authority suggests a significant role for international law in the management of international conflict. It also demonstrates that H.L.A. Hart oversimplified when he described the international legal system as a system of primary rules without what he terms secondary rules conferring authority and regulating the processes of prescription and application.[17] The reality of the international legal system seems to be a great deal

16. McDougal, Lasswell & Reisman, *The World Constitutive Process of Authorative Decision,* 19 J. LEGAL ED. 253, 403 (2 pts. 1967).
17. See H.L.A. HART, note 7 *supra,* at 208-209.

more complex than previous techniques at analysis have enabled us to see.

The Impact of the International System
on the Development of International Law

A number of international relations theorists have focused on the impact of the international milieu in shaping the role of international law. Most notably they include Morton Kaplan and Nicholas Katzenbach in their famous study of "The Political Foundations of International Law"[18] and Stanley Hoffmann in a series of provocative articles on international systems and international law.[19] Because of their detailed discussion of what Hoffmann regards as the limitations on the role of international law inherent in the present international system, his articles are particularly important. Hoffmann hypothesizes that the present international system is a revolutionary as opposed to a stable system, and that one characteristic of a revolutionary system is to drastically restrict the role of international law. According to Hoffmann:

> A stable system is one in which the stakes of conflict are limited; relations among the actors are marked by moderation in scope and means. Whatever the system's basic structure and the state of the technology of conflict, the units act so as to limit the amount of harm they could inflict upon one another. In a revolutionary system, this moderation disappears. When one major actor's decision to discard it coincides with or brings about a revolution in the technology of conflict or a change in the basic structure of the world (or both), the system is particularly unstable. In other words, in a stable system, the life or essential values of the basic units are not constantly in question, and the main actors agree on the rules according to which competition among them will take place; in a revolutionary system, the incompatibility of purposes rules out such agreement.[20]

18. M. KAPLAN & N. KATZENBACH, THE POLITICAL FOUNDATIONS OF INTERNATIONAL LAW (1961).
19. See the articles by Hoffmann set out in note 5 *supra*.
20. Hoffmann, "International Systems and International Law," in S. HOFFMANN, THE STATE OF WAR 88, 93 (1965).

In a revolutionary system the lack of consensus on goals and the prevalence of revolutionary and revisionist ideologies prevents the fundamental agreement necessary for the effective functioning of international law. Hoffmann also discusses this difficulty from the perspective of national policy-makers caught up in the international system. Policy-makers may pursue long-run milieu goals concerning the shape and stability of the international order or international legal order or short-run possession goals in pursuit of other national interests. In a revolutionary system, the policy-makers adhering to revolutionary ideologies are characteristically likely to pursue revolutionary visions at the expense of long-run milieu goals, and the pressure of the competitive struggle drives even conservative powers to neglect the pursuit of long-run milieu goals.[21]

Hoffmann's analysis is a brilliant explanation of the unfortunately too frequently observable lack of concern of national policy-makers for the long-range health of the international legal system. Like all generalizations, however, it may overstate the case in some respects and mislead in others. Hoffmann's focus on the goals and subjectivities of national policy-makers rather than simply on power relations is an important perspective. But the option to pursue long-run milieu goals is not conditioned simply by assessment of risk of reciprocal non-compliance and loss of system stability as Hoffmann implies, but may also be conditioned by widespread community expectations concerning "international law" in the sense of compliance with expectations about authority. Action which violates such expectations may entail a high cost even if it does not lead to dramatic sanctions. The Soviet invasion of Czechoslovakia, though a paradigm of unsanctioned action in the traditional sense, was achieved only at a real and perhaps intolerably high cost to Soviet leadership in the communist and third-world nations. The cost was not merely attributable to immediate self-interest or moral revulsion but was in significant measure a product of violation of fundamental community expectations concerning the authoritativeness of such unilateral acts.

In short, by failing to focus on the very real international con-

---

21. Hoffmann, "International Law and the Control of Force," in K. DEUTSCH & S. HOFFMANN, THE RELEVANCE OF INTERNATIONAL LAW 21, 36-46 (1968).

stitutive process of authoritative decision, Hoffmann understates the substantial pressures for compliance with international law even in a revolutionary system. Moreover, some of these pressures are greatest in the areas of war-peace issues dealing with national sovereignty and self-determination, areas which we sometimes mistakenly assume are subject only to minimal control from the international system. To dismiss these pressures as only "international public opinion" neither clarifies their nature (particularly their basis in authority) nor adequately takes account of their convertibility into power relations.

Second, if Hoffmann's model is accurate (largely a question of emphasis) one might expect greater international adventurism than has actually been the case. A characteristic of most major public order disputes since World War II—the Greek civil war, the Quemoy-Matsu dispute, Berlin, the recurrent India-Pakistan conflict, the four Arab-Israeli wars, Indo-China, and Cuba—however, has been the uncertainty and complexity of the legal issues. Most have related either to legal claims arising from World War II settlements or some aspect of the inadequately regulated internal conflict problem or both. Even Korea, perhaps the paradigm counter-example, was part of the general intractable divided-nation problem created by uneasy settlements flowing from World War II. For the most part, conflict has arisen at precisely those points in the system where the legal issues and expectations of authority were least well-defined. This suggests that international law is playing a significant role in preventing conflict, and that strengthening authoritative expectations in poorly regulated areas may be an important strategy of conflict avoidance.

Third, Hoffmann's analysis may understate the perceived interest in cooperation for the preservation of inclusive and exclusive common interests in the present international system. The nuclear test ban treaty, the non-proliferation agreement, the Soviet-West German non-aggression pact, the peace-keeping actions undertaken by the United Nations in the Middle East, the Congo, and Cyprus, as well as the continuing strategic arms limitations talks between the United States and the Soviet Union all attest a not insignificant perceived common interest in stability of the international system.

Fourth, even if for the reasons Hoffmann suggests international law were unable to significantly deter major conflict, it does not follow that it would not provide useful concepts and institutions for the management and containment of conflict. The continuing and highly significant role of the United Nations in the Arab-Israeli wars is a case in point even though the conflict has not to date been resolved by the United Nations.

Lastly, Hoffmann's analysis of why international law may have a restricted role in the international system may easily be misinterpreted as a prescription for action in the national interest. Though there is nothing in Hoffmann's analysis which suggests that long-run milieu goals concerning the legal order should be downgraded, the failure to develop the case why such goals may be strongly in the national interest, even in the face of intense competition from revolutionary and revisionist actors, leaves one with a general and false sense of the unimportance of international law in the search for the national interest.

In short, though Hoffmann's analysis is insightful in recognizing the generally deleterious effect of a revolutionary international system on the development of international law, it may greatly understate the role of international law in the present system and its importance for national decision-makers. This may in part be attributable to the international relations theorists' understandable preoccupation with the impact of the international system on international law rather than the role of international law in the international system.

The Role of International Law in the International System

Just as international relations theorists have generally focused on the impact of the international system on the development of international law, international lawyers have largely focused on the role of international law in the international system. One of the best recent studies has been that of Louis Henkin, in *How Nations Behave*,[22] in which he explores the role of international law in the Suez crisis of 1956 and the Cuban missile crisis of 1962 and concludes that international law plays a significant role in

22. L. HENKIN, HOW NATIONS BEHAVE (1968).

moderating state conduct. More recently, a series of studies edited by Scheinman and Wilkinson have painted a much more limited picture of the role of international law in moderating international conflict.[23] One difficulty with most of these studies is that they focus on extreme contexts in which the stabilizing effect of international law has already largely been overcome. A second difficulty is their primary reliance on the episodic statements of national decison-makers rather than on a more comprehensive inquiry into the pre-conflict, conflict, and post-conflict roles of international law. For example, it is quite possible and even probable that national decision-makers are frequently insensitive to the real costs of international law violation and to the uses of an international-legal perspective for conflict management.[24]

Though empirical research into the role of international law in the management of international conflict is highly important, the following structure would seem to offer a more useful basis for inquiry. With respect to each role, it might be useful to describe both the actual operation of international law and the perceptions of national and international decison-makers about the operation and utility of international law.

Pre-Conflict

   I. International law contributes to conflict-avoidance by stabilizing expectations concerning value production and allocation and by clarifying community common interest.

  II. International law contributes to the avoidance of conflict by contributing to solution of conflict-generating international problems.

III. International law contributes to the avoidance of conflict by providing rules of the game which minimize unintended conflict.

23. See L. SCHEINMAN & D. WILKINSON, INTERNATIONAL LAW AND POLITICAL CRISIS (1968).

24. Since World War II, the prevailing attitude among foreign policy decision-makers of every political persuasion and at every decision level has been one of skepticism toward international law. Empirical studies which focus on the rhetoric of such decision-makers are likely to be self-fulfilling prophecies. To be effective such studies must also focus on other indicia of the effect of international law.

Conflict

IV. International law moderates extreme behavior of states:
    a. by facilitating recognition of the national interest in the stability of the international milieu;
    b. by imposing costs for violation of authoritative expectations limiting state discretion to resort to force;
    c. by the integration of international law regulating contexts of violence into domestic law;
    d. by the effect of the law habit on official behavior.
    e. *Caveat*: the possibility that in some contexts international law may inflame conflict.

V. International law provides alternative techniques for conflict-minimization:
    a. techniques of conflict-avoidance;
    b. techniques of conflict-moderation;
    c. techniques of dispute settlement.

VI. International law provides a medium for diplomacy and communication.

Post-Conflict

VII. International law provides a normative basis for assessing state conduct.

VIII. International law contributes to alteration of the international system by providing world order models for conflict-minimization.

Consider briefly each of these ways in which international law may contribute to the management of international conflict.

First, international law may contribute to conflict-avoidance by stabilizing expectations concerning value production and allocation, and by clarifying community common interest. It is commonplace that the operation of complex societies requires a minimum degree of stability of expectations. The high level of interaction present in the international system could not effectively take place in the absence of an effectively functioning international constitutive process. It thus seems likely that the international legal system contributes to avoidance of conflict in facilitating international interdependence and in maintaining a minimal stability of expectations. It may also contribute to avoidance of conflict by clarifying areas of shared common interest. The current concern for defining a regime for the exploitation of the resources of the deep ocean floor and the substantial Soviet-United States agreement on space law are examples of this potential conflict-avoidance role of international law.

Second, international law may abet the avoidance of conflict by contributing to solution of conflict-generating international problem. In a recent article in *Science*, John Platt attempts to rank many of the most critical problems facing man and his global environment.[25] In addition to nuclear war, they include environmental pollution, overpopulation, resource depletion, and problems in bureaucratic management of our increasing numbers and increasing complexity. Each of these problems, as well as the more traditional problems of hunger, ignorance, disease, exploitation, and racism, has a substantial potential for generating conflict. To the extent that international law assists in ameliorating these problems it may play a significant role in conflict-avoidance. Professor Wolfgang Friedmann has already described the substantial international law of cooperation which has emerged during the last century to deal with such functional problems.[26] It seems likely that international law may already play a significant role in conflict-reduction through social action on a global scale. The problems of the future, of course, may require far more attention to these aspects of international law, quite apart from their function in controlling conflict.[27]

Third, international law may contribute to the avoidance of conflict by providing rules of the game which minimize unintended conflict. For example, for the most part states adhere to the reasonably clear provisions of the Geneva Conventions on the Law of the Sea in refraining from exercising jurisdiction over foreign flag vessels outside of their territorial sea and contiguous

25. See Platt, *What We Must Do*, 166 SCIENCE 1115 (Nov. 28, 1969).
26. W. FRIEDMANN, THE CHANGING STRUCTURE OF INTERNATIONAL LAW (1964).
27. See Falk, note 2 *supra*, at 930-32; Nelson, *We Need a New Global Agency to Confront the Environment Crisis*, 10 WAR/PEACE REPORT 3 (May, 1970).

zone, and *a fortiori* from seizing foreign warships even if engaged in espionage activities. The rules are well known and as such they work remarkably well to prevent unintended conflict. What conflict there is from violation of the rules usually stems from a deliberate decision, as for example North Korea's seizure of the *Pueblo*. And even in areas where international agreement is lacking, as for example on the width of the territorial sea, wide deference is generally accorded to claims of other states. Thus, the United States in practice tends to observe the twelve-mile limit claimed by most communist nations and it chooses to provide indemnity to United States fishermen seized in the extraordinarily large contiguous zones claimed by the Latin American states rather than protest too much. Conversely, in areas where international law may be unclear, the danger of unintended confrontation may increase. For example, the lack of precedent and authoritative expectations concerning the recovery of material released into the sea during underwater firing of the Polaris missiles (one can make a superficially plausible case that such cover material is salvage and recoverable by the first to take effective possession) may have been a contributing factor in encouraging recent Soviet attempts to recover such materials.[28] Similarly, the major uncertainty surrounding the political settlement provisions of the 1954 Indo-China settlement was probably a significant factor in the outbreak of a second Indo-China War. This is not to simplistically suggest that all that is needed for a peaceful world is a comprehensive "Restatement of International Law." At least one obstacle to such a solution is that legal uncertainty is frequently caused because the parties cannot agree. The 1954 Indo-China settlement may be an example. It is to suggest, however, that uncertainty in the rules of the game may create increased risk of unintended and escalating conflict, and that where such uncertainty can be narrowed to do so may reduce the potential for conflict.

Fourth, for a number of reasons, international law may moderate extreme behavior of states. Since the international law of the Charter stresses the common interest in avoiding coercion, it seems likely that international law is an important source of sub-

28. See N.Y. Times, Aug. 4, 1970, at 1, col. 5.

jectivities concerning the national interest in the stability of the international milieu. Should states violate the authoritative prescriptions of international law, they are encouraging reciprocal violation and contributing to an authority deflation of the relevant norms. Their own assessment of the undesirability of such a loosening of reciprocally beneficial normative restraints can sometimes be expected to override their pursuit of short-run national "possession" objectives. The international system also imposes what can be substantial costs for violation of norms prohibiting recourse to aggressive use of force, quite apart from the interest in a stable international milieu and the fear of legitimizing reciprocal conduct. The prescriptions concerning use of force are among the most fundamental norms of the international legal system. Violation of those norms in a reasonably clear context, as for example the recent Soviet invasion of Czechoslovakia, may result in a very real drop in diplomatic or ideological influence. The Soviet loss of influence in many foreign communist parties following the Czechoslovak intervention is an example. In an age in which nations spend vast sums in an avowed effort to win men's minds, it seems shortsighted to fail to take into account the potentially disastrous impact on ideological influence because of failure to adhere to fundamental norms of international law.

To some extent, international law regulating contexts of violence has been integrated into domestic law, and to the extent that it forms a recognized part of domestic law, national decision-makers may be particularly influenced. In some nations, international law in general has been constitutionally received as part of the law of the land.[29] Even in the United States, in which existing decisions support the power of the Executive and Congress to override valid treaties,[30] a significant amount of international law has been woven into the fabric of domestic law. One example relevant to conflict management is the provisions of the 1949 Geneva Conventions regulating the laws of war. For United States Army personnel the provisions of FM 27-10[31] incorporate

29. See Basic Law for the Federal Republic of Germany, Chapter II, Art. 25; The Constitution of Japan, Chapter X, Art. 98, § 2.
30. See Chae Chan Ping v. United States, 130 U.S. 581 (1889); Whitney v. Robertson, 124 U.S. 190 (1888).
31. ARMY FIELD MANUAL FM 27-10, THE LAW OF LAND WARFARE (1956).

the Hague and Geneva Conventions into domestic law, and the difficulty in invocation and application is that of domestic law. Finally, adherence to international law may simply result from the law habit of bureaucratic officials. No one wishes to admit to law violation, particularly bureaucratic officials who fear alienation of large groups holding views strongly in favor of adherence to law. As a possibly illegal decision is made at routine levels or is particularly blatant, national officials may feel strong tugs toward protection by avoiding illegality, even should their own predilections be otherwise.

Though there are a number of reasons suggesting that international law may frequently moderate extreme state behavior, Stanley Hoffmann has suggested that law may sometimes be counter-productive for world order and detrimental to the nation that invokes it. He is concerned that the extreme rhetoric of states in seeking to legally justify their doubtful actions will debase the currency of international law, that much of contemporary international law authorizes states to increase their power, and that premature attempts to enforce or strengthen international law may further weaken the system.[32] Though extreme rhetoric in attempted justification of unjustifiable conduct may to some extent debase the currency, if the international constitutive process is sufficiently healthy it should be able to separate the wheat from the chaff. The "Brezhnev Doctrine" of "socialist self-determination" does not seem to have been even minimally accepted by the international community as a justification for the Soviet invasion of Czechoslovakia and is a case in point. In any event, the argument is not one that illustrates an immediate danger to the international system from the use of international law but only a danger to the preservation of the efficacy of international law itself.

Hoffmann's second point, that much of contemporary international law authorizes states to increase their power, is in its emphasis simply untrue, at least in the area regulating the control of unauthorized coercion. The most fundamental principle of the

32. See Hoffmann, *Introduction* to SCHEINMANN & WILKINSON, INTERNATIONAL LAW AND POLITICAL CRISIS xi, xvi-xvii (1968).

Charter is that states should not resort to unilateral force as a modality of major change. It is hard to see how this is a "perfect recipe for chaos." Although Hoffmann's last point concerning the danger of premature efforts at enforcing international law is certainly a valid one, it should be balanced by recognition of the danger of failing to use international law and institutions to effectuate conflict management. International organizations can suffer an authority deflation as much from under-use as over-use, and one suspects that under-use of the United Nations may be a greater contributor to its present malaise than premature efforts to use it.[33] Hoffmann's third point also concerns preservation of the integrity of the international legal system itself, and does not illustrate international law as an independent source of conflict. In short, though Hoffmann's first and third points do point out the dangers of unjustified or kneejerk reliance on international law, they do not demonstrate a serious state of affairs, in which international law may increase rather than decrease conflict. A more persuasive possibility, which Hoffmann suggests in another context, is that international law may sometimes increase the stakes of conflict.[34] After a formal treaty has been breached or an adversary's conduct has been characterized as aggression, the issue becomes one of preservation of international law as well as redress of the national injury. This tendency of formal legal obligations to escalate the stakes might conceivably be a potent source of conflict. Against this tendency, however, one would have to weigh the beneficial effect for conflict-avoidance of having rules concerning *pacta sunt servanda* and non-aggression. Adding up these possibilities of increased conflict arising from the use of international law, the present inadequacy of international law concerning the regulation of intervention of internal conflict and the relationship of regional and global international organizations for the maintenance of peace and security would seem to be more

33. The problems precipitated for the United Nations by the Congo and financing crises are examples to the contrary.
34. "A legal norm communicates a solemn commitment, and establishes a trip-wire that begs for, and can set off, a conspicuous crisis when crossed." Hoffmann, "International Law and the Control of Force," in K. DEUTSCH & S. HOFFMANN, THE RELEVANCE OF INTERNATIONAL LAW 21, 41 (1968).

potent sources of conflict.[35] It is probably no accident that most major public order disputes since World War II have fallen into one or another of these gaps in the Charter. The road to improvement seems to be development of a more complete international law rather than its abandonment. Again, this is not to suggest that international law is an independent variable in the control of international conflict. It is to suggest that a focus on the effect of international law on the control of conflict may sometimes yield significant dividends.

Fifth, international law may provide useful techniques for conflict minimization. The international legal process, broadly conceived to include the panoply of relevant international institutions, offers a host of techniques and options for conflict avoidance, conflict moderation, and dispute settlement. During the *Pueblo* crisis the United States made effective use of referral to the United Nations Security Council as an alternative to forceful reprisal against North Korea. Similarly, in the recent Honduras-El Salvador border dispute the Organization of American States provided effective machinery for conflict resolution as had the Organization of African Unity in the earlier Algeria-Morocco conflict.[36] United Nations assistance in peace-keeping and mediating efforts are legend,[37] and theories of the international system which focus only on its failures, as well as those which focus only on its successes, are incomplete. International law also offers a host of more traditional techniques for dispute settlement such as international arbitration, the International Court of Justice, mediation, and good offices. One of the problems of the present international system is that such traditional techniques seem to be utilized less frequently than formerly. Stanley Hoffmann's thesis of the difficulty of international law in an increasingly revo-

---

35. See Moore, *The Control of Foreign Intervention in Internal Conflict*, 9 VA. J. INT'L L. 209 (1969); Moore, *The Role of Regional Arrangements in the Maintenance of World Order*, III C. BLACK & R. FALK, (EDS.), THE FUTURE OF THE INTERNATIONAL LEGAL ORDER: CONFLICT MANAGEMENT 122 (1970).

36. See Moore, *The Role of Regional Arrangements in the Maintenance of World Order*, note 35 *supra*.

37. See, *e.g.*, R. HIGGINS, UNITED NATIONS PEACEKEEPING 1946-1967 (1970); D. WAINHOUSE & OTHERS, INTERNATIONAL PEACE OBSERVATION: A HISTORY AND FORECAST (1966).

lutionary system may be a partial explanation for this decline. Even so, institutional alternatives offered by the legal system have continued to play a significant role in conflict management.

Sixth, international law may provide a medium for diplomacy and communication. Existing international institutions, particularly the United Nations, provide a significant forum for diplomatic interaction which may assist in conflict management. Apparently both the nuclear test ban treaty and the non-proliferation treaty (as well as the United States-Soviet promoted agreement on space law) were hammered out by representatives of the principal powers within a forum provided by the United Nations. The interrelation of the four-power efforts at peace in the Middle East with the mission of United Nations mediator Gunnar Jarring is another case in point. In addition to providing additional forums for communication, the language of international law may also serve as a medium of communication in crisis bargaining or in diplomatic efforts at conflict-avoidance.[38]

Seventh, international law provides a normative basis for assessing state conduct. The history, agreement, custom, state practice, and scholarly writing which make up "international law" represent a condensed and valuable repertory of human experience bearing on normative judgment of state behavior. Though other disciplines such as theology or economics are also relevant in making normative judgments about international conduct, the law is frequently specialized to precisely the issue at hand. A comparison of the present "just war" doctrine predominant in theological approaches to normative assessment of war, with the detailed and laborious evolution of the international law norms regulating use of force, illustrates the point. International law moved from early "just war" notions to concentration on regulation of minor coercion and the conduct of hostilities through the procedural checks of the League Covenant to the present institutional and normative system of the Charter.[39] Even with its sub-

---

38. Stanley Hoffmann adverts to this role as well as the danger that some forms of international-legal communication may make the competition fiercer. See Hoffmann, note 32 *supra*, at xii-xiii.
39. For a brief history of the international law of conflict management see M. Kaplan & N. Katzenbach, "Resort to Force: War and Neutrality," in THE POLITICAL FOUNDATIONS OF INTERNATIONAL LAW 198-228 (1961), *re-*

stantial gaps, the present international law of conflict-management offers a highly useful basis for normative appraisal of state conduct. As a nation we do not live by assessment of the national interest alone. Even if it could be convincingly demonstrated that it would be in the national interest to usurp the values of a smaller state, notions of international law and morality are likely to still give us pause. Since ultimately our beliefs about right and wrong are more or less translated into action politics, this role alone would make international law a highly important discipline.

Eighth, international law may contribute to alteration of the international system by providing world order models for conflict-minimization. Complex institutions and ideas rarely spring fullblown into the world. Rather, they more often result from slow accretion through repeated insight and experience. Efforts at modifying the international system are no exception. The League of Nations built heavily on the experience of the Hague Conferences and the earlier functional agencies, and the United Nations built heavily on the experience of the League and the International Labor Organization.[40] (One of the problems of international organization is that each generation seems to perfect institutions to deal with the problems of earlier eras rather than its own.) Despite its shortcomings, international law provides one of the principal sources of thought concerning either minor tinkering or utopian modification of the international system. Law is in essence an instrumental tool, and the legal literature, particularly that infused with the dynamism of the legal realist movement, tends to reflect that role. For example, the most thoroughly developed alternative world order model today is the Clark-Sohn plan for World Peace Through World Law,[41] developed by two highly creative international lawyers. Though utopian, it fulfills a valuable role in promoting thought on alternative models of the international system.

This brief sketch of some of the roles played by international

printed in II R. FALK & S. MENDLOVITZ, THE STRATEGY OF WORLD ORDER 276 (1966).

40. See generally, I. CLAUDE, SWORDS INTO PLOW-SHARES (1956).

41. G. CLARK & L. SOHN, WORLD PEACE THROUGH WORLD LAW (2d ed. 1962).

law in the international system is intended as an illustration of the range of ways in which international law is a reality to be reckoned with on war-peace issues. Almost certainly it does not exhaust the diverse roles actually played by international law in the management of international conflict. To the extent that empirical research is possible on these roles, it would be helpful if future research could more systematically explore each of the roles suggested.

The Role of International Law In National Security Decisions

Much of the legalist/anti-legalist debate concerns the role which international law has played and ought to play in national security decisions. The criticism of legalistic-moralistic approaches to foreign policy made by George Kennan in his *American Diplomacy—1900-1950* has been typical of anti-legalist views echoed since. In a now famous passage, Kennan wrote:

> I see the most serious fault of our past policy formulation to lie in something that I might call the legalistic-moralistic approach to international problems. This approach runs like a red skein through our foreign policy of the last fifty years. It has in it something of the old emphasis on arbitration treaties, something of the Hague Conferences and schemes for universal disarmament, something of the more ambitious American concepts of the role of international law, something of the League of Nations and the United Nations, something of the Kellogg Pact, something of the idea of a universal "Article 51" pact, something of the belief in World Law and World Government. But it is none of these, entirely. Let me try to describe it.
>
> It is the belief that it should be possible to suppress the chaotic and dangerous aspirations of governments in the international field by the acceptance of some system of legal rules and restraints. This belief undoubtedly represents in part an attempt to transpose the Anglo-Saxon concept of individual law into the international field and to make it

applicable to governments as it is applicable here at home to individuals.[42]

A blunter statement from the same perspective was made by Dean Acheson at the 1963 Annual Meeting of the American Society of International Law:

> I must conclude that the propriety of the Cuban quarantine is not a legal issue. The power, position and prestige of the United States had been challenged by another state; and law simply does not deal with such questions of ultimate power— power that comes close to the sources of sovereignty.[43]

There is a substantial measure of truth in both the Kennan and Acheson statements. A fuzzy and too idealistic focus on World Law, an overestimation of the capacity of international organizations, and a neglect of hard power realities can obscure the national interest in a cloud of rhetoric and moral precept. But in the measure of their omission, the Kennan and Acheson statements are as fuzzy and unrealistic as the world views which they criticize, an omission made all the more serious by the victory of the Kennan-Acheson view in United States foreign-policy making circles during the past decade. In his Hague lectures of 1957, Hardy Dillard has taken Kennan to task for failing to make clear that international law has a place in determining the national interest and for a "conception of 'law' as something 'static' which binds states to a rigid set of rules. . . ."[44] The Acheson statement has also been the subject of rebuttal from international lawyers, most of it justified. In referring to the Acheson and other recent anti-legalists' statements, Professor Richard Falk points out:

> What is disturbing about the simpler statements of the anti-legalist position is its double confusion: first, an inaccurate and simplistic presentation of the legal tradition and, second, a false depiction of the relationship between "a characteris-

---

42. G. KENNAN, AMERICAN DIPLOMACY 1900-1950 95 (1951). Kennan's views about the role of international law seem to have mellowed somewhat since his classic criticism in *American Diplomacy 1900-1950*.
43. Remarks of the Honorable Dean Acheson, 1963 PROC. AM. SOC'Y INT'L L., 13, 14 (1963).
44. See H. C. DILLARD, note 12 *supra*, at 452.

tic legalism" and certain recent extravagances in American foreign policy.[45]

Rather than enter the fray over the accuracy of the conception of international law held by Kennan, Acheson, and other anti-legalists, I think that it may lead to a more sophisticated model, which will assist in refining agreement and disagreement, first to briefly explore the role of international law in conflict management from the perspective of the national security manager, and then to explore briefly risks and dangers inherent in the use of international law. From the perspective of the national security manager, the principal roles of international law in the management of international conflict would seem to include the following:

Pre-Conflict

I. International law is useful as an instrumental device for solution of international problems prior to their conflict-generation.

II. International law and its focus on the long-run stability and quality of the international milieu should enter into the determination of national interests and goals.

Conflict

III. An international-legal perspective can suggest a range of options and strategies for conflict management.

IV. Since violation of international law may be associated with substantial costs, particularly authority deflation, an international-legal approach is useful in appraising the costs of alternative actions and in maximizing the national authority position.

V. International law may assist in predicting responses to national action, in communicating intention, and in avoiding unintended escalation.

Post-Conflict

VI. International law provides a normative basis for assessing the international conduct of one's own and other states.

45. Falk, note 2 *supra*, at 924.

Briefly exploring each of these roles, one sees that, first, international law is useful as an instrumental device for solution of international problems prior to their conflict generation. As Richard Falk has eloquently argued, national policy-makers must be increasingly concerned with such international problems as overpopulation, resource conservation, pollution control, and the increasing gap between developed and developing nations.[46] Such problems are severe in their own right, but they may also be major contributors to international conflict. In addition, problems associated with strategic and conventional arms control and other more directly conflict-linked issues may have a dynamism of their own in contributing to increased conflict. International law and institutions provide an important instrumental tool for alleviating such international problems prior to their violent explosion. Recent examples have included the work of the functional agencies and the World Bank, the nuclear test ban treaty, and the nuclear non-proliferation treaty.

Second, international law and its focus on the long-run stability and quality of the international milieu should enter into the determination of national interests and goals. Stanley Hoffmann has pointed out that the national interest may include long-run milieu goals as well as more short-run possession goals. Though he has also argued that competitive pressures in a revolutionary international system tend to influence national decision-makers of even conservative states to downgrade the long-run milieu goals, it does not follow that the relative neglect of milieu goals is a good strategy for national decision-makers of either revolutionary or conservative powers.[47] Particularly in a nuclear and increasingly interdependent age, the kind of world order we would like to see established is an important part of the national interest. In fact,

46. Falk, note 2 *supra*, at 930-32.
47. See Hoffmann, note 34 *supra*, at 36-46. Hoffmann's later conclusion that: "the circumstances of the present system suggest a *downplaying* of formal law in the realm of peace-and-war issues, and an *upgrading* of more flexible techniques, until the system has become less fierce," does not necessarily follow from his analysis. At most he has simply demonstrated that the characteristics of the present international system contribute to the inadequacy of the present international law of conflict management. See Hoffmann, note 32 *supra*, at xviii-xix; Hoffmann, note 34 *supra*, at 31-32.

it seems probable that the most effective strategy for a conservative power in a revolutionary system is to emphasize world order goals even at the expense of short-run "possession" losses. This does not mean that the national interest requires pursuit of a policy of policeman for the world regardless of capability and power realities, but only that the stability and quality of the international system are an important part of the national interest. During the last decade, United States foreign policy has probably erred too much on the side of neglecting important long-run milieu interests rather than, as Kennan charged with reference to an earlier period, being preoccupied with a legalistic approach to world order. For example, the steady decline of the United Nations as an effective instrument for conflict management might have been substantially lessened, or even reversed, by an imaginative and more milieu oriented American foreign policy.

Third, an international-legal perspective can suggest a range of options and strategies for conflict management. National decision-makers who neglect a range of options for conflict avoidance and management would certainly not be as likely to perform satisfactorily as those who consider the full range of options. Yet failure to take an international-legal perspective into account has precisely that effect. A quick perusal of the literature of international law and international relations shows that the international lawyer is for the most part concerned with a different set of alternatives and strategies for world order than is the international relations theorist. That concern is typically characterized by a focus on long-run community common interest and on institutional alternatives. The international lawyer is concerned with the uses of the United Nations Secretary General, Security Council, and General Assembly, and with the potential of regional systems such as the Organization of American States or the Organization of African Unity.[48] He may also focus on third-party

48. Even while downplaying the role of international law in the Cuban missile crisis, Dean Acheson recognized its usefulness as a strategy for conflict management. Thus he pointed out:
  [I]n the action taken in the Cuban quarantine, one can see the influence of accepted legal principles. These principles are procedural devices designed to reduce the severity of a possible clash. Those devices cause wise delay before drastic action, create

techniques for dispute settlement and for alternatives to uni-lateral action. As such, an international-legal perspective offers access to an important range of options and strategies for con-flict management. It is also frequently a repository of past experi-ence in dealing with international problems which can shed sig-nificant light on current issues and help avoid resolving all issues anew. That some tools in the international lawyers' kit are rusty or impractical does not mean that others may not be effective and frequently preferable alternatives for conflict management.

Fourth, since violation of international law may be associated with substantial costs, particularly authority deflation, an inter-national-legal approach is useful in appraising the costs of al-ternative actions and in maximizing the national authority posi-tion. Violation of international law can have both long-run and short-run costs: long-run costs in undermining the stability and quality of the international milieu and in encouraging reciprocal non-compliance, and short-run costs particularly in international and domestic authority deflation translatable into a reduction in power. A central feature of the international-legal system is rec-iprocity. As a result, arguments used by the United States in the Cuban missile crisis may also be available to the Soviet Union in complaining of nuclear missiles in Turkey or West Germany. An international-legal perspective should provide a sensitivity to pos-sible reciprocal claims and to the common interest in long-run stability and quality of the international order.[49]

Even in the short run, however, violation of international law can have real costs. First, there is always the possibility of effec-tive community action against the law-breaker, though as a result of their great influence and their "veto" in the United Nations

---

a "cooling off" period, permit the consideration of others' views. The importance of the Organization of American States was also procedural, and emphasized the desirability of collective action, thus creating a common denominator of action. Some of these desirable consequences are familiar to us in the domestic indus-trial area.

Remarks of the Honorable Dean Acheson, note 43 *supra*, at 14.

49. The best statement of the importance of sensitivity to reciprocal claims in framing national policy is Ehrlich, *The Measuring Line of Occasion,* 3 STANFORD JOURNAL OF INTERNATIONAL STUDIES 27 (1968).

Security Council, this risk would be remote with respect to the superpowers. In the absence of any such dramatic sanction there are nevertheless other costs associated with violation of authoritative community expectations. Chief among them is the domestic and international authority deflation usually associated with international-law violation. If there are widespread domestic expectations that national decision-makers have acted illegally, the consensus and ultimately the power base for the national action may be eroded. It is not superfluous that critics of particular national actions attempt to escalate their criticism to claims of illegality. The anti-war Lawyers Committee on American Policy Toward Vietnam ran an advertisement in *The New York Times* seeking to persude a mass audience that United States action in Vietnam was illegal.[50] Conversely, governmental spokesmen sometimes sought to override arguments against United States policy by arguing that the United States was legally obligated to defend South Vietnam by the SEATO Treaty. Whatever the merits of their arguments, the point is that critics and government spokesmen alike perceived that domestic perceptions of authority were a real source of power.

Internationally, violation of international law has the same effect. For example, it seems probable that one of the reasons President Kennedy backed down at the time of the abortive United States-sponsored Bay of Pigs invasion was his realization of the weakness of the United States authority position in a blatantly illegal posture. International perceptions of authority are translatable into power relations in a host of ways, including the amount of assistance from allies and the amount of assistance to opposition forces. There *is* a functioning international constitutive process of authoritative decision, and national decision-makers who ignore it or imprecisely dismiss it as "mere public opinion" may not be as realistic as they believe.

Even when national action is lawful, an international-legal perspective may be indispensable in maximizing the national authority position. Since rhetoric and claims of illegality can be tools of adversary argument, a government which neglects interna-

---

50. See the nearly full-page advertisement "U.S. Intervention in Vietnam is Illegal," N.Y. Times, Jan. 15, 1967, at E 9.

tional-legal considerations in the exploration and execution of its policies is unnecessarily weakening its position. This may have been one of the greatest costs to United States foreign policy from the failure to systematically take into account an international-legal perspective. The recent Cambodian operation, though lawful, provides an excellent example of costs unnecessarily incurred through failure to adequately focus on an international-legal perspective, particularly in the neglect to obtain an explicit and public prior Cambodian consent to the action and in the omission of reasons rooted in international-legal considerations in public explanations of the action.[51]

Fifth, international law may assist in predicting responses to national action, in communicating intention, and in avoiding unintentional escalation. Since one of the functions of international law is to establish stability of expectations in transnational interactions, the relative compliance of a policy option with international law may assist in predicting other actors' perceptions and likely responses should it be adopted. Though the multiplicity of factors relevant to third-party response would make myopic reliance on international-legal rights alone a dangerous exercise, in general, action which is unambiguously unlawful would seem more likely to draw a counter-reaction than action which is unambiguously lawful. The language of international law may also be useful in communicating important national interests and limited objectives of national action in order to minimize unintended conflict. Treaties such as NATO (and even SEATO) convey a conception of national interest indicating likely counter-reaction from encroachment and such communications, once made, assume an additional credibility by the reciprocally perceived need to back up one's most formal signals in order not to denigrate the future credibility of such signals. Needless to say, this effect also suggests the need to be particularly thoughtful and cautious in sending such signals and conversely not failing to send them when they actually reflect national policy (as may have been a contributing factor in inducing the Korean war). The language of international law may also make clear that one's objectives are

---

51. See the discussion of these costs in Moore, *Legal Dimensions of the Decision to Intercede in Cambodia*, 65 AM. J. INT'L L. 38 (1971).

limited, thus reducing the possibility of escalation through an opponent's miscalculation of objectives. On the advice of the State Department Legal Adviser, the United States naval action in the Cuban missile crisis was referred to as a "quarantine" rather than as a "blockade," in order to reduce the risk that the action would be perceived as an act of war. Similarly, clear characterization of the United States Cambodian incursion as "interdiction of unlawful belligerent activities on neutral territory" might have assisted in communicating the limited objectives of the incursion.[52]

Sixth, international law provides a normative basis for assessing the international conduct of one's own and other states. Though other perspectives are useful, if not indispensable, in assessing international conduct, international law frequently provides a rich background of practice and thought relative to normative judgment of state conduct. Its reference is to long-run community common interest, and its sources transcend the parochial identifications of policy-makers from any one nation.

These six ways in which international law is important from the perspective of the national decision-maker suggest that the anti-legalists have overstated the case in dismissing or even condemning an international-legal perspective. To complete the picture, however, it may be useful to articulate more fully the dangers with which the anti-legalists are concerned, and to see if any fundamental inconsistency remains. The principle dangers in unsophisticated application of an international-legal approach seem to be:

1. preoccupation with long-run milieu interests (or more simplistically preoccupation with legal rhetoric) at the expense of more complete assessment of national interests and capabilities, both short- and long-term;

2. pursuit of policies or goals which are unattainable or otherwise unrealistic in the present international system (for example, advocacy of submission of the Vietnam dispute to the International Court of Justice);

3. overzealous adherence to "legalism" when such adherence would damage the international system (for example, too in-

52. See the discussion of this point in Moore, note 51 *supra*.

sistent pursuit of the Article 19 loss of vote for arrears in financial contributions when continued insistence would damage the United Nations more than non-compliance with Article 19);

4. the simplistic equating of the lawfulness of a course of action with action in the national interest;

5. reliance on pre-realist conceptions of international law which conceive international law as a static body of rules and which overemphasize the patterns of control available for enforcement of authoritative community expectations;

6. the danger that perceptions (or misperceptions) concerning international legal rights will serve to inflame or sustain conflict, as for example when both sides perceive the other as an aggressor and the conflict becomes one for vindication of international law.

Most of these dangers are suggested by a sympathetic reading of Kennan, Morgenthau, Acheson, Kissinger, and Hoffmann, and they undoubtedly have substance. In fact, some legalist writing continues to exhibit most of these tendencies. The critical point, however, which the anti-legalists have not made, is that none of these defects, with the possible exception of the last, is inherent in a reasonably sophisticated legal approach such as is the daily grist in most of our major law schools today. They are simply dangers in *unsophisticated* application of an international-legal approach. It would not seem difficult to compile a comparable list of the dangers inherent in unsophisticated application of systems or historical-sociological approaches to international relations. A mix of perspectives would seem healthier for the national security process than the dominance of any one tradition.

The anti-legalists were correct in warning of the dangers in simplistic preoccupation with an international-legal approach. Nevertheless, the conclusions which they drew as to the irrelevance of an international-legal perspective were as erroneous as the extreme legalism which they condemned. More precise focus on both the importance and the limitations of international law is a more reliable guide to exploration of the proper role of international law in national security decisions.

*The Structure of the National Security Process
for Effectively taking an International-Legal
Perspective into Account*

If an international-legal perspective is a useful perspective in considering national security issues, some attention should be given to the mechanism by which it is taken into account in the national security process. Partly through lack of advertence to the problem and perhaps also partly through widespread acceptance of the anti-legalist position among senior policy-planners, at the present time there is no way in which international law is systematically introduced into the policy-planning process, although international relations and military and economic traditions are more or less systematically heard. This is not to suggest that as a nation we have less concern for international law than other nations. Failure to structure the foreign policy process to systematically take account of international-legal perspectives seems to be the norm among nations. It is, however, to suggest that we are needlessly and seriously weakening our foreign policy and our national security by failing to take action to correct the situation. Recently Richard Falk has suggested an Attorney General for International Affairs who would provide legal advice to the President at the cabinet level.[53] For reasons elaborated elsewhere, it has seemed to me that a more useful and realistic way of systematically introducing an international-legal perspective would be to upgrade the State Department Legal Adviser to Under-Secretary of State for International Legal Affairs, and to place him on the National Security Council as an *ex officio* member. It would also seem useful to create a new presidential advisory position whose incumbent might be called "Assistant to the President for International-Legal Affairs," and to add similar advisers to the staffs of the Senate and House Foreign Relations Committees.[54] Finally, it would probably be worth while to undertake a review of the adequacy of international legal services at lower levels in the national security process, particularly with respect to the ade-

53. See Falk, note 2 *supra*, at 930.
54. See Moore, *The Control of Foreign Intervention in Internal Conflict*, 9 VA. J. INT'L L. 209, 310-314 (1969).

quacy of coordination of effort and the ways in which such perspectives are systematically presented to policy-makers.[55]

Alternative Approaches to International Law

An important undercurrent in the debate about the role of international law in the management of international conflict has been the controversy concerning alternative approaches to international law. One consequence of this controversy has been that assessment of the role and importance of international law tends to be significantly shaped by one's assessment of the state of international-legal theory and one's commitment to the viability of one or another jurisprudential tradition. Stanley Hoffmann cites as one major factor in the decline in the study of international law by social scientists:

> A sense of the futility of traditional methods of teaching international law. Social scientists are impatient with a discipline that seems to focus exclusively either on a closed universe of norms—their logical consequences, their hierarchy, their interconnections—divorced from the political and social universe in which they appear and which they try to regulate, or on doctrinal interpretations and desiderata that, while they take political and social purposes into account, represent only the idiosyncratic views of irrelevant if respectable writers.[56]

Hoffmann's statement reflects the post-legal-realist vision predominant in the United States since the 1940s and echoes the legal realists from the great German jurist Von Jhering,[57] who thoughtfully equipped lawyers' heaven with a hair-splitting machine, to Myres S. McDougal, who stresses the study of law in its political

55. For example, it might be worthwhile to examine the kinds of issues which do or should receive Legal Adviser clearance within the Department of State and the coordination between the Legal Adviser's office in the State Department and other departments such as the Defense Department.
56. Hoffmann, *The Study of International Law and the Theory of International Relations*, 1963 PROC. AM. SOC'Y INT'L L., 26 (1963), *reprinted* in S. HOFFMANN, THE STATE OF WAR 123, 123-24 (1965).
57. See VON JHERING, IM JURISTISCHEN BEGRIFFSHIMMEL, IN SCHERZ UND ERNST IN DER JURISPRUDENZ 245 (11th ed. 1912).

and social context.[58] As such, his concern with "traditional methods of teaching international law" is in significant measure out of date, at least as applied to the teaching of international law in major law schools in the United States. Though there are pockets of Kelsenian holdouts, most international lawyers would agree that international law and its study should be functional, in the sense that law should be explicitly policy- and goal-oriented; contextual, in the dual sense that law should be studied as part of its political and social context and that law should be analyzed by isolating issues which raise common policies and conditioning factors (perhaps the most important insight of the legal realists); inter-disciplinary, in the sense that legal research and analysis should be consciously data-sharing; and process-oriented, in the sense that law can most usefully be treated as a process rather than a hierarchical set of rules. It is no accident that what is perhaps the most important contemporary jurisprudential tradition in international law in the United States, the approach of Myres S. McDougal and Harold Lasswell, embodies these insights more systematically than other approaches.[59]

The McDougal-Lasswell system would seem to be broadly compatible with Hoffmann's own interest in a historical-sociological approach, interdisciplinary collaboration between international lawyers and international relations theorists, impatience with a focus on "a closed universe of norms," and call for stress on "underlying political realities."[60] Surprisingly though, Hoffmann indicates an uneasiness with the McDougal-Lasswell approach,[61] an uneasiness which is articulated more completely by Richard Falk, a former student of McDougal, when he says:

> The point of this excursion into the vulnerability of international law to *ex parte* manipulation is to give some sense of what is involved in affirming or repudiating a modernist

---

58. See, *e.g.*, Lasswell & McDougal, *Legal Education and Public Policy*, 52 YALE L.J. 203 (1943); McDougal, *Jurisprudence for a Free Society*, 1 GEORGIA L. REV. 1 (1966).

59. For an introduction to the jurisprudence of Myres McDougal and Harold Lasswell see Moore, *Prolegomenon to the Jurisprudence of Myres McDougal and Harold Lasswell*, 54 VA. L. REV. 662 (1968).

60. See Hoffmann, notes 20 and 56 *supra*.

61. See, *e.g.*, Hoffmann, note 34 *supra*, at 31.

approach of the sort advocated by McDougal. It becomes clear that a stress on openness accentuates the potentiality for plausible manipulation of legal rights and duties by powerful, anarchistic, or desperate states. At the same time such openness impairs the capacity of legal criteria to provide the organized international community with impartial yardsticks by which to measure its response to crisis and conflict, and thereby to legitimize its own role in resolving international disputes and to make possible a clear decision achieved after minimum debate. The Kelsenian image of law as a restraint system generating relatively clear criteria to assess legality serves well, it would seem, certain of the most crucial needs of international life, especially those arising out of the use of force by one state against another. In contrast, the McDougalian image is at once too complex and too vague to provide guidance either to national actors or to global institutions.[62]

It is understandable that the rigor and unfamiliarity of the McDougal-Lasswell jurisprudence, coupled with McDougal's own outspoken defense of many United States policies, might lead to an uneasiness concerning the manipulative potential of the system. Nevertheless, the uneasiness of Hoffmann and Falk is misplaced; worse, by unwillingness to accept their own premises concerning the dangers in closed rule systems, they encourage regression to a less useful conception of international law. Falk's statement suggests that there is somehow greater certainty and less chance of partisan manipulation in a Kelsenian rule-orientation than in an explicitly policy-oriented system. Though superficially plausible, a principal message of the legal realist movement was that in general this simply is not so. In fact, Professor Brainerd Currie won the first Order of the Coif Prize awarded for outstanding legal scholarship (roughly the equivalent of a hypothetical Pulitzer prize for law) for his work in demonstrating that the certainty offered by the rigid *Restatement* approach to

---

62. Falk, "The Relevance of Political Context to the Nature and Functioning of International Law: An Intermediate View," in K. DEUTSCH & S. HOFFMANN, THE RELEVANCE OF INTERNATIONAL LAW 132, 140 (1968).

conflict of laws was only illusory and that his more flexible "governmental interest analysis" approach was a preferable alternative.[63] Moreover, McDougal simply offers a more sophisticated range of analytic tools. If it is concluded that certain features of a problem require a limited number of hard and fast rules, there is nothing in the system which would prevent it. Falk's example of the rule prohibiting resort to force as one which requires such a Kelsenian approach, however, is an unpersuasive choice. For example, an absolute rule focusing on initial resort to armed territorial incursion would be of rather negligible value in deterring or assessing impermissible conduct in the context of the 1967 Arab-Israeli war. The whole history of the attempt at a simple definition of aggression divorced from context suggests the folly of the traditional approaches to which Falk would return. It should be remembered that any jurisprudential approach may be used for either scholarship or advocacy. The real test is whether the approach offers real potential for intellectual clarification when used for scholarship. In this, the McDougal-Lasswell approach excels.

The point of this excursion into jurisprudential intricacy is not to defend a particular jurisprudential system, however defensible, but to point out that maximization of the role of international law in world affairs is linked with discarding outmoded notions about law and adopting the principal insights of the post-legal-realist mainstream, whether incorporated into the McDougal-Lasswell jurisprudence or some other. Hoffmann is right that upgrading the role of international law in the management of international conflict is importantly linked with a viable jurisprudence of international law. International lawyers now have the tools for such a jurisprudence and happily are increasingly putting them to work.

63. See B. CURRIE, SELECTED ESSAYS IN THE CONFLICT OF LAWS (1963). Professor Falk's own creative, contextual and policy-oriented approach suggests that he is not really persuaded of the superior merits of a Kelsenian system. See, *e.g.*, Falk, *The Beirut Raid and the International Law of Retaliation*, 63 AM. J. INT'L L. 415 (1969); Falk, *International Law and the United States Role in the Viet Nam War*, 75 YALE L.J. 1122 (1966).

Conclusion

The controversy surrounding the role of law in the management of international conflict involves not one but a series of inter-related issues.[64] Both legalists and anti-legalists have contributed important insights to the understanding of these issues, but both extremes have pictured an incomplete model of the role of law. The legalists have tended to preoccupation with international adjudication and have often failed to take into account the realities of the international system. Despite these excesses, there are a range of important roles which international law plays in the present international system and should play in the consideration of national security issues. On the other hand, the anti-legalists have often attacked only caricatures of the legal system and have not sufficiently focused on the effects of violation of widespread authoritative expectations as controls on law-breaking. Their message of the dangers of abuse in unsophisticated application of international law, however, has merit. The development of more sophisticated and particularized models of the role of international law should assist in refining the agreement and disagreement between the two camps. In the process, it is to be hoped that traditional lines between international law and international relations will be increasingly discarded and that a meaningful cross-disciplinary dialogue can begin.

64. In addition to the authorities relied on throughout this Chapter see R. FALK, LAW, MORALITY AND WAR IN THE CONTEMPORARY WORLD (1963); R. FISHER, INTERNATIONAL CONFLICT 151-177 (1969); E. ROSTOW, LAW, POWER, AND THE PURSUIT OF PEACE (1968); Q. WRIGHT, THE ROLE OF INTERNATIONAL LAW IN THE ELIMINATION OF WAR (1961); Deutsch, "The Probability of International Law," in K. DEUTSCH & S. HOFFMANN, THE RELEVANCE OF INTERNATIONAL LAW 57 (1968); Fisher, "Bringing Law to Bear on Governments," in II R. FALK & S. MENDLOVITZ, THE STRATEGY OF WORLD ORDER, 75-85 (1966); Kaplan & Katzenbach, "Law in the International Community," in II R. FALK & S. MENDLOVITZ, THE STRATEGY OF WORLD ORDER, 18-44 (1966); Kelsen, "The Essence of International Law," in K. DEUTSCH & S. HOFFMANN, THE RELEVANCE OF INTERNATIONAL LAW 85 (1968).

CHAPTER II

Prolegomenon to the Jurisprudence of
Myres McDougal and Harold Lasswell*

IF a Benjamin Cardozo or a Jerome Frank were to spend a few weeks browsing in any of today's good law schools, he would be enthusiastic about the rising tide of "social consciousness." The trend in legal education and student interest is toward involvement with such major social problems as the inequality of treatment accorded the black man, poverty, war and revolution, urban blight, crime and reform of the criminal process, and the challenges to human dignity presented by an exploding technology.[1] Law has begun unmistakably, even if erratically, a fundamental transition from a self-contained and sometimes irrelevant discipline to a socially conscious discipline which has the potential to play a leading role in the amelioration of major social concerns. Though our observers might be justifiably exasperated at the slowness of the transition, which was also underway in their day, they would find the recent acceleration of the trend encouraging. But in another respect they would almost certainly be disappointed, for law today largely lacks the jurisprudential spark and excitement that prevailed at the height of the legal-realist movement during the 1920s and 1930s. Today there is little disagreement that judges are men, that legal rules do not automatically decide cases, and that law is a tool for achieving social goals rather than a brooding omnipresence in the sky. And, from the perspective of the law teacher, the teaching of "black letter law" has become a sign of academic inferiority, except (as myth has it) for a few Harvard holdouts. But most of this realism, no

*Thanks are due to Professor Thomas F. Bergin of the University of Virginia Law School, Professor Mary Ellen Caldwell of the Ohio State College of Law, and Professor W. Michael Reisman of the Yale Law School, all of whom read the manuscript of this chapter and offered helpful suggestions.

1. See generally *Report of the Committee on Curriculum*, 1968 PROCEEDINGS OF THE AALS 7 (1968); *Report of the Curriculum Committee*, 1966 PROCEEDINGS OF THE AALS 37 (1966).

matter how necessary, has been nihilistic. And the very success of an essentially negative legal realism has led to a puzzlement about where we go from here that has infected most of the legal world. All too often the answer seems to be that a diffuse and ill-defined policy approach replaces a rigorous but frequently irrelevant analytic approach.

There are a few legal scholars today, however, whose creative work offers positive direction and an exciting jurisprudential challenge.[2] Perhaps the most influential of these scholars are

2. As the principal sources of jurisprudential excitement today, I would list the McDougal-Lasswell policy-oriented jurisprudence, the "new analytical school" and the "new natural law school." And, though not a school of jurisprudence, certainly the related "neutral principles" and "political question" debates concerned with the justification and limits of judicial review should be included in this list. Of the "schools," it seems to me that all offer significant insights. For that reason it does not seem that a choice need be made among them. The principal problem common to all "schools" may be how to increase the interaction among them.

With respect to the "new analytical school" see, *e.g.*, *Symposium, The Philosophy of H.L.A. Hart*, 35 U. CHI. L. REV. 1 (1967); R. Summers, *The New Analytical Jurists*, 41 N.Y.U.L. REV. 861 (1966); R. Dworkin, *Does Law Have a Function? A Comment on The Two-Level Theory of Decision*, 74 YALE L.J. 640 (1965).

With respect to the "new natural law school" see, *e.g.*, L. FULLER, THE MORALITY OF LAW (1964); H. DILLARD, SOME ASPECTS OF LAW AND DIPLOMACY (1957), *reprinted from* 91 HAGUE ACADEMY RECUEIL DES COURS 447 (1957); Dillard, *Law and Conflict: Some Current Dilemmas*, 24 WASH. & LEE L. REV. 177 (1967); *Symposium, The Morality of Law*, 10 VILL. L. REV. 624 (1965).

With respect to the "neutral principles" debate see, *e.g.*, Wechsler, *The Myth of Neutrality in Constitutional Adjudication*, 73 HARV. L. REV. 1 (1959); Pollak, *Racial Discrimination and Judicial Integrity: A Reply to Professor Wechsler*, 108 U. PA. L. REV. 1 (1959); Miller & Howell, *The Myth of Neutrality in Constitutional Adjudication*, 27 U. CHI. L. REV. 661 (1960). With respect to the "political question" discussions see, *e.g.*, A. BICKEL, THE LEAST DANGEROUS BRANCH (1962); Scharpf, *Judicial Review and the Political Question: A Functional Analysis*, 75 YALE L.J. 517 (1966).

There are, of course, as always individual scholars who do not fit neatly into any of these "schools" but whose creative work offers exceptional insight and stirs considerable excitement. Brainerd Currie's "governmental interest analysis" theory in conflict of laws is a prime example. And to mention a few recent articles in this catagory from one area with which I am familiar see Michelman, *Property, Utility, and Fairness: Comments on the Ethical Foundations of "Just Compensation" Law*, 80

Myres S. McDougal and Harold D. Lasswell, who, in a distinguished series of major books with a number of talented colleagues, have put together a comprehensive jurisprudence which has had a profound impact on post-legal-realist thinking.[3]

The philosophical underpinnings of the McDougal-Lasswell jurisprudence are broadly eclectic. Among the principal influences, however, would certainly be listed the entire legal-realist movement and the work being carried on in a host of social science disciplines, particularly work in description of social process, decision theory, and communication theory. The McDougal-Lasswell jurisprudence is broader than the traditional schools of

---

HARV. L. REV. 1165 (1967); Reich, *The New Property*, 73 YALE L.J. 733 (1964).

3. Myres S. McDougal is Sterling Professor of Law at Yale Law School and is a former president of the Association of American Law Schools and the American Society of International Law. Harold D. Lasswell is Phelps Professor of Law and Political Science at Yale Law School, is a former president of the American Political Science Association and is the current president of the American Society of International Law. The principal books using the McDougal-Lasswell system are: M. McDOUGAL, H. LASSWELL & J. MILLER, THE INTERPRETATION OF AGREEMENTS AND WORLD PUBLIC ORDER (1967); L. CHEN & H. LASSWELL, FORMOSA, CHINA, AND THE UNITED NATIONS (1967); B. MURTY, THE IDEOLOGICAL INSTRUMENT OF COERCION AND WORLD PUBLIC ORDER (1967); D. JOHNSTON, THE INTERNATIONAL LAW OF FISHERIES (1965); M. McDOUGAL, H. LASSWELL, & I. VLASIC, LAW AND PUBLIC ORDER IN SPACE (1963); M. McDOUGAL & W. BURKE, THE PUBLIC ORDER OF THE OCEANS: A CONTEMPORARY INTERNATIONAL LAW OF THE SEA (1962); R. ARENS & H. LASSWELL, IN DEFENSE OF PUBLIC ORDER (1961); M. McDOUGAL & F. FELICIANO, LAW AND MINIMUM WORLD PUBLIC ORDER: THE LEGAL REGULATION OF INTERNATIONAL COERCION (1961); M. McDOUGAL & ASSOCIATES, STUDIES IN WORLD PUBLIC ORDER (1960); H. LASSWELL & A. KAPLAN, POWER AND SOCIETY (1950).

Other books are in the works now, notably a book on the world constitutive process of authoritative decision with Harold Lasswell and Michael Reisman. For an introduction see McDougal, Lasswell & Reisman, *The World Constitutive Process of Authoritative Decision*, 19 J. LEGAL ED. 253, 403 (1967).

See also M. McDOUGAL & D. HABER, PROPERTY, WEALTH, LAND: ALLOCATION, PLANNING AND DEVELOPMENT (1948). The McDougal and Haber book is to my knowledge the only casebook explicitly using the system although many casebooks have been influenced by the system. Though the book has never been widely adopted it is still in many ways ahead of its day twenty years after it was written.

jurisprudence and encompasses not only a theory about law, but also a means of describing social process and the role of law within it, techniques for systematic research into legal problems, and a framework for analysis of theories about law. It is made up of a variety of different insights and analytic tools which together are usually termed the McDougal-Lasswell "system," but which individually often have a life of their own.[4]

An overriding characteristic of the system is the use of a meta-linguistic terminology for assistance in carrying out the sophisticated tasks performed by the system. This use of a precise meta-language for analysis is both one of the greatest strengths of the system and one of the greatest causes of popular misunderstanding of the system.[5] A meta-language in its classic sense is a linguistic system for precise definition of another language. Though the lawyer has had little occasion to become familiar with the con-

---

4. Probably the best introductory treatments of the McDougal-Lasswell jurisprudence are: McDougal, *Jurisprudence for a Free Society*, 1 GA. L. REV. 1 (1966); Lasswell & McDougal, *Jurisprudence in Policy-Oriented Perspective*, 19 U. FLA. L. REV. 486 (1967); McDougal, Lasswell & Reisman, *supra* note 3; Feliciano, *Book Review*, 68 YALE L.J. 1039 (1959).

Other basic writings about the system are McDougal & Reisman, *"The Changing Structure of International Law" Unchanging Theory for Inquiry*, 65 COL. L. REV. 810 (1965); McDougal, *The Ethics of Applying Systems of Authority: The Balanced Opposites of a Legal System* in H. LASSWELL & H. CLEVELAND, THE ETHICS OF POWER (1962); McDougal, *Some Basic Theoretical Concepts about International Law: A Policy-Oriented Framework of Inquiry*, 4 JOURNAL OF CONFLICT RESOLUTION 337 (1960); McDougal & Lasswell, *The Identification and Appraisal of Diverse Systems of Public Order*, 53 AM. J. INT'L L. 1 (1959); Lasswell, *The Public Interest: Proposing Principles of Content & Procedure*, NOMOS V: THE PUBLIC INTEREST 54 (1962); McDougal, *Law as a Process of Decision—A Policy-Oriented Approach to Legal Study*, 1 NATURAL LAW FORUM 53 (1956); Lasswell, *The Interrelations of World Organization and Society*, 55 YALE L.J. 870 (1946); Lasswell & McDougal, *Legal Education and Public Policy: Professional Training in the Public Interest*, 52 YALE L.J. 203 (1943); McDougal, *Fuller v. The American Realists*, 50 YALE L. REV. 827 (1940-41).

5. The best introduction to the meta-language of the McDougal-Lasswell system is an unpublished learning program in the Yale Law Library called "The Scharpf Learning Program." The introductory treatments of the system cited in note 4 *supra* also provide an introduction to the meta-language. For greater detail see also H. LASSWELL & A. KAPLAN, POWER AND SOCIETY (1950).

cept, in other disciplines it has become an indispensable tool. For example, the computer programmer relies heavily on a meta-language called Backus Normal Form to achieve precise syntactic description of the programming language by which he instructs the computer. The use of this BNF language has become indispensable for achieving the precision required in his task. The McDougal-Lasswell system utilizes a specialized vocabulary for theorizing about law and for exploring and analyzing the role of law in social process, a vocabulary which is closely analogous to a meta-language. In fact, one of the insights of the system is to insist on clarity of distinction between theories about law and theories of law, which is another way of expressing this distinction between a language or theory used for analysis and the language or system being analyzed.

An example of this meta-linguistic usage is the breakdown of "law" into patterns of "authority" and patterns of "control." "Authority" is used to signify community expectations about how decisions should be made and about which established community decision-makers should make them. Decisions made in conformance with community expectations about proper decision and proper decision-makers, as distinguished from decisions based on mere naked power, are said to be authoritative.[6] "Control" is used to signify that a decision is backed by effective sanction. Using these terms some of the classic jurisprudential debates about the nature of "law" can be recast as whether there can be law without authority (e.g., was Nazi law really law in the absence of widespread expectations about proper decision?) or whether there can be law without control (e.g., is the international norm prohibiting the use of force as an instrument of national policy really law in the absence of a controlling sanction?). The analytic concepts "authority" and "control," which are key decision concepts of the McDougal-Lasswell system, expose these dimensions of the traditional debate as largely sterile. Whether or not one postulates any particular combination of authority and control as the most useful definition of law for a particular pur-

6. For a somewhat related analysis of the meaning of authority see Friedrich, *Authority, Reason, and Discretion* in AUTHORITY (Friedrich ed. 1958).

pose, the observer of the legal system must be concerned both with patterns of authority and patterns of control. The traditional debate obscured this distinction. Explicit focus on the distinction has already had a substantial liberating influence on legal scholars concerned with international law.

Similarly, the meta-linguistic concepts "perspectives" and "operations" provide a valuable tool for evaluation of theories about law. "Perspectives" are defined to include the rules or norms of the legal system. "Operations" are the actual practices of that system. Armed with these concepts, the legal-realist-positivist debates about the meaning of law are sharpened. Were the legal-realists so concerned with "what courts do in fact," i.e., "operations," that they downgraded too much the effect of rules in influencing decision? Or were the positivists too concerned with rules and wordplay, i.e., "perspectives," to understand the law as applied by judges who were always faced with the necessity of choice not dictated by any logical system?

Another important tenet of the system is that law is a process. That is, law is not merely rules, it is not merely judges or courts, or, as Holmes suggested, what courts do in fact. Instead, if our concern is understanding and accurately describing the role of law in society, the most useful conception of law is a broad one encompassing the entire process by which judges, legislators, litigants, and many others pursue particular values through the whole panoply of authoritative community decision-making. This tenet is used with the key decision concepts of authority and control and perspectives and operations to provide a basis for appraisal of theories about law (schools of jurisprudence).

McDougal and Lasswell also emphasize that law as an on-going process is located in a larger social context. Law as a normative and social science is concerned with social interaction, and legal problems are generally attributable to the broader social setting in which they always occur. Yet traditional legal parlance and modes of legal analysis provide no tools for systematically describing social process and the role of law within it. As a result, McDougal and Lasswell have constructed a framework consisting of interpenetrating processes to facilitate more accurate description and analysis of the role of law in society. Their starting point for description of social process is "the world community process" or the total "big blooming ongoing confusion" which is the reality of global interaction. For convenience in study, this global process, which may be thought of as the total pie of social interaction, may be sliced by value processes such as the "wealth" or "power" processes and further subdivided politically as, for example, by the "national power process." Each process is marked off for convenience in study, and it is recognized that in other ways such division may be arbitrary.

It is further recognized that other ways of slicing the pie may also be useful depending on what one intends to study. Since legal scholars and political scientists are concerned particularly with the application of community power, the most useful slice for their study is "the effective power process," or that part of the ongoing social process concerned with making and enforcing decisions of community wide effect. And since legal scholars are also particularly concerned with patterns of "authority" as this term is used in its meta-linguistic sense, the system marks off for special study within "the effective power process," a process termed the process of authoritative decision. The authoritative decision process is the on-going authoritative application of power we call law. And within this process, the system marks off the process by which this authoritative decision process is created, maintained, modified, and terminated. This last process is termed the "constitutive process of authoritative decision."[7] The concept of "constitutive process" is a fundamental insight which permits more sophisticated analysis of such problems as the classic problem of the sources of international law. Instead of focusing only on the incomplete generalities of Article 38 of the Statute of the International Court of Justice for an understanding of the sources of international law, the scholar is offered a map of the world constitutive process detailing the range of participants in the making of international law and their characteristics.

Decisions which establish or otherwise affect the authoritative decision process are "constitutive decisions." Decisions without constitutive impact which flow from the constitutive process and

7. For a detailed description of the "constitutive process" see M. Mc-Dougal, H. Lasswell & M. Reisman, *supra* note 3.

which affect other value allocations in the community, i.e., which affect other slices of the pie, are termed "public order decisions." Hence the "public order" designation in the title of many of the books using the system. Though delineation of these interpenetrating processes tends to look artificial, in fact it provides an invaluable tool for understanding law by locating legal process in its broadest social context.

In addition to the schematization of interpenetrating social processes, McDougal and Lasswell have also developed techniques for describing any inter-personal interaction. These techniques result from the same need for an adequate description of social process which can most usefully be adapted to legal problems. Though as individuals we talk about particular interactions every day (for example the seizure of the *Pueblo* by North Korea), we are sadly lacking in adequate language in everyday speech for systematically describing them. As a result, systematic inquiry into social interaction requires that an appropriate language be formulated to call attention to the range of relevant variables evident in any such interaction. The principal workhorses of the system for meeting this need are "value analysis" and "phase analysis," each of which may be more or less useful for analysis of a particular interaction. Like the schematization of the interpenetrating processes, each looks artificial and arbitrary unless one is aware of its function as a checklist for the systematic analysis of context. Value analysis breaks down a process of interaction by reference to the principal values sought, of which eight are currently employed: power, enlightenment, wealth, well-being, skill, affection, respect, and rectitude. The eight categories have no magical quality and are chosen for their convenience in analysis of social process. Phase analysis breaks down a process of interaction by component elements and sequence. The phases in current use are eight: the *participants* in the process; the *perspectives* of the participants; the *situations*, geographical and temporal, in which the participants are interacting; the means or *base values* which the participants have available for achieving their objectives; the manner or *strategies* by which these means are employed by the participants; the immediate *outcomes* of the process of interaction; the longer range *effects* of the interaction;

and the broader context of *conditions* in which the process of interaction takes place. Again, there is nothing magical about these categories. They are selected for their broad utility in describing any process of interaction.[8]

8. The concept of phase analysis is particularly flexible and has substantial utility even apart from other features of the system. Legal rules may be said to be a relationship between context (some feature of the real-world) and consequence. As such they may be cast in "if-then" form. That is, "if X then Y," where X represents some feature of the real-world and Y represents the consequence flowing from its presence or absence. When in "if X then Y" form, legal rules are good or bad depending at least on whether or not the feature of the context chosen to represent X is a feature whose presence or absence is important or decisive for policy realization. But all too frequently complex legal problems are approached with a kind of single factor analysis which implicitly assumes that only one feature is important for policy realization. Such analysis may lead to over-simplified legal rules such as the classic rule of international law that it is always lawful to render military assistance to a widely recognized government or the current response advocated by some contemporary scholars, who are rightly concerned with the abuses of the traditional rule, that neither side engaged in civil strife can lawfully be aided. "X" in the traditional norm represents the single contextual feature of recognition. The resulting rule neglects the great range of other contextual variables which are important for policy realization with respect to community "intervention" norms, and it is not surprising that the rule is under assault. Similarly the newer neutral non-intervention norm does not escape the undue emphasis on the widely recognized government-insurgents distinction of the traditional rule and is also suspect.

Systematic application of phase analysis to the process of intervention reveals the great range of variables which may be important in formulating a more responsive normative framework. For example, who the participants are is certainly important for determination of legitimacy. Is the intervention under the auspices of the United Nations, collective intervention pursuant to a regional arrangement, or unilateral? Certainly the objectives of the intervening parties are important. Is assistance rendered for territorial conquest, protection of nationals, or humanitarian concern with the slaughter of minorities? What are the strategies employed in the intervention? Are they economic aid or military advisers or regular combat troops? And similarly, the arenas, base values, outcomes, effects and conditions of the process may suggest other features important for policy realization. Recognition of the government assisted turns out on close analysis to be only one such feature (it would be picked up under the heading base values) in a systematic phase analysis of the process of intervention.

Because legal rules depend on their relationship to context, a tool such as phase analysis which expedites systematic exploration of context is a

Though some of the terminological difficulty of the McDougal-Lasswell system stems from the techniques for slicing social process and for evaluating theories about law, probably the greatest source of confusion for the uninitiated is this use of "phase analysis" and "value analysis." This may be because much of the rest of the meta-language of the system can easily be misunderstood as simply a pedantic use of language with which the reader is familiar. But since "phase" and "value analysis" are often used in outline form as headings, no such false comfort is available, and the terms are frequently rejected out of hand as arbitrary, repetitive, and proof positive of a Benthamite language difficulty. "Phase" and "value analysis," however, are intended as analytic tools for exploration of context, and their utility is substantial.

In addition to phase and value analysis, a third method of slicing a process of interaction used by McDougal and Lasswell is the slicing of the decision process by "authority functions." This breakdown is a refined and much more useful counterpart of Montesquieu's famous institutional division of legislative, executive, and judicial. One of the difficulties of the Montesquieu division always has been that there is a substantial overlap in functions performed by each branch. No branch of government has performed solely a making or an applying or an enforcing function. When the emergence of new governmental institutions in the early part of this century threatened to blur the traditional institutional distinction, a fourth category, "administrative," was added in frank recognition of this fact. But more fundamentally, the Montesquieu division, even as modified by the administrative category, did not achieve any real focus either on the range of functions being performed in the legal process or on the diversity of the institutions performing those functions. This failure was far more than a failure to focus on the justification and limits of judicial review which in recent years has stimulated such useful debate and which certainly has transcended the Montesquieu framework.

particularly useful tool for the legal scholar. Again, we tend to dismiss such techniques as what we have been doing all along, but there is a vast difference between episodic awareness of context and the deliberate, systematic exploration of context in search of features important for policy realization.

Rather it was a failure to locate the major institutional branches of government in their broader social context and a failure to focus on decision functions other than making, applying, and enforcing.

To meet the failure, the McDougal-Lasswell system breaks down the decision process into seven "authority functions" which also correspond sequentially with the functioning of the legal process. The seven "authority functions" are: *intelligence-gathering*, the obtaining and supplying of information to the decision maker; *promotion*, the recommendation of policy; *prescription*, the promulgation of norms—as in legislation; *invocation*, the provisional application of a prescription—as by a grand jury indictment; *application*, the final application of a prescription—as by an appellate decision; *termination*, the ending of a prescription; and *appraisal*, the evaluation of the degree of policy realization achieved. Like phase analysis, this functional breakdown may have many uses. One of the immediate insights from functional analysis when it is applied to the traditional range of concerns of legal education is that legal education has been concerned almost exclusively with the "application" and "prescriptive" functions. Interestingly, in the recent concern with police and prosecutorial discretion, however, legal educators are showing signs of interest in the "invocation" function. And in the increasing awareness of the value of law revision commissions the legal profession is showing signs of a long overdue awakening of the need for a continuing "appraisal" function.[9] Since the process of making, applying, and enforcing law is more complex than the traditional focus has enabled us to see, it is probable that this trend toward greater interest in the whole range of authority functions will continue. In any event, explicit recognition of these authority functions is a useful insight for increasing awareness of the greater range of decisions with which the legal scholar must be concerned.

---

9. See the recent article by Harold Lasswell calling for continuing exercise of the appraisal function. Lasswell, *Toward Continuing Appraisal of the Impact of Law on Society*, 21 RUTGERS L. REV. 645 (1967). The American Law Institute has sometimes performed an appraising function.

The McDougal-Lasswell system is also characterized by a concern with law in terms of value production and allocation and by its insistence that all law be investigated in these terms. The system is pragmatic and value-oriented; its concern with law is a normative concern. As with the legal realists, law is seen as an instrument for effectuating community policies and is good or bad according to its effectiveness in realization of those policies. Though realization of community policy is seen as the ultimate justification for legal norms, the system carefully avoids intellectual confusion between the is and the ought; the most rational clarification of policies requires the systematic performance of all intellectual tasks. Clarification of the classic debate in legal philosophy over the separation of is and ought is achieved by careful description of the intellectual tasks necessary for decision. The crucial distinction is that between the intellectual task of accurate description of the law (i.e., community expectations about authority and control which may include community expectations about ought) and clarification of an observer's policy preferences, which, though they build upon past experience, may express new goals.[10] The emphasis on the intellectual tasks necessary for decision also provides a pragmatic outline for systematic analysis of legal problems.

In simplest form the McDougal-Lasswell decision theory postulates that rational decision requires the performance of five intellectual tasks: clarification of goals, description of past trends, analysis of conditions affecting past trends, projection of future trends, and invention and evaluation of policy alternatives.[11] These tasks are performed by all of us, implicitly or explicitly, when we make any decision. We perform them, for example, when we decide whether to buy a house or rent. Though we tend to dismiss such clarification about decision-making as something we have been doing all along, explicit reflection on how decisions

10. A related insight of the system which is a substantial aid to intellectual clarification is the insistence on clarification of observational standpoint. Is the observational standpoint that of observer, authoritative decision-maker, advocate, or some other?

11. For an introduction to decision theory see I. Bross, Design For Decision (1959); Mayo & Jones, *Legal-Policy Decision Process: Alternative Thinking and the Predictive Function*, 33 Geo. Wash. L. Rev. 318 (1964).

are made can have and is having great impact in improving performance in government, business, and other aspects of our daily lives. In fact, similar systematic applications of decision theory have given rise to the discipline of "systems analysis" which is an effort to apply decision theory to solution of concrete problems.[12] A dramatic example of the impact of systems analysis is the McNamara revolution in the Pentagon following the adoption of a planning-programming-budgeting system.

Since policy-oriented jurisprudence has a pragmatic concern for problem solving, the basic outline of each of the recent McDougal-Lasswell studies is designed to facilitate systematic performance of each of these five intellectual tasks. Characteristically, the first chapter of books using the system defines the prob-

---

12. For an introduction to systems analysis see C. Hitch, *An Appreciation of Systems Analysis*, The RAND Corp., P-699 (Aug. 1955). Also of general interest are: R. McKean, Efficiency in Government Through Systems Analysis (1958); P. Don Vito, *Annotated Bibliography on Systems Cost Analysis*, The RAND Corp., RM-4848-PR (Feb. 1966); E. Quade, *Systems Analysis Techniques for Planning-Programming-Budgeting*, The RAND Corp., P-3322 (March 1966); The President's Commission on Law Enforcement and the Administration of Justice, Task-Force Report: Science and Technology (prepared by the Institute for Defense Analysis 1967).

One should not overestimate the ability of systems analysis, PPBS, or decision theory to solve all problems. As Robert Millward points out about PPBS:

One must conclude that PPBS has many shortcomings, although its attempts at normative decision-making may be desirable. There is no disagreement about the need for new decision-making tools, only a caution that the PPBS framework alone will not solve the immense problems facing us. It is hoped that working with PPBS will result in a greater awareness of ends, means, consequences, needs, and resources, all of which will facilitate decision-making within agencies. Its attempt at quantification of costs and benefits may lead to more sophisticated comparative efforts, particularly the use of mathematical models. Perhaps the basic advantage of PPBS is in the forced examination of ongoing activities in problem terms, in direct contrast to the present approach of incrementalism, where we do not evaluate what has already been approved and is operational. Such an examination is bound to reveal problems heretofore unrecognized.

Millward, *PPBS: Problems of Implementation*, 34 J. Am. Institute of Planners 88, 93 (1968). Also see Kaplan, *Some Limitations on Rationality*, Nomos VII: Rational Decision 55 (1964).

lem in its broadest context, including the relevant features of the processes of claim and decision by which the problem is presented to the decision-maker and decided. The second chapter then clarifies the goals and policies at stake in deciding the problem, a number of intermediate chapters systematically and exhaustively explore each major type of dispute by analysis of past trends and conditions affecting past trends, and the final chapter evaluates the possible alternatives. This overall outline is a thorough-going aid to problem solving and is particularly helpful in presenting an overview of a problem, in focusing attention on the goals at stake, and in enabling comparison of trends through time and across national boundaries. It encourages research which is pragmatic, contextual, systematic, and policy oriented.

Though the McDougal-Lasswell system is a substantial help in avoiding intellectual confusion and in problem solving, as with any methodology no matter how elaborate or perceptive it cannot automatically solve problems. Variations in value input and difficulties in accurately predicting the impact of varying alternatives see to that. But just as one should not imbue a methodology with the ability to solve problems, one also should not underestimate the effect which a methodology can have on problem solving. The great strength of the McDougal-Lasswell system is its ability to clarify what are otherwise real intellectual difficulties in thinking about law and legal problems, to stimulate creativity by getting outside traditional modes of thought about law, to successfully utilize inter-disciplinary techniques, and to assist legal research by arming it with a variety of analytic techniques.

It may assist in understanding the McDougal-Lasswell system to briefly identify the three most commonly articulated criticisms of its authors' approach.

The first, and perhaps most common criticism, and one sometimes taken to naive extreme,[13] runs: "Their writing is filled with

---

13. A recent book review of McDougal, Lasswell & Vlasic's LAW AND PUBLIC ORDER IN SPACE contains this attempt to translate a condensed and precise passage from the book into the reviewer's own language:
   In order to know what the authors attempt in *Law and Public Order in Space* we need only wrestle with their own statement:
   The basic design of our book is the modality of policy-oriented

insight but why don't they write in English?" This criticism stems from a genuine difficulty in understanding the specialized terminology of their policy-oriented jurisprudence. Perhaps it also stems from a natural suspicion, nurtured by a jargon-filled world, of that which is not understood. But the terminological suspicion of policy-oriented jurisprudence is not well-founded. The terminology which causes the greatest difficulty for the uninitiated is a necessary part of the approach and is itself responsible for many of the insights. Though policy-oriented jurisprudence is characterized by a diversity of techniques, central to the approach is a focus on the intellectual tasks necessary for problem solving and a method of systematically exploring social context in aid of decision. Both of these objectives require a meta-language for maximum success. Phase analysis, value analysis, concepts for evaluating theories about law and the role of legal process in society, and the decision theory outlined above are some of the responses to this need. Moreover, this terminology is not an isolated phenomenon springing full-blown from the heads of McDougal and Lasswell but is a synthesis of specialized lin-

---

jurisprudence: we first seek to identify the major recurring types of problems—that is, types of contraposed claims to authoritative decision which raise common issues in policy and which are affected by common conditioning factors—and to locate these problems in their most comprehensive context of community process; we then proceed to explore each major type of problem by employing the various relevant intellectual techniques of policy-oriented inquiry, including the detailed clarification and recommendation of general community policies, the description of past trends in decision on comparable problems, appraisal of the factors which appear to have affected past decision, the projection of probable future conditioning factors and decisions, and the recommendation of alternatives in policy content and procedures more appropriately designed to secure overriding community goals.

What the authors are trying to tell us is that: (1) they will define jurisprudence as a policy regime; (2) they will characterize problems accordingly; and (3) they will analyze these problems with a view to ascertaining whether or not policy should override precedent.

Scafuri, Book Review, 18 VAND. L. REV. 863, 864-65 (1965). The attempt, which does not remotely restate anything the authors were talking about, stands as a monument to the danger of believing that what one doesn't understand doesn't say anything.

guistic systems developed in a host of component social science disciplines. Much of their terminology is the daily grist of the political scientist, statistician, economist, systems analyst, or sociologist. As Professor Falk points out:

> I would argue that the stylistic criticism is unfounded. McDougal strives to achieve clear and precise expression. His sentences are almost always impossible to improve upon. Their complexity stems from an insistence upon nuance and accuracy, not from an infatuation with German metaphysics, or some inborn quality of verbal ineptitude. McDougal, with the substantial help of Harold D. Lasswell, is engaged in the formidable task of developing and applying a jurisprudence that takes *systemic account* of all aspects of social reality relevant to the processes and structures of making *rational* decisions about legal policy alternatives. This is a complicated endeavor and requires an elaborate intellectual apparatus. It would not occur to anyone to complain about Einsteinian theories of physical reality on the ground that they were abstruse and not readily susceptible to lay understanding. Well, it is time that we appreciate that theories about social reality are also likely to be comparably complicated if they are to render service. Our expectations seem quite wrong. Why should a reader be entitled to grasp McDougal's ideas on international law without special effort and training? We confront an insidious form of anti-intellectualism whenever we meet the argument that legal analysis must be carried on in a fashion that requires its meaning to be evident to the uninitiated or hurried reader. All that it is proper to demand is that legal analysis bring added knowledge and understanding to the adept. McDougal and Feliciano overfulfill this demand.[14]

To Falk's eloquence should be added the observation that those who doubt that the scope of a medium sets limits on its usefulness

---

14. Falk, *International Legal Order: Alwyn V. Freeman vs. Myres S. McDougal,* 59 Am. J. Int'l L. 66, 70-71 (1965).

   A quick reading of most of the reviews of the books using the system indicates that few recognized scholars familiar with the objectives of the McDougal-Lasswell system make the terminological criticism.

should try to multiply 867 by 493 using Roman numerals.[15] Without most of the specialized terminology of the system it would be awkward if not impossible to achieve its objectives.

A second criticism is that the system somehow depends on a particular value orientation which may or may not be shared by others, and that it is not useful if one has a different value orientation or is concerned with reconciling competing values (between, for example, communist and non-communist states). This criticism seems to be triggered principally by a misunderstanding of two features of the system: "value analysis" and the insistence on policy clarification as a necessary task in decision.[16] Perhaps also it reflects the disagreement of some critics with McDougal's position on such major public order issues as the lawfulness of the hydrogen bomb tests.

This second criticism is also unwarranted. "Value analysis" is an analytic tool for exploration of context. The eight current value headings have proven useful for systematic research. They do not carry any "value" overtones for decision. The emphasis on policy clarification as a necessary task in decision does of course result in policy choice. But the policy choices are explicitly and candidly revealed as distinguished from the inevitable policy choices which may go unrevealed under other methodologies. Moreover, the policy plugged into the system is largely independent of the system. The analytic tools of the system will, like a computer, function equally well should someone postulate a public order of human indignity rather than the public order of human dignity espoused by McDougal and Lasswell. Policy choices are

15. See generally M. McLuhan, Understanding Media: The Extensions of Man (1964).
16. Perhaps the value criticism also stems from the illusion that policy-oriented or even analytic systems can be tools for automatic decision. Arthur Corbin points out that the same criticism plagued Wesley Hohfeld's analytic system of "fundamental legal conceptions."

> Hohfeld's articles disturbed the mental complacency of professors of law as well as of students. This was due not only to the fact that mastery of his work is a severe disciplinary process, but also to the fact that they got the erroneous impression that his analysis of concepts and terms was offered as a method of determining social and legal policy. . . .

A. Corbin, Foreword to W. Hohfeld, Fundamental Legal Conceptions xi (1964).

inevitable in any decision process; the great advantage of the system is precisely its ability to focus attention on the necessity of goal definition and to make final choices explicit for appraisal by others. Its use does not guarantee that equally talented and sincere scholars would not disagree, for example, on such issues as the "admission" of Communist China to the United Nations.[17]

McDougal and Lasswell, however, are no mere technicians fashioning a series of neutral tools for legal analysis. On the contrary, they insist that all law be investigated in terms of value production and allocation. Their "policy-oriented jurisprudence" has perhaps gone farther than any other in recommending values and in developing techniques for dealing with values. As a starting point they insist that goal values be systematically clarified whatever their derivation. This emphasis on explicit value clarification is poles apart from the haphazard "balancing" or "absolutist" position which is the usual extent of the law student's exposure to value problems. And since McDougal and Lasswell go farther in explicit clarification of their own values they are much more vulnerable to criticism than those who obscure their own value choices in the "phonograph" theory of the law. The inevitability of value choice in decision and the desirability of decision-makers and scholars making their value choices explicit is a major theme of the Swedish political economist Gunnar Myrdal and many others of the best thinkers of our age.[18]

In dealing with policy clarification, McDougal and Lasswell also recommend that the more reliable technique is for reference to proceed from highest level generalization to more concrete

---

17. *Compare* L. CHEN & H. LASSWELL, FORMOSA, CHINA, AND THE UNITED NATIONS (1967), *with* McDougal & Goodman, *Chinese Participation in the United Nations*, 60 AM. J. INT'L L. 671 (1966).

18. Gunnar Myrdal . . . places great importance on the idea that social scientists should work from explicit value premises; that is to say, a person should set out his personal preferences and predilections as clearly as possible when dealing with social data. By so doing, he will enable one who reads his exposition to evaluate what he says in the light of those preferences. It is only in this way, according to Myrdal, that any manageability and real intelligibility may be attained in handling social phenomena.
Miller & Howell, *The Myth of Neutrality In Constitutional Adjudication*, 27 U. CHI. L. REV. 661, 669 (1960).

statement, and not *vice versa*. For example, their own highest level abstraction, "human dignity," is given more specific policy content at lower levels of abstraction when dealing with particular problems in context. Reasonable men can, of course, still disagree at lower levels of abstraction about, for example, whether the interdictive attacks on facilities in North Vietnam may ultimately minimize or increase coercive use of the military instrument, but whatever one's persuasion the policy justification for or against particular action is not most usefully made in terms of the highest level abstractions "human dignity" or "morality."

At a time when some social scientists are disclaiming any ability to deal with values, it seems particularly important for legal scholars, operating in an essentially normative discipline, to sharpen their skills for dealing with values. Value technique, meaning a technique for clarification and justification of value choice, is an area of jurisprudence which is barely embryonic today but which seems destined to become an area of major concern.

A variation of the criticism that the system somehow depends on a particular value orientation is the criticism that the system facilitates chauvinistic manipulation of the law. This criticism has sometimes been hinted at by international law scholars who disagree with the conclusions of McDougal or other writers using the system on major public order issues such as Vietnam or the Dominican Republic.[19] The fatal flaw in the criticism is its concealed premise that rules automatically decide cases and that a positivist or analytic approach somehow mystically avoids the necessity of choice. Anyone with experience with the kinds of legal norms involved in controversies such as Vietnam, or the Cuban missile crisis, or the Arab-Israeli war, however, realizes that rules often provide only minimal guidance. Among other

---

19. See, *e.g.*, Anderson, *A Critique of Professor Myres S. McDougal's Doctrine of Interpretation By Major Purposes*, 57 Am. J. Int'l L. 378, 382 (1963); Wright, *Review of Studies In World Public Order*, 39 U. Det. L.J. 145, 149 (1961). For a recent exchange raising this charge see Friedmann, *Law and Politics in the Vietnamese War: A Comment*, 61 Am. J. Int'l L. 776 (1967); Moore, *Law and Politics in the Vietnamese War: A Response to Professor Friedmann*, 61 Am. J. Int'l L. 1039, 1050-52 (1967).

problems, they may be at a high level of abstraction, or normatively ambiguous, or travel in complementary opposites.[20] For example, aggression is impermissible under Article 2(4) of the Charter; collective defense is permissible under Article 51 of the Charter. But these complimentary standards contain no external referent as to how a particular use of force is to be characterized.

Moreover, international law, perhaps more than most law, is limited by gaps and tears in the legal fabric and even by controversies concerning identification of "controlling" legal norms. In a system with these characteristics, an approach which relies on "black letter rules," without consideration of context or function, itself carries the greater risk of manipulation. Such reliance on asserted positive law carries with it even greater chance of obfuscation in that no hint of the necessity of choice among rules or policies need be revealed. That is, the footwork of the positivist approach is largely covert rather than overt. This is particularly dangerous for the lay observer who tends to be more legalistic

20. The notions of "complementarity" and "normative ambiguity" in legal rules are other insights of the McDougal-Lasswell approach. "Complementarity" is a refined version of the legal realists' observation that frequently legal norms travel in pairs of complementary opposites such as self-defense-aggression or the famous Karl Llewellyn arrangement of the canons of construction in opposing columns labeled "thrust" and "parry." For example, "THRUST: Statutes in derogation of the common law will not be extended by construction; PARRY: Such acts will be liberally construed if their nature is remedial." K. LLEWELLYN, THE COMMON LAW TRADITION 522 (1960). "Normative ambiguity" refers to the observation that many key legal terms are used ambiguously to refer both to operative facts and to purported legal consequences. One example is the term "delivery" in the law of gifts which is sometimes used to refer to some operative feature of the real-world such as manual transfer of an object and sometimes is used as a conclusory legal term to indicate that a gift will be upheld despite lack of manual transfer. Another form of normative ambiguity is the use of a term such as "intervention" to refer simultaneously to what is, what will be and what ought to be. Much of the trouble the international lawyer experiences in trying to define "intervention" arises from this ambiguity. The antidote is careful separation of the intellectual tasks necessary for decision. Public international law issues suffer from an abundance of both complementarity and normative ambiguity.

For a somewhat related and extremely useful insight into the choice points in judicial decision-making see Allen & Caldwell, *Modern Logic and Judicial Decision Making: A Sketch of One View*, 28 LAW & CONTEMP. PROB. 213 (1963).

than the most black letter of lawyers. The so-called "Lawyers Committee Memorandum," condemning United States assistance in Vietnam as illegal by invocation of a series of asserted "rules of international law" (an example of one of these "rules" is the assertion that it is illegal to assist South Vietnam under Article 51 of the Charter because Vietnam is not a member of the United Nations), is a prime example of the dangers of manipulation present in a black letter approach.[21] Policy-oriented jurisprudence, on the other hand, provides the intellectual tools to focus attention on the competing norms, reveal the choice characteristics of the system, separate expectations about law from personal policy preference, and explicitly reveal the preference of the writer. Both positivist and policy-oriented systems can be used to accomplish chauvinistic aims, as can any system of jurisprudence. It is naive to believe that the use of any particular system will inevitably end in the one true result. And it is equally naive to believe that all approaches offer the same possibilities of intellectual clarification.[22]

A third criticism sometimes leveled at the system is that it is uneconomic to apply these admittedly sophisticated techniques to practical decisions that must be made by lawyers and judges in the everyday operation of the legal system. The answer is that the system provides a series of precise, analytical tools for analysis of legal and jurisprudential problems. Just as it may be uneco-

21. *Memorandum of Law of the Lawyers Committee on American Policy Toward Vietnam*, 112 CONG. REC. 2552 (daily ed., Feb. 9, 1966).
22. Professor Lissitzyn hit the nail on the head when he wrote:
    Professor McDougal frequently stresses the fact that norms usually come in pairs of "complementary opposites." Decision-makers who desire to make rational and lawful decisions will be helped rather than hindered in their task by the clarification of the nature and function of law. There is always, of course, some danger of "flexible" interpretations of the law being misused as ostensible justification for socially undesirable conduct, but this danger is diminished rather than increased by a wider understanding of the factors and processes involved."
    Lissitzyn, *Review of Law and Minimum World Public Order*, 76 HARV. L. REV. 668, 670 (1963). *See also* Dillard, *Combined Review of Four Books in the System*, 40 VA. Q. REV. 629 (1964), *reprinted in* 19 VA. READING GUIDE 56 (1964); Falk, *Review of Law and Minimum World Public Order*, 8 NATURAL L.F. 171, 175-77 (1963).

nomic to use a computer to make out one's weekly grocery list and highly efficient to use it to make out a large payroll, so too the nature of the task will dictate when the system or sub-skills of policy-oriented jurisprudence may be efficiently used. No one, however, would downgrade the computer because it is not a useful device for the task of making the weekly grocery list.

With respect to some legal tasks, it will not, of course, be economic to use the Lasswell-McDougal system. One of the common errors of the neophyte is that he is tempted to apply the system in ways and on tasks in which it is uneconomic. Another more annoying error is the use of the meta-language in attempting to communicate with audiences who have had no exposure to it. The system and its meta-language are rigorous; their use requires a systematic analysis which may entail some repetition in the final product and which is always achieved at a cost in time and a sacrifice in wide communication. Sensitivity to function is the only guide to profitable use. The system itself subsumes this answer to the third criticism in what McDougal and Lasswell term the principle of economy.[23]

A variation of the third criticism asks whether the meta-linguistic structure and the elaborate systematic method of inquiry are really worthwhile in any context. Or sometimes it is said that interdisciplinary work is fine in theory, but in practice it just does not work. The answer from one who has spent his share of confused hours becoming familiar with the system is that there is simply no question of its *great* utility in legal problem solving and in clarifying jurisprudential issues. It is no accident that the books utilizing the system, such as *Law and Minimum World Public Order, The Public Order of the Oceans, Law and Public Order in Space,* and *The Interpretation of Agreements,*[24] provide substantially greater insight into the range of problems within their compass than the usual treatises. One has but to search the literature on use of force or treaty interpretation or the admission of Communist China to the United Nations to realize how great the contribution of the works using the system really is. The comment heard so often, that the books are great but would be better if they did not use an abstruse language, is understandable but

23. See note 33 *infra*.   24. See the books listed in note 3 *supra*.

naive. For it is in large measure the use of the language which enables the thorough analysis of problems and the outstanding issue and policy clarification achieved.

As examples of the utility of the system for clarifying major areas of concern, it may be useful to examine the application of the system to two major problems of international law: first, by a brief sketch of the McDougal-Feliciano approach to the determination of "aggression," and second, by an analysis of the recent McDougal, Lasswell, Miller book dealing with the interpretation of international agreements. Both problems are of fundamental and longstanding concern to international law theorists, and their clarification has been significantly aided by use of the McDougal-Lasswell system. In fact, the impact of the McDougal-Lasswell jurisprudence has been particularly heavy in international law, an area in which McDougal and his associates have done most of their recent writings. As an aid in understanding the system, the reader is urged to refer to the *Interpretation of Agreements* book in conjunction with the analysis of the research techniques employed.

Major use of force is prohibited as an instrument of national policy by the United Nations Charter.[25] On the other hand, defense against aggression (or in the language of Article 51 "armed attack") is permissible at least until the Security Council takes action. The problem of appraising lawfulness of the use of force, then, is largely one of separating aggression from defense. Traditional approaches to this problem either have attempted to define a list of hostile acts, any one of which would constitute aggression, or have declared that little could be said in the absence of the *ad hoc* circumstances of a particular case. Both approaches have proven either illusory or of little help in making concrete determinations. In their book *Law and Minimum World Public Order*,[26] McDougal and Feliciano offer a more meaningful

---

25. To what extent does this statement refer to both patterns of "authority" and patterns of "control" in the McDougal meta-language?
26. "Minimum public order" is a meta-linguistic term of art used to denote absence of high order coercion. The concern is with at least a minimum stability of expectations of freedom from non-authoritative use of force as a prerequisite to maximum shaping and sharing of all public order values.

method of analysis: first, clarification of the community goals at stake, principally avoidance of intense coercion as an instrument of international change—that is, avoidance of intense coercion for purposes of value extension rather than value conservation; and second, the orderly examination of context with reference to the characteristics of the participants, the nature of the objectives (extension or conservation of values and the degree of consequentiality of the values protected), the modalities of response, the conditions of use of force (reasonable expectations of necessity), and the effects of the use of force (the degree of intensity and scope of the responding coercion and the necessity of its use to achieve permissible objectives). This approach provides a means of operationalizing the community policy against aggression by reference to more specific community policies relevant to each feature of the process of coercion. Though the McDougal-Feliciano method of analysis does not guarantee instant agreement about aggression-defense characterizations, it does offer both greater realism than the definitional approach and greater guidance than the *ad hoc* approach. To test the potentiality of the various methods of analysis, try analyzing the recent Arab-Israeli war in the "who did what to whom first" format of the 1954 Draft Resolution on the Definition of Aggression[27] and then in the McDougal-Feliciano policy-oriented contextual framework.

The *Interpretation of Agreements and World Public Order*, written by McDougal, Lasswell, and James Miller, is aimed primarily at another major problem in international law. The book sets forth a viable theory of interpretation which surpasses the sensitivity of the legal realists both in describing the system as it operates and in making sound positive recommendations for practical guidelines to interpretation. It also graphically demonstrates the benefits from real interdisciplinary collaboration, for an eminent legal scholar, an outstanding political scientist, and a talented young psychologist were capable of integrating their specialized skills in search of a solution to a particularly prickly legal problem. But the *Interpretation of Agreements* is not only a practical book with practical suggestions about an important

---

27. Reprinted in L. SOHN, BASIC DOCUMENTS OF THE UNITED NATIONS 106-08 (2d ed. 1968).

problem of international law and a practical demonstration of interdisciplinary work; it is also a book with enormous jurisprudential significance that far transcends the interpretation of international agreements. The basic approach conceives the task of interpreting international agreements and prescriptions as a problem in communication, and lends itself with some adaptation to the interpretation of prescriptive communications at all levels of social organization, including constitutions, statutes, case holdings, contracts, wills, and even something as elusive as custom.

Traditional debate about interpretation of agreements has tended to polarize around the textualists, who would substantially restrict the decision-maker as to the sources he might legitimately look to in the process of interpretation, and the extreme realists, who deny that very much useful can be said about the process of interpretation.[28] Typically, the extreme textualists emphasize the "plain and natural meaning rule," argue that interpretation is largely automatic, and deny the legitimacy of reliance on *travaux preparatoires* as an aid in interpretation. Equally typically, the extreme realists denigrate the canons of construction by arguing that they travel in pairs of complementary opposites which serve only a rationalizing function. The McDougal, Lasswell, Miller approach effectively transcends the limited frames of reference of both schools by approaching the problem of interpretation primarily as a problem in communication and by using the analytic tools and interdisciplinary findings which are the hallmark of the McDougal-Lasswell jurisprudence.

The *Interpretation of Agreements* follows the general outline of decision tasks used by the authors in other studies, except that in the interest of economy the past trends in decision chapters are organized around the features of the process of agreement and decision rather than by types of disputes (claims). Extended use

28. Though the generalization about these polar camps is useful, as Ronald Dworkin points out with respect to the much maligned "mechanical jurisprude," it would probably be difficult "to cage and exhibit" a pure representative of either camp. See Dworkin, *The Model of Rules*, 35 U. CHI. L. REV. 14, 16 (1967).

For an excellent discussion on the merits see P. Liacouras, *The International Court of Justice and Development of Useful "Rules of Interpretation" in the Process of Treaty Interpretation*, 1965 PROCEEDINGS AM. SOC. INT'L L. 161.

of phase analysis is made both to analyze the processes of agreement and decision, and to recommend principles of content appropriate to each of the phases of the process of agreement.

In the first chapter the authors make a systematic contextual analysis of the process of agreement, claim, and decision which encompasses all phases of the processes by which parties reach agreement, and by which their claims about agreements are presented to and decided by authorized community decision-makers. The purpose of this chapter is to demonstrate the great range of features which are relevant to policy realization in the process of interpretation and application. In locating the problem of interpretation in its broadest context, the authors effectively debunk the automatic interpretation school and demonstrate that some interpretation is always necessary.

Chapter two makes explicit the goals and strategies of interpretation. The primary or initial goal is postulated as the ascertainment of the shared expectations of the parties in order to give effect to genuine agreement. Where the search for genuine shared expectation fails because of gaps, contradictions, or ambiguities in the agreement, the authors recommend as a secondary goal that the agreement be "supplemented" by reference to basic policies of the community and basic objectives of the parties. And as a tertiary goal, in those few cases in which the genuine shared expectations of the parties are subversive of basic community policies, the authors recommend that the decision-maker "police" the agreement by application of overriding community policies. An example of policing, by analogy to domestic contract law, would be the refusal to enforce contracts for prostitution, no matter how clearly spelled out, in deference to an overriding community policy against prostitution.

This tripartite goal, consisting of first a disciplined search for genuine shared expectations using the findings of modern communications theory, then the "supplementing" of gaps or contradictions by reference to the parties' purposes and community policies, and finally "policing" the agreement if necessary by application of any overriding community policies, is a simple but profound insight into legal process. Because the starting point in many legal problems is ascertainment of intent or relied-upon expectation, this tripartite division is useful in a number of contexts. For example, most of the material taught in the course in trusts and estates, to use a "private law" course with which I am particularly familiar, could profitably be located within a related framework. Much of the content of the course is concerned with effectuating the expectations of a donor with regard to the transmission of wealth at his death. The wills acts, the statute of frauds, and to a substantial degree even the intestate succession laws are intended to give effect to genuine expectations. On the other hand, such problems as "death without issue," the problem of implied survivorship, and the doctrine of worthier title are, to the extent that they perform any real function, largely intended to serve the secondary goal of "supplementing" gaps and contradictions. And finally, such rules as the statutory forced share, the Rule in Shelley's case, and the rule against perpetuities are invoked as "policing" rules which override intent presumably because of some more or less pressing community policy. The use of such a tripartite goal structure impels attention to the function, or lack thereof, of these and related rules, and can materially assist in appraisal of the efficacy of the process for transmission of property on death. Using such a framework to organize our thoughts on the goals being served by all these rules would produce greater insight into the causes of the popular dissatisfaction with the administration of estates that enables a form book to become a best seller.[29]

McDougal, Lasswell, and Miller also recommend a detailed and comprehensive strategy of interpretation for implementation of their goals. Their recommendation includes principles of both content and procedure. Principles of content are defined as recommendations concerning the subject matter which the decision-maker should take into account in interpreting an agreement.

---

29. See N. DACEY, HOW TO AVOID PROBATE (1965), reviewed in 46 BOST. L. REV. 417 (1966). The significance of this book for the legal profession is that if a rather dull form book can become a best seller it would seem to be proof positive that there is widespread dissatisfaction with the legal processes for transmission of wealth on death. The causes of this dissatisfaction rather than Dacey's book might profitably be studied. The success of the book also suggests the need for institutions to provide continuing appraisal of the efficacy of legal systems. See Lasswell, *supra* note 9.

Principles of procedure are defined as recommendations as to how the decision-maker should go about taking them into account. The most basic of these principles of content and procedure is the contextual principle that the decision-maker utilize the context as a whole as a basis for ascertaining shared expectations and "that he use procedures calculated to bring all relevant content to the focus of his attention in the order best adapted to exhibiting relevance."[30] This principle stems from the diffuseness of the process of communication itself which makes it dangerous arbitrarily to weight any one feature of the context prior to examination of the context as a whole. More detailed principles of content are then formulated for each of the phases of the processes of agreement and decision. For example, "the principle of the distinctive phase of agreement" is postulated as: "When sources of equal credibility give contradictory results concerning the expectations that prevailed at the preoutcome and outcome phases of the agreement process, assign priority to the expectations shared at the outcome phase."[31] This principle of content is based on the relevance of the outcome phase of the process of agreement for achieving the goals of interpretation. And similarly "the principle of explicit rationality" is postulated as: "For the guidance of future agreement-makers and interpreters, as well as for their own guidance and self-knowledge, decision-makers should make as explicit as possible the principles of interpretation and application which influence their decision."[32] This principle of content is based on the relevance of the strategies of the process of decision concerned with interpreting and applying agreements. An example of a principle of procedure is the "historical operation." Decision-makers undertaking "the historical operation" are urged to "consider the focal agreement in the light of the context by moving attention back to the period of negotiating the agreement and forward to date."[33]

---

30. M. McDougal, H. Lasswell & J. Miller, The Interpretation of Agreements and World Public Order 65 (1967).

31. *Id.* at 58.   32. *Id.* at 64.

33. *Id.* at 67. One of the principles of procedure which is particularly worth noting is "the operation of adjusting effort to importance." This is described by the authors as: "Adjust the time and facilities devoted to the act of interpretation according to the importance of the values at stake

Interpretation buffs will be familiar with Karl Llewellyn's famous arrangement of the traditional canons of construction in pairs of opposites labeled "thrust and parry."[34] The McDougal, Lasswell, Miller principles of content and procedure are no mere canons of construction in this traditional sense. They offer instead a series of recommendations about what is important for the interpreter to look at, based on every phase of the process of agreement, the negotiation (preoutcome), the agreement (outcome), and subsequent conduct (postoutcome), and based on every phase of the process of decision. They also offer a series of recommendations about how the decision-maker should most efficiently go about serving community goals in the interpretation and application of the agreement. These recommendations are soundly rooted in communication theory, semantics, propositional calculus, and other relevant information from the social sciences. As guidelines for interpretation they offer a whole new world to the episodic insights of the traditional canons of construction or to the nihilistic "realism" which despaired of any interpretative guides.

Chapters one and two, defining the problem of interpretation and clarifying the basic goals and strategies of interpretation, contain the basic conceptual framework and recommendations of the authors. Chapters three through five contain what would traditionally be the "meat" of the subject. These chapters offer a panorama of the past practices and trends in interpretation, pinpoint each of the existing rules and canons on a larger canvas, and discuss the relevance (or lack of relevance) of each. They also present an exhaustive and scholarly analysis of the existing case law and the writings of publicists, and contain a timely and forceful critique of the recent International Law Commission Draft Articles on Treaty Interpretation, which they criticize for retrogressing to textuality rather than taking a more balanced ap-

---

in the controversy and to community policies." *Id.* at 65. This principle carries its own answer to those who argue that the systematic methods of interpretation set out require the decision-maker to make an uneconomic exertion.

34. K. LLEWELLYN, THE COMMON LAW TRADITION, DECIDING APPEALS 521-35 (1960). See note 20 *supra*.

proach emphasizing all relevant features of the process of agreement in a search for genuine shared expectations of the parties.[35] A final chapter completes the intellectual tasks for decision with a comprehensive summation of the recommendations of the authors.

The tripartite goal structure postulated for the interpretation and application of agreements[36] and the materials dealing with the lexical and logical operations bear close scrutiny.[37] This latter material relies on modern social science findings in semantics and syntactics which demonstrate an impressive utility for interpretation, again with a great promise of carry-over value to many other aspects of legal process. Much of this discussion of syntactics builds on the contributions of Laymen Allen in the application of modern logic to legal problems.[38]

The *Interpretation of International Agreements* is the most recent major application of the McDougal-Lasswell system of jurisprudence. It is an excellent example of the results such a system can achieve[39] and demonstrates again the system's extraordinary capacity for intellectual clarification. It should be clear by now, however, that before one can obtain maximum benefit from the system, he must dig in and obtain the necessary background. The purpose of this necessarily oversimplified introduction is to stimulate more digging and to suggest that the jurisprudential yield from such digging is among the highest in law today.

35. M. McDougal, H. Lasswell & J. Miller, *supra* note 30, at 88-90. See also McDougal, *The International Law Commission's Draft Articles Upon Interpretation: Textuality Redivivus*, 61 Am. J. Int'l L. 992 (1967).
36. M. McDougal, H. Lasswell & J. Miller, *supra* note 30, at 39-45.
37. *Id.* at 67-73, 319-43.
38. See, *e.g.*, Allen, *Some Uses of Symbolic Logic in Law Practice*, 1962 M.U.L.L. 119.
39. For an almost immediate practical application of the Interpretation of International Agreements framework to a problem of great contemporary concern, see Hannon, *A Political Settlement For Vietnam: The 1954 Geneva Conference and Its Current Implications*, 8 Va. J. Int'l L. 4 (1967).

PART TWO

WORLD ORDER PERSPECTIVES

Introduction

FROM the perspective of the future of world order, the problem of intervention in internal conflict is potentially one of the most serious in the present international system. Although the Indo-China conflict cannot be accurately generalized solely in terms of internal conflict (the North Vietnamese invasion of Cambodia is more meaningfully characterized as an armed attack than as intervention), to some extent the fighting within Laos, Cambodia, South Vietnam, and between North and South Vietnam has overtones of the internal conflict problem. In fact, a major portion of the public order disputes since World War II have had at least overtones of the problem. They would include the Greek civil war, the Korean war (in the divided-nation aspect of the problem), the continuing Arab-Israeli conflict, Indian intervention in Bangla Desh, Soviet intervention in Hungary and the Congo, United States intervention in Guatemala, Lebanon, Cuba, and the Dominican Republic, the multi-nation intervention in the Nigerian-Biafran civil war, United Nations actions in Cyprus and the Congo, and a host of lesser interventions cutting across every ideological grouping. In a revolutionary international system constrained by the fear of mutual nuclear annihilation, proxy wars, indirect aggression, and other forms of covert and limited coercion have become the principal modes of violent conflict. Revolutionary and revisionist powers have actively sought extension of their values through such strategies, and the pressure of the competition has frequently induced the more conservative powers to respond in kind. The problem of control has been compounded by the diversity and complexity of internal conflict settings and by the lack of normative guidance as to permissible state action in the range of settings. International-legal theory, like international-relations theory, has been largely unprepared for the pressures of the present era. Prior to the Indo-China conflict, only relatively little had been written on internal conflict problems, and to a substantial degree the structure of the United Nations was normatively and institutionally unresponsive to the problem. Chapters III and IV, "Intervention: A Monochromatic Term for a

Polychromatic Reality" and "The Control of Foreign Intervention in Internal Conflict," are preliminary efforts at filling this important gap with a theory of an international law of non-intervention.[1]

Chapter IV is the later and more complete statement of my position, but Chapter III suggests an alternative method of analysis which may also offer merit. Though the multiplicity of claims concerning intervention in internal conflict makes distillation of general rules enormously difficult, there is a strong presumption that unilateral authority-oriented intervention in internal conflict should be impermissible. International law should not justify foreign maintenance of the *status quo* against genuine internal demands for change. Hungary is a good example of the dangers of such a policy. But if international law should not countenance repressive foreign maintenance of the *status quo*, it does not follow that it should blind itself to indirect aggression and covert forms of external domination. Thus, a principal exception permits proportional counter-intervention on behalf of a widely recognized government in the event of prior unlawful foreign assistance to or sponsorship of insurgents. This counter-intervention exception may be analogized to the Article 51 exception in the Charter permitting individual or collective defense against an armed attack.

The problem of building a viable national foreign policy in an era of indirect aggression and competitive intervention is the national counterpart of the general problem of control of foreign intervention. Chapter V, "The Elephant Misperceived: Intervention and American Foreign Policy," briefly sets out some of the

1. The American Society of International Law sponsors a continuing Panel on the Role of International Law in Civil Wars which is broadly concerned with clarification of the international law of non-intervention. Several volumes of case studies sponsored by the Panel and concerning the role of international law in internal conflicts have been published by the Johns Hopkins Press. See R. FALK (ED.), THE INTERNATIONAL LAW OF CIVIL WAR (1970). A third volume of essays tentatively entitled "Law and Civil War in the Modern World" is scheduled for publication in late 1972 or early 1973. The additional volume will be edited by John Norton Moore, will include essays by a wide range of international law and international relations scholars and is intended to contribute to an interdisciplinary analysis of current problems and prospects in intervention theory.

issues involved in retooling American foreign policy for the world order threats of the present system. The context is a review of a widely influential book by Richard Barnet, which sets out a revisionist view of intervention and American foreign policy. Though likely to appeal to the widespread *mea culpa* instinct in America (and making some valid points), in the measure of their omission the Barnet and other revisionist writings on American intervention are dangerously simplistic. United States foreign policy since World War II seems much more explainable as a response to competitive pressures from rhetorically and genuinely revolutionary powers than from economic imperialism or "the police idea" in American foreign policy. Instead of beating our breast, we need to set about the difficult task of implementing a foreign policy which will project an intellectually powerful image of world order. We also need to carefully reassess both the national interest and the national capability in interventionary settings. If the domino theory is a poor guide for national action, cries that any assistance to nations beleaguered by foreign intervention will inevitably lead to a Vietnam war (the currently fashionable reverse domino theory) are equally poor.

The outline of a more viable American foreign policy for the seventies should have two principal characteristics. First, it should demonstrate a commitment to a model of world order which is sensitive to the nuances of the international law of nonintervention. Rather than submit to the competitive pressures of a revolutionary system and encourage response in kind, it would seem preferable to vigorously promote a powerful view of world order which is in the common interest of all nations. In other words, it may be considerably more in the national interest for the United States, which is essentially a conservative power in the international system, to actively promote the stability of the international milieu rather than to muddle through from one short-term crisis to another or to respond to revolutionary and revisionist pressures in kind. Second, within a coherent model of world order, the United States should develop a policy more sensitive to national capabilities and the costs of action and inaction. In this regard, a policy which sharply differentiates economic and military assistance from the commitment of regular United States armed forces has considerable merit. Though not an absolute, the line has special meaning in interventionary contexts both in the dynamics of internal conflict and in the limitation of cost. Cost and the invention of more viable alternatives when cost is too high are frequently as important as determining whether a particular goal is in the national interest. The tragedy of the fashionable revisionist rhetoric on intervention and American foreign policy is that for the most part it does not meaningfully come to grips with these hard issues.

Chapter VI, "The Role of Regional Arrangements in the Maintenance of World Order," develops the relationship between global and regional arrangements in the maintenance of world order. Along with the problem of control of intervention in internal conflict, the issues posed by the interrelation of the United Nations with regional security arrangements have posed the second major normative gap in the Charter structure as applied in the contemporary international system. They include such questions as when should the United Nations defer to the exercise of regional jurisdiction? Under what circumstance can regional arrangements initiate coercive action without Security Council authorization? And what procedures are necessary for the United Nations to authorize or terminate regional action? Chapter VI attempts to provide a general framework for the analysis of these and other issues in the relationship of regional organizations to the United Nations. An international law of conflict management adequate for the future must deal satisfactorily with these issues as well as those posed by the control of intervention and the substantial interrelation between the two sets of issues.

CHAPTER III

Intervention: A Monochromatic Term for a Polychromatic Reality

IT HAS become increasingly evident over the last few years that the control of international involvement in real or pretended domestic upheaval is one of the central problems of peace in our time. Since World War II the world has witnessed major international involvement in conflicts within Greece, Korea, and now Vietnam, and numerous lesser involvements in such conflicts as Laos, Malaysia, Cyprus, Guatemala, Hungary, Yemen, Cuba, Lebanon, Venezuela, Bolivia, the Dominican Republic, Thailand, Czechoslovakia, Nigeria, Pakistan, Northern Ireland, and the Congo. This development, while never wholly absent from the international scene, seems to have been stimulated after World War II by the parameters of a nuclear confrontation, a shift from a stable to a revolutionary international system, an accelerating rate of social change in the developing countries with a concomitant decrease in stability, and a militancy of some new leaders who advocate use of force for the expansion of ideology.

International law has been slow to respond to the challenge of these new developments and in doing so has been hampered by an antiquated set of intellectual tools which has threatened to make international law scholars amateurs of the irrelevant. In this vacuum legal scholars either have tended to take a super legalistic approach by the deification of simplistic all-encompassing norms or have capitulated to the not so real reality of the *realpolitik* school.[1]

1. Happily, in recent years there has been a growing list of thoughtful treatments of intervention. For a general introduction to the problems of intervention see: J. ROSENAU (ED.), INTERNATIONAL ASPECTS OF CIVIL STRIFE (1964); R. STANGER (ED.), ESSAYS ON INTERVENTION (1964); A. THOMAS & A. THOMAS, NON-INTERVENTION: THE LAW AND ITS IMPORT IN THE AMERICAS (1956); THE DOMINICAN REPUBLIC CRISIS 1965 (The Ninth Hammarskjöld Forum, 1967); Cabranes, *Human Rights and Non-Intervention in the Inter-American System*, 65 MICH. L.R. 1147 (1967); Falk, *The United States and the Doctrine of Non-Intervention in the Internal Affairs*

One of the principal roadblocks to clarity has been the failure to define the rainbow of events obscured by the intervention—non-intervention proscription. As Professor Burke has observed, the term intervention is used ambiguously to refer both to operative facts and to purported legal consequences.[2] Moreover, it is used indiscriminately to refer to a range of practices as diverse as student exchange programs and the dispatch of Soviet tanks to the streets of Budapest. Used in this fashion the term intervention obscures the fact that the critical nexus between the operative facts of transnational interaction and the normative force of non-intervention lies in the coerciveness of the interaction. This does not mean that use of armed forces is the only intervention problem. If the principal community concern is with the degree of coercion in transnational interactions, we should recognize that undesirable levels can be reached through a range of strategies. This recognition is implicit in Article 15 of the OAS Charter, which gives the doctrine of non-intervention one of its broadest formulations. Article 15 provides that:

> No State or group of States has the right to intervene, directly or indirectly, for any reason whatever, in the internal or external affairs of any other States. The foregoing principle prohibits not only armed force but also any other form of interference or attempted threat against the personality of the State or against its political, economic and cultural elements.

---

of Independent States, 5 HOW. L.J. 163 (1959); Falk, *International Law and the United States Role in the Viet Nam War*, 75 YALE L.J. 1122 (1966); J. N. Moore, *International Law and the United States Role in Viet Nam: A Reply*, 76 YALE L.J. 1051 (1967); Falk, *International Law and the United States Role in Viet Nam: A Response to Professor Moore*, 76 YALE L.J. 1095 (1967); Farer, *Intervention in Civil Wars: A Modest Proposal*, 67 COL. L.R. 266 (1967); Fenwick, *Intervention and the Inter-American Rule of Law*, 53 AM. J. INT'L L. 873 (1959); Friedmann, *Intervention, Civil War and the Role of International Law*, 59 PROC., AM. SOC'Y INT'L L. 67 (1965); Henkin, *Force, Intervention and Neutrality in Contemporary International Law*, 57 PROC., AM. SOC'Y INT'L L. 145 (1963).

2. Burke, *The Legal Regulation of Minor Coercion: A Framework of Inquiry*, in STANGER, *supra* note 1, at 87, 88.

One task facing the international law scholar is to pour content into the community aspirations reflected by this and similar provisions. That means the explicit recognition that undesirable levels of coercion can be achieved by use of the economic, diplomatic, or ideological instruments as well as by the more dramatic use of "volunteers" or marines. It also means the exploration of limiting norms with respect to these strategies. Such exploration would have as one guideline ascertainment of the coerciveness of a particular transnational interaction, whatever its modality. Such exploration should also clarify that coercive economic or ideological strategies may sometimes be in conformance with community policy, for example as seems to have been true of OAS economic sanctions against Trujillo, and as may be true of some restrictions on foreign aid designed to induce needed social reforms. Professor Friedmann's sensitive discussion of some of the forms of "economic intervention"[3] (a term which fails to distinguish objectives from modalities) indicates both the complexities of drawing these lines in a world filled with transnational interactions and the relatively primitive state of normative and procedural control in this area. The future legal order, however, probably will and should have a great deal to say about the coercive limits on employment of the economic and ideological instruments. For example, in a world increasingly polarized between have and have not nations, to what extent should economic sanctions such as trade or travel restrictions be available to the have nations to secure political objectives? To what extent do political restrictions on foreign aid result in unacceptable levels of economic coercion? For the moment, however, the focus remains on control of armed forces, a modality of interaction which characteristically involves high-order coercion, and which for that reason is the most pressing concern.

Here again talk of intervention has obscured the great diversity of situations characterized by transnational uses of armed force and as a result existing norms have tended to place all such uses into a single undifferentiated category.

3. Friedmann, "Intervention and the Developing Countries," 16-32 (Paper delivered at the Princeton Conference on Intervention and the Developing Countries Nov. 10-11, 1967).

A use of armed forces which was perhaps central to the notion of intervention during much of the nineteenth and the early part of the twentieth centuries was the use of troops or naval bombardment to collect debts or to enforce asserted breach of agreement or violation of international law. In United States foreign policy this took the form of the Roosevelt Corollary to the Monroe Doctrine, an assertion of the right of outright military occupation throughout Latin America to forestall European intervention. This period witnessed the military occupation of Haiti, Cuba, Nicaragua, and the Dominican Republic, and the Latin American reaction in the form of the Drago doctrine and the principal of absolute non-intervention.

At the Seventh International Conference of American States in 1933, however, the United States accepted in principle the non-intervention doctrine and in effect repudiated the right to enforce non-forceful breach of international obligations by force.[4] This principle, that force not be used as a modality of major change or to provide a remedy for non-forceful breach of agreement, has subsequently become one of the cornerstones of the United Nations Charter.[5]

The use of armed forces, which is perhaps central to the largest contemporary invocation of intervention, centers around external participation in real or pretended domestic upheaval. Some of the instances are cold-war conflicts in the sense that they are fought between communist and non-communist factions over form of government or ideology.[6] Frequently, the battleground is the developing nations with the competing factions more or less proxies of a particular system or sub-system. In their ideological orientation and structural objectives, such conflicts are closer to the ideological conflict of the Spanish civil war than to the armed

4. See THOMAS & THOMAS, *supra* note 1, at 61-64; Cabranes, *supra* note 1, at 1153.
5. See generally, M. MCDOUGAL & F. FELICIANO, LAW AND MINIMUM WORLD PUBLIC ORDER (1961).
6. It is peripheral but perhaps useful to point out that the recognition of a "cold war" or of contending public order systems does not depend on acceptance of dogma about "monolithic Communism." Similarly, one can applaud the attempted shift from cold war containment to a policy of "peaceful engagement" in United States trade relations with the Soviet Union and its Eastern European allies.

intervention for the collection of debts characteristic of an earlier era.[7] Though the distinction is one of degree, and earlier military interventions were never free of political overtones, there does seem to have been a significant shift in the pattern of intervention over the last fifty years. Not all civil strife since World War II, however, neatly fits this pattern. In recent years, civil strife has included a wide range of different types of conflicts: "wars of national liberation" or proxy wars represented by the conflicts in Vietnam, Greece, Thailand, Malaysia, Laos, and Bolivia, anticolonial wars as in Algeria and Angola, wars of secession as in Nigeria and the Congo, and conflicts primarily involving a breakdown of law and order as in Cyprus, the Dominican Republic, and the Congo. This great range of conflicts is also matched by the great range of modalities of external participation or nonparticipation. Such external reactions may range from premature recognition, through propaganda support, to commitment of military advisory units or tactical troops. Other features of the process of intervention reflect this same diversity. As a result, though the varieties of cold war intervention are probably the primary concern today, a fundamental reality of the process of intervention is the great diversity of situations in which the issue is raised.

Given this diversity, it is not surprising that the norms of intervention have been controversial. For traditional legal theory has sought one rule applicable to all forms of intervention in all forms of civil strife.

The traditional view has been that it is lawful to aid a widely recognized government but not insurgents.[8] More recently, some

---

7. The Spanish Civil War was particularly significant for the development of norms of intervention in that it served as one of the major triggering events for writing in this area. See Borchard, *'Neutrality' and Civil Wars*, 31 AM. J. INT'L L. 304 (1937); Garner, *Questions of International Law in the Spanish Civil War*, 31 AM. J. INT'L L. 66 (1937); O'Rourke, *Recognition of Belligerency and the Spanish War*, 31 AM. J. INT'L 398 (1937).

8. See Farer, *supra* note 1, at 271-72. Professor Friedmann states: "What is probably still the prevailing view is that the incumbent government, but not the insurgents, has the right to ask for assistance from foreign governments, at least as long as insurgents are not recognized as 'belligerents or insurgents.'" Friedmann, *Intervention, Civil War and the Role of International Law*, 1965 PROC. AM. SOC'Y INT'L L. 67. Professor Friedmann also criticizes this rule.

scholars have urged a "neutral non-intervention rule" to the effect that a foreign power may not aid either side engaged in purely civil strife once some threshold of indigenous conflict is exceeded.[9]

The principal dangers of the traditional rule are that it may serve as a Maginot line for vested privileges, deterring necessary reforms in feudal or totalitarian societies, and that it may be invoked by recognizing a puppet government as in the Soviet-Finnish war or the Soviet intervention in the 1956 Hungarian uprising. A principal danger of the newer "neutral rule" is that by focusing its normative weight on the more visible overt response it may provide a shield for aggressive takeover through covert attack. The fate of the 1936 Non-Intervention Pact in the Spanish civil war illustrates in a somewhat different context the danger of an unrealistic "neutral" rule. The effectiveness of the "neutral" norm is also substantially impaired by the almost unanimous acceptance of authorization of counter-intervention and by the difficulty of limiting pre-insurgency assistance. Both rules are largely unresponsive to the range of significant variables involved in external participation in intrastate conflict in the present world, although both may intuitively reflect valid policies in particular contexts.

The basic principle of the United Nations Charter that force not be used across international boundaries as an instrument to remedy non-forceful international violations or to compel political change is of overwhelming relevance to many non-consensual interventions. But in many other situations of external participation in intrastate conflict, the armed attack-defense abstractions of Articles 2(4) and 51 offer little guidance. A principal reason is the ambiguity in determining whether a genuine request has been made for external assistance and the ambiguity in appraising the legitimacy of the requesting faction. Interestingly, the OAS Charter and associated agreements, purportedly dealing more explicitly with intervention, also reflect this complementarity of the armed attack-defense abstractions of the Charter.

9. See W. FRIEDMANN, THE CHANGING STRUCTURE OF INTERNATIONAL LAW 265-66 (1964); Wright, *United States Intervention in the Lebanon*, 53 AM. J. INT'L L. 112 (1959).

On the one hand, Articles 15 and 17 of the OAS Charter reflect a purportedly absolute non-intervention doctrine, and on the other hand Articles 19 and 25 of the Charter, Article 6 of the Rio Pact, and the 1962 Punta del Este Resolution reflect the need for mutual security and declare communism incompatible with the principles of the Inter-American system. Sadly, but perhaps understandably, the OAS Charter and the Rio Pact offer only minimal guidance to the resolution of value conflicts when mutual security may be threatened by events which are otherwise primarily internal.

As an alternative to the traditional search for a single norm to regulate intervention, and in the absence of complete guidance in the charters of existing international institutions, it may be useful to first attempt greater clarification of the community policies at stake. That is, to explore as explicitly as possible the reasons why the international community regards certain practices labeled intervention as undesirable. And second, in the light of these policies, to try to clarify the features of the process of intervention which are critical for normative and procedural control.

As is characteristic of many legal norms, whether international or domestic, "intervention" suffers from a definitional problem. The answer to the problem of defining "intervention," though, lies not in a quixotic search for a new verbal test but in careful analysis of the functions to be served by the norms of intervention. As any systems analyst would agree, a starting point for clarification is goal definition. Goal definition alone, however, is only part of the job of operationalizing the concept of intervention. A second necessary step is the anchoring of policies in context by isolation of features crucial to policy realization. Since the traditional norms of intervention tend to be single-factor oriented it would seem particularly useful to attempt this anchoring by a systematic method of inquiry. The next two sections of this chapter are a preliminary attempt to adapt this method to the problem of intervention, first by attempting a preliminary clarification of community policies to be served by the norms of intervention and second by systematic analysis of the critical features of the process of intervention. In suggesting this method, my purpose is to demonstrate the diversity of intervention problems and to attempt preliminary clarification, and is not to formulate a definitive normative framework.

Similarly, though strategic questions in achieving national objectives are an important concern, this analysis is not directed primarily at clarifying the problem of intervention and the national interest, though some features suggested as critical may also be critical for evaluating the chances of "success" by intervention. The identification sought, instead, is that of the scholar concerned with the broadest question of long-run global common interest.

External Participation in Intrastate Conflict: A Clarification of Community Policies

One of the strengths of an approach to international relations which takes account of international law is the almost unique opportunity for focus on long-run community common interest. Moreover, to the extent that clarified community policies are actually reflected in community perspectives about authority, these community subjectivities represent an important reality in predicting and altering events. The principal policies relevant to decision about the permissibility of external participation in intrastate conflict seem to be self-determination and the maximization of human rights, the maintenance of peace and avoidance of destructive coercion, a preference for centralized community decision-making in situations involving transnational use of force, the desirability of mutual assistance in an interdependent world, and perhaps also a preference for a culturally pluralistic world community.

Self-determination, the right of peoples within an entity to choose their own institutions and form of government, is a basic community policy reflected in the principle of equality of states and community condemnation of colonialism. This policy is set out in Article 1, section 2, of the Charter as one of the fundamental purposes of the United Nations.

Somewhat greater difficulty is encountered in defining self-determination at a lower level of abstraction when it is asked what is meant by the right of peoples within an entity to choose their own institutions and form of government. A simplistic answer espoused by Hall[10] identifies self-determination with anything that happens in an entity. According to this view, if aid to the recognized government were legitimate then it would impair the right to revolution, and if aid to the insurgents were legitimate it would violate independence by interfering with the regular organ of the state. This judgment that self-determination requires that neither the recognized government nor insurgents can ever be aided conceals the erroneous assumption that whatever takes place within the confines of a territorial entity is pursuant to genuine self-determination of peoples. Such simplistic deductive notions that territorial entities should in all circumstances be left alone ignore the reality that minorities can through terror, sabotage, and the control of the military establishment capture or maintain control of governmental machinery. The Hall view seems to adopt a kind of Darwinian definition of self-determination as survival of the fittest within the national boundaries, even if fittest means most adept in the use of force. To be meaningful, the right to revolution must be limited to the right to overthrow an unrepresentative government when avenues of peaceful change are foreclosed. It is not a right to minority military takeover whenever another political system is preferred. And similarly, in the converse situation, self-determination does not mean the right of minority maintenance of power by imposition of totalitarian controls.[11]

In place of the Hall rigidity, and despite the formidable obstacles in empirical translation of self-determination, it seems preferable to treat the policy of self-determination as one which turns on the genuine identifications and demands of a populace rather than on territorial isolation. The results of free elections provide probably the best criterion for ascertaining these subjectivities, but there are others as well. Thus, the amount of popular support received by an insurgency, the number of prominent leaders of a society attracted to its cause, responses to calls for

10. See W. HALL, INTERNATIONAL LAW 287 (6th ed. 1909); W. HALL, INTERNATIONAL LAW 347 (8th ed. 1924).
11. See the Resolution by the Eighth Meeting of Consultation of the Ministers of Foreign Affairs held at Punta del Este January 22-31, 1962, Art. IV (adopted by a vote of 20 to 1).

general strikes (such as provided substantial indication of popular feeling for independence in Algeria), opinion polls, demonstrations, the commentary of a more or less free press, and the willingness of the participants—including intervening parties—to agree to free elections, all provide a useful indication of the genuine identifications and demands of the people.

Perhaps the point of the self-determination policy in evaluating external assistance is simply that we do not want external coercive imposition of a particular political ideology against the genuine demands of the people of an entity. But in evaluating what kinds of external interactions produce this effect, it is neither realistic nor philosophically sound simply to draw a line around the boundaries of a state and say that within these boundaries anything goes.

With respect to the policy of maximization of human rights—even apart from its self-determination aspects—the recent events in Rhodesia and the more dramatic events in Indonesia, Biafra, and the Sudan suggest a role for community intervention to preserve a minimum level of human rights or at least to prevent mass starvation.

A second policy relevant to decision about the permissibility of external participation in intrastate conflict is the maintenance of peace and avoidance of destructive coercion. This might be broadly termed the requirements of minimum world public order, after a phrase made familiar by Harold Lasswell and Myres McDougal. In relation to the permissibility of intervention this requirement of minimum world public order embodies a series of relevant policies.

In its broadest sense, it reflects the need in a nuclear world for maintenance of a certain stability and balance of power in what Morton Kaplan hypothesizes as a loose bipolar system.[12] If the danger of prolonged conflict or nuclear disaster is greater when external coercive change is sought in nations committed to an opposing bloc, or in nations located in the primary security zone of an opposing power, or in the "unfriendly" half of a cold-war divided nation, then resulting norms of intervention should en-

12. See Kaplan, *Intervention in Internal War: Some Systemic Sources,* in J. ROSENAU, *supra* note 1, at 92.

able clearer focus on the peculiar danger of such strategies. As both Korea and Vietnam demonstrate, one of the greatest threats to world order today is external intervention seeking coercive change across a boundary separating the *de facto* halves of a cold-war divided country. This is a major reason why it is crucial that international legal scholars clearly condemn the strategy of Hanoi in seeking coercive change across such a cold-war dividing line.[13]

Although not decisive of legitimacy, the need for minimum bloc security and the dangers perceived by national decision-makers in sudden and unpredictable shifts within "committed" areas (particularly within primary security zones, perhaps as given empirical content by reference to such factors as the need to prevent an opposing power from achieving a nuclear first strike capability) provide a strong motivating force for intervention within these zones to prevent sudden shifts to an opposing bloc or sub-bloc. United States actions with respect to Guatemala, Cuba, and the Dominican Republic, and Soviet reactions when faced with insurgencies in East Germany and Hungary, although differing in other crucial aspects, were in part similarly motivated by this perceived need for stability. In fact, the failure of the United States to prevent the sudden shift in its primary security zone in Cuba, a "failure" caused largely by a perception (initially accurate) of the Cuban civil strife as a personnel rather than a structural conflict, did result in direct confrontation between the major powers in the later Cuban missile crisis. When the Soviets secretly and unexpectedly pressed advantage from the sudden shift by emplacement of offensive nuclear missiles in Cuba, the resulting perceived shift in deterrence capabilities precipitated an unusually dangerous inter-bloc confrontation. An unanswered question is to what extent it is legitimate, if at all, to reflect this kind of danger from sudden shifts in "committed" areas in the norms of intervention. Obvious dangers of over-

13. For development of this point see J. N. Moore, *The Lawfulness of Military Assistance to the Republic of Viet Nam*, 61 AM. J. INT'L L. 1 (1967); J. N. Moore, *International Law and the United States Role in Viet Nam: A Reply*, 76 YALE L.J. 1051 (1967); J. N. Moore, *Law and Politics in the Vietnamese War: A Response to Professor Friedmann*, 61 AM. J. INT'L L. 1039 (1967).

emphasis of such a policy include legitimation of intervention against the genuine demands of self-determination, as for example Soviet intervention in Hungary and Czechoslovakia, uncertainty as to Chinese claims to a "sphere of influence," and a return to a Roosevelt Corollary for Latin America. But though, standing alone, this policy is a doubtful one for legitimation of intervention, its converse is crucial in condemning intervention for the purpose of maintaining or achieving change in areas long "committed" to an opposing system or sub-system.

Minimum public order also reflects the Charter principle that use of force as a modality of major change or for dispute settlement is outlawed. The danger and disruptiveness of coercive change in today's world strongly militates for strict adherence to the Charter proscription that force may not be used except in defense against an armed attack. Clearly it is impermissible for either communist or non-communist nations to use major force as a means of expanding ideology or remedying asserted non-forceful breach of international obligations. In a nuclear world, the international system cannot tolerate major use of force as a modality of major change, whether by the United States in Cuba, North Vietnam in South Vietnam, or either Israel or the Arab states in the Middle East. This is perhaps the principal attractiveness of outlawing all assistance to insurgents as under the traditional approach.

Lastly, minimum public order reflects the range of policies for minimization of destruction of all values with respect to on-going coercion. For example, in evaluating the Dominican Republic operation it is relevant to consider the extent, if any, which United States and later OAS actions contributed to damping down destructiveness and avoiding a prolonged bloodbath in the Dominican Republic. Similarly, a major policy concern with regard to the Vietnam conflict is the major destruction of Vietnamese society involved in the decision to wage a protracted defense within Vietnam. Policies involved in minimizing the destructiveness of on-going coercion also include those of proportionality in tailoring the amount of force employed to that necessary to achieve lawful objectives with the least cost to all participants.

A third policy concerning external participation in intrastate conflict is the preference for inclusive community decision-making in situations involving transnational use of force. The problem of auto-interpretation of events and the dangers of major power involvement on opposite sides of intrastate conflict are such that there is a strong community preference for centralized decision-making with respect to transnational use of force. This policy is reflected in the United Nations Charter, which makes unilateral use of force subject to later community review, and in the provisions of the OAS Charter and the Rio Pact, which call for collective regional determination in situations endangering the peace of the Americas.

Presumably, the more inclusive the participation in the decision to intervene the greater the likelihood that the intervention will reflect fundamental community policies. This premise is felt to be so decisive when the level of decision-making becomes global that Article 39 of the Charter gives the Security Council great discretion to determine the existence of a "threat to the peace, breach of the peace, or act of aggression," and Articles 40-42 provide the Security Council with equal discretion in choosing the modality of response. At the intermediate regional level of decision-making, for example, OAS decisions, there is greater controversy as to the permissible discretion to intervene. Doctrinally, the controversy centers on the meaning of "enforcement action" in Article 53 of the U.N. Charter, but functionally the problem is one of allocation of competence to initially employ transnational coercion in situations not involving an armed attack within the meaning of Article 51.

Insofar as this policy favoring institutional decision-making is based on greater likelihood that a particular decision will reflect fundamental community policies, it is also applicable to interventions other than by the use of armed force. For example, political restrictions on foreign aid to the developing states designed to promote needed social reforms might be better imposed by a global or regional organization more representative of inclusive interests.

A fourth policy evident in external participation in intrastate conflict, and in fact in any kind of transnational interaction, is the desirability of mutual assistance in an interdependent world. Like the policy for inclusive community decision-making in situations involving use of force, the policy of mutual assistance is not entirely separate from the demands of self-determination and minimum world public order. But it is perhaps useful to state it as an additional policy in order to focus on the felt interdependence in the world today, both in matters of defense and otherwise. The many regional defense treaties, such as NATO, CENTO, the Rio Pact, SEATO, the Warsaw Pact, and the Arab League, to name a few, demonstrate the real defense interdependency felt in a world which though not composed of monolithic blocs, East or West, is divided between fundamentally different and actively competing public order systems and sub-systems. Given this evidence of interdependency, it may be relevant to ask to what extent focus on self-determination of a single entity is realistic or desirable in situations in which the impact of intrastate conflict is substantial in third states. A tentative answer is that it is still fundamentally necessary to emphasize the genuine demands of the peoples of the entity undergoing the intrastate strife, but that the decision-maker may also be legitimately concerned with the genuine demands of the people of a wider area which may be affected by the outcome.

With respect to interests other than defense, there is a great interdependency also, and it is certainly a widely shared community policy that the developed nations should assist the developing nations in attaining higher economic outputs and a wider distribution of goods and services. It is the tension with these real interdependencies, defense and otherwise, which makes it impossible and undesirable to adopt easy line-drawing solutions to shut out external interactions, and which makes modern day isolation unthinkable.

Lastly, perhaps the norms of intervention reflect a preference for a culturally pluralistic world community. The sociologists tell us that it is frequently the surface superficiality and more undesirable cultural traits that are the first to be transmitted from one culture to another. And the cultural anthropologist has provided greater insights into the values of other cultures that are all too frequently characterized on superficial knowledge as backward. These findings suggest the desirability of restraining missionary zeal in attempts to foster transnational cultural or political change. The excesses of the early missionaries provide ample proof of the dangers of cultural imperialism even for the most beneficent of motives. Perhaps Article 13 of the OAS Charter reflects this preference for cultural pluralism when it provides that: "Each State has the right to develop its cultural, political and economic life freely and naturally."[14]

Necessarily, however, this policy preference for cultural pluralism is difficult to implement in an era when the level of transnational interactions is such that we may accurately speak of a world community. And necessarily, the focus of policies against intervention will remain the more coercive strategies of change.

This preliminary analysis of the policies involved in decision about the permissibility of external participation in intrastate conflict is not intended to be exhaustive. Rather, it is an attempt to isolate the more fundamental reasons why we regard intervention as right or wrong so that resulting norms will be more responsive to the functions they are intended to serve and to encourage a dialogue on the community values at stake. Even an analysis of all operative policies is not a clear chart to wisdom. For in a concrete instance policies may be conflicting. But without such clarification, sound decision becomes little more than chance.

Elsewhere I have attempted to analyze the principal existing norms of intervention with respect to the major policies of self-determination and minimum public order, and have concluded that existing norms are too oversimplified to be meaningfully policy-responsive in the wide range of situations in which they are applied.[15] Nevertheless, existing norms, such as the traditional view that assistance could be rendered to widely recognized gov-

14. Similarly, section 2 (e) of the draft recommendation adopted on April 22, 1966 by the Special Committee on Principles of International Law Concerning Friendly Relations and Co-operation Among States provides that: "Each State has the right freely to choose and develop its political, social, economic and cultural systems." U.N. Doc. A/6230 at 176, 183 (1966).

15. See Moore, *supra* note 13, 61 AM. J. INT'L L., at 28-32; 76 YALE L.J. at 1080-88. See also my brief recommendation of a framework for inquiry about non-intervention norms in the 1967 PROC. AM. SOC'Y INT'L L. 75.

ernments only, may intuitively reach sound results in particular contexts. For example, the traditional view that a widely recognized government may be lawfully aided and that insurgents may not seems on analysis to have some merit in the cold-war divided nation context. Considerations which suggest this conclusion are the desirability of focusing on the great threat to peace in providing sustained assistance to insurgents across cold-war boundaries, the difficulty of appraising covert assistance in externally sponsored "wars of national liberation," the perceived threat to the balance of power from sudden shifts in committed areas, and realism about contraints felt by opposing bloc powers to support existing friendly regimes, as evidenced by the events in Hungary, East Germany, Malaysia, Korea, Greece, and now Vietnam.

But since this chapter is a preliminary inquiry into method, instead of repeating a policy analysis of the existing norms or formulating a new set of non-intervention norms, it seems more useful in light of the great diversity of situations subsumed under intervention to attempt to clarify the critical features of the process of intervention. The features selected as "critical," of course, are "critical" from the standpoint of one or more of the community policies just explored. Focusing on these critical features of the process is a way of operationalizing the community policies served by the non-intervention proscription. Hopefully, this exposition of a systematic method for anchoring non-intervention policies in context might aid in eventual formulation of a more responsive normative framework for controlling intervention. And in the short run, it seems a substantial improvement to at least move from certainty for the wrong reasons to uncertainty for the right reasons.

The Critical Features of the Process of Intervention: Some Unanswered Questions

The critical features of the process of intervention can be most conveniently explored by systematic analysis of the process with regard to the participants involved, the objectives sought by the participants, the situations spatially and temporally of the intervention, the resources or base values available to the participants, the strategies pursued by the participants, the immediate outcomes of the process, the longer-range effects of the intervention on the international system, and the conditions of the system shaping the process. This method of analysis is intended to focus attention on the range of variables in the process which may be useful for normative judgment and to suggest the disutility of attempting the formulation of norms for all contexts by reference to a single feature of the process of intervention.

PARTICIPANTS

One important feature of the process of intervention is the degree of collectivization of the action. Because of the community policy favoring inclusive decision-making in situations involving transnational coercion, it is highly relevant to judgment about such transnational interactions whether the principal decision was made at a global level by the United Nations, or at a regional level by perhaps the OAS, or unilaterally.

The Charter provides wide competence to the United Nations Security Council to take action, including the use of force to take measures to deal with "any threat to the peace, breach of the peace, or act of aggression." Moreover, this competence is specifically excluded from the Article 2 prohibition against intervention "in matters which are essentially within the domestic jurisdiction of any state." The community policies militating for a broad United Nations competence to intervene "whenever civil strife threatens world peace or whenever gross abuses of fundamental human rights take place" have been eloquently stated by Professor Falk earlier.[16] Since then, the substance of Professor Falk's thesis "that the United Nations should be authorized on a selective basis to coerce domestic social changes" has been adopted in the limited form of United Nations sanctions against Rhodesia.[17]

An unanswered question which must also be met even by those

16. Falk, *The Legitimacy of Legislative Intervention by the United Nations,* in STANGER, *supra* note 1, at 31.
17. See McDougal & Reisman, *Rhodesia and the United Nations: The Lawfulness of International Concern,* 62 AM. J. INT'L L. 1 (1968); Rabinowitz, *U.N. Application of Selective, Mandatory Sanctions Against Rhodesia: A Brief Legal and Political Analysis,* 7 VA. J. INT'L L. 147 (1967).

applauding the Rhodesian sanctions, however, is whether Security Council competence to intervene under Chapter VII of the Charter is to be absolute, limited only by the necessity of permanent member assent and the requisite vote of seven members, or whether it is to be limited by other substantive community policies. The answer, it would seem, should lie in the further exploration and application of the broad community policies explored in the preceding section. Since one of those policies is a preference for inclusive decision-making in situations involving transnational use of force or threatening the stability of world order, it seems desirable that the United Nations have a broad competence along the lines suggested by Professor Falk whenever an otherwise "domestic" question is a threat to the stability of the international system. The Rhodesian situation is such a case. Effective exercise of this competence in conformance with inclusive community concern presupposes the maintenance within the United Nations of effective representation of inclusive interests.

When the decision to intervene is made at a regional level, for example by the OAS, the institutionalization and collectivization of the actions do increase the legitimacy of those actions. One reason for this increase is the greater assurance that such actions represent legitimate inclusive interests. But since by definition regional actors do not share the global representation of the United Nations, they should not have the degree of discretion available to the global organization. Moreover, a factor militating against wide regional discretion to use major force is the danger that regional action poses for major power confrontation, since regional action does not need the concurrent vote of all major powers voting, as is true of Security Council authorization. Again, however, the answer to the degree of competence of regional actors is suggested not so much by an analysis of the "enforcement action" language of the U.N. Charter as by careful analysis of the community values at stake in any particular type of action, particularly the effect on self-determination and the danger to minimum public order.

Though individual or collective action which falls short of regional or global authority does not share the greater assurance offered by the wider collectivization and institutionalization of regional and U.N. action, the imperfections of existing global and regional peace-keeping machinery make it inevitable that a substantial area of individual discretion be retained, subject to later community review. This is particularly true of the need for an effective right of individual and collective defense, but may also extend to other actions in conformance with basic community policies. The effect of timing of institutional consent, whether prior approval or later ratification of unilateral action, may also reflect important policy consequences worth further contextual exploration.

Other features which might be explored with respect to intervening participants include the resources available for the intervention, geographic distance from the intervention, and degree of particiption in a regional bloc or movement.

OBJECTIVES

A particularly relevant feature of the process of intervention, though often one of the most difficult to appraise, is the objectives with which the participants initiate and sustain an intervention.

Anti-colonial wars such as the Algerian war may evidence objectives which are basically in conformance with widely shared community notions about self-determination. The totalitarian pattern of "wars of national liberation," on the other hand, if carried on by a minority using terrorist tactics, may be the antithesis of genuine self-determination, despite rhetoric about democracy and anti-colonialism.

In the Vietnam conflict, Hanoi's sustained assistance to the insurgents in the South seems to be given with the more or less long-run objective of territorial and political unification of a *de facto* divided country. This at times self-proclaimed objective of Hanoi in intervening in South Vietnam is a highly relevant feature in assessing the legitimacy of third-party assistance to the government of South Vietnam.

A somewhat different objective evidenced in the American Civil War, the Congo strife, and the Nigerian civil war is the desire for secession. Analysis of the requirements of self-determination here raise such imponderables as how to define an "entity" as a starting point for appraisal of self-determination. This question, which is crucial to many situations of civil strife, is conspicuously neglected by the non-intervention literature. Presumably inquiry aimed at this question might consider the desirability of existing boundaries in terms of geographic, historic, economic, political, and ethnic factors.

Major intervention by military force which evidences as an objective the collection of asserted debts or which seeks to impose sanctions for asserted breach of international law not amounting to an "armed attack" offers no justification either in terms of the requirements of self-determination or minimum public order, and as such should be condemned. The joint British-French-Israeli invasion of Suez would seem a recent example of intervention in which such objectives played a substantial role.

On the other hand, limited use of force for the protection of the lives of nationals or for "humanitarian intervention" may serve community policies and should be accepted if narrowly confined to these objectives. For example, even those critical of later stages of the Dominican Republic operation seem to have conceded the propriety of landing limited American forces for the protection of the lives of nationals in a situation of near anarchy, though they dispute to what extent the lives of American nationals were threatened. Although perhaps more controversial, I would place the November 1964 joint U.S.-Belgian Congo intervention for the protection of civilian hostages, nationals of at least eighteen foreign countries, in the same category. The much needed Biafran relief, if aimed at avoiding mass starvation rather than establishing a second state, would also fall in this category.

The point is that the objectives evidenced by intervening powers and by national participants in civil strife vary widely, and as objectively appraised by both conduct and statement, such objectives provide a highly relevant feature in assessing permissibility of intervention. It is inaccurate to take the absolutist position that all intervention is identical and should be impermissible. The truth is that some interventions promote community policies while others do not, and a quest for a "neutral" rule which ignores these policies may be self-defeating.

Of course, just because a particular action is consistent with self-determination does not mean that it should be legitimate.

Other community policies, particularly the maintenance of minimum public order, may also be threatened. Where the risk of major conflict is slight, grave and continuing denial of self-determination may outweigh dangers of the use of coercive strategies of change. But where such risk is grave, minimum public order may be the most important consideration.[18]

SITUATIONS

One feature of the process of intervention which has been almost entirely overlooked in traditional treatments but which seems highly relevant in evaluating the consequences of intervention with respect to minimum public order is the location of the intervention in relation to major power security.

The risk that intervention will trigger major or prolonged conflict is much higher for interventions aimed at altering the *status quo* in the primary security areas or among the committed nations of a competing bloc. And the risk is much less for interventions aimed at maintaining the *status quo* within the corresponding areas of the intervening power. For example, regardless of their substantial dissimilarities, the Soviet interventions in Hungary and Czechoslovakia, and the United States interventions in Guatemala and the Dominican Republic, ran substantially low risks of major power conflict or prolonged war. And each was at least partially a reaction to a perceived threat (erroneously perceived or not) to the stability of the defensive posture of the intervening power. If intervention does not threaten to alter the primary security interests of opposing major powers, there is even less threat to the global implications of minimum public order. Indian intervention in Goa and a hypothetical British intervention in Rhodesia would seem to offer examples of this. On the other

18. James N. Rosenau's classification of internal wars as personnel wars, authority wars, and structural wars is a useful characterization based principally on the objectives of the participants. Of these, the structural wars, which he defines as "those which are perceived as being not only contests over personnel and the structure of political authority, but also as struggles over other substructures of the society . . . or its major domestic and foreign policies," could be expected to be the most disruptive of the international system and the most likely to invite external participation. See Rosenau, *Internal War as an International Event*, in J. ROSENAU, *supra* note 1, at 45, 63.

hand, the Egyptian and Saudi Arabian intervention on opposing sides in the Yemen illustrates that minimum public order in its other senses may still be a major value at stake even if the global threat is minor.

Perhaps the clearest example of this geographic principle is provided by the Korean and Vietnam conflicts, where North Korea and North Vietnam sought change by, in the one case overt and in the other covert, use of the military instrument across lines clearly separating the major contending public order systems. Probably few interventions possess the potential for major and escalating conflict as such interventions across the cold-war demarcation lines in these divided countries. Both Korea and Vietnam amply demonstrate this danger. And though it would seem desirable in many ways for the contending cold-war camps to recognize the real-world division of these divided countries in Germany, Korea, China, and Vietnam, it is *imperative* that rhetoric about "one nation" used by both sides not conceal the great community interest in at least clearly recognizing the separateness of such entities for the purpose of assessing the legitimacy of the use of force across the boundaries and cease-fire lines separating them.

Similarly, though the problem of how to define an "entity" may be considerably more complex with reference to the requirements of self-determination, when the principal policy at stake becomes minimum public order the criterion is essentially *de facto* separateness.

Again, this geographic feature of the process of intervention is not necessarily decisive, primarily because other important community values may be at stake. But intervention clearly within the "committed" area of another major power presents a grave threat to world public order which should usually be enough *ipso facto* to render such intervention impermissible. Even within one's own bloc, however, intervention which blatantly denies self-determination should be impermissible. Thus, in analyzing the Hungarian uprising it would seem that the requirements of self-determination made it impermissible for the Soviets to intervene to crush the revolt (and *a fortiori* impermissible in Czechoslovakia) and that the requirements of minimum public order made it impermissible for the United States to intervene to assist the revolt against the Soviet-imposed regime. In circumstances like the Hungarian uprising, intervention by either party would threaten fundamental community policies, though for different reasons, and should not be undertaken.

BASE VALUES

The single feature emphasized in the traditional non-intervention norm is whether external assistance was requested by a recognized government. This feature of the process of intervention— whether assistance was rendered to insurgents or at the request of a widely recognized government—conceals a number of important questions which may be relevant to normative clarification. In fact, because the traditional norm largely conceals the real importance of the recognized government-insurgent distinction with respect to policies both of self-determination and minimum public order, it has obscured its own real relevance, an obfuscation which has made it unnecessarily vulnerable to the seeming attractiveness of the "neutral" non-intervention norm. It is not suggested, however, that this traditional norm is policy responsive in a broad range of contexts.

More explicitly, the question is whether there are any real differences between insurgents and a widely recognized government which make a difference in impact on community policies whether assistance is rendered to one or the other.

On analysis, the distinction between widely recognized governments and insurgents does seem to reflect important differences, but these differences may be more precisely stated by reference to degree of authority and control exercised by each faction, by reference to which faction controls the organized military apparatus, and by reference to which faction may have the greater communicated expectation of international support.

A government whose credentials are undisputed is usually characterized both by widespread expectations, internal and external, of its authority, and by effective control of its territory and population. To the extent that either authority or control, or both, is lacking, a government's legitimacy in requesting external assistance is reduced. The degree to which insurgents or the widely recognized government possess authority, both internal and external, in the sense of expectations as to their "rightness" to govern, is relevant from the standpoint of self-determination in determining which faction may be assisted. And the degree to which insurgents or the widely recognized government exercise effective control over territory and population is relevant from the standpoint of minimum public order in determining which faction may be assisted. In fact, the traditional law of civil strife contains the label "belligerent" for insurgents who exercise greater effective control, and when they are so labeled accords them greater international status. Thus, one relevant aspect of the recognized government-insurgent distinction is really a question of where each faction falls on a continuum of authority and control. Assistance to a faction which exercises little authority and control is essentially nothing but an external attack (which may or may not rise to the level of an "armed attack" within the meaning of Article 51 of the Charter), if provided against a faction which exercises substantial authority and control. Real nakedness of authority and control cannot be cured by puppet governments or instant recognition. For example, the Soviet creation of an instant government which invited them in to the Russo-Finnish War, and the same Soviet ruse in the 1956 Hungarian uprising, did not in any but a propaganda sense render Soviet actions more permissible. The 1968 invasion of Czechoslovakia was even more blatant. And on the other hand, assistance at the request of a widely recognized government which exercises substantial authority and control is not "intervention" in any primary sense.

On the whole, it can be expected that a government which is widely recognized over a significant period of time can be expected to exercise substantial authority and control, and, as such, the traditional rule may often reflect an important feature, albeit intuitively.

A second important feature underlying the recognized government-insurgency dichotomy is the question of control of the organized military apparatus. It seems to be particularly important in predicting the consequences for minimum public order if sustained military assistance is rendered to a faction which does not control the organized military. A comparison of such diverse situations as Hungary and Lebanon with Algeria and Vietnam indicates that sustained assistance to an insurgency which is opposed by the organized military is likely to lead to a prolonged costly struggle. One of the reasons for the "success" of the United States Guatemalan intervention was that the low-level assistance to the insurgents was premised on the organized military switching to the insurgent cause of Castillo Armas. When the organized military did switch from Arbenz to Armas the brief fight was over.[19] And conversely, one of the principal reasons for the failure of the Bay of Pigs venture was its effective opposition by the organized military which seemed to have little inclination toward a shift in loyalties. The failure of the attempted Maoist coup in Indonesia may be partly attributable to this same factor. Similarly, one of the principal reasons for the prolonged war in Vietnam is that the organized military is perhaps the principal opposition to the insurgent cause. The decision by North Vietnam to provide sustained assistance to an insurgency opposed by the organized military is another factor making such a decision extremely dangerous for world order, and which one suspects may have resulted from a persistent miscalculation about political collapse in the South or the degree of United States support to be expected.

To the extent that widely recognized governments more often command the loyalties of the organized military apparatus, sustained assistance to insurgents is likely to be an intervention which is particularly dangerous to world peace.

A third factor underlying the recognized government-insurgency dichotomy, and there may be others, is the degree to which a faction has, and communicates expectations of having, access to external support. One manifestation of such support might be a preexisting treaty of guarantee against external attack or internal subversion. The SEATO Treaty is a common example of a loose agreement of this type.[20] To the extent that assistance is rendered

19. See WESTERFIELD, THE INSTRUMENTS OF AMERICA'S FOREIGN POLICY 422-42 (1966).

20. There has been considerable controversy surrounding the weight to be given the SEATO "obligation" to defend South Vietnam. On balance it would seem that SEATO has been neither all-important nor inconsequential. One of the ways in which SEATO is relevant is simply

to a faction opposed by an elite which is party to such an agreement, or which otherwise has expectations of external assistance, the conflict stands a substantial likelihood of being internationalized in a dangerous fashion. To the extent, then, that widely recognized governments are more likely to have access to such external support, sustained assistance to insurgents runs a greater risk of dangerous international escalation of the conflict. To some extent, these expectations of access to external support may also be said to be a function of the external authority position of a particular faction. Thus, degree of external authority may be important with respect to the minimum public order policy as well as with respect to the self-determination policy.

STRATEGIES

The strategies or modalities of intervention may range from propaganda support of one faction or another through diplomatic recognition, economic assistance, supply of military hardware, shows of force, commitment of advisory and training forces, and commitment of troops in tactical operations. Moreover, failure to provide assistance or withdrawal of assistance previously begun with respect to each of these modalities may also have internal effects which are sometimes characterized as intervention.

Though this feature of the process of intervention seems highly relevant to the permissibility of intervention, traditional theory has accorded it little weight. Recently, however, Tom Farer has suggested, in a provocative reevaluation of the norms of intervention, that there should be "a flat prohibition of participation in tactical operations, either openly or through the medium of advisors or volunteers."[21] This proposal has considerable merit. It is particularly sensitive to the need for reducing the danger of great power confrontation on opposing sides of civil strife and

---

its function as a manifestation of expectations of international assistance for the Saigon government. The existence of such a communication is a relevant feature in predicting the danger to minimum world public order of a decision to provide sustained assistance to insurgents aimed at the structural overthrow of established elites.

21. Farer, *Intervention in Civil Wars: A Modest Proposal*, 67 COL. L. REV. 266, 275 (1967).

also has the substantial merit of ruling out one of the most coercive forms of interaction.

Like the norms which preceded it, however, this proposal is keyed to only one feature of the process of intervention and as such is incomplete. It is highly questionable, for example, whether in light of the applicable community policies it is desirable to legitimate all external assistance by any participant for any objective in any situation and to any faction which falls short of the threshold of participation in tactical operations. For example, continuing supply of military hardware by the United States to insurgents in Hungary or such continuing supply from Taiwan to insurgents in mainland China or from North Korea to South Korea would also seem to carry substantial risk of escalation.

Presumably also the rule breaks down unless reciprocity is accorded when one side resorts to tactical operations. And as Vietnam demonstrates, this transition may provide a difficult line to draw when the operations of one side are largely covert. Like the "neutral" non-intervention rule, there is some danger that this tactical operations rule will be largely focused on the overt response rather than the precipitating covert assistance.

Despite my reservations about this proposal as a panacea, however, it is probably the single most useful normative suggestion which has been made for dealing with the intervention problem and provides a long overdue focus on the possibility of using the modality of intervention as a normative base. Perhaps its major shortcoming is that there is simply too broad a range of intervention situations to be adequately dealt with by one rule.

OUTCOMES

Another significant feature of the process of intervention, which might be usefully employed as a normative base and which has been largely ignored in formulating the traditional rules, is the question of whether an external participation is followed by genuine elections or some other means of ascertaining the requirements of self-determination. Since this feature of the process of intervention may more directly reflect the requirements of genuine self-determination than any other feature of the process, it would certainly be worthwhile to explore to what extent the permissibility of particular types of intervention might be conditioned on holding supervised elections.

EFFECTS

The relatively long-run consequences for world order of a particular intervention or type of intervention may also be a relevant factor in formulating normative restraints on intervention. One such feature might be that the state in which intervention takes place has itself been widely intervening by fostering and supporting insurgencies, as for example is true of the activities of Castro's Cuba in a number of Latin American countries, though, as Che Guevara's death indicates, probably with a generally unfavorable prognosis. A related question at an earlier stage of the process would be whether the dominant myth espoused by a particular faction engaged in civil strife includes revolutionary assistance to insurgencies elsewhere.

One relatively long-run effect of insurgency is particularly interesting and may suggest some questions relevant to the norms of intervention. That is, the degree to which successful insurgencies foster more insurgencies. George Modelski has described what he terms a "diffusion effect" in the international system by which the prevailing subjectivities and myths of the time are translated into such movements as a wave of colonial wars or a movement toward democratic regimes, as occurred immediately after World War II, or a noticeable trend toward fascist governments as was true throughout the world between 1938 and 1941.[22]

It is conceivable in some cases that the subjectivities, demands, and identifications fostered by a decision to intervene or not to intervene may even be the most important single feature of the process of intervention in terms of effects on world order. The underestimation of this kind of psychological factor, the subjectivities involved in the process, is a consistent error of the *realpolitik* school. If this factor is an important feature of the process of intervention it may be useful to inquire to what extent the principal revolutionary myths today are anti-colonial wars and "wars

22. Modelski, *The International Relations of Internal War*, in J. ROSENAU, *supra* note 1, at 14, 32.

of national liberation," and what the consequences of this, if any, should be for the norms of intervention.

CONDITIONS

The broader context of conditions in which the process of intervention takes place is also of importance for the formulation of norms of intervention.

Conditions of particular relevance to this process have been implicit in much of the discussion thus far. Perhaps the overriding condition is the presence in the world of competing but loosely coordinated public order systems maintaining a precarious nuclear balance of terror.

This condition renders minimum world public order of crucial dimension. In this context, norms which reduce the possibility of direct inter-bloc conflict and which place a premium on the stability of the international system may well be more important than norms which evince great sensitivity to other community policies but which perform poorly in terms of minimum public order.

Another general condition affecting the process of intervention is the great interdependency of nations today and the high level of interaction achieved on a global level. The rapid transformation of communications and transportation technology in the last fifty years has shrunk the world as never before. This interdependency and high level of interaction intensifies the effect of internal war on the international system and the effect of system change on internal war. At the same time, the knowledge and technology explosions tend themselves to promote rapid social change which, lacking other outlets, may take the form of revolution. The combination of factors produces an unusually high number of intrastate conflicts, with resulting intensified instability in the international system, and tends to make the developing countries a battleground for competing public order systems. These conditions suggest the need for international legislative competence to ease explosive change and for institutions and practices which protect the developing countries from cold-war tensions.

It is also of great concern that the international system currently offers only a low level of institutionalization for the control of intrastate conflict. What has been termed by Abram Chayes "the process side" of the control of external participation in such conflict is extremely primitive.[23]

Lacking to a greater or lesser degree are readily available and reliable fact-finding institutions for ascertaining the level and occurrence of covert external participation, effective mediating agencies, agencies for conducting elections, and other forms of desirable process controls.

Internal war is most tractable to settlement and least dangerous in early stages, and it is in these early stages that an effective international process should intervene to secure settlement. The existing process controls, however, show little sign of functioning before a high order of chaos is reached. And though regional organizations such as SEATO and the OAS have performed some fact-finding functions, SEATO to a lesser extent in Vietnam and the OAS more forcefully in Venezuela, the potentiality even of these "committed" organizations to secure and publish facts has largely gone untapped. It would be particularly helpful if reasonably reliable permanent fact-finding agencies were available at a global level. The willingness of one faction or another to resort to the agency could be a relevant factor in evaluating assistance to that faction.

It is particularly important that the role of the U.N. in damping down dangerous intrastate conflict, already begun in the Congo and Cyprus, and the existing potentiality of the U.N. to provide some of the suggested process tools, be strengthened. In fact it is probable that development of this "process side" offers greater hope for control than does normative clarification. Certainly attention should be directed at creating and strengthening the kinds of institutions needed. But as perhaps the controversy surrounding the Congo operation demonstrates, "process" is a means to a goal, not a substitute for goal definition. Normative clarification remains necessary for direction and for evaluation.

This preliminary analysis of the critical features of the process

---

23. This is a term which caught my fancy during the panel discussion of the "Norms of Intervention" at the 1967 Annual Meeting of the American Society of International Law.

of intervention is intended to call attention to the broad range of contextual features which may be important in formulating a normative framework for the control of external participation in intrastate conflict and to suggest the importance of several critical features of the process of intervention. It is not intended as a definitive formulation of a normative framework or as a complete analysis of all the relevant features. Undoubtedly there are other important factors which might also be profitably analyzed in a thorough systematic analysis of the process of intervention.

An Appraisal

The traditional approach to the norms of intervention has sought one rule applicable to all forms of civil strife. Characteristically, that rule has focused on only a single feature of the process of intervention. The great diversity of situations in which intervention is invoked, however, and the variety of critical features of the process of intervention have rendered such rules hopelessly over-simplified. It is not surprising that they have not been widely observed. Furthermore, since the traditional rules usually lacked policy clarification, what function they have performed has been largely intuitive. The traditional controversy between the legitimacy theory and the so-called neutral non-intervention norm, for example, has distracted attention from a meaningful search for other normative bases, such as limitations on types of assistance, area limitations, international procedural processes, or conditioning the lawfulness of external assistance on willingness to hold free elections. The mechanical application of these rules has also obscured focus on the community policies at stake in situations of intervention. The traditional dialogue must move beyond controversy about these rigid rules and give way to more flexible and thoroughgoing inquiry.

As an alternative method for clarifying policy choices with respect to the control of intervention, it is recommended that we first seek greater clarification of the function to be served by the norms of intervention. Such clarification offers standards which may then be used for the isolation of critical features for each major type of civil strife which in turn may provide a base for more effective normative refinement.

Empirical research may not support some of these contextual features as crucial for policy realization, and thorough analysis may reveal other critical features. But the important point is that the method of inquiry should serve as a way of operationalizing the non-intervention proscription for a badly needed more responsive and realistic normative structure.

CHAPTER IV

The Control of Foreign Intervention in Internal Conflict*

I. Delimitation of the Problem

INTERVENTION IN INTERNAL CONFLICT AS A MAJOR PUBLIC ORDER CONCERN

The nuclear arms race, the economic gap between the have and have not nations, and the weakness of international organization have long been recognized as major public order concerns. During the last few years it has become increasingly evident that intervention in internal conflict is also a major concern. The recent events in the Congo, Cyprus, Czechoslovakia, the Dominican Republic, Hungary, Israel, Laos, Lebanon, Nigeria, Northern Ireland, Pakistan, Vietnam, and Yemen make this concern self-evident. The problem, though, may be more pervasive than these dramatic incidents suggest, for our world is both increasingly revolutionary and increasingly interdependent.

Professor C. E. Black has predicted "ten to fifteen revolutions a year for the foreseeable future in the less developed societies."[1] Former Secretary of Defense Robert McNamara reported a few years ago that while "at the beginning of 1958 there were 23 prolonged insurgencies going on around the world, as of February, 1966, there were 40. Further, the total number of outbreaks of violence has increased each year: in 1958 there were 34; in 1965 there were 58."[2] And Professors Leiden and Schmitt, in their summary of revolution in the modern world, assert that "even a cursory view of recent history forces an acknowledgment that we are living in a new era of revolution . . . ; the last third of the twentieth century promises to be a period of almost constant

---

* I am indebted to Hardy C. Dillard, Rosalyn Higgins, Myres S. McDougal, and W. Michael Reisman for their many helpful suggestions on an earlier draft of this chapter.
1. C. BLACK, THE DYNAMICS OF MODERNIZATION 166 (1966).
2. R. McNAMARA, THE ESSENCE OF SECURITY 145 (1968).

revolutionary turmoil. . . ."[3] This increase in violent revolutionary activity is a complex phenomenon about which little is known except that it is almost certainly a result of interaction among a number of systemic and psychological variables. Among the more likely causative factors are the great increase in newly independent and underdeveloped nations of the third world, resulting from the accelerated process of decolonization after World War II; a widening economic gap between the have and have not nations, coupled in some areas with an actual decrease in per capita income (described by Oran Young as an "asymmetrical distribution of values" in the system or the "so-called North-South problem");[4] an accelerating rate of social change, resulting from technological and communications explosions; the parameters of a nuclear balance of terror that may sometimes encourage limited and proxy wars; a fragmentation into competing factions of an international system which was once divided between more monolithic blocs; an intense ideological competition (the so-called East-West problem); and strong revolutionary and nationalistic myths shared by many communist and non-communist reformers.

Many of these same factors, particularly the continued high level of cold-war confrontation and the continuation of colonial and racially divided regimes in a world increasingly aspiring to genuine self-determination, have also encouraged more frequent intervention. Since a number of these trends contributing to increased revolutionary and interventionary activity may be accelerating, it seems possible that the control of intervention in internal conflict may become an even more critical problem in the future.

We have arrived at this critical point in the upswing of revolutionary and interventionary activity without either accepted norms differentiating permissible from impermissible external interference or international machinery well suited for the control of intervention. The history of efforts to manage international

3. C. LEIDEN & K. SCHMITT, THE POLITICS OF VIOLENCE: REVOLUTION IN THE MODERN WORLD 212 (1968).
4. Young, *Intervention and International Systems*, 22 J. INT'L AFFAIRS 177, 179 (1968).

conflict is the twin history of normative clarification and the development of international organization; but such efforts typically have been mere responses to the public order problems which acted as triggering events.[5] Since the problem of intervention in internal war has developed into a core public order problem chiefly since World War II, neither the present normative structure for control of coercion nor the institutional capacity of present international organizations is well suited to its control.

It is true, of course, that the post-Napoleonic period in Europe and the Spanish civil war both triggered concern with the problem of intervention, but these earlier efforts lacked the sophistication of current dialogue; and for the most part what lessons were learned were never effectively assimilated into the international law of conflict management.[6] Thus, the United Nations, which is the central structure for the control of international conflict, is largely a reaction to situations of overt aggression, particularly World War II. As a result, the armed attack-defense abstractions of the Charter provide little guidance as to permissibility of assistance to either a widely recognized government or insurgents in a situation of internal war. Article 2(4) of the Charter prohibits the use of force in international relations but does not bar the use of force internal to a state. The difficulty is in determining when

5. For a brief history of the international law of conflict management see M. Kaplan & N. Katzenbach, *Resort to Force: War and Neutrality*, in The Political Foundations of International Law 198-228 (1961), *reprinted in* II R. Falk & S. Mendlovitz, The Strategy of World Order 276 (1966).

6. The Spanish Civil War was particularly significant for the development of intervention theory in that it was one of the major triggering events stimulating writing about intervention. See Borchard, *"Neutrality" and Civil Wars*, 31 Am. J. Int'l L. 304 (1937); Garner, *Questions of International Law in the Spanish Civil War*, 31 Am. J. Int'l L. 66 (1937); O'Rourke, *Recognition of Belligerency and the Spanish War*, 31 Am. J. Int'l L. 398 (1937).

The Vietnam War has been another such triggering event; in the last few years there has been a flood of writing about revolution and intervention. See generally I & II R. Falk (ed.), The Vietnam War and International Law (Vol. I, 1968, Vol. II, 1969). Volume III of The Vietnam War and International Law will be published in 1972 and together the three volumes give some indication of the intense current interest in intervention. The volumes are sponsored by the American Society of International Law.

external assistance to one side or another in internal war threatens "the territorial integrity or political independence" of a State as proscribed by Article 2(4). Similarly, Article 51 preserves the right of individual and collective defense against an armed attack. But when is assistance to one side or another an armed attack and when is it collective defense? The abstractions of the Charter also provide little guidance in determining the legitimacy of some non-authority-oriented interventions, such as the classic "humanitarian intervention," where objectives are other than the influencing of authority structures. Finally, customary international law, with its focus on the now largely defunct distinctions between rebellion, insurgency, and belligerency, and with its simplistic insistence on the sanctity of military assistance to a widely recognized government, is equally inadequate. Contemporary discussion about the definition of aggression still reflects most of these ambiguities.

The institutional side of the Charter is also deficient in dealing with intervention in internal war. A central problem in appraising most interventions is the need for impartial fact-finding and disclosure. We need answers to such questions as: What is the extent of Hanoi's involvement in insurgencies in Laos, Thailand, and Vietnam? What was the chronology of external intervention on behalf of the competing factions in Vietnam? What was the role of the United States with regard to the competing factions in the Dominican and Stanleyville operations?

While sometimes useful, as in Laos, Lebanon, and Yemen, the Charter machinery for fact-finding is *ad hoc*, subject to cold war currents, and frequently unavailable when most needed. In addition, the only real reporting requirements of the Charter relate to action taken in defense against an armed attack or as enforcement by regional agencies; and since assistance to one side or another in internal conflict may frequently be neither of these, such assistance often goes unreported. This was the case in Vietnam during the five years prior to the Tonkin Gulf incident of 1964, despite a sustained high level of conflict. Moreover, the Charter structure is equally lacking in machinery to catch internal war in its early and more malleable stages, before positions harden and a lasting political solution becomes next to impossible.

The increase in interventionary and revolutionary activity, coupled with the poorly developed responsive capability of the international system, suggest that the development of normative and institutional controls on intervention in internal war is an urgent task for those concerned with public order problems. To be most useful this development should be compatible with the broader Charter framework, which has been a major evolutionary step in conflict management, and should build on the effective features of existing international institutions.

SOME INTELLECTUAL TRAPS IN THEORIZING ABOUT INTERVENTION

Before outlining a suggested approach to the control of intervention it is useful to enumerate some of the common sources of intellectual confusion in theorizing about intervention. The two principal sources seem to be terminological confusion and the contextual fallacy.

TERMINOLOGICAL CONFUSION

Terminological confusion has been a major cause of the intellectual rigor-mortis which has characterized much of the discussion about intervention. The confusion stems from the different senses, at least four in number, in which the term intervention is commonly used in discourse about international relations.[7]
These are:

as a synonym for transnational interaction or influence;
as a statement that a particular transnational interaction violates authoritative community expectations about permissible international conduct;

7. That the confusion is still with us is suggested by the Editor's Foreword to a recent symposium on intervention which identifies the cause of conceptual confusion about intervention as the "result of the dual usage of the term . . . as an *analytical* concept by political scientists and as an *operational* concept by diplomats and strategists." *Editor's Foreword*, 22 J. INT'L AFF. ix (1968). Though the referents are vague, the *analytical* usage probably refers to the fourth meaning of the term as a nominal definition of a problem for study and the *operational* usage probably refers to the first meaning of the term as a synonym for transnational interaction or influence. The *operational* usage, however, may refer to any of the first three senses of the term.

as a personal policy judgment that a particular transnational interaction is wrong; and

as a definition of a problem for study.

Although there is an interrelation among these four senses, failure to separate them and to recognize that two of the four are value-charged is to court needless intellectual confusion.[8]

The first sense in which intervention is used, as a synonym for transnational interaction or influence, may be illustrated by an excerpt from a classic article on intervention by Professor Wolfgang Friedmann: "The relevant question for the international lawyer is at what point the manifold forms and degrees of intervention may be said to amount to an act of unlawful interference with the sovereignty of another country."[9]

In this excerpt, Professor Friedmann uses intervention to refer to a whole range of transnational interactions by which states influence the actions of other states. Used in this sense, intervention is not intended to carry normative overtones as to legitimacy of conduct, but is intended simply to refer to a range of transnational interactions. *Unless otherwise clear from the context, intervention is used throughout this chapter in this first sense.*

The second sense in which intervention is used, as an assertion that a particular transnational interaction violates authoritative community expectations about permissible international conduct, is simply an assertion about what we might loosely call international law. In this sense, intervention refers to the scientific task of describing authoritative community expectations; and as such it can be used accurately or inaccurately. When used in this sense,

8. In a recent article on *The Concept of Intervention* Professor James N. Rosenau may have identified a fifth meaning of the term. That is, as a statement about how the term is popularly or specially used based on empirical observation of linguistic usage. Although such observation might be useful in determining community expectations, this sense does not seem sufficiently common to justify major treatment. See Rosenau, *The Concept of Intervention*, 22 J. INT'L AFF. 165, 175 (1968).

9. Friedmann, *Intervention, Civil War and the Role of International Law*, 1965 PROC. AM. SOC. INT'L L. 67, 69. Professor David A. Baldwin consciously equates intervention with influence. Baldwin, *Foreign Aid, Intervention, and Influence*, 21 WORLD POLITICS 425, 426 (1969).

intervention is strictly an assertion about a state of affairs and thus need not be a value-charged statement; but as a practical matter an observer's own value preferences often intrude.

The third sense in which intervention may be used, as a personal policy judgment that a particular transnational interaction is wrong, refers to an observer's own judgment as to the permissibility of a particular interaction. Used in this sense, the term merely signifies that an interaction is viewed by the observer as impermissible. Intervention is often used this way in everyday speech and is, of course, value-charged when so used. Symptomatic of this expression of a negative value judgment, *Webster's* defines intervention in terms of the pejorative "interference" instead of the neutral "influence."[10] All recommendations as to what the rules of intervention ought to be must necessarily make a value judgment. Thus, when used in this sense, we should insist on the observer's making his policy preferences explicit for appraisal by others, and we should prefer the more particular statements of policy preference to high level generalizations.

The fourth sense in which intervention is used, as a definition of a problem for study, delimits a range of transnational interactions with which the declarant is expressing interest or concern. Such uses of the term intervention are neither true nor false but only more or less useful. Their usefulness depends on the relevance of the declarant's area of concern to real world problems and the degree of selectivity (inclusive of the relevant and exclusive of the irrelevant with respect to the declarant's professed concern) in transactions chosen for study. Used in this sense intervention need say nothing about whether a particular interaction is good or bad. It is important to recognize, however, that the delimitation of a particular range of events for study is not value free. A scholar is faced with a potentially infinite range of problems on which to lavish his attentions. His choice of a particular range of interactions assumes the value importance of those interactions. As Jones and Mayo remind us, the recognition of a

10. "[A]ny interference in the affairs of others; especially, interference of one state in the affairs of another." WEBSTER'S NEW WORLD DICTIONARY 765 (College ed. 1966).

"problem" assumes nonfulfillment of value demands, that is, a gap between value demands and their realization.[11] As such, the identification of a problem is necessarily value-charged.

Several common confusions among these four senses illustrate the danger of terminological confusion. Richard Falk calls attention to the importance of distinguishing between the first and second senses of intervention when he says:

> As William Burke shows well in his excellent treatment of minor coercion, it is important to distinguish between the facts alleged to constitute intervention and the legal determination of these facts as intervention. Does a documented assertion that United States military aid to South Viet Nam constitutes "intervention" make it "intervention" in a legal sense?[12]

But then in his own definition of intervention he fails to make clear whether he is using it in the second, third or fourth sense. According to Falk: " 'Intervention' refers to conduct with an external animus that credibly intends to achieve a fundamental alteration of the state of affairs in the target nation."[13]

Aside from the considerable difficulties in determining the referent of "external animus" and "fundamental alteration," does the definition indicate that Professor Falk believes that all such transnational interactions are illegal, that they ought to be illegal, or that they constitute the range of interactions with which he is concerned? From the context, I believe that he means the last, although the reader cannot be sure. In any event, explicit focus on the sense in which the definition was being offered would, I believe, have enabled Professor Falk to further refine his definition.

Similarly, the key to the seeming paradox of the famous Talleyrand description of non-intervention as "a mysterious word that

11. Mayo & Jones, *Legal-Policy Decision Process: Alternative Thinking and the Predictive Function*, 33 GEO. WASH. L. REV. 318, 327 (1964).
12. R. FALK, LEGAL ORDER IN A VIOLENT WORLD 343 (1968). Professor Falk was referring to Burke, *The Legal Regulation of Minor International Coercion: A Framework of Inquiry*, in ESSAYS ON INTERVENTION 87, 88-89 (R. Stanger ed. 1964).
13. *Id.*

signifies roughly the same thing as intervention,"[14] seems to lie in the confusion of senses in which intervention may be used. Literally, Talleyrand must have been using the term in its first sense, meaning interactions having transnational impacts. As such, there is little difficulty in the assertion that in an interdependent world nonaction can produce effects in a third state as realistically as can action. But the paradox is introduced when the statement is interpreted as saying something about intervention in the second or third sense. It is certainly a contradiction to maintain that an interaction both violates and does not violate authoritative community expectations, or to maintain that an interaction is both right and wrong at the same time. Yet sometimes the Talleyrand statement seems to be invoked in these latter senses to justify any coercive interaction or to condemn alike any foreign policy of action or inaction. James Rosenau points out the absurdity of following this seemingly logical position when he says:

> the height of definitional vagueness is occasionally reached when inaction is regarded as intervention. Having defined intervention as the impact that one state has on the affairs of another, logic leads some observers to classify inaction as intervention whenever consequences follow within a state from the failure of another to intrude upon its affairs. Such a conception, for example, leads to the absurd conclusion that the United States avoidance of the conflict in Indochina in 1954 and its extensive involvement in that part of the world a decade later both constitute intervention.[15]

Another common form of terminological confusion is the failure to distinguish between intervention in its second and third senses, that is, between an assertion about authoritative community ex-

---

14. See Modelski, The International Relations of Internal War 9 (Research Monograph No. 11, Center of International Studies, Princeton University, 1961).

15. J. Rosenau, The Concept of Intervention 12 (paper delivered at the Conference on Intervention and the Developing States, sponsored by the Princeton International Law Society and held at Princeton, N.J., on November 10-11, 1967).

pectations as to permissible conduct on the one hand, and personal policy preference on the other. When one asserts that Soviet action in Czechoslovakia is impermissible intervention, does it mean that such action contradicts the writer's personal policy preference, that it violates community expectations about lawful conduct, or both? The operation called for here is not the separation of "is" and "ought" but clear focus on the separate intellectual tasks of either describing trends in community expectations as to permissible conduct or giving the writer's personal policy preference.

Confusion between the fourth sense in which intervention is used and either the second or third sense may also be a potent source of confusion. At the Princeton Conference on Intervention and the Developing States in November, 1967, substantial audience skepticism greeted an outstanding paper on intervention by James Rosenau.[16] I believe this skepticism stemmed largely from confusion between the third and fourth senses of the term. Rosenau was formulating a particularly thoughtful definition of intervention for the purpose of delimiting events for empirical study. Many in the audience mistook this limited definition as implying that the speaker approved of all interactions falling outside his definition. Since many in the audience held strong views on the impermissibility of interactions outside the delimited area, they rejected the considerable insights in the paper simply because of an intellectual confusion about what the author meant.

A second source of audience skepticism about the paper, which also has its genesis in terminological problems, is, I believe, more justified. Professor Rosenau defined intervention for purposes of "operationalizing" the concept (i.e., in the fourth sense) as interactions which are both convention-breaking and authority-oriented.[17] This definition contains impressive insight as to the importance of these two factors. But since it was rooted more in a search for the core meaning of intervention in linguistic usage and in factors making for convenience in study, rather than in relevance to values at stake in some real world problem, it could

16. See Rosenau, *supra* note 8, at 165.
17. See Rosenau, *supra* note 8, at 167.

not be a sufficiently inclusive definition for study of the full range of intervention problems. The simple truth is that the same values at stake in this "core definition" are also at stake in other situations not included in the definition, that intervention is therefore popularly alleged in other situations, and that these other situations are also worthy of study. To be most useful, the criterion of relevance for determining inclusiveness and exclusiveness in operationalizing a problem in this fourth sense must be rooted in the policies at stake which justify recognition and study of a problem, not simply in linguistic usage or in convenience in study. This is not to say that Rosenau's definition is not useful. It is impressively insightful in calling to our attention two important variables in interventionary situations; but it is not a definition inclusive of the range of interactions which are shaped by common' policies and common conditioning factors, and which therefore justify analysis together.

In an article, written subsequent to the Princeton Conference, Professor Rosenau recognizes the audience skepticism toward his definition of intervention and defends his initial formulation. In doing so, he identifies what he takes to be the chief source of the confusion: "the root of the problem seems to be that two basic and interrelated distinctions were overlooked—namely, the distinction between the common-sense and operational meanings of intervention on the one hand and between intervention as an empirical phenomenon and an analytic concept on the other."[18] Although both sources of confusion may have contributed to the misunderstanding, I believe that by far the principal source of confusion (and one which underlies both of the above reasons given by Rosenau) resulted from failure to adequately identify the value problems inherent in talking about intervention. First, it was not clear to the audience that the defining of events for study did not mean that all events so defined were impermissible and everything else permissible. Second, the definition, no matter how precise, was not explicitly related to the values at stake in interventionary situations, and as such was overly narrow. Both sources of confusion are inevitable unless we keep our eye on the

18. See Rosenau, *supra* note 8, at 173.

four senses in which intervention is commonly used and unless we insist on relating the utility of a definition of intervention to the values at stake in interventionary situations.

THE CONTEXTUAL FALLACY

A second major source of confusion in theorizing about intervention can conveniently be termed the contextual fallacy. The contextual fallacy is the failure clearly to recognize the diversity of issues and contexts in which intervention is alleged and to formulate a framework for inquiry which organizes these diverse claims according to features of the context which raise common issues of policy and are shaped by common conditioning factors. The legal realists repeatedly demonstrated that as the legal issue changes the result too may change. Legal doctrines which purport to decide more than one issue will usually be unstable. For example, traditional discussion about internal conflict characterizes revolutionary activity as rebellion, insurgency, or belligerency without providing sufficient sharpness to indicate that these characterizations are often conclusary terms which vary with the legal issue. Thus, the issues may include such diverse problems as the rights of neutral shipping, the applicability of conventions regulating the treatment of prisoners of war, recognition, and permissibility of military assistance to a contending faction. Moreover, intervention has been claimed across a broad spectrum of activities, including student exchange programs, conditions on economic aid, the free Quebec statements of former French President De Gaulle,[19] efforts to provide relief supplies to civilians in Biafra, and the subjugation of Prague by Soviet tanks. Most of these allegations raise different intervention issues.

Even when the issue is kept relatively stable, theorists frequently approach the problem of control of interventionary conduct as if claims of intervention were asserted in one or two homogeneous contexts capable of policy responsive regulation by one or two all-encompassing rules. In fact, though, both the situations in which claims are made as well as the types of claims vary widely. In dealing with claims of military intervention in internal conflict, for example, claims range through use of the military instrument in the territory of a third state for the protection of

19. See N.Y. Times, July 25, 1968, at 1, col. 2.

human rights, use of the military instrument against the territory of a state providing assistance to an opposing faction, assistance to one-half of a divided nation engaged in a struggle with the other half, and at least eighteen other types.[20]

A symptom of the contextual fallacy is the tendency to define intervention in high level generalizations without careful separation of issues and contexts. An example, which evinces terminological confusion as well, is Oppenheim's definition: "dictatorial interference by a State in the affairs of another State for the Purpose of maintaining or altering the actual condition of things."[21] Such definitions are by themselves so devoid of content that any real meaning they convey is little more than pseudo-knowledge comparable to saying that sleeping pills put one to sleep because they contain a dormative agent. A healthy antidote to this form of the contextual fallacy is to remember that definitions are never true or false, only more or less useful. Perhaps even more to the point, unless serving an explicit *raison d'être* definitional exercises about intervention frequently seem to divert energy from the performance of the intellectual tasks necessary for fruitful problem solving.

Contextuality means more precise specification of intervention issues, and with respect to each, a map of features of the context which may affect policy. Thus, to avoid the contextual fallacy, a framework for control of intervention must carefully separate the types of intervention claims which present common policies and common conditioning factors. The problem of intervention can be adequately clarified only by more precisely differentiating the relevant claims.

The Outlines of a Policy Responsive Approach

the problem for study

In a world in which it is meaningful to speak of a global community, there is by definition a high level of transnational interac-

---

20. For a full breakdown of these claims see part IV of this chapter.
21. I Oppenheim, International Law 305 (8th ed. Lauterpacht 1955). Brierly's widely quoted definition is at an only slightly lower level of abstraction. His definition is: "dictatorial interference in the domestic or foreign affairs of another state which impairs that state's independence." J. Brierly, The Law of Nations 402 (6th ed. Waldock, 1963).

tion. Events in Léopoldville and decisions made in Washington, Tel Aviv, or Moscow may be felt around the world, sometimes in a matter of hours or even minutes. It is obviously too broad, then, if one is defining intervention for purposes of delimiting the problem for study, to include all actions having impact abroad. The totality of transnational interactions is neither an economical nor a policy-responsive basis for study.

In narrowing this range of interaction for purposes of defining events for study, the most useful approach is to relate the definition to the reasons for our concern about intervention. That is, in order to get a useful handle on intervention, the interactions chosen for study should be those potentially most destructive of the values at stake, the threatened loss of which prompted the allegations of intervention. As will be examined in a later section, the policies principally at stake in the intervention context seem to be self-determination, the protection of human rights, and the maintenance of world order.[22] Since these policies are most acutely affected by coercive interactions, it would seem that coercive transnational interactions constitute the broadest intervention concern. Coercive interactions, by whatever method—military, economic, or ideological—would in this approach be considered as intervention for purposes of delimiting the broadest problem for study. This broadest definition of intervention is not watertight; for example, some forms of "cultural imperialism" might not be included even though they raise important questions of community policy. But no definition will ever be watertight; and the defining of intervention in terms of coercive transnational interaction does seem to identify the most critical community concern.

Intervention in its broadest sense, then, encompasses the full range of claims on a continuum of major-minor coercion by all methods and with respect to all values. There is no bright-line distinction on the basis of motivation for coercion, method of coercion, or values affected by coercion; and to pursue such a distinction is to miss the point of the concept of intervention. For purposes of economy of effort, however, it is useful to further delimit the range of interactions for study. Accordingly, this

22. These policies are developed in part III of this chapter.

chapter will be concerned principally with coercive actions by one international actor aimed at the authority structures of another and effectuated through military strategies. Non-authority-oriented claims, such as humanitarian intervention, will also be considered if they involve claims to use military strategies and are currently recurring problems.

Claims concerning authority structures are particularly important since the control of authority structures provides a base for coercion with respect to a wide range of values. And claims concerning military strategies are important because of their characteristically high coercive impact. The sending of Soviet tanks to Czechoslovakia, the landing of United States marines in the Dominican Republic, and the supplying of arms to Nigeria or Biafra are generally more coercive and have greater consequences for important community policies than economic assistance to those states. Moreover the community consensus is generally greater with respect to claims concerning authority structures and military strategies than with respect to claims concerning economic assistance programs or foreign exploitation of natural resources. These latter claims, couched in the rhetoric of "neo-colonialism" and "economic imperialism," are likely to become increasingly important and certainly deserve attention,[23] but at the present time the control of intervention in internal conflict seems both to be the more pressing problem and to reflect greater community consensus about impermissible conduct.

The problem of intervention in internal conflict may also be conceptualized in conventional legal terms as one of defining aggression. Although such high level generalizations as "aggression" and "coercive transnational interaction" can be useful, if we are to achieve the working degree of specificity necessary to avoid the contextual fallacy, it is important to keep in mind that the real questions for study are formulated only at a more specific level in the section of this chapter discussing recurrent claims presenting common policies and conditioning factors.

The use of the term "internal conflict" instead of the prevailing "civil strife" or "civil war" is a deliberate choice intended to include both external sponsorship of conflict and external partici-

23. See generally Baldwin, *supra* note 9.

pation in indigenous conflict. The two are important for study; yet the "civil war" terminology popularly carries overtones which both confuse location of conflict with sponsorship and beg the question by suggesting normative conclusions. The use of this "civil war" terminology has given rise to such veiling of the policy issues as the representation of the central issue in the dispute about the legality of the Vietnam War as whether the war should be regarded "as 'civil war' or as a peculiar modern species of international war."[24] While the term "internal conflict" is not free from such overtones, it is sufficiently more free of them to justify its use whenever there is danger of normative confusion.

THE METHODOLOGY

As a useful technique for clarifying policy choices, this chapter will follow an outline which facilitates explicit performance of the intellectual tasks in decision.[25] That is, definition of the problem for study, description of the problem in its broadest context, clarification of policies, description and analysis of past trends, and invention and evaluation of policy alternatives.

24. 1 THE VIETNAM WAR AND INTERNATIONAL LAW, *supra* note 6, at 4. Professor Falk has elsewhere shown a perceptive awareness of the danger in the use of the term "civil war." In his innovative study of *The International Law of Internal War* he points out:

> The term "internal war" is consciously selected as a substitute for the usual designation: civil war. This is done to facilitate an accurate perception of the modern phenomena of intrastate political violence. It is especially important to appreciate the extent to which external actors participate in internal wars so as to distract the mind from a predisposition to view internal war as a domestic matter.

Falk, *Janus Tormented: The International Law of Internal War*, in INTERNATIONAL ASPECTS OF CIVIL STRIFE 185, 217 (J. Rosenau ed. 1964).

Linda Miller also considers the terminology problem and rejects "internal war" for "internal conflict," "internal violence," and "internal disorder." She points out that: "Many significant internal disorders, for example the recurring violence in the former Belgian Congo, are not 'wars.'" L. MILLER, WORLD ORDER AND LOCAL DISORDER: THE UNITED NATIONS AND INTERNAL CONFLICTS 3 (1967).

25. The methodology of this essay loosely follows the policy-oriented approach recommended by Myres McDougal and Harold Lasswell which I have found to be a helpful analytic tool. I also owe an intellectual debt to the "new analytical school" for the section on terminological confusion. See, *e.g.*, Summers, *The New Analytical Jurists*, 41 N.Y.U.L. REV. 861 (1966).

Behavioral approaches to the problem of intervention usually seek to avoid normative appraisal. No such comfort is available to the international lawyer, however, as normative appraisal is a principal stock in trade. This normative aspect of the problem makes it imperative that scholars concerned with the appraisal of intervention set out the basis for their appraisal as explicitly as possible. As the Swedish political economist Gunnar Myrdal has indicated, social scientists should work from explicit value premises to enable appraisal by others.[26] The third section of this essay seeks to develop the basic community policies at stake in intervention and is an installment on this duty.

It is also helpful to keep in mind that to date only beginning efforts have been made at scientific study of the causes of revolution and the effects of intervention. In this state of the art, disagreements about interventionary activities may frequently turn as much on differing or insufficient data for predicting effects on

26. Gunnar Myrdal, the Swedish political economist, places great importance on the idea that social scientists should work from explicit value premises; that is to say, a person should set out his personal preferences and predilections as clearly as possible when dealing with social data. By so doing, he will enable one who reads his exposition to evaluate what he says in the light of those preferences. It is only in this way according to Myrdal, that any manageability and real intelligibility may be attained in handling social phenomena.
Miller & Howell, *The Myth of Neutrality in Constitutional Adjudication*, 27 U. CHI. L. REV. 661, 669 (1960).
See also Thompson, *Normative Theory in International Relations*, in THEORY AND REALITY IN INTERNATIONAL RELATIONS 94 (J. Farrell & A. Smith eds., Colum. paperback ed. 1968).
The complexities of the international scene and the urgency of current problems heighten the need for normative thinking. It would be reassuring to say that the literature abounds with serious writing on normative problems. The truth is that discussion of normative problems appears to lag both in status and prestige. It does not figure extensively in listings of research awards. Its spokesmen constitute no more than a handful of observers. Numerically superior by far are the so-called value-free social scientists. Behaviorist approaches to international-relations theory are currently in vogue.
Nevertheless, the need for serious and exacting normative thinking is ever more clear.
Id. at 105.

values as on value disagreement. With better data, apparent value conflicts may sometimes be narrowed. Behavioral approaches to the problem of intervention are perfectly compatible with the recommended framework, and more policy responsive results will doubtless await better data about revolution and intervention.

To avoid the contextual fallacy and to accurately describe past trends, it is important to classify the separate claims which present common policies and common conditioning factors. The classification of claims recommended in the fourth section of this chapter is intended to meet these needs and to provide a useful tool for clarifying policy choices. The complexity of the recommended classification simply reflects the complexity of the real world; approaches which fail to focus on this complexity will inevitably oversimplify the problem.

It does not follow, however, that because the problem is complex one must recommend a large number of intervention rules or adopt an *ad hoc* approach. A balance must always be struck between many detailed rules which are policy responsive for a larger number of contexts, and the common requirement of all legal systems that the rules offer certainty and ease of application. In striking this balance, one must guard against both overemphasis of illusory certainty and recommendation of only incidentally policy responsive rules on the one hand and against an *ad hoc* approach offering little guidance on the other. All approaches must deal with this danger that rules will be either too general to be policy responsive or too specific to be useful; there is nothing incompatible between definite rules and a policy-oriented approach.

The recommended approach also seeks an appropriate balance between normative and institutional concerns. The problem of control of intervention is inescapably related to normative clarification about permissible intervention. No amount of procedural control or international organization can transcend the necessity of making value judgments about interventionary activities. But control of intervention also requires development of the procedures and institutions for securing compliance with non-intervention rules. Concern with the institutional weaknesses of the international system affecting the control of intervention is particularly important in view of the inadequacy of present institutions and the relative neglect of the institutional side of the problem.

In accordance with these suggestions, it will be helpful, first, briefly to orient ourselves in the current theory concerning the causes, conditions, and course of intrastate change, the systemic factors influencing external interference, and the organization of the world community to respond to claims of intervention; second, to attempt clarification of the basic community policies at stake in intervention; next, to discuss the principal interventionary problems organized by claims which raise common policies and are affected by common conditioning factors; then to examine the institutional weaknesses of the international system affecting the control of intervention and to make recommendations for improvement; and finally, to evaluate past standards and proposals for the control of intervention and to suggest new alternatives.

II. The Processes of Intrastate Change, External Interference, and Decision as Context

The broadest context in which claims of intervention in internal conflict are presented and decided includes the process of intrastate change, the process of external interference, and the international legal process. A brief thumbprint of each is presented here more by way of illustration of the range of relevant variables than as a detailed exploration of all the important features of the context.

THE PROCESS OF INTRASTATE CHANGE

For convenience in analysis, the process of intrastate change will be explored in terms of the *participants* in intrastate change, the *objectives* of the participants in seeking change, the *situations* in which the change takes place, and the *strategies* by which the changes occur.

PARTICIPANTS

A threshold problem concerning the process of intrastate change is deciding when change is internal to a state and when it is international. For example, was the Algerian war internal to France or international? Is the Vietnamese war internal to Vietnam or international between North and South Vietnam? Was the Nigerian war internal to Nigeria or international between Nigeria and Biafra? Similarly, problems of delimiting the relevant entity arise with respect to events in Anguilla, the Congo, Rhodesia, and the divided states of Germany, China, and Korea. Since characterization as internal or international may have important legal consequences, it should be rooted in the policies at stake in interventionary situations. That is, characterization for a particular legal purpose should be based on the effect on self-determination, protection of human rights, and maintenance of world order resulting from the characterization. For example, in the Nigerian war the most critically affected policy seemed to be self-determination, and consequently the principal issue was substantially one of the genuine demands and identifications of the people of Biafra balanced against the impact a separate Biafra would have on the remainder of Nigeria (minimum human rights may also have been seriously threatened in the Nigerian war). In divided country conflicts, on the other hand, the most critically affected policy seems to be the maintenance of world order, and consequently the principal issue is more the threat to the stability of the international system in treating the two competing entities as one.[27]

OBJECTIVES

The objectives of the participants in the process of intrastate change vary widely. In pursuit of maximization of their values they may be a small group of adventurers competing for personal power, idealists seeking modernization of a neo-feudal system or an end to a social system based on racial discrimination, governmental officials seeking greater internal decision-making autonomy, or political activists dedicated to major structural changes through implementation of a political ideology. In many of the nations of the underdeveloped world, as well as in some nations of the developed world, government may be autocratic or totali-

---

27. For development of this point in the context of the Vietnam War, see Moore, *International Law and the United States Role in Viet Nam: A Reply*, 76 YALE L.J. 1051, 1055 (1967).

tarian, socially unresponsive to the needs of the people, unconcerned with minimum human rights, or only incompletely centralized. The presence of a large number of governments in one or more of these categories assures the generation of great demand for internal change.

SITUATIONS

Situations in which intrastate changes in authority structures frequently occur and may conveniently be grouped include the breakaway colony, the war of secession, the cold-war divided nation conflict, and the competition for internal authority structures. This last category includes such diverse situations as the palace coup, the sudden collapse of organized government, and the prolonged revolution against the governing elite. The range of situations in which major internal structural changes occur suggests the futility of seeking to control intervention in internal conflict through one all-encompassing rule.

STRATEGIES

It is useful to remind ourselves in a study of intervention in internal conflict that probably most intrastate change occurs non-violently through economic, political, and ideological change. It is commonplace for political power to shift peacefully through elections or other institutional procedures; and certainly such non-coercive change should be preferred. But since intervention frequently takes place in revolutionary situations and involves claims of interference with the right to self-determination through revolution, it is important that we understand the nature of revolution and civil violence. Although there are still great gaps in our understanding, an increasing number of works provide useful insight into the revolutionary process.[28]

28. See generally H. ARENDT, ON REVOLUTION (1963); C. BRINTON, THE ANATOMY OF REVOLUTION (rev. ed. 1965); C. JOHNSON, REVOLUTIONARY CHANGE (1966); C. LEIDEN & K. SCHMITT, THE POLITICS OF VIOLENCE: REVOLUTION IN THE MODERN WORLD (1968); G. PETTEE, THE PROCESS OF REVOLUTION (1938); Gottschalk, *Causes of Revolution*, 50 AM. J. SOC. 1 (1944); Gurr, *Psychological Factors In Civil Violence*, 20 WORLD POLITICS 245 (1967); *Hearings on The Nature of Revolution, Before the Senate Comm. on Foreign Relations*, 90th Cong., 2d Sess. (1968).

Crane Brinton, in his classic study of the English, French, Russian, and American revolutions, first published in 1938, approaches the problem of revolution from a historical perspective.[29] Rather than attempting isolation of the causative factors in civil violence, Brinton describes the phases of revolution evident in these four instances. He cautions, however, that the type of revolution exemplified by these four is but one type, and that generalizations on the basis of this type may not prove accurate in dealing with other types.[30] He also points out that not all revolutions are movements on the left, citing the fascist revolutions in Germany and Italy which brought Hitler and Mussolini to power.[31]

Brinton describes five symptoms of revolutionary societies which emerge as tentative uniformities from the English, French, Russian, and American revolutions.[32] First, the societies were economically on the move and the revolutionaries were not suffering from crushing oppression. Rather, "revolutionary movements seem to originate in the discontents of not unprosperous people who feel restraint, cramp [and] annoyance. . . ."[33] Second, revolutions have an element of class conflict. It is not just a simplistic have and have-not conflict, but more an expectations gap. Paradoxically, revolutions are more likely when social classes are rather close together than when they are far apart. Third, there is a widespread disaffection of the intellectuals from the governing elite. Fourth, for whatever the reason, whether corruption or rapid change in the environment, existing governmental machinery is inefficient. And fifth, the established elite suffers disaffection from within and increasing political ineptitude.

Apparently in the ripples they spread, revolutions can have a major unsettling effect on the international system. Brinton points out that revolutions are frequently accompanied by a kind of messianic zeal spilling over into foreign wars to spread the gospel.[34] And with respect to the role of force in successful revolutions Brinton says:

29. C. BRINTON, THE ANATOMY OF REVOLUTION (rev. ed. 1965).
30. *Id.* at 262.
31. *Id.*
32. *Id.* at 250-53.   33. *Id.* at 250.   34. *Id.* at 213.

[W]e may suggest in very tentative and hypothetical form the generalization that no government has ever fallen before attackers until it has lost control over its armed forces or lost the ability to use them effectively—or, of course, lost such control of force because of interference by a more powerful foreign force, as in Hungary in 1849 and in 1956, and conversely that no revolutionists have ever succeeded until they have got a predominance of effective armed force on their side.[35]

Louis Gottschalk, writing in 1944, postulated three complexes of factors which may cause revolution.[36] First, "a demand for change, . . . itself the result of (a) widespread provocation and (b) solidified public opinion . . . ,"[37] second, "a hopefulness of change, which is itself the result of (a) a popular program and (b) trusted leadership,"[38] and third, which was regarded as the necessary immediate causes of revolution, the weakness of the governing elite.[39] Gottschalk stressed the multiple causation of revolution and particularly made the point that "provocations alone do not create revolutions. If they did, we should always be having revolutions, for some of them are constantly to be found in human society. . . ."[40]

Chalmers Johnson, in a recent book on *Revolutionary Change*,[41] approaches the problem from a social systems perspective. He seeks to identify "a theoretical formulation of the necessary and sufficient causes of a revolution and . . . to know why revolutions, when they do occur, sometimes succeed and sometimes fail."[42] Johnson answers this query with a theoretical formulation which postulates two necessary causes and a third sufficient cause of revolution. The first necessary cause is "a disequilibrated social system—a society which is changing and which is in need of further change if it is to continue to exist."[43] The change can occur in the values of society or in its environment, and can be either progressive or regressive, but must lead to a dissynchronization

---

35. *Id.* at 89-90.
36. Gottschalk, *Causes of Revolution*, 50 Am. J. Soc. 1 (1944).
37. *Id.* at 7.   38. *Id.*   39. *Id.*   40. *Id.* at 5.
41. C. Johnson, Revolutionary Change (1966).
42. *Id.* at 90-91.   43. *Id.* at 91.

between values and environment. Johnson also indicates that the one characteristic of a disequilibrated social system which most contributes to revolution is "power deflation," or the lessening of the power based on popular expectation of legitimacy of the status-holders in society and the resulting increased necessity to resort to force to maintain the system.[44] Although it largely contradicts the popular myth, Johnson suggests, as does Gottschalk, that social problems alone or a social system in disequilibrium can never in themselves be sufficient causes of revolution.[45]

A second cluster of necessary causes is described by Johnson as

> the quality of the purposeful change being undertaken while a system is disequilibrated. This quality depends upon the abilities of the legitimate leaders. If they are unable to develop policies which will maintain the confidence of non-deviant actors in the system and its capacity to move toward resynchronization, a *loss of authority* will ensue. Such a loss means that the use of force by the elite is no longer considered legitimate, although it does not necessarily mean that a revolution will occur at once.[46]

Johnson's third and "sufficient" cause of revolution "is some ingredient, usually contributed by fortune, which deprives the elite of its chief weapon for enforcing social behavior (e.g., an army mutiny), or which leads a group of revolutionaries to *believe* that they have the means to deprive the elite of its weapons of coercion."[47] He refers to these causes as "accelerators," and indicates that they are the principal factors affecting whether or not the revolutionaries will succeed.[48] The three types of accelerators given by Johnson are factors directly influencing the effectiveness of a system's armed forces, ideological beliefs about an effective way to overcome the elite's armed forces, and special operations launched against the armed forces by a band of revolutionaries.[49]

Another useful theoretical treatment of civil violence is that of Ted Gurr, who explores the psychological factors in civil violence from a frustration-aggression perspective.[50] Although Gurr does

44. *Id.* 45. *Id.* at 92. 46. *Id.* at 91.
47. *Id.* 48. *Id.* at 91-92. 49. *Id.* at 99.
50. Gurr, *Psychological Factors In Civil Violence*, 20 WORLD POLITICS 245 (1967).

not reject the relevance of the theoretical work based on critical features of the social structure, he takes the position that the most fruitful model of civil violence will be based on the psychological characteristics of man's reaction to society.[51] Using such a model Gurr advances eleven propositions for predicting the likelihood and magnitude of civil violence. The eleven are divided into two principal groupings. These groupings are propositions about *"instigating variables,* which determine the magnitude of anger, and . . . *mediating variables,* which determine the likelihood and magnitude of overt violence as a response to anger."[52] The interrelationship between the two groupings determines the likelihood and magnitude of violence.

Propositions in the first grouping are related to Gurr's basic premise that "the necessary precondition for violent civil conflict is relative deprivation, defined as actors' perception of discrepancy between their *value expectations* and their environment's apparent *value capabilities.*"[53] Propositions in this grouping include: severity of relative deprivation increases the likelihood of violence;[54] strength of anger varies "inversely with the extent to which deprivation is held to be legitimate";[55] and strength of anger varies "directly with the proportion of all available opportunities for value attainment with which interference is experienced or anticipated."[56]

Propositions in the second grouping are related to Gurr's observation that civil violence as a response to anger can be influenced by a number of mediating variables reflecting the degree of social control or facilitation of violence.[57] Propositions in this category include: "Any decrease in the perceived likelihood of retribution tends to increase the likelihood and magnitude of civil violence";[58] the likelihood of violence varies "inversely with the availability of institutional mechanisms that permit the expression of nonviolent hostility";[59] and the likelihood of violence varies "directly with the availability of common experiences and beliefs that sanction violent responses to anger."[60]

51. *Id.* at 245-47, 251. 52. *Id.* at 251. 53. *Id.* at 252-53.
54. *Id.* at 254. 55. *Id.* at 260. 56. *Id.* at 263.
57. *Id.* at 263-65. 58. *Id.* at 265. 59. *Id.* at 269.
60. *Id.* at 271.

In simplified form, Gurr's model for predicting the likelihood and magnitude of civil violence has as principal inputs the society's value expectations, including intensity of commitment to values and legitimacy of deprivation, the society's value capabilities, including degree of deprivation and proportion of opportunities interfered with, the society's control of violence, including retribution and institutionalization of peaceful channels of protest, and the society's facilitation of violence, including its beliefs and traditions sanctioning violence.[61] Both the relative deprivation inputs and control of violence inputs are critical.

Though Johnson and Gurr approach the problem of revolution from the different perspectives of macro- and micro-theory, they seem to be in substantial agreement on a number of critical causative factors. Both seem to agree that a gap between value expectation and realization is an important causative factor, that expectations about legitimacy of deprivation or authority of the depriving elite's use of force are significant, and that perception of the likelihood of the application of effective control measures is a critical variable. An important tenet of both theories is that civil violence is not simply a function of poor material conditions or an underdeveloped society producing few goods and services, but is related in a number of critical ways to the psychological attitudes of the participants. These attitudes include subjectivities about relative deprivation, legitimacy of the ruling elite's use of force, legitimacy of the revolutionaries' use of force, and appraisal of the revolutionaries' chances to escape punishment or overcome the control resources of the ruling elite. Gottschalk's and Brinton's work would also seem to substantially support these conclusions.

Although current theories of civil violence are useful, there is much of relevance to the control of intervention that they do not answer.[62] For example, what is the likelihood of minority seizure

61. *Id.* at 252.
62. Ted Gurr does suggest that his frustration—aggression model provides a ready model for investigation of the effects of foreign intervention. And he hypothesizes that:
> intervention on behalf of the deprived is likely to strengthen group support . . . and may, as well, heighten and intensify value expectations. . . . Foreign assistance to a threatened regime is

of control in revolutions and what factors predispose to minority control? Must a majority of the populace support the revolutionaries for the revolution to succeed? Under what conditions might outside assistance alter this? What conditions lead to prolonged conflicts highly destructive of societal values instead of swift victories or palace coups? What is the effect of external assistance by various methods to one side or the other in terms of effect on destructive violence or minority seizure of control? To what extent do successful or unsuccessful revolutions foster other revolutions by a demonstration effect? What effect do revolutions have on the stability of the international system? The answers to these and other questions as yet only imperfectly understood might materially assist in formulating control measures for intervention.

There is also a growing body of data on the conditions for successful guerrilla insurgency and counter-insurgency operations.[63] Although insurgency theory is interrelated with revolution theory, since insurgency may be externally initiated, the two theories need not be congruent. It is widely agreed that successful counter-insurgency operations require a ratio of government forces to insurgents of at least 10 to 1. The force ratio in the British counter-insurgency operation in Malaysia is said to have been on the order of 50 to 1. Fidel Castro is even said to have maintained that the Cuban insurgents became invincible when they reached a ratio of 500 government soldiers to 1 insurgent.[64]

---

most likely to raise retribution levels . . . , but may also alter aspects of value capabilities . . . and strengthen justification for violence among the deprived, insofar as they identify foreigners with invaders. . . .

Id. at 277.

63. See, *e.g.*, R. DEBRAY, REVOLUTION IN THE REVOLUTION? (1967); J. PAGET, COUNTER-INSURGENCY OPERATIONS (1967); Kinley, *Development of Strategies in a Simulation of Internal Revolutionary Conflict*, 10 AMERICAN BEHAVIORAL SCIENTIST 5 (November, 1966); Pye, *The Roots of Insurgency and the Commencement of Rebellions*, in INTERNAL WAR 157 (H. Eckstein ed. 1964). Since the perspectives from which they are written vary from the revolutionary to the counter-revolutionary, studies on insurgency theory are often more polemical than the literature on civil violence. Régis Debray's *Revolution in the Revolution*, which has been described as a primer for Marxist insurrection, is an example.

64. R. DEBRAY, *supra* note 63, at 76.

It also seems to be generally accepted insurgency theory that insurgent operations against an entrenched elite backed by a modern army will be a long drawn out conflict. The prolonged insurgencies in Algeria, Malaya, Yugoslavia, and Vietnam would seem to bear this out. In addition, it is generally accepted that nonmilitary strategies may also have a critical bearing on the resolution of an insurgency, whether employed on behalf of the insurgents or the government. In fact the importance of political and social reform in successful counter-insurgency operations is so much a part of the dominant myth about insurgency that it may be in danger of being overemphasized.

THE PROCESS OF EXTERNAL INTERFERENCE: SOME SYSTEMIC FACTORS

Just as change within a state is a product of the totality of forces at work internally, the process of external interference occurs within a broader context and is shaped by the systemic variables of the international system.[65] In time, it may be expected that a theory of intervention comparable to those of revolution for the internal arena, which will seek to explain interventionary phenomena in terms of critical systemic variables, will emerge. In fact, Oran Young and several others have already suggested a number of systemic factors which seem to have a high correlation with periods of greater interventionary activity. Young defines intervention nominally (in the fourth sense) as "organized and systematic activities across recognized boundaries aimed at affecting the political authority structures of the target."[66] He divides systemic factors contributing to high levels of intervention within a system into those making for *opportunities* and those making for *motivation*. As opportunity factors he includes disparity in effective power among the international actors, the structure of the international system (unipolar, multipolar, or other), the internal viability of the actors, and the level of interdependence within the system. He also indicates that the

---

65. See generally INTERNAL WAR, *supra* note 63; INTERNATIONAL ASPECTS OF CIVIL STRIFE (J. Rosenau ed. 1964).
66. Young, *Intervention and International Systems*, 22 J. INT'L AFF. 177, 178 (1968).

impact of the structure of the international system may be altered by the degree of collusion among major powers and by the nature of prevailing military technology.[67] As motivational factors he includes asymmetrical distribution of values, more rapid change in effective power than in other values, the existence of crusading ideologies, and high levels of competition among competing public order systems.[68]

Because of the pervasive influence of the larger international context on the processes of intrastate change and external interference, it seems useful briefly to examine the features of the present international system most relevant to the control of intervention in internal conflict. For convenience in analysis, these features will be explored in terms of the *participants* in the system, the *objectives* with which the participants act, the *situations*, spatial and temporal, in which the interaction takes place, the *base values* or resources available to the participants, the *strategies* employed by the participants in their interactions, the immediate *outcome* of the process of interaction, the longer range *effects* of the interaction on the international system, and the broader context of *conditions* in which transnational interactions take place.

PARTICIPANTS

A few years ago, Morton Kaplan hypothesized a model of "a loose bipolar system" which seemed to describe the then international system.[69] Today it might be more accurate to speak of a loose bipolar system getting looser. The East-West split between the Soviet Union and the United States remains the dominant feature of the system, but the two camps no longer look as monolithic as they once did. In the communist camp, Peking and to some extent even such smaller nations as Cuba and Yugoslavia go their own way and peddle their own brand of ideology. In fact, the Moscow Conference of Communist Parties in 1969 declared "there is no longer a center of the Communist movement."[70] Simi-

---

67. *Id.* at 180-82.   68. *Id.* at 182-84.
69. See Kaplan, *Intervention in Internal War: Some Systemic Sources*, in INTERNATIONAL ASPECTS OF CIVIL STRIFE, *supra* note 65, at 92, 93.
70. TIME, June 27, 1969, at 26.

larly, in the Western camp, the increased nationalism of De Gaulle's and Pompidou's France has at least temporarily driven a wedge into the alliance of the Western democracies. The Soviet invasion of Czechoslovakia seems temporarily to have retarded this centrifugal force in the Western camp, but what its long range effect will be remains to be seen.

Somewhat qualifying this break-up of the monoliths is the question of the degree of cooperation on vital issues, despite ideological differences, among the members of each camp. If the myth of monolithic communism has unduly influenced American foreign policy, we should be careful lest we create a counter-myth which fails to take into account cooperation on vital issues and even increased competition against the West.

The international system is also characterized by the emergence of new power blocs, particularly in Asia and Africa, and by a proliferation of new actors. The 51 original members of the United Nations have grown in only 26 years to 132, and a large number of mini-states are still in the wings. Most of these newly independent states are former colonies still largely underdeveloped and still undergoing political and economic growing pains. Many, reflecting their background of crazy-quilt colonial development, may never be economically or politically viable as presently constituted. Even the more fortunate seem to have a built-in social disequilibrium accentuated by extreme poverty and efforts at rapid modernization.

The impact of these features and the level of intervention is substantial. The great increase in the number of third world nations, coupled with their instability, practically ensures a high level of civil violence and a high turn-over in authority structures. Many simply await the "accelerator" factors before bursting into violence. Furthermore, the high level of competition between the ideologies of the East and West, and even among the participants within each grouping, tends to turn such nations into ideological battlegrounds.

Another feature of the international system which is particularly important for the control of intervention is the present imperfect level of international organization. The United Nations and regional organizations such as the Organization of American

States (OAS), the Organization of African Unity (OAU), the North Atlantic Treaty Organization (NATO), the Southeast Asian Treaty Organization (SEATO), the Central Treaty Organization (CENTO), the Arab League, and the Warsaw Pact nations may play important roles both as intervening actors and as institutions for the control of impermissible intervention. The United Nations, however, mirrors the existing splits within the world community and in dealing with serious public order issues is substantially dependent upon great power unanimity. To date, its major role in internal conflict, as typified by the United Nations Operation in the Congo (ONUC) and by the United Nations Peace-Keeping Force in Cyprus (UNFICYP), has been dependent as well on the consent of the state concerned and has been fairly rigidly limited to peace-keeping rather than peace-making operations. Although it has played some role in most interventionary situations, such as those in Hungary, Czechoslovakia, Lebanon, Yemen, and the Dominican Republic, for the most part it has not been able to deal effectively with either these situations or the more dangerous major power competitive interventions as in Greece, Laos, and Vietnam.

Even as now constituted, though, the United Nations may have a number of important roles in the control of intervention which are just emerging. For example, the General Assembly resolutions in effect authorizing members to assist insurgents in Southern Rhodesia,[71] South Africa, and South-West Africa,[72] and the Portuguese colonies[73] suggest an important legitimizing role in recognizing one or another competing faction. There is also precedent for UN fact-finding missions in situations of internal conflict, as in the Greece, Laos, Lebanon, and Yemen investigations, but as yet the record is far from satisfactory in this task. Finally, of course, the office of the Secretary-General has unique capability for mediation and settlement assistance.

71. G.A. Res. 2262, 22 U.N. GAOR, Supp. 16, at 45-46, U.N. Doc. A/6716 (1967).
72. G.A. Res. 2307, 22 U.N. GAOR, Supp. 16, at 19-20, U.N. Doc. A/6716 (1967) (South Africa); G.A. Res. 2372, 22 U.N. GAOR, Supp. 16A, at 1-2, U.N. Doc. A/6716/Add.1 (1968) (South-West Africa).
73. G.A. Res. 2270, 22 U.N. GAOR, Supp. 16, at 47-48, U.N. Doc. A/6716 (1967).

In evaluating proposals for the control of intervention one should be on guard against claims that either assume an unrealistic omnipotence for the United Nations out of an excess of idealistic zeal or ignore the real potential for control which the organization already possesses or which could be cultivated with a little effort.

Since regional organizations reflect a less universal and more homogeneous membership than does the United Nations, and since they are more apt to be dominated by a great power, there is a substantial and largely unresolved question as to the limits of legitimate independent action by such organizations. Certainly the Arab League or the OAS cannot justify coercive action against Israel or Cuba simply on the basis of collective regional determination, and no one is impressed with assertions of greater legitimacy in the invasion of Czechoslovakia simply because the collective machinery of the Warsaw Pact was employed. In many situations short of these "horribles," however, regional organizations may have a significant role to play in the control of internal conflict. Although the parameters of legitimate regional action and the relationship of regional organizations to the United Nations are as yet unclear, interventionary claims by regional organizations, as with the OAS in the Dominican Republic and the OAU in Rhodesia, seem to be here to stay.

OBJECTIVES

A critical feature of the present international system is the existence of fundamentally different public order systems and sub-systems. Each is espoused by its champion in Washington, Paris, Moscow, Peking, or Havana. This intense ideological competition between east and west, and among the communist states, is a principal motivation for what is probably the most spectacular and dangerous form of intervention today. Some of these cold-war interventions are prompted by an aggressive proselytizing spirit, as is illustrated by Havana's attempts to foster guerrilla insurgencies throughout Latin America, and others by a determined defensive stance, as seems the case with the United States policy of containment.

One feature of the present world which suggests the likelihood of even higher levels of interventionary activity is the contemporary growth in militant revolutionary and interventionary ideology. This growth in militance seems in part a product of competition among the major communist centers of ideology in Moscow, Peking, and Havana, and in part a worldwide growth in attitudes condoning use of violence for attainment of social justice. Régis Debray's exposition of the Havana ideology in his *Revolution in the Revolution*[74] illustrates the revolutionary fervor of some Marxist theorists who argue for abandonment of united front tactics in favor of uncompromising protracted guerrilla insurrection. The Soviet "Brezhnev Doctrine"[75] upholding the right of intervention to maintain the ideological purity of any socialist regime, although radically different from that of Régis Debray, further indicates the growth in interventionary attitudes. It remains to be seen whether this new Soviet doctrine of "socialist self-determination" is an aberrational doctrine and whether it is intended for countries other than those in Eastern Europe already dominated by the Soviet Union.

A second major contemporary ideological motivation for intervention is anti-colonialism. Themselves products of the breakdown of the colonial system after World War II, the third world nations have called for assistance to insurgent groups in colonial areas. Algeria may be classified as an example of an anti-colonial struggle which received substantial assistance in this manner. Areas of current applicability include South-West Africa and the Portuguese colonies in Africa.

A third source of motivation for contemporary intervention, which sometimes overlaps anti-colonialism, is the existence of regimes which deny self-determination on a racial basis. The activities of African states and the OAU in assisting insurgencies within Rhodesia, South Africa, and South-West Africa are perhaps the chief contemporary examples.

Other sources of motivation for civil violence and intervention include regional or religious unity, as in the Pan-Arab movement; modernization of feudal societies, as was a factor in Egyptian

---

74. R. DEBRAY, *supra* note 63.
75　See Pravda Article Justifying Intervention in Czechoslovakia, 7 INT'L LEG. MAT. 1323 (1968).

military assistance to the Republicans in Yemen; the desire for increased influence or access to oil resources or other wealth, as perhaps was the case with the alleged French aid to Biafra; and a crazy-quilt pattern of newly independent states lacking homogeneous ethnic, linguistic, or cultural backgrounds.

SITUATIONS

The level of interdependence in the global community is high and rising. The transportation and communications revolutions of recent decades have increased the level of global interaction explosively. Felt interdependencies are real, as is reflected by the mutual security arrangements with forty-two countries to which the United States is currently a party.[76] If fortress America concepts were attractive in an earlier day, they are totally unrealistic in the kind of world in which we now find ourselves, and the same is true for other major powers. To suggest that there is no turning back from broad international involvement, however, is not to suggest neglect of the hard questions as to what interests are legitimate and how legitimate interests may best be protected, whether they be those of the United States or of any other country. Thus, the issue is not whether the Viet Cong will stage an amphibious landing in Los Angeles unless stopped in Vietnam, but is instead a fundamental question of how the United States can best protect legitimate interests elsewhere which may have real effects within the United States.

The increasing interdependence throughout the world seems to be a significant factor in the increase of foreign involvement in internal conflicts. It also seems to carry with it cultural and technological exchange that probably accelerates social change, which in turn increases the likelihood of civil violence. It may also widen the expectations gap as persons in southern underdeveloped countries become increasingly aware of the standard of living in the more industrialized societies of the northern hemisphere.

The degree of protection which the international system accords to legitimate interests, and the institutional structures available for achieving needed change peacefully, are factors which

76. STAFF OF HOUSE COMM. ON FOREIGN AFFAIRS, 90TH CONG., 1ST SESS., COLLECTIVE DEFENSE TREATIES 1 (Comm. Print 1967).

also seem significant for the level of interventionary activity within a system. Although the present system has a plethora of specialized international agencies which do make an impact on both the protection of legitimate interest and needed social change, present institutions are rudimentary given the magnitude of the problems. The history of present functional agencies and regional communities is a recent one, though; and the degree of international cooperation achieved by them is a bright spot, so much so that the functional school of international law theorists emphasizes an "international law of co-operation."[77] As specialized and regional organizations expand their competence and are able to cope more effectively with needed change, they may work a significant reduction in interventionary activity.

BASE VALUES

One feature which Oran Young suggests may be an important factor in the extent of interventionary activity within an international system is the degree of discrepancy in effective power among the actors. The contemporary international system exhibits a great range in this regard. Major actors, such as the United States and the Soviet Union, maintain a military establishment far larger than that of other actors in the system, although it may also be true that in terms of usable power many other states maintain a military apparatus sufficient to deter or at least discourage military action against them. The armies of North Vietnam, North Korea, and Cuba are but three examples. Moreover, it is arguable that much of the intervention which otherwise might result from substantial discrepancies in effective power is prevented by competitive pressures among the superpowers. In areas of greater freedom of action, as in Eastern Europe for the Soviet Union and Latin America for the United States, there may be greater likelihood of such overt intervention as occurred in Hungary and Czechoslovakia in Eastern Europe, and Cuba and the Dominican Republic in the Caribbean. In other areas of the globe where competitive pressures are more evident, the result may be an increase in covert intervention but a great reluctance to intervene

---

77. See W. Friedmann, The Changing Structure of International Law 60-64 (1964).

openly. The observation that the most dangerous type of intervention is the competitive intervention between superpowers not only seems accurate but is also mirrored in the patterns of intervention of the superpowers. The growth of the guerrilla insurrection as a strategy of intervention also seems to have increased the actors able to engage in interventionary activities, for the resources allocated to such indirect forms of intervention need not be major.

A second factor in resource allocation which may play an important role in the amount of interventionary activity is the pattern of distribution of all other values, particularly wealth, within the international system. The present international arena exhibits an asymmetrical distribution of values, a pattern which affects all regions, but which is most noticeably a north-south split between the relatively industrialized nations of the north and the third world nations of Africa, Asia, and Latin America. If the relative gap between have and have-not nations continues to widen with the resulting increase in unrealizable expectations, it can be expected to foster increased demands for drastic restructuring which may lead to increased revolutionary and interventionary activity.

The degree of internal stability of the actors within the international system seems to be another factor affecting the degree of interventionary activity. In this regard, the built-in functional disequilibrium of many third world states and the concern over the viability of existing colonial boundaries heighten the problem. It is particularly relevant that the widespread African antipathy to secessionist movements, as in Biafra and Katanga, reflects the almost universal African concern that if a secessionist movement succeeds anywhere on the continent it may set off a chain reaction affecting a host of other vulnerable entities only nominally nations. The African concern is also heightened because present fragmentation on the continent may already be greater than can be supported by economic realities.

It may also be relevant to observe that rigid implementation of totalitarian controls, as is the pattern in most communist countries (Yugoslavia and briefly Czechoslovakia to the contrary), seems to have effectively prevented revolutionary change. Spain and Haiti are non-communist examples. In the current east-west ideological conflict, the thoroughgoing totalitarian regimes have so far exhibited relative immunity to guerrilla strategies.

STRATEGIES

The international system exhibits a wide range of interventionary strategies. If intervention is defined broadly as any coercive transnational interaction, then such interactions may be carried out by any method, military, diplomatic, economic, or ideological. But by its nature military intervention remains the most critically coercive. Patterns of military intervention in the contemporary system include arms sales or grants, military training missions at home and abroad, initiation of or assistance to guerrilla insurgencies, aid to exile groups, assistance of military advisory or transportation units, the commitment of regular combat units as by both sides in Vietnam, and outright invasion as in Czechoslovakia.

One development in strategies affecting the likelihood of interventionary activity is the shift advocated by some Marxist theorists from emphasis on political efforts, typified by the united front, to emphasis on the guerrilla insurgency. Régis Debray, who seems to be a spokesman primarily for the Cuban style of revolution, demonstrates this shift when he writes:

> [A]t the present juncture, the principal stress must be laid on the development of guerrilla warfare and not on the strengthening of existing parties or the creation of new parties.
>
> That is why insurrectional activity is today the number one political activity.[78]

It should not be assumed that this militant Havana line is necessarily that of Moscow, or even of Peking. The point is simply to highlight one insurrectionary line which calls for widespread guerrilla insurgency as the first order of business. Such attitudes can, as Chalmers Johnson theorizes, provide a powerful "accelerator" effect which may trigger revolution. The insurrectionary movements in Guatemala, Colombia, and Venezuela seem to owe

78. R. DEBRAY, *supra* note 63, at 116.

their existence, at least in part, to this newer line. Recent events in Uruguay, where a small band of revolutionaries is harassing the militarily weak Uruguayan government, suggest an even newer strategy of urban rather than rural guerrilla activity which may have even more profound implications for the spread of insurrectionary activity. This shift toward guerrilla insurrections as a strategy for assuming power also seems to have been greatly influenced by the guerrilla successes in Yugoslavia, China, Algeria, Cuba, and North Vietnam.

OUTCOMES

The outcome of this process of external interference is the high level of intervention, both in frequency and intensity, noted at the outset of this chapter. Though military intervention for the purpose of collecting debts or enforcing international obligations may have declined since the nineteenth century, military intervention motivated by ideological competition for political authority seems to have substantially increased. This is an increase to which all major international actors as well as the newly independent third world nations have contributed. Their patterns of participation, though, have varied widely, ranging through retention of former colonies, preservation of spheres of influence, mutual defense, anti-colonialism, and militant proselytizing of a particular political system.

EFFECTS

Intervention can itself be a significant factor affecting the level of interventionary activity within a system. Successful or even protracted guerrilla movements (as in Vietnam today) may foster other guerrilla movements by demonstration, an effect similar to the wave of fascist regimes which came to power just prior to World War II or the trends toward democratic regimes and against colonialism shortly after the war.[79]

The interventionary conduct of actors in the system may also affect the level of interventionary activity in that the conduct of

79. For a brief discussion of this "demonstration effect," see Deutsch, *External Involvement In Internal War*, in INTERNAL WAR, *supra* note 63, at 100-01.

states is one of the prime sources of authoritative expectations as to the permissibility of conduct within the system. To intervene in one situation is to concede the legitimacy of reciprocal conduct engaged in by one's competitors. If used without critical examination of what cases are alike, this reciprocity principle may cloud the illegitimacy of even an unlike intervention. Thus did Senator Eugene McCarthy deemphasize Soviet actions in Czechoslovakia by reference to American actions in Vietnam and the Dominican Republic.[80]

Intervention may also alter the balance of power in such a way as to increase the chances of future intervention, as Czechoslovakia may have done. It may result in intervention subsidiary to an on-going conflict, as currently seems to be the case with North Vietnamese forces in Laos and Cambodia and the insurgency in Thailand. And it may result in the coming to power of militantly interventionist regimes. In fact, with the exception of Yugoslavia, regimes which have come to power by a protracted guerrilla war in which they received at least some outside assistance seem to be among the most militantly interventionist regimes. They include North Vietnam, China, Algeria, and Cuba.

CONDITIONS

One overriding condition affecting the international system which has critical consequences for the control of intervention is the present nuclear stalemate. The development of nuclear weapons and systems for their delivery against major population centers has rendered all-out war an unthinkable event which might both wipe out a substantial portion of mankind and wreak destructive genetic aftereffects into the distant future. With the deployment of ABM and MIRV systems the nuclear arms race may be entering an even more dangerous and unstable period. Yet the nuclear balance is such that it is unlikely that any major participant will develop a first-strike capability; in fact the maintenance of the system may depend on this. In the absence of critically needed agreement on effective arms control the nuclear stalemate is likely to continue.

The effect of this stalemate on interventionary practices has

80. See N.Y. Times, Aug. 22, 1968, at 22, col. 1.

been mixed. On the one hand, the threat of all-out nuclear war has probably deterred interventions in high risk areas felt to be under the hegemony of a nuclear adversary, as seems to be the case with United States policy in Eastern Europe and Soviet policy in Latin America. But on the other hand, it has also provided a nuclear umbrella which may have encouraged some forms of limited war and indirect confrontation. Clearly, the danger of escalation has also rendered the competitive intervention between nuclear adversaries or their proxies the most dangerous form of contemporary intervention. The existence of this nuclear threat and the particularly acute danger of competitive interventions between nuclear adversaries suggests the overriding importance of the need both to avoid nuclear war as a first priority goal of non-intervention norms, and to formulate special rules aimed at high risk areas, such as the cold war divided nations.

Although the global legal process does not exhibit the degree of centralization and control characteristic of national systems, there is an effective global constitutive process which creates authoritative expectations concerning the legitimacy of interventionary activities.[81] This more diffuse legal system is shaped by the practices of states, resolutions of the United Nations, the writings of publicists, and statements of the representatives of nation states and international organizations. The structure of the international legal system and the expectations of legitimacy which flow from it are themselves conditioning factors which influence the level of interventionary activity within the international system and which must be taken into account in formulating rules for the regulation of intervention. The next section will briefly explore the organization of this international legal process and the framework of rules which have emerged for the control of intervention in internal conflict.

The Organization of the International Legal Process to Respond to Claims of Intervention

The international legal process is marked by a lack of centralization and, with respect to major public order issues, a weak

81. The most comprehensive description of this global constitutive process is McDougal, Lasswell & Reisman, *The World Constitutive Process of Authoritative Decision* (pts. 1-2), 19 J. Legal Ed. 253, 403 (1967).

sanctioning process. The lack of centralization extends through the range of authority functions which must be performed by any complete legal system. Thus, with respect to the prescribing function there is no central legislature with the authority of those to which we are accustomed in the domestic legal order. With respect to the applying function there is only a judiciary lacking in compulsory jurisdiction and which at least in major public order disputes is usually ignored. And with respect to the sanctioning process there is no powerful executive controlling an international police force. But these great differences between the international and domestic legal systems should not obscure the great similarity of functions being performed in both. That the international system is more diffuse does not make it any less real, only weaker in some respects and harder to describe in all.[82]

Claims of unlawful intervention flowing from the processes of intrastate change and external interference may be presented to a range of decision-makers, including the United Nations, regional organizations, the officials of nation states, international legal scholars, and many others. Within the United Nations, claims may be presented to the Security Council, the General Assembly, or the Secretary-General. To the extent that the Security Council is able to respond, members and non-members alike may be bound by its determinations. For the most part, however, the Security Council has not been able to respond in instances of major power disagreement. The aberrational response in the Korean situation resulted from Soviet absence because of a dispute over the exclusion of Communist China from the United Nations; the Congo operation resulted from an initial shared perception by the major powers that United Nations intervention would prove advantageous to their interests. Czechoslovakia and the Bay of Pigs demonstrate the inability to respond against the strong interests of a major power despite clearly unlawful interventions.

The General Assembly of the United Nations has played, through the machinery of the Uniting for Peace Resolution, a modest role in responding to claims of intervention, as the Hungary and Lebanon-Jordan cases illustrate. But the Soviet-French

82. For development see McDougal, Lasswell & Reisman, *supra* note 81.

refusal to pay for the Suez and Congo operations illustrates the limitations of an enlarged General Assembly peace-keeping competence. More importantly, in the Greek and Oman cases the General Assembly called for cessation of assistance to a particular faction in internal conflict, and in recent resolutions concerning Rhodesia, South Africa, South-West Africa, and the Portuguese colonies, the General Assembly has been playing a new role in legitimating assistance to one or another faction in internal conflict.

The Secretary-General may also function as a decision-maker responding to claims of unlawful intervention. He may investigate on his own authority (by implication from Article 99 of the Charter), as did Trygve Lie in Greece and Dag Hammarskjöld in Laos and Lebanon, or he may carry out fact-finding or observation missions on instructions from the Security Council or General Assembly (pursuant to Article 98), as did U Thant in Yemen and the Dominican Republic. U Thant's peace proposals for the Vietnam War also illustrate a dimension of the decision-making capabilities of the Secretary-General in internal conflict situations.[83]

The United Nations framework in theory provides for community review of breaches of the peace or acts of aggression. For the most part, however, the various organs of the United Nations have demonstrated only modest capabilities in providing community review of allegations of unlawful intervention. The touchstone of effective UN action remains major power agreement, at least in the area of major power concern.

Regional organizations such as the OAS and the OAU add some degree of community review and fact-finding capability, but their committed membership, and in some cases their domination by a superpower, severely limit the usefulness of their determinations.

Suggestions for institutional change which seek to strengthen the present inadequate community review and fact-finding procedures constitute a critical part of any comprehensive framework for dealing with intervention. But in the absence of greater centralization in the international system, the officials of nation

---

83. See generally L. GORDENKER, THE UN SECRETARY-GENERAL AND THE MAINTENANCE OF PEACE (1967).

states will remain the major decision-makers responding to claims of intervention. This creates a severe auto-interpretation problem in which national decision-makers must frequently pass on the legitimacy of their own actions. The auto-interpretation problem should not cause us to throw up our hands in despair, however. There is no escape from the problem short of more effective community review; in the absence of such review scholars can attempt to clarify the community interest at stake and can recommend rules and procedures for improved control. International-legal scholars and political theorists have in fact been contributing dramatically in the last few years to an understanding of the problem of control of intervention, and their areas of agreement probably overshadow their areas of disagreement. The writings of publicists are a source of relatively disinterested community review of allegations of unlawful intervention and as such contribute to community expectations as to impermissible conduct. The extreme *realpolitik* argument that the international system provides no control of intervention both understates the capacity and avoids personal responsibility for appraisal of the community of the international system to respond to claims of intervention interest.

In response to the claims of unlawful intervention presented for decision, the international legal process has established at least two major sets of rules which to some extent vie with one another. The selection of the relevant set of rules is frequently a critical choice point in legal argument about the permissibility of a particular intervention, and their reconciliation is one of the major tasks for intervention theorists.

The first set of rules stems from the United Nations Charter. Basically, the Charter provides that unilateral force may not be used across international boundaries except in defense against an armed attack threatening major values.[84] This Charter proscription embodies the substantial insight of the Kellogg-Briand Pact, critical in the nuclear age, that force not be used in international affairs as an instrument of national policy no matter how great the non-forceful grievance. This framework, although of great impor-

---

84. For refinement of this generalization see M. McDougal & F. Feliciano, Law and Minimum World Public Order (1961).

tance in condemning the unilateral export of revolution as an instrument of national policy, does not always provide adequate guidance for other interventionary situations. For example, given some degree of indigenous insurgency, the armed attack-defense abstractions of the Charter provide little guidance as to the legitimacy of external assistance at the request of either the recognized government or insurgents. A principal reason is the difficulty involved in determining which faction represents the people of the state. Similarly, the armed attack-defense abstractions provide little guidance in determining the legitimacy of consensual use of force in situations where objectives are other than the influencing of authority structures. The armed attack test of Article 51 of the Charter does seem to have its principal relevance for control of intervention in determining at what point external intervention becomes a covert invasion justifying response against the territory of the intervening state.[85] As a result, the useful reporting requirement of Article 51 has been largely bypassed by states intervening in internal conflict on request. There are, of course, other Charter principles which may provide guidance for some of these situations, such as subjecting unilateral use of force to subsequent community review in the Security Council and the obligation embodied in Article 33 of the Charter to seek peaceful solution to problems.

The second set of international law rules applicable to intervention antedated the Charter and has continued to develop under the Charter as a more specific response to the areas in which the Charter provides little guidance. These are the norms of intervention of customary international law. Again, however, like the sometimes complementary Charter generalities, customary law frequently provides little guidance for solution of concrete cases. A principal reason for this is the ambivalence toward intervention within the international system. This ambivalence results in seemingly contradictory proscriptions, such as the General Assembly resolutions proscribing intervention in the affairs of third states and those of African sponsorship recommending intervention to assist insurgent movements in Rhodesia and South-West Africa;

85. See Moore, *supra* note 27, at 1068.

Soviet sponsorship of definitions of aggression which proscribe military intervention while promulgating the principle of "socialist self-determination" in the invasion of Czechoslovakia; Indian repudiation of intervention while intervening in Goa for the stated purpose of eliminating colonialism; and OAS non-intervention norms broadly prohibiting intervention in the affairs of states within the hemisphere while proclaiming communism incompatible with the basic principles of the Organization. These conflicting pronouncements reflect real clashes of interest which distort development of consistent norms.

A lack of "neutral principles" is not wholly the cause of the confusion, however. It is also a lack of clarification of criteria for identifying like cases which should be treated alike (which is perhaps really the heart of what Professor Wechsler was saying in his famous "neutral principles" article).[86] For example, General Assembly resolutions and the work of the International Law Commission on intervention provide few criteria for characterization of like cases, leave most of the hard questions unanswered, and have a tendency to beg the question by relying on such conclusory terms as "aggression," "intervention," and "civil strife." Thus the General Assembly said in Resolution 380 (V) in 1950:

> *The General Assembly* . . . condemning the intervention of a State in the internal affairs of another State for the purpose of changing its legally established government by the threat or use of force,
>
> 1. Solemnly reaffirms that, whatever the weapons used, any aggression, whether committed openly, or by fomenting civil strife in the interest of a foreign Power, or otherwise, is the gravest of all crimes against peace and security throughout the world. . . .[87]

In a more specific though still incomplete and over-simplistic vein the International Law Commission provided in the 1954 Draft Code of Offenses Against the Peace and Security of Mankind:

86. Wechsler, *Toward Neutral Principles of Constitutional Law*, 73 HARV. L. REV. 1 (1959).
87. G.A. Res. 380, 5 U.N. GAOR, Supp. 20, at 13-14, U.N. Doc. A/1775 (1950).

Article 2. The following acts are offenses against the peace and security of mankind: . . .

(4) The organization, or the encouragement of the organization, by the authorities of a State, of armed bands within its territory or any other territory for incursions into the territory of another State, or the toleration of the organization of such bands in its own territory, or the toleration of the use by such armed bands of its territory as a base of operations or as a point of departure for incursions into the territory of another State, as well as direct participation in or support of such incursions.

(5) The undertaking or encouragement by the authorities of a State of activities calculated to foment civil strife in another State, or the toleration by the authorities of a State of organized activities calculated to foment civil strife in another State.

(6) The undertaking or encouragement by the authorities of a State of terrorist activities in another State, or the toleration by the authorities of a State of organized activities calculated to carry out terrorist acts in another State. . . .[88]

And in 1965 the General Assembly simplistically declared in the Declaration on Inadmissibility of Intervention:

Considering that armed intervention is synonymous with aggression and, as such, is contrary to the basic principles on which peaceful international co-operation between States should be built,

Considering further that direct intervention, subversion and all forms of indirect intervention are contrary to these principles and, consequently, constitute a violation of the Charter of the United Nations, . . .

1. No State has the right to intervene, directly, or indirectly, for any reason whatever, in the internal or external affairs of any other State. Consequently, armed intervention and all other forms of interference or attempted threats

88. 9 U.N. GAOR, Supp. 9, at 11-12, U.N. Doc. A/2693 (adopted by the International Law Commission July 28, 1954).

against the personality of the State or against its political, economic and cultural elements, are condemned.

2. . . .[N]o State shall organize, assist, foment, finance, incite or tolerate subversive, terrorist or armed activities directed towards the violent overthrow of the régime of another State, or interfere in civil strife in another State. . . .[89]

The General Assembly and International Law Commission are not the only bodies making vague pronouncements about nonintervention. One of the broadest and vaguest is Article 18 of the Revised Charter of the Organization of American States which provides:

No State or group of States has the right to intervene, directly or indirectly, for any reason whatever, in the internal or external affairs of any other State. The foregoing principle prohibits not only armed force but also any other form of interference or attempted threat against the personality of the State or against its political, economic and cultural elements.[90]

In addition to the vagueness, incompleteness, and complementarity of such authoritative pronouncements on intervention, another reason for the lack of guidance provided by customary international law is the lack of agreement among publicists as to what the norms are or ought to be. The traditional rule is said to be that it is lawful to assist a widely recognized government at its request, at least until belligerency is attained.[91] Presumably once

---

89. G.A. Res. 2131, 20 U.N. GAOR, Supp. 14, at 11-12, U.N. Doc. A/6014 (1965).

90. L. SOHN, BASIC DOCUMENTS OF THE UNITED NATIONS 140, 143 (2d ed. rev. 1968).

91. See Borchard, *"Neutrality" and Civil Wars*, 31 AM. J. INT'L L. 304, 306 (1937); Garner, *Question of International Law in the Spanish Civil War*, 31 AM. J. INT'L L. 66, 68 (1937); O'Rourke, *Recognition of Belligerency and the Spanish War*, 31 AM. J. INT'L L. 398, 410 (1937). Professor Friedmann wrote a few years ago:

What is probably still the prevailing view is that the incumbent government, but not the insurgents, has the right to ask for assistance from foreign governments, at least as long as insurgents are not recognized as 'belligerents' or 'insurgents.'

belligerency is attained it is lawful to aid either side if the assisting state is willing itself to become a belligerent. A competing rule first espoused by Sir William Hall at about the turn of the century,[92] and subsequently echoed by a number of contemporary scholars,[93] is that it is unlawful to assist either the recognized government or insurgents once an insurgency breaks out and the outcome is uncertain. Newer theories espoused by a few scholars or officials also include those proscribing all intervention absent prior United Nations authorization,[94] proscribing tactical assistance only,[95] and legitimating intervention for purposes of wars of national liberation,[96] modernization,[97] anticolonialism,[98] or "socialist self-determination."[99] The impact of the Charter on the

---

Friedmann, *Intervention, Civil War and the Role of International Law,* 1965 PROC. AM. SOC'Y INT'L L. 67, 72.

92. W. HALL, INTERNATIONAL LAW 287 (6th ed. 1909); W. HALL, INTERNATIONAL LAW 347 (8th ed. 1924).

93. See W. FRIEDMANN, *supra* note 77, at 264-67; Wright, *United States Intervention in the Lebanon,* 53 AM. J. INT'L L. 112, 121-22 (1959).

94. See R. BARNET, INTERVENTION AND REVOLUTION: THE UNITED STATES IN THE THIRD WORLD 278-80 (1968).

95. See Farer, *Harnessing Rogue Elephants: A Short Discourse on Foreign Intervention in Civil Strife,* 82 HARV. L. REV. 511 (1969); Farer, *Intervention in Civil Wars: A Modest Proposal,* 67 COLUM. L. REV. 266, 272 (1967).

96. A view particularly associated with Communist theorists in China, Vietnam and Cuba.

97. See K. Boals, The Role of International Law in the Internal War in Yemen: An Interpretative Essay 69-76 (unpublished paper prepared for the American Society of International Law Study Group on Civil Strife, 1969).

98. A view particularly associated with the newly independent states of Africa and Asia. See R. FALK, THE NEW STATES AND INTERNATIONAL LEGAL ORDER 51, 64-65 (1966), *reprinted from* 118 HAGUE ACADEMY RECUEIL DES COURS 1 (1966). See also the discussion of the "use of force in self-defense against colonial domination" in the Report of the Special Committee on Principles of International Law Concerning Friendly Relations and Cooperation Among States, 23 U.N. GAOR, Agenda Item No. 87, at 37-38, 63-64, U.N. Doc. A/7326 (1968), and the discussion of "the right of peoples to receive assistance in their struggle against colonialism" in the Report of the 1966 Special Committee on Principles of International Law Concerning Friendly Relations and Co-operation Among States, 21 U.N. GAOR, Annexes, Agenda Item No. 87, at 22, 96-97, U.N. Doc. A/6230 (1966).

99. See the Pravda Article Justifying Intervention in Czechoslovakia, *supra* note 75.

customary law or on these newer proposals has largely been ignored—a strange testament to the duality of the framework for appraisal of intervention.

III. The Basic Community Policies at Stake in Intervention

To be useful, non-intervention standards must be relevant to the community policies which they are intended to serve. Yet far too often they seem to be rooted only in a logical spiral in the sky. Though policy differences and difficulty in fully articulating community policies ensure that there will not be universal agreement, appraisal of the reasons why the international community regards some kinds of intervention as wrong is a useful first step. Identification of the policies at stake in intervention, of course, will not provide a clear chart to wisdom, as in particular cases major policies may conflict. But without such identification policy choices simply go unperceived.

For purposes of appraising non-intervention standards the community policies at stake in intervention should be clarified from the perspective of the scholar identified with the broadest global community. The identification should not be that of the advocate interested in maximization of one nation's interest. This latter perspective is also useful, but if dialogue about international law is to add anything, it should be based on shared community interest.[100]

The basic policies at stake in intervention seem to be self-determination, the preservation of minimum human rights, and the maintenance of minimum public order. To these three principal policies, the process principles applicable in choosing effective non-intervention standards might also be added.

SELF-DETERMINATION

ITS REFERENT

Self-determination refers to the freedom of a people to choose their own government and institutions and to control their own

---

100. For an excellent statement of the utility of a legal perspective on foreign relations see Falk, *Law, Lawyers, and the Conduct of American Foreign Relations*, 78 YALE L.J. 919 (1969).

resources.[101] Thus Article One of the International Covenant On Civil And Political Rights, adopted by a 1966 resolution of the General Assembly and typical of a host of community pronouncements, provides:

> All peoples have the right of self-determination. By virtue of the right they freely determine their political status and freely pursue their economic, social and cultural development . . . [and] freely dispose of their natural wealth and resources. . . .[102]

Self-determination may be denied by either external or internal coercion. As against external coercion, the philosophical underpinnings of self-determination rest on an amalgam of the historical importance of the nation state and the democratic principle that persons primarily affected by decision should have the right to participate in the decision process. It is quite natural, then, that when one state seeks to force a decision on another in an area regarded as primarily internal to the latter, the coercion will be widely regarded as illegitimate intervention. This feeling of illegitimacy is heightened when the coercion is applied against internal authority structures which control a wide range of decisions about internal value production and allocation. Perhaps for this reason, there is a strong community consensus against colonialism, in which internal authority structures are controlled by another state. Sporadic intervention for the purpose of policing the form of government of another state, and even external domination of economic resources, may also seriously deny self-determination. In fact, self-determination may be threatened by external domination of any value. Charges of neo-colonialism are sometimes leveled in these situations of non-authority-oriented coercion.

101. See generally H. JOHNSON, SELF-DETERMINATION WITHIN THE COMMUNITY OF NATIONS (1967); T. Mensah, Self-Determination Under United Nations' Auspices (unpublished J.S.D. dissertation in the Yale Law Library, 1963); Report of the 1966 Special Committee on Principles of International Law Concerning Friendly Relations and Co-operation Among States, *supra* note 98, at 91-99.
102. G.A. Res. 2200, 21 U.N. GAOR, Supp. 16, at 52-58; U.N. Doc. A/6316 (1966).

As against internal coercion, self-determination is the freedom of the people of an entity, with respect to their own government, to participate in the choice of authority structures and institutions and to share in the values of society. Totalitarian or discriminatory regimes which deny their peoples self-determination in this sense may do so as effectively as the most thoroughgoing colonial regime. Thus, perhaps the strongest area of community consensus about self-determination today is that the discriminatory regimes of South Africa and Rhodesia deny their black populations self-determination.

Since history teaches that self-determination, whether denied by external or internal coercion, is sometimes attainable only through revolution, there is nothing in the principle of self-determination which excludes revolutionary change. The United Nations has indicated in the revolutionary situations in Algeria, Hungary, Rhodesia, South Africa, South-West Africa, and the Portuguese colonies that the principle of self-determination need not be sacrificed to the *status quo*.

If self-determination includes freedom to overthrow an unrepresentative government, or to break away from a colonizing state, it also includes freedom from coercive externally sponsored revolutions. The referent must always be to the genuine demands and identifications of the people. The "Brezhnev Doctrine" of "socialist self-determination,"[103] intended as a justification for the Soviet invasion of Czechoslovakia, must be rejected precisely because the referent of self-determination is not to the genuine demands and identifications of the people of Czechoslovakia, as events since then have amply confirmed. In fact, one will look in vain in the "Brezhnev Doctrine" for any referent of "socialist self-determination" other than preservation of Soviet interests in Eastern Europe.

Similarly, "modernization" is sometimes asserted to be a basic community policy at stake in intervention. One writer has even taken this so far as to suggest that the legitimacy of intervention should rest on its effect on modernization.[104] There is certainly

103. See the Pravda Article Justifying Intervention in Czechoslovakia, *supra* note 75.
104. See K. Boals, *supra* note 97, at 69-76.

significant support in the international community for the proposition that centralized and production-oriented societies are preferred to traditional, decentralized, and agrarian societies. But for this desire for modernization not to contradict that for self-determination it must be a genuine preference of the people of the entity. For others to coercively impose their own notions about the value of "modernized" society smacks of the paternalism of nineteenth-century missionaries and the "white man's burden." "Modernization," then, is more usefully regarded as one aspect of the general principle of self-determination.

THE SCOPE OF PEOPLES TO WHOM IT IS APPLIED: THE PROBLEM OF DEFINING SELF

A second question concerning self-determination is the scope of the peoples to whom it is applied. The question can also be stated as one of defining the self which is to have the right of determination.[105] For most purposes, this question is definitively answered in the international system by invoking the boundaries of the nation state, although philosophically one might be on sounder ground to answer it by reference to the principle that those affected by decision should have a voice in decision. In some contexts, however, the issue of the scope of an entity becomes acute. For example, in wars of secession, such as the Nigerian civil war or the Congo crisis, are Biafra and Katanga to be considered as separate entities for purposes of self-determination or are they to be included in the larger whole? The same issue may be raised in anti-colonial wars. Thus, was Algeria to be considered part of France or one or more separate entities for purposes of self-determination? The issue was also presented in the Indonesian-Netherlands dispute concerning West Irian, where Indonesia viewed West Irian as part of Indonesia, and is presented by the Vietnam War, where determination of whether the relevant entity is South Vietnam or all Vietnam is a major choice point in disagreement about the war. In making this characterization in Vietnam, though, considerations of minimum public order may be even more important than self-determination. Other in-

---

105. See H. JOHNSON, *supra* note 101, at 112-135; T. Mensah, *supra* note 101, at 282-329.

ternal conflict situations which raise, at least in part, this scope of entity issue include the American Civil War, the Sudan, Anguilla, and Quebec.

Criteria which could be applied in making the determination about scope of entity include constitutional boundaries, geographic boundaries, historical relation, economic viability, and sociological and psychological factors.[106] Have the people historically constituted a nation? Do they share a common ethnic, religious, or linguistic identity? Are the old and new entities economically viable? Do the people live within a common geographic area? Do they share common institutions and political authority or common awareness as a people?

It is probably best to begin this determination by including everyone affected. That is, to ask which characterization would best maximize the values at stake for everyone affected and then to apply whatever criteria seem to be most relevant to the particular case. While it is probably impossible to fix any criteria which will always be most responsive to the values of everyone affected, the demands and identifications of all the people and the economic consequences for both entities seem to be particularly important factors.

THE PROBLEM OF DETERMINATION

A third question of particular relevance for choice among non-intervention standards is how genuine self-determination is determined. Given the referent to the genuine demands and identifications of the people of an entity, rather than to some mystical territorial notion, how are those demands and identifications ascertained? In some cases the situation may be clear enough or the community consensus great enough for General Assembly resolution. And whether an accurate reflection of self-determination or not, at least such General Assembly resolutions are an authoritative community decision. Situations of internal conflict in which General Assembly pronouncements about self-determination (or cessation of intervention) have been made include Greece, Hungary, the Congo, Algeria, Southern Rhodesia, the Portuguese

---

106. These criteria are suggested by Thomas Mensah. See T. Mensah, *supra* note 101, at 289-329.

colonies, Oman, South Africa, and South-West Africa.[107] The fairness of such resolutions, of course, depends on their accordance with the genuine demands of the people of the entity and with consistency in treating like cases alike. In the absence of such community determinations, the ascertainment of genuine self-determination during the course of internal conflict presents both a severe auto-interpretation problem and a severe measurement problem.[108] These problems suggest that in the absence of prior external assistance, partisan military intervention in authority-oriented internal conflict should be impermissible. *A fortiori*, the deliberate unilateral export of revolution or use of force for the imposition of authority structures presents the gravest of dangers to genuine self-determination.

In some contexts internationally supervised free elections may be a useful technique for ascertaining the genuine demands of a populace. For example, non-partisan intervention in situations involving a breakdown of order might usefully be conditioned on genuine free elections. The elections following the United States-OAS intervention in the Dominican Republic seemed to produce an outcome at least as consistent with genuine self-determination as was promised by continuation of the anarchy prior to the intervention, although neither alternative will necessarily lead to long-run political stability. The election and plebiscite are cer-

---

107. See G.A. Res. 109, 2 U.N. GAOR 12-14, U.N. Doc. A/519 (1947); G.A. Res. 193, 3 U.N. GAOR 18-21, U.N. Doc. A/810 (1948); G.A. Res. 288A, 4 U.N. GAOR 9-10, U.N. Doc. A/1251 (1949); G.A. Res. 382, 5 U.N. GAOR, Supp. 20, at 14 U.N. Doc. A/1775 (1950) (Greece); G.A. Res. 1133, 11 U.N. GAOR, Supp. 17A, at 1, U.N. Doc. A/3572/Add.1 (1957) (Hungary); G.A. Res. 1474 (Emer. Sess. IV), U.N. GAOR, Supp. 1, at 1, U.N. Doc. A/4510 (1960) (the Congo); G.A. Res. 1573, 15 U.N. GAOR, Supp. 16, at 3, U.N. Doc. A/4684 (1960) (Algeria); G.A. Res. 2262, 22 U.N. GAOR, Supp. 16, at 45-46, U.N. Doc. A/6716 (1967) (Southern Rhodesia); G.A. Res. 2270, 22 U.N. GAOR, Supp. 16, at 47-48, U.N. Doc. A/6716 (1967) (the Portuguese colonies); G.A. Res. 2302, 22 U.N. GAOR, Supp. 16, at 49-50, U.N. Doc. A/6716 (1967) (Oman); G.A. Res. 2307, 22 U.N. GAOR, Supp. 16, at 19-20, U.N. Doc. A/6716 (1967) (South Africa); G.A. Res. 2372, 22 U.N. GAOR, Supp. 16A, at 1-2, U.N. Doc. A/6716/Add.1 (1968) (South-West Africa).

108. Tom Farer has colorfully illustrated the difficulty in ascertaining genuine self-determination during the course of internal conflict. See Farer, *Harnessing Rogue Elephants: A Short Discourse on Foreign Intervention in Civil Strife, supra* note 95, at 513-18.

tainly imperfect tools for ascertaining subjectivities, but if conducted and supervised fairly, with opportunity for major competing factions to be heard, they are the best techniques we have for providing large numbers of persons a voice in decision. As such, it is not surprising that there has been strong support within the United Nations to adopt the plebiscite "as a regular international instrument" for ascertaining self-determination.[109]

MINIMUM HUMAN RIGHTS

Although minimum human rights are also a part of self-determination, they are separate to the extent that there are strong community policies for their protection regardless of the majority sentiment within an entity. The Universal Declaration of Human Rights, approved by a resolution of the General Assembly in 1948,[110] sets forth a number of such human rights on which there is at least nominal international agreement. Among those set forth are rights to be free from discrimination on the basis of race or sex, rights to life, liberty, and the security of the person, and rights to be free from slavery, torture, or inhuman treatment. The 1966 International Covenant on Civil and Political Rights reaffirms these rights.[111]

The Convention on the Prevention and Punishment of the Crime of Genocide, in force since 1951, is one of the most specific and important guarantees of minimum human rights. Article 1 of the Convention defines genocide as:

> . . . [A]ny of the following acts committed with intent to destroy, in whole or in part, a national, ethnical, racial or religious group as such.

Article II specifies the prohibited acts:

(a) Killing members of the group;
(b) Causing serious bodily or mental harm to members of the group;

109. See H. JOHNSON, *supra* note 101, at 64.
110. G.A. Res. 217A, 3 U.N. GAOR 71-77, U.N. Doc. A/810 (1948). See generally E. SCHWELB, HUMAN RIGHTS AND THE INTERNATIONAL COMMUNITY (1964).
111. G.A. Res. 2200, 21 U.N. GAOR, Supp. 16, at 52-58, U.N. Doc. A/6316 (1966).

(c) Deliberately inflicting on the group conditions of life calculated to bring about its physical destruction in whole or in part.[112]

These and other community pronouncements about minimum human rights suggest that there may be room within appropriate safeguards for retention of something approximating the traditional categories of "humanitarian intervention" and "intervention for the protection of nationals."

Minimum Public Order

The common interest in minimum public order is an interest in maintaining an orderly world in which cooperation can proceed with respect to all values.[113] In its most general meaning, minimum public order includes the need to maintain the stability of the international system and to avoid a general nuclear exchange. In an era of massive overkill the avoidance of nuclear war is the most important concern of the world community. Because of its importance, situations which particularly threaten major power conflict, such as assistance to insurgents across cold-war boundaries separating the divided nations, should be singled out for special treatment. Similarly, adventures in a competing major power sphere of influence, whether justified by self-determination or not, as for example a hypothetical United States assistance to insurgents in Czechoslovakia, are much too dangerous. Situations threatening major power conflict always run the risk of escalation to a general nuclear exchange or, in its absence, a prolonged limited war.

The policy of minimum public order also reflects a preference for change by peaceful processes rather than by coercion. Coercive change can be destructive of a wide range of values and can deter gain through cooperation. Unilateral export of revolution

112. 78 U.N.T.S. 277 (1951). The Convention came into force on January 12, 1951, in accordance with Article XIII. *See Status of Multilateral Conventions*, U.N. Doc. ST/LEG/3, Rev. 1. See generally McDougal & Arens, *The Genocide Convention and the Constitution*, 3 VAND. L. REV. 683 (1950).

113. For a comprehensive statement of the principle of minimum public order see M. McDougal & F. Feliciano, *supra* note 84, at 121-260.

or external use of force for the imposition of internal authority structures may present a dangerous threat to this policy.

A third policy included within minimum public order is minimization of destruction within a contested entity. As internal conflict is prolonged by lack of settlement machinery or by competitive interventions, it may lead to increased destruction within the entity. Similarly, inadequate laws of warfare or failure to abide by the laws of war may needlessly increase the destruction within an internal conflict. The reduction of the level of destruction within internal conflict must be a major concern of intervention controls.

The UN Charter reflects these policies in its proscription of unilateral force in international relations as a modality of major change or as a technique for dispute settlement. As corollaries to this proscription, the Charter provides in letter or spirit that the unilateral use of major force against the territory of another entity is permissible only in response to an armed attack, must be proportional, and is subject to community review by the Security Council. Military strategies are wasteful and disruptive even in the absence of a major threat of nuclear escalation, and the strong community preference must be for minimization of their use. In a world without a perfectly effective centralized peace-keeping machinery, however, there are real defense interdependencies. As such, the individual or collective use of force in defense against an armed attack, as authorized by Article 51 of the Charter, is an important feature of the international system. Any non-intervention framework likely to be widely accepted must preserve this defensive right. This suggests a need for allowing pre-insurgency assistance to a widely recognized government, since such assistance may be required for adequate defense against external attack. It also suggests a need for allowing counter-intervention on behalf of a widely recognized government, at least if necessary to counter covert armed attack.

PROCESS CRITERIA FOR EFFECTIVE NON-INTERVENTION STANDARDS

The policies of self-determination, minimum human rights, and minimum public order seem to be the principal community policies at stake in intervention. In recommending non-intervention standards for effectuating these policies, however, other critiera relating to the effectiveness of rules are also applicable. The principal such process criterion seems to be that non-intervention standards should be reasonably acceptable, workable, certain, and effective.

Acceptable refers to the likelihood that government actions will tolerably conform to the standard. In a system which relies partly on governmental action for the development of customary law, often repeated governmental action may have a law-creating role. A high incidence of foreign office conformance, then, will in turn strengthen the authority of the standard. A low incidence of conformance, on the other hand, may detract from both the authority of the standard and the authority of international law in general. In a world with only a rudimentary sanctioning process, however, acceptability can easily be overemphasized at the expense of policy-responsiveness. The most acceptable standard in terms of real-world compliance may be no standard at all. Thus, on balance, acceptability is a valid concern, but it should not be taken to the extreme of major sacrifice of policy-responsiveness.

The second criterion for effectiveness is that a standard be reasonably workable. Workable refers to the realism with which a standard treats the features of the international system. For example, unless covertly announcing an absolute non-intervention standard, it would be unworkable in the present system to premise permissible intervention on prior Security Council approval.

The third criterion is that a standard be reasonably certain. Certainty refers to the reliability with which a standard can be usefully applied to specific cases. To be certain in this sense, a standard must be reasonably definite and reasonably complete. To the extent that a standard is uncertain it neither provides guidance for decision nor serves the fundamental principle of fairness in all law that like cases should be treated alike. As has been seen, the traditional international law of non-intervention suffers from an abundance of vagueness, incompleteness, and complementarity in the initial choice of normative systems. Perennial problems in definiteness include the identification of a "recognized government," the point at which internal violence reaches a level requiring a freeze on external assistance, and the point at which external assistance to insurgents justifies counter-intervention.

The final and most important criterion, interrelated with all of the others, is that a standard be reasonably effective. Effectiveness refers to the responsiveness of a standard to community policies at stake. A standard which is acceptable, workable, and certain is of little use if it is not also reasonably policy-responsive. There is a temptation, too frequently indulged in recommending non-intervention standards, to overemphasize the value of acceptability and certainty at the expense of policy-responsiveness. A balance of emphasis seems more likely to produce meaningful standards.

IV. Intervention in Internal Conflict: Claims Presenting Common Policies and Conditioning Factors

An essential element of policy-responsive non-intervention standards is clarification by claims presenting common policies and common conditioning factors. The great diversity of situations in which claims of intervention are raised makes this problem of classification critical. Frequently, however, no effort is made to identify like cases presenting common policies and affected by common conditioning factors, and it is often assumed that a single rule will be policy responsive for the entire range of intervention. Scholars almost mystically continue to pursue this will-o'-the-wisp of a single non-intervention rule, even though they would not dream of one rule for all jurisdiction, treaty-interpretation, or tort law. Furthermore, when classification has been attempted, though some of the schemes have been insightful, they have not presented the most useful classification for formulating policy-responsive rules for the full range of intervention phenomena. At the present stage of intervention theory a comprehensive policy-responsive classification of intervention situations is badly needed.

The most insightful past classifications have included the following. Linda Miller has divided internal conflict into "colonial wars," "internal conflicts involving a breakdown of law and order," and "proxy wars and internal conflicts involving charges of external aggression or subversion."[114] This breakdown is useful for a focus on *The United Nations and Internal Conflict*, but it does not subsume the full range of intervention in internal conflict. Neither does it achieve a clear focus on the different claims presented within each category.

As an analytic tool for clarification of policy choices, Professor Richard Falk has postulated a fourfold division of internal conflict into "civil strife without significant foreign intervention," "civil strife with foreign intervention by states other than great powers or their surrogates," "civil strife with foreign intervention by the great powers or their surrogates," and "civil strife in which the foreign intervention is alleged to take the form of an 'armed attack.'"[115] This classification by source and amount of external involvement, although useful in describing world order consequences, begs the question for normative clarification about when external involvement is permissible.

In a more behavioral definition, Professor James Rosenau divides internal strife into personnel wars, authority wars, and

114. L. MILLER, WORLD ORDER AND LOCAL DISORDER: THE UNITED NATIONS AND INTERNAL CONFLICTS 4-7 (1967). Linda Miller demonstrates a sensitive awareness of the need for comprehensive classification.

Inquiry into internal disorders remains in a "pre-theoretical" stage. As Eckstein argues, it is necessary to develop "descriptive categories in terms of which the basic features of internal wars can be identified, in terms of which their nuances and broader features can be depicted in general structural concepts, classes (or types) constructed, and resemblances of cases to one another or to types can be accurately assessed." Only after such categories have been established will social scientists begin to comprehend the preconditions of internal violence, the courses such disorders take, and the long-term consequences of their evolution.

Id. at 4.

Categories useful for analyzing internal conflicts from one perspective may not be useful for other purposes. Thus the present study, the first concerned with the role of the United Nations in contemporary internal conflicts, employs categories chosen for their value in assessing the Organization's record. The writer does not suggest that these categories are adequate for a theoretical approach to the international relations of internal violence.

Id. at 6.

115. See R. FALK, *supra* note 98, at 67-68.

structural wars. Personnel wars are those "perceived as being fought over the occupancy of existing roles in the existing structure of political authority . . ."; authority wars are those "perceived as being fought over the arrangement (as well as the occupancy) of the roles in the structure of political authority . . ."; and structural wars are those "perceived as being not only contests over personnel and the structure of political authority, but also as struggles over other substructures of the society. . . ."[116] Although particularly insightful in calling attention to the great range of international effects of the diverse types of internal conflict, and in establishing operational categories for study of these effects, the Rosenau division is too general for normative clarification.

Neither these nor any other classification scheme suggested to date has achieved a comprehensive classification of claims of intervention in internal conflict presenting common policies and common conditioning factors. As an alternative classification the following six major categories are suggested, subject to appropriate contextual breakdown of the claims subsumed under each: type I situations, claims not relating to authority structures; type II situations, claims relating to anti-colonial wars; type III situations, claims relating to wars of secession; type IV situations, claims relating to indigenous conflict for control of internal authority structures; type V situations, claims relating to the use of external force for imposition of internal authority structures; and type VI situations, claims relating to cold-war divided nation conflicts. Together these six situations make up an intervention-in-internal-conflict spectrum which might be represented by the following continuum:

I	II	III	IV	V	VI
Non-authority-oriented intervention	Anti-colonial wars	Wars of secession	Indigenous conflict for control of internal authority structures	External imposition of authority structures	Cold-war divided nation conflicts

116. Rosenau, *Internal War as an International Event* in INTERNATIONAL ASPECTS OF CIVIL STRIFE 45, 63-64 (J. Rosenau ed. 1964).

Although the spectrum is roughly one of increasing threat to community values as one moves from the lower to higher categories, the correlation is only approximate and some conflicts in lower categories might present greater threats than others in higher categories. For example, a war of secession in the United States or the Soviet Union would be likely to present a greater world order threat than the conflict in Yemen for control of internal authority structures.

With more complete contextual breakdown these six situations include the following claims:

Type I Situations: Claims Not Relating to Authority Structures.
    A. Claims to provide military assistance to a widely recognized government in the absence of internal disorders.
    B. Claims to assist a widely recognized government in controlling non-authority-oriented internal disorders.
    C. Claims to use the military instrument in the territory of another state for the protection of human rights.

Type II Situations: Claims Relating to Anti-Colonial Wars.
    A. Claims to assist a colonial power in an anti-colonial war.
    B. Claims to assist the break-away forces in an anti-colonial war.
    C. Claims by an administering authority to use the military instrument to prevent break-away.

Type III Situations: Claims Relating to Wars of Secession.
    A. Claims to assist the federal forces in a war of secession.
    B. Claims to assist the secessionist forces in a war of secession.
    C. Claims that external assistance to an opposing faction justifies assistance.

Type IV Situations: Claims Relating to Indigenous Conflict for the Control of Internal Authority Structures.
    A. Claims to assist a widely recognized government in a struggle for control of internal authority structures.
    B. Claims to assist an insurgent faction in a struggle for control of internal authority structures.

C. Claims to assist any faction in a struggle for control of internal authority structures where a widely recognized government cannot be distinguished.

D. Claims that external assistance provided to an opposing faction justifies assistance.

E. Claims to use the military instrument in the territory of another state for the purpose of restoring orderly processes of self-determination in conflicts over internal authority structures involving a sudden breakdown of order.

F. Claims to use the military instrument against the territory of a state providing assistance to an opposing faction.

Type V Situations: Claims Relating to External Initiation of the Use of Force for the Imposition of Internal Authority Structures.

A. Cold-war claims for the use of the military instrument in the territory of another state for the purpose of maintaining or imposing "democratic" or "socialist" regimes.

B. Claims for the use of the military instrument in the territory of another state for the purpose of altering internal authority structures which deny self-determination on a racial basis.

C. Claims to assist exile or refugee groups for the purpose of restoring self-determination.

Type VI Situations: Claims Relating to Cold-War Divided Nation Conflicts.

A. Claims by one-half of a cold-war divided nation to take over the authority structure of the other half or to assist an insurgent faction in a struggle for control of internal authority structures.

B. Claims to assist the widely recognized government of a cold-war divided nation to resist takeover of its authority structures by the other half of the divided nation or to counter assistance provided to an insurgent faction by the other half.

C. Claims to use the military instrument against the territory of one-half of a cold-war divided nation which is providing assistance to an insurgent faction in the other half.

A full development of participation claims would also include claims to participate because of special treaty rights.[117] In most situations, however, such treaties should not be a source of additional rights, because if they were, any non-participation standard could easily be avoided by the simple expedient of concluding a treaty with the government. Moreover, since self-determination is a principal reason for non-participation, there is some difficulty in allowing one government to conclude an external arrangement to guarantee itself against revolution. Perhaps because of this sensitivity to self-determination, most mutual defense treaties guarantee only against external attack. Nevertheless, there may be some special circumstances, such as treaties with associated or protected mini-states or treaties resulting from the establishment of a state, for example, the 1960 Greece-Turkey-United Kingdom Treaty of Guarantee with Cyprus,[118] which may complicate the picture.

Although undoubtedly others, in addition to claims to participate because of special treaty rights, may be added, this classification into twenty-one claims includes most of the basic claims concerning foreign participation in internal conflict. Many of these participation claims might also be further broken down by type of assistance. That is, was the claim to participate a claim to provide economic assistance, organization and political skills, armaments (by grant, cash sale, or sale on long-term credits), military training or advisory missions, territorial sanctuary, citizen volunteers, or regular combat troops? Although certainly relevant, for the most part this additional precision in the division of claims does not seem to be sufficiently helpful to justify the further breakdown.

A complete description of claims concerning internal conflict would also include, in addition to these participation claims, the full range of claims concerning the conduct of internal war (that is, claims concerning the regulation of hostilities), and the full

117. For the extraordinary looseness with which at least pre-Charter customary international law regarded claims to intervene on the basis of an alleged treaty right see Oppenheim's list of seven reasons for which intervention was permissible. I OPPENHEIM, INTERNATIONAL LAW 306-10 (8th ed. Lauterpacht 1955).

118. 382 U.N.T.S. 3 (1960).

range of claims concerning relations with third states (including claims concerning recognition).

It might also be pointed out that some conflicts include claims in more than one situation or suggest claims cutting across several situations. For example, the Congo crisis presented type I claims to assist in controlling non-authority-oriented disorders and for the protection of human rights, a type III claim to assist the federal forces in a war of secession with Katanga province, and a type IV claim for the purpose of restoring orderly processes of self-determination. Similarly, the British invasion of Anguilla suggests a type II claim by Britain as an administering authority to use the military instrument to prevent breakaway and a type III claim by Britain to assist the forces of the St. Kitts-Nevis-Anguilla federation in a war of secession with Anguilla. Depending on the degree of authority in fact retained by Britain over her former colony either or both claims could be applicable. The point is that the six situations are not intended as watertight compartments, but only as a useful framework for development of claims. And as in the case of the British invasion of Anguilla, the more specific claims should provide a useful technique of analysis for most situations which may arise.

Each of the twenty-one participation claims will be considered in turn. On each I will attempt to isolate the important conditioning factors, explore existing community expectations, and suggest appropriate policy-responsive standards.

TYPE I SITUATIONS: CLAIMS NOT RELATING TO AUTHORITY STRUCTURES

This category is intended to focus on claims which have only an incidental effect on authority structures; that is, claims which only peripherally affect the political and social institutions of an entity even though they may be highly coercive in their limited impact. As such, this category really includes a broad range of minor coercion claims, including claims of reprisal and even the now largely defunct claim to use coercion for collection of alleged international debts. The most relevant sub-categories for a current study of foreign participation in internal conflict, however, seem to be claims to provide military assistance to a widely recognized government in the absence of internal disorders, claims to assist a widely recognized government in controlling non-authority-oriented internal disorders, and claims for the protection of human rights. Since these three claims are by definition non-authority-oriented, they generally present only a low order threat to self-determination. All three claims may also constitute permissible pre-insurgency assistance, as developed in the discussion of type IV claims to assist a widely recognized government, and the first two are by definition always permissible pre-insurgency assistance under the suggested criteria for determining an insurgency. It should be noted also that the last two of these type I claims frequently depend on the deployment of external combat units in small scale tactical operations.

A. CLAIMS TO PROVIDE MILITARY ASSISTANCE TO A WIDELY RECOGNIZED GOVERNMENT IN THE ABSENCE OF INTERNAL DISORDERS

There seems to be no question that in the absence of internal disorders military assistance may be provided to a widely recognized government. Most military assistance programs fall into this category and such programs are commonplace. Legitimate defense interdependencies against external threats justify such assistance and in the absence of internal disorder such assistance does not really present an intervention in internal conflict problem.

The problem, however, is determining when the level of internal conflict is such as to require cessation of assistance or a prohibition of increased assistance in order to avoid participation in internal conflict. If the threshold is too low, military assistance programs would be frequently interrupted by the low-level internal violence endemic to many developing nations. On the other hand, if the threshold is too high, the non-participation requirement would be compromised. Despite the possibility of confusion with the traditional doctrine, "insurgency" seems the best term to indicate this non-participation threshold. Because of acute involvement with the type IV claim to assist a widely recognized government in an indigenous conflict for the control of internal authority structures, the development of criteria for determining the insurgency threshold will be deferred until the type IV situation is discussed. It is sufficient at this point to indicate that pre-insurgency assistance to a recognized government is widely regarded as permissible.

B. CLAIMS TO ASSIST A WIDELY RECOGNIZED GOVERNMENT IN CONTROLLING NON-AUTHORITY-ORIENTED INTERNAL DISORDER

This category includes military assistance by one state for the purpose of restoring order in another state when the disorder stems essentially from causes other than competition for control of internal authority structures. Although few internal disorders are totally devoid of authority overtones, some are sufficiently non-authority-oriented to justify separate emphasis. Perhaps the clearest examples of events in this category include the pre-Matadi Congo crisis in July, 1960, and the Tanganyika (now Tanzania), Uganda, Kenya disorders in 1964.

Essentially, all of these disorders were sparked by a mutiny of African soldiers against their European officer corps for higher pay or Africanization of the corps. In the Tanganyika mutiny, which led to general rioting, President Jullius Nyerere requested military assistance from Britain. A force of 500 British Royal Commandos restored order at a cost of one man dead and two injured and quickly left the country. Ethiopian and Nigerian troops, which replaced the British Commandos, stayed about a year. Events in Uganda and Kenya followed a similar course.[119]

Although the Tanganyika crisis had political overtones and was at least psychologically related to the Zanzibar coup which immediately preceded it, at the time the British flew in troops from Aden it was not primarily an authority-oriented disorder aimed at the Nyerere regime. Reaction in the United Nations to the Tanganyika, Uganda, Kenya operations indicated that the British actions were regarded as legitimate by the world community.

In its early stages of sporadic mutiny against the Belgian officer corps the Congo crisis seems to have had still fewer political overtones. One commentator has even suggested that had the United

119. See Lefever, *The Limits of U.N. Intervention in the Third World*, 30 REV. OF POLITICS 3, 11-12 (1968).

States provided immediate military assistance when requested by the Congo government on July 12, the costly subsequent crisis could have been avoided in a manner similar to the later Tanganyika, Uganda, Kenya crisis.[120]

There are no bright-line distinctions between authority-oriented and non-authority-oriented disorders, but the Tanganyika experience suggests the desirability of preserving an area of unilateral competence to assist in quelling non-authority-oriented internal disorders at the request of the widely recognized government. Many of the newer states have inadequate internal police forces and may easily be unable to deal with internal disorders, particularly those resulting from breakdowns in Army discipline. Powerful bandit groups and private armies may also be a continuing threat in many poorly centralized societies, and there seems to be little reason why a widely recognized government should not be allowed to receive foreign assistance to control such groups. Burma and Southern Thailand provide examples of internal conflicts partly resulting from such bandit armies.

Although it might be suggested that competence to intervene in non-authority-oriented disorders should rest exclusively with the United Nations, the contrast between the Congo and the Tanganyika crises suggests that such a limitation might be undesirable. As much as we would like the greater security of a more centralized response, the political realities of the present United Nations severely limit its ability to provide a reliable and flexible response.

Lastly, since non-authority-oriented internal conflicts are not insurgencies, consistency with the principle allowing pre-insurgency assistance suggests that it should be permissible to assist a widely recognized government to control such disorders.

C. CLAIMS TO USE THE MILITARY INSTRUMENT IN THE
TERRITORY OF ANOTHER STATE FOR THE
PROTECTION OF HUMAN RIGHTS

Customary international law recognized a right to use the armed forces in the territory of another state both for humani-

120. *Id.* at 15-18.

tarian intervention and for the protection of nationals.[121] Humanitarian intervention encompassed use of force for the protection of persons other than nationals from gross denial of fundamental human rights and was frequently a collective undertaking. According to Professor Richard Lillich, the doctrine is "so clearly established under customary international law that only its limits and not its existence are subject to debate."[122]

Some scholars have argued that Article 2(4) of the Charter, proscribing "the threat or use of force against the territorial integrity or political independence" of another state, terminated this customary law right.[123] Others have urged that when construed together Article 55, providing for respect for human rights, and Article 56, pledging all members "to take joint and separate action . . . for the achievement of the purposes set forth in Article 55," reinforce the customary law right of humanitarian intervention.[124] The truth seems to be that the Charter speaks in complementary policies on the one hand of restricting unilateral force as an instrument of national policy, and on the other of urging action for the protection of human rights. Consequently, both interpretations are plausible on a major purposes rationale. The real difficulty seems to be, as is true with respect to many intervention claims, that the Charter is simply not responsive to the problem. For example, it is certainly open to argument that humanitarian intervention does not threaten "territorial integrity or political independence." As a result, arguments made on the basis of the Charter seem more useful as exercises in logical derivation than as criteria for decision.

The major recent instances of claims in this category include the 1964 joint Belgian-United States rescue operation in the

121. See, *e.g.*, I OPPENHEIM, *supra* note 117, at 309, 312-13.
122. R. Lillich, Intervention to Protect Human Rights 8 (unpublished paper presented at a Regional Meeting of the American Society of International Law at Queen's University on November 22-23, 1968).
123. See I. BROWNLIE, INTERNATIONAL LAW AND THE USE OF FORCE BY STATES 433 (1963); Wright, *The Legality of Intervention Under the United Nations Charter*, 51 PROC. AM. SOC'Y INT'L L. 79, 88 (1957).
124. See McDougal & Reisman, *Response by Professors McDougal and Reisman*, 3 INT'L LAWYER 438, 444 (1969).

Congo, the initial landing of a small contingent of United States marines during the disorders in the Dominican Republic in 1965, and perhaps the initial brief introduction of Belgian troops after the July 1960 breakdown of order in the Congo. In each case the claim was made that a breakdown of order or a deliberate violation of human rights threatened the lives of nationals of the intervening state and that the intervention was requested by the lawful government. In the joint Stanleyville rescue mission the action was undertaken at the request of the widely recognized Congolese government, and over 2,000 civilian hostages of over eighteen nationalities were rescued within a four-day period. In the Dominican Republic the operation was at least nominally requested by a faction engaged in authority-oriented internal conflict; and in the 1960 Belgian dispatch of troops to the Congo the action was taken apparently without the consent of Prime Minister Lumumba but with the permission of Foreign Minister Bomboko.

In the absence of insurgency, of course, if a widely recognized government requests foreign assistance for the protection of human rights, such assistance should be permissible just as is other pre-insurgency assistance. Even in other circumstances, however, some such interventions should be permissible if carefully safeguarded.

There is some danger that actions which go beyond pre-insurgency assistance may conceal authority-oriented claims, as has been alleged in both the Congo and Dominican Republic operations. But despite this danger, it seems undesirable to prohibit all external assistance for the purpose of preserving fundamental human rights if such assistance is narrowly confined to humanitarian objectives. In most of these situations there is practically no real interference with meaningful self-determination and only low levels of violence or threats to international peace. Moreover, the recognition of such a competence would seem to encourage at least a minimum level of respect for fundamental human rights. When widespread loss of human life is at stake because of arbitrary action, it would seem mere sophistry to argue that community policies or legalities prevent effective action.

Other factors suggesting preservation of some unilateral interventionary competence, even beyond pre-insurgency assistance, are the present lack of international machinery for the enforcement of human rights and the necessity to take quick decisive action in what is usually a crisis situation; international organizations are simply not able to respond with the same dispatch as individual states. For these and other reasons, a number of scholars have recently affirmed the legitimacy of a limited right of humanitarian intervention "as a minimum enforcement measure to protect human rights."[125] Scholars recently affirming this right include Professor Myres S. McDougal and Dr. Michael Reisman,[126] and Professor Richard Lillich.[127] Sir Hersh Lauterpacht is also associated with this position.[128] In fact, some such right is probably present international law.

Intervention for the protection of human rights which goes beyond pre-insurgency assistance, however, should be adequately limited to ensure that it serves community policies. In the most comprehensive review of these claims to date, Professor Richard Lillich has suggested five useful criteria for judging the permissibility of interventions for the protection of human rights. They are: (1) the immediacy of violation of human rights, (2) the extent of violation of human rights, (3) an invitation from appropriate authorities to use forcible self-help, (4) the degree of coercive measures employed, and (5) the relative disinterestedness of the intervening state.[129]

To these criteria might be added a minimal effect on authority structures, a prompt disengagement consistent with the purpose of the action, and immediate full reporting to the Security Council and appropriate regional organizations. If the protection of

---

125. See R. Lillich, *supra* note 122, at 4.
126. See McDougal & Reisman, *supra* note 124.
127. See R. Lillich, *supra* note 122, at 4; Lillich, *Forcible Self-Help by States to Protect Human Rights*, 53 IOWA L. REV. 325 (1967).
128. See H. LAUTERPACHT, INTERNATIONAL LAW AND HUMAN RIGHTS 120-21 (1950); I OPPENHEIM, *supra* note 117, at 312-13 (Lauterpacht ed.).
129. See Lillich, *Forcible Self-Help by States to Protect Human Rights, supra* note 127, at 347-51; R. Lillich, Intervention to Protect Human Rights, *supra* note 122, at 16.

human rights requires the overthrow of authority structures, it would seem best to require United Nations authorization as a prerequisite for action. To allow unilateral action in such cases would be to permit all manner of self-serving claims for the overthrow of authority structures.

With respect to the extent of the threat to human rights which justifies intervention, the answer largely seems to depend on the extent of values threatened by the intervention. A threat of widespread loss of human life would seem to be the clearest justification and seems to have constituted most of the past instances in this category.

Although an invitation to use forcible self-help may be important in reducing the coercion necessary to effectuate the protection of human rights, it does not seem necessary as a sine qua non for humanitarian intervention. The Dominican operation is an example of a situation in which such an invitation did not seem particularly meaningful.[130] Biafra may have been another.

To summarize, intervention for the protection of human rights should be permissible if made prior to the outbreak of insurgency at the request of a widely recognized government. In addition, some interventions for the protection of human rights which go beyond pre-insurgency assistance should be permissible. Criteria for determining legitimacy of interventions which go beyond pre-insurgency assistance include:

(1) an immediate and extensive threat to fundamental human rights, particularly a threat of widespread loss of human life;

(2) a proportional use of force which does not threaten greater destruction of values than the human rights at stake;

(3) a minimal effect on authority structures;

(4) a prompt disengagement, consistent with the purpose of the action;

(5) immediate full reporting to the Security Council and appropriate regional organizations.

130. See the description of the circumstances surrounding the invitation in the Dominican operation in Nanda, *The United States' Action in the 1965 Dominican Crisis: Impact on World Order*, 43 DENVER L. REV. 439, 465-67 (1966).

TYPE II SITUATIONS: CLAIMS RELATING TO ANTI-COLONIAL WARS

Anti-colonial wars are conflicts to establish the independence of internal authority structures from foreign authority and control. Examples have been the American Revolution, the Netherlands-Indonesian war, the Algerian war, the first Vietnamese war (in part), and at the present time the insurrections in Angola, Mozambique, and Portuguese Guinea.

Anti-colonial wars differ from wars of secession in the lesser degree to which internal authority structures of the break-away regime have participated in decision-making for the entity and in the greater clarity of separation of the dominant and subordinate entities prior to break-away. They are also frequently associated with racial or developmental differences between the two entities. The distinction is one of degree rather than bright-line clarity, but the consequences of the distinction are great. For unlike the difficulties in ascertaining which way self-determination cuts in the war of secession, there is a strong community consensus against colonialism. This consensus is demonstrated most dramatically in the Declaration on the Granting of Independence To Colonial Countries and Peoples first adopted by the General Assembly in 1960. The vote then was 90 for, none against, and 9 abstentions. A subsequent vote in 1961 reaffirmed the Declaration and established a Special Committee of Seventeen to oversee its implementation. The vote was 97 for, none against, and 4 abstentions. And in 1962 the General Assembly increased the membership of the Committee of Seventeen to a Committee of Twenty-Four and again reaffirmed the Declaration, this time by a vote of 101 for, none against, and 4 abstentions.[131] Professor Egon Schwelb points out that because of this overwhelming adoption without substantive dissent the Declaration of 1960 amounts to an assertion about present international law.[132]

The Declaration provides in pertinent part:

The General Assembly . . . solemnly proclaims the necessity of bringing to a speedy and unconditional end colonialism in

131. E. SCHWELB, *supra* note 110, at 66-69.
132. E. SCHWELB, *supra* note 110, at 70.

all its forms and manifestations; And to this end *Declares* that:

1. The subjection of peoples to alien subjugation, domination and exploitation constitutes a denial of fundamental human rights, is contrary to the Charter of the United Nations and is an impediment to the promotion of world peace and co-operation.

2. All peoples have the right to self-determination; by virtue of that right they freely determine their political status and freely pursue their economic, social and cultural development. . . .

4. All armed action or repressive measures of all kinds directed against dependent peoples shall cease in order to enable them to exercise peacefully and freely their right to complete independence, and the integrity of their national territory shall be respected.

5. Immediate steps shall be taken, in Trust and Non-Self-Governing Territories or all other territories which have not yet attained independence, to transfer all powers to the peoples of those territories, without any conditions or reservations, in accordance with their freely expressed will and desire, without any distinction as to race, creed or colour, in order to enable them to enjoy complete independence and freedom. . . .

7. All States shall observe faithfully and strictly the provisions of the Charter of the United Nations, the Universal Declaration of Human Rights and the present Declaration on the basis of equality, non-interference in the internal affairs of all States, and respect for the sovereign rights of all peoples and their territorial integrity.[133]

A. CLAIMS TO ASSIST A COLONIAL POWER IN AN
ANTI-COLONIAL WAR

Because of the strong community consensus against colonialism and the usually stronger status of the colonial power vis-à-vis the colony, claims to assist a colonial power have been rare.

Two instances which are somewhat aberrational are those of

133. G.A. Res. 1514, 15 U.N. GAOR, Supp. 16, at 66-67, U.N. Doc. A/4684 (1960).

United Nations support for Britain in the non-armed struggle with the break-away regime in Rhodesia and United States support for France during the first Indo-China war. The Rhodesian instance was aberrational because of the racial policies of the break-away Ian Smith regime, which promoted a kind of internal colonialism along racial lines; the first Indo-China war was aberrational because United States support was not provided in sympathy with France's continuing colonial aspirations, but in a spirit of containment of communism. As such, the United States consistently pressured France to grant greater autonomy to the non-communist Vietnamese nationalists. The United States position, though, was consistently compromised by the colonial aspects of the war.

The strong community feeling against colonialism suggests that assistance to a colonial power in an anti-colonial war should be illegitimate in the absence of some unusual circumstances such as the Rhodesian racial policies prompting collective authorization by the United Nations.[134] One difficulty with this generalization is that some conflicts, such as the first Indo-China war, raise other claims such as assistance to a faction engaged in authority-oriented internal conflict, perhaps complicated further by external assistance to an opposing faction. The only guide to clarification in such cases presenting multiple claims would seem to be awareness of all of the claims presented and classification by major policies at stake.

B. CLAIMS TO ASSIST THE BREAK-AWAY FORCES IN AN ANTI-COLONIAL WAR

Although assistance to the break-away forces in an anti-colonial war may frequently support genuine self-determination (Rhodesia being a counter-example), such assistance may have serious adverse consequences on minimum public order. The support of a guerrilla movement, regardless of how much it promotes self-determination, can have severe destructive effects and should not be undertaken lightly. Moreover, even though a struggle is in its broadest outlines one of anti-colonialism, there are frequently competing insurgent factions espousing different public order

---

134. On the Rhodesian case see McDougal & Reisman, *The Lawfulness of International Concern*, 62 AM. J. INT'L L. 1 (1968).

systems. The consequences of assistance to one of these insurgent groups may be as much an interference with self-determination as colonialism itself. For these reasons it seems preferable to proscribe all assistance to break-away forces in an anti-colonial war until the United Nations authorizes individual or collective assistance to a particular faction, although in practice the Afro-Asian world may not accept this restriction. Collective United Nations authorization has the substantial advantages of deterring counter-assistance to the other side, providing community judgment about the legitimacy of competing demands for self-determination and the necessity of the use of force, and minimizing the danger of self-serving classification for parochial motives. There is already precedent in United Nations practice to support such collective determinations authorizing individual states to provide assistance to break-away forces in an anti-colonial war. On November 17, 1967, the General Assembly passed resolution 2270 which says:

The General Assembly,...

Appeals again to all States to grant the peoples of the Territories under Portuguese domination the moral and material assistance necessary for the restoration of their inalienable rights. . . .[135]

The resolution also requested all states to withhold military assistance from Portugal.[136] And on June 12, 1968, the General Assembly adopted a resolution calling upon:

all States to provide the necessary moral and material assistance to the Namibian [South-West African] people in their legitimate struggle for independence. . . .[137]

Although such resolutions still raise questions of fairness in applicability and reasonable efforts to avoid resort to coercion, collec-

135. G.A. Res. 2270, 22 U.N. GAOR, Supp. 16, at 47, 48, U.N. Doc. A/6716 (1967) (Article 12). The General Assembly repeated this provision in a 1968 resolution on the Question of Territories Under Portuguese Administration, G.A. Res. 2395, 23 U.N. GAOR, Supp. 18, at 59, U.N. Doc. A/7218 (1968) (Article 5).

136. G.A. Res. 2270, 22 U.N. GAOR, Supp. 16, at 47, U.N. Doc. A/6716 (1967) (Article 8).

137. G.A. Res. 2372, 22 U.N. GAOR, Supp. 16A, at 1, 2, U.N. Doc. A/6716/ Add.1 (1968) (Article 10).

tive authorization is far preferable to individual determination with its danger of self-serving characterization.

It would seem desirable, then, to prohibit all external assistance to any faction in an anti-colonial war until the United Nations authorizes individual or collective assistance to one or the other faction, as it has done both in the case of South-West Africa and the Portuguese colonies of Angola, Mozambique, and Portuguese Guinea. The consensus in the world community seems sufficiently opposed to colonialism to ensure that the General Assembly will authorize assistance in most instances where it would genuinely promote self-determination.

C. CLAIMS BY AN ADMINISTERING AUTHORITY TO USE THE MILITARY INSTRUMENT TO PREVENT BREAK-AWAY

The primary policy in appraising claims by an administering authority to prevent the break-away of a colony, protectorate, or trust territory is again self-determination. Self-determination, however, may occasionally be offset by the complementary principle of responsibility, as in cases where a territory is so small that complete independence is impractical. The rapidly declining number of trust territories under the international trusteeship system suggests that this latter category may be very small indeed. General Assembly or Trusteeship Council determination seems to be the most reliable guide to the legitimacy of claims in this category. In fact, both the Trusteeship Council and the General Assembly Committee of Twenty-Four have been active in assessing the legitimacy of relationships between administering powers and their dependencies. In the absence of special treaty rights or United Nations recognition of the continuing legitimacy of an arrangement, then, community policies against colonialism suggest that such claims should be impermissible. This conclusion is strongly supported by section four of the Declaration on the Granting of Independence to Colonial Countries and Peoples which provides that: "All armed action or repressive measures of all kinds directed against dependent peoples shall cease . . . and the integrity of their national territory shall be respected."[138]

138. G.A. Res. 1514, 15 U.N. GAOR, Supp. 16, at 66-67, U.N. Doc. A/4684 (1960).

TYPE III SITUATIONS: CLAIMS RELATING TO WARS OF SECESSION

Wars of secession are conflicts over permanent territorial division of a territory formerly consolidated under a unitary internal authority structure. In popular parlance they are particularly likely to be called civil wars. Examples in this category include the American Civil War, the attempted Katanga secession and the Nigerian-Biafran civil war. Although cold-war divided nation conflicts may have overtones of wars of secession, because of their unique position in the international system they also present other policies and conditioning factors requiring their separate treatment.

Wars of secession could certainly present a major threat to the stability of the international system if, for example, they occurred in a major nuclear power or if major powers intervened on opposing sides. The greatest threat to minimum public order in most wars of secession, however, seems to be that outside intervention will prolong the struggle and unnecessarily increase the internal suffering. British assistance to the South in the American Civil War is one example and alleged French aid to Biafra may have been another. In every case, however, wars of secession present a major problem in self-determination. The major self-determination issue, discussed previously in the section on basic community policies, is the scope of the peoples to whom self-determination should be applied. In the Nigerian civil war should one have looked to the Biafran demands only or to the demands of the people of Nigeria as a whole? Was the principal criterion the economic effect of split-off, the tribal antagonism between the Ibos and other Nigerians, the effect on the stability of other African boundaries which also crosscut tribal rivalries, or something else?

The danger of competing interventions prolonging the struggle and the complexity of identifying the scope of peoples to whom self-determination is to be applied in such struggles strongly suggest that unilateral assistance to either faction in a war of secession should be prohibited without a collective United Nations decision as to which faction may be aided. One question for inquiry might be the extent to which regional determination of legitimacy of assistance to a faction should be available in addition to United Nations determination. The strong African opposition to the secession of Katanga and Biafra and the danger of further African balkanization might suggest sufficient regional concern in these cases to justify regional determination by the OAU.

A. CLAIMS TO ASSIST THE FEDERAL FORCES IN A WAR OF SECESSION

Examples of claims in this category include United Nations assistance to the central Congo government to resist the secession of Katanga,[139] and British assistance to the Nigerian federal government.

The principal problem in the application of a "non-participation without collective authorization" standard to claims to assist the federal government is that the federal government is likely to have been receiving arms from friendly powers prior to the secession attempt. To require termination of this assistance after creating a military supply dependency may well work as intervention in favor of the secessionist forces. Although there is no neutral solution to this problem, perhaps the best practical solution, in the absence of collective authorization, is to limit the military assistance provided the federal government to the sources and amount of assistance being provided immediately prior to the secession attempt. Collective United Nations authorization (and possibly regional authorization), however, could permit increased assistance to the federal forces or require cessation of all assistance.

B. CLAIMS TO ASSIST THE SECESSIONIST FORCES IN A WAR OF SECESSION

A classic example of assistance to the secessionist forces was the British aid provided to the Confederate states during the American Civil War. Since the *Alabama* claims arbitration in 1872, growing out of United States claims against Britain for deprivations inflicted by the *Alabama* and other Confederate cruisers

---

139. With respect to the U.N. Congo operation see generally E. LEFEVER, UNCERTAIN MANDATE: POLITICS OF THE U.N. CONGO OPERATION (1967); L. MILLER, *supra* note 114, at 66-116.

built in Britain, such assistance has been regarded as illegal.[140] Section six of the Declaration on the Granting of Independence to Colonial Countries and Peoples provides contemporary evidence of this illegality. Section six declares:

> Any attempt aimed at the partial or total disruption of the national unity and the territorial integrity of a country is incompatible with the purposes and principles of the Charter of the United Nations.[141]

An example of a claim to assist secessionist forces was the French aid allegedly provided the Biafran forces in the Nigerian civil war. Absent a collective community determination that Biafra should have been aided, all such assistance only prolonged the war, was highly suspect in seeking to answer the scope of peoples' problem by external coercion, and should have been prohibited. Humanitarian assistance intended to prevent widespread civilian starvation, and not intended as authority-oriented assistance, of course, is quite another matter and should be vigorously encouraged.[142]

C. CLAIMS THAT EXTERNAL ASSISTANCE TO AN OPPOSING FACTION JUSTIFIES ASSISTANCE

A recent study of the rhetoric of intervention shows that two of the most common justifications put forth by governments in support of their interventions are that assistance was requested by the lawful government and that prior external assistance justifies counter-intervention.[143] If factually accurate, the claim of counter-intervention on behalf of federal forces probably ought

140. For the opinion of the tribunal in the *Alamaba* claims arbitration see W. BISHOP, INTERNATIONAL LAW 864 (2d ed. 1962) (the actual decision rested narrowly on the duties of a neutral toward a belligerent).

141. G.A. Res. 1514, 15 U.N. GAOR, Supp. 16, at 66-67, U.N. Doc. A/4684 (1960).

142. See R. Lillich, *supra* note 122, at 13-14; W. M. Reisman, Memorandum Upon Humanitarian Intervention to Protect the Ibos 15-16 (unpublished paper written in collaboration with Professor Myres S. McDougal).

143. Bohan, American and Soviet Justifications of Armed Intervention: A Study in Law and Propaganda (unpublished paper delivered at the Regional Meeting of the American Society of International Law on Bloc Law and Intervention, Tallahassee, Florida, March 27-29, 1969).

to be allowed. Once significant external assistance is being provided to the secessionist forces, there is little in one-sided isolation of the conflict which inspires confidence that self-determination will necessarily result. The right of counter-intervention would mean that if significant military assistance is being provided to secessionist forces, comparable military assistance may be provided to federal forces even in excess of pre-secession levels. In order not to create an endless series of escalating claims by competing powers aiding opposing factions, however, it seems wise to restrict the right of counter-intervention to assist on behalf of federal forces. This restriction would seem to accord with prevailing expectations as to the illegitimacy of assisting secessionist forces.

TYPE IV SITUATIONS: CLAIMS RELATING TO INDIGENOUS
CONFLICT FOR THE CONTROL OF INTERNAL
AUTHORITY STRUCTURES

This category includes all conflicts for control of internal authority structures which have substantial indigenous origin and support, whether personnel wars, authority wars, or structural wars. Again, however, the cold-war divided nation context is excluded for separate treatment even though it may have overtones of similar claims. Representative conflicts in this category, most of which have involved unilateral or collective intervention, include the Spanish civil war, the Greek civil war, Malaysia, Lebanon, Yemen, Guatemala, Laos, the Congo, Cyprus, the Dominican Republic, and Hungary.

Claims relating to indigenous conflict for the control of internal authority structures are easily the most difficult non-intervention claims to deal with as they present serious policy clashes sometimes suggesting contradictory solution. Resulting standards must uneasily reconcile revolutionary change reflecting genuine internal demand with the need to proscribe imported revolution and to maintain minimum public order. Moreover, claims in this category are usually motivated by ideological considerations, often reflecting deeply divisive splits in the world community. Because of the cold-war overtones of many interventions in this category and the difficulty of political solution, it is unrealistic to expect much effective United Nations involvement. Where cold-war aspects are subordinate, of course, as in the Congo, Cyprus, and Yemen conflicts, a United Nations presence may be possible.

Some claims concerning conflicts in this category are not claims to assist a particular faction, but are claims to restore order or to restore conditions allowing the people free choice between competing factions. Examples of conflicts involving such claims include Cyprus and the second stage of the Dominican Republic operation. Since these are not claims of assistance to either faction, some such interventions may be consistent with a rule that neither faction may be aided. Consequently, these claims will be examined as a separate sub-category.

A. CLAIMS TO ASSIST A WIDELY RECOGNIZED GOVERNMENT IN A STRUGGLE FOR CONTROL OF INTERNAL AUTHORITY STRUCTURES

There is considerable uncertainty today as to the legality of military assistance to a widely recognized government in a struggle for control of internal authority structures. Under what is generally said to be the traditional view, a widely recognized government is in a privileged position vis-à-vis an insurgent faction, at least until the status of belligerency is reached.[144] Even after belligerency is reached, it is not clear that the traditional view does anything more than require a choice between ending assistance and loss of neutrality with respect to the new belligerent party. Unquestionably, state practice catalogues many instances of assistance to a widely recognized government engaged in an insurgency, and the rhetoric of state practice shows that a request by the lawful government is perhaps the principal justification given for intervention. A growing number of scholars, however, have urged that assistance to both sides should be prohibited when an insurgency breaks out.[145] The 1965 General Assembly Declaration on Inadmissibility of Intervention, which provides that "no State shall . . . interfere in civil strife in another State . . . ," lends support to this position.[146]

Though the stability of the international system might some-

144. See the authorities collected at note 91 *supra*.
145. See the authorities collected at notes 92-94 *supra*.
146. G.A. Res. 2131, 20 U.N. GAOR, Supp. 14, at 11-12, U.N. Doc. A/6014 (1965).

times be promoted by a rule which permitted assistance to a widely recognized government engaged in a struggle for control of internal authority structures, in the usual type IV situation the possible denial of self-determination in thwarting popular demands for change seems too high a price to pay. Hungary is a good example. Accordingly, once an indigenous insurgency breaks out and the ruling elite are faced with a serious challenge to their authority, it seems preferable to prohibit external military assistance even to a widely recognized government. This prohibition, however, should permit an exception allowing comparable assistance to a widely recognized government whenever impermissible external assistance is provided to an insurgent faction, and an exception allowing pre-insurgency levels of assistance to continue.

In a world divided between intensely competing world order systems this non-intervention rule entails considerable risk that one side will adhere to it while others do not. Under conditions of guerrilla warfare, which are said to require a favorable government force ratio of from 10 to 1, it may be easier to evade the "no assistance to insurgents" requirement than the "no assistance to widely recognized government" requirement. Such a rule may also be self-defeating in those cases in which an armed minority seeks takeover of a government. The difficulty of determining which way genuine self-determination cuts, however, probably justifies this standard absent detectable foreign intervention on behalf of insurgents.

As in type III situations, since withdrawal of pre-existing military support may amount to intervention on behalf of insurgents, continuation of levels of assistance provided to a widely recognized government prior to the outbreak of conflict should be permissible. Today many recognized governments are likely to be receiving external military aid on a continuing basis, and creation of a military supply dependency may even be the objective of such aid. In these circumstances it might unfairly advantage the insurgent to require total cessation of military aid to the widely recognized government.

The greatest problem with the suggested standard prohibiting increased military assistance to a widely recognized government after an insurgency breaks out is in determining when the critical threshold has been reached. Did Che Guevara's operation in Bolivia constitute an insurgency requiring a freeze on military assistance to the Bolivian government? Do the estimated 1,000 terrorists in Uruguay require a freeze on military assistance to the Uruguayan government?[147] When did the 1956 Hungarian uprising require a freeze? If the insurgency threshold is too low, and includes sporadic or small-scale civil violence, the high prevalence of such violence in many undeveloped and relatively decentralized societies suggests that the rule will be neither acceptable nor workable. On the other hand, if the threshold is too high it may be largely ineffective. For the most part, scholars urging the applicability of the non-intervention standard to the recognized government have unaccountably neglected this critical problem of ascertaining the threshold requiring a freeze on military assistance. One test for determining this threshold, suggested by Quincy Wright, is whether the outcome is in doubt.[148] Professor Wright, however, does not provide any criteria for determining when the outcome is in doubt. Another possibility is the criteria for recognition of belligerency. Lauterpacht gives these criteria as:

> the existence of a civil war accompanied by a state of general hostilities; occupation and a measure of orderly administration of a substantial part of national territory by the insurgents; [and] observance of the rules of warfare on the part of the insurgent forces acting under a responsible authority. . . .[149]

147. See N.Y. Times, Jan. 23, 1969, at 12, col. 4.
148.   Some writers have taken the view that only if civil strife has been generally recognized as "belligerency," obliging outside states to be "neutral," are such states forbidden to give military assistance to either faction, but where belligerency has not been recognized, and the situation is one merely of "insurgency," military aid may be given to the recognized government but not to the insurgents. The predominant opinion, however, follows the view stated by Hall, that in respect to military intervention, the critical line is not recognition of belligerency, but the uncertainty of the outcome.
Wright, *supra* note 93, at 122.
149. II OPPENHEIM, INTERNATIONAL LAW 249 (7th ed. Lauterpacht 1952).

This classic belligerency test served to create a duty of neutrality toward the contending belligerents (unless a state was itself willing to become a belligerent), and to regulate a host of legal relations between the contending factions. Although the test is slightly responsive to the problem of non-participation, it is vague, outdated for current internal conflict, and suspect in that belligerency was never really intended as an absolute bar to participation.

Still another possibility for determining the non-participation threshold is the "convenient criteria" for "distinguishing a genuine [internal] . . . conflict from a mere act of banditry or an unorganized and shortlived insurrection," set out in the Final Record of the Geneva Diplomatic Conference of 1949. These criteria are:

(1) That the Party in revolt against the *de jure* government possesses an organized military force, an authority responsible for its acts, acting within a determinate territory and having the means of respecting and ensuring respect for the Convention.

(2) That the legal Government is obliged to have recourse to the regular military forces against insurgents organized as military and in possession of a part of the national territory.

(3) (a) That the *de jure* Government has recognized the insurgents as belligerents; or

(b) that it has claimed for itself the rights of a belligerent; or

(c) that it has accorded the insurgents recognition as belligerents for the purposes only of the present Convention; or

(d) that the dispute has been admitted to the agenda of the Security Council or the General Assembly of the United Nations as being a threat to international peace, a breach of the peace, or an act of aggression.

(4) (a) That the insurgents have an organization purporting to have the characteristics of a State.

(b) that the insurgent civil authority exercises *de facto* authority over persons within a determinate territory.

(c) that the armed forces act under the direction of the

organized civil authority and are prepared to observe the ordinary laws of war.

(d) that the insurgent civil authority agrees to be bound by the provisions of the Convention.[150]

The difficulty with these criteria is that they were not developed for the purpose of requiring a freeze on military assistance,[151] and that they make extensive use of the inappropriate recognition of belligerency standard. Nevertheless, they do suggest some useful factors, such as the necessity of the recognized government to make use of its regular military forces, which might be incorporated into more responsive criteria.

150. 10 M. WHITEMAN, DIGEST OF INTERNATIONAL LAW 40-41 (1968). I owe the discovery of this interesting test to Rosalyn Higgins.

151. It is helpful to keep in mind that the insurgency threshold problem is also a critical problem for the applicability of rules regulating the conduct of internal conflict. Although my suggested criteria may have some carryover value for this regulation of conduct issue, they are primarily responsive to the participation issue. These Geneva Conference criteria, on the other hand, are directed at the regulation of conduct issue; that is, at the applicability of the Geneva Conventions regulating the conduct of hostilities. Article three of each of the four Geneva Conventions of 1949 provides:

> In the case of armed conflict not of an international character occurring in the territory of one of the High Contracting Parties, each Party to the conflict shall be bound to apply, as a minimum, the following provisions:
> . . . .

Comment on this article in the Final Record of the Geneva Conference points out:

> . . . What is meant by "armed conflict not of an international character?"
> That was the burning question which arose again and again at the Diplomatic Conference. . . . The expression was so general, so vague, that many of the delegations feared that it might be taken to cover any act committed by force of arms—any form of anarchy, rebellion, or even plain banditry. For example, if a handful of individuals were to rise in rebellion against the State and attack a police station, would that suffice to bring into being an armed conflict within the meaning of the Article? In order to reply to questions of this sort, it was suggested that the term "conflict" should be defined or, which would come to the same thing, that a certain number of conditions for the application of the Convention should be enumerated. . . .

Id. at 39-40.

Although a completely satisfactory answer may have to depend on the total context in light of the purposes of the restriction, the following four criteria are suggested as useful for determining whether internal conflict has reached a level which requires a freeze on military assistance to the recognized government.

(1) the internal conflict must be an authority-oriented conflict aimed at the overthrow of the recognized government and its replacement by a political organization controlled by the insurgents;

(2) that the recognized government is obliged to make continuing use of most of its regular military forces against the insurgents, or a substantial segment of its regular military forces have ceased to accept orders;

(3) that the insurgents effectively prevent the recognized government from exercising continuing governmental authority over a significant percentage of the population; and

(4) that a significant percentage of the population supports the insurgent movement, as evidenced by military or supply assistance to the insurgents, general strikes, or other actions.

It would certainly seem that a *prima facie* case for a freeze on further assistance has been made out when these four criteria are present. The first criterion, that the internal conflict must be an authority-oriented conflict, should be a necessary condition of an insurgency. Thus when internal conflict is non-authority-oriented, it is not an insurgency requiring a freeze on assistance. The second criterion, that the recognized government is making use of most of its regular military forces against the insurgents, also seems particularly responsive, since if the government has most of its military resources in reserve, additional external assistance to the government forces seems less critical.

Applying these criteria to the Bolivian and Uruguayan cases, although the first criterion is met, there does not seem to be sufficient satisfaction of any of the last three criteria to justify characterization as an insurgency. On the other hand, the 1956 Hungarian uprising quickly satisfied all four conditions.

B. CLAIMS TO ASSIST AN INSURGENT FACTION IN A STRUGGLE FOR CONTROL OF INTERNAL AUTHORITY STRUCTURES

Existing expectations as to the lawfulness of assistance to an insurgent faction are predominantly against lawfulness in the absence of collective United Nations authorization. Both those writers, such as Hall, who advocate treating recognized governments and insurgents alike, and those who take the traditional position allowing assistance to a widely recognized government, regard assistance to insurgents as unlawful. Moreover, General Assembly resolutions on non-intervention and proposed drafts defining aggression uniformly proscribe such assistance to insurgents.[152] The practice of states, however, has not always been consistent with this view. Thus the United States is alleged to have intervened covertly on behalf of an insurgent faction in Guatemala in 1954 and to a lesser extent in Iran in 1953,[153] and the Soviet Union, Peking, North Vietnam, and Cuba have frequently sponsored or supported wars of national liberation. This assistance to insurgents varies from the relatively minor United States activities in Iran to the major North Vietnamese involvement in Laos and South Vietnam. In recent years the Afro-Asian states have been willing to regard assistance to insurgents in states maintaining racially discriminatory regimes as permissible, but the substantial community consensus against such regimes and the General Assembly determinations authorizing assistance to the insurgent forces set these instances apart.

One of the principal dangers in allowing assistance to insurgents is that assistance may be aggressively provided to spread the world view of the intervening power. In fact, it may simply conceal external sponsorship of what amounts to a covert armed attack; for if a faction assisted has only negligible internal support, then military assistance to it is functionally very close to an external attack. The United States sponsorship of the Bay of Pigs invasion and Havana's sponsorship of the guerrilla insurgency in Bolivia are good examples of this. As such, these situations are

---

152. See, *e.g.*, the Soviet Draft Definition of Aggression, 9 U.N. GAOR, Annexes, Agenda Item No. 51, at 6-7, U.N. Doc. A/C.6/L.332/Rev. 1 (1954).
153. See R. BARNET, *supra* note 94, at 225-36.

really type V situations concerning external initiation of force for the imposition of internal authority structures, rather than type IV situations.

Because of the dangers involved in permitting assistance to insurgents, in the absence of collective United Nations authorization such assistance should be prohibited.

C. CLAIMS TO ASSIST ANY FACTION IN A STRUGGLE FOR CONTROL OF INTERNAL AUTHORITY STRUCTURES WHERE A WIDELY RECOGNIZED GOVERNMENT CANNOT BE DISTINGUISHED

In most internal conflicts, it is readily apparent which side is the incumbent and which the insurgent. Such factors as wide diplomatic recognition, historic continuity of political authority, continuing exercise of administrative functions, control of the regular military apparatus, representation in international organizations, and continuing control of major cities and ports set the two factions apart. The characterization "widely recognized government" which is used in this essay is shorthand for indicating an incumbent faction strongly satisfying these conditions. The legal effect of this characterization is to permit pre-insurgency assistance and counter-intervention on behalf of the faction so characterized.

In some internal conflicts, however, there may be no incumbent government, or the competing factions may have roughly similar credentials to represent the incumbent. For example, at the time of the breakdown of order which precipitated the United States Dominican intervention, neither faction in the Dominican conflict could be meaningfully identified as a widely recognized government.[154] Similarly, I would characterize the Yemen conflict as one in which a "widely recognized government" cannot be distinguished, although United Nations seating of the Republicans makes this less clear. Certainly at the time the external assistance to both factions began, it was meaningless to factually charac-

---

154. See note 130 *supra.* United States claims in the Dominican operation, however, were predominantly not claims to assist a particular faction.

terize the Republicans and Royalists as either incumbent or challenger. According to Kathryn Boals' account of the conflict:

> The internal war in Yemen began in September, 1962 when a group of army officers carried out a palace coup against the ruling Imam and proclaimed the Yemen Arab Republic in place of the Kingdom of Yemen. The ousted Imam and his supporters immediately began organizing a counter-revolution, recruiting northern Yemeni tribesmen and requesting help from Saudi Arabia in the form of training bases, arms, money, and supplies. Meanwhile the Republicans asked the United Arab Republic for technical and military assistance.
>
> With Saudi Arabia helping the Royalists and the United Arab Republic aiding the Republicans, fighting between the two sides began in October, 1962. . . .[155]

Subsequently, a number of states recognized the Republican forces, including the Soviet Union, the United Arab Republic, and the United States. And the day following United States recognition, the General Assembly voted to seat the Republican delegation as the representative of Yemen.[156] These factors cut for permitting counter-intervention on behalf of the Republican forces. Diplomatic recognition, however, is frequently based more on political than on objective criteria, and this seems to have been the case in Yemen. As such, diplomatic recognition alone, at least when the recognition pattern is significantly mixed, should not be decisive. The collective community endorsement of the Republicans by the United Nations credentials decision was perhaps more significant. But although such an endorsement deserves considerable weight, it is not the same thing as specific United Nations authorization of intervention on behalf of a particular faction. Despite the subsequent community recognition of the Republicans, the early commencement of intervention prior to substantial recognition, the lack of effective Republican control, the leadership of the insurgents by the ousted incumbent, and the substantial authority and control exercised by the ousted Imam and his supporters suggest that neither faction qualified as a

155. See K. Boals, *supra* note 97, at 4.
156. See K. Boals, *supra* note 97, at 6-8.

widely recognized government and that external assistance to either faction should be impermissible.

In contexts such as the Yemen and Dominican conflicts, where the incumbent and insurgent forces cannot be readily distinguished, it seems desirable to treat both sides as if they were insurgents and prohibit all partisan military assistance to both. Where government and insurgent forces are factually indistinguishable there is no reason to allow either pre-insurgency assistance or counter-intervention to either faction. In such conflicts the dangers to self-determination of permitting partisan external assistance strongly suggest a flat prohibition of military assistance to either side, absent collective United Nations authorization. In such cases also, recognition of one side or the other, if premature, may itself constitute an impermissible intervention.[157]

D. CLAIMS THAT EXTERNAL ASSISTANCE PROVIDED TO AN OPPOSING FACTION JUSTIFIES ASSISTANCE

Most commentators have regarded assistance to government forces, provided to offset external assistance to insurgents, as lawful.[158] To regard such counter-intervention as unlawful might be to deprive a state subject to a covert external attack of its right to collective defense under Article 51 of the Charter. And even if external assistance is provided to an indigenous insurgent movement the success of the insurgency certainly carries little meaning for determining the genuine demands of the people. The rhetoric

---

157. See II OPPENHEIM, *supra* note 149, at 250.
158. The only specific statement to the contrary seems to be that of Professor Quincy Wright who argues:
> It would appear that illegal intervention in the domestic jurisdiction of a state should not be made the occasion for counter-intervention but should be dealt with by the United Nations as it was in the Congo. Intervention to prevent civil strife from developing into international hostilities is within the legal competence of the United Nations. Only in this way can illegal counter-intervention designed to stop illegal intervention by another state be avoided.

Wright, *Non-Military Intervention*, in THE RELEVANCE OF INTERNATIONAL LAW 5, 16-17 (K. Deutsch & S. Hoffmann eds. 1968). In addition, Richard Barnet's proposed "prohibition on unilateral assistance" standard would also bar counter-intervention. See R. BARNET, *supra* note 94, at 278-80.

and practice of states and United Nations practice also support this claim. For example, during the 1948 Greek civil war external assistance was provided to the Greek insurgents, primarily by Yugoslavia.[159] Offsetting assistance was provided to the Greek government by the United States and was clearly regarded as lawful by the General Assembly.

If the counter-intervention exception is not to be totally open-ended, permitting powers intervening on both sides to make escalating claims that each is simply responding to increases in assistance by the other, it would seem desirable to limit the exception to the widely recognized government side. And since military assistance programs to government forces are legitimate prior to the critical insurgency threshold, if the exception were available on the insurgent side, as a practical matter military assistance to insurgents would never be lacking for rationalization.

If counter-intervention is permissible only on behalf of a widely recognized government, the United States would have been able to provide offsetting assistance to the widely recognized government during the Greek civil war but would not have been able to provide assistance in 1956 to offset the Soviet assistance to the Hungarian rebels. Although harsh in terms of self-determination, this result seems entirely consistent with the demands of system stability.

It should be pointed out that the counter-intervention exception is only necessary after the critical insurgency threshold requiring a freeze on assistance to recognized government forces has been passed. Below that threshold military assistance to a widely recognized government is permissible in its own right.

Once above the insurgency threshold there is a major issue as to how much external military assistance to insurgents is necessary to justify counter-intervention and how much counter-intervention is in turn justified. Rather than treat this problem as one of assistance thresholds, the most effective approach seems to be to allow the recognized government to receive military assistance comparable to that being provided to insurgents. When assistance to insurgents stops, then comparable assistance to the government forces should be stopped. This requirement that assistance be

159. See R. BARNET, *supra* note 94, at 111-12.

comparable does not require a one-to-one troop count, or a one-to-one weapons count, but means that the political and military effect of the offsetting assistance be proportional, taking into account the balance of forces required in an insurgent conflict and the difficulty of estimating covert assistance to insurgents.

E. CLAIMS TO USE THE MILITARY INSTRUMENT IN THE
TERRITORY OF ANOTHER STATE FOR THE PURPOSE OF
RESTORING ORDERLY PROCESSES OF SELF-DETERMINATION
IN CONFLICTS OVER INTERNAL AUTHORITY STRUCTURES
INVOLVING A SUDDEN BREAKDOWN OF ORDER

This claim differs from the last four in that it is not a claim to provide partisan assistance to a particular faction. And unlike the claim to assist a widely recognized government in controlling non-authority-oriented disorders of the type I situation it is made in a type IV situation of a conflict for the control of internal authority structures. The principal examples of claims in this category are the second stages of the United States Dominican Republic operation and the United Nations Cyprus and, in part, Congo operations.

This category includes perhaps the most likely internal conflict situations for a United Nations peacekeeping presence. There is little difficulty in establishing the lawfulness of such a collective presence, at least when the United Nations is acting with the permission of the widely recognized government. But unilateral actions in this category, such as the Dominican Republic operation prior to meaningful OAS involvement, are highly controversial and present a much more difficult question.[160] On the one hand, there is a serious risk that claims of neutrality might mask support for a particular faction; and even if good faith neutrality is pursued, it is almost impossible to achieve, as normally one side will benefit more from cessation of hostilities. On the other hand, pressures for such interventions stem from the genuine interdependencies among nations which sometimes create strong interests in

160. The most comprehensive analysis of the legal issues raised by the Dominican operation is Nanda, *The United States' Action in the 1965 Dominican Crisis: Impact on World Order—Part I*, 43 DENVER L. REV. 439 (1966), *Part II*, 44 DENVER L. REV. 225 (1967).

avoiding minority seizure of control of one's neighbors. Conflicts involving a sudden breakdown of order in a small state may present a particular danger of such minority seizure of control, both because of the weakness of effective military opposition and the small size of the force necessary to successfully seize power. And if good faith neutrality among factions is pursued, and genuinely free elections are substituted for armed conflict, self-determination may well be promoted. Another substantial benefit which may result from a successful intervention in this category, of course, is the ending of the destruction and loss of life involved in the usual civil authority struggle.

As a tentative resolution of claims in this category, I would permit such claims if sufficiently safeguarded to ensure that they are not merely self-serving operations masking external imposition of authority structures. In doing so, I recognize that interventions in this category present a serious danger of self-serving action, and if in practice the suggested safeguards prove unworkable, then such interventions should be prohibited in the absence of collective United Nations authorization. Conditions which such claims should meet to be adequately safeguarded are: (1) a genuine invitation by the widely recognized government, or, if there is none, by a major faction; (2) relative neutrality among factions, with particular attention to neutrality in military operations; (3) immediate initiation of and compliance with the decision machinery of appropriate regional organizations;[161] (4) immediate full reporting to the Security Council and compliance with United Nations determinations; (5) a prompt disengagement, consistent with the purpose of the action; and (6) an outcome consistent with self-determination. Such an outcome would be defined as one based on internationally observed elections in which all factions are allowed freely to participate on an equal basis, which is freely accepted by all major competing factions, or

161. Such claims, of course, must also be consistent with the more particularized requirements of applicable regional arrangements, Article 20 of the Revised Charter of the Organization of American States, for example, casts some doubt on the permissibility of such claims in the absence of agreement by the Organ of Consultation acting under Article 6 of the Inter-American Treaty of Reciprocal Assistance. See L. SOHN, *supra* note 90, at 118-20, 140, 143.

which is endorsed by the United Nations. System stability suggests that such interventions should also not take place in an area committed to an opposing bloc.

A state contemplating such an intervention must plan in advance on meeting these conditions and must in fact successfully meet them. If these conditions are met, claims in this category would largely conform to the basic standard for type IV situations, which is that partisan military assistance, other than pre-insurgency assistance to a widely recognized government, may not be provided to any faction engaged in indigenous conflict for the control of internal authority structures absent unauthorized military assistance to insurgents or collective United Nations authorization.

F. CLAIMS TO USE THE MILITARY INSTRUMENT AGAINST THE TERRITORY OF A STATE PROVIDING ASSISTANCE TO AN OPPOSING FACTION

The principal instances in which one assisting state has made the claim that assistance to an opposing faction justifies the use of the military instrument against the territory of another assisting state seem to be the French bombing of the Tunisian frontier village of Sakiet Sidi Youssef during the course of the Algerian war,[162] Egyptian bombing raids against Saudi Arabian villages during the Yemen conflict,[163] Portuguese bombing of areas in Zambia allegedly being used as bases for guerrilla activities against Portuguese Africa,[164] and the United States bombing of North Vietnam during the Vietnam war.[165] Although not itself just an assisting state, the Israeli raids against Jordan and Lebanon in retaliation for their assistance to Palestinian refugee

---

162. See M. CLARK, ALGERIA IN TURMOIL—THE REBELLION: ITS CAUSES, ITS EFFECTS, ITS FUTURE 363-66 (1960).
163. See Boals, *supra* note 97, at 23; N.Y. Times, Aug. 17, 1969, at 16, col. 4, 5-6.
164. See N.Y. Times, Dec. 2, 1968, at 2, col. 4.
165. For joinder of issue on the question of permissibility of United States bombing of North Vietnam during the Vietnam War see Moore, *International Law and the United States Role in Viet Nam: A Reply*, 76 YALE L.J. 1051, 1073-78 (1967); Falk, *International Law and the United States Role in Viet Nam: A Response to Professor Moore*, 76 YALE L.J. 1095, 1126-27, 1140-42 (1967).

groups attacking Israel are in many ways similar.[166] Of these instances, only the Egyptian raids occurred in an unequivocal type IV situation. The French bombing occurred in a type II anticolonial war, the American in a type VI divided nation conflict, and the Israeli and Portuguese in a situation with type V external initiation of force overtones. Since these instances for the most part raise similar issues, they will be treated together here rather than repeating this claim in each situation where it occurs. Because of its importance, however, the Vietnam claim will be deferred to the discussion of the type VI divided nation situation.

The first step in appraising these claims is to ascertain the lawfulness of the claimant's participation in the internal conflict. Since in some cases the claimant's participation is itself unlawful, as was Egyptian participation in Yemen, *a fortiori* the use of the military instrument against the territory of a state providing assistance to an opposing faction is unlawful. The French and Portuguese claims are at least questionable on this same score.

If the claimant's participation is otherwise lawful, then the principal issue is squarely presented. Under the Charter, the criterion for resolution of this issue is simply whether the assistance to the opposing faction amounts to an armed attack within the meaning of Article 51. If it does, then the claimant may respond proportionally to the attack. If not, such a response is unlawful. This resolution of the issue adopts the restrictive view of self-defense which limits it to response against an armed attack under Article 51 of the Charter. There would be some scholars who would urge the less restrictive interpretation not limiting the right of self-defense to that of Article 51.[167] Professor Richard Falk, on the other hand, has pointed out that there is a strong community interest in discouraging geographic escalation of internal conflict. Thus he argues that unilateral reply against the territory of an assisting state should always be impermissible if

---

166. See generally Falk, *The Beirut Raid and the International Law of Retaliation*, 63 AM. J. INT'L L. 415 (1969).

167. See *e.g.*, D. BOWETT, SELF-DEFENSE IN INTERNATIONAL LAW 184-93 (1958); M. MCDOUGAL & F. FELICIANO, LAW AND MINIMUM WORLD PUBLIC ORDER 233-41 (1961); J. STONE, AGGRESSION AND WORLD ORDER 92-101 (1958).

assistance is covert.[168] Since most assistance to a genuine indigenous faction would not amount to an armed attack, avoiding geographic escalation is for the most part consistent with the requirements of Article 51 of the Charter. If, however, assistance to insurgents is massive and intense, and threatens major values in the target state, such assistance may constitute an armed attack under Article 51 of the Charter. Similarly, if intervention takes the form of initiation of the insurgent movement, and is simply a type V situation of indirect armed attack, then Article 51 may be invoked if major values are threatened. Such instances can be expected to occur infrequently. Even when they do occur, for reasons of strategy assisting nations will rarely choose to respond against the territory of another assisting state. But it is unrealistic to restrict the right of defense to situations in which armed attack is overt. The terrorist bomb can as substantially threaten fundamental values as armies on the march.

In its recent work on defining aggression, the United Nations Special Committee on the Question of Defining Aggression adverted to this claim of reply against the territory of an assisting state. Paragraph eight of a thirteen-power draft provides:

> When a State is a victim on its own territory of subversive and/or terrorist acts by irregular, volunteer or armed bands organized by another State, it may take all reasonable and adequate steps to safeguard its existence and its institutions, without having recourse to the right of individual or collective self-defense against the other State under Article 51 of the Charter. . . .[169]

Senator John Sherman Cooper, the United States representative to the General Assembly, objected to this paragraph both on the

---

168. See Falk, *supra* note 165, at 1125, 1140-43.
169. Report of the Special Committee on the Question of Defining Aggression, 23 U.N. GAOR, Agenda Item No. 86, at 9, U.N. Doc. A/7185/Rev. 1 (1968). With slight changes in wording, paragraph eight has become paragraph seven in the latest 13-power draft proposal. See Report of the Special Committee on the Question of Defining Aggression, 24 U.N. GAOR, Supp. 20, at 8, U.N. Doc. A/7620 (1969), *reprinted* in 8 INT'L LEG. MAT. 663, 664 (1969).

ground of its ambiguity and on the ground that as an absolute it would unduly restrict the right of individual and collective defense. Senator Cooper pointed out:

> Now, there can be no doubt that the acts enumerated in this paragraph may involve the use of force within the meaning of Article 2(4) of the Charter. If we understand the foregoing paragraph correctly, its effect is thus that so far as the United Nations Charter is concerned, whether a state may defend itself against force employed by another state to destroy its population, change its government, or inflict physical damage upon its people or territory, depends simply on the techniques of force selected. In practical terms this means that for a large—and perhaps at present the most dangerous—class of aggressions, the victim must deal with the aggressor only in the victim's own territory and must deal with the aggressor alone and unassisted, regardless of the level of intensity to which the illegal force used against the victim may rise. This paragraph appears to us, therefore, to be seriously at variance with the Charter, and we doubt that on reflection the principle of conduct it contains would commend itself to governments. Its practical effect could be to protect an aggressor. . . .
>
> [W]hat I have said assumes that the "reasonable and adequate steps" referred to in the paragraph are intended to be purely internal; i.e., confined to the territory of the victim state. It is worth noting that such a provision is not a part of international law. . . .[170]

Senator Cooper would seem to be correct both in noting that there is no present international law requirement prohibiting reply against the territory of an assisting state if such assistance amounts to an armed attack, and in rejecting such a prohibition as an unwarranted restriction on the right of individual and collective defense. The real test is not a simplistic *a priori* geographic rule, but whether external involvement, covert or overt, is so extreme as to amount to an armed attack.

170. Cooper, *U.N. Legal Committee Discusses the Question of Defining Aggression*, 59 DEP'T STATE BULLETIN 664, 670-71 (1968).

Type V Situations: Claims Relating to External Initiation of the Use of Force for the Imposition of Internal Authority Structures

Type V situations are those in which there is little or no indigenous conflict for the control of internal authority structures; that is, the conflict is externally initiated. One factor which may be indicative (but not necessarily decisive) of a type V situation is the participation of personnel of the allegedly assisting entity in leadership positions and in tactical operations. Claims in this category are that a state may use its military instrument to externally impose its choice of internal authority structures on another state. In their baldest form, such claims simply assert a right of external choice of government. In their less candid form, they are sometimes masked as assistance to an indigenous faction or as counter-intervention. Examples are the puppet government set up by the Soviets during their 1939 invasion of Finland, the United States use of Cuban exiles in the Bay of Pigs invasion, and the alleged government request to combat "foreign forces hostile to socialism" in the 1968 Soviet invasion of Czechoslovakia.[171] None of these instances reflects genuine indigenous conflict.

There is little doubt that in the absence of United Nations authorization such claims are generally regarded as violations of international law; but in recent years such claims are being made with increasing frequency and have been predicated on the requirements of self-determination. One group of claims is made by the African states, which assert a right to overthrow discriminatory regimes in South Africa, South-West Africa, and Rhodesia.[172] The claims are implemented by the external fostering of insurgencies in those countries (as well as by the assisting of internal insurgencies).

A second recent claim is that made by the Soviets in their overt invasion of Czechoslovakia. In the now famous "Brezhnev Doc-

---

171. *Compare* the Tass Statement on Military Intervention *with* the Declaration of the Presidium of the Central Committee of the Czechoslovakian Communist Party in 7 Int'l Leg. Mat. 1283-84, 1285 (1968).
172. See generally R. Falk, *supra* note 98; R. Taubenfeld & H. Taubenfeld, Race, Peace, Law, and Southern Africa (The Tenth Hammarskjöld Forum 1968).

trine," published in Pravda and intended to justify the Czechoslovakia intervention, the Soviets argue:

> It has got to be emphasized that when a socialist country seems to adopt a "non-affiliated" stand, it retains its national independence, in effect, precisely because of the might of the socialist community, and above all the Soviet Union as a central force, which also includes the might of its armed forces. The weakening of any of the links in the world system of socialism directly affects all the socialist countries, which cannot look indifferently upon this. . . .
>
> Naturally the Communists of the fraternal countries could not allow the socialist states to be inactive in the name of an abstractly understood sovereignty, when they saw that the country stood in peril of antisocialist degeneration.[173]

In Czechoslovakia there could be no claim of assistance to a widely recognized government to defeat an insurgency, for there was neither invitation nor insurgency at the time of the Soviet invasion; rather, it was the very changes pressed by the Czechoslovakian government itself which the Soviets sought to roll back. Indeed, there seems to have been little concern even with the appearance of invitation from the government, although an official Tass statement did allege a Czechoslovakian government request.[174] Under the "Brezhnev Doctrine" of intervention to preserve "socialist self-determination," the Soviets are essentially asserting a legal right to external imposition of government in the socialist countries of Eastern Europe.

A third recent claim asserting a right of external imposition of authority structure is that made by the Arab countries in justifying continuing guerrilla activity against Israel. Although the Arab-Israeli conflict has a complex history in which the Arabs have many legitimate grievances, the Arabs are essentially asserting a right to overthrow the government of Israel for the purpose of restoring self-determination to Palestinian Arabs.[175]

173. See the Pravda Article Justifying Intervention in Czechoslovakia, *supra* note 75, at 1323-24.
174. See the Tass Statement on Military Intervention, *supra* note 171, at 1283-84.
175. For a summary background of the Arab-Israeli conflict see SENATE COMM.

Because of the danger that such claims may merely mask a self-serving export of one's own demands, as Czechoslovakia amply demonstrates, as well as the serious public order threat they present, these claims must be regarded as impermissible in the absence of broad community support evidenced by United Nations endorsement. Even with UN endorsement, some would argue that such import of revolution is a violation of state sovereignty. If we are to deter self-serving individual claims and to recognize legitimate demands for self-determination, however, it seems appropriate to accord the community as a whole, acting through the United Nations, the competence to authorize initiatives to restore self-determination. The responsibility for such authorization should not be taken lightly and should fairly consider alternative peaceful modes of change and the likelihood of a major public order threat from the authorization of the use of force.

Military interventions in type V situations which do not have United Nations authorization and which seriously threaten major values, such as political and territorial integrity, may constitute an armed attack under Article 51 of the Charter giving rise to the right of individual and collective defense.

A. COLD WAR CLAIMS FOR THE USE OF THE MILITARY
INSTRUMENT IN THE TERRITORY OF ANOTHER STATE
FOR THE PURPOSE OF MAINTAINING OR IMPOSING
"DEMOCRATIC" OR "SOCIALIST" REGIMES

Claims in this category, particularly if undertaken in a crusading spirit in the committed area of an opposing bloc, present an acute public order threat. Since these claims are unlikely to receive United Nations approval, they should be regarded as clearly impermissible.

The most flagrant example of intervention in this category is the Soviet invasion of Czechoslovakia. The United States sponsored Bay of Pigs invasion of Cuba, however, and the Che Guevara operation in Bolivia present essentially the same claim. In none of these cases was there any significant internal insur-

ON FOREIGN RELATIONS, 90TH CONG., 1ST SESS., A SELECT CHRONOLOGY AND BACKGROUND DOCUMENTS RELATING TO THE MIDDLE EAST (Comm. Print. 1967). For more extensive analysis see J. N. MOORE (ED.), THE ARAB-ISRAEL CONFLICT (Vols. I-III 1972).

gency at the time the military instrument was employed. All represent a fairly bald attempt at external imposition of a favored form of government and all are impermissible under international law.

B. CLAIMS FOR THE USE OF THE MILITARY INSTRUMENT IN THE TERRITORY OF ANOTHER STATE FOR THE PURPOSE OF ALTERING INTERNAL AUTHORITY STRUCTURES WHICH DENY SELF-DETERMINATION ON A RACIAL BASIS

One factor justifying separate treatment of claims for the purpose of altering authority structures which deny self-determination on a racial basis is the extraordinary community consensus against such denial. This consensus is evidenced by the United Nations Declaration on the Elimination of All Forms of Racial Discrimination adopted by the General Assembly in 1963. The Declaration provides in part:

The General Assembly,...

Alarmed by the manifestations of racial discrimination still in evidence in some areas of the world, some of which are imposed by certain Governments by means of legislative, administrative or other measures, in the form, *inter alia*, of *apartheid*, segregation and separation, as well as by the promotion and dissemination of doctrines of racial superiority and expansionism in certain areas,

Convinced that all forms of racial discrimination and still more so, governmental policies based on the prejudice of racial superiority or on racial hatred, besides constituting a violation of fundamental human rights, tend to jeopardize friendly relations among peoples, co-operation between nations and international peace and security. . . .

Convinced further that the building of a world society free from all forms of racial segregation and discrimination, factors which create hatred and division among men, is one of the fundamental objectives of the United Nations,

1. *Solemnly affirms* the necessity of speedily eliminating racial discrimination throughout the world, in all its forms and manifestations, and of securing understanding of and respect for the dignity of the human person;

2. *Solemnly affirms* the necessity of adopting national and international measures to that end. . . .[176]

The greatest danger in type V situations is probably self-serving definition of self-determination. There can be little doubt, however, that in view of the General Assembly Declaration on the Elimination of Racial Discrimination there is a broad community consensus that self-determination is denied to the black African in South Africa and Rhodesia. The same is true, though complicated by the problem of colonialism, in South-West Africa and the Portuguese colonies of Angola, Mozambique, and Guinea. But though these denials of self-determination of the black African are extreme, there are also other peoples of the world deprived of self-determination; for example, the peoples of Czechoslovakia and Hungary following the Soviet invasions or the peoples of Haiti under the regime of François Duvalier. In each case, even if a collective community decision is reached that force is necessary and justified for achieving self-determination, we must still be concerned with the destructiveness of coercive change and the threat to minimum public order of attempted coercive change. In the case of western assistance to insurgents in Hungary or Czechoslovakia, the public order threat seems intolerably high. In southern Africa it is lower but still of substantial concern; and in Haiti it seems still lower.

Because it reflects a wide range of interests cutting across the cold-war, collective United Nations determination seems the best way to lessen both the danger of self-serving claims about self-determination and the danger of cold-war clashes resulting from intervention in a committed area. It is unlikely that the United Nations will authorize western assistance to insurgents in Hungary or Czechoslovakia. The United Nations, however, has authorized individual use of force in Southern Rhodesia, South Africa, South-West Africa, and the Portuguese colonies.

The Southern Rhodesian resolution of November 7, 1968, is only a little stronger than most such second generation General Assembly resolutions authorizing individual use of force on be-

176. G.A. Res. 1904, 18 U.N. GAOR, Supp. 15, at 35-37, U.N. Doc. A/5515 (1963).

half of insurgents fighting against colonial or discriminatory regimes. The Rhodesian resolution urges

all States, as a matter of urgency, to render all moral and material assistance to the national liberation movements of Zimbabwe [Southern Rhodesia], either directly or through the Organization of African Unity. . . .[177]

The Resolution also condemns

the illegal intervention of South African forces in Southern Rhodesia and calls upon the United Kingdom, as the administering Power, to ensure the immediate expulsion of all South African armed forces, including the police, from Southern Rhodesia and to prevent all armed assistance to the racist minority regime. . . .[178]

And the South African resolution of December 13, 1967, provides:

The General Assembly . . .
Noting with grave concern that the racial policies of the Government of South Africa have led to violent conflict and an explosive situation,
Convinced that the situation in the Republic of South Africa and the resulting explosive situation in southern Africa continue to pose a grave threat to international peace and security, . . .
8. *Appeals* to all States and organizations to provide appropriate moral, political and material assistance to the people of South Africa in their legitimate struggle for the rights recognized in the Charter. . . .[179]

The 1968 Report of the Special Committee on the Policies of *Apartheid* of the Government of the Republic of South Africa removes any doubt that this language is a call for military assistance

177. G.A. Res. 2383, 23 U.N. GAOR, Supp. 18, at 58, U.N. Doc. A/7218 (1968) (Article 14). A 1967 Southern Rhodesia resolution contained an identical provision. See G.A. Res. 2262, 22 U.N. GAOR, Supp. 16, at 45-47, U.N. Doc. A/6716 (1967) (Article 16).
178. G.A. Res. 2383, 23 U.N. GAOR, Supp. 18, at 58, U.N. Doc. A/7218 (1968) (Article 10).
179. G.A. Res. 2307, 22 U.N. GAOR, Supp. 16, at 19-20, U.N. Doc. A/6716 (1967).

to insurgents in South Africa (or for external initiation of insurgency). In referring to this provision the Committee reports:

> The Special Committee takes note of the view of the liberation movement of South Africa that the policies and actions of the South African Government have obliged it to seek the achievement of the legitimate rights of the people by means including an armed struggle. The primary responsibility for the present violent conflict rests on the South African Government, since it has defied decisions by the United Nations, rejected a peaceful solution of the situation in conformity with the principles of the United Nations and tried to impose its inhuman racist policies by brutal repression. . . .
>
> In view of recent developments, the Special Committee feels that the General Assembly should strongly reaffirm its recognition of the legitimacy of the struggle of the people of South Africa and urge all States and organizations to provide greater moral, political and material assistance to them in this legitimate struggle.[180]

In the short run the Rhodesian, South African, and similar resolutions are unlikely to be successfully implemented against the effective military forces of most of these regimes. But they do represent an important community determination that self-determination is denied sufficiently to justify resort to force. In making such determinations, it seems incumbent on the General Assembly to carefully consider non-forceful alternatives for achieving self-determination and to be aware of the adverse public order consequences from authorizing use of force. Absent such specific United Nations authorization, claims in type V situations for external initiation of force to secure self-determination should be impermissible.

C. CLAIMS TO ASSIST EXILE OR REFUGEE GROUPS FOR THE PURPOSE OF RESTORING SELF-DETERMINATION

Arab claims to overthrow the State of Israel for the purpose of restoring self-determination to Palestinian Arabs are the most

---

180. Special Committee on the Policies of *Apartheid* of the Government of the Republic of South Africa, Report, 23 U.N. GAOR, Agenda Item No. 31, at 31, U.N. Doc. A/7254 (1968).

important claims in this category. Regardless of the legitimacy of Arab grievances, such claims to use force on behalf of refugee groups should be impermissible absent collective United Nations authorization of the use of force. At this point in time there is no reason to prefer the self-determination of the Arab refugees to that of the Israelis, and the continuation of a state of belligerency seems inconsistent with the basic principle of the United Nations Charter.

Other situations presenting claims in this category, though not as clearly, are the United States assistance to Cuban refugees in the Bay of Pigs invasion, the abortive 1968 Cap-Haitien landing of Haitian exiles rumored to be operating from the Bahamas (if in fact the small-scale operation received any governmental assistance), and the North Vietnamese training and infiltration of South Vietnamese cadres who went north at the time of the Geneva settlement in 1954. Regardless of which way self-determination seems to cut, the danger of self-serving claims and the threat to minimum public order suggest that all such claims to assist refugee or exile groups should be impermissible absent collective United Nations authorization. Moreover, the Bay of Pigs and Vietnamese instances involved such third-party initiation and sponsorship that in reality the claims to restore self-determination to exile groups were merely covers for cold-war claims for the purpose of imposing "democratic" or "socialist" regimes.

A related question, presented over a range of claims but particularly critical with respect to claims to assist refugee or exile groups, is the question of duty to prevent such groups from operating from one's territory. The Arab states' acquiescence in, if not encouragement of, the operations of the Arab guerrilla organizations from their territory is a particularly acute example. This question, however, is complicated by doubts whether some of the Arab states are politically or militarily strong enough to prevent such use of their territory.

In any event, at least the impermissibility of toleration of one's territory as a base for armed activities against another state seems reasonably clear in theory. The 1965 General Assembly Declaration on Inadmissibility of Intervention is representative of many authoritative pronouncements when it provides:

[N]o State shall organize, assist, foment, finance, incite or *tolerate* subversive, terrorist or armed activities directed towards the violent overthrow of the regime of another State. . . . [Emphasis added].[181]

TYPE VI SITUATIONS: CLAIMS RELATING TO COLD-WAR DIVIDED NATION CONFLICTS

Claims relating to the cold-war divided nations of China, Germany, Korea, and Vietnam have overtones of conflicts from types I through V, but because of their peculiar features and their acute involvement with the major cold-war public order problem, they can most usefully be treated separately. That these divided nations present an acute public order problem is evidenced by the least critical two, Korea and Vietnam, having precipitated the two major wars since World War II. The other two divided nations, China and Germany, have constituted a continuing source of cold-war tension.

One peculiar feature of the divided nations is the fiction, carefully maintained by both halves, that each is really the legitimate government of the entire nation. In each case both halves are clearly *de facto* entities in their own right, with separate social and political institutions, military forces, and diplomatic representation. Moreover, each of the divided nations is linked through a series of treaty commitments with the cold-war bloc which supports it; and major powers feel a strong commitment to stand by these undertakings, partly because of legitimate fear about loss of credibility in the other divided nation situations. These factors have combined to make the cold-war divided nations perhaps the most acute public order threat in the international system. Under such circumstances it must be regarded as the gravest of transgressions for one half of a cold-war divided nation to attack the other half or to assist an insurgency in the other half. For the purpose of maintaining world public order, the halves of these divided nations are really more than separate countries, and should certainly not be regarded as simply one nation. The civil war

181. G.A. Res. 2131, 20 U.N. GAOR, Supp. 14, at 11-12, U.N. Doc. A/6014 (1965).

label is particularly misleading in concealing the dominant public order concern of these conflicts.[182]

Internal conflicts within the divided nations which do not involve participation of the other half may be classified much as any other internal conflict, and for that reason this separate section contains only claims concerning conflict involving both halves.

A. CLAIMS BY ONE HALF OF A COLD-WAR DIVIDED NATION TO TAKE OVER THE AUTHORITY STRUCTURE OF THE OTHER HALF OR TO ASSIST AN INSURGENT FACTION IN A STRUGGLE FOR CONTROL OF INTERNAL AUTHORITY STRUCTURES

The two principal examples of such claims have been North Korean claims in the invasion of South Korea and North Vietnamese claims in what has at least been substantial assistance to an insurgency in South Vietnam. Apparently North Korea has also periodically infiltrated guerrillas into South Korea.[183]

The North Korean claim in the invasion of South Korea was decisively rejected by the United Nations in a collective defense action which has remained the paradigm of UN action in response to a breach of the peace.[184] The Vietnam case has remained controversial, complicated by such factors as an uncertain international settlement, significant indigenous support for the Viet Cong, and the covert nature of the attack.[185]

Despite the ambivalent response of the world community in the second Vietnam war, however, public order considerations evidenced by the very existence of the war make it imperative that the use of the military instrument by one-half of a divided nation against the territory of the other be prohibited, whether constituting an all-out attack or simply covert assistance to an insurgency. And this should be so regardless of the legitimacy or justice of any non-forceful grievance which one half has against the other. It is likely that the Chinese and Soviet blocs would feel justifiably aggrieved at sustained military assistance provided from

182. For development of this point in the context of the Vietnam War see Moore, *supra* note 165, at 1054-58.
183. See N.Y. Times, Jan. 9, 1969, at 4, col. 5.
184. See generally L. SOHN, CASES ON UNITED NATIONS LAW 474-90, 509-27 (2d ed. rev. 1967).
185. See I THE VIETNAM WAR AND INTERNATIONAL LAW (R. Falk ed. 1968).

Taiwan to an insurgency on mainland China or from West Germany to an insurgency in East Germany. And what works one way in international law must also work the other.

This prohibition of involvement of one half of a divided nation in conflict in its twin simply treats the two halves as separate international entities (which in view of the policies at stake is a minimum characterization), and applies what is essentially the prohibitions of the type IV and V situations. It should be emphasized, though, that the reasons for the prohibition of assistance may be much more important in the divided nation context.

B. CLAIMS TO ASSIST THE WIDELY RECOGNIZED GOVERNMENT
OF A COLD-WAR DIVIDED NATION TO RESIST TAKEOVER OF
ITS AUTHORITY STRUCTURES BY THE OTHER HALF OF THE
DIVIDED NATION OR TO COUNTER ASSISTANCE PROVIDED TO
AN INSURGENT FACTION BY THE OTHER HALF

Public order considerations and *de facto* realities strongly suggest that the two halves of the cold-war divided nations should be treated as separate states.[186] As such, one half of a divided nation subjected to an attack from the other half should have all the rights of individual and collective defense under the Charter of the United Nations. In fact, that has been the case in both Korea

186. McDougal and Feliciano point out:
> In the Korean conflict, neither of the initial participants—the Republic of Korea and the North Korean People's Republic—recognized the other as a state. The Soviet Union argued to the United Nations that the exercise of violence in Korea could not be characterized as unlawful coercion since the conflict was an internal or civil one and the Charter prescriptions are not applicable to coercion between two groups within a single state. The decisions reached by the United Nations in the Palestine and Korean cases suggest that conflicts involving a newly organized territorial body politic, or conflicts between two distinct territorial units which the community expects to be relatively permanent, are, for purposes of policy about coercion, to be treated as conflicts between established states. Thus, the applicability of basic community policy about minimum public order in the world arena and competence to defend against unlawful violence are not dependent upon formal recognition of the technical statehood of the claimant-group by the opposing participant.

M. McDougal & F. Feliciano, Law and Minimum World Public Order 221 (1961).

and Vietnam, with the United Nations in Korea and the United States and a number of its allies in Vietnam assisting in collective defense of the entity under attack. Moreover, since North and South Korea and North and South Vietnam are separate international entities for purposes of the lawfulness of the use of force, assistance by North Korea or North Vietnam to insurgents in the south triggers a right of counter-assistance to the widely recognized government under the situation IV (d) standard. Not to allow counter-assistance would tie the hands of the government forces and prevent effective sanction against covert attempts at takeover.

C. CLAIMS TO USE THE MILITARY INSTRUMENT AGAINST THE TERRITORY OF ONE HALF OF A COLD-WAR DIVIDED NATION WHICH IS PROVIDING ASSISTANCE TO AN INSURGENT FACTION IN THE OTHER HALF

There is no doubt that in cases of overt invasion across national boundaries, as in the Korean war, the right of defense includes the right to proportional response against the territory of the invading state. There is less authority, however, on the question of response against the territory of a state which is providing assistance to an insurgent faction. Apparently the only major precedent in the divided nation context is the United States response against the territory of North Vietnam.

Richard Falk has argued strongly in the Vietnam context against the permissiveness of such response outside of the territory of the state undergoing internal conflict on the grounds that the discretion available to nation states should be curtailed in ambiguous covert attack situations and that the danger of escalation from such response is too great.[187] Though these arguments are persuasive in some contexts, they do not sufficiently take account of the functional equivalence of overt invasions and some massive covert attacks. Moreover, they overemphasize the difficulty of appraisal of such claims. In most cases assistance to an indigenous insurgent faction would simply not amount to an armed attack. But if in the cold-war divided nation context such assistance is massive and intense, threatens major values in the

187. See Falk, *supra* note 165, at 1125-26, 1140-43.

target state, and is rendered with a more or less long-run objective of territorial unification, then it would seem that it does constitute an armed attack under Article 51 of the Charter justifying a proportional defensive response against the territory of the assisting entity. Persistent claims by both halves of the cold-war divided nations that each represents the entire nation heighten the probability that sustained assistance to insurgents in one half by the other half represents a take-over attempt. *A fortiori*, if the assistance really amounts to an externally initiated insurgency masking a covert invasion, then if major values are threatened in the target state a defensive response is justified. Whether such a response against the territory of the attacking entity is an effective strategy, however, is another question, and perhaps one carrying a substantial burden of persuasion.

V. Institutional Weaknesses of the International System Affecting the Control of Intervention and Some Recommendations for Improvement

A. Problems and Prospects

The history of efforts in international conflict management shows that both normative and institutional developments are important for progress.[188] It is essential to have standards for appraisal as well as institutional mechanisms for their effectuation. Publicists, however, have been largely preoccupied with the normative appraisal of intervention and have woefully neglected the institutional side. And as has been seen, existing international organizations were largely a response to conventional war and are poorly equipped for the control of intervention in internal conflict.

New and untried international machinery should not be thought of as a panacea for the control of intervention. As the founders of the League of Nations learned, attitudes and beliefs about the settlement of international conflict may play a critical

---

188. See M. Kaplan & N. Katzenbach, *Resort to Force: War and Neutrality,* in The Political Foundations of International Law 198-228 (1961), *reprinted* in II R. Falk & S. Mendlovitz, The Strategy of World Order 276 (1966).

role.[189] But it can be confidently predicted that given the present infancy of institutional machinery for coping with intervention, institutional development holds great promise.

A number of intervention problems recur with sufficient frequency to suggest major institutional needs. First, most decisions to intervene are unilateral decisions and as such pose a greater threat of impermissible action than collective decisions. Although there is no guarantee that collective decisions will always promote the community interest, the greater the community participation the more likely that decisions will transcend the purely national interests of any one nation. Additionally, collective decision which includes the rival superpowers offers greater assurance of conflict avoidance. For these reasons, collective decision should be preferred. A related problem is the complementary need to establish effective institutions for collective authorization in areas of needed change.[190] If a general non-intervention proscription is to be workable, then such effective agencies for community authorization are a necessity.

Second, there is a significant fact-finding and disclosure problem in the appraisal of most interventions. Was the Stanleyville mission simply a non-authority-oriented humanitarian intervention or was it also aimed at the Gbnye regime? What was the participation of Yugoslavia and Albania in the 1947 Greek civil war? What was the extent of Syrian and Egyptian military involvement in the 1958 Lebanon crisis? What is the role of Hanoi in insurgencies in Laos, South Vietnam, and Thailand? Were the French providing military assistance to the Biafran government in the Nigerian civil war, and if so what was the extent of the assistance? Were United States military operations in the Dominican Republic in fact relatively neutral among the competing factions? Was the election of Balaguer a fair election? What was the extent of Cuban military assistance to insurgents in Venezuela? Techniques which may be useful in dealing with these fact-find-

---

189. See I. CLAUDE, SWORDS INTO PLOWSHARES (2d ed. 1959).
190. See R. FALK, *On Legislative Intervention by the United Nations in the Internal Affairs of Sovereign States*, in LEGAL ORDER IN A VIOLENT WORLD 336 (1968).

ing problems include reporting requirements and an international agency for observation and disclosure. In a recent General Assembly resolution, the Assembly recognized the importance of fact-finding in the settlement of international disputes and urged states "to make more effective use of the existing methods of fact-finding. . . ."[191] Unfortunately, however, existing methods of fact-finding are not wholly responsive to the problem of intervention.

Third, both the problem of intervention in internal conflict and the problem of intensification of internal conflict (as well as the problem of proliferation of nuclear weapons) are worsened by the burgeoning arms race in conventional weaponry and in military assistance programs. The magnitude of these programs today is so great that it is appropriate to speak of a military assistance race. The secrecy of such programs and the growing demand for conventional weaponry may lead to an escalating spiral of competitive armament, miscalculation, and conflict. The Middle East provides a dramatic example.

Fourth, settlement of internal conflict is a difficult problem at best, but it seems particularly intractable in the later stages of a prolonged conflict. The problem of settlement in Vietnam provides vivid illustration. The continuation of the Yemen and Cyprus conflicts adds additional testimony. There is clearly a major need in internal conflict for early invocation of settlement machinery and for the creation of more effective techniques of settlement.

Fifth, there is a need for greater agreement on standards for appraisal of intervention and for a greater role for such standards in national decision processes. Too often the only perspective which seems to be represented in national decision processes is a kind of spur-of-the-moment *realpolitik*. Reversal of this dominance requires a concerted effort by scholars concerned with intervention to clarify areas of agreement as well as disagreement.

191. G.A. Res. 2329, 22 U.N. GAOR, Supp. 16, at 84, U.N. Doc. A/6716 (1967) (Article 1). This resolution also requested:
> the Secretary-General to prepare a register of experts in legal and other fields, whose services the States parties to a dispute may use by agreement for fact-finding in relation to the dispute. . . .
>
> *Id.* at Article 4.

The American Society of International Law sponsors a panel for the study of internal conflict,[192] and one planned feature of its keystone study is a summation of such agreement. The effort to distill at least a minimum consensus on the standards for appraisal of intervention is worthwhile and is likely to be more productive than the rhetoric of debating scholars would suggest. Reversal of the dominance of *realpolitik* requires as well concern for how non-intervention standards are fed into national decision processes, and proposals for their more effective input.

In partial response to these problems, the following recommendations for institutional improvement seem to offer promise. Though some are presented more specifically than others, I am not as wedded to the details as to the general ideas.

B. RECOMMENDATIONS FOR IMPROVEMENT IN THE INTERNATIONAL CONSTITUTIVE PROCESS

THE GENERAL ASSEMBLY AS AN AUTHORIZING AGENCY

One of the problems with proscribing partisan intervention in internal conflict is that some such interventions may promote genuine self-determination, as might be the case in Rhodesia and Haiti. The danger of leaving such judgments to unilateral determination, though, is a strong reason for proscribing such intervention. Yet to be truly acceptable and effective, a system for the control of intervention must provide for legitimate demands for change. One solution to this problem is to strengthen the role of the General Assembly as an authorizing agency. This strengthening should be accompanied by non-intervention standards which clearly proscribe partisan assistance in internal conflict absent General Assembly authorization.

General Assembly authorization could take the form of recommending assistance to a faction, of recommending a particular kind of assistance, or of recommending withdrawal of assistance. In any event the General Assembly's role need not take the form of ordering or supervising collective military action, but simply of authorizing member states to take action individually. General Assembly resolutions which simply recommend action avoid the

192. Study Group on the Role of International Law in Civil Wars (Civil War Project of the American Society of International Law).

debilitating financial problems of the Congo and Middle East operations as well as the considerable political difficulties in maintaining a consensus for collective action. Of course, General Assembly authorization also has the very substantial advantage of avoiding the veto.

There is already precedent for such General Assembly recommendations in the 1967-68 Rhodesia, South Africa, South-West Africa, and Portuguese territories resolutions calling for assistance to the national liberation movements in those countries.[193] As these resolutions suggest, General Assembly authorization is a workable prerequisite for action in cases in which there is a strong community consensus. Lacking such consensus, intervention is suspect both in terms of self-determination and in the danger of conflict escalation resulting from major power disagreement.

One difficulty with this proposal is that as presently constituted the General Assembly is grossly malapportioned, both in terms of population and in terms of effective power.[194] This malapportionment increases the likelihood of an abuse of power. But this danger of abuse seems slight in comparison with the normless present in which individual states are asserting competence to make such determinations unilaterally. Moreover, because of the greater influence exercised by major powers, the present malapportionment is not as extreme as it might seem.

A second difficulty with this proposal, also not fatal, is the constitutional objections under the Charter. The two principal objections would be that such General Assembly recommendations "intervene in matters which are essentially within the domestic jurisdiction" of a state contrary to Article 2(7), and that they constitute action which may be taken only by the Security Council.[195] These constitutional objections should be appraised in the perspective of the trend of effective power away from the Security

193. See text at notes 135-37 and 177-80 *supra*.
194. See L. SOHN, *supra* note 184, at 248-90.
195. With respect to constitutional limits on Security Council action, Article 24 may limit Security Council authority to "the Maintenance of international peace and security." See Sohn, *The Role of the United Nations in Civil Wars*, in III R. FALK & S. MENDLOVITZ, THE STRATEGY OF WORLD ORDER 580, 582 (1966).

Council and to the General Assembly (perhaps slowed down or reversed in recent years). The reasons for this trend are many, but chief among them are the failure to sustain the wartime cooperation among the major powers, resulting in the abuse of the veto and inability to effectuate an Article 43 agreement, and the great increase in membership of the General Assembly.[196]

With respect to the "intervention in domestic jurisdiction" objection, in the Spanish,[197] Rhodesian, South African, South-West African, and Portuguese territories resolutions the General Assembly recommended action on the basis of a general consensus that a particular regime denied self-determination. Arguably, the South-West African and Portuguese territories resolutions rested on the special authority of the General Assembly in colonial and trusteeship matters. Certainly, the "domestic jurisdiction" limitation is weakest in resolutions concerning colonial and trust areas.[198] And the Rhodesian resolution may be a special case in that the Security Council had already found that the Rhodesian situation constituted a threat to international peace and security. The application of enforcement measures under Chapter VII of the Charter is an exception to the "domestic jurisdiction" limitation of Article 2(7). But even so, taking all of these resolutions together, particularly the South African resolution, there is precedent for a broad interpretation of General Assembly competence which would support the suggested authorizing role. The real test, of course, would be a recommendation solely on the authority of the General Assembly in a situation such as Haiti, which is not a trust or colonial area.

With respect to the objection that General Assembly recommendations, which could include recommendations for military assistance, constitute action which may be taken only by the Secu-

---

196. See Goodrich, *The UN Security Council*, in III R. FALK & S. MENDLO-VITZ, *supra* note 195, at 169.
197. G.A. Res. 39, 1 U.N. GAOR 63-64, U.N. Doc. A/64/Add.1 (1946).
198.   [T]he United Nations has in the past shown constant interest in revolts of non-self-governing peoples against the colonial Powers, and regardless of objections raised against interference in matters of domestic jurisdiction, it can be said that a "colonial revolution is now legally as well as practically a matter of concern to the whole community."
   Sohn, *supra* note 195, at 580.

rity Council, the Spanish, Rhodesian, South African, South-West African, and Portuguese territories resolutions could again be cited as precedent for a broad General Assembly competence. The resolution in the Spanish case, however, did not go so far as to authorize military assistance, but only recommended severance of diplomatic relations; and in the Rhodesian case the Security Council had previously branded the Rhodesian situation as constituting a threat to international peace and security. Additional precedents for General Assembly recommendations concerning internal conflict are the resolutions passed in 1947 and 1948 calling upon Albania, Bulgaria, and Yugoslavia to withhold assistance from the Greek guerrillas,[199] the 1949 resolution recommending that all states "refrain from the direct or indirect provision of arms or other materials of war to Albania and Bulgaria until the [United Nations] . . . has determined that the unlawful assistance of these States to the Greek guerillas has ceased . . . ,"[200] the 1960 resolution calling on all states to refrain from intervention in the Congo,[201] and the 1967 resolution calling for the removal of British troops from Oman.[202] Although these resolutions strongly support a General Assembly competence to call for withdrawal of assistance (even from an incumbent government), admittedly the recent Rhodesian, South African, South-West African, and Portuguese territories resolutions, authorizing military assistance to national liberation movements in those countries,[203] go a step farther.[204]

199. G.A. Res. 109, 2 U.N. GAOR 12-14, U.N. Doc. A/519 (1947); G.A. Res. 193, 3 (1) U.N. GAOR 18-21, U.N. Doc. A/810 (1948).
200. G.A. Res. 288A, 4 U.N. GAOR 9-10, U.N. Doc. A/1251 (1949).
201. G.A. Res. 1474 (Emer. Sess. IV), U.N. GAOR, Supp. 1 at 1, U.N. Doc. A/4510 (1960).
202. G.A. Res. 2302, 22 U.N. GAOR, Supp. 16, at 49-50, U.N. Doc. A/6716 (1967).
203. The Rhodesian, South African, South-West African and Portuguese territories resolutions all contain the language "moral and material assistance" in calling for assistance to national liberation movements in those countries. The Oman resolution also calls for assistance but uses less specific language. The resolution appeals: "to all Member States to render all necessary assistance to the people of the Territory [Oman] in their struggle to obtain freedom and independence. . . ." Id. at Article 9.
204. For purposes of constitutional analysis it is useful to focus on the precise claim which the resolution raises. For example, a resolution calling

The 1950 Uniting for Peace resolution specifically authorizes General Assembly recommendations for "collective measures" and for "the use of armed force."[205] Though the Uniting for Peace machinery is based on the Security Council's inability to act because of lack of unanimity of the permanent members,[206] the constitutional capacity of the General Assembly which it evidences lends support to General Assembly power to recommend the use of armed forces.

Finally, the 1962 Advisory Opinion of the International Court of Justice in the *Certain Expenses of the United Nations* case[207] also lends some support to a broad General Assembly authorizing role. In the *Certain Expenses* case a majority of the Court upheld the power of the General Assembly to initiate the United Nations peace-keeping operation in the Middle East (UNEF). The Court emphasized that the action was taken with the consent of the host government and was thus not "enforcement action."[208] Resolutions recommending national military assistance to liberation movements seem to present a stronger case for the constitutionality of General Assembly competence than the UNEF case in that they do not constitute collective action under the United Nations flag, but they present a weaker case for constitutionality in that they recommend coercive measures without the consent of the government.

Though the issue is not free from doubt, existing authority seems to support a broad General Assembly competence with respect to internal conflict, including authority to recommend to member nations the use of military measures on behalf of an insurgent faction, as long as such recommendations are consistent with the purposes and principles of the Charter. General Assem-

---

for cessation of assistance to insurgents is more clearly constitutional than a resolution calling for assistance to insurgents to overthrow a widely recognized government.

205. G.A. Res. 377A, 5 U.N. GAOR, Supp. 20, at 10-12, U.N. Doc. A/1775 (1950).

206. Apparently also recommendation of the use of armed force under the Uniting for Peace resolution is authorized only "in the case of a breach of the peace or act of aggression." *Id.* at Article 1.

207. [1962] I.C.J. 151.   208. *Id.* at 164-66, 170, 177.

bly authorization, like all exercises of power, is subject to abuse. But on balance the development of a broad General Assembly authorizing competence, if coupled with a clear proscription of partisan military assistance absent such authorization, promises to be a significant advance in the control of intervention in internal conflict.

A PROPOSAL FOR INTERNATIONAL REPORTING OF MILITARY ASSISTANCE

International reporting of military assistance would serve a number of purposes. First, it would serve a "blue-sky" function, developing community awareness of the magnitude of the military assistance race, exposing individual interventionary activities, and inviting community appraisal. Second, it would assist in fact-appraisal of interventionary situations. For example, if non-intervention standards require a freeze on military assistance to the government forces once the insurgency threshold is reached, reporting of military assistance would enable appraisal of the permissible level of continuing assistance. Third, reporting could serve as an early-warning device for spotting conflicts in an early stage when they may be most amenable to settlement. Thus, if a sudden increase in military assistance indicated the outbreak of conflict, and if reporting were to the Secretary-General, he might pursue diplomatic initiatives or refer the dispute to the Security Council. Finally, reporting might prevent an arms spiral resulting from miscalculation of a competitor's assistance.

Despite these substantial advantages, the international system does not even have rudimentary reporting machinery applicable to intervention in internal conflict. There is no general arrangement for reporting arms transfers or other forms of military assistance. And the only real reporting requirements in the Charter, Articles 51 and 54, have proven only peripherally relevant to the internal conflict problem. Article 54 provides that:

> The Security Council shall at all times be kept fully informed of activities undertaken or in contemplation under regional arrangements or by regional agencies for the maintenance of international peace and security.

But this reporting requirement is vague, applies only to regional agencies or arrangements, and in practice has not proven of substantial benefit in the internal conflict context. Article 51 provides that "Measures taken by Members in the exercise of . . . [the] right of self-defense [if an armed attack occurs] shall be immediately reported to the Security Council. . . ." But in practice the antecedent "self-defense if an armed attack occurs" seems to have been interpreted as applying to military response against the territory of a hostile state rather than to assistance in internal conflict. The pattern of United States reporting in the course of the Vietnam war demonstrates this interpretation; the first explicit reporting to the Security Council seems to have been in response to the Tonkin Gulf raids on the north and the commencement of the regular bombing of the north.[209] It is a tragic commentary on the adequacy of present reporting requirements that neither side in the Vietnam war meaningfully reported its actions to the Security Council for almost three years after significant hostilities were commenced. In other instances of intervention, such as the 1964 British assistance in Kenya, the joint Belgian-United States rescue mission in the Congo, and military assistance programs in the absence of internal conflict, the armed attack antecedent is not even relevant. The reporting requirement of Article 51, then, has not proven responsive to the internal conflict problem.

In the last few years there have been several proposals for limited reporting arrangements, but perhaps because there is not yet full commitment to the need for such arrangements, little seems to have come of them. In December, 1965, Malta sponsored a resolution in the First Committee of the General Assembly which called for "establishment of a system of publicity through the United Nations" for the transfer of armaments.[210] The resolution

209. See Public U.S. Communications to the Security Council and Secretary-General in *Hearings on S. 2793 Before the Senate Committee on Foreign Relations*, 89th Cong., 2d Sess., pt. 1, at 634-35 (1966).

210. 20 U.N. GAOR, Annexes, Agenda Item No. 28, at 1, U.N. Doc. A/C.1/ L.347 (1965). In support of the resolution, Mr. Pardo, the delegate from Malta said:

   Malta did not question the right of any country to request arms for the protection of its security or of any State to grant such requests; however, the secrecy surrounding many transactions of that kind . . . could endanger world peace. . . .

was defeated 19 to 18 with 39 abstentions, but apparently the vote was taken on short notice and was not a true indication of the support which might have been mustered had such a plan been properly presented.[211] And in his June, 1967, speech on the Middle East, President Johnson proposed that "the United Nations immediately call upon all of its members to report all shipments of all military arms into this area and to keep those shipments on file for all the peoples of the world to observe."[212] The proposal was never implemented.

In view of the usefulness of a reporting arrangement and the inadequacy of present machinery, the United States should take the initiative in the United Nations to draft a multilateral treaty for the reporting of military assistance to the Secretary-General. The scope of the treaty would be subject to negotiation but might include:

(1) all governmental and private transfers of military armaments to another country and the terms of the transfer—grant, sale, sale on credit, etc.;

The United Nations had no reliable information on the arms traffic; yet the accumulation and transfer of armaments were matters which might threaten the maintenance of international peace and security. . . .

Malta realized that publicity alone would not solve the urgent problem of the international traffic in armaments; it might, however, mitigate some of the dangerous consequences of that trade by enabling the United Nations to be apprised of and to discuss dangerous situations before armed conflicts erupted.

20 U.N. GAOR, First Comm. 222-23 (1965).

211. 20 U.N. GAOR, First Comm. 240 (1965). The United States did not actively support the proposal but indicated that it might well support "some variant of the proposal." Mr. Foster, the United States delegate, said:

Regional competition in conventional arms among the smaller Powers posed a grave threat to world peace and frequently diverted funds away from the urgent needs of economic development. The United States would welcome any initiatives for the control and reduction of conventional arms, which might well include some variant of the proposal made by the representative of Malta.

Id. at 236.

212. N.Y. Times, June 20, 1967, at 18, col. 1, 7.

(2) the transfer of military or para-military personnel from one country to another;

(3) foreign military training and assistance missions;

(4) domestic military training programs for foreign nationals; and

(5) foreign para-military groups enjoying sanctuary.

The duty of reporting would be on the assisting state. To avoid the difficulties of the League of Nations arms registration plan, it should be made clear that the treaty would only establish a reporting arrangement and would not limit or prohibit military assistance.[213]

The treaty might also provide for an annual report from the Secretary-General to the Security Council which would summarize military assistance activity and possibly even catalog instances of non-reporting. Another possibility might be the establishment of a reporting agency responsible to the Secretary-General.

If it is felt that secrecy in military operations should be preserved in cases of collective defense against an armed attack, the treaty might contain a provision allowing a statement of assistance in lieu of detailed reporting whenever a claim is made that assistance is being provided in collective defense against an armed attack. Such a claim would only be allowed on behalf of a widely recognized government and, as a result of the statement of claim and assistance, would be subject to community appraisal.

A multilateral treaty endorsed by the General Assembly seems a better procedure for effectuation than a General Assembly resolution alone. If the substantial traffic in private arms is to be included, then domestic implementing legislation will probably be necessary. A prior treaty may make this domestic implementation politically easier.[214] More importantly the multilateral treaty

---

213. Article VIII (6) of the League Covenant provided for "full and frank" interchange of information concerning the scale of national armaments. This provision, however, was associated in Article VIII with a comprehensive plan for reduction of national armaments to be formulated by the Council of the League. See generally II OPPENHEIM, INTERNATIONAL LAW 122-26 (7th ed. Lauterpacht 1952).

214. Though there seems to be plenty of constitutional basis for federal implementing legislation, a prior treaty would also strengthen the con-

technique followed in approval of the Nuclear Non-Proliferation Treaty provides an opportunity for nations principally concerned to shape the final arrangement and assures greater likelihood of compliance.[215] A bargaining process seems essential if the arrangement is to be effective, since the United States will certainly need the agreement of the Soviet Union. Because of the complexity of the issues and the political difficulty of Charter amendment, implementation by amendment of the Charter seems out of the question.

A principal objection which might be raised to a reporting requirement is that some nations may refuse to sign the treaty or may continue secret military assistance. Admittedly, if the scope of the treaty is broad, as it should be for maximum responsiveness to the internal conflict problem, a significant number of violations may go undetected. Further, if the scope is too broad, the number of signatories to the treaty may fall off drastically. But these difficulties do not seem any greater than those which accompany all worthwhile arms control proposals, including both the Nuclear Test Ban and the Nuclear Non-Proliferation Treaties. And since compliance is voluntary, the ultimate protection of reciprocal non-compliance is always available.

There are at least three reasons which suggest that such a treaty might work. First, the military assistance race is expensive and dangerous and there are some indications that at least the major powers are becoming increasingly aware of their common interest in its control.[216] Second, once some nations begin report-

---

stitutional underpinnings of legislation in implementation of the treaty. See Missouri v. Holland, 252 U.S. 416 (1920).

215. On the legislative history of the Nuclear Non-Proliferation Treaty see M. WILLRICH, NON-PROLIFERATION TREATY: FRAMEWORK FOR NUCLEAR ARMS CONTROL 61-64 (1969). For the General Assembly resolution commending the Treaty and urging the widest possible adherence see G.A. Res. 2373, 22 U.N. GAOR, Supp. 16A, at 5, U.N. Doc. A/6716/Add.1 (1968).

216. The interest in control is strongly shared by the developing nations as well. Mr. Pardo, the delegate from Malta, pointed out in presenting his proposal for a publicity system for arms transfer that: "the *per capita* rates of military expenditure of some of the poor countries were among the highest in the world, and much of that expenditure went for arms imports." 20 U.N. GAOR, First Comm. 222 (1965). A recent

ing, world opinion may exert pressure on other nations to report. Major violations would be likely to be discovered and would focus attention on the impermissibility of covert operations. Third, even if we reported and our adversaries did not, it is not clear that we would be in any worse position than we are in now. In fact, that was precisely the position in which the United States found itself under the International Control Commission reporting arrangements during the early years of the Vietnam War. Most major assistance is known quickly, and there might even be an advantage in openly reporting instead of suggesting improper motives by covert operations. For these reasons, a multilateral treaty for the reporting of military assistance seems well worth the try.

FACT-FINDING IN THE INTERVENTION CONTEXT: SUGGESTIONS FOR INTERNATIONAL OBSERVATION AND DISCLOSURE

In some kinds of international disputes, fact disagreement may be a significant causative factor. For example, the dispute between the German and Netherlands governments about responsibility for the sinking of the Dutch steamer *Tubantia* in 1916 was in large part a dispute about whether in fact the *Tubantia* was torpedoed by a German submarine. After an International Commission of Inquiry reported that the sinking was probably caused by a German submarine, the German government paid compensation for the loss.[217] Similarly, border disputes may sometimes turn

---

article in the *New York Times* on the military expenditures of the developing nations points out that: "Military expenditures of the underdeveloped countries are rising faster than their gross national products. . . ." N.Y. Times, Aug. 18, 1969, at 1, col. 5, 6.

It is interesting to speculate on the effect that a multilateral treaty for the reporting of military assistance might have had on the Cuban missile crisis. It is even possible that such a treaty might have deterred the Soviets from attempting to secretly emplace nuclear missiles in Cuba and thereby have prevented the crisis.

217. See the Report of the Secretary-General on Methods of Fact-Finding, 20 U.N. GAOR, Annexes, Agenda Items 90 and 94, at 1, 10-11, U.N. Doc. A/5694 (1965).

See generally with respect to international fact-finding machinery, Report of the Secretary-General on Methods of Fact-Finding, *supra;* Franck & Cherkis, *The Problem of Fact-Finding in International Disputes,* 18 W. Res. L. Rev. 1483 (1967); Note, *UN Fact-Finding as a Means of Settling Disputes,* 9 Va. J. Int'l L. 154 (1968).

on fact disagreements which may be settled by submission to international fact-finding. Generally, however, disputes underlying internal conflict are not caused by fact disagreements and will not be settled by submission to international fact-finding. Most such conflicts are competitive authority struggles in which the ultimate issue is the success of one or another faction. This is true of interventions as well, most of which seem to result from a political commitment to one side or another. Some interventions, of course, might be deterred by more accurate factual information as, for example, counter-intervention resulting from misperception of aggression. But for the most part, the core fact problem in the intervention context is more a fact-disclosure than a fact-finding problem. The chief value of fact-disclosure lies not in enabling immediate settlement of conflict but in establishing a basis for appraisal and in deterring impermissible assistance by exposing it. Probably the principal need for fact-disclosure as a deterrent is for disclosure of assistance to insurgents. Such disclosure may be helpful in deterring both impermissible assistance to insurgents and impermissible claims of counter-intervention made on behalf of incumbents. Disclosure of assistance to incumbents is also important, but such assistance is more often openly provided.

Examples of international fact-disclosure are the United Nations Special Committee on the Balkans, the United Nations Special Committee on Hungary, the Secretary-General's Special Representative to Oman, the United Nations Observation Group in Lebanon, the Security Council Sub-Committee on Laos, and the 1959 OAS investigations of the situations in Panama and Nicaragua.[218]

A second form of fact-finding which may be useful in the process of settlement of internal conflict is international observation of elections or supervision of a cease-fire. Unlike fact-disclosure missions, such observation and supervision missions usually depend on prior agreement between the parties to the dispute. Examples of observation and fact-finding in this category include the United Nations Temporary Commission on Korea, the United Nations Truce Supervision Organization, the United Nations

218. See the Report of the Secretary-General on Methods of Fact-Finding, *supra* note 217, at 28 (the Balkans), 32 (Hungary), 43 (Oman), 41 (Lebanon), 42 (Laos), and 47 (Panama and Nicaragua).

Emergency Force, the Security Council Committee on the Indonesian Question, the United Nations Observation Mission in Yemen, the United Nations Malaysia Mission,[219] and the International Commission for Supervision and Control in Vietnam.[220]

A third concern of fact-finding in the intervention context is investigation of an internal situation as a basis for community appraisal of self-determination or denial of human rights. Examples in this category include the United Nations Commission on the Racial Situation in the Union of South Africa, the General Assembly Sub-Committee on the Situation in Angola, the General Assembly Special Committee for South-West Africa, the General Assembly Special Committee on the Policies of *apartheid* of the Government of the Republic of South Africa, and the United Nations Fact-Finding Mission to South Vietnam.[221] Both the Trusteeship Council and the Special Committee on the Granting of Independence to Colonial Countries have also been actively engaged in fact-finding concerning self-determination.[222]

As these examples indicate, there is an abundance of international fact-finding machinery useful in the intervention context. Most of it, however, is *ad hoc* machinery invoked by the General Assembly, Security Council, Secretary-General, or Council of the OAS in particular cases and as such is subject to political pressures and cold-war tensions. Aside from those established for special situations, the only standing bodies for general fact-finding are the Panel for Inquiry and Conciliation created by the General Assembly in 1949,[223] which has never been used;[224] the Peace Observation Commission created in 1950 pursuant to the Uniting

219. See the Report of the Secretary-General on Methods of Fact-Finding, *supra* note 217, at 28 (Korea), 40 (UNTSO), 31 (UNEF), 39 (Indonesia), 42 (Yemen), and 44 (Malaysia).

220. See Hannon, *The International Control Commission Experience and the Role of an Improved International Supervisory Body in the Vietnam Settlement*, 9 VA. J. INT'L L. 20 (1968).

221. See the Report of the Secretary-General on Methods of Fact-Finding, *supra* note 217, at 30 (South Africa), 33 (Angola), 34 (South-West Africa), 35 (*apartheid*), and 35 (Viet-Nam).

222. See Franck & Cherkis, *supra* note 217, at 1505-08.

223. See the Report of the Secretary-General on Methods of Fact-Finding, *supra* note 217, at 25-27.

224. Note, *supra* note 217, at 173.

for Peace Resolution, used in connection with the Balkan situation in 1951;[225] and the register of experts to be established by the Secretary-General pursuant to a unanimous General Assembly resolution in 1967.[226] The Panel for Inquiry and Conciliation is essentially a list of available experts maintained by the Secretary-General. Although not wholly clear, apparently it may be used by any organ of the United Nations or by a joint request from any two or more states party to a controversy. The Peace Observation Commission is invoked by a two-thirds vote of the members of the General Assembly present and voting "if the Security Council is not exercising the functions assigned to it by the Charter with respect to the matter in question."[227] It is thus subject to even stronger political pressures and cold-war tensions than are other *ad hoc* bodies. The non-use of this standing machinery for fact-finding suggests both a strong preference for flexible response and the inadequacy of this permanent machinery. Because of this inadequacy, the Netherlands in 1966 proposed a permanent fact-finding organ, limited "to the establishment of facts," and which could be invoked by "the United Nations and the specialized agencies . . . [and any] two or more States."[228] The Netherlands suggested that the proposal be implemented by General Assembly resolution.[229] To date the proposal has not been implemented.

A common deficiency of all of this machinery, existing and proposed, is that it requires invocation by United Nations action, with all of the resulting political disability, or invocation by at least two states party to a dispute, which, if fact-disclosure is the goal, is usually unrealistic. If the substantial advantages of fact-disclosure in the intervention context are to be maximized, there is a need for permanent international machinery shielded from political pressure and available to any state which wishes to use

225. See the Report of the Secretary-General on Methods of Fact-Finding, *supra* note 217, at 27.
226. G.A. Res. 2329, 22 U.N. GAOR, Supp. 16, at 84, U.N. Doc. A/6716 (1967).
227. G.A. Res. 377A, 5 U.N. GAOR, Supp. 20, at 10-12, U.N. Doc. A/1775 (1950) (Article 3).
228. 21 U.N. GAOR, Annexes, Agenda Item No. 87, at 111, 112, U.N. Doc. A/6373 (1966).
229. *Id.* at 113.

it. It should not be necessary or sufficient to rely on self-serving "white papers" in support of claims of impermissible assistance to insurgents or permissible counter-intervention. Such international machinery might also be a useful way of implementing Article 51 by establishing the facts in situations of alleged armed attack.

Without too strongly recommending any particular institutional structure,[230] it seems useful to explore the possibility of a permanent fact-disclosure agency available to any state wishing to use it for the investigation of an alleged armed attack or intervention in internal conflict. If it is felt desirable to narrow the range of states which might invoke it, it might be made available only to states requesting investigation of military assistance or the use of the military instrument in their own territory. The agency should also be available to any organ of the United Nations. It would be limited solely to the establishment of facts and would be purely voluntary. The experience of the United Nations Special Committee on the Balkans and the United Nations Commission on the Racial Situation in the Union of South Africa suggests

---

230. See the exploration of the strengths and weaknesses of various structures for international fact-finding machinery in Note, *supra* note 217, at 173-78.

In the context of an article appraising the Dominican crisis, Professor Ved Nanda has called for the establishment of permanent regional and international fact-finding organs. He points out:

[I]n the Dominican situation or any other similar situation, the criteria of necessity and proportionality to determine permissibility of the use of coercive measures will have a meaningful reference only if the "facts" are known. Therefore, it is imperative that independent fact-finding bodies on regional and international levels be established. It is suggested that as a preliminary step, regional organizations such as the OAS should set up a permanent fact-finding organ with its representatives stationed in the capital of each member state. The mechanics of setting up such an operation should not pose too much of a problem. It is realized that this suggestion involves the risk of a major power in a regional organization exercising a preponderance of influence and control in such an agency, and thus the reported "facts" may be colored; however, as a first step, it is still preferable to the present situation wherein a state assumes the competence of unilaterally defining the character of a situation and subsequently justifying its response by reference to the character so defined.

Nanda, *supra* note 160, Part I, at 479.

that even when a voluntary agency is denied access to the territory of a state under investigation it can still make a useful report.[231] The agency would be composed of a diplomatically protected staff recruited from relatively neutral countries, such as Sweden, India, Canada, and Yugoslavia, and perhaps also recruited from as wide a geographic base as possible, and would be equipped to respond promptly to an appropriate request. Establishment of the agency could be by either General Assembly or Security Council resolution,[232] but in view of the veto problem and the need to encourage the General Assembly role as an authorizing agency, General Assembly creation and supervision seems preferable. Since existing fact-finding machinery does not specifically include a standing observation of elections capability, it might also be worth considering the feasibility of establishing a second chamber with an observation capability.

Regardless of institutional structure, whether *ad hoc*, permanent, or hybrid, there is a need for greater fact-disclosure capability in the international system. New institutions should be relatively insulated from political pressures and should be available to any state seeking to justify either a claim of impermissible assistance to insurgents or of permissible counter-intervention.

PROSPECTS IN SEARCH OF DEVELOPMENT

In addition to strengthening the role of the General Assembly as an agency for community review of intervention, promoting agreement on the international reporting of military assistance, and encouraging international observation and disclosure, at least three other prospects for improvement in the international constitutive process deserve serious inquiry for possible development.

The first of these is a technique for collective recognition.[233]

231. See the Report of the Secretary-General on Methods of Fact-Finding, *supra* note 217, at 28 (the Balkans), and 30-31 (South Africa).
232. For discussion of the competence of the Security Council or General Assembly to create a permanent fact-finding body see Note, *supra* note 217, at 178-81.
233. "Community procedures for recognition of status" are suggested by Rosalyn Higgins as a useful technique for dealing with internal conflict problems. See Higgins, *Internal War and International Law* in III C:

Counter-intervention is available only on behalf of a faction readily identifiable as the widely recognized government. For purposes of this standard, a "widely recognized government" may be identified by a range of factors, such as historic contiguity of political authority, continuing control of the administrative apparatus, control of the regular military apparatus, representation in international organizations, continuing control of major cities and ports, and particularly wide diplomatic recognition relative to competing factions. Since wide diplomatic recognition is particularly helpful, collective community recognition would greatly assist in making the "widely recognized government" characterization. As such, collective recognition should be thought of in the internal conflict context as one aspect of the general problem of centralized legitimation of assistance. Although, as the Yemen case illustrates,[234] legitimation of assistance should probably not depend solely on UN credentials decisions, the General Assembly should be encouraged to expand its competence in dealing with recognition problems, already demonstrated with respect to Iraq, Yemen, and the Congo.

A second prospect deserving development is Senator Edward Kennedy's proposal for a permanent United Nations emergency relief force to assist victims of conflicts like the Nigerian civil war.[235] It is an international disgrace that the United Nations has not even been able to bring into existence a permanent force for humanitarian assistance to victims of natural and political disasters. Since such a force would not provide military assistance and need not necessarily have a military capability, forceful sponsorship of such a proposal by one of the major powers would seem

---

BLACK & R. FALK, THE FUTURE OF THE INTERNATIONAL LEGAL ORDER: CONFLICT MANAGEMENT 81, 114 (1971).

234. See the discussion of the Yemen case under the type IV (c) claim to assist any faction in a struggle for control of internal authority structures where a widely recognized government cannot be distinguished.

235. See N.Y. Times, Feb. 9, 1969, at 1, col. 4.

Such a force would be endowed with a staff of international relief experts, with funds and emergency supplies and would be ready to move quickly to any part of the world on invitation to help victims of disaster.

Id.

to have a significant chance of success. It is important that the United Nations be strengthened whenever possible by exploitation of just such areas of shared concern.

The third prospect in need of development is thorough revision of the conventions on the laws of war, protection of civilians, and treatment of prisoners for greater responsiveness to internal conflict.[236] Just as existing international organizations are largely a response to conventional war and are inadequate for dealing with internal conflict, so too present conventions on the conduct of war are largely a response to conventional war. As a result of an uneasy compromise, the Geneva Conventions of 1949 purport to require at least minimum humanitarian standards "in the case of armed conflict not of an international character,"[237] but in practice the ambiguity as to who is bound by the Conventions and the limited protection which they offer have rendered them less than satisfactory. Moreover, the excesses with which both sides in the Vietnam war have conducted hostilities, and the outmoded technological basis of most of the conventions on the laws of war, also suggest a strong community interest in thorough revision. The conclusion of the Vietnam war might be an opportune time to press for such revision. Specific problems which might be addressed include criteria for determining the threshold of internal conflict for applying the laws of war (the old belligerency test is hopelessly uncertain), the identification required of combatants in order to be protected, the responsibility of an assisting state for the treatment of prisoners of war, the limits of permissible guerrilla strategies, and the limits of permissible weapons systems and military targets in combatting an insurgency.

Institutional changes in the international constitutive process should not be thought of as panaceas for the control of intervention. The creation of new agencies and procedures is not likely to significantly alter underlying political and economic realities. But where there is a need for institutional change, new agencies and

---

236. See generally Petrowski, Law and the Conduct of Internal War (unpublished paper, 1967, prepared for Phase III of the American Society of International Law Civil War Studies Project); Note, *The Geneva Convention and the Treatment of Prisoners of War in Vietnam*, 80 HARV. L. REV. 851 (1967).
237. See note 151 *supra*.

procedures may significantly aid in moderating and even avoiding conflict. Present international institutions are so unresponsive to the problems of intervention in internal conflict that institutional changes appear to offer significant promise for the control of intervention.

RECOMMENDATIONS FOR IMPROVEMENT IN THE NATIONAL CONSTITUTIVE PROCESS: THE SYSTEMATIC INCLUSION OF INTERNATIONAL LAW AS AN INPUT IN FOREIGN POLICY PLANNING

For the past twenty years a debate has raged within the United States between the legalists and anti-legalists.[238] The anti-legalists have criticized an approach to American foreign policy which they allege has obscured the national interest in a cloud of legal rhetoric and moral precept. The legalists in turn have intensified their call for world peace through law and have for the most part dismissed the anti-legalists as latter day Machiavellis. Though both camps have some truth on their side, much of the argument has that air of unreality which comes from debate without dialogue. The anti-legalists are probably correct in their charge that the rhetoric of legal obligation and world order frequently conceals a failure to make a tough-minded assessment of the national interest. Their own engagement with this enterprise is a promising development. But in their attack on the legalists, the anti-legalists may have engaged in an overkill which itself obscures the real contribution which the legalist tradition can make to the defining of the national interest.

The national interest is more than simply barrels of oil per day or military potential; it also includes the kind of world order which we would like to see established. An international law approach, if rooted firmly in the usually harsh realities of the international system, has an important and complementary role to play in defining the national interest.[239] Much of the legalist tradition,

238. See Falk, *Law, Lawyers, and the Conduct of American Foreign Relations*, 78 YALE L.J. 919. I owe the useful "legalist" "anti-legalist" terminology to Professor Falk.

239. See Moore, *supra* note 165, at 1088-89.

which the anti-legalists justly condemned, was a pre-legal realist approach which, perhaps because of the influence of the continental jurists, seemed to hang on longer in international law. Although today there are still some amateurs of the irrelevant, most international lawyers are as concerned with power realities and the interrelation of law and society as is the staunchest proponent of the *realpolitik* school. The lawyer and the international relations theorist frequently achieve a different and complementary focus, however. The international relations theorist tends to be concerned with power relations and the consequences of national action for those relations. The international lawyer tends to emphasize normative appraisal, the clarification of community common interest, and institutional techniques for implementing the kind of world order espoused. In a world in which reciprocity is a principal sanction, the clarification of areas of common interest is necessarily a part of the national interest. And if rooted firmly in the real world, one can hardly fault international lawyers for attempting to use law and institutional development as tools for social change.

If international law has suffered in the legalist-anti-legalist debate, it has suffered even more from lack of representation in the national foreign policy process. In fact, a good argument can be made that a major cause of the superficial use of international law by national foreign policy planners is the failure to systematically include international law as an input in the policy planning process. The sad truth is that there is no way in which international law is systematically introduced in policy planning within the present structure of the foreign policy process in the United States. In contrast, political, economic, military, and international relations inputs are introduced in a score of more or less institutionalized ways from Cabinet level representation to Assistants to the President for National Security Affairs. This is not to say that international law and lawyers have not sometimes influenced policy planning, as they most assuredly have. To use the example of the Cuban missile crisis, Leonard Meeker, the then Deputy Legal Adviser of the Department of State, George Ball, the Under Secretary of State, Nicholas Katzenbach of the Justice Department, and former Secretary of State Dean Acheson were all called on to present an analysis of the legal issues.[240] But in view of the strong interest in securing systematic inclusion of international law in the foreign policy process, reliance on episodic participation of influential lawyers, some of whom may even represent the anti-legalist tradition,[241] is grossly inadequate.

Professor Richard Falk has proposed a new Cabinet level position, Attorney General for International Affairs, as a response to this problem.[242] While I endorse the reasons for his proposal, I doubt whether in practice an Attorney General for International Affairs is a workable solution. My doubt stems principally from the political unreality of creating a new cabinet position for international affairs in competition with the Secretary of State. There is also a substantial question whether extensive new foreign policy machinery is the best way to respond to the problem. The Jackson Subcommittee on National Policy Machinery concluded in 1961, after lengthy hearings on the problem of foreign policy making, that "radical additions to our existing policy machinery are unnecessary and undesirable."[243] Moreover, given the skepticism with which international law is widely regarded, it seems unrealistic to expect a new cabinet position solely for advice on international law. Although the proposal has the substantial merit of encouraging independence and impartiality in international legal advice, it is no bargain if achieved at the cost of political impossibility.

As an alternative proposal, and one which hopefully is work-

240. See E. ABEL, THE MISSILE CRISIS 59, 73 (Bantam ed. 1966). Leonard Meeker, who later became the Legal Adviser of the Department of State, is said to have originated the suggestion to call the United States action a "defensive quarantine" instead of a "blockade." *Id.* at 59.

241. Dean Acheson is said to have taken the position during the deliberations in the Cuban missile crisis that "legal niceties were so much pompous foolishness in a situation where the essential security of the United States, its prestige, its pledged word to defend the Americas, was threatened." *Id.* at 59. See also *id.* at 73.

242. See Falk, *supra* note 238, at 13-14.

243. Concluding statement by Senator Henry M. Jackson, in THE NATIONAL SECURITY COUNCIL 65, 66 (H. Jackson ed. 1966). See also Hilsman, *Improving the Foreign Policy "Machinery,"* in THE PRESIDENTIAL ADVISORY SYSTEM 271 (T. Cronin & S. Greenberg eds. 1969).

able while still effecting a significant improvement, I suggest that the office of Legal Adviser of the Department of State be upgraded to Under Secretary of State for International Legal Affairs and that the new Under Secretary be made a permanent *ex officio* member of the National Security Council.[244] The statutory description of the new office should indicate that a principal duty is to participate in the foreign policy planning process and to provide impartial advice to both the Secretary of State and the National Security Council on the basis of international law. The National Security Council is the principal advisory agency to the President on major public order issues and should provide an adequate forum for the Legal Adviser to participate in the process.[245] As with the present Legal Adviser, the new Under Secretary would be appointed by the President, with the advice and consent of the Senate.[246] In choosing the appointee, independence of judgment and background in newer approaches to international law should be stressed. The present office of the Legal Adviser ranks equally with the eleven Assistant Secretaries of State.[247] This proposed change would put the office on a par with that of Under Secretary of State for Political or Economic Affairs, which ranks immediately below the Under Secretary.[248]

One advantage of this proposal is that it encourages the systematic inclusion of international law in the foreign policy process without requiring major governmental reorganization. In doing so, it builds on the office of Legal Adviser, which is the governmental office most involved in providing legal advice on major

244. Existing law provides that Under Secretaries may become members of the National Security Council to serve at the pleasure of the President "when appointed by the President [to the National Security Council] . . . with the advice and consent of the Senate. . . ." 50 U.S.C. § 402(a) (7) (1964).

245. See *id.* at 31, 39, and 293. The statutory authority for the National Security Council is 50 U.S.C. § 402 (1964).

246. The statutory authority for the office of Legal Adviser of the Department of State is 22 U.S.C. § 2654 (1964) (Supp. III, 1968).

247. 22 U.S.C. § 2653 (1964) (Supp. III, 1968). See also 5 U.S.C. § 5315 (1964) (Supp. IV, 1969).

248. See 22 U.S.C. § 2653 (1964) (Supp. III, 1968); 5 U.S.C. §§ 5313-14 (1964) (Supp. IV, 1969).

foreign policy issues.[249] The Legal Adviser has the substantial resource base of the Department of State and, because he may have to defend it later, a personal stake in decision. In recent years, there seems to be a trend toward greater emphasis on the role of the Legal Adviser in the policy planning process and in general, since the establishment of the office in 1931, there has been a strong tradition of the appointment of Legal Advisers well qualified in international law.[250] In fact, the present Legal Adviser, John R. Stevenson, is a past President of the American Society of International Law.

Two limitations on the proposal are that the President may sometimes bypass the National Security Council and that even as upgraded the new Under Secretary would still be subordinate to the Secretary of State. An example of the first problem occurred during the Cuban missile crisis when President Kennedy relied most heavily on an *ad hoc* group of advisers which later came to be known as the Executive Committee of the National Security Council.[251] If the enabling act which makes the new Under Secretary a permanent member of the National Security Council stresses that the purpose of the addition is to facilitate his participation in the foreign policy planning process, however, it may at least serve as a reminder of the importance of including the new Under Secretary in any *ad hoc* advisory group. Moreover, the purpose is not to put the President in a procedural strait jacket, and any proposal which attempts to do so should be avoided. In any event, since President Nixon has affirmed his intention to rely on the National Security Council as the principal arm of the President in foreign policy planning, perhaps this limitation is largely imaginary.[252] With respect to the second problem, that of sub-

---

249. For a thorough analysis of the work of the Legal Adviser's Office see Bilder, *The Office of the Legal Adviser: The State Department Lawyer and Foreign Affairs*, 56 Am. J. Int'l L. 633 (1962). Professor Bilder points out that "most Legal Advisers . . . have become heavily involved in high-level policy questions having legal implications." *Id.* at 638.

250. See the list of Legal Advisers *id.* at 635 n.5. The immediate predecessor of John Stevenson was Leonard Meeker.

251. See E. Abel, *supra* note 240, at 99; R. Kennedy, Thirteen Days: A Memoir of the Cuban Missile Crisis 30-31 (1969).

252. See *The National Security Council System: Responsibilities of the Department of State*, 60 Dep't State Bulletin 163 (1969).
    To assist him in carrying out his responsibilities for the con-

ordination to the Secretary of State, the new Under Secretary will participate directly in the work of the National Security Council as well as report to the Secretary of State. If it is clear from the enabling act creating the new office that the inclusion of impartial judgment about international law is the principal purpose of the new office, a competent Under Secretary should be able to successfully interject international law into the decision process from his base on the National Security Council.

In addition to the proposal to upgrade the office of Legal Adviser to that of Under Secretary of State for International Legal Affairs and to make the new Under Secretary a member of the National Security Council, it might also be useful to pursue less institutionalized techniques for including international law in the foreign policy process. One possibility might be for the President to add to his staff an Assistant to the President for International Legal Affairs, a position in some ways similar to that of Assistant to the President for National Security Affairs, now held by Dr. Henry Kissinger.[253] It might also be useful for the Senate Foreign Relations Committee to add a similar position to its staff. Whatever the technique, efforts aimed at restructuring the national decision process to make it more sensitive to the common interest in an effective international-legal order may be quite useful in implementing normative agreement about the control of intervention.

VI. Toward Policy Responsive Control: An Evaluation of Past Standards and Recent Proposals and a Summary of Tentative Recommendations

EVALUATION OF PAST STANDARDS AND RECENT PROPOSALS

Past standards for the control of intervention have been deficient principally because they failed to clarify the community

---

duct of national security affairs, the President has designated the National Security Council as the principal forum for consideration of national security policy issues requiring Presidential decision. *Id.* at 165.

253. The responsibility of the Assistant for International Legal Affairs, however, would largely be to advise the President concerning national security issues and he would not oversee a national security staff. See THE NATIONAL SECURITY COUNCIL, *supra* note 243, at 302-03.

policies which they sought to promote,[254] failed to focus on the full range of intervention claims, and overemphasized normative appraisal at the expense of institutional development. As a result, past standards have been overly simple and only episodically policy responsive. Recent proposals, though largely suffering from these same difficulties, have been based on a generally more sophisticated awareness of the total context than past standards. But despite this rising level of sophistication, the field continues to be dominated by the snipe hunt for one all-encompassing non-intervention rule.

THE TRADITIONAL STANDARD

The traditional standard is said to be that it is lawful to assist a widely recognized government at its request and unlawful to assist insurgents, at least until belligerency is attained.[255] Once belligerency is attained, apparently it is lawful to aid either side if the assisting state is willing to itself become a belligerent. In practice, this may still be the most widely accepted standard, as is evidenced by the frequency with which an invitation from a widely recognized government is advanced as a justification for intervention. Its philosophical underpinnings, however, have been thoroughly discredited.

A principal drawback of the traditional standard is that it may serve as a Maginot Line for the *status quo*. That is, it may be used to justify suppression of indigenous revolutionary movements. The 1956 Soviet invasion of Hungary to assist government forces in suppressing the genuine internal revolution is a good example. Similarly, self-determination may sometimes suggest assistance to insurgents, as in South-West Africa and Haiti. The traditional rule seems more rooted in self-contained notions of sovereignty than in the requirements of genuine self-determination.

Other difficulties with the traditional standard are that it is non-responsive for conflicts in which there is no clearly recogniz-

---

254. Professor Tom Farer's proposal for a prohibition of participation in tactical operations, however, is rooted in an explicit statement of his understanding of community policies. See Farer, *Harnessing Rogue Elephants: A Short Discourse on Foreign Intervention in Civil Strife*, 82 HARV. L. REV. 511, 513-22 (1969).

255. See authorites cited note 91 *supra*.

able government side,[256] and that the vague belligerency threshold for permitting assistance to either side seems to be out of step with the Charter limitations on use of force.

On the other hand, the traditional standard did have some strengths. If insurgents could not lawfully be aided prior to belligerency, there was no difficulty in distinguishing foreign initiation of insurgency as a form of covert armed attack from assistance to an indigenous insurgency. There might also be some advantage in promoting stability of government, although if stability is achieved only by denial of self-determination this would certainly be suspect. Moreover, the traditional standard may sometimes have been more policy responsive to the needs of war prevention than contemporary proposals. As Korea, Vietnam, Cuba, Czechoslovakia, Hungary, and most of the major power conflicts since World War II demonstrate, major powers are particularly sensitive to shifts perceived as upsetting the stability of the international system and are likely to intervene to preserve the *status quo.* A standard which prohibits assistance to insurgents across such cold-war boundaries and permits assistance to widely recognized governments may sometimes serve to prevent major power clashes and to preserve system stability. In differentiating between insurgents and widely recognized government, the traditional standard may also have reflected a number of differences between them which are important for policy realization. Thus, incumbents are likely to control the organized military and may be a party to international agreements guaranteeing their government or protecting against external attack. Both of these factors may make military assistance to insurgents more dangerous than assistance to incumbents.

On balance, however, the traditional standard is unsatisfactory. It is not necessary in responding to the acute danger of major power intervention on behalf of insurgents across cold-war boundaries, or to the generally greater risk to world order of providing assistance to insurgents, to legitimate repressive assistance to incumbents. And unless one is willing to carve up the world into major power spheres of influence and recognize a right of

256. For example, what guidance does it provide for the Dominican Republic or Yemen cases?

self-determination within each sphere only at the pleasure of the major power, the traditional standard presents too great a danger of self-serving interference with genuine internal demands for revolutionary change. The traditional standard also fails to provide criteria for appraisal of the full range of intervention claims and fails to focus on institutional machinery for control.

THE NEUTRAL NON-INTERVENTION STANDARD

A second standard, first enunciated by William Hall,[257] and subsequently championed by Quincy Wright,[258] is that it is impermissible to aid either faction in a struggle for control of authority structures once the outcome is uncertain. Presumably prior to the "outcome in doubt" threshold it is permissible to assist the widely recognized government. The principal advantage of this neutral non-intervention standard is that it better serves self-determination by lessening the opportunities for self-serving claims masking external interference. An underlying premise is that unilateral external interference presents a greater threat to self-determination than does allowing genuine indigenous conflict to run its course. Even though intervention on either side is not necessarily disruptive of self-determination, the difficulty in determining the demands of self-determination and the danger of unreviewable external claims on balance probably support this premise. For this reason, the neutral non-intervention standard has been attracting an increasing following in recent years.[259] In fact, the 1965 General Assembly Declaration on Inadmissibility of Intervention seems to embody this standard, and a good case can be made for the proposition that it is present international law.

The principal drawback with the neutral non-intervention standard as developed to date is that its proponents have not provided workable criteria for determining when assistance to incumbents must be frozen to pre-insurgency levels. Frequently, incumbents may be receiving military assistance as part of an on-

257. W. HALL, INTERNATIONAL LAW 287 (6th ed. 1909); W. HALL, INTERNATIONAL LAW 347 (8th ed. 1924).
258. See, *e.g.*, Wright, *United States Intervention in the Lebanon*, 53 AM. J. INT'L L. 112, 122 (1959).
259. See W. FRIEDMANN, THE CHANGING STRUCTURE OF INTERNATIONAL LAW 264-67 (1964).

going aid program prior to the outbreak of an insurgency. Since the prohibition of all such assistance would deny genuine defense interdependencies against external attack and would be completely unacceptable in practice, the neutral non-intervention standard must distinguish such assistance from partisan assistance in internal conflict. Moreover, since cessation of an on-going military aid program may amount to intervention on behalf of insurgents, there is strong reason for permitting continuation of assistance at the pre-insurgency level. These difficulties do not appear to be insoluble,[260] and elsewhere in this chapter I suggest criteria for determining when a level of conflict is reached which requires a freeze on partisan assistance.[261]

A second problem with the standard, which is also not fatal but

260. Professor Tom Farer, in his critique of the neutral non-intervention standard, offers the following hypothetical which he says "illustrates one feature of the presently insoluble definitional difficulties" associated with the neutral non-intervention standard:

> On January 1, 1965, country I becomes independent. Country C immediately offers massive economic and military assistance, which is accepted. In 1967, armed civil strife breaks out in I and quickly reaches dimensions which threaten the survival of the incumbent government. Is country C an interventionary power if it fails to terminate its aid program?

Farer, *supra* note 254, at 530. Adverting to the dilemma that both withdrawing and continuing aid might critically affect the internal authority struggle (particularly in view of the quasi-dependent status of many underdeveloped states) he concludes that "the concept of nonintervention cannot be made operational in any form that might conceivably be acceptable to the international community." Farer, *supra* note 254, at 530-31. Although a valid criticism of the typical formulation of the neutral non-intervention rule, which did not clearly focus on the need to permit pre-insurgency assistance to be maintained, Farer's criticism does not take sufficient account of the difference between freezing all assistance (military and economic) at pre-insurgency levels and allowing an unlimited increase in all assistance. This third alternative of freezing assistance at pre-insurgency levels, while not purporting to have zero effect on the internal authority struggle, may well promote community policies by isolating the conflict and minimizing the effect of external assistance. The real problem, and one on which critics and supporters of the rule alike have not focused, is the need to develop workable criteria for determining when assistance to incumbents must be frozen.

261. See the discussion with respect to the type IV (a) claim to assist a widely recognized government in a struggle for control of internal authority structures.

which in practice is cause for concern, is that it frequently seems to obscure legitimacy of counter-intervention on behalf of a widely recognized government. There is little merit in arguing that the auto-interpretation problem prevents partisan assistance to a widely recognized government if unlawful external assistance is already being supplied to insurgents. Non-intervention as a requirement of self-determination is much too suspect in these circumstances. And if the standard is taken to the point of condemning assistance to a widely recognized government in meeting what amounts to a covert armed attack, then it loses all justification. There is some danger that in these situations writers relying on this standard will focus on the relatively open responsive assistance to the widely recognized government and ignore or minimize the covert assistance to the insurgents. In fact, this seems to be the case in Professor Wolfgang Friedmann's treatment of the Vietnam war.[262] It may be that similar non-intervention feeling played a role during the Spanish Civil War in discouraging intervention by the western democracies on behalf of the recognized Spanish government despite the substantial intervention of Hitler and Mussolini on behalf of the insurgents.[263] The cost of the non-intervention by the democracies was an insurgent win by the Franco forces. The antidote to this problem, however, is simply clear focus on the legitimacy of counter-intervention on behalf of a widely recognized government.

A third difficulty with the neutral non-intervention standard is that like the traditional standard it fails adequately to deal with the full range of intervention claims or to focus on institutional machinery for control. This deficiency is particularly acute with respect to non-authority-oriented intervention, and in this category the standard should probably not be followed. The standard is also suspect in non-partisan interventions in authority-oriented conflicts. In both these categories other criteria for control may be more responsive to community policies than the non-intervention standard.

262. *Compare* Friedmann, *Law and Politics in the Vietnamese War: A Comment*, 61 Am. J. Int'l L. 776 (1967), *with* Moore, *Law and Politics in the Vietnamese War: A Response to Professor Friedmann*, 61 Am. J. Int'l L. 1039 (1967).
263. See generally H. Thomas, The Spanish Civil War (1961).

Despite these difficulties, if incorporated into comprehensive recommendations for control which focus on the pre-insurgency, counter-intervention, non-authority-oriented, and non-partisan-assistance problems, the neutral non-intervention standard provides probably the most useful normative base of any generally accepted standard.

Professor Richard Falk has suggested a standard which, although it achieves a different focus, approximates the neutral non-intervention standard. He divides violent conflict into type I conflict, involving "the direct and massive use of military force by one political entity across a frontier of another"; type II conflict, involving "substantial military participation by one or more foreign nations in an internal struggle for control"; type III conflict, involving "internal struggle for control of a national society, the outcome of which is virtually independent of external participation"; and type IV conflict, involving an authorization by "a competent international organization of global (IVa) or regional (IVb) dimensions . . . [for] the use of force."[264] Falk postulates that in type I conflict it is permissible to reply against the territory of the attacking state as in response to an armed attack under Article 51 of the Charter; in type II conflict it is only "appropriate to take offsetting military action confined to the internal arena"; in type III conflict "it is inappropriate for a foreign nation to use military power to influence the outcome"; and in type IV conflict international authorization or prohibition "resolves the issue of legality," at least if the authorizing organization is the United Nations.[265]

Falk's recommendation for his type III conflict is essentially the neutral non-intervention rule. His recommendation for his type II conflict, however, introduces a new claim; that is, the claim to use the military instrument against the territory of a state providing assistance to an opposing faction. His recommendation that counter-intervention be confined to the internal arena is intended to minimize the auto-interpretation problem and the danger of escalation.

---

264. See R. FALK, LEGAL ORDER IN A VIOLENT WORLD 227-28 (types I, II, and III), and 273 (type IV) (1968).
265. *Id.*

For reasons given more fully elsewhere in this chapter,[266] this *a priori* geographic rule seems undesirable in cases in which covert external assistance amounts to an armed attack. But despite my disagreement with Falk's suggestion when writ large, it expresses an important distinction between the right to counter-intervention and the right to reply against the territory of an assisting state. The two claims are separate and the second requires a finding of an armed attack. In all situations, reply against the territory of an assisting state represents a serious escalation and should be permissible only after a clear finding of extreme foreign involvement amounting to an armed attack.

Professor Falk's recommendation for his type II conflict is ambiguous; but if it means that counter-intervention should be available on behalf of insurgents as well as the widely recognized government then it seems undesirably broad. To allow counter-intervention on behalf of insurgents is to sanction a spiral of escalation on both sides, and would as a practical matter reduce the non-intervention standard to a non-rule. Allowing counter-intervention on behalf of a widely recognized government and not on behalf of insurgents does not treat the competing factions equally; but this lapse of neutrality in favor of the incumbents is strongly called for by the danger of competing counter-interventions, the need to permit pre-insurgency assistance to the widely recognized government coupled with the problem of ascertaining the insurgency threshold, the need to preserve the Article 51 right of collective defense against an armed attack, and the greater danger to world order in providing assistance to insurgents.

A PROHIBITION OF PARTICIPATION IN TACTICAL OPERATIONS

In recent articles in the *Columbia*[267] and *Harvard Law Reviews*,[268] Professor Tom Farer has suggested a "flat prohibition of participation in tactical operations, either openly or through the medium of advisors or volunteers"[269] as a single rule for the control of intervention in internal conflict. Under this rule Farer

---

266. See the discussion of the type IV (f) and VI (c) claims.
267. Farer, *Intervention in Civil Wars: A Modest Proposal*, 67 COL. L. REV. 266 (1967).
268. Farer, *supra* note 254.   269. Farer, *supra* note 267, at 275.

postulates that all military assistance is permissible except assistance involving the personnel of the assisting state in combat.[270]

Farer's proposal is an imaginative departure and has a number of advantages over the traditional and neutral non-intervention standards. Perhaps the most important advantages are relative ease of detection of violation and relative neutrality between contending factions. Other important underpinnings of the proposal relate to the greater danger of tactical assistance. Thus Farer cautions that the commitment of troops to tactical operations may psychologically commit an assisting state and convert an indigenous struggle for control of internal authority structures "into a defense of international law."[271] He also points out that foreign casualties occasioned by external participation in tactical operations may increase the likelihood of escalation[272] and that foreign participation in tactical operations may greatly increase the physical and cultural damage to the society in which the conflict occurs.[273] All of these factors suggest that tactical assistance should have a special burden in contexts in which they may be operative. Farer's approach is also noteworthy in that it is premised on an explicit statement of his understanding of community policies and a good identification of the core problem of intervention. Reasons given for concentrating on military assistance are that it has the most intense impact on the community policies at stake and offers a broader community consensus for regulation.

Despite these strong points, however, Farer's proposal is fatally deficient and if adopted as a single standard for the control of military intervention would be a serious regression. It is fatally deficient in that it is too permissive in legitimating some forms of serious military intervention not involving participation in tactical

270. The crucial distinction is the possibility of combat; the rule would prohibit any entry by foreign personnel into areas in which both incumbent and rebel units were known to be active. A foreign power would, on the other hand, be legally free to provide any type or amount of aid other than that which would be at all likely to involve its personnel in combat.
Farer, *supra* note 254, at 532.
271. Farer, *supra* note 254, at 532.
272. Farer, *supra* note 254, at 532-33.
273. Farer, *supra* note 254, at 535.

operations now widely regarded as unlawful. As a result, it is unlikely to receive wide acceptance. The proposal also seems questionable in that it condemns some relatively benign forms of intervention, such as non-authority-oriented intervention, simply because they involve participation in tactical operations. Moreover, it seems heavily dependent on several questionable assumptions about its acceptability, the nature of process criteria for effective legal rules, and the outcome of internal conflict absent external participation in tactical operations. Finally, just as is true of the traditional and neutral non-intervention standards, the Farer proposal fails to provide criteria for appraisal of the full range of intervention claims and fails to focus on institutional machinery for control.

The first deficiency, that the test is too permissive in legitimating some forms of intervention seriously threatening community policies, is the most serious. Examples of interventions which would be permissible under the proposal because not involving participation in tactical operations, and which nevertheless seem to seriously threaten community policies, include: the deliberate initiation by Hanoi and Peking of a rebellion in Thailand; French military assistance to the secessionist Biafran regime; the indirect United States invasion of Cuba at the Bay of Pigs by training, supplying, and instigating Cuban exiles (there may have been minimal U.S. participation in tactical operations); Cuban provisioning of communist rebels in Venezuela; Chinese training of communist rebels in Indian border areas; Saudi Arabian assistance to the Royalists in Yemen; and Arab and Soviet assistance to Palestinian refugees in guerrilla attacks on Israel. The rule would also legitimate hypothetical West German training and supplying of East German or Czechoslovakian insurgents, United States provisioning of Hungarian freedom fighters, Taiwanese training and provisioning of refugee mainland Chinese for guerrilla operations on the mainland, and North Korean instigation of guerrilla operations in South Korea utilizing native South Koreans trained in the north. Regardless of the success or failure of such intervention attempts, they would certainly pose a serious threat to minimum public order. Why should the international community ignore the external encouragement of guerrilla operations or terrorist murder squads as an instrument of national policy? A little reflection shows that some of these interventions even pose a threat of nuclear confrontation. It is also significant that these activities would be characterized as aggression under the most widely used tests for aggression,[274] and that they would be regarded as impermissible under every major non-intervention standard except Professor Farer's. That Professor Farer would regard these activities as permissible suggests a serious insensitivity to minimum public order. And if he is really covertly seeking to promote greater fluidity so that popular rebellions will succeed, he should be careful lest he promote too much fluidity at the cost of success for unpopular foreign-inspired insurgencies and a dangerous increase in the number of violent conflicts.

A second and lesser difficulty with Professor Farer's proposal is that it is too restrictive in condemning interventions simply because they involve participation in tactical operations. For example, if humanitarian intervention for the prevention of gross abuse

---

274. See M. McDOUGAL & F. FELICIANO, LAW AND MINIMUM WORLD PUBLIC ORDER 143-48 (1961). Professor Farer's proposal would also legitimate activities proscribed by both the Soviet and United States draft definitions of aggression currently before the United Nations Special Committee on the Question of Defining Aggression. The Soviet draft definition of aggression provides:

> The use by a State of armed force by sending armed bands, mercenaries, terrorists or saboteurs to the territory of another State and engagement in other forms of subversive activity involving the use of armed force with the aim of promoting an internal upheaval in another State or a reversal of policy in favour of the aggressor shall be considered an act of indirect aggression.

Report of the Special Committee on the Question of Defining Aggression, 24 U.N. GAOR, Supp. 20, at 4, 5, U.N. Doc. A/7620 (1969) [Section 2 (C)]. The six-power draft jointly sponsored by the United States provides:

> The uses of force which may constitute aggression include . . . :
> (6) organizing, supporting or directing armed bands or irregular or volunteer forces that make incursions or infiltrate into another State;
> (7) organizing, supporting or directing violent civil strife or acts of terrorism in another State; or
> (8) organizing, supporting or directing subversive activities aimed at the violent overthrow of the Government of another State.

Id. at 8, 9 (Section IV).

261

of human rights is ever permissible, it seems likely that it will usually need to be effectuated by the regular military units of a foreign power participating in tactical operations in the rescue or protection effort (or at least participating in a zone in which there is a substantial possibility of combat). Although this is not the core problem which Farer has addressed, he does not make clear whether his rule is intended to apply to such situations.

Another situation in which I believe Farer's rule to be too restrictive is intervention on invitation for the purpose of controlling non-authority-oriented internal disorders. An example is the Tanganyika disorder in 1964 in which the British responded to President Julius Nyerere's request for assistance by landing 500 British Royal Commandos. Though casualties were minimal, I suppose that the British participated in tactical operations (or a zone of combat) at least as meaningfully as did the United States marines in Lebanon who were greeted on the beaches by Coca-Cola salesmen.[275] Yet the British assistance was generally accepted in the United Nations and did not seem to compromise community values.

Perhaps the most important context in which the Farer rule may be too restrictive is in providing military assistance to a widely recognized government to offset impermissible external assistance provided to insurgents. In this counter-intervention context, Farer's point, that the commitment of regular troops to tactical operations may psychologically commit a nation to conflict and increase the chances of escalation, is a good one. His concern with the level of destruction within the entity undergoing internal conflict is also important, as the decision to commit foreign forces to tactical operations may well intensify the destructiveness of the conflict. Both the Spanish Civil War and the Vietnam war illustrate this. But if an insurgency in its initiation and continuation simply amounts to a covert armed attack, it would seem a questionable limitation of the defensive right in Article 51 of the Charter to prohibit defensive assistance amounting to participation in tactical operations. Farer is probably right that if a government is viable, most of the time such tactical assistance should not be necessary. But I am not convinced that that is al-

275. See R. BARNET, INTERVENTION AND REVOLUTION 268 (1968).

ways the case, as, for example, when an entity is an economically poor nation with only small internal security forces, or a newer nation which has not yet had an opportunity to build up an experienced army. Under such conditions it does not seem implausible that an insurgent minority with foreign sanctuary and an unlimited draw on foreign training and supply could bring down a more broadly representative government which is slow to respond in seeking or obtaining foreign assistance. If that is the case, a later infusion of foreign troops may sometimes be the only way to protect the more representative government against foreign sponsorship of a less representative insurgent. Vietnam seems to me to have some of the elements of such a case. Certainly during the early stages of the conflict the South Vietnamese army was poorly trained and equipped, and many observers have reported that the situation had deteriorated badly before the magnitude of the insurgency was officially recognized and greater United States assistance was triggered.[276] More importantly, if counter-intervention is adequately to preserve defensive rights it would seem necessary to recognize explicitly a right to proportional counter participation in tactical operations whenever external assistance to insurgents amounts to participation in tactical operations. Farer does not indicate whether his proposal is intended to include such a reciprocity exception.

In addition to being too permissive for some interventions and too restrictive for others, Farer's approach to the problem of control of intervention is not the most useful for clarifying problems in achieving control in different intervention situations. Non-authority-oriented interventions, anti-colonial wars, wars of secession, indigenous conflicts for control of internal authority structures, external imposition of authority structures, and cold-war divided nation conflicts reflect the great diversity in intervention situations. Clarification of the problem of control of intervention requires recognition of this diversity and the exploration of conditioning factors and policies at stake in each different context. Failure to deal explicitly with this diversity is a principal reason that Farer's proposal is frequently not policy responsive.

The Farer proposal also seems heavily dependent on several

276. See, *e.g.*, A. Schlesinger, The Bitter Heritage 15-16, 19, 20-31 (1966).

questionable assumptions. The first is an explicit assumption about the acceptability of the proposal.[277] Yet it was not followed by Germany or Italy in the Spanish Civil War, by the Soviets in Hungary or Czechoslovakia, by Britain in Tanganyika or Malaya, by Cuba in Bolivia, by North Vietnam in Laos and South Vietnam, by Egypt in Yemen, and by the United States in Lebanon, the Dominican Republic, and Vietnam. This list suggests that nations which correctly or incorrectly perceive that they have the military capability will intervene to the point of participation in tactical operations when they feel that their vital interests are at stake or when they feel the risk is small. There is little in the international system to suggest that this will not continue to be the case. Moreover, the widespread community concern with intervention, as evidenced by Latin American sensitivities embodied in the sweeping Article 18 of the Revised Charter of the OAS, also suggests that the free-wheeling Farer proposal will not be widely accepted. Even the Soviets and militantly anti-colonial powers are likely to reject the proposal as too sweeping. Since the proposal is less restrictive than the neutral non-intervention standard it may in fact more often coincide with the generally anarchic state practice than does the neutral non-intervention standard. Nevertheless, this hardly seems a very persuasive argument for its adoption.

A second questionable assumption which Farer makes is in overemphasizing the weight accorded certainty at the expense of policy effectiveness as a criterion in selecting a standard for the control of intervention.[278] Definiteness of standard and ease of detection of violation are certainly important criteria for rule selection, and it is probably easier to identify serious violations under Farer's test. But the certainty of Farer's test can be easily overstated in a setting which by its nature encourages adversary interpretation of the facts. It is worth remembering that despite substantial evidence there is still considerable controversy about

277. Farer, *supra* note 267, at 271, 276-78.
278. See Farer, *supra* note 267, at 271, 275-79; Farer, *supra* note 254, at 522-26, 541. "A sacrifice of normative flexibility seems required in order to facilitate the always onerous task of effective legal characterization of state behavior." Farer, *supra* note 254, at 541.

whether regular North Vietnamese troops were engaged in tactical operations in South Vietnam prior to the commencement of regular bombing of the north in February, 1965. There is even greater uncertainty as to the timing and role of native North Vietnamese cadres in participation in tactical operations in the south. How many cadres must participate and in what capacity to violate the rule or to justify counter-intervention by participation in tactical operations? I am suggesting that though the rule ranks fairly high in enabling detection of violation, the covert nature of insurgent operations in an adversary setting (and sometimes of government operations as well) still leaves a not inconsiderable fact-finding and disclosure problem. Moreover, though Farer's test scores high on certainty, it frequently rates an unsatisfactory on policy effectiveness. Yet certainly the most important process criterion for rule selection is policy effectiveness with respect to self-determination, minimum human rights, and minimum public order. Out of concern with these policies we rightly reject an intervention standard which says that intervention is always permissible, even though such a standard is more certain and may reflect the actual practice of states to a greater degree than Farer's proposal. Felix Cohen has long since shown that the more certain rule of awarding a newborn mule to the first roper is an insufficient reason for adopting the first roper test as the legal rule of ownership.[279] Fortunately, the choice among norms of intervention is not, as Farer seems to suppose, an either-or choice between *ad hoc* characterization offering little guidance and his proposed test.[280] Careful delineation of the major intervention claims, with development of a few policy effective standards, is another alternative which, though it may not yield rules as certain as Farer's, may be considerably more policy responsive at a not intolerable cost in definiteness of application.

A third questionable assumption which Farer makes is that

any government which enjoys significant support from substantial sections of the populace will defeat any insurgency

279. See Cohen, *Dialogue on Private Property*, 9 RUTGERS L. REV. 357, 367 (1954).
280. See Farer, *supra* note 254, at 522-36.

if it has an unlimited draw on material and foreign training facilities for its officers and administrators.[281]

To be complete Farer should add that to support his proposal this must also be so where the insurgents have an unlimited draw on material and foreign training facilities for their officers and administrators and enjoy foreign sanctuary for their bases and combat missions. Phrased completely, the assumption is that a representative government with external assistance will always win in a conflict with insurgent forces with external assistance as long as all assistance to both sides is below the "participation in tactical operations" threshold. Farer supports this critical assumption as an "empirical conclusion" based on the outcomes of the "insurgencies in Greece, Colombia, Venezuela, Peru, the Philippines, and Burma."[282] Aside from the fact that in none of these insurgencies did the insurgents enjoy an unlimited draw on material and foreign training plus foreign sanctuary (Greece came closest to it but was still a long way from the kind of external assistance that might have been rendered to the insurgents if Stalin had clearly supported them),[283] to generalize about all possible insurgencies from these six is quite a leap of faith. The assumption seems questionable in situations where a country has only a small security force, where a country is newly independent and has not yet built up an efficient military, and where the insurgent training and build-up catches the government by surprise and there is not time for an effective training and assistance program to begin to pay off on the government side. Vietnam has demonstrated that there is no such thing as an instant army, regardless of unlimited draw on foreign dollars and training facilities.

Though government forces often have a number of inherent advantages over insurgents, such as ability to employ armor and air power, to secure resupply through regular channels, and to control the administrative and patronage apparatus, it is also pertinent to advert to some of the disadvantages. These include

281. Farer, *supra* note 267, at 277.
282. Farer, *supra* note 267, at 277.
283. See R. BARNET, *supra* note 275, at 110-12, 121. Barnet quotes Stalin as telling the Yugoslav Vice-Premier: "The uprising in Greece must be stopped, and as quickly as possible." R. BARNET, *supra* note 275, at 121.

the responsibility of the government to maintain essential services throughout the society, and the need for a force ratio for successful counter-insurgency operations of at least ten to one. Terrorist activities in Uruguay illustrate this difficulty. Guerrilla activities there have been estimated to be the work of about 1,000 well organized guerrillas in a population of more than 2.5 million; yet they have been able to pose a significant threat to the stability of democratic processes in that militarily weak country.[284] The Uruguayan government is said to have only one police station for every 400 square miles and only 200 soldiers for every 4,000 square miles.[285] Interestingly, Uruguay has a reasonably democratic government and, according to the *New York Times*, "only 6 per cent of Uruguay's voters favored Marxist-Leninist candidates in the last election in 1966. . . ."[286]

Even if Farer's assumption were accurate it is still beside the point whenever a widely recognized government is unable to secure external assistance. In such situations Farer's rule legitimates external initiation of insurgency without the check of counter-participation on the government side. In fairness to Farer's proposal, however, it seems unlikely that many widely recognized governments will be unable to secure external assistance, and if they cannot perhaps it says something about their representativeness. But in a post-Vietnam world in which being a world policeman may seem an unattractive role, the possibility of a widely recognized government's being unable to secure external assistance to combat a foreign inspired insurgency is a major flaw in Farer's argument. The problem exists in any event, but other standards do not legitimate assistance to insurgents.

Whether for these or other reasons, at a regional meeting of the American Society of International Law in March, 1969, Professor Farer indicated some "modulation" away from his proposal to a more general non-intervention standard.[287] It is to be hoped that this will be a lasting "modulation."

284. See N.Y. Times, Jan. 23, 1969, at 12, col. 4.
285. *Id.* at col. 7.   286. *Id.* at col. 8.
287. The meeting was the Regional Meeting of the American Society of International Law on *Bloc Law and Intervention*, at Tallahassee, Florida, March 27-29, 1969. "Modulation" is Professor Farer's term.

A PROHIBITION ON UNILATERAL INTERVENTION

In an influential book entitled *Intervention and Revolution*[288] Richard Barnet suggests a flat "prohibition on unilateral intervention."[289] According to Barnet, only collective intervention by the United Nations should be permissible.[290] Going a step farther, Barnet implies that his proposal is required by Articles 39-44 and 51 of the Charter.[291] There are, of course, obvious advantages to a rule prohibiting unilateral intervention. Chief among them is avoidance of the auto-interpretation problem which makes each nation the judge of its own actions. In addition, collective action not only increases the likelihood that intervention will serve community goals, but it also reduces the risk of major power involvement on opposing sides. But in spite of these substantial advantages, Barnet's suggestion is simplistic and unworkable.

A first difficulty with the suggestion is that it fails to take account of the problem of differentiating permissible military assistance programs from intervention in internal conflict. That is, it fails to provide criteria for delimiting the critical insurgency threshold above which additional assistance becomes impermissible. In a world with substantial defense interdependencies it is obviously too broad to prohibit all unilateral military assistance programs whether or not there is internal conflict. As a practical matter, then, any non-intervention standard must come to grips with this pre-insurgency threshold problem. That Barnet's suggestion fails to deal with this problem does not make it theoretically unsound, but only less useful.

A second difficulty, however, which does go to the soundness of the suggestion, is that it would prohibit unilateral counter-intervention on behalf of a widely recognized government. As has already been pointed out, the basis for the neutral non-intervention rule collapses once it is established that substantial external assistance is being supplied to one of the competing factions. It is hard to see how "the internal dynamics of revolution itself provide an important measure of the popularity of the contending forces"[292] in a situation in which one side is receiving substantial

---

288. R. Barnet, Intervention and Revolution (1968).
289. *Id.* at 280.   290. *Id.* at 278-80.   291. *Id.* at 278-79.
292. *Id.* at 280.

external assistance. Whatever validity there is in the notion of self-determination resulting from "the internal dynamics of revolution," this reason for denying assistance collapses once it is established that substantial external assistance is being provided to one of the competing factions. Similarly, if the principal reason for non-intervention is the difficulty in determining genuine self-determination and the consequent danger of self-serving claims by an intervening power, then this reason also collapses if a foreign power is already intervening. Moreover, if counter-intervention is impermissible, the suggestion may effectively deny the Article 51 defensive right in situations of covert rather than open invasion.[293] And contrary to Barnet's understanding, there is nothing in Article 51 of the Charter limiting "armed attack" to open invasions.[294] In fact, some scholars question whether self-defense under the Charter is even limited to the Article 51 right of defense against an armed attack.[295]

Professor Quincy Wright, the leading proponent of the neutral non-intervention standard, has also recently adopted the position that counter-intervention should be prohibited in the absence of collective United Nations action.[296] In the present cold-war atmosphere, however, it is completely unrealistic to rely on collective United Nations action as the sole response to impermissible intervention. Counter-intervention is one of the major claims put

293. Barnet would prohibit unilateral "foreign intervention in a civil war" but would permit "collective defense against a foreign invasion. . . ." *Id.* at 279. He fails to take account, however, of the sometimes considerable difficulty in characterizing a particular conflict as civil war or foreign invasion. A case in point is Barnet's characterization of the Vietnam War as a civil war, a characterization which many, including the writer, find unpersuasive. *Id.* at 218. This difficulty in characterization, really a difficulty in reconciling defensive rights under the Charter with the duty of non-intervention, is one of the factors suggesting preservation of the right of counter-intervention on behalf of a widely recognized government.

294. *Id.* at 278-79.

295. See authorities cited note 167 *supra*.

296. See Wright, *Non-Military Intervention*, in THE RELEVANCE OF INTERNATIONAL LAW 5, 16-17 (K. Deutsch & S. Hoffmann eds. 1968). "It would appear that illegal intervention in the domestic jurisdiction of a state should not be made the occasion for counter-intervention but should be dealt with by the United Nations as it was in the Congo." *Id.* at 16.

forth by states in justification of intervention, and Barnet's and Wright's proposal to deny it is unlikely to be widely accepted.

A third difficulty with the Barnet suggestion is that like all other single rule approaches it fails adequately to focus on the full range of intervention claims. Consequently, the suggestion seems overly restrictive with respect to non-authority-oriented interventions. Some such interventions, for example humanitarian intervention for the prevention of widespread loss of life, may actually promote community policies and may require faster action than is possible from a politically charged multi-national organization.

Barnet's proposal also seems to be premised on three questionable assumptions. The first is an assumption about the dynamics of revolution and intervention in which he seems to go far beyond even the questionable assumption made by Tom Farer. Farer postulates that a representative government with external assistance will always win in a conflict with insurgent forces with external assistance as long as all assistance to both sides is below the "participation in tactical operations" threshold.[297] Barnet, however, comes close to suggesting that if a government is representative no amount of foreign assistance to insurgents can topple it;[298] and he does say that if counter-intervention is necessary "no amount of repressive force short of wholesale murder and resettlement of the population has a chance of achieving lasting success."[299] While I agree with Barnet that the prognosis for exporting revolution where the conditions are not ripe is poor, as witnessed by the fate of Che Guevara and his band, to conclude that if a government is representative no amount of foreign assistance can topple it is absurd. It is also inconsistent with Barnet's criticism (whether right or wrong) of United States activities on behalf of insurgents in Iran and Guatemala, which according to Barnet's own account overthrew popular governments with only a minimum of foreign involvement.[300] Further, the suppression

297. See text note 281 supra.
298. See R. BARNET, supra note 288, at 280.
299. R. BARNET, supra note 288, at 280.
300. See R. BARNET, supra note 288, at 225-29 (Iran), 229-36 (Guatemala). Arbenz's [the President of Guatemala] general popularity was probably down from his peak strength in the last election, but

of the insurgents in Malaya with British assistance, and in Greece with United States assistance, demonstrates that Barnet exaggerates when he says that if counter-intervention is necessary it will only be successful if it constitutes "wholesale murder."

A second questionable assumption which seems to underlie Barnet's suggestion is an overemphasis on the present capacity of the United Nations for collective action in internal conflict. The Congo and Cyprus operations demonstrate an important United Nations capability for collective action in the control of internal conflict; but they also demonstrate just how cumbersome present United Nations machinery is for such operations.[301] The United Nations financial crisis should remind us of the precariousness of the consensus for such operations even when they seem to involve a minimum of East-West conflict.[302] In fact, the lack of agreement on the financing of major peace-keeping operations, such as ONUC and UNEF, suggests that such operations may have even less chance of approval today. In these circumstances, rather than stressing collective United Nations action, it seems more fruitful to focus on the General Assembly as an agency for authorizing or proscribing individual national actions. This is not to suggest that the potential of the United Nations for effective action should be neglected, but rather that it is important to distinguish between collective action and collective authorization, and that at the present time the strengthening of the General Assembly as an agency for community review may be particularly fruitful for internal

---

> there is no evidence that popular feeling had turned decisively against him. His downfall was the direct result of the defection of the army under the stimulus of a foreign invasion financed and directed by the United States.
>
> R. Barnet, *supra* note 288, at 235.

301. See generally A. Cox, Prospects for Peacekeeping (1967); E. Lefever, Uncertain Mandate: Politics of the U.N. Congo Operation 207-22 (1967); L. Miller, World Order and Local Disorder: The United Nations and Internal Conflicts 65-148, 201-14 (1967); R. Russell, United Nations Experience with Military Forces: Political and Legal Aspects 135-45 (Brookings Staff Paper 1964); Lefever, *The Limits of U.N. Intervention in the Third World*, 30 Review of Politics 3 (1968).

302. For a review of the problem of financing peace-keeping see L. Sohn, Cases on United Nations Law 763-818 (2d ed. rev. 1967).

conflict problems. In any event, it smacks of the unreality of the legalist tradition at its worst to overemphasize the present institutional capacity for the control of intervention.

The third questionable assumption Barnet makes is that his suggestion is a present requirement of international law.[303] As has been pointed out, nothing in the Charter definitively answers the question whether a widely recognized government may be assisted at its invitation in an internal struggle for control. Barnet cites no evidence that the framers of the Charter adverted to the problem of changing what had been widely assumed to be the traditional rule of customary international law, that a widely recognized government could be assisted at its request. Although an argument could be made that the principle of self-determination in Article 1 of the Charter requires a neutral non-intervention standard, the implication from Barnet's work that Articles 39-44 and 51 of the Charter require his rule is sheer fantasy.

MODERNIZATION AS A TOUCHSTONE

In a recent essay on the role of international law in the conflict in Yemen, Kathryn Doherty Boals suggests "a principle of modernizing legitimacy . . . [for appraising all] intervention by one society in the internal affairs of another. . . ."[304] Under this principle the sole test of legitimacy is whether "a state's intervention . . . [has] a reasonable possibility of contributing to the modernization of the society in which it . . . [takes] place."[305] Modernization, in the sense of self-sustaining economic growth and centralization of authority, does seem to be a widely shared community goal.[306] To make it the touchstone of legitimacy, how-

---

303. See R. BARNET, *supra* note 288, at 278-79.
304. K. Boals, The Role of International Law in the Internal War in Yemen: An Interpretative Essay 69, 74-75 (unpublished paper prepared for the American Society of International Law Study Group on Civil Strife, 1969).
305. *Id.* at 74. "Modernizing legitimacy" is also defined as:
   legitimacy measured in terms of the relative capacity of the contending groups to develop the consciousness, creativity, institutionalized power, and justice necessary for coping with the revolution of modernization.
   Id. at 69.
306. See Farer, *supra* note 254, at 521-22.

ever, seems both unwise and unworkable. The principal faults with the proposal are that it fails to take into account the full range of community policies at stake in intervention and that it is hopelessly uncertain in application.

Modernization may be an important aspect of self-determination, but to legitimate intervention by its effect on modernization is to run a substantial risk of validating external denial of self-determination. The referent of genuine self-determination must be the demands of the people of the entity in question. If the people prefer other values to modernization, then coercive external imposition of modernization would be a denial of self-determination. Self-determination in all of its aspects would make a more complete touchstone than modernization alone.[307] Yet because of the difficulty of determining the genuine demands of a people, and the consequent danger of self-serving claims, even self-determination as a touchstone has yielded to a non-intervention standard. This should certainly be the case when, in addition to the uncertainty of determination, the touchstone itself may deny self-determination. For the people of one entity to set themselves up as benevolent judges of the proper amount of modernization to be coercively imposed upon others smacks of the nineteenth-century paternalism which was the principal justification for colonialism.

The modernization touchstone also fails adequately to consider the policy of minimum public order. As postulated by Kathryn Boals, the principle of modernizing legitimacy would not focus on "preventing intervention as such but [on] preventing interventions which do not foster modernization."[308] In other words, as long as "intervention . . . [has] a reasonable possibility of contributing to the modernization of the society in which it . . . [takes] place,"[309] it should be permissible and perhaps even encouraged regardless of the threat to world order. Just as Tom Farer's prohibition on participation in tactical operations seems to result from preoccupation with the Vietnam war, Kathryn

307. For development of the full range of claims to self-determination see T. Mensah, Self-Determination Under United Nations' Auspices 31-44 (unpublished J.S.D. dissertation in the Yale Law Library, 1963).
308. K. Boals, *supra* note 304, at 75.
309. K. Boals, *supra* note 304, at 74.

Boals' principle of modernizing legitimacy seems to result from preoccupation with the Yemen war. But even though the Yemen war presents only a relatively small threat to world order, external intervention may well have intensified the loss of life and internal destruction. Minimum public order in all of its senses is frequently a critical policy at stake in intervention. It is only a small step from downgrading it to justify wars of modernization to downgrading it to justify cold-war claims for the purpose of imposing "democratic" or "socialist" regimes.

A second fault with the principle of modernizing legitimacy is that it is hopelessly uncertain. Assuming that modernization may be given a specific meaning which will command wide support, an assumption not without considerable doubt, how does one evaluate the impact on modernization of a particular intervention? For example, which way does modernization cut in Algeria, the Congo, the Dominican Republic, Lebanon, Nigeria, Rhodesia, and Vietnam? Might modernization sometimes result simply from the cultural shock attendant on massive military intervention in a quasi-feudal society regardless of the faction supported? Is the choice of one or another competing faction ever a sufficiently significant cause of modernization to justify a test of modernizing legitimacy? In view of these and other uncertainties, the danger of self-serving claims that an intervention promotes modernization seems too great to support a modernization test.

SUMMARY OF TENTATIVE RECOMMENDATIONS

Intervention is truly a monochromatic term for a polychromatic reality.[310] Because of this diversity, recommendations for the control of intervention must provide a technique for adequately focusing on the wide range of issues. As a tentative classification of issues concerning foreign participation in internal conflict, it is recommended that intervention be divided into six basic situations, each situation in turn being divided into more specific claims. The six situations are: type I situations, claims not relating to authority structures; type II situations, claims relating to anti-colonial wars; type III situations, claims relating to wars of secession; type IV situations, claims relating to indigenous conflict for

310. See Chapter III.

control of internal authority structures; type V situations, claims relating to the use of external force for imposition of internal authority structures; and type VI situations, claims relating to cold-war divided nation conflicts. These six situations are then further divided into the twenty-one more specific claims developed in the course of this chapter.

This classification of issues concerning foreign participation in internal conflict into six basic situations and twenty-one claims is not intended as a slot machine for mechanical solution of intervention problems. It is offered instead as a useful technique for contextually identifying like cases and for formulating standards for appraisal. The complexity of intervention is a complexity of the real world. The suggested classification merely reflects that complexity in the interest of obtaining a useful handle on it. As Professors McDougal and Feliciano point out, a principal task in clarifying policy choice is

> that of presenting to the focus of attention of the various officials who must reach a decision about the lawfulness or unlawfulness of coercion, the different variable factors and policies that, in differing contexts and under community perspectives, rationally bear upon their decisions. . . .[311]

Recommendations for control must also take into account that the institutional framework for international conflict management is gravely unresponsive to the problems of control of intervention in internal conflict. The United Nations was structured in response chiefly to conventional aggression, and even that structure has in large measure gone unimplemented. Recommendations for control must take this institutional weakness into account and should achieve a balance of emphasis between recommendations for appraisal and recommendations for institutional improvement.

RECOMMENDATIONS FOR THE APPRAISAL OF INTERVENTION

The need for community review of intervention claims and for institutional mechanisms for change suggest that both the General Assembly and the Security Council should be recognized as hav-

311. M. McDougal & F. Feliciano, *supra* note 274, at 151.

ing authority to deal with claims of unauthorized intervention or of denial of self-determination. There is a danger of abuse in such centralized authority, particularly in view of a General Assembly which sometimes demonstrates a disturbing schizophrenia in dealing with claims of Western colonialism in Asia and Africa and communist colonialism in Eastern Europe. Unless the *status quo* is to be frozen, however, the alternative seems to be preservation of a more dangerous unilateral competence. In practice, UN action is likely only in cases of wide community agreement shared by the superpowers, and examples to date, such as the Rhodesia and South-West Africa resolutions, have borne this out. The absence of United Nations action in the Vietnam War, where the superpowers were on opposing sides, demonstrates the reverse side of the coin. The danger of abuse of power, though, does suggest that for either authorizing or proscribing interventions a resolution specifically concerned with use of force should be required.

In the absence of UN action, non-participation should be the basic standard for appraisal of intervention in authority-oriented internal conflict. That is, it should be impermissible to intervene for the purpose of maintaining or altering authority structures in another state. This standard, however, must be qualified by the need to take account of pre-insurgency assistance to a widely recognized government and by the need to permit counter-intervention on behalf of a widely recognized government. In addition, it seems justifiable in the present institutionally weak system to qualify the non-participation standard to sometimes permit carefully safeguarded non-partisan participation for the purpose of restoring orderly processes of self-determination.

For an intervention standard to be acceptable and workable it must permit assistance to a widely recognized government prior to insurgency. Nations have legitimate defense interdependencies against external attack, and in the absence of internal conflict, assistance to a widely recognized government is clearly permissible. If internal conflict is minor or is non-authority-oriented, this privilege of external assistance to the government should be continued. Such assistance may enable a militarily weak state to suppress a powerful band of bandits or to control non-authority-oriented rioting. Moreover, since low-level internal violence is endemic in many third world nations, it would be unworkable to require termination of assistance on every occasion of internal violence. A prerequisite of a workable non-participation standard, then, is criteria for determining the threshold of internal conflict requiring non-participation.

In the recommendations which follow, four criteria for determining the non-participation threshold are suggested. Because it is a necessary condition, the first criterion deserves particular attention. It is that "the internal conflict must be an authority-oriented conflict aimed at the overthrow of the recognized government and its replacement by a political organization controlled by the insurgents." This means that assistance may be provided at the request of a widely recognized government to suppress a bandit group or to quell a non-authority-oriented internal disorder as in the Tanganyika, Uganda, Kenya disorders of 1964. This criterion emphasizes the policy choice that the basic non-participation standard should be limited to authority-oriented internal conflict.

After a conflict becomes an insurgency requiring non-participation, the danger that cessation of assistance to the government may work as an intervention on behalf of insurgents suggests that it should be permissible to continue pre-insurgency levels of assistance.

The second qualification of the basic non-participation standard is that assistance to a widely recognized government should be permissible to offset impermissible assistance to insurgents. If the principal reason for the non-participation standard is the difficulty of determining genuine self-determination, with a resulting preference for allowing indigenous conflict to run its course, the force of the standard collapses if impermissible foreign assistance is already being supplied to insurgents. Allowing counter-intervention on behalf of a widely recognized government and not on behalf of insurgents does not treat the competing factions equally, but this lapse of neutrality in favor of the incumbents is strongly called for by the danger of competing counter-interventions, the permissibility of pre-insurgency assistance to the widely recognized government, the need to preserve the right of collective defense against an armed attack, and the generally greater threat to world order of assistance to insurgents.

Counter-intervention on behalf of a widely recognized government should be comparable to the impermissible assistance being supplied to insurgents. That is, the political and military effect of the offsetting assistance should be proportional, taking into account the balance of forces required in an insurgent conflict and the difficulty of estimating covert assistance to insurgents. In addition, counter-intervention should be restricted to the territory of the state undergoing internal conflict unless the impermissible assistance to insurgents is so substantial as to amount to an armed attack under Article 51 of the Charter. This recommendation rejects both Professor Falk's proposal that it is always impermissible to reply against the territory of a covertly attacking state and the view that self-defense under the Charter is not restricted to defense against an armed attack. As an absolute, Professor Falk's proposal is an unwarranted restriction on the right of individual and collective defense. And not to restrict the right of reply against the territory of an assisting state to responses against an armed attack would be much too open-ended for the frequently ambiguous internal war context. Factors which are important in determining whether impermissible assistance to insurgents is so substantial as to constitute an armed attack include the degree of external initiation, whether intervention is motivated by an objective of territorial expansion, and the amount and kind of external support, particularly the involvement of foreign personnel in tactical operations.

The third qualification to the basic non-participation standard would sometimes permit non-partisan participation for the purpose of restoring orderly processes of self-determination in conflicts involving a sudden breakdown of order. This qualification is intended to differentiate situations in which intervention in authority-oriented conflict is not rendered on behalf of a particular faction but is instead a non-partisan operation intended to substitute free elections or negotiated settlement for continued conflict. Because of the difficulty in maintaining neutrality and the consequent danger of self-serving claims by a participating power, the justification for this third qualification is not as clear as that for the first two. Nevertheless, some such interventions may promote community policies by ending internal conflict and restoring orderly processes of self-determination, and if carefully safeguarded an exception seems justified.

If none of these three qualifications is present, it should be impermissible to assist any faction in an authority-oriented internal conflict or to otherwise use the military instrument against another state for the purpose of affecting authority structures. Prohibited assistance should include economic as well as military aid and outright arms sales as well as grants or sales on long-term credit. Arguably, outright sales of military armaments should not be considered assistance. But the difficulty of distinguishing outright sales from various credit arrangements, the desirability of minimizing the level of internal violence, and the reciprocity of the non-participation standard suggest that even outright sales should be prohibited.

In addition to the three qualifications to the basic non-participation standard, non-authority-oriented intervention for the protection of human rights should sometimes be permissible. Of course, if such intervention is at the request of a widely recognized government prior to insurgency it is permissible under the first exception to the non-participation standard, at least to the same extent as other pre-insurgency assistance. But even if made in other circumstances, the importance of the protection of fundamental human rights, the lack of adequate institutional protection for human rights, and the small threat to community policies of most such interventions suggest that if carefully safeguarded such interventions should be permissible. There is strong recent support from the scholarly community for the continued validity of such a limited right of humanitarian intervention.[312]

312. See McDougal & Reisman, *Response by Professors McDougal and Reisman*, 3 INT'L LAWYER 438, 444 (1969); Lillich, *Forcible Self-Help by States to Protect Human Rights*, 53 IOWA L. REV. 325 (1967); R. Lillich, Intervention to Protect Human Rights (unpublished paper presented at a Regional Meeting of the American Society of International Law at Queen's University on November 22-23, 1968).

The following three recommendations summarize these normative suggestions. Although they are personal policy recommendations for the appraisal of intervention, in each case there are strong community expectations supporting them. In fact, with the possible exception of the qualification for non-partisan participation in authority-oriented conflict, a good case can be made that these recommendations summarize the present international law of non-intervention in internal conflict as well as present community consensus permits.

I. An intervention in internal conflict is permissible if specifically authorized by the General Assembly or Security Council, even though in the absence of such authorization it would be impermissible. Conversely, if the General Assembly or Security Council specifically calls for cessation of a particular intervention, continuation is impermissible even though in the absence of such prohibition it would be permissible.

II. It is impermissible to assist a faction engaged in any type of authority-oriented internal conflict or to use the military instrument in the territory of another state for the purpose of maintaining or altering authority structures. The three qualifications to this basic non-intervention standard are:

(A) Assistance to a widely recognized government is permissible prior to insurgency. After a conflict becomes an insurgency, it is impermissible to increase but permissible to continue the pre-insurgency level of assistance. Criteria for determining insurgency, for this purpose of permitting pre-insurgency assistance, include:

  (1) that the internal conflict must be an authority-oriented conflict aimed at the overthrow of the recognized government and its replacement by a political organization controlled by the insurgents;

  (2) that the recognized government is obliged to make continuing use of most of its regular military forces against the insurgents, or a substantial segment of its regular military forces have ceased to accept orders;

     (3) that the insurgents effectively prevent the recognized government from exercising continuing governmental authority over a significant percentage of the population; and

     (4) that a significant percentage of the population supports the insurgent movement, as evidenced by military or supply assistance to the insurgents, general strikes, or other actions.

(B) Assistance to a widely recognized government is permissible to offset impermissible assistance to insurgents; if assistance to insurgents or the use of the military instrument against another state constitutes an armed attack within the meaning of Article 51 of the Charter, it is permissible to reply proportionally against the territory of the attacking state.

(C) The use of the military instrument in the territory of another state for the purpose of restoring orderly processes of self-determination in an authority-oriented conflict involving a sudden breakdown of order is permissible if it meets the following conditions:

     (1) a genuine invitation by the widely recognized government, or, if there is none, by a major faction;

     (2) relative neutrality among factions, with particular attention to neutrality in military operations;

     (3) immediate initiation of and compliance with the decision machinery of appropriate regional organizations;

     (4) immediate full reporting to the Security Council and compliance with United Nations determinations;

     (5) a prompt disengagement, consistent with the purpose of the action; and

     (6) an outcome consistent with self-determination. Such an outcome is one based on internationally observed elections in which all factions are allowed freely to participate on an equal

basis, which is freely accepted by all major competing factions, or which is endorsed by the United Nations.

III. Non-authority-oriented intervention for the protection of human rights may sometimes be permissible. Criteria for determining legitimacy include:

(A) an immediate and extensive threat to fundamental human rights, particularly a threat of widespread loss of human life;

(B) a proportional use of force which does not threaten greater destruction of values than the human rights at stake;

(C) a minimal effect on authority structures;

(D) a prompt disengagement, consistent with the purpose of the action;

(E) immediate full reporting to the Security Council and appropriate regional organizations.

At a time when the United Nations is concerned with the problem of defining aggression,[313] the activities termed "impermissible" in these recommendations may be conceptualized as "aggression." There seems to be little advantage in using the aggression terminology, however, and it may even obscure the consequences of classification.

RECOMMENDATIONS FOR INSTITUTIONAL IMPROVEMENT

The history of efforts at international conflict management shows that both normative and institutional developments are important for progress. It is essential to have standards for appraisal as well as institutional mechanisms for their effectuation. Existing international organizations, however, are largely a re-

313. In December, 1967, "noting that there is still no generally recognized definition of aggression," the General Assembly passed a resolution establishing a thirty-five member Special Committee on the Question of Defining Aggression. The Special Committee has issued several reports and is currently considering a number of draft definitions of aggression. See G.A. Res. 2330, 22 U.N. GAOR, Supp. 16, at 84-85, U.N. Doc. A/6716 (1967); Report of the Special Committee on the Question of Defining Aggression, 23 U.N. GAOR, Agenda Item No. 86, U.N. Doc. A/7185/Rev.1 (1968); Report of the Special Committee on the Question of Defining Aggression, 24 U.N. GAOR, Supp. 20, U.N. Doc. A/7620 (1969).

sponse to conventional aggression and are poorly equipped for the control of intervention in internal conflict. Major institutional needs include the strengthening of collective community decision-processes for authorizing needed change and for responding to claims of unauthorized coercion, development of a reliable observation and disclosure capability, measures for control of the military assistance race, mechanisms for settlement of internal conflict in early, more tractable stages, and a strengthening of the role of international law in national decision-processes.

In partial response to these institutional weaknesses, it is recommended that the General Assembly be strengthened as an agency for community review of intervention, that the United States should sponsor a multilateral treaty for the reporting of military assistance, that the General Assembly should establish a permanent observation and disclosure agency available to any state which wishes to use it for the investigation of intervention in internal conflict, and that other institutional changes in the international constitutive process, particularly machinery for collective recognition, a UN emergency relief force, and revision of conventions on the conduct of war, should be explored. It is also recommended, with respect to the domestic constitutive process, that the Legal Adviser of the Department of State be upgraded to Under Secretary of State for International Legal Affairs and made a permanent member of the National Security Council.

The recommendation that the General Assembly should be strengthened as an agency for community review of intervention is interrelated with the first recommendation for the appraisal of intervention. Although there is a danger of abuse in strengthening General Assembly competence, the danger seems slight in comparison with the normless present in which individual states are asserting unilateral competence to take action to effectuate preferred change. Moreover, General Assembly action seems unlikely in the absence of wide community agreement shared by the superpowers. Recognition that General Assembly authority extends to authorizing as well as proscribing intervention is simply recognition of an authority already exercised by the Assembly in the 1967-68 Rhodesia, South Africa, South-West Africa, and Portuguese territories resolutions. Such a General Assembly authorizing competence is not constitutionally clear under the Charter, particularly in other than colonial situations, but on balance the precedents seem to support it.

International reporting of military assistance would develop community awareness of the magnitude of the military assistance race, expose interventionary activities, assist in fact appraisal, serve as an early-warning device for initiating settlement efforts in the early, more easily manageable stages of internal conflict, and assist in avoiding miscalculations of intention. Despite these benefits of reporting, however, there is no international machinery for reporting military assistance at the present time. The best procedure for implementation of such reporting machinery seems to be a multilateral treaty endorsed by the General Assembly. Such a procedure would provide an opportunity for nations principally concerned to shape the final agreement and would assure greater likelihood of compliance. Though some nations might refuse to sign such a treaty or might continue secret military assistance, the common interest of the major powers in controlling the military assistance race, the pressure of world opinion on non-complying states once some nations begin to report, and the reduction of the credibility gap by open reporting suggest that such a treaty would have a reasonable chance of success.

For the most part, disputes underlying internal conflict are competitive authority struggles which cannot be settled by submission to international fact-finding. There is, however, a real need for international observation and disclosure to establish a basis for appraisal and to deter impermissible assistance by exposure. Although existing international machinery has been useful in this regard, there is a need for new machinery, relatively insulated from political pressure and available to any state seeking to invoke it. One possibility is a permanent observation and disclosure agency available on a voluntary basis to any state which wishes to use it for the investigation of an alleged armed attack or intervention in internal conflict. Such an agency would be limited solely to the observation and disclosure of facts, would be composed of a diplomatically protected staff from neutral countries, and would be established and supervised by the General Assembly.

With regard to institutional changes in the national constitutive process, it is recommended that the office of Legal Adviser of the Department of State be upgraded to Under Secretary of State for International Legal Affairs and that the new Under Secretary be made a permanent *ex officio* member of the National Security Council. This recommendation is intended to systematically introduce an international law perspective into the foreign policy planning process. Although political, economic, and military considerations are now introduced in a score of more or less institutionalized ways, there is no systematic way in which international law is taken into account. By making the new Under Secretary a member of the National Security Council, the principal foreign policy advisory agency, and by specifying in the enabling act that one of his principal duties is to provide impartial advice on the basis of international law, it is hoped that the strength of the international law tradition can also be brought to bear on foreign policy planning.

The following five recommendations summarize these suggestions for improvement in the international and domestic constitutive processes. They are not advanced as panaceas for the control of intervention; new agencies and procedures are not likely to significantly alter underlying political realities. They are advanced, however, as suggestions which offer both real promise for improvement and a reasonable chance for implementation.

I. The General Assembly should be strengthened as an agency for community review of intervention. General Assembly authority should be recognized as extending to authorizing as well as proscribing intervention.

II. The United States should take the initiative in the United Nations to sponsor a multilateral treaty for the reporting of military assistance. The scope of the treaty would be subject to negotiation but might include:

  (A) all governmental and private transfers of military armaments to another country and the terms of the transfer —grant, sale, sale on credit, etc.;
  (B). the transfer of military or para-military personnel from one country to another;

(C) foreign military training and assistance missions;

(D) domestic military training programs for foreign nationals;

(E) foreign para-military groups enjoying sanctuary.

III. The General Assembly should establish a permanent observation and disclosure agency available to any state which wishes to use it for the investigation of armed attack or intervention in internal conflict. Such an agency would be limited to observation and disclosure of facts, would be purely voluntary, and would be under the supervision of the General Assembly.

IV. Additional changes in the international constitutive process deserving study include:

(A) machinery for collective recognition;

(B) a permanent UN emergency relief force to assist victims of natural and political disasters;

(C) revision of conventions on the laws of war, the protection of civilians, and the treatment of prisoners of war for greater responsiveness to internal conflict.

V. As a recommendation for improvement of the national constitutive process, the office of Legal Adviser of the Department of State should be upgraded to Under Secretary of State for International Legal Affairs, and the new Under Secretary should be made a permanent *ex officio* member of the National Security Council. The statutory description of the office should indicate that a principal duty of the new Under Secretary is to participate in the foreign-policy planning process and to provide impartial advice on the basis of international law to both the Secretary of State and the National Security Council.

CHAPTER V

The Elephant Misperceived:
Intervention and American Foreign Policy*

THE vigorous reexamination of American foreign policy triggered by the Vietnam War has thrust forward two competing·models of American intervention since World War II. The first model pictures American intervention as a necessary response to an expansionist and centrally directed communist drive for control of the third world. According to this model, American counter-intervention has served to contain aggressive communist regimes, to prevent the domino-like fall of third world countries, and to meet the newest strategy of communist aggression—the war of national liberation. The second model is radically different. It pictures American intervention as part of a global campaign to crush needed revolutionary change in dictatorial and quasi-feudal societies. America is seen as the guardian of the *status quo* acting much as a traditional imperialist power to preserve and extend its military and economic interests. The communist threat central to the first model is deemphasized as fragmented, largely rhetorical, and perhaps in any event beneficial for the modernization of underdeveloped societies. Although it might be difficult to cage and exhibit a pure representative of either camp, each serves to illustrate the core of a widely held view of American foreign policy.

In *Intervention and Revolution*, Richard Barnet emerges as a leading true believer of the second camp. The surprising endorsement of Barnet's thesis by Karl Hess, the Goldwater speechwriter who coined the slogan "extremism in the defense of liberty is no vice,"[1] suggests that in a post-Vietnam world this second camp

---

* This Chapter was originally published as a review of Richard J. Barnet's influential book *Intervention and Revolution: The United States in the Third World* (1968). Richard J. Barnet is the Co-Director of the Institute for Policy Studies, Washington, D.C.

1. Acceptance speech by Senator Goldwater, Republican Nat'l Convention, July 16, 1964, in N.Y. Times, July 17, 1964, at 10, col. 8.

may have wide appeal to Americans of differing persuasions.[2] But like the blind men who described an elephant to each other as resembling either a tree or a snake depending on whether they felt the elephant's leg or his trunk, both camps misperceive a more complex reality. Thus, despite an engaging literary style and occasional flashes of genuine perception, Barnet's book is rather more a polemical overstatement than a searching analysis of the real shortcomings of American foreign policy. If a reflex anticommunism has been a poor guide for national action, it does not follow, as Barnet suggests, that the United States is the greatest force of repression in the world,[3] bent on "a crusade against revolution,"[4] or that it acts as an imperialist power "to exploit the rest of mankind."[5]

In part one of *Intervention and Revolution*, Barnet argues that the principal ideological clash in American foreign policy is no longer between the United States and the Soviet Union (which he likens to the ideological competition between Ford and General Motors) but between the "National-Security Managers" and "the Revolutionaries who guide insurgent movements."[6] According to Barnet, the national security managers' perception of communist revolution as necessarily imported by agents of a foreign power leads them to attempt to contain "the master planners of the Kremlin and Peking"[7] by suppressing revolution and radical social change wherever it occurs in the third world. The revolutionary, on the other hand, sees the underdevelopment of his society as a product of internal and external exploitation with the United States as the principal exploiter.

Barnet convincingly demonstrates that for the most part revolutionaries are indigenous nationals, justly or unjustly aggrieved by a ruling elite, and that revolutions succeed or fail because of local conditions rather than a global scheme for the export of revolution. In keeping with this thesis, he focuses on Soviet and Chinese efforts to purvey revolution and concludes that such

2. See the review of *Intervention and Revolution* by Karl Hess in The Washington Post, Jan. 7, 1969, at B4, col. 3.
3. See R. BARNET, INTERVENTION AND REVOLUTION: THE UNITED STATES IN THE THIRD WORLD 14-19, 34, 257 (1968).
4. *Id.* 14, 119, 276.   5. *Id.* 278.   6. *Id.* 23-24.
7. See *id.* 26-27, 48.

efforts have been principally rhetorical. The major impact of these efforts, he asserts, has been to furnish a model for successful revolutionary change. Accordingly, the national security mangers' preoccupation with the threat of centrally orchestrated communist revolution is unrealistic, arising from an amalgam of "the police idea" in American foreign policy attended by economic imperialism and the momentum of the security bureaucracy.[8]

In part two Barnet examines these propositions in the light of American interventions in Greece, Lebanon, the Dominican Republic, and Vietnam, and what he describes as "the subversion of undesirable governments" in Guatemala, Iran, Indonesia, British Guiana, and the Congo.[9] Not surprisingly, he concludes that the United States has indeed embarked on a global campaign against revolution and that American intervention has largely been counter-productive.

In a final chapter, Barnet summarizes his views of American actions toward the third world:

> The United States has sought to apply the imperial model to the postimperial world. If the earth were still a place where a relatively few governments could speak for the billions of inhabitants, and the business of international politics were limited to a competition among them for the right to exploit the rest of mankind, one would have to predict a glorious history for the American Empire.[10]

In place of what he feels to be a futile attempt to maintain an American Empire on an imperial model, Barnet urges exclusive recourse to the United Nations, which, he asserts, rules out unilateral intervention.[11]

Barnet's description of the elephant does describe an important part of the reality. He rightly focuses on the response to internal conflict as a central problem for American foreign policy in the next decade. He convincingly shows that American foreign policy planners have overemphasized the danger of communist export of revolution and have underestimated the difficulty of successful counter-intervention. Both reflex anti-communism without analy-

8. See *id.* 3-93.   9. See *id.* 225-54.   10. *Id.* 278.
11. See *id.* 278-80.

sis of local conditions and a willingness to employ subversive tactics against disapproved regimes have weakened the credibility of American actions and may have been counter-productive. Moreover, there has been a disturbing lack of consistency in American foreign policy, demonstrated most dramatically by the moral outrage at the Soviet invasion of Czechoslovakia in contrast to the *realpolitik* approach toward the United States-sponsored Bay of Pigs invasion. Despite these valid thrusts, however, in the measure of its omission Barnet's model is as misleading as that of the largely imaginary national security manager with which he tilts.

While United States foreign policy may have sometimes opposed revolutionary change, it has also frequently supported it, sometimes despite the real disgruntlement of our allies. Examples include support for Indonesian independence from the Netherlands, support for the coup which brought Nasser to power in Egypt, opposition to Duvalier, Trujillo, and the military coup which ousted Bosch, and a sympathetic attitude toward independence for Algeria and the plight of blacks in southern Africa. That the United States has not intervened more actively for social change does not prove that the national security managers have been happy with the slow pace of reform throughout much of the world. To the contrary, the Alliance for Progress and other foreign assistance programs demonstrate a real commitment to social change. That the United States failed to intervene militarily in violation of the United Nations Charter every time it felt that the pace of change was too slow is hardly a persuasive argument for condemnation of American foreign policy! If there has been a reflexive "anti" running through American foreign policy, it has certainly been anti-communism and not anti-revolution or anti-social change.

Furthermore, like other cold-war revisionists,[12] the frame which Barnet uses may be too small. There have been major communist interventions in Greece, Laos, Cambodia, and Vietnam,

12. Barnet's judgment that "[i]t is certainly at least as plausible that the North Koreans attacked to forestall an attack from the South as that this was a case of Hitler-like aggression," *id.* 67, suggests a revisionist view.

and significant interventions in the Congo, Venezuela, Thailand, Bolivia, Nicaragua, and a host of other nations. That they have not been centrally orchestrated from Moscow or Peking is hardly a persuasive argument for justifying or minimizing them. In fact, it is precisely the smaller communist countries such as North Vietnam and Cuba which seem to be the most enthusiastic merchants of revolution. Though most attempts at the export of revolution seem doomed to fail of their own unrealism, the box score of communist success might be considerably higher had the United States not demonstrated a willingness to provide assistance to counter foreign intervention.

Although Barnet catalogues all the arguments against American intervention in defense of the *status quo*, he largely neglects the reasons against unilateral intervention by communist or third world states for purported revolutionary goals. This one-sided treatment may be attributable to his justifiable concern with modernization and meaningful social change in the developing states. A central reason for non-intervention, whether communist or non-communist, however, is to protect the rights of the people of every nation to choose their own government and institutions. Just because an intervention may contribute to modernization or social change does not provide moral license externally to coerce development or to impose a particular political system which may or may not encourage a reluctant people to modernize. The unpopular interventions of Egypt in Yemen and Cuba in Bolivia expose the myth that such "benevolent" interventions are necessarily welcomed. Self-determination refers to the genuine wants of the people of a nation, not the imposition of foreign wants, however beneficently motivated. Other factors not emphasized by Barnet also support the critical importance of non-intervention on behalf of revolutionary as well as counter-revolutionary factions. These factors include the difficulty in ascertaining the real motive for external intervention, the open question whether choice of political system is ever a substantial factor in modernization, the threat to world order in providing license for unilateral export of a favored political system, the possible escalation in human suffering, and the difficulty in ascertaining which of the competing revolutionary factions, if any, represents the people of the state.

Barnet's rejection of all intervention other than United Nations collective action is simplistic despite the substantial advantages of a normative scheme which would proscribe unilateral action. Non-intervention in internal authority struggles must be the basic international standard which applies to the United States as well as to the Soviet Union and third world countries. Once foreign assistance is already being provided to an insurgent faction, however, there is little reason for requiring non-intervention on behalf of the government under attack. Accordingly, almost all international-law scholars support a right of counter-intervention on behalf of a widely recognized government to offset impermissible assistance supplied to insurgents.[13] Furthermore, it is not essential that the insurgency be externally initiated or controlled as Barnet emphasizes,[14] but only that it be externally assisted.[15]

Barnet's recommendation also vastly overstates the present capacity of the United Nations to respond constructively to impermissible intervention in internal conflict. The post-Congo financial crisis and the inability of the United Nations to play a significant role in Vietnam suggests that the present UN is not able to shoulder the full responsibility of deterring impermissible intervention. Though the UN has an important role to play in legitimating needed change, as evidenced by the recent resolutions authorizing members to assist insurgents in South Africa,[16] Rho-

13. See Borchard, *"Neutrality" and Civil Wars*, 31 AM. J. INT'L L. 304, 306 (1937); Friedmann, *Intervention, Civil War and the Role of International Law*, 1965 PROC. AM. SOC'Y INT'L L. 67, 72; Garner, *Questions of International Law in the Spanish Civil War*, 31 AM. J. INT'L L. 66, 68 (1937); O'Rourke, *Recognition of Belligerency and the Spanish War*, 31 AM. J. INT'L L. 398, 410 (1937). *But see* Farer, *Harnessing Rogue Elephants: A Short Discourse on Foreign Intervention in Civil Strife*, 82 HARV. L. REV. 511 (1969); Farer, *Intervention in Civil Wars: A Modest Proposal*, 67 COLUM. L. REV. 266, 272 (1967).

14. See R. BARNET, *supra* note 3, at 52.

15. For a discussion of the competing non-intervention norms and the right of counter-intervention, see Moore, *The Control of Foreign Intervention in Internal Conflict*, 9 VA. J. INT'L L. 205, 279-80, 315-42 (1969).

16 G.A. Res. 2307, 22 U.N. GAOR, Supp. 16, at 19-20. U.N. Doc. A/6716 (1967) (South Africa); G.A. Res. 2372, 22 U.N. GAOR, Supp. 16A, at 1-2, U.N. Doc. A/6716/Add. 1 (1968) (South West Africa).

desia[17] and the Portuguese colonies,[18] it smacks of the legalist tradition[19] at its worst to overemphasize its present capacity.

A subtle but far more pervasive problem with *Intervention and Revolution* is its polemical tone. Thus, Barnet invokes images of American "imperialism,"[20] "exploitation,"[21] "suppression,"[22] and "empire,"[23] and to pick a typical example, he ascribes to the national security managers the view "that there is no way for a great country to relate to a small one other than as manipulator or exploiter."[24] National security managers, Machiavelli-like, ask their critics: "What's wrong with imperialism or unilateralism? Is there anything better?"[25] A more serious indication, however, is that Barnet's accounts of American interventions are consistently onesided. A notable example is the complete omission of any reference to the massive North Vietnamese intervention in Laos in violation of the 1962 Laotian Accords despite criticism of American intervention in Laos.[26] And if Barnet does see legitimate American security interests abroad, he does not indicate even *en passant* where they are.

It is a pity that a scholar of Barnet's distinction and ability should be content to indulge in an attack on familiar straw men rather than to focus on the real questions facing American foreign policy. The need is for clarification, not abuse; specifically, three major questions must be faced. First, when is American or any other intervention consistent with the international common interest? Second, when is intervention which is consistent with the international common interest also justified by the national interest? Third, and closely related to the second, when is intervention which is otherwise justifiable likely to be successful?

The first question suggests a need for a principled framework

17. G.A. Res. 2262, 22 U.N. GAOR, Supp. 16, at 45-46, U.N. Doc. A/6716 (1967).

18. G.A. Res. 2270, 22 U.N. GAOR, Supp. 16, at 47-48, U.N. Doc. A/6716 (1967).

19. For a description of the useful "legalist" and "anti-legalist" terminology, see Falk, *Law, Lawyers, and the Conduct of American Foreign Relations*, 78 YALE L.J. 919 (1969).

20. See, *e.g.*, R. BARNET, *supra* note 3, at 30-31, 264.

21. See, *e.g.*, *id.* 262.   22. See, *e.g.*, *id.* 9, 60, 267, 281.

23. See, *e.g.*, *id.* 14, 259, 263, 278.   24. *Id.* 262.

25. *Id.* 264.   26. See *id.* 209-11.

for appraisal of intervention and a consistent American foreign policy which takes it into account. If the United States is to be able convincingly to condemn the Soviet invasion of Czechoslovakia, it must not intervene on behalf of non-communist insurgents in Cuba. Clarifying international common interest is the traditional concern of international law, but thus far international law has developed neither a comprehensive framework for appraisal of intervention nor adequate institutional mechanisms for control.[27] The development of both, particularly the strengthening of the United Nations for greater responsiveness to intervention, provides an opportunity for American leadership which should not be missed. And certainly American foreign policy must be sensitive to the widespread demand for modernization and social change.

The second question requires a hard assessment of the consequences for the United States of action or inaction in each case, divorced from the generalities of Munich analogies and falling dominoes or the rhetoric of imperialism. Vietnam has demonstrated that protracted intervention can have profound effects domestically as well as on the achievement of other foreign policy goals. Assessment of these effects may involve a weighing of imponderables, but nevertheless, the full range of risks must be considered before the commitment of American blood and treasure.

The third question requires greater realism in the assessment of usable power and greater understanding of the requisite conditions for effective action. It should not be automatically assumed that American nuclear or industrial power is translatable to a counter-insurgency capability in every foreign land. On the other hand, it should not be assumed in a kind of reverse domino thinking that the difficulties of Vietnam will be writ large in every exercise of power. For example, if the ability to isolate an area from an aggressive regime is critical for successful counter-intervention, Laos and Uruguay should not be lumped together. And if the strength of the indigenous communist party, the ambiguity of an uncertain international settlement, and the absence of viable

27. For a review of the inadequacies of the present international framework for the control of unauthorized intervention and some suggestions for improvement, see Moore, *supra* note 15.

political alternatives were debilitating factors in the American intervention in Vietnam, Cambodia and Thailand may or may not present the same difficulties.

The newness and complexity of these issues cast doubt on popular stereotypes of American intervention and suggest a need for inquiry rather than enmity. Whatever the final answers to these critical questions, half of the elephant is an unreliable basis for finding them.

CHAPTER VI

The Role of Regional Arrangements in the Maintenance of World Order

Introduction

As the United Nations ends its first quarter-century, two flaws in its normative structure have become increasingly apparent. The first and perhaps more important of these is the unresponsiveness of the Charter to the problem of control of foreign intervention in internal conflict.[1] The second is the ambiguity surrounding the role of regional arrangements in the maintenance of world order. Unlike the problem of control of unauthorized intervention, the framers of the Charter were largely aware of the problems in the interrelation of regional arrangements and the United Nations. The clash of competing regional and universal interests, however, resulted in an ambiguous resolution of the issues. That ambiguity has been magnified as the original expectations of an effectively functioning Security Council were shattered on the rocks of the cold-war. Today there is general agreement that the United Nations has the ultimate responsibility for the maintenance of international peace and security, but there are major uncertainties surrounding the initial exercise of regional jurisdiction, the authority of regional arrangements to initiate coercive action, and, where necessary, the procedure for United Nations authorization of regional action.

Though the problem of control of unauthorized intervention has received increasing attention in the last few years, the ambiguous interface between the United Nations and regional arrangements has remained largely neglected.[2] Clarification of

---

1. See Chapters III and IV.
2. Some of the better recent studies of the role of regional arrangements are J. NYE, JR., INTERNATIONAL REGIONALISM (1968); C. FENWICK, THE ORGANIZATION OF AMERICAN STATES (1963); THE INTER-AMERICAN INSTITUTE OF INTERNATIONAL LEGAL STUDIES, THE INTER-AMERICAN SYSTEM (1966); A. THOMAS & A. THOMAS, JR., THE ORGANIZATION OF AMERICAN

the role of regional arrangements in the maintenance of peace and security is important if the Charter structure is to be made a more viable tool for conflict management. Clarification is also important from a purely national perspective. National actions which seek legitimacy through regional action can succeed only to the extent of underlying regional legitimacy. Moreover, to the extent that such actions are widely regarded as illegitimate, they may weaken the authority of the regional system itself. Whatever its other merits, the OAS action initiated by the United States in the 1965 Dominican situation may have resulted in some deflation of OAS authority from such a feedback.[3] It is important, then, that the pursuit of short-run national goals should not be permitted to obscure a perhaps greater national and international interest in the integrity of regional systems.

It has been customary to distinguish three kinds of regional

STATES (1963); R. MACDONALD, THE LEAGUE OF ARAB STATES, (1965); Frey-Wouters, *The Prospects for Regionalism in World Affairs*, in I R. FALK & C. BLACK (EDS.), THE FUTURE OF THE INTERNATIONAL LEGAL ORDER 463 (1969); Miller, *The Prospects for Order Through Regional Security*, in I R. FALK & C. BLACK, (EDS.) THE FUTURE OF THE INTERNATIONAL LEGAL ORDER, 556 (1969); Korbonski, *The Warsaw Pact*, INT'L CONCILIATION No. 573 (May 1969); Claude, *The OAS, the UN, and the United States*, INT'L CONCILIATION No. 547 (March 1964); Boutros-Ghali, *The Addis Ababa Charter*, INT'L CONCILIATION No. 546 (Jan. 1964); Boutros-Ghali, *The Arab League: 1945-55*, INT'L CONCILIATION, No. 498 (May 1954); Nanda, *The United States Action in the 1965 Dominican Crisis: Impact on World Order Part II*, 44 DENVER L.J. 225 (1967); Halderman, *Regional Enforcement Measures and the United Nations*, 52 GEO. L.J. 89 (1963); Slater, *The Limits of Legitimization in International Organizations: The Organization of American States in the Dominican Crisis*, 23 INT'L ORGAN. 48 (1969); Wild, *The Organization of African Unity and the Algerian-Moroccan Border Conflict: A Study of New Machinery for Peacekeeping and for the Peaceful Settlement of Disputes Among African States*, 20 INT'L ORGAN. 18 (1966); Wilcox, *Regionalism and the United Nations*, 19 INT'L ORGAN. 789 (1965); Padelford, *The Organization of African Unity*, 18 INT'L ORGAN. 521 (1964); Meeker, *Defensive Quarantine and the Law*, 57 AM. J. INT'L L. 515 (1963); Bebr, *Regional Organizations: A United Nations Problem*, 49 AM. J. INT'L L. 166 (1955).

The article by Professor Inis Claude on "The OAS, the UN and the United States" is the best starting place.

3. Slater, *supra* note 2, at 67.

organizations: first, the so-called "functional" organizations focused on regional economic integration or transnational community-building, such as the British Commonwealth, the European Community, the Council for Mutual Economic Assistance and the Latin American Free Trade Association; second, the postwar multilateral defense organizations created pursuant to Article 51 of the Charter and focused on extra-regional threats, such as the North Atlantic Treaty Organization, the Southeast Asian Treaty Organization, the Central Treaty Organization, the ANZUS Pact, and the Warsaw Pact; and third, the "genuine" regional arrangements created pursuant to Chapter VIII of the Charter and focused on intra-regional threats, meaning pre-eminently the Organization of American States but also including the Organization of African Unity and the Arab League. Although these distinctions have enabled a useful focus, they have also been a potent source of confusion. One reason for the confusion is that all regional organizations are functional in some sense and most are multi-functional. Thus, though NATO and SEATO focus on defense, they also perform related economic and political functions. Conversely, though the British Commonwealth focuses on economic and political integration, it also exercises a security function. Moreover, though the Article 51 organizations focus primarily on regional defense against external threats, they may sometimes become involved in intra-regional disputes, an example being the NATO involvement in the Cyprus conflict. And conversely, the so-called Chapter VIII organizations, though focusing more heavily than the Article 51 organizations on management of intra-regional disputes, may perform the same functions as Article 51 organizations in defense against external threats. The Inter-American system is a paradigm example of an organization structured for the handling of both intra-regional and extra-regional security threats.[4]

An even more potent source of confusion stemming from the

---

4. For an analysis of the Inter-American system, see generally Fenwick, *supra* note 2; The Inter-American Institute of International Legal Studies, *supra* note 2; Thomas & Thomas, *supra* note 2; Claude, *supra* note 2; and Nanda, *supra* note 2.

usual classification trilogy is the temptation to let legal conclusions concerning relations with the United Nations be dictated by *a priori* characterization of an organization as either an Article 51 organization or a Chapter VIII organization. In its most extreme form the argument is that if an organization is an Article 51 organization rather than a Chapter VIII organization, its actions could not be "enforcement action" requiring Security Council approval pursuant to Article 53. *Vice versa*, if an organization is a Chapter VIII organization, its actions must be "enforcement action." Though the claim that particular regional action is "enforcement action" may or may not be sound, such reasoning by *a priori* organizational characterization is nonsense.

To avoid these confusions, it seems preferable to recognize that regional organizations are located on a series of functional continua. Thus, though the EEC is intensely concerned with economic integration, and to a lesser extent with the promotion of human rights, the OAS and even SEATO may perform some of the same functions. With respect to the peace and security function, it is useful to construct two continua, one for focus on intra-regional settlement of disputes and one for focus on concern with external threats. Both NATO and OAS would be high on the external threat continuum, but they would be far apart on the intra-regional dispute continuum. Even more important, for purposes of normative clarification we need a more specific functional breakdown by types of issue. Such a breakdown, rather than any classification by types of regional security organization, seems best calculated to assist in clarification.

This chapter will attempt to provide a framework for analysis of the role of regional arrangements in the maintenance of world order. In doing so, an effort will be made first to isolate the initial understandings and misunderstandings behind the Charter framework and the major trends and conditioning factors affecting the development of regional arrangements, then to develop general policy criteria for allocating competence between the United Nations and regional security arrangements, and finally to develop a functional framework for appraising regional security claims.

The Development of Regional Arrangements
under the Charter

THE INITIAL UNDERSTANDINGS AND MISUNDERSTANDINGS:

Early wartime planning concerning postwar international organization was principally concerned with whether such organization should follow the Churchillian conception of regional councils or place primary emphasis on a universal organization.[5] Secretary of State Cordell Hull's arguments for a strong universal organization eventually won out and were reflected in both the Moscow Declaration and the Dumbarton Oaks Proposals. The Dumbarton Oaks Proposals did not preclude regional organizations but they cautiously stipulated that regional enforcement action should not be undertaken without the approval of the Security Council and that the Council should be kept informed of regional action relating to peace and security.[6] In a more pro-regional vein they also provided for Security Council encouragement and utilization of regional arrangements for the settlement of local disputes.[7] This strong universalist position clashed head on at the San Francisco Conference with the determination of the Latin Americans to ensure a largely autonomous inter-American system. Latin American dissatisfaction, supported by Senator Arthur Vandenburg, focused on two issues: the desire to free regional action from the veto implicit in the Dumbarton Oaks Proposals requiring regional enforcement action to be approved by the Security Council, and the desire to achieve primary jurisdiction for regional agencies with respect to local disputes, that is, to require an exhaustion of regional remedies before Council involvement. The resulting compromise was ambiguous on both issues, allowing spokesmen for both universalist and regionalist viewpoints to claim victory.

5. Claude, *supra* note 2, at 4-5; II C. HULL, THE MEMOIRS OF CORDELL HULL 1639-48 (1948).
6. See Articles 2 and 3 of Section C, Chapter VIII, of the Dumbarton Oaks Proposals for the Establishment of a General International Organization in R. RUSSELL & J. MUTHER, A HISTORY OF THE UNITED NATIONS CHARTER 1026 (1958).
7. See Articles 1 and 2 of Section C, Chapter VIII, of the Dumbarton Oaks Proposals. RUSSELL & MUTHER, *supra* note 6, at 1026.

The compromise on the first issue resulted in the addition of Article 51 to Chapter VII of the Charter. Article 51 provides that

> Nothing in the present Charter shall impair the inherent right of individual or collective self-defense if an armed attack occurs against a Member of the United Nations, until the Security Council has taken measures necessary to maintain international peace and security. . . .

Article 53, embodied in Chapter VIII, however, retained the rhetoric of Dumbarton Oaks that "no enforcement action shall be taken under regional arrangements or by regional agencies without the authorization of the Security Council. . . ."

The issue of primary jurisdiction was even more ambiguously resolved by the inclusion of the complementary Articles 52(2) and 52(4). Article 52(2) provides that members of regional arrangements

> shall make every effort to achieve pacific settlement of local disputes through such regional arrangements or by such regional agencies before referring them to the Security Council.

But Article 52(4) provides that nothing in Article 52 "impairs the application of Articles 34 and 35," which give authority to the Security Council to "investigate any dispute, or any situation which might lead to international friction . . . ," and provide that "any Member of the United Nations may bring . . . [such a dispute or situation] to the attention of the Security Council or . . . General Assembly." Article 52(3) further confuses the compromise on the issue of primary jurisdiction. It provides:

> The Security Council shall encourage the development of pacific settlement of local disputes through such regional arrangements or by such regional agencies either on the initiative of the states concerned or by reference from the Security Council.

The Dumbarton Oaks principle that the Security Council should "be kept fully informed of activities undertaken or in contemplation under regional arrangements or by regional agencies for the maintenance of international peace and security"[8] was embodied in Article 54 of the Charter.

Though the final outcome of the San Francisco Conference clearly recognized a role for regional organizations in the maintenance of international peace and security the specifics of that role were obscure. As Professor Inis Claude has observed:

> The decision of the San Francisco Conference . . . provided no precise indication of the contemplated division of competence and responsibility between it [the United Nations] and regional agencies, much less a firm basis for predicting the nature of the relationships that would emerge in the dynamic interplay of the United Nations and regional organizations during the next two decades.[9]

MAJOR TRENDS AND CONDITIONING FACTORS IN THE DEVELOPMENT OF REGIONAL AUTHORITY:

The ambiguous compromise at San Francisco meant that the authority of regional arrangements would be largely shaped by the forces of the international arena. At least seven conditioning factors seemed to have played a significant role in this development. They were the post-war division between competing public order systems with the consequent breakdown in Chapter VII effectiveness, the increasing influence of the smaller states within the United Nations, major power dominance of key regional organizations, the paramountcy of the OAS in testing regional authority, the increase in revolutionary and interventionary activity within the international system, the trend to regional economic and political integration, and the nuclear arms race. Present trends with respect to each of these factors can be expected to have a continuing impact on the future development of regional authority.

PERHAPS the principal factor affecting the development of regional arrangements has been the breakdown of the wartime co-

---

8. See Article 3 of Section C, Chapter VIII, of the Dumbarton Oaks Proposals. RUSSELL & MUTHER, *supra* note 6, at 1026.
9. CLAUDE, *supra* note 2, at 3. The preceding discussion of the initial understandings and misunderstandings draws heavily on Claude's pioneering work.

operation between the major powers and its replacement by the continuing conflict of the cold-war. Within the United Nations this breakdown in the envisaged cooperation of the major powers resulted in inability to conclude an Article 43 agreement which was to have made contingents of national forces available to the Security Council. Moreover, the cold-war was reflected in the frequency with which the Soviet Union exercised the veto in the Security Council. The result was substantially reduced Chapter VII effectiveness. In turn, this limited Security Council effectiveness coupled with the high level of East-West conflict provided a major stimulant to the formation of multilateral defense arrangements pursuant to Article 51, since such arrangements would not be subject to Council veto in initial defensive planning or action. This post-war period witnessed the formation of the Rio Treaty (1948), NATO (1949), the Pacific Security Treaty or ANZUS Pact (1952), the Collective Security Pact of the Arab League (1952), SEATO (1955), the Warsaw Pact (1955), and the Baghdad Pact (1955), which became CENTO in 1959.[10] Although there was some initial questioning whether such organizations were compatible with the Charter,[11] the wide participation in

---

10. See KEESING'S TREATIES AND ALLIANCES OF THE WORLD 144 (The Rio Treaty), 98-99 (NATO), 186 (The ANZUS Pact), 170 (The Arab League), 187 (SEATO), 120 (The Warsaw Pact), 174 (CENTO) (1968). See also *Staff on House Comm. on Foreign Affairs, 90th Cong., 1st Sess., Collective Defense Treaties* (Comm. Print 1967).

11. Differing from Article 53, the so-called inherent right of the individual or collective self-defence is what may be termed an emergency right. It is conceived as a spontaneous, temporary re-action to a sudden, illegal armed attack, and it becomes operative only and solely after the event. Hence, differing from Article 53, the proper interpretation of Article 51 precludes regional organs of the States signatories to the North Atlantic Treaty, to elaborate strategic plans, and to co-ordinate their military forces under a combined High Command before an armed attack has occurred.

Schick, *The North Atlantic Treaty and the Problem of Peace*, 62 JURID. REV. 26, 49 (1950). For a discussion of Soviet objections to NATO see Kulski, *The Soviet System of Collective Security Compared with the Western System*, 44 AM. J. INT'L L., 453 (1950). See also Bebr, *supra* note 2, at 173; Kelsen, *Is the North Atlantic Treaty A Regional Arrangement?*, 45 AM. INT'L L. 162, 164 (1951); Heindel, Kalijarvi, Wilcox, *The North Atlantic Treaty in the United States Senate*, 43

such organizations of states on both sides of the cold-war firmly established their legitimacy.

A second major effect of the cold-war and the breakdown of Chapter VII effectiveness was to shift the United States position from the largely pro-universalist position of Cordell Hull toward the pro-regionalist position of the Latin American delegates at the San Francisco Conference. The United States, which exercised great influence within the OAS, now saw regional autonomy (meaning largely OAS autonomy) as a way of avoiding the veto in the Security Council. Accordingly, in the 1954 Guatemalan case and the 1960 Cuban case the United States urged that the dispute should first be submitted to the OAS pursuant to Article 52(2).[12] Similarly, the United States began to urge a narrow definition of "enforcement action" in order to increase the regional autonomy of the OAS. The position of the Soviet Union and the communist states, on the other hand, has generally been in opposition to increased regional autonomy for Chapter VIII arrangements (meaning largely OAS autonomy) in order to maximize the power of the Soviet veto and their own influence within the United Nations.

The trend to greater regional autonomy, supported by the United States, is also reflected in the trend to increased General Assembly authority evidenced in the Uniting for Peace Resolution and the trend to increased Secretary-General authority as evidenced by a host of initiatives, particularly under Secretary-General Dag Hammarskjöld. All three trends are partly attributable to the decreased effectiveness of the Security Council as the result of cold-war tension.

Although in the long run a rapprochement between the Soviet Union and the United States could conceivably reverse the pressures for increased regional autonomy, Peking's recent entry into the United Nations and seat on the Security Council might provide another strong impetus toward increased regional autonomy.

Though there are too many variables to make a confident prediction, it seems likely that in the immediate future the Security

---

AM. J. INT'L L. 633 (1949); Van Kleffens, *Regionalism and Political Pacts*, 43 AM. J. INT'L L. 4, 666 (1949).

12. See Claude, *supra* note 2, at 21-43.

Council will continue to have only limited effectiveness and that those centrifugal forces for increased regional autonomy which result from the breakdown in Security Council effectiveness will continue strong.

A SECOND factor affecting the development of regional organizations has been the increasing influence of the smaller states within the United Nations. The great increase in United Nations membership resulting from the large influx of new states since World War II and the resulting increase in 1965 in the size of the Security Council from eleven to fifteen members have effected this change. In the case of the United States, the decrease in control has been dramatic. Prior to about 1960, United States influence within the General Assembly was so great that it was appropriate to speak of an automatic majority. Though United States and major power influence still remains high within the United Nations, today no other major power exercises influence comparable to that of the earlier United States influence. It seems likely that this decline in major power influence within the United Nations will contribute to continued support for regional autonomy by those major powers which are in a position to benefit from increased regional autonomy. Conversely, it can be expected that many smaller states may continue to prefer a United Nations forum.

A THIRD factor affecting the development of regional organizations has been the continued dominance in many such organizations by a major power. The Warsaw Pact seems to have had as one purpose the continued exercise of Soviet control over Eastern European satellites following de-Stalinization.[13] The Southeast Asia Treaty Organization was essentially an instrument of United States foreign policy intended to assist in the containment of communism.[14] And even the venerable institutions of the inter-American system were subject to disproportionate United States influence.

13. See Korbonski, *supra* note 2, at 11-12.
14. See generally R. FIFIELD, SOUTHEAST ASIA IN UNITED STATES POLICY, 113-58 (1963).

This major power dominance of key regional organizations produced a number of effects on the development of regional authority. First, it compounded the effects of the cold-war on regional authority by ensuring that regional autonomy would be a cold-war issue. Because it identified increased regional autonomy with a United States cold-war position, the Soviet Union consistently opposed United States efforts to increase regional autonomy, at least with respect to Chapter VIII issues. The United States, on the other hand, had substantial influence over the principal Chapter VIII regional organization, the OAS, and thus sought to increase Chapter VIII autonomy.

A second effect of major power dominance has been to decrease the legitimacy of regional action in the eyes of the smaller states. Since the smaller states were subject to the veto of the major powers in the Security Council, it might have been expected that they would take a pro-regional position similar to that of the Latin American states at the San Francisco Conference. Major power dominance of some regional organizations, however, prompted the smaller states to champion the United Nations forum in preference to regional arrangements dominated by a major power. Thus, within the OAS there has been a substantial shift in the position of many of the Latin American states who now champion tighter United Nations control of regional action. The position of other Latin American states is an ambivalent one which fluctuates between a desire for regional autonomy on local issues and the preservation of a United Nations forum as a counterweight to United States hegemony in the OAS. This desire of the smaller nations to maintain United Nations control over regional action and to maximize what many perceive as an advantageous forum provides a counterweight to centrifugal forces favoring increased regional autonomy.

The withdrawal of France from NATO, the weakness of SEATO in the Vietnam conflict, the disaffection of Albania and to a lesser extent Czechoslovakia and Romania within the Warsaw Pact, and the narrow margin of support within the OAS for United States initiatives in the Dominican conflict suggest a steady lessening of major power influence within regional organizations. In fact, as a result of the authority deflation in the OAS resulting from the 1965 Dominican operation it seems likely that the United States must move toward full cooperative partnership on OAS peace and security decisions if the OAS is to remain effective. The Soviet invasion of Czechoslovakia may have temporarily retarded these forces in both NATO and the Warsaw Pact, but it seems unlikely to alter the long-run political trend.[15] Any pronounced trend toward genuine partnership within the OAS and other regional arrangements now dominated by a major power would provide a powerful incentive toward increased regional authority.

A FOURTH factor significantly affecting the development of regional organizations is the paramountcy of the OAS in testing regional authority. Although most regional organizations focus on intra-regional problems to some extent, only three such organizations are sufficiently directed at intra-regional disputes to have presented much opportunity for testing the full range of problems in the relationship between regional organizations and the United Nations. They are the OAS, the OAU, and the Arab League. Unlike the Arab League and the OAU which date from 1945 and 1963 respectively, the OAS is the latest version of a working inter-American system which traces its origins to the International Union of American Republics established in 1889. The OAS also provides more elaborate machinery for settlement of intra-regional problems and brings a substantial history of involvement with regional peace and security issues to its task. Moreover, as has been seen, most of the pressure for increased regional autonomy at the San Francisco Conference came from the desire of the Latin Americans to preserve a vigorous inter-American system. Under the circumstances, it is not surprising that the OAS has provided most of the test cases for determining regional authority.

The consequences of this OAS paramountcy have been substan-

15. See generally *Staff of Senate Subcommittee on National Security and International Operations, 91st Cong., 1st Sess. Czechoslovakia and the Brezhnev Doctrine* (Comm. Print 1969).

tial. Since the major tests of regional authority have involved a regional organization identified with a major cold-war power, tests of regional authority have been perceived by all concerned primarily in cold-war terms. The United States tends to equate regional autonomy with OAS autonomy and presses for broad regional authority. And the Soviet Union equates regional autonomy with autonomy of a United States-dominated OAS and opposes increased regional autonomy. As a result, the general issue of regional versus universal authority tends to be subordinated to more immediate cold-war interests.

In the future, it is possible that African demands for increased autonomy for the OAU or Arab demands for increased autonomy for the Arab League or even demands for increased autonomy for some new regional organization may introduce new forces into the development of regional autonomy and end the equation that regional autonomy equals OAS autonomy. For the time being, however, the African and Arab states are internally split on objectives and without dominant regional leadership, do not have the power to achieve major objectives regionally, and for the most part receive a sympathetic forum within the United Nations. As long as these factors continue to exert substantial influence, African and Arab pressures for increased regional autonomy may develop only slowly if at all.

A FIFTH factor significantly affecting the development of regional authority has been the increase in revolutionary and interventionary activity within the international system. Former Secretary of Defense Robert McNamara reported a few years ago that while "at the beginning of 1958 there were 23 prolonged insurgencies going on around the world, as of February, 1966, there were 40. Further, the total number of outbreaks of violence has increased each year: in 1958 there were 34; in 1965 there were 58."[16] The trend seems to be more than a passing phenomenon. Professors Leiden and Schmitt, in their summary of revolution in the modern world, assert that "even a cursory view of recent history forces an acknowledgement that we are living in a new era of revolution . . . ; the last third of the twentieth century promises

16.   R. MC NAMARA, THE ESSENCE OF SECURITY 145 (1968).

to be a period of almost constant revolutionary turmoil. . . ."[17] As the events of recent years in Czechoslovakia, the Congo, the Dominican Republic, Laos, Nigeria, Vietnam, and Yemen illustrate, this increase in revolutionary activity has also been accompanied by an increase in interventionary activity. The United Nations Charter, however, was primarily structured in response to the kind of overt aggression which triggered World War II. Although there had been earlier experiences with intervention in internal conflict, notably during the Spanish Civil War, for the most part the lessons learned were not assimilated into the Charter structure. Consequently, as intervention in internal conflict developed into a core public order problem the Charter contributed only an inadequate response. For example, the Article 2(4) proscription of "the threat or use of force against the territorial integrity or political independence of any state," provides little guidance as to permissibility of assistance to either a widely recognized government or insurgents in a situation of internal war. Similarly, when is assistance to one side or another either an armed attack or collective defense within the meaning of Article 51? The principal difficulty in both cases, of course, is in determining which faction represents the state.[18]

These Charter ambiguities and gaps also affect the delineation of regional authority, since regional authority is delineated in the Charter by reference to these same provisions. Thus, is regional action which provides assistance to one or another faction on request an "armed attack" or "enforcement action" within the meaning of Articles 51 or 53? Are regional peacekeeping operations such as the Inter-American Peace Force in the Dominican Republic, which are undertaken at the request of a major faction, "enforcement action"? These ambiguities have also contributed to regional support of liberation movements, such as Arab League support of the Palestine Liberation Organization and OAU establishment of a Liberation Committee to support liberation movements directed against the remaining colonial regimes in Africa. These uncertainties and gaps in the Charter concerning the con-

17. C. LEIDEN & K. SCHMITT, THE POLITICS OF VIOLENCE: REVOLUTION IN THE MODERN WORLD 212 (1968).
18. See generally Moore, *supra* note 1, at 210-11, 242.

trol of intervention in internal conflict coupled with the pressing need to deal with the increased revolutionary and interventionary activity have resulted in increased regional autonomy. Present trends in the frequency of intervention and internal conflict suggest that this factor will continue to exert a significant influence on the development of regional authority.

A SIXTH factor significantly affecting the development of regional arrangements has been the strong post-war trend to regional economic and political integration. Both the Arab League and the OAU are in part products of this trend. The early enthusiasm for "Arab solidarity," "Pan-Africanism," and regional economic integration has somewhat waned as the difficulties have become more apparent. To the extent that regions are primarily affected by particular decisions or otherwise share common interests, however, regional autonomy seems a likely long-run development. If a significant number of new regional arrangements directed at regional peace and security issues emerge or if existing arrangements become more viable, it will probably strengthen regional autonomy and further generalize the issue of regional versus United Nations authority.

IN ANY listing of factors affecting the development of regional arrangements it is prudent to include the nuclear arms race. The enormous economic and technological requirements for maintaining a competitive nuclear position necessarily limit that status to a few superpowers. In matters of nuclear defense, this factor could be expected to encourage a proliferation of regional defense arrangements as smaller powers seek to cluster around the competitive nuclear powers. On the other hand, the magnitude of the nuclear threat may itself destroy the credibility of such arrangements and reduce their importance. In any event, it seems probable that within regional arrangements the disparity in nuclear power increases dependence on major power initiatives, particularly when the issue itself involves a nuclear threat, as in the Cuban Missile Crisis of 1962. The disparity in nuclear power, then, provides a built-in dependence in those regional organizations such as the OAS which include a major power participant.

The Cuban Missile Crisis illustrates another effect of the nuclear condition. That is, the pressure to enlarge the concept of armed attack when fundamental defense interests are perceived as threatened by sudden shifts in nuclear deployment. That nuclear defense matters may be subject to different rules which reflect the immense importance of the stakes is suggested by the virtual absence of Security Council debate challenging OAS action in the Missile Crisis. In such cases, the interest in avoiding a nuclear war overshadows the problem of allocation of competence between the United Nations and regional organizations.

A NUMBER of long-range trends suggest an increased autonomy and importance for regional arrangements in the maintenance of international peace and security. These include the probable continued limited effectiveness of the Security Council, the decrease in major power influence within both the United Nations and regional arrangements, and the trend to increased identification of regional common interest evident in the movements for regional economic and political integration. In the short run, however, continued cold-war pressures combined with small power preference for a United Nations forum may somewhat restrict regional autonomy. The length of the debate in the Security Council on the 1965 Dominican operation, which was longer than all prior Security Council discussion on the issues of regional autonomy combined,[19] and the resultant Security Council resolution taking action parallel to the OAS action while the OAS was still seized with the situation, suggest that the latter trend may already be underway.

Community Policies for Allocating Authority between Regional and Universal Security Organizations

There is surprisingly little discussion in the literature of regional arrangements concerning criteria for optimum allocation of authority between regional and universal security organizations.[20] During the wartime planning for post-war international

19. See Nanda, *supra* note 2, at 254-55.
20. What discussion there is focuses on a choice between international organization based on either regional arrangements or a universal or-

organization there was some debate within the Allied camp as to whether emphasis should be given to regional councils or a universal organization. The Churchillian emphasis on regional councils was opposed by Secretary of State Cordell Hull on the ground that emphasis on competing regional councils might create a system conducive to war between regions and that it might encourage great power hegemony within regions.[21] Hull also argued that emphasis on regional councils might create "a haven for the isolationists, who could advocate all-out United States cooperation in a Western Hemisphere council on condition that we did not participate in a European or Pacific council."[22] Within the framework of the United Nations Charter, which adopts a structure of both universal and regional organizations but assigns ultimate responsibility for the maintenance of peace and security to the universal organization, the arguments of Hull do not seem very helpful as criteria for determining the precise role of regional arrangements. In fact, with the partial breakdown in the centralized collective security system envisaged for the United Nations and the consequent proliferation of Article 51 collective defense arrangements, Hull's first and second points have largely been realized, despite the initial emphasis on universal rather than regional organizations. And his second point concerning a haven for isolationists seems more appropriate to the League era than the present.

Most of the more recent debate following the adoption of the Charter has been heavily influenced by cold-war currents which frequently obscure the criteria for optimum allocation of authority. In the absence of more useful discussion of these issues the following discussion of policies favoring universalism and policies favoring regionalism are necessarily tentative formulations. The background assumption is that both universal and regional organ-

---

ganization rather than an optimum allocation of authority between regional and universal organizations in a system made up of both. See S. GOODSPEED, THE NATURE AND FUNCTION OF INTERNATIONAL ORGANIZATION 567-70 (1967). HULL, *supra* note 5, at 1639-48. There is some discussion of policy criteria for regional authority under the Charter, however, in Wilcox, *supra* note 2, at 807-11.

21. HULL, *supra* note 5, at 1644.
22. HULL, *supra* note 5, at 1645.

izations may have a role in the maintenance of peace and security and that the real issue is allocation of authority between them in the most policy-responsive manner.

THE principal policies favoring universalism seem to be that states affected by decision should have an opportunity to participate in the decision-making, that effective decision may require that competing major powers be included in security decisions, that wider decision is more likely to reflect community common interest, and the corollary of this principle that major power dominance of regional organizations may sometimes result in assertion of special interests.

The first of these, that states affected by decision should have an opportunity to participate in making those decisions, is a widely shared community policy. To the extent that peace and security issues affect the whole community of states, the whole community has an interest in participating in their resolution. And in the kind of interdependent world in which we live today the quality of the international peacekeeping machinery is of concern to every nation. This policy strongly suggests that at least final authority for the maintenance of world order should be vested in a universal organization.

A second policy is the desirability of representation of competing major powers in security decisions. This policy reflects the importance of avoiding conflict between the competitive nuclear powers and of ensuring effective power to implement collective decisions. To the extent that world order decisions are approved by all major powers there is less likelihood of a major power clash. There is also greater likelihood that decisions will be effectively implemented. Moreover, participation in the decision process might moderate positions even if agreement is not possible. As Francis Wilcox puts it:

> regional organizations are not capable of bridging the gap between the East and West—or the North and South for that matter—nor are they able to transcend the Cold War in a search for a common ground for the solution of great-power differences.[23]

23. Wilcox, *supra* note 2, at 811.

The permanent seats for the major powers in the Security Council reflect these realities.

A third policy is that wider decision is more likely to reflect community common interest. There is, of course, no guarantee that a universal organization will always make just or rational decisions. The United Nations is a political arena with characteristics similar to other such arenas, and it is a mistake to idealize its decisions just because they are collective. Nevertheless, on a continuum from unilateral to universal decision there is greater likelihood that the wider the participation in decision the more the decision will reflect community common interest. As a corollary to this principle, since major powers exert disproportionate influence in a number of regional organizations, United Nations authority should be preferred as a check on assertion of special interests.

POLICIES favoring regional authority include the principle that those with greater values at stake in decision ought to have greater participation in decision, the advantages of utilization of local expertise and interest, the principle of effectiveness, and deference to consensual arrangements submitting local disputes to regional authority.

The first of these, the principle that those with greater values at stake in decision ought to have greater participation in decision, reflects the differential impact of decisions. If a decision affects only a particular region, then that region ought to participate in decision to the exclusion of non-regional participants. It is self-evident that in matters other than peace and security there are large areas of exclusive interests in which decision is and should be made unilaterally or regionally. Although few interests are that clearly exclusive if the issue is one affecting peace and security, nevertheless, even peace and security issues may have differential impact. Thus, the El Salvador-Honduras "soccer war" (really a population pressures war) presented a greater threat to the security of other Central American states than to the security of European or Asian states.[24] Similarly, it may have posed a

24. For a history of OAS action in the El Salvador-Honduras conflict see *Documents Concerning Conflict Between El Salvador and Honduras*, 5

greater threat to the integrity of regional peacekeeping machinery than to the structure of the United Nations. Accordingly, it seems reasonable to accord the regional machinery of the OAS the initial competence to deal with the situation.

A second policy favoring regional authority is the desirability of taking advantage of local expertise, interest, and capabilities. The inter-American system, the OAU, and to a lesser extent the Arab League embody dispute-settlement machinery which may be highly efficient in settling intra-regional conflicts. The relatively quick and efficient OAS handling of the El Salvador-Honduras conflict is a case in point. Had the OAS been unsuccessful in obtaining a withdrawal of Salvadorian troops, then the greater effective power of the Security Council might have been required. But in the first instance at least, the OAS was almost certainly a more efficient forum for dealing with such a localized intra-regional dispute than would have been the United Nations Security Council. Another case which illustrates this regional peacemaking competence is the OAU handling of the Algerian-Moroccan border conflict. It is particularly significant in the Algeria-Moroccan conflict that the major western powers preferred the OAU forum to the United Nations in order to minimize the chances of cold-war involvement.[25] Francis Wilcox develops several aspects of this second policy for regional authority when he points out:

> Clearly a smaller organization, such as the OAS or the OAU, which is restricted geographically to nations in relatively close proximity to each other, can create the kind of machinery its members need to cope with their common problems more effectively than a world organization. States located several thousand miles away from each other, separated by vast differences in historical background, culture, language, and political and economic interests, may find it difficult to appreciate as fully as they should the mutual problems that afford them a common basis for cooperative action. Even

---

INT'L LEG. MATERIALS 1079-1148 (1969); Fenwick, *Procedure under the Rio Treaty of Reciprocal Assistance*, 63 AM. J. INT'L L. 769 (1969).
25. Wild, *supra* note 2, at 28.

more important, most states have not accepted the idea that world peace is indivisible. Insofar as collective action to repel aggression is concerned, they are inclined to respond with far greater speed and vigor to a security threat in their own area than to a distant danger whose focal point is far from their own frontiers.[26]

A third policy favoring regional authority is the principle of effectiveness. Article 1(1) of the Charter sets forth as a principal purpose of the United Nations the maintenance of "international peace and security, and to that end . . . [the taking of] effective collective measures for the prevention and removal of threats to the peace, and for the suppression of acts of aggression or other breaches of the peace. . . ." To the extent that this purpose has been frustrated by the breakdown of the original conception of collective security, particularly the impotence of the Security Council, interpretation by major purposes may suggest a broader role for regional arrangements. Similar reasoning has been responsible for the growth of General Assembly and Secretary-General authority during the last two decades. This policy supports enlarged regional competence only to the extent that regional arrangements are in fact more effective in achieving the major purposes of the Charter.

A fourth policy favoring a regional role is the desirability of deference to consensual arrangements which submit local disputes to regional authority. The allocation of competence between regional and universal organizations ought not place arbitrary limits on the inventiveness of man. Consensual arrangements freely arrived at should not be overturned unless in conflict with clearly articulable community policies. The paradigm case in which this policy would seem applicable is when all parties to a dispute genuinely prefer a regional forum for dispute

26. Wilcox, *supra* note 2, at 807. Similarly, Cordell Hull reported that Churchill:

> attached great importance to the regional principle, because it was only the countries whose interests were directly affected by a dispute that could be expected to apply themselves with sufficient vigor to secure a settlement. Only vapid and academic discussion would result from calling in countries remote from a dispute.

HULL, *supra* note 5, at 1642.

settlement. Under those circumstances, unless truly compelling community policies suggest otherwise, the universal forum should defer to the regional forum chosen by the parties. Security Council deference to the OAS in the Haitian and Panamanian cases in 1963 and 1964 reflects this policy. In both cases all parties consented to initial reference to OAS machinery, though in both cases the reference seemed to imply residual Security Council authority. The policy favoring consensual arrangements is less clear but may still be applicable under circumstances in which the parties to a dispute have agreed as a condition for joining a regional organization to first submit local disputes to regional dispute-settlement machinery. Article 2 of the Rio Treaty and Article 23 of the Revised Charter of the OAS, both of which purport to create an obligation for members to first submit regional disputes to the machinery of the inter-American system before referring them to the United Nations, present this question squarely. Whatever the resolution in other contexts, in view of the possibility of assertion of special interests inherent in the disproportionate United States influence in the OAS, and the rejection of the purported obligation by many Latin American states, it seems preferable to restrict the principle to situations in which all parties to a dispute genuinely prefer a regional forum. In limiting the effect of these provisions in the inter-American system, reliance can be placed on Article 10 of the Rio Treaty, Article 137 of the Revised OAS Charter, and Article 103 of the United Nations Charter, which make United Nations rights and obligations preeminent when in conflict with the provisions of the inter-American system.

THERE are strong reasons for urging that a universal organization should have ultimate authority for the maintenance of peace and security. In the interdependent world in which we live, most issues of peace and security affect all of the members of the world community. Moreover, a universal forum is a more broadly based forum for the resolution of security issues, both in the sense of greater assurance that decision will reflect community common interest, and in the sense of greater effectiveness by inclusion of the major powers in the decision process. A universal security organization should encourage regional settlement of disputes, however, in situations in which the interests at stake are primarily regional, in which regional machinery offers more effective conflict management, or in which the parties to a dispute genuinely prefer a regional forum.

Claims Concerning the Authority of Regional Arrangements in the Maintenance of World Order

Study of the present and potential role of regional arrangements in the maintenance of world order can most usefully proceed by reference to the full range of specific issues presented for decision. In the absence of a comprehensive scheme for classification of these specific issues the study of regional authority necessarily remains episodic and pre-theoretical. Unfortunately, however, although a number of studies have perceptively focused on some of the major issues, there is still no adequate conceptual framework for inquiry into the full range of claims concerning regional authority. The following enumeration of claims is offered as a tentative foundation for such a framework.

A. *Claims Concerning Participation In Regional Organizations*
 1. Claims that organization for collective defense is impermissible.
 2. Claims that participants must have a common geographic, ethnic, or religious base.
B. *Claims Concerning Regional Jurisdiction of a Dispute or Situation*
 1. Claims that the regional organization has primary jurisdiction.
    a. Claims that members of regional organizations must first exhaust regional remedies.
    b. Claims that the United Nations may not interfere with the initial exercise of regional jurisdiction.
 2. Claims that the regional organization has exclusive jurisdiction.
 3. Claims that the regional organization has concurrent jurisdiction.

4. Claims that the United Nations should defer to regional machinery even though the United Nations has jurisdiction.

5. Claims that the United Nations may terminate regional jurisdiction.

C. *Claims Concerning Regional Authority to Initiate Non-Coercive Action*

D. *Claims Concerning Regional Authority to Initiate Coercive Action*

1. Claims to use the military instrument in response to an armed attack.

2. Claims to use the military instrument in situations not amounting to an armed attack.

   a. Claims that regional action which authorizes but does not require coercive action by member states is not "enforcement action" requiring Security Council authorization.

   b. Claims that regional action not directed against a state is not "enforcement action" requiring Security Council authorization.

   c. Claims that regional assistance to insurgent groups for the purpose of restoring self-determination is not "enforcement action" requiring Security Council authorization.

3. Claims to use economic or diplomatic sanctions.

E. *Claims Concerning Procedures By Which the United Nations May Authorize or Terminate Regional Action*

1. Claims that Security Council authorization of "enforcement action" need not be prior authorization.

2. Claims that Security Council authorization of "enforcement action" need not be express authorization.

3. Claims that regional jurisdiction has been revoked by United Nations action.

F. *Claims Concerning the Obligation of Regional Arrangements to Report Activities to the Security Council*

The following brief exploration of each of these claims is offered more by way of illustration than as a thumbprint of all prior instances of each claim. On each I will attempt to illustrate the problem and to suggest appropriate policy-responsive conclusions.

A. CLAIMS CONCERNING PARTICIPATION IN REGIONAL ORGANIZATIONS

Claims in this category concern the lawfulness of the existence of a particular regional organization or the lawfulness of a particular state's participation in a regional organization. Two specific claims have been made concerning participation, neither of which has been generally accepted. They are claims that organization for collective defense is impermissible and claims that participants must have a common geographic or ethnic base.

CLAIMS THAT ORGANIZATION FOR COLLECTIVE DEFENSE IS IMPERMISSIBLE

During the period of greatest activity in the formation of regional organizations oriented toward Article 51 collective defense there was some opposition to such organizations on the ground that they were unconstitutional under the Charter.[27] NATO in particular was subject to attack on this ground. The principal criticism was summarized by Grayson Kirk during an address delivered at the 1950 Annual Meeting of the American Society of International Law:

> there is potentially, and perhaps actively, a considerable amount of conflict between the principle of regional arrange-

27. See note 11 *supra*; Gerhard Bebr writes:
> Statements have been made denying the right of the United Nations Members to form any regional organization in advance of armed attack and make appropriate military preparations on the basis of the right of collective self-defense. The Soviet note protesting the conclusion of the North Atlantic Treaty argued along those lines in its attempt to show the incompatibility of the NATO with the United Nations Charter. Such "reasoning" is clearly untenable, given the present development of the technology of war. There is no indication, either in the Charter or the discussions, which would even remotely support such a view.

Bebr, *supra* note 2, at 173.

ments for security purposes and the general principle of collective security as it has usually been thought of in the past. Certainly I do not need to remind the people in this room that one of the driving forces for the principle of collective security as it was developed in the League of Nations and in connection with the creation of the United Nations was the conviction that limited groups, historically called alliances, would inevitably tend to breed counter-alliances and that a world in which alliances bred counter-alliances was an unstable world in terms of political and military security and a world in which, in all probability, controversy would end in conflict.[28]

The breakdown in effectiveness of the Security Council and the participation by all major powers in multilateral treaty arrangements for collective defense, however, resulted in general acceptance of collective defense arrangements. In view of the probable continued limited effectiveness of the Security Council, renewed challenge to multilateral collective defense arrangements such as NATO, SEATO, CENTO, and the Warsaw Pact seems unlikely.

CLAIMS THAT PARTICIPANTS MUST HAVE A COMMON GEOGRAPHIC, IDEOLOGICAL, ETHNIC, OR RELIGIOUS BASE

Egypt proposed at the San Francisco Conference that regional arrangements should be defined as:

> organizations of a permanent nature grouping in a given geographical area several countries which, by reason of their proximity, community of interests, or cultural, linguistic, historical or spiritual affinities, make themselves jointly responsible for the peaceful settlement of any disputes which may arise . . . as well as for the safeguarding of their interests and the development of their economic and cultural relations.[29]

The proposal was rejected by a subcommittee of Committee III/4 that seems to have been motivated in part by feelings that the list-

28. Kirk, *Comment*, 1950 PROC. AM. SOC'Y INT'L L. 22-23.
29. RUSSELL & MUTHER, *supra* note 6, at 705.

ing of factors was too narrow and in part by fear of reopening the difficult negotiations which had led to agreement on the regional provisions.[30] From time to time since then, there have been similar claims raised that participation by a particular state in a regional organization is impermissible absent common geographic, ideological, ethnic, or religious ties. Thus, the claim was raised by "The Lawyers Committee on American Policy Toward Vietnam" in criticizing American sponsorship and participation in SEATO.[31] Although it might be expected that heterogeneous organizations without common geographic, ideological, ethnic, or religious ties might be poor performers in dealing with local disputes, there seems to be nothing in the Charter that limits "regional" organizations (much less Article 51 organizations) to states with a common geographic, ideological, ethnic, or religious base. The United States participation in SEATO is perhaps the clearest example of this practice, but British participation in CENTO and Turkish participation in NATO are additional examples. The extent to which members of a particular grouping share a genuine common interest, of course, may be decisive in the efficient functioning of the organization. The collapse of SEATO demonstrates that such interests cannot be pressure-cooked simply by promoting a multilateral arrangement. But there is no reason to believe that genuine common interests cannot be shared across geographic, ideological, ethnic, or religious boundaries.

30. See RUSSELL & MUTHER, *supra* note 6, at 706.
31. Lawyers Committee on American Policy Toward Vietnam, *Memorandum of Law*, 112 CONG. REC. 2665, 2668 (February 9, 1966). The claim that regional organizations may only include states with common ideological or geographic ties has been explicitly rejected by a number of commentators. See Van Kleffens, *supra* note 11, 670-71; Kulski, *supra* note 11, 466-67.

    Robert Strausz-Hupe points out the fallacy of overemphasizing geographic ties when he says:
      Were the idea of Pan Americanism based exclusively upon the facts of geography—the continental relationships of North, Central, and South America—it would hardly be an important factor in world politics. The Americas are not a region.
    Robert Strausz-Hupe, "Regionalism in World Politics," in *The Americas and World Order*, INT'L CONCILIATION 117, 118 No. 419 (March 1946).

B. Claims Concerning Regional Jurisdiction of a Dispute or Situation

The issue of regional jurisdiction was one of the two major issues of regional authority argued at the San Francisco Conference. During the Conference the Latin American states vigorously championed broad jurisdiction for the inter-American system. Although the United States position was not completely clear, in theory at least the United States supported strong United Nations control of regional activities. The outcome at San Francisco was a perhaps deliberately ambiguous compromise reflected in Articles 52(2) and 52(4) which could be variously interpreted to fit the position of the interpreter. Thus Professor Inis Claude reports:

> At the meeting of Committee III(4), which approved the package of proposals designed to meet the pro-regionalist demands of the Latin Americans, a Peruvian spokesman articulated his concern that the changes did not clearly preclude the Security Council from asserting jurisdiction over intra-regional disputes at any stage; he was disappointed that the exclusiveness of regional responsibility for dealing initially with local disputes had not been recognized and safeguarded. The president of the Committee, speaking for Colombia, offered reassurance. He saw no problem of double jurisdiction, but believed that the newly adopted provisions established the rule that the Security Council must leave initial efforts at peaceful settlement of local disputes to regional agencies; the Council might investigate to determine whether such disputes threatened international peace, but it could not intrude upon the regional settlement process unless and until the latter had failed.[32]

In the twenty-five years since the San Francisco Conference, the breakdown of Security Council effectiveness contributed to a United States shift to advocacy of broader primary jurisdiction for regional organizations. At the same time, what many Latin

32. Claude, *supra* note 2, at 11.

323

American states viewed as United States dominance of the OAS and consequent assertion of special interests caused many of them to champion United Nations jurisdiction as a check on United States hegemony within the OAS. Today, although there are still occasional statements to the contrary by some United States officials and Latin American spokesmen, there is overwhelming support for a Charter interpretation that the United Nations has jurisdiction over all matters affecting international peace and security, and that deference to regional jurisdiction is a matter of pragmatic judgment rather than Charter requirement. The issues have been settled almost exclusively in a context of OAS action, though, and it is possible that as the equation regional autonomy means OAS autonomy breaks down the issues may again be raised and the lines in the debate redrawn. But in view of the present strong consensus for United Nation control it seems likely that the present resolution of the issues will stick.

CLAIMS THAT THE REGIONAL ORGANIZATION HAS PRIMARY JURISDICTION

The heart of the jurisdictional dispute is the issue of primary jurisdiction. Primary jurisdiction involves two related claims: claims that members of regional organizations must first exhaust regional remedies and claims that the United Nations may not interfere with the initial exercise of regional jurisdiction. Frequently the two are inextricably mixed together.

Claims that members of regional organizations must first exhaust regional remedies: Although it is frequently not clear whether this claim is one of prior submission or exhaustion of remedies, the usual implication is that members of regional organizations must exhaust the remedies of the regional system prior to referral to the United Nations. Support for this view may be found in Article 52(2) which provides:

> The Members of the United Nations entering into such arrangements or constituting such agencies shall make every effort to achieve pacific settlement of local disputes through such regional arrangements or by such regional agencies before referring them to the Security Council.

In addition, the inter-American system contains provisions in Article 2 of the Rio Treaty and Article 23 of the Revised Charter of the OAS which purport to create an obligation for members to first submit obligations to the inter-American system before resorting to the United Nations. These provisions were inserted in the inter-American treaties in order to strengthen Charter interpretations taking a broad view of regional jurisdiction. The overriding question, of course, is the interpretation to be given Article 52(2) in the light of Article 52(4), for if the Charter recognizes the right of member states to bring a dispute before the Security Council regardless of regional machinery, then Article 103 of the Charter, Article 10 of the Rio Treaty, and Article 137 of the Revised OAS Charter require that the Charter right prevail.

Though the issue was initially hotly disputed, present United Nations practice strongly supports the right of member states to appeal to the United Nations at any time.[33] Thus, the United States and Colombia argued in the 1954 Guatemalan case that Guatemala had a duty to first submit the dispute to the OAS. Similarly, in the 1960 Cuban case, Britain, France, and the United States made a similar contention with respect to Cuba. The argument, however, seems never to have been generally accepted in United Nations discussion of the Guatemalan and Cuban complaints. And in his Annual Report for 1953-54 the Secretary-General seems to have adopted a position in favor of the right of member states to appeal to the United Nations at any time, although his language was somewhat ambiguous:

> . . . a policy giving full scope to the proper role of regional agencies can and should at the same time fully preserve the right of a Member nation to a hearing under the Charter.[34]

During the ninth General Assembly a number of Latin American states explicitly expressed their understanding that nothing in the inter-American system could restrict their right to have recourse

33. Claude, *supra* note 2, at 21-46.
34. Introduction to the Annual Report of the Secretary-General on the Work of the Organization, 1 July 1953-30 June 1954, U.N. GAOR supp. 1, at xi, U.N. DOC. A/2663 (9th Sess. 1954).

at any time to the United Nations.[35] This interpretation seems to have been generally accepted within the United Nations during the Haitian case of 1963, the Panamanian case of 1964, and the Dominican case of 1965 despite the fact that the OAS exercised the principal initiative in all three cases. Even if there were an exhaustion of remedies requirement, the requirement should not be interpreted to require a futile appeal to a hostile regional organization. It would seem that the Guatemalan and Cuban appeals could have been decided on this ground alone, since in both cases the regional organization was clearly hostile to the position of the complaining state and in the Cuban case it was the hostile action of the regional organization itself which Cuba sought to raise.

Though the OAS has been the principal crucible for testing the right of regional member states to appeal at any time to the United Nations, one somewhat inconclusive case arose in an OAU context. During the Algerian-Moroccan border conflict of 1963, Morocco sought a hearing within the United Nations rather than the OAU. Eventually she agreed to the OAU forum but the reason was largely lack of political support for a United Nations hearing rather than any victory for a "try OAU first" principle.[36] Although as these cases illustrate, it may frequently be desirable for the United Nations to in fact adopt an exhaustion of regional remedies rule, it seems unwise to constitutionally require such a rule. And certainly any such rule should not require an exhaustion of regional remedies which would obviously be futile.

Claims that the United Nations may not interfere with the initial exercise of regional jurisdiction: This claim is slightly differ-

---

35. Claude, *supra* note 2, at 33-34. The United States continues to support an exhaustion of remedies rule though conceding United Nations "competence to deal with any situation which might threaten international peace and security." See Adlai E. Stevenson, *Principles of U.N.-OAS Relationship in Dominican Republic*, 52 DEP'T STATE BULLETIN 975, 976 (1965). Stevenson took the position that:

> the members of the United Nations pursuant to Articles 33 and 52 of the Charter should seek to deal with threats to the peace within a geographical region through regional arrangements before coming to the United Nations.

Id. at 976.
36. Wild, *supra* note 2, at 28.

ent from the claim that members of regional organizations must first submit disputes to regional machinery. For under Article 35 any member of the United Nations, whether a member of the regional arrangement or not, can bring a dispute or situation to the attention of the Security Council. Thus, it is possible for regional members to resort only to regional machinery and still have the issue raised in the Security Council. Similarly, any state might raise the issue in the General Assembly. The prior submission and interference with initial jurisdiction claims are usually not differentiated, however, and as a result their development has been similar. Arguments were made in both the Guatemalan and Cuban cases that the Security Council could not exercise jurisdiction while the OAS was seized of the dispute, and in the Cuban case this argument was made despite Cuba's not having filed a complaint with the OAS. The arguments were closely linked to arguments concerning the duty of OAS member states to first resort to regional machinery, and like that claim did not seem to be accepted by the Council. Thus, in the same Annual Report in which he referred to "the right of a member nation to a hearing under the Charter" the Secretary-General also said:

> in those cases where resort to . . . [regional] arrangements is chosen in the first instance, that choice should not be permitted to cast any doubt on the ultimate responsibility of the United Nations.[37]

The jurisdiction of the Security Council to consider a dispute or situation concerning international peace and security despite regional exercise of jurisdiction seems to have been largely unchallenged since the Guatemalan and Cuban cases. Security Council competence was implicit in both the 1963 Haitian case and the 1964 Panamanian case. And it was explicit in the 1965 Dominican case in which the Security Council took parallel action by creating a United Nations Mission in the Dominican Republic while the OAS was still actively involved in dispute-settlement efforts.[38]

37. Introduction to the Annual Report of the Secretary-General on the Work of the Organization, 1 July 1953-30 June 1954, *supra* note 34, at xi.
38. See Nanda, *supra* note 2, at 257.

Moreover, in arguing that the United Nations should not interfere with the actions of the OAS in the Dominican Republic, Ambassador Stevenson conceded for the United States that the question of United Nations competence to deal with the situation was not even in issue.[39] That lingering, though seemingly unfounded, doubts remain, however, is illustrated by the declaration of the Inter-American Bar Association at its Fourteenth Conference in May, 1965:

> . . . the Organization of American States has original jurisdiction over the situation in the Dominican Republic and no other international organization has competence to interfere in the case until the O.A.S. submits it to the U.N. Security Council.[40]

CLAIMS THAT THE REGIONAL ORGANIZATION HAS EXCLUSIVE JURISDICTION

Claims that the regional organization has primary jurisdiction only assert regional priority. That is, regional disputes must first be submitted to regional agencies, and the United Nations must refrain from taking jurisdiction until regional efforts have failed. Sometimes, though, there has been a hint in the debates on primary jurisdiction that what is really being asserted is that the United Nations has no jurisdiction at all to deal with disputes within the region of a regional organization. That is, that the regional agency has exclusive jurisdiction. The United States position in the 1960 Cuban case, in which Cuba had not even referred the dispute to the OAS, is a case in point. The overtones of the debate might be interpreted to indicate a total denial of United Nations jurisdiction over events within the OAS region.[41] If that was the United States position, Ambassador Stevenson's remarks in the 1965 Dominican case indicate that it no longer is.

A second case in which there has been a hint of a claim that regional jurisdiction is exclusive was the 1963 Algerian-Moroc-

39. Stevenson, *supra* note 35, at 976.
40. As reported by Eleanor Finch. Finch, *Inter-American Bar Association*, 40 AM. J. INT'L L. 80, 81 (1966).
41. This seems to have been the Soviet interpretation of the United States position. The interpretation, however, requires a not inconsiderable stretching. See Claude, *supra* note 2, at 34-43.

can case. In that case the OAU Council of Ministers adopted a resolution which hinted at OAU supremacy in cases of breach of the peace in Africa. The pertinent language was:

> Considering the imperative necessity to settle differences by peaceful means and in a *strictly African framework*; . . .
>
> Reaffirms the . . . determination of African States to seek constantly, through negotiations and *within the framework of principles and institutions established by the O.A.U. Charter*, a peaceful and fraternal solution to all differences which may arise among them; . . .[42]

In any event, the claim of exclusive regional jurisdiction seems never to have been accepted, if in fact it has ever been made. To accept such a claim would be a giant step toward complete reversal of the decision to give overriding responsibility for resolution of peace and security issues to the United Nations.

CLAIMS THAT THE REGIONAL ORGANIZATION HAS
CONCURRENT JURISDICTION

Although claims that regional organizations have primary or exclusive jurisdiction have been largely rejected, there seems to be a general understanding that regional organizations may exercise concurrent jurisdiction, at least in the absence of United Nations action terminating regional jurisdiction. The 1965 Dominican case, in which both the United Nations and the OAS were simultaneously engaged in field operations, is an example. Coercive action by regional agencies, of course, may raise claims that the action is "enforcement action" requiring prior Security Council approval.

CLAIMS THAT THE UNITED NATIONS SHOULD DEFER TO
REGIONAL MACHINERY EVEN THOUGH THE UNITED NATIONS
HAS JURISDICTION

Claims in this category are easily and frequently confused with primary jurisdiction claims. Unlike primary jurisdiction claims,

---

42. Wild, *supra* note 2, at 30. Patricia Wild says of this resolution: "The wording . . . appeared to establish the primacy of OAU institutions over the United Nations in case of a breach of the peace in Africa." *Id.* at 30. It is not at all clear, however, that the resolution was intended to announce anything stronger than an exhaustion of remedies rule.

however, these claims are based on pragmatic rather than formal jurisdictional grounds for deferring to regional machinery. That is, the primary jurisdiction claims are claims that the United Nations *must* constitutionally defer to regional authority. The pragmatic claims, on the other hand, are based on the premise that such deference is permissive rather than required. And unlike the general rejection of the primary jurisdiction claims, these claims for deference on pragmatic grounds have been highly persuasive. Thus, the United Nations in effect deferred to regional action in the 1954 Guatemalan case, the 1960 Dominican case, the 1960 Cuban case, the 1963 Algerian-Moroccan case, the 1963 Haitian case, and the 1964 Panamanian case. In the 1954 Guatemalan case the Security Council did pass a resolution calling on all states to refrain from giving assistance to the attackers, but subsequent Security Council inaction in fact left the issue to the OAS. Even the Cuban complaint in the Bay of Pigs invasion resulted in an equivocal United Nations response.[43] The 1965 Dominican case is apparently the only case in which the United Nations has actually taken parallel action in the face of a claim that a regional dispute should be left to a regional agency. In the Dominican case, however, the parallel action did not go significantly beyond a call for a strict cease-fire and the establishment of a United Nations Mission to the Dominican Republic for the purpose of keeping the Security Council informed of the situation. Even this minimal exercise of concurrent jurisdiction stirred up a hornet's nest of opposition from the OAS. Garcia Amador, the Director of Legal Affairs of the Pan American Union, labeled the Security Council action an "abuse of power," and both the OAS Special Committee and the Inter-American Bar Association issued strong condemnations of the United Nations action.[44]

In evaluating claims for United Nations deference to regional machinery, it is useful to distinguish those cases in which the regional forum was chosen because all parties genuinely preferred regional action, because of genuine regional expertise or because the interests at stake were primarily regional, from those which were simply cold-war efforts to avoid United Nations con-

43. See Claude, *supra* note 2, at 21-34 (Guatemala), 40-43 (Cuba).
44. See Nanda, *supra* note 2, at 259-61.

sideration of questionable conduct. Those in the first category, such as the consensual deferrals to the OAS in the 1963 Haitian and 1964 Panamanian cases, were largely non-controversial. Cold-war efforts to avoid UN consideration, though, primarily the 1954 Guatemalan and the 1960 Bay of Pigs instances, faced rougher going. The 1965 Dominican case seems to have some elements of both categories and may foreshadow a tougher United Nations attitude toward deference to regional action. It would seem that claims in this category ought to be decided by reference to the policy criteria whether the interests at stake are primarily regional, whether regional machinery offers more effective conflict management, and whether the parties to the dispute genuinely prefer a regional forum.

CLAIMS THAT THE UNITED NATIONS MAY TERMINATE REGIONAL JURISDICTION

The Security Council would seem to have authority under Articles 24, 25, 39, 51, 52, and 53 taken together to revoke regional jurisdiction in the handling of any issue affecting international peace and security. Of particular significance, Article 24 confers "on the Security Council primary responsibility for the maintenance of international peace and security. . . ." Although claims that the United Nations may terminate regional jurisdiction seemed implicit in the Soviet position in the 1954 Guatemalan and 1960 Cuban cases, the United Nations seems never to have terminated regional jurisdiction over a dispute or situation. That it has not done so even though general authority may be assumed is not surprising in view of the difficulties in obtaining Security Council approval of such a course of action, which can frequently be expected to be in opposition to the position of a major power.

C. CLAIMS CONCERNING REGIONAL AUTHORITY TO INITIATE NON-COERCIVE ACTION

The principal Charter provision concerning non-coercive regional action is Article 52(1) which requires regional activities to be "consistent with the Purposes and Principles of the United Nations." To date there seem to have been no major claims concerning regional authority to initiate non-coercive action. Since it is clear that non-coercive action is not "enforcement action" within the meaning of Article 53, such authority seems to be assumed in the absence of an allegation of a purpose inconsistent with that of the Charter. In fact, this category probably includes the most likely situations for Security Council referral to regional agencies, as is suggested by Article 52(3) of the Charter.

D. CLAIMS CONCERNING REGIONAL AUTHORITY TO INITIATE COERCIVE ACTION

Regional authority to initiate coercive action without prior Security Council approval, and thus without initial exposure to the possibility of a veto, was the second major issue in regional authority at the San Francisco Conference. The result of the compromise reached at San Francisco was the addition of Article 51. Article 51 provides:

> Nothing in the present Charter shall impair the inherent right of individual or collective self-defense if an armed attack occurs against a member of the United Nations, until the Security Council has taken the measures necessary to maintain international peace and security. . . .

Article 53, however, embodies a requirement that "no enforcement action shall be taken under regional arrangements or by regional agencies without the authorization of the Security Council. . . ." Regional action in response to an armed attack, then, need not have Security Council authorization but "enforcement action" must. Major doctrinal issues in clarifying regional authority with respect to coercive action, then, are the identification of the breadth of the defensive right and the identification of "enforcement action." In addition, pursuant to Article 52(1), coercive action, like non-coercive action, must be consistent with the purposes and principles of the Charter. If, of course, the Security Council authorizes a regional agency to take coercive action for the maintenance of international peace and security, then under Articles 39-42, 48, and 53 such action is clearly valid. Absent prior Security Council authorization, however, the parameters of regional authority to take coercive action are less clear.[45]

45. See generally Claude, *supra* note 2, at 47-60; Halderman, *supra* note 2; Meeker, *supra* note 2, at 520-22; Nanda, *supra* note 2, at 251-54.

CLAIMS TO USE THE MILITARY INSTRUMENT IN
RESPONSE TO AN ARMED ATTACK

Since the essence of the compromise at San Francisco provided for collective defense against armed attack without the need for prior Security Council authorization, it is clear that regional action in defense against an armed attack is permissible. As such, the major controversies concerning defensive action by regional arrangements center on the meaning of armed attack, particularly in relation to external involvement in internal conflict, and whether valid defensive action is limited to situations in which there is a prior armed attack.

The Charter is in large measure unresponsive to the problems of control of unauthorized intervention in internal conflict. On a major purposes rationale, however, it would seem that the defensive exception of Article 51 should be interpreted to permit proportional counter-intervention on behalf of a widely recognized government to offset impermissible external assistance to insurgents. Not to permit such counter-intervention on behalf of a widely recognized government would be to insulate covert aggression from defensive response.[46] This interpretation should be applicable to regional as well as unilateral action.

Perhaps the potentially most divisive issue in delineating valid defensive regional action is the question of whether such action is limited to situations in which there is a prior armed attack. The Cuban Missile crisis of 1962 presented this issue since the secret emplacement of Soviet missiles in Cuba could not be classified as a prior armed attack, and there was no prior Security Council authorization for the quarantine. A number of scholars have urged in this context that the "defensive quarantine" authorized by the OAS was permissible defensive action under the Charter, and that if such action otherwise meets the requirements of the "inherent" right of defense it is not limited by the armed attack requirement of Article 51.[47] Their interpretation, however, which

46. See Moore, *supra* note 1, at 279-80, 328-29, 337.
47. See Halderman, *supra* note 2, at 111-16; Mallison, *Limited Naval Blockade or Quarantine-Interdiction: National and Collective Defense Claims Valid Under International Law*, 31 GEO. WASH. L. REV. 335, 360-64 (1962).
    For a restrictive interpretation of the defensive right, limiting it to response against an "armed attack," see, *e.g.*, P. JESSUP, A MODERN LAW OF NATIONS 165-67 (1948).

parallels a long-standing dispute about the scope of the defensive right under the Charter, remains controversial.

CLAIMS TO USE THE MILITARY INSTRUMENT IN SITUATIONS NOT AMOUNTING TO AN ARMED ATTACK

Claims to use the military instrument otherwise than in response to an "armed attack," or arguably otherwise than in response to a broader inherent defensive right, raise questions of both whether such action is "enforcement action" requiring Security Council approval and whether such action is otherwise consistent with the Charter.

The meaning of "enforcement action" is disputed. One interpretation is that it refers to all coercive action by any modality (other than defensive action) and does not include non-coercive action.[48] Another interpretation is that it refers only to action which is obligatory on member states as opposed to action which is merely recommended.[49] One scholar indicates that because of the breakdown in Security Council effectiveness some states seem to be tacitly assuming a Charter amendment doing away with the requirement of Security Council approval for enforcement action.[50] Any such assumption, however, would certainly meet widespread opposition within the United Nations.

Claims that regional action which authorizes but does not require coercive action by member states is not "enforcement action" requiring Security Council authorization: Leonard Meeker, the then Deputy Legal Adviser of the Department of State, argued with respect to the lawfulness of the OAS action in the Cuban quarantine that " 'enforcement action' does not include action . . . which is not obligatory on all the members."[51] Thus, since Article 20 of the Rio Treaty provides that "no State shall be required to use armed force without its consent," the military measures authorized by the OAS could not amount to "enforce-

---

48. See Claude, *supra* note 2, at 48-53; Halderman, *supra* note 2, at 96.
49. Meeker, *supra* note 2, at 520-22. Professor Abram Chayes suggests that he shares this view when he indicates that "enforcement action" has been treated "as a rigorously narrow category." See Chayes, *Law and the Quarantine of Cuba*, 41 FOREIGN AFFAIRS 550, 556 (1963).
50. Halderman, *supra* note 2, at 91-92, 105-11.
51. Meeker, *supra* note 2, at 521.

ment action." The argument is based principally on a distinction between "a Security Council measure which is obligatory and constitutes 'action,' on the one hand, and a measure which is recommended either by the Council or by the General Assembly, on the other. . . ."[52] Although at least one scholar disputes this distinction as a delimitation of enforcement action even as applied to allocation of authority between the General Assembly and the Security Council,[53] the real issue seems to be whether such a definition of "enforcement action" for the purpose of allocating responsibility between the General Assembly and the Security Council should be applied for the purpose of allocating responsibility between the United Nations and regional agencies. It seems doubtful whether the restriction argued in the one context should be applied literally to the other. The consequence of such an interpretation would be that Security Council authorization of regional action would not be required even for coercive use of the military instrument as long as the regional body merely recommended and did not require that its members take action. Such action, of course, would still have to be consistent with the purposes and principles of the Charter, but for all practical purposes this restrictive interpretation would virtually eliminate the "enforcement action" requirement of Article 53. As long as the OAS remains the only regional organization seriously asserting regional autonomy, the United States may have a continued incentive to assert this narrow construction of "enforcement action." The possibility of the narrower interpretation's being invoked by the Warsaw Pact nations in taking military action in Eastern Europe or by the Arab League in taking such action against Israel, however, suggests some of the dangers in adopting this interpretation.

Claims that regional action not directed against a state is not "enforcement action" requiring Security Council authorization: During the course of the Security Council debates on the 1965 Dominican action, the United States took the position that the action was peace-keeping action not directed against a state and

52. Meeker, *supra* note 2, at 521.
53. Halderman, *Regional Enforcement Measures and the United Nations,* 52 GEO. L.J. 89, 97-105 (1963).

as such was not "enforcement action." The Cuban representative disputed this contention and argued that the "very presence of foreign military forces in a sovereign state constituted an act of a coercive nature and made the measure 'an enforcement action.' "[54] In its broadest formulation "enforcement action" refers to all coercive action other than valid defensive action. The Cuban argument implicitly seems to adopt this view. In its broadest formulation, then, the issue is whether a peace-keeping force (or if the first stage of the Dominican operation is in question, a force for the protection of nationals) undertaken with the permission of the government amounts to coercive action. If the purpose of the force is to restore orderly processes of self-determination and is not simply to render assistance to one side or another in an internal conflict, then there would seem to be a good case for saying that such action is not directed against a state and is thus not "enforcement action." In view of the United Nations financial crisis stemming from and further inhibiting United Nations peace-keeping operations, it seems desirable to permit regional peace-keeping operations without prior Security Council approval. Such operations, of course, should be neutral operations conducted within safeguards designed to ensure genuine self-determination and should be subject to subsequent United Nations review.

An interpretation of "enforcement action" which permits regional peace-keeping actions or humanitarian intervention undertaken at the request of a widely recognized government is also supported by the 1962 Advisory Opinion of the International Court of Justice in the *Certain Expenses of the United Nations* case.[55] The Court held that the peace-keeping action authorized by the General Assembly in the Middle East was not "enforcement action," in part because it was not directed against the sovereignty of any state and was undertaken with the permission of the Egyptian government.[56] Although the issue in the *Certain Expenses* case was the authority of the General Assembly rather than the authority of

54. As reported by Professor Nanda. Nanda, *The United States Action In the 1965 Dominican Crisis: Impact on World Order—Part II*, 44 DENVER L. REV. 225, 265 (1967).

55. [1962] I.C.J. 151.   56. [1962] I.C.J. 151, 164-66, 170, 177.

regional arrangements, many of the same considerations seem applicable on the issue of regional authority.

Claims that regional assistance to insurgent groups for the purpose of restoring self-determination is not "enforcement action" requiring Security Council authorization: The ambiguity surrounding intervention in internal conflict and the critical political interests at stake have prompted both the OAU and the Arab League to give collective assistance to national liberation movements without Security Council authorization. One of the purposes of the Charter of the OAU is "to eradicate all forms of colonialism from Africa. . . ."[57] To that end the OAU established a Commission on Liberation Movements which has been active in assisting insurgents in Angola, Mozambique and South Africa.[58] And the Arab League has supported the Palestine Liberation Organization in its struggle with Israel.[59] Such assistance raises both the issue of lawfulness of assistance to insurgent groups, whether unilateral or regional action, and whether such action, if collective regional action, amounts to "enforcement action" requiring Security Council authorization. On the first issue, the prevailing view seems to be that absent United Nations authorization assistance to insurgent groups is unlawful.[60] The Arab League action against Israel seems unlawful even on this first ground. But in the last few years the General Assembly has passed a series of resolutions authorizing assistance to insurgent movements directed against the colonial and racially discriminatory regimes of Southern Africa, and arguably such resolutions would support OAU intervention in Southern Africa.[61] Since re-

---

57. Article II (1d) of the Charter of the Organization of African Unity, *reprinted* in B. Boutros-Ghali, *The Addis Ababa Charter*, INT'L. CONCILIATION 53, 54, No. 546 (Jan. 1964).

58. See Boutros-Ghali, *supra* note 57, at 31-33; Padelford, *The Organization of African Unity*, 18 INT'L. ORGAN. 521, 536-37 (1964); Wilcox, *Regionalism and the United Nations*, 19 INT'L. ORGAN. 789, 802-803 (1965).

59. See *Keesing's Treaties and Alliances of the World, supra* note 10, at 172.

60. See authorities collected in J. N. Moore, *The Control of Foreign Intervention in Internal Conflict*, 9 VA. J. INT'L. L. 209, 276-77, 315-32 (1969).

61. See G.A. RES. 2262, 22 U.N. GAOR, Supp. 16, at 45-46, U.N. DOC. A/6716 (1967) (Southern Rhodesia); G.A. RES. 2307, 22 U.N. GAOR, Supp. 16, at 19-20, U.N. DOC. A/6716 (1967) (South Africa); G.A. RES. 2372, 22 U.N.

gional "enforcement action" requires Security Council approval, however, there is still some question whether such General Assembly authorization would be sufficient authorization for collective regional intervention. Although it seems anomalous that General Assembly action might suffice to authorize unilateral but not regional intervention, it would also seem anomalous to characterize assistance to insurgents as something other than "enforcement action." The issue seems never to have been raised and remains one of many submerged icebergs on the vast and only slightly charted sea of intervention.

CLAIMS TO USE ECONOMIC OR DIPLOMATIC SANCTIONS

There can be little doubt that claims to employ economic or diplomatic sanctions in response to an armed attack (or possibly any other situation triggering an inherent defensive right) are as lawful as claims to respond with the military instrument. The recent OAS action in the Honduras-El Salvador conflict indicates that the threat of economic and diplomatic sanctions may be all that is necessary to ensure compliance with regional peace-making efforts. Certainly such sanctions should be as lawful as the more coercive use of the military instrument.

If economic and diplomatic sanctions are employed in the absence of an armed attack, however, then regional authority is less certain. The difficulty, of course, is whether such action amounts to "enforcement action" requiring Security Council approval. One interpretation of "enforcement action" is that such action is restricted to military measures and does not include economic or diplomatic sanctions.[62] In support of this interpretation

---

GAOR, Supp. 16A, at 1-2, U.N. DOC. A/6716/Add. 1 (1968) (South-West Africa); G.A. RES. 2270, 22 U.N. GAOR, Supp. 16, at 47-48, U.N. DOC. A/6716 (1967) (Portuguese colonies).

62. See Halderman, *supra* note 53, at 96. Francis Wilcox suggests that this position has merit though "its historical roots" are unimpressive:

The United States' argument that Security Council approval should be limited to enforcement action that involves the use of military power and should not be required for the limited kind of political or economic sanctions the OAS invoked against the Dominican Republic certainly has some merit. Clearly it is within the power of *any* sovereign state—without violating the Charter—to sever diplomatic or economic relations or to interrupt its comit is argued that since individual states are not restricted from breaking diplomatic relations or imposing trade or other economic restrictions, states acting collectively within a regional organization may also take such action without Security Council approval. On the other hand, at least one scholar urges that the proper distinction is not between military and non-military measures, but between coercive and non-coercive measures, whatever the modality of coercion.[63] In support of this position, Articles 41 and 42 of the Charter refer alike to both non-military and military actions as "measures" which the Security Council may take "to maintain or restore international peace and security" under Article 39. And Professor Inis Claude refers to some evidence from both the San Francisco Conference and the formation of the Rio Treaty that "enforcement action" was thought to cover collective imposition of non-military as well as military sanctions.[64] Although none of these arguments on either side of the debate appears decisive, there is strong support in United Nations practice for an interpretation which does not consider economic or diplomatic sanctions as "enforcement action."

The first case in which the issue arose seems to have been the 1960 Dominican case in which the OAS condemned the Dominican Republic for "acts of intervention and aggression" against Venezuela and instituted diplomatic and partial economic sanctions against the Dominican Republic. Although the Soviet Union did not oppose the sanctions against Venezuela, it requested a meeting of the Security Council to consider authorizing the OAS sanctions. During the ensuing debate the United States took the position that diplomatic and economic measures of the kind being applied against the Dominican Republic did not constitute "enforcement action." The Soviet Union, on the other hand, argued that all such actions were "enforcement action" within the mean-

---

munications with another state. Why, then, should UN approval be necessary for the same kind of action undertaken by a few states individually or by a *group* of states acting together?
Wilcox, *supra* note 58, at 800.

63. Halderman, *supra* note 53, at 96, 116-18.
64. Claude, *The OAS, the UN and the United States*, INT'L. CONCILIATION, 50-51, No. 547 (March 1964).

ing of Article 53. Despite the adoption of a United States resolution that the Security Council merely acknowledge the OAS report and "take note" of the sanctions, the Dominican case seems merely to have indicated the lack of agreement on whether "enforcement action" includes non-military measures.

If the 1960 Dominican case was not decisive, however, Security Council action in the March, 1962, phase of the Cuban case seems to have been a clear victory for the view that non-military measures were not to be considered "enforcement action." The March, 1962, action in the Cuban case was in response to a complaint by Cuba that the OAS measures taken against Cuba at Punta del Este constituted illegal enforcement action in the absence of Security Council approval. Cuba also sought to refer the issue of whether such sanctions constituted "enforcement action" to the International Court of Justice. During the debate, however, only four members of the Security Council denied or questioned the interpretation advanced by the United States that "enforcement action" did not include non-military measures. Claude says of this case; "Thus the victory that the United States had proclaimed at the close of the Dominican case became belatedly a fact."[65] That the victory was fairly conclusive is suggested by Ved Nanda's observation that:

> following the decision of the Ninth Meeting of Consultation to apply even more severe diplomatic and economic measures than had been previously imposed against the Cuban government, the Secretary General of the OAS, pursuant to Article 54, informed the Security Council of this decision, and the Council never even discussed the issue.[66]

The economic boycott of Israel instituted by the Arab League is a non-OAS example of regional non-military sanctions. As is true of OAS non-military sanctions, the Arab League boycott seems to have been generally accepted despite the absence of formal Security Council authorization.[67] Another non-OAS example is the OAU economic and diplomatic sanctions against South

65. *Id.*, at 56.   66. Nanda, *supra* note 54, at 254.
67. For a brief discussion of the Arab League boycott see Wilcox, *supra* note 58, at 799.

Africa and Portugal. Since the OAU nations have also pressed their case within the United Nations, and since the racial and colonial issues at stake largely transcend the cold-war, the OAU has not been faced with a major jurisdictional challenge from this action.[68]

Collective non-military sanctions, such as severing diplomatic relations or taking coercive economic measures, do seem to involve more than unilateral state action. As such, the principle that what states are free to do individually they may also do collectively may sometimes prove too much. Realistically, non-military sanctions may sometimes be as coercive as military sanctions, particularly if instituted by a multinational initiative. United Nations practice, however, seems to support a narrow definition of "enforcement action" which does not include non-military measures.

E. Claims Concerning Procedures by which the United Nations May Authorize or Terminate Regional Action

The debate in the Security Council on the OAS action in the Cuban missile crisis was drastically curtailed by the overriding concern to avoid a nuclear confrontation between the United States and the Soviet Union. Subsequent discussion of the lawfulness of the "defensive quarantine," however, has raised a number of important issues concerning procedures by which the United Nations may authorize regional "enforcement action." There is no question, of course, that such action may be authorized in advance by an express Security Council resolution. The issues which have been raised concern whether such authorization must be prior authorization and whether it must be express authorization. Although there seem to have been no claims to date concerning the revocation of regional jurisdiction, a separate category is included to consider the related procedural claims.

claims that security council authorization of "enforcement action" need not be prior authorization

Abram Chayes and Leonard Meeker, both former Legal Advisers of the Department of State, have argued in evaluating the OAS actions during the missile crisis that it is reasonable to in-

68. See Wilcox, *supra* note 58, at 802.

terpret Article 53 to mean that Security Council authorization of "enforcement action" need not be prior authorization.[69] In support of this interpretation, both scholars rely on the 1960 Dominican case in which the Soviet Union proposed Security Council authorization of OAS sanctions against the Dominican Republic after those sanctions had already been imposed by the OAS. Thus Leonard Meeker says:

> On this point it is illuminating to recall a 1960 precedent. In September of that year the Security Council had met, on Soviet request, to consider diplomatic and economic measures voted against the Dominican Republic by the Foreign Ministers of the American Republics meeting at San Jose the preceding month. The U.S.S.R. asked the Council to approve these measures after they had been taken. The Soviet theory quite evidently was that the Council could appropriately give its "authorization" after the fact.[70]

In evaluating this claim it is useful to distinguish the question whether the Security Council may approve regional enforcement action at any time either before or after regional action is taken, from the question whether regional enforcement action is valid until Council authorization is given. On the first question the Soviet position in the Dominican case was clearly that the Security Council could authorize regional enforcement action even after regional action had been taken. On the second question, however, the Soviet Union equally clearly took the position that: "Without authorization from the Security Council, the taking of enforcement action by regional agencies would be contrary to the Charter. . . ."[71] There seems to be no policy reason why the Security Council cannot authorize regional enforcement action at any stage, whether before or after such action has been taken. Moreover, if regional action is subsequently authorized it would seem reasonable to accord the Security Council authority to authorize it retroactively to the time when such measures were initiated. In

69. L. Meeker, *Defensive Quarantine and the Law*, 57 AM. J. INT'L L. 515, 520 (1963); Chayes, *supra* note 49, at 556.

70. Meeker, *supra* note 69, at 520.

71. U.N. SCOR, 15th year, 893 meeting at 4, U.N. DOC. S/PV. 893 (1960).

fact, unless the Security Council states otherwise, such retroactive authorization seems implicit in subsequent authorization. That authorization may be subsequent, however, does not mean that regional enforcement action is valid without any authorization at all. Until the Security Council authorizes such action it remains unauthorized enforcement action.

CLAIMS THAT SECURITY COUNCIL AUTHORIZATION OF "ENFORCEMENT ACTION" NEED NOT BE EXPRESS AUTHORIZATION

Chayes and Meeker also argue in evaluating the "defensive quarantine" in the missile crisis that in light of the paralysis of the Security Council and the consequent constitutional evolution of the United Nations it is reasonable to interpret Article 53 to mean that Security Council authorization of regional enforcement action need not be express authorization.[72] During the missile crisis the United States placed the situation before the Security Council and called for an urgent meeting of the Council. The Council met before the "defensive quarantine" was instituted and the Soviet Union introduced a resolution condemning the quarantine. The Soviet resolution, though, was not brought to a vote. In this context Leonard Meeker urges:

> The Council let the quarantine continue, rather than sup-plant it. While the quarantine continued, and with knowledge of it, the Council encouraged the parties to pursue the course of negotiation between the United States and the Soviet Union. Thus, if it were thought that authorization was necessary (which was not the view of the United States), such authorization may be said to have been granted by the course which the Council adopted.[73]

It is only a short step to Abram Chayes' formulation that:

> surely it is no more surprising to say that failure of the Security Council to disapprove regional action amounts to authorization within the meaning of Article 53 than it was to say

72. Meeker, *supra* note 69, at 522; Chayes, *supra* note 49, at 556-57.
73. Meeker, *supra* note 69, at 522.

that the abstention and even the absence of a permanent member of the Security Council met the requirement of Article 27(3) for "the concurring votes of the permanent members. . . ."[74]

But surely it would be surprising if failure to disapprove regional enforcement action amounted to authorization. The contention turns the Article 53 authorization requirement into an Article 51 subsequent review requirement. Whereas under the generally accepted interpretation of Article 53 the veto can be used to prevent authorization of regional enforcement action, in the Chayes view the veto could be used to prevent disapproval of regional enforcement action.[75]

For all practical purposes, then, the Chayes view amounts to an interpretation that regional action is valid unless disapproved by subsequent Security Council action. If that position is to be taken, it does seem necessary to call it a tacit Charter amendment stemming from changed circumstances rather than a reasonable interpretation of the initial intent of the San Francisco Conference. And as to the Article 27(3) analogy, the interpretation which Chayes refers to seems much stronger on a major purposes rationale than his Article 53 interpretation.[76] In any event, the consequences of accepting this interpretation would seem to be a quite undesirable loosening of Security Council control over regional action. What works for the OAS must also work for the Warsaw Pact, the Arab League, and the OAU.

74. Chayes, *supra* note 49, at 556.
75. See Halderman, *supra* note 53, at 105-11.
76. The interpretation that abstention or absence of a permanent member does not constitute a "veto" within the meaning of Article 27(3) prevents a permanent member from destroying the Security Council by prolonged absence. Moreover, it does not deprive the permanent members of the "veto" should they choose to exercise it. The Chayes interpretation of Article 53, however, reverses the original understanding regarding Security Council approval of regional "enforcement action" and for all practical purposes deprives the permanent members of the "veto" with respect to regional "enforcement action." For arguments for and against the Article 27(3) interpretation and a discussion of the policy issues raised see McDougal & Gardner, *The Veto and the Charter: An Interpretation for Survival*, 60 YALE L.J., 258 (1951); Gross, *Voting in the Security Council: Abstention From Voting and Absence From Meetings*, 60 YALE L.J. 209 (1951).

It should be kept in mind that the "enforcement action" requirement of Article 53 has both a positive and a negative aspect. Negatively it is a limitation on regional action in addition to the requirement that such action must be consistent with the purposes and principles of the Charter. As such, unauthorized regional action, even if it does not constitute "enforcement action," must still have an independent basis in the Charter. Positively, however, Security Council authorization of regional "enforcement action" is an independent basis for regional action which carries its own authorization. A loosening of the procedures for Security Council authorization of regional action, then, may have far more anarchic consequences than a narrowing of the definition of "enforcement action."

CLAIMS THAT REGIONAL JURISDICTION HAS BEEN REVOKED BY UNITED NATIONS ACTION

Apparently no regional action has been revoked by the Security Council pursuant to its authority to do so. Revocation which took the form of an express resolution condemning the regional action would seem fairly clearly to terminate authority. It might also be argued that Security Council action inconsistent with regional action would revoke regional authority. Just as in the case of Security Council authorization of regional authority, though, it seems preferable to require express Council action.

F. CLAIMS CONCERNING THE OBLIGATION OF REGIONAL ARRANGEMENTS TO REPORT ACTIVITIES TO THE SECURITY COUNCIL

Both Articles 51 and 54 create an obligation for regional arrangements to report certain of their activities to the Security Council. Thus, Article 51 provides:

> Measures taken by Members in the exercise of this right of self-defense shall be immediately reported to the Security Council. . . .

And Article 54 provides:

> The Security Council shall at all times be kept fully informed of activities undertaken or in contemplation under regional

345

arrangements or by regional agencies for the maintenance of international peace and security.

Though these two articles create a fairly comprehensive duty to report regional actions concerning international peace and security, in practice that duty does not always seem to have been satisfactorily met.[77] A principal difficulty has been regional involvement in internal conflict. Both the Arab League and the OAU appear to have engaged in assisting favored insurgent groups without reporting such assistance. And SEATO did not meaningfully report its assistance to the South Vietnamese government until several years after such assistance was initiated.[78] If the Security Council is to assert more meaningful control over regional activities affecting international peace and security, it would seem important to make the reporting requirement more responsive to the problem of internal conflict and to more effectively police its effectuation.

The Future Role of Regional Arrangements

The World War II debate focusing on a choice between universal and regional security organizations no longer seems relevant. Both universal and regional organizations are here to stay, and rather than an either/or choice the issues for the future are the precise interrelations between regional and universal authority. To date, these judgments concerning specific allocation of competence have tended to be made largely on the basis of the cold-war positions of the protagonists. The result is that discussion of criteria for optimum allocation of authority is long overdue. As a tentative beginning, the pervasiveness of peace and security issues suggests that the United Nations should have ultimate authority with respect to all such issues. It should encourage regional action, however, in situations in which the interests at stake are primarily regional, in which regional machinery offers more effective conflict management (for example, avoidance of cold-war entanglements), or in which the parties to a dispute gen-

77. See Wilcox, *supra* note 58, at 799.
78. See Moore, *supra* note 60, at 211-12, 300-301.

uinely prefer a regional forum. These criteria support the general expectation that the United Nations has jurisdiction of any dispute or situation likely to endanger "the maintenance of international peace and security,"[79] but that in particular cases regional jurisdiction may be preferred on pragmatic grounds. It should be emphasized that these pragmatic grounds for deference to regional action may, in a particular case, be quite compelling, and that there are persuasive policy reasons for encouraging strong regional arrangements. If nothing else, the necessity of making security decisions with a high differential impact would strongly support some decentralization of international machinery for dealing with peace and security issues. Greater regional effectiveness in conflict management and deference to genuine preferences for a regional forum for dispute settlement are additional reasons for preferring regional arrangements which have demonstrated real merit. When policies suggest a regional arrangement as the more appropriate forum for dispute settlement, the Security Council should be encouraged to work explicitly through the regional arrangement. There have been too few instances of Security Council authorization or support of regional action when such authorization or support seemed called for. The United Nations should not, however, defer to regional arrangements when deference is sought simply as a technique for insulating regional action from community appraisal. Both the Guatemalan and Bay of Pigs incidents (and the Arab League action against Israel which somehow escaped Security Council scrutiny) suggest an abdication of United Nations responsibility.

In the absence of explicit Security Council authorization, regional action should be tested by conformance with the purposes and principles of the Charter. In addition, coercive regional action may constitute "enforcement action" requiring Security Council authorization. Though some arguments advanced for drastically narrowing the meaning of "enforcement action," such as the argument that regional action which authorizes but does not require coercive action by member states is not "enforcement action," seem to cut too broadly, the real question is why regional

79. Articles 24 and 34 of the United Nations Charter.

action should be more restricted than unilateral action.[80] Theoretically at least, since regional action is less likely to reflect special interests than unilateral action, it would seem that regional action should have broader latitude than unilateral action. Since the "enforcement action" requirement of Article 53 applies only to regional action, however, under the present Charter framework regional action is more restricted than unilateral action. This discrepancy has given rise to a strained narrowing of "enforcement action" to exclude coercive diplomatic or economic action largely on the ground that states are free to take such action unilaterally. It also raises such anomalous possibilities as General Assembly authorization of unilateral intervention while regional intervention, lacking Security Council authorization, would be prohibited "enforcement action," or certain unilateral humanitarian interventions being legal while the same action, if regionally initiated, would be unauthorized "enforcement action." Although, because of the greater coercive effect of regional action, coercive regional action should arguably be more restricted than coercive unilateral action, the argument proves too much. In the era of the superpower some unilateral action may be far

80. The United Kingdom Representative urged during the Security Council debate on the 1962 Punta del Este resolution that "enforcement action" should be interpreted "as covering only such actions as would not normally be legitimate except on the basis of a Security Council resolution." The argument for this interpretation was:

> There is nothing in international law, in principle, to prevent any State, if it so decides, from breaking off diplomatic relations or instituting a partial interruption of economic relations with any other State. These steps, which are the measures decided upon by the Organization of American States with regard to the Dominican Republic, are acts of policy perfectly within the competence of any sovereign State. It follows, obviously, that they are within the competence of the members of the Organization of American States acting collectively.

U.N. SCOR, 15th year 893d meeting at 16, U.N. DOC. S/PV. 893 (1960). See also Halderman, *supra* note 53, at 95-96.

This United Kingdom test might be rephrased more explicitly as "collective regional action is lawful (and thus does not constitute 'enforcement action') whenever comparable unilateral action would be lawful." Though such a test lacks historical basis, as a policy matter there is a case to be made for it. The test for individual and collective action is the same, of course, under Article 51.

more coercive than regional action. For the future, there seems to be little policy reason for appraising regional action by a stricter standard than that applied to comparable unilateral action. It seems likely, then, that pressures for a narrow definition of "enforcement action" will continue strong.

Perhaps the major policy issue for the future is whether and to what extent regional arrangements should be authorized specific areas of coercive competence which would go beyond unilateral competence, for example competence in authority-oriented humanitarian intervention.[81] The present dominance of key regional organizations by the major powers and their resulting cold-war involvement, as well as the use of the Arab League to wage regional warfare, though, suggest that for the intermediate future such an expanded regional authority not predicated on United Nations authorization in a particular case would be unwise. The challenge for the future is to revitalize the legitimacy of regional arrangements so that regional authority might be expanded to capitalize on their real potential in the maintenance of world order.

81. For an explanation of the possibility of using regional action as a halfway house between undesirable unilateral and unattainable United Nations intervention see Miller, *Regional Organization and the Regulation of Internal Conflict,* 19 WORLD POLITICS 582 (1967).

PART THREE

INTERNATIONAL LAW AND
THE INDO-CHINA WAR

Introduction

THE debate within the United States on the legal issues presented by the Indo-China War has been as insistent as that on other aspects of the conflict. A principal· choice point in the debate has been whether the United States participation in the Vietnam War should be viewed as a response to an armed attack or as intervention in an internal conflict. If the United States participation is properly characterized as collective defense against a prior armed attack, as it is characterized by the State Department memorandum, then the action would be lawful pursuant to Article 51 of the Charter. But even if it were more usefully characterized as intervention in internal conflict, as some scholars have urged, it by no means follows that it would be unlawful. International law strongly supports a right of counter-intervention against prior assistance to insurgents, and the evidence supports such a characterization as a minimum description of Hanoi's activities in South Vietnam. A more complete view is that the conflict is inherently ambiguous and has some features of "aggression from the North," as suggested by the State Department White Paper model, and some features of civil strife within South Vietnam and between North and South Vietnam, as suggested by critics of the action. For purposes of assessing world order considerations, then, it seems more useful to deal with the conflict in its full factual setting rather than in either/or terms. If it must be categorized, it seems most appropriately located in a unique category of divided nation conflicts.

Whatever the characterization, in its basic outline, as opposed to some incidents in clear violation of the laws of war as in the Son My massacre, the United States participation in the war would seem to have been in accordance with international law and the United Nations Charter.

The central point of international law relevant to assessment of the Indo-China War is that force should not be used in international relations as a technique of value extension. This principle was the basis of the Kellogg-Briand Pact and has since become a cornerstone of the United Nations Charter. It seems difficult to escape the assessment that North Vietnam, in pursuit of a revolutionary and nationalistic vision, is seeking value extension in waging war in South Vietnam, Laos, and Cambodia, and that the United States has been reluctantly pulled into a defense of its interests in that area. "Victory" for the United States essentially means maintenance of a non-communist regime in South Vietnam, but "victory" for Hanoi would mean a variety of changes favorable to North Vietnam. As such, the North Vietnamese action is in direct violation of the Charter, whether or not their perceptions of grievances arising from the failure to implement the Geneva Accords are accepted. On this the Charter is unambiguous. Force may not be used as a modality of international change regardless of the perceived justice of the cause. The basic force of this principle can be easily illustrated by application to other contemporary public order disputes such as the Arab-Israeli conflict. Application of the Charter principle to the existence of the present State of Israel seems more conducive to world order than encouraging competing Arab and Israeli conceptions of the justice of Israel's structure and existence. It is principally the failure to focus clearly on this basic Charter principle and the unconscious regression to the earlier and potentially disastrous "just war" notion that has marred the analysis of many of the legal critics of the war.

Perhaps more importantly than conclusion on the legal issues of the Indo-China War, the war and the debate have taught some important lessons. First, the inadequacy of the international law of non-intervention has pointed up the critical need for a comprehensive theory of non-intervention.[1] As a corollary, the war has pointed up the particular danger of divided nation conflicts. Of the nations precariously divided between the principal contending ideological systems, Korea, Vietnam, China, and Germany (perhaps Laos should also be included), two of them, Korea and Vietnam, have precipitated the two principal wars since World

1. The discussion in Chapter eight of "External Participation in Intra-State Conflict: A Policy Inquiry" is a preliminary policy analysis of a theory of non-intervention suggested by Professor Richard A. Falk. For a more recent effort at development of a viable theory of non-intervention see Chapter four "The Control of Foreign Intervention in Internal Conflict."

War II.[2] Efforts at accommodation of these disputes, such as the Soviet-West German non-aggression pact, would seem particularly worthwhile. It is also important in such settings to focus on the extreme danger of revisionist policies which seek to alter the *status quo* in such areas.

Second, the war has pointed up the need for revision and strengthened application of the laws of war. North Vietnam's blatant refusal to observe the Geneva Convention in its treatment of American prisoners of war and the excesses with which both sides have conducted the war, particularly in relation to the protection of civilians, indicate that revision and greater efforts at implementation of existing Conventions are long overdue.[3] Not surprisingly, a principal problem has been that the Conventions have been generally aimed at traditional warfare between nations rather than the peculiar difficulties of internal conflict, proxy wars, and indirect aggression. It might be useful at the conclusion

2. The recent disturbances in Northern Ireland also reflect lingering overtones of the divided nation problem as well as the more visible human rights and social issues.

3. For an analysis of the applicability of the 1949 Geneva Convention Relative to the Treatment of Prisoners of War to American servicemen held by North Vietnam see the Memorandum prepared by the State Department Assistant Legal Adviser for Far Eastern Affairs, George Aldrich, on the Applicability of the Geneva Convention of 1949 Relative to the Treatment of Prisoners of War to American Military Personnel Held by North Vietnam (July 13, 1966) in 10 M. WHITEMAN, DIGEST OF INTERNATIONAL LAW 231 (1968), *reprinted* as appendix B, and the article by Charles W. Havens III, *Release and Repatriation of Vietnam Prisoners*, 57 ABAJ 41 (1971). Quite aside from the applicability of minimum guarantees of the Convention, the Convention itself is inadequate for achieving its humanitarian objectives in internal conflict and limited war settings. For example, there should be an unambiguous right to direct repatriation of prisoners of war after prolonged captivity on condition that the repatriated prisoners of war not engage in further belligerent activities or other actions in aid of the war effort.

With respect to United States compliance with the laws of war in the Indo-China conflict see T. TAYLOR, NUREMBERG AND VIETNAM: AN AMERICAN TRAGEDY (1970). Although the United States has generally sought to adhere to the laws of war and the 1949 Geneva Conventions, adherence has been marred by inadequate efforts at implementation and by overly rigid reliance on Conventions which extend inadequate protection in mixed international-internal settings.

of the conflict to encourage the United Nations and the International Committee of the Red Cross to promote revision of the laws of war and their implementation in internal conflict settings. Such consideration might be aimed at revised and strengthened general conventions for the protection of civilians and prisoners of war. There are beginning to be hopeful signs of movement in this direction.

Third, international law should more seriously concern itself with the willingness of belligerents to negotiate in good faith rather than focusing its normative weight exclusively on initial assessment of lawfulness. Article 33 of the United Nations Charter binds all states which are parties to a dispute "the continuance of which is likely to endanger the maintenance of international peace and security" to seek a solution by peaceful means. Little adverse attention, however, seems to be focused on unreasonable negotiating positions or even outright refusals to negotiate. In view of the complexity of most public order disputes, extreme demands such as those made by North Vietnam or the Palestinian Liberation Organization as a condition for cessation of hostilities would seem to be inconsistent with Article 33 of the Charter. In this regard, reasonableness might be determined by willingness to compromise, by whether the settlement would result in value extension or conservation, and by reference to United Nations assessment of the requirements of self-determination. Perhaps the next stage in the evolution of the international law of conflict management is to meaningfully pour content into this principle in addition to continuation of the normative emphasis on non-use of force as a modality of major change. It would also seem particularly useful to attempt to increase institutional techniques and pressures for assisting in settlement.

Fourth, the Indo-China War has graphically illustrated the dangers of ambiguous and poorly-structured peace treaties. A principal point in chapters VIII and IX is that the Geneva settlement of 1954 was ambiguous in several key respects and that that ambiguity made it misleading to overemphasize the literal language of the Accords in emphasizing the justice of the cause of either side. Since these articles on Vietnam were written, Robert Randle's thorough study of the Geneva Accords and their surrounding context has strongly supported an interpretation of the essential ambiguity of the Accords in key areas of apparent agreement.[4] It seems likely that this ambiguity was a substantial contributing factor to the present Indo-China War. The experience illustrates the importance of spelling out the principal details of any political settlement or at least the procedures by which such details are to be agreed upon, of making sure that the agreement unambiguously binds all of the parties to the dispute (whether recognized or not), and that international control procedures are endowed with real power, financing, and recourse to a continuing international body such as the United Nations.[5] Political realities may prevent satisfying each of these recommendations, but to the extent that they are not realizable their potential cost should be clearly understood.

4. See R. RANDLE, GENEVA 1954: THE SETTLEMENT OF THE INDOCHINESE WAR (1969).
5. See Hannon, *The International Control Commission Experience and the Role of An Improved International Supervisory Body in the Viet Nam Settlement*, 9 VA. J. INT'L L. 20 (1968).

CHAPTER VII

The Lawfulness of Military Assistance to the Republic of Vietnam*

THE major thrust of contemporary international law is to restrict coercion in international relations as a modality of major change. The use of force as an instrument of change has always been wasteful, disruptive, and tragic. In the nuclear era the renunciation of force as a method of settlement of disputes has become an imperative. These necessities have resulted in a widely accepted distinction between lawful and unlawful uses of force in international relations which is embodied in the United Nations Charter. Force pursuant to the right of individual or collective defense or expressly authorized by the centralized peacekeeping machinery of the United Nations is lawful. Essentially all other major uses of force in international relations are unlawful.[1] These fundamental proscriptions are designed to protect self-determination of the peoples of the world and to achieve at least minimum world public order. As such, they reflect the basic expectations of the international community. Since they are aimed at prohibiting the unilateral use of force as a modality of major change, they have con-

---

* This Chapter draws heavily on a more comprehensive paper entitled "The Lawfulness of United States Assistance to the Republic of Viet Nam," written by the author and James L. Underwood in collaboration with Myres S. McDougal, and distributed to Congress by the American Bar Association. This joint study is summarized by Senator Javits at 112 CONG. REC. 13232-33 (daily ed., June 22, 1966), and is reprinted in full at 112 CONG. REC. 14943 (daily ed., July 14, 1966). The joint study also includes an analysis of the lawfulness of United States assistance under internal constitutional processes.

   For different perspectives on the problem treated in this chapter, see Standard, *United States Intervention in Vietnam Is Not Legal*, 52 A.B.A.J. 627 (1966); Wright, *Legal Aspects of the Viet-Nam Situation*, 60 AM. J. INT'L L. 750 (1966). See generally Finman and Macaulay, *Freedom to Dissent: The Vietnam Protests and the Words of Public Officials*, 1966 WIS. LAW REV. 632.

1. See generally M. MCDOUGAL & F. FELICIANO, LAW AND MINIMUM WORLD PUBLIC ORDER 121-260 (1961).

sistently authorized the use of force in individual or collective defense at least "until the Security Council has taken the measures necessary to maintain international peace and security." This defensive right is, at least at the present level of effectiveness of international peacekeeping machinery, necessary to the prevention of unilateral use of force as an instrument of change. The fundamental distinction between unlawful unilateral force to achieve major change and lawful force in individual or collective defense against such coercion is the structural steel for assessment of the lawfulness of the present military assistance to the Republic of Vietnam.

Assessed against this fundamental structure, defensive assistance to the Republic of Vietnam is lawful under the most widely accepted principles of customary international law and the United Nations Charter. The unilateral use of coercion by the Democratic Republic of Vietnam (the D.R.V.)—North Vietnam—against the territorial and political integrity of the Republic of Vietnam (the R.V.N.) is unlawful. Analysis placing principal emphasis on minimum world public order and genuine self-determination as basic community policies indicates that, for purposes of assessing the lawfulness of the use of force, the Republic of Vietnam and the Democratic Republic of Vietnam are separate international entities, that there is an unlawful armed attack on the R.V.N. by the D.R.V., that third states may lawfully assist in the collective defense of the R.V.N., and that the response of the R.V.N., the United States, and other assisting nations is reasonably necessary to the defense of the R.V.N.

For Purposes of Assessing the Lawfulness of the Use of Force the Republic of Vietnam and the Democratic Republic of Vietnam are Separate International Entities

It is often asserted that the Vietnam conflict is merely a civil war between North and South Vietnam, with the implication that North Vietnam may lawfully use the military instrument against South Vietnam and that defensive assistance to the R.V.N. is intervention in a civil war. Such arguments are not new. Similar assertions were made by the U.S.S.R. during the Korean conflict.[2] Although, as in Korea, there are a number of similarities between the Vietnam conflict and a civil war, for the purpose of assessing the lawfulness of the use of force by the D.R.V. against the R.V.N. and the lawfulness of responding defensive military assistance to the R.V.N. there can be no question but that the R.V.N. is a separate international entity. McDougal and Feliciano point out in their treatise *Law and Minimum World Public Order*:

> The decisions reached by the United Nations in the Palestine and Korean cases suggest that conflicts involving a newly organized territorial body politic, or conflicts between two distinct territorial units which the community expects to be relatively permanent, are, for purposes of policy about coercion, to be treated as conflicts between established states. Thus, the applicability of basic community policy about minimum public order in the world arena and competence to defend against unlawful violence are not dependent upon formal recognition of the technical statehood of the claimant-group by the opposing participants. . . .[3]
>
> Our emphasis here is merely that rational community policy must be directed to the coercive interactions of territorially organized communities of consequential size, whatever the "lawfulness" of their origin and whatever the prior niceties in the presence or absence of the ceremony of recognition.[4]

Since disputes about the legality of the origin of territorial entities or exercises of authority over territory are common, it would greatly undermine the basic prohibition on unilateral use of force in international relations to allow unilateral resort to force to change a continuing *de facto* exercise of authority. The R.V.N. and the D.R.V. have at least been separate *de facto* international entities for the more than sixteen-year period since the Geneva Accords of 1954. Professor Friedmann points out this reality

2. H. KELSEN, THE LAW OF THE UNITED NATIONS 930, note 6 (1964); MC DOUGAL & FELICIANO, *supra*, note 1, at 221.

3. MC DOUGAL & FELICIANO, *supra* note 1, at 221.

4. *Id.* at 222.

when he says: "It may be conceded that North and South Vietnam are today *de facto* separate states, even though the Geneva Agreement of 1954 spoke of 'two zones.' "[5] In fact, the evidence indicates that the R.V.N. is a state under international law and that today there are substantial expectations that the D.R.V. and the R.V.N. are separate and independent states under international law.[6] On three separate occasions, once prior to the Accords, and twice since then, the General Assembly of the United Nations has found that the R.V.N. or its predecessor, the state of Vietnam, is a state entitled to admission to the United Nations. On each occasion the "veto" of the U.S.S.R. has defeated the Security Council resolution calling for admission.

The status of the R.V.N. as a state under international law is confirmed by the recognition presently accorded it by about 60 nations. It is also presently a member of at least 30 international organizations including 12 specialized agencies of the United Nations, has a permanent observer at the United Nations, and has participated in a large number of international conferences. The R.V.N. is a member of as many specialized agencies of the United Nations as is the Republic of Korea and is a member of more such agencies than are Albania, Cambodia, Cuba, Czechoslovakia, and the U.S.S.R., among others. With respect to the D.R.V., its claims to statehood are strengthened by the recognition presently accorded it by about 24 nations, and its participation in a number of international conferences. The substantial expectations that the D.R.V. and the R.V.N. are separate and independent states under international law are also evidenced by the package-deal proposal of the U.S.S.R. in 1957 to admit the D.R.V., the R.V.N., and both Koreas to the United Nations as four separate states.[7]

5. Friedmann, *United States Policy and the Crisis of International Law,* 59 AM. J. INT'L L. 857, 866 (1965).

6. For more detailed treatment of the evidence, see Moore & Underwood, *The Lawfulness of United States Assistance to the Republic of Viet Nam,* 112 CONG. REC. 14943, 14944-48 (daily ed., July 14, 1966).

7. During the debates on this and the other draft resolutions calling for the admission of the R.V.N., the three Soviet delegates said between them:

    [B]oth in Korea and in Viet-Nam two separate States existed, which differed from one another in ˙political and economic structure. . . .

Today, more than sixteen years after the Geneva Accords of 1954, it denies reality to assert that there are not at least two continuing *de facto* international entities in Vietnam.[8] The D.R.V. and the R.V.N. unmistakably function as separate entities in the international arena. They have separate governments, separate international representation, separate constitutions, separate territories, separate populations, separate armies, and have developed for a substantial period of time along separate ideological lines. Whether or not the D.R.V. and the R.V.N. are full fledged *de jure* states under international law, and there are substantial expectations that they are, they are at least separate international entities with respect to the lawfulness of the use of force. In these circumstances the D.R.V. may not unilaterally resort to force against the R.V.N. consistent with the vital expectations of the peoples of the world about the preservation of minimum world public order and the minimization of destructive modes of change.

A favorite argument of those who characterize the Vietnam

The fact was that there were two States in Korea and two States in Viet-Nam. . . .

The realistic approach was to admit that there were two States with conflicting political systems in both Korea and Viet-Nam. In the circumstances, the only possible solution was the simultaneous admission of the four countries constituting Korea and Viet-Nam.
. . .

[T]wo completely separate and independent States had been established in each of those countries, [Korea and Vietnam] with different political, social and economic systems. *Id.* at 14947.

8. Professor Lauterpacht listed both Vietminh and Vietnam as separate states under international law apparently even prior to the Accords. Under the heading "States At Present International Persons," Professor Lauterpacht listed among others "Vietminh, Vietnam, North Korea and South Korea." I. L. OPPENHEIM, INTERNATIONAL LAW 255-58 (8th ed., Lauterpacht, 1955). See also B. MURTI, VIETNAM DIVIDED 171-72, 172, note 7 (1964).

As Dr. B. S. N. Murti, an Indian scholar who was actively associated with the International Commission For Supervision and Control in Viet-Nam, has written in 1964: "Two independent sovereign States, claiming sovereignty over the whole country, came into existence in Viet Nam and the division of the country seems permanent. . . ." *Id.* at v. "Both the States are completely independent with full-fledged Governments of their own owing no allegiance to the other." *Id.* at 176.

conflict as a civil war is to invoke the language of the Accords to the effect that "the military demarcation line is provisional and should not in any way be interpreted as constituting a political or territorial boundary."[9] Under the Geneva Accords a principal purpose of the agreements was a military cease-fire making the use of force by one zone against the other unlawful. If nothing else, the two zones were at least intended as separate international entities with respect to the lawfulness of the use of force. To get comfort from the Accords for the proposition that force by the D.R.V. against the R.V.N. is not unlawful is to stand the agreements on their head. The Geneva Accords of 1954 affirm for Vietnam the norm of customary international law that force by one international entity against another is unlawful as a method of settlement of political disputes. Clearly, the use of force as an instrument of political settlement across an international cease-fire line is not civil strife for purposes of assessing its lawfulness under international law.[10]

9. William Standard, in a recent article in the *American Bar Association Journal* invokes this language to indicate that "It cannot be asserted that South Vietnam is a separate 'country' so far as North Vietnam is concerned." Standard, *United States Intervention in Vietnam Is Not Legal*, 52 A.B.A.J. 627, 630 (1966). The group known as the "Lawyers Committee on American Policy Toward Vietnam," of which Standard is Chairman, make much the same point. *Memorandum of Law of the Lawyers Committee on American Policy Toward Vietnam*, 112 CONG. REC. 2552, 2555-56 (daily ed., Feb. 9, 1966).

Aside from the very considerable uncertainties as to whom the Geneva Accords bound and the reasonable expectations of the participants with respect to the Geneva settlement, Standard and the Lawyers Committee miss the point. The issue is not whether North and South Vietnam are separate countries, although there are substantial expectations today that they are, despite this language, but whether they are separate international entities for purposes of assessing the lawfulness of the use of force.

10. As Professor Quincy Wright pointed out in the 1959 PROC. AM. SOC'Y INT'L L.:

Another complication may result from the protracted functioning of a cease-fire or armistice line within the territory of a state. While hostilities across such a line by the government in control of one side, claiming title to rule the entire state, seems on its face to be civil strife, if such lines have been long continued and widely recognized, as have those in Germany, Palestine, Kashmir, Korea, Vietnam and the Straits of Formosa, they assume the char-

It is also not tenable to suggest that the use of force by the D.R.V. against the R.V.N. is civil strife on the theory that the Accords ceased to have legal validity when elections were not held in 1956. Regardless of the failure to hold elections in 1956, and whether or not the Accords have continuing validity, in reality there are two, at least *de facto*, separate international entities in Vietnam. If the major framework of contemporary international law as reflected in the United Nations Charter is to have efficacy, one such entity cannot resort to unilateral use of force to achieve settlement of a political dispute against another, regardless of asserted unlawfulness of its origin or continuation. The argument made by some, that the Accords ceased to function when elections were not held and that the D.R.V. could then lawfully employ force against the R.V.N., sanctions unilateral determination to resort to force against another at least *de facto* international entity to remedy an asserted political grievance or breach of treaty. As Lord McNair points out, a breach of treaty as such can never amount to an "armed attack" justifying the resort to force.[11] The argument also seems to assume that, if the Accords ceased to have legal validity, the situation would revert to the pre-Accords state. In view of the separate reality of two functioning international entities after—and to some extent even prior to—the Accords, it is at least equally credible to assume that cessation of legal validity of the Accords would sanction the *status quo* and provide yet another indication of two separate *de jure* states in Vietnam.

In any event, the evidence strongly indicates that the military demarcation line in Vietnam *is* of continuing validity despite the failure to hold elections in Vietnam in 1956. There is no provision

---

acter of international boundaries. Hostilities across them immediately constitute breaches of *international* peace, and justify "collective defense" measures by allies or friends of the attacked government, or "collective security" measures by the United Nations. If this were not so, armistice and cease-fire lines would have no meaning at all. . . .
Wright, *International Law and Civil Strife*, 1959 PROC. AM. SOC'Y INT'L L. 145, 151.

11. A. MC NAIR, LAW OF TREATIES 577, note 1 (1961). See also D. BOWETT, SELF-DEFENCE IN INTERNATIONAL LAW 189 (1958).

in the Accords which indicates that the military cease-fire line would cease to have validity should the elections not be held. In fact, the continued functioning of the International Control Commission (I.C.C.) after 1956 and the official messages of the Co-Chairmen of the Conference suggest that the failure to hold elections did not affect the continuing legal validity of the international cease-fire line in Vietnam.[12] Moreover, there is evidence that both the D.R.V. and the R.V.N. regard the Accords as having continuing legal validity, as their continuing complaints to the International Control Commission indicate.[13] As the "Four Point" proposals[14] of the D.R.V. aptly demonstrate, assertions that the Accords ceased to have legal validity when the 1956 elections were not held would seem to be more rationalization than accurate reflection of the D.R.V. attitude toward the Accords or of contemporary community expectations.[15]

12. See Moore & Underwood, *supra* note 6, at 14971, note 71. In an official message from the British and Soviet Co-Chairmen, which adverted to the possibility of non-implementation of the election provisions, the Co-Chairmen said: "Pending the holding of free general elections for the reunification of Viet-Nam, the two Co-Chairmen attach great importance to the maintenance of the cease-fire under the continued supervision of the International Commission for Viet-Nam." Documents relating to British Involvement in the Indo-China Conflict (Misc. No. 25 [1965], Command Paper 2834) 96-99, at 97.

13. See Moore & Underwood, *supra* note 6, at 14971, note 70. "The commission receives an average of one note daily from North Vietnam protesting alleged violations of the Geneva agreements. . . ." New York Times, Aug. 6, 1966, p. 3, col. 6 (city ed.).

14. The "Four Points" state the public position of the D.R.V. with respect to negotiation of the Vietnam conflict. They rest heavily on unilateral U.S. compliance with the Geneva Accords of 1954 as interpreted by Hanoi. See the April 8, 1965, speech by Mr. Pham Van Dong excerpted in Recent Exchanges Concerning Attempts to Promote a Negotiated Settlement of the Conflict in Viet-Nam (Viet-Nam No. 3 [1965], Command Paper 2756), at 51.

15. For the stress that the D.R.V. places on the Accords, see Moore & Underwood, *supra* note 6, at 14978. Hanoi also invokes the Geneva Accords as the principal reason why United Nations "intervention" is inappropriate. *Id.* The D.R.V. position on whether Vietnam is one or two international entities is not the simple "civil war after elections were not held" argument put forward by some. By way of example, Ho Chi Minh's letter to heads of state on January 28, 1966, said: "U.S. imperialists have massively increased the strength of the U.S. expeditionary corps and sent in troops from a number of their satellites to wage direct ag-

To allow the D.R.V. to make the unilateral determination that the Accords are no longer in effect and that it may use force to aggressively achieve its objectives in a non-defense situation is a negation of the principal structure of contemporary international law as embodied in the United Nations Charter. The fundamental proscription prohibiting unilateral force as a modality of major change prohibits such use despite any number of political grievances, whether they be legitimate or illegitimate. Any justification of unilateral action because of asserted political grievances would substantially destroy the present structure of world public order. The only condition for lawful unilateral use of force—and then only "until the Security Council has taken the measures necessary to maintain international peace and security"—is individual or collective defense. If that condition is absent, unilateral force by the D.R.V. against the territorial and political integrity of the R.V.N. is unlawful and an armed attack gives rise to appropriate defensive rights in the R.V.N. to meet that illegality. If there is an armed attack on the R.V.N. by the D.R.V., the R.V.N. may lawfully take measures to defend itself consistent with the right of individual or collective defense recognized under contemporary international law and the United Nations Charter.

There Is an Unlawful Armed Attack on the Republic of Vietnam by the Democratic Republic of Vietnam

In addition to the fundamental community proscription that unilateral resort to coercion is unlawful as an instrument of major change, the strong community interest in restricting coercion limits the right to use intense coercion in individual or collective defense to, generally speaking, very serious situations in which there is no reasonable alternative to the use of force for the protection of major values. This community policy is reflected in the famous "necessity" test of the *Caroline* case, and in the language of Article 51 of the United Nations Charter, which expressly reserves the right of individual and collective self-defense if there

---

gression in South Vietnam. They have also launched air attacks on the D.R.V., Democratic Republic of Vietnam, an independent and sovereign country, and a member of the Socialist camp." N.Y. Times, Jan. 29, 1966, at K, col. 5 (city ed.).

is an "armed attack." By such verbal tests, contemporary international law expresses the judgment that minor encroachments on sovereignty, political disputes, frontier incidents, the use of non-coercive modalities of interference, and generally aggression which does not threaten fundamental values, such as political and territorial integrity, may not be defended against by major resort to force against another entity. These tests are simply representative of the community interest in restricting intense responding coercion in individual or collective defense to those situations where fundamental values are seriously threatened by coercion. Such tests have few magic qualities for making these determinations, and decision must depend on the context. As McDougal and Feliciano indicate:

> [T]he coercion characterized as "permissible" and authorized by the general community in the cause of "self-defense," should be limited to responses to initiating coercion that is so intense as to have created in the target state reasonable expectations, as those expectations may be reviewed by others, that a military reaction was indispensably necessary to protect such consequential bases of power as "territorial integrity" and "political independence." . . .[16]

This is the real issue in making the characterization as to whether there is an "armed attack" on the R.V.N. by the D.R.V. or whether the responding coercion was "necessary."

In arguing that there is no "armed attack" against the R.V.N. justifying a defensive response by the R.V.N., William Standard and the group known as the "Lawyers Committee on American Policy Toward Vietnam" apparently assume that the only right of defense under the United Nations Charter is spelled out in Article 51 and is limited by the "armed attack" test, presumably a somewhat more restrictive test.[17] There is a substantial body of opinion among international legal scholars, however, that the Charter was not intended to restrict the right to initially take defensive action in any way, and that Article 51, drafted for the purpose of accommodating regional security organizations, did not

16. MC DOUGAL & FELICIANO, *supra* note 1, at 259.
17. See references *supra* note 9.

restrict that right, whether by an "armed attack" requirement or any other.[18] Even if the restrictive interpretation of the Charter is accepted, accurate characterization of the evidence with reference to the policy of this language indicates that there is unquestionably an "armed attack" by the D.R.V. against the R.V.N. Among other evidence of this "armed attack":

On June 2, 1962, the International Control Commission, composed of representatives from India, Canada, and Poland and established pursuant to the Geneva Accords, issued a Special Report which considered allegations of aggression and subversion on the part of the D.R.V. against the R.V.N. In this Special Report, the first report so designated since the commencement of the I.C.C.'s reporting in 1954, the Commission, with the Polish representative dissenting, adopted the following findings of the Legal Committee:

> Having examined the complaints and the supporting material sent by the South Vietnamese Mission, the Committee has come to the conclusion that in specific instances there is evidence to show that armed and unarmed personnel, arms, munitions and other supplies have been sent from the Zone in the North to the Zone in the South with the object of supporting, organizing and carrying out hostile activities, including armed attacks, directed against the Armed Forces and Administration of the Zone in the South. These acts are in

18. See, *e.g.*, D. BOWETT, SELF-DEFENCE IN INTERNATIONAL LAW 184-93 (1958); MCDOUGAL & FELICIANO, *supra* note 1, at 233-41; J. STONE, AGGRESSION AND WORLD ORDER 92-101 (1958). The restrictive interpretation advocated by some scholars that the right of defense under the U.N. Charter is limited by the language of Art. 51 differs principally in practical effect from the above interpretation in assessing the lawfulness of anticipated defense and the lawfulness of response to attacks not involving the use of the military instrument. Since the D.R.V. aggression against the R.V.N. utilizes the military instrument as the principal strategy and since the response of the R.V.N. and the United States does not even remotely raise questions of anticipatory defense, there would seem to be little doubt that an "armed attack" has taken place even under this more restrictive view of the Charter. For scholars advocating the more restrictive view see, *e.g.*, P. JESSUP, A MODERN LAW OF NATIONS 165-67 (1948); Wright, *International Law and Civil Strife*, 1959 PROC. AM. SOC'Y INT'L L. 145, 148, 152.

violation of Articles 10, 19, 24 and 27 of the Agreement on the Cessation of Hostilities in Viet-Nam.

In examining the complaints and the supporting material, in particular documentary material sent by the South Vietnamese Mission, the Committee has come to the further conclusion that there is evidence to show that the PAVN [The People's Army of Vietnam—the Army of the D.R.V.] has allowed the Zone in the North to be used for inciting, encouraging and supporting hostile activities in the Zone in the South, aimed at the overthrow of the Administration in the South. The use of the Zone in the North for such activities is in violation of Articles 19, 24, and 27 of the Agreement on the Cessation of Hostilities in Viet-Nam. . . .[19]

In adopting these findings of the Legal Committee, the Commission said: "The Commission accepts the conclusions reached by the Legal Committee that there is *sufficient evidence to show beyond reasonable doubt* that the PAVN has violated Articles 10, 19, 24 and 27 in specific instances."[20]

In a February, 1965, report, the Canadian representative to the I.C.C. said in a dissenting statement:

It is the considered view of the Canadian Delegation that the events which have taken place in both North and South Vietnam since February 7 are the direct result of the intensification of the aggressive policy of the Government of North Vietnam. In the opinion of the Canadian Delegation, therefore, it should be the chief obligation of this Commission to focus all possible attention on the continuing fact that North

---

19. Special Report to the Co-Chairmen of the Geneva Conference on Indo-China (Vietnam No. 1 [1962], Command Paper 1755). Great Britain Parliamentary Sessional Papers, XXXIX (1961/62), at 6-7.

20. *Id.* at 7 (emphasis added). The Commission also found after recording this armed aggression from the D.R.V. that the R.V.N. had violated Arts. 16, 17 and 19 of the Geneva Agreements by receiving military assistance. *Id.* at 10. It is erroneous to merely "balance" the violations recorded against both sides in this report. The kinds of violations recorded against the two sides are crucially different. For a fuller exploration of this point and a discussion placing the Commission findings in the broader context of the Geneva settlements and the norms regulating the use of coercion, see the discussion in Section VI below.

Vietnam has increased its efforts to incite, encourage, and support hostile activities in South Vietnam, aimed at the overthrow of the South Vietnamese administration. These activities are in direct and grave violation of the Geneva Agreement and constitute the root cause of general instability in Vietnam, of which events since February 7 should be seen as dangerous manifestations. The cessation of hostile activities by North Vietnam is a prerequisite to the restoration of peace in Vietnam as foreseen by the participants in the Geneva Conference of 1954.[21]

A number of leading journalists have reported in the *New York Times* that the evidence indicates a high degree of initiation and control of the conflict from Hanoi. They also report that since late 1964 North Vietnamese regular army units have been moving into the R.V.N., a movement which has intensified since then and which has resulted in North Vietnamese regular army troops making up a substantial proportion of those fighting in the R.V.N.[22] According to the United States Department of State:

21. Special Report to the Co-Chairmen of the Geneva Conference on Indo-China, February 13, 1965 (Vietnam No. 1 [1965], Command Paper 2609), at 14-15.

22. New York Times correspondent Neil Sheehan, in an article in the May 2, 1966, *New York Times*, points out that:

> The available evidence strongly indicates that the war was actually initiated on orders from Hanoi. . . . The instrument for the renewal of guerrilla warfare was the clandestine organization that had been deliberately left behind when the bulk of the Communist-led Vietminh troops, who fought the French and were the predecessors of the Vietcong, were withdrawn to the North in 1954.
>
> The existence of such a clandestine Communist party organization in the South has been documented. In this regard, analysts also point out a fact often little understood in the West, that there is only one Communist party in Vietnam and that its organizational tentacles extend throughout both the North and the South. At no time since the mid-nineteen-forties, when the struggle against the Japanese, and then the French began, has the politburo of the party lost control over its branch in the South. . . .
>
> By 1960, the evidence indicates, Hanoi decided that some instrument was necessary to lend an aura of legitimacy and to disguise Communist control over the guerrilla warfare its cadres had fostered in the South [leading to a call for the formation of the N.L.F.]. . . .

In the three-year period from 1959-1961, North Viet Nam infiltrated an estimated 10,700 men into South Viet Nam. . . . The aggression by Hanoi became substantial in 1959 and had intensified to dangerous proportions by late 1961. . . .

It is now estimated that by the end of 1964 North Viet Nam had infiltrated over 40,000 men into South Viet Nam.

[T]he Liberation Front does not control the Vietcong armed forces, despite its claims to the contrary. Documentary evidence, interrogation of prisoners and other intelligence data indicate that the guerrilla units are directed by an organization known as the Central Office for South Vietnam, or Cosvin as it is commonly called here.

Cosvin is believed to be the senior Communist headquarters in the South, reporting directly to the reunification department of the Communist party in Hanoi and thus to the politburo. Through its military affairs department, Cosvin acts as a high command for the Vietcong guerrilla units. . . .

N.Y. Times, May 2, 1966 at 1, col. 2 (city ed.).

Similarly, Takashi Oka, a former Far East correspondent for the Christian Science Monitor, wrote in the *New York Times Magazine*:

Ho Chi Minh's Laodong party, with the intense, single-minded Le Duan as secretary general, was the Communist party for all of Vietnam until the Geneva Accords of 1954 divided the country into Communist North and non-Communist South. It retained its clandestine network in the South, and began expanding party membership there in earnest soon after the Third Party Congress (Hanoi, September, 1960), which decided on the "liberation" of South Vietnam. When it changed its name in the South to People's Revolutionary party, it was following the Communist scenario of an insurrection independent of Hanoi. . . .

The Communist chain of command begins in Hanoi, where the Laodong party's central committee openly maintains a reunification department headed by Maj. Gen. Nguyen Van Vinh. Analysts in Saigon believe that the reunification department is an agency for transmitting orders from the Laodong politburo to the South. Policy-making is the sole prerogative of the politburo, with Le Duan himself probably playing a major role.

From the reunification department in Hanoi, orders go out to C.O.S.V.N., which is at the same time the central committee of the People's Revolutionary party.

Takashi Oka, "The Other Regime in South Vietnam," *New York Times Magazine*, July 31, 1966, p. 9, at 46.

In a recent article about General Vo Nguyen Giap, Commander of the North Vietnamese Army, the *New York Times* reported: "Late in 1964 General Giap apparently decided, with the concurrence of party leaders, to move to phase three [mobile warfare] in the war in South

Most of these men were infiltrated through the territory of Laos in plain violation of the 1962 Geneva Agreement on the Neutrality of Laos. Native North Vietnamese began to appear in South Viet Nam in large numbers in early 1964, and in December 1964 full units of the regular North Vietnamese Army began to enter the South. The latest evidence indicates that elements of the 325th PAVN division began to prepare for the move south in April 1964. . . .[23]

Although there is certainly evidence that the conflict in the R.V.N. also has internal support, the totality of evidence—whether or not the above evidence is accepted in its entirety—strongly indicates that the campaign to overthrow the recognized govern-

---

Vietnam. So he began moving North Vietnamese regular army units down the Ho Chi Minh Trail." N.Y. Times, July 31, 1966, at 2, col. 5 (city ed). According to the Mansfield Report, "Infiltration of men from North Vietnam through Laos has been going on for many years. It was confined primarily to political cadres and military leadership until about the end of 1964 when North Vietnam Regular Army troops began to enter South Vietnam by this route." Mansfield, Muskie, Inouye, Aiken & Boggs, *The Vietnam Conflict: The Substance and the Shadow— Report to the Senate Committee on Foreign Relations*, 112 CONG. REC. 140, 141 (daily ed., Jan. 13, 1966). Times Saigon correspondent, Charles Mohr, recently reported that according to informed sources the latest intelligence estimates indicated that "of the 177 enemy combat battalions in South Vietnam, 81, or 46 per cent, are now North Vietnamese. . . ." N.Y. Times, Aug. 10, 1966, p. 1, col. 4, at p. 5, col. 5 (city ed.).

These figures are not far from those released by General William Westmoreland at a press conference on Aug. 14, 1966, when he indicated that:

> At the present time there are approximately 280,000 Vietcong. This consists of about 110,000 main-force North Vietnamese regular army troops; approximately 112,000 militia or guerrilla forces; approximately 40,000 political cadre, and approximately 20,000 support troops. Regular troops have been, in recent months, moving down from North Vietnam to South Vietnam in great numbers.
>
> Since the first of the year, we estimate that at least 30,000 regular troops have moved down, and perhaps as many as 50,000. You are well aware that several weeks ago a regular army North Vietnamese division crossed the demilitarized zone. This is the latest intrusion.

N.Y. Times, Aug. 15, 1966, p. 2, col. 4, at col. 7 (city ed.).

23. The Basis for United States Actions in Viet Nam Under International Law 5 (Mimeograph, U.S. Dept. of State).

ment of the R.V.N. by intense coercion receives at least substantial military assistance and direction from the D.R.V. and suggests that prior to any significant increase in the United States assistance, D.R.V. initiative was a critical element in the conflict. There can be little doubt from the evidence that this was so prior to the commencement of bombing of military targets in the D.R.V. in February, 1965, and the introduction of United States combat units in the spring of 1965. This use of the military instrument by the D.R.V. against the R.V.N. is not a minor aggression nor one effectuated by non-coercive means such as propaganda. It is not a mere political dispute and it is not a minor frontier incident. Nor does the attack raise questions of the right to prevent an armed attack before it occurs. Instead, the attack, whether initiated and controlled by the D.R.V. or merely substantially assisted by the D.R.V., is a serious, sustained, and determined attack on the territorial and political integrity of the R.V.N. The totality of the context, characterized by use of military force as the principal strategy, constitutes intense coercion creating in the target state reasonable expectations that it must use the military instrument to preserve its fundamental values.

Whether or not the "armed attack" language of Article 51 of the Charter places restrictions on the right of individual or collective self-defense, the intense and sustained attack aimed at the political and territorial integrity of the R.V.N. and employing the military instrument as the predominant strategy unquestionably gives rise to rights of individual and collective defense. As an analysis of the purpose of this "armed attack" language indicates, an "armed attack" is not limited to the overt Korean type of invasion. Professor Kelsen points out:

> Since the Charter of the United Nations does not define the term "armed attack" used in Article 51, the members of the United Nations in exercising their right of individual or collective self-defense may interpret "armed attack" to mean not only an action in which a state uses its own armed force but also a revolutionary movement which takes place in one state but which is initiated or supported by another state. In this case, the members could come to the assistance of the legiti-

mate government against which the revolutionary movement is directed.[24]

And Professor Brownlie writes:

> [I]t might be argued that "armed attack" in Article 51 of the Charter refers to a trespass, a direct invasion, and not to activities described by some jurists as "indirect aggression." But providing there is a control by the principal, the aggressor state, and an actual use of force by its agents, there is an "armed attack."[25]

The evidence suggests that D.R.V. initiative in the use of the military instrument goes significantly beyond such descriptions.

This armed attack by the D.R.V. against the R.V.N. is unlawful. The actions of the D.R.V. are neither pursuant to authority of the United Nations nor individual or collective defense. A study of the I.C.C. reports with respect to the grievances asserted by the D.R.V. demonstrates that the D.R.V. has no legitimate claim to justify its aggression against the R.V.N. as defense. The principal D.R.V. allegations of R.V.N. breach of the Accords are failure to consult on the holding of elections in 1956, reprisals against resistance leaders, inadequate cooperation with I.C.C. controls, and entering into a military alliance with and receiving military assistance from the United States. Since none of these principal asserted grievances of the D.R.V. constitutes a legitimate defense situation, even if all of these grievances were legally justified and the R.V.N. were bound by the applicable provisions of the Geneva Accords, the D.R.V. in its attack on the R.V.N. would still be acting contrary to the fundamental community norms on the regulation of coercion. Its activities constitute unilateral use of force as an instrument of political change and as such are unlawful.

In the perspective of the community framework for the regulation of coercion in international relations, the unilateral armed at-

24. Kelsen, *Collective Security under International Law*, 49 INTERNATIONAL LAW STUDIES 88 (1956).
25. I. BROWNLIE, INTERNATIONAL LAW AND THE USE OF FORCE BY STATES 373 (1963).

tack by the D.R.V. on the political and territorial integrity of the R.V.N. is unlawful and gives rise to the right of individual and collective self-defense.

The United States May Lawfully Assist in the Collective Defense of the Republic of Vietnam

The right of collective defense is recognized under both customary international law and the United Nations Charter. That right is the right to assist or be assisted by another state on invitation of a state which is subjected to unlawful attack. In a world with only limited expectations as to the effective competence of the existing centralized peacekeeping machinery, such a right has been regarded as necessary to prevent weaker states from becoming the victims of more powerful states. Moreover, in a global era in which we may accurately speak of a "world community," interdependencies among states suggest real interests, defense and otherwise, in what transpires in other parts of the globe. Article 51 of the Charter recognizes these factors when it refers to "the inherent right of individual and collective self-defense."

The fundamental community interest in restricting coercion has qualified the right of individual or collective defense by establishing an overriding competence in the centralized peacekeeping machinery of the United Nations to deal with the situation as it sees fit in the interest of world peace and security. But since the United Nations Security Council may be delayed in its response, may be paralyzed by the "veto," or may otherwise be unable to act for political reasons, the Charter clearly contemplates that the right of individual or collective defense exists in the first instance until qualified by the Security Council acting in a particular case. The language of Article 51 of the Charter reflects this understanding when it says "until the Security Council has taken the measures necessary to maintain international peace and security." In effect the structure of the Charter reaffirms the right of individual or collective defense but makes it subject to possible later community review by the existing, but unfortunately imperfect, centralized peacekeeping machinery. The initial determination as to when an attack justifies responsive measures in individual

375

or collective defense has always been left for individual determination and nothing in the Charter was intended to or does vary this necessity.[26] Specifically, such defensive measures are not predicated on a finding by the Security Council of a breach of the peace or aggression or armed attack under Article 39 or 51 or any other provision of the Charter. The argument of William Standard and the Lawyers Committee that some such United Nations action is required before the United States may lawfully assist the R.V.N. is erroneous.[27] Neither the R.V.N., the D.R.V., nor the United States has the right to be final judge in its own case. But this is not the issue. Their action, of course, is properly subject to community review. But it is lawful for the United States to assist in the collective defense of the R.V.N. at least until, in the language of Article 51, "the Security Council has taken the measures necessary to maintain international peace and security." To date the Security Council has not taken the measures necessary to maintain international peace and security in Vietnam. In the absence of such measures, the right of the United States to par-

26. D. BOWETT, SELF-DEFENCE IN INTERNATIONAL LAW 193, 195 (1958); J. BRIERLY, THE LAW OF NATIONS 319-20 (5th ed., 1955); P. JESSUP, A MODERN LAW OF NATIONS 164-65, 202 (1948); H. KELSEN, THE LAW OF THE UNITED NATIONS 800, 804, note 5 (1964); Kelsen, *Collective Security under International Law*, 49 INTERNATIONAL LAW STUDIES 61-62 (1956); M. MCDOUGAL & F. FELICIANO, LAW AND MINIMUM WORLD PUBLIC ORDER, 218-19 (1961); J. STONE, LEGAL CONTROLS OF INTERNATIONAL CONFLICT 244 (1954); A. THOMAS & A. THOMAS, NON-INTERVENTION 171 (1956); Kelsen, *Collective Security and Collective Self-Defense under the Charter of the United Nations*, 42 AM. J. INT'L L. 783, 791-95 (1948).

27. Professor Kelsen indicates the correct doctrine when he says:

Since within a more or less centralized system of international security the exercise of the right of individual and collective self-defense must be permitted because the central organ of the organization cannot interfere immediately after an illegal use of armed force has taken place, the question of whether or not the use of armed force which has actually taken place is illegal must be decided by the state which claims to be exercising the right of individual or collective self-defense. However, this is true only as long as the central organ of the security organization does not interfere. As soon as it does, this central organ must decide that question, and it may decide that question in another way than the state which claims to be exercising its right of self-defense.

Kelsen, *Collective Security under International Law*, *supra* note 24, at 61-62 (1956).

ticipate in the collective defense of the R.V.N. continues unimpaired.

With major emphasis, Standard and the Lawyers Committee assert that, because Article 51 speaks of "an armed attack against a member of the United Nations," the United States may not lawfully assist in the collective defense of the R.V.N., a non-member of the United Nations.[28] As has been pointed out, there is a substantial body of opinion among international legal scholars that the United Nations Charter was not intended to restrict the right to initially take defensive action in any way, and that Article 51 did not restrict that right. In any event, the above restrictive interpretation of Article 51 with respect to non-members has been almost universally rejected by legal scholars. Professor Kelsen says that ". . . according to an almost generally accepted interpretation of Article 51, the right of collective self-defense may also be exercised in case of an armed attack against a non-member state."[29] Professor Brownlie points out:

> It has been suggested by some writers that a literal interpretation of Article 51 would permit members to act in collective defence only when another member state has been attacked. This hypothesis is of doubtful validity for several reasons. There is no evidence that this was the intended effect of the Charter provisions and many members of the United Nations have participated and still participate in mutual security pacts which include non-members. Kelsen asserts that such restriction of collective defence is inconsistent with Article 2, paragraph 6. Finally, the Security Council resolutions of 25 and 27 June and 7 July relating to the Korean hostilities employ wording reminiscent of Article 51 in the context of recommending states to give assistance to a non-member.[30]

Most, if not all, legal scholars who have answered this question have agreed that the United Nations Charter does not restrict a

---

28. Standard, *supra* note 9, at 628.
29. Kelsen, *Collective Security under International Law, supra* note 24, at 88.
30. BROWNLIE, *supra* note 25, at 331.

member from participating in the collective defense of a non-member.[31] Article 51 was drafted largely to reassure the Latin American delegates that collective defense pursuant to regional arrangements would not be disturbed. Since the principal concern was that of the Latin American states worried about the status of their right to receive collective defense under the Act of Chapultepec if they were to join the United Nations, the language of Article 51 quite naturally was concerned with preserving the rights of members to receive collective defense protection. Noth-

31. In addition to the discussion by Professors Kelsen and Brownlie cited in notes 29 and 30 above, see BOWETT, supra note 26, at 193-95; J. BRIERLY, LAW OF NATIONS 305 (6th ed., Waldock, 1963); Heindel, Kalijarvi & Wilcox, *The North Atlantic Treaty in the United States Senate*, 43 AM. J. INT'L L. 633, 657-58 (1949). See also MC DOUGAL & FELICIANO, supra note 26, at 233-41; C. POMPE, AGGRESSIVE WAR AN INTERNATIONAL CRIME 66 (1953); THOMAS & THOMAS, supra note 26, at 171.

    Scholars indicating in the context of the Vietnam debate that the U.N. Charter does not restrict a member from participating in the collective defense of a non-Member include Professor Myres S. Mc-Dougal, Sterling Professor of Law at Yale, Professor Louis B. Sohn, Bemis Professor of International Law at Harvard, and Professor Quincy Wright, Professor of International Law at the University of Virginia.

    The only authority cited by Standard and the Lawyers Committee for the proposition that U.N. Members may not assist in the collective defense of non-Members is an excerpt from STONE, supra note 26, at 244 to the effect that "the license of Article 51 does not apparently cover even an 'armed attack' against *a non-Member*." Standard has not done his homework. Professor Stone is one of the scholars taking the position that the right of individual and collective defense under customary international law is not impaired by Art. 51. Although, as the quotation by Standard illustrates, Professor Stone does take a narrow view of the right of Members to assist in the collective defense of non-Members when acting under the license of Art. 51, he does not take the position, necessary for Standard's argument, that the U.N. Charter restricts a Member from participating in the collective defense of a non-Member. In fact, in his more recent book, *Aggression and World Order*, Professor Stone indicates that a consequence of the extreme restrictive interpretation of the U.N. Charter would be that a Member could not assist in the collective defense of a non-Member, and terms such a result an absurdity and injustice. He clearly opts against what he terms this "extreme" view. See J. STONE, AGGRESSION AND WORLD ORDER 92-98, at 97 (1958). Professor Stone's interpretation of Art. 51 seems to be based solely on the literal text and is also open to the criticism discussed above.

ing in the history of the article suggests that it was intended to restrict the rights of members to collectively assist non-members.[32]

It should also be pointed out that such a restrictive interpretation of Article 51 is merely one interpretation, and is not logically required by the text of that article. If Article 51 is to be interpreted to prohibit the right of a member state to assist a non-member state, the phrase "if an armed attack occurs against a member of the United Nations" must be interpreted as meaning "if *and only if* an armed attack occurs against a member of the United Nations." Syntactically these interpretations are quite different. No plausible policy rationale has as yet been offered— much less any policies offered by the framers of Article 51—as to why members should be permitted to assist in the collective defense of other members but not of non-members. The distinction is specious. It would mean, for example, that, today, East Germany, West Germany, North Korea, South Korea, Switzerland, and the People's Republic of China as well as the R.V.N. and the D.R.V. could not be collectively assisted by members of the United Nations if subjected to attack. And in the past it would have raised doubts about collective assistance to Indonesia or Israel for example. Such an interpretation is unlikely to have wide appeal to any ideological grouping, as the practice of both East and West in concluding regional defense treaties with non-members indicates. Since the major purpose of Article 51 was essentially to reaffirm the right of individual and collective defense, the verbal quibble restricting that right is contrary to the major purpose of the article. This argument, a favorite in the attack on the lawfulness of United States assistance to the R.V.N., is reminiscent of what Judge Jerome Frank called preoccupation with "word magic."[33] It cannot be taken seriously.

Collective defense, whether pursuant to Article 51 or not, does not require a pre-existing regional defense agreement.[34] This

32. See, generally, MC DOUGAL & FELICIANO, *supra* note 26, at 235; R. RUSSELL & J. MUTHER, A HISTORY OF THE UNITED NATIONS CHARTER 688-712 (1958).
33. J. FRANK, LAW AND THE MODERN MIND 24-82 (Anchor Book ed., 1963).
34. See H. KELSEN, THE LAW OF THE UNITED NATIONS 795-96 (1950); C. POMPE, AGGRESSIVE WAR AN INTERNATIONAL CRIME 66 (1953); A. THOMAS & A.

means that the United States may lawfully assist in the collective defense of the R.V.N. whether or not that action is taken by virtue of the SEATO Treaty. As has been discussed, collective defense under either customary international law or the United Nations Charter does not require prior United Nations authorization of any kind. This is so regardless of whether the collective defense measures are pursuant to a regional defense arrangement or not. Standard, however, asserts that "the United States actions also violate Article 53 of the United Nations Charter . . . which unequivocally prohibits enforcement action under regional arrangements except with *previous* Security Council authorization."[35] The Lawyers Committee makes the same argument.[36] This argument, for which they cite no authority, is erroneous when applied to the Vietnam context. Although international legal scholars differ as to whether particular collective defense treaties are "regional arrangements" within Chapter VIII of the Charter, they are in agreement that collective defense activities, whether termed pursuant to a regional arrangement, a collective defense treaty or something else, are not subject to the prior authorization and reporting requirements of Articles 53 and 54 of the Charter.[37] For the very purpose of Article 51 was principally to preserve the right of individual and collective defense when the Latin American countries were concerned lest the major Power "veto" in the Security Council would deprive them of that right. The clear understanding of the framers of the Charter was that action in individual or collective defense, whether pursuant to a

---

THOMAS, NON-INTERVENTION 172 (1956); Kunz, *Individual and Collective Self-Defense in Article 51 of the Charter of the United Nations*, 41 AM. J. INT'L L. 872, 874 (1947).

35. Standard, *supra* note 9, at 633.

36. *Memorandum of Law, supra* note 9, at 2557.

37. See P. JESSUP, A MODERN LAW OF NATIONS 208 (1948); H. KELSEN, THE LAW OF THE UNITED NATIONS 792-95, 921-27 (1950); Kelsen, *Collective Security under International Law*, 49 INTERNATIONAL LAW STUDIES 264 (1956); M. MCDOUGAL & F. FELICIANO, LAW AND MINIMUM WORLD PUBLIC ORDER 245 (1961); J. STONE, LEGAL CONTROLS OF INTERNATIONAL CONFLICT 248-51 (1954); A. THOMAS & A. THOMAS, NON-INTERVENTION 187 (1956); Heindel, Kalijarvi and Wilcox, *The North Atlantic Treaty in the United States Senate*, 43, AM. J. INT'L L. 633, 639 (1949); Kelsen, *Is the North Atlantic Treaty a Regional Arrangement?*, 45 AM. J. INT'L L. 164-166 (1951).

regional arrangement or not, would not be subjected to a requirement of prior approval from the Security Council, although such action would be subject to later review by the United Nations. This understanding is evidenced not only in western defense treaties such as NATO and SEATO, but also in the 1955 Warsaw Treaty of Friendship, Cooperation and Mutual Assistance between the Soviet Union and Communist East European nations, and the 1950 Joint Defense and Economic Cooperation Treaty of the Arab League. Senator Mansfield, a member of the United States Delegation to the conference which established SEATO, evidenced the relation of SEATO to Article 51 when he told the Senate:

> The Southeast Asia Collective Defense Treaty is consistent with the provisions of the United Nations Charter. The treaty would come under the provisions of Article 51, providing that nothing contained in the United Nations Charter shall deprive one of the states from the individual or collective right of self-defense.[38]

Senator Mansfield further noted in the same speech that measures taken under Article 51 "do not need prior approval of the Security Council. . ."[39]

The United States at the request of the R.V.N. is assisting in the collective defense of the R.V.N. against armed attack. That assistance is lawful, whether taken by virtue of the SEATO Treaty or not. The actions of the United States, the R.V.N., and the D.R.V. are subject to later community review by the Security Council, which may take "measures necessary to maintain international peace and security" as it sees fit. The periodic efforts of the United States and the R.V.N. to secure such review have to date

---

38. 101 CONG. REC. 1055 (1955).
39. *Id.* Ruth Lawson has summarized this understanding:
> The relationship of contemporary regional and global organizations is worthy of special comment. The collective defense organizations based on the North Atlantic Treaty and the Rio, Manila, Baghdad, and Warsaw pacts are ultimately grounded in Article 51 of the United Nations Charter, which with notable prescience legitimized collective defense against armed attack without Security Council authorization.

R. LAWSON, INTERNATIONAL REGIONAL ORGANIZATION vi (1962).

been unsuccessful. They have been consistently opposed by the D.R.V. and the People's Republic of China, which continue to maintain that the United Nations has no right to examine the question.[40]

The Response of the United States and the Republic of Vietnam Is Reasonably Necessary to the Defense of the Republic of Vietnam

The fundamental community interest in restricting coercion as a modality of change carries with it a requirement that defensive action should not involve greater coercion than is reasonably necessary for the defense of the fundamental values under attack. This is the issue often subsumed under the "proportionality" test.[41] Disciplined answer to whether a particular responsive coercion is reasonably necessary to the preservation of the fundamental values under attack will not be provided by a simple comparison of types of coercion used by both sides, or counting of units committed to the field by the opposing participants. Nor will it be solved by the verbal magic of the *Caroline* or "proportionality" tests. Instead, meaningful characterization must depend on all of the relevant features of the context, including the scope and intensity of the attack as well as the response.

There is little doubt that the scope and intensity of the attack on the R.V.N. has presented a grave threat to its territorial and political integrity. That attack has been characterized by wide-

---

40. See Moore & Underwood, *supra* note 6, at 14955-56, 14977-79.

41. As MC DOUGAL & FELICIANO indicate:

> Proportionality in coercion constitutes a requirement that responding coercion be limited in intensity and magnitude to what is reasonably necessary promptly to secure the permissible objectives of self-defense. For present purposes, these objectives may be most comprehensively generalized as the conserving of important values by compelling the opposing participant to terminate the condition which necessitates responsive coercion. . . . Thus articulated, the principle of proportionality is seen as but one specific form of the more general principle of economy in coercion and as a logical corollary of the fundamental community policy against change by destructive modes.

Supra note 37, at 242-43.

spread terror and assassination, guerrilla raids, and sabotage, and more recently by mobile warfare involving large-size regular army units of the D.R.V. In its early stages it was principally characterized by infiltration of armed and unarmed personnel in support of guerrilla activities, and from about late 1964 it involved the use of regular PAVN army units in large-unit "mobile warfare." According to the Mansfield Report, by early 1965 the situation had become so serious that the R.V.N. was in imminent danger of total collapse.[42] Militarily, the situation had deteriorated to the point where there was serious concern that the R.V.N. would be cut in two.

The United States and R.V.N. response to this attack has been reasonable under the circumstances. That response divides imperfectly but most usefully into three major periods: prior to 1961, from mid-1961 to February, 1965, and from February, 1965, to the present.[43] Prior to 1961, the United States had no military casualties and had only a very limited Military Assistance Advisory Group in the R.V.N.—probably not more than about 800-900, with figures somewhat lower in earlier years. Infiltration and military assistance from the D.R.V. apparently were initiated as a significant factor during the latter part of this period. Beginning about mid-1961, in response to increased infiltration from the D.R.V., the United States began a moderate buildup of United States military advisory personnel, reaching roughly 12,000 by mid-1962 and about 23,000 by January, 1965. An indication of the relatively minor combat exposure of United States advisory personnel during much of this period is evidenced by the fact that as late as September 2, 1963, President Kennedy indicated that as few as 47 Americans had been killed in combat in Vietnam. It was not until after the D.R.V. had significantly stepped up infiltration and other assistance and had begun the introduction of their regular army units into the R.V.N. pursuant to the escalation of the conflict to the third "mobile warfare" phase of guerrilla strategy, and after the R.V.N. had reached the stage of imminent collapse, that the United States and the R.V.N. in February, 1965, began

42. Mansfield, Muskie, Inouye, Aiken and Boggs, *supra* note 22, at 140.
43. See Moore & Underwood, *supra* note 6, at 14974, note 124.

regular air strikes against military objectives in the D.R.V., and that the United States in the spring of 1965 began an introduction of regular combat units.[44]

Operations within the R.V.N. and most supporting air strikes have been carried out carefully and have been relevant to reasonably necessary military objectives. Air strikes on populated areas resulting in civilian casualties should not be undertaken in contexts in which civilian casualties may be out of proportion to the legitimate and reasonably proximate military effect. Some such incidents have occurred and every effort should be made to prevent them from recurring.

With respect to the use of the military instrument by the D.R.V.-Vietcong, the evidence suggests that the scope and intensity of the attack on the R.V.N. have increased and that the use of the military instrument is not primarily related to reasonably necessary defensive measures. The use of coercion by the D.R.V.-Vietcong has also been characterized by deliberate terrorism against civilian and political targets. In this context, the United States and R.V.N. response has been measured and reasonable. That response is necessitated by the continuing intense attack on the political and territorial integrity of the R.V.N. It has been gradual, limited, and reasonably necessary to the permissible objective of the defense of the R.V.N.

Vietnam and the Requirements of Minimum World Public Order

In the welter of charges and countercharges growing out of the Vietnam conflict it is easy to lose sight of fundamentals in a preoccupation with legalistic arguments or the ambiguities of the situation. Some are surprised and dismayed to learn that both sides assert grievances. It is easy to take another step and assume that both sides are responsible for initiating and continuing the use of the military instrument, or that the conflict is a just one because of the existence of grievances, or that questions of lawfulness are irrelevant. But probably most conflicts are fought over

44. According to the Mansfield Report, as late as May, 1965, U.S. regular combat units were still not engaged on the ground. Mansfield, Muskie, Inouye, Aiken and Boggs, *supra* note 22, at 141.

grievances which the parties consider just. The existence of asserted grievances, whether just or unjust, is not surprising and is not the point. The central issue facing the international community is the regulation of coercion. That issue has resulted in the outlawing of unilateral coercion as a modality of major change, regardless of asserted grievances. The policies behind this legal norm, the minimization of destructive modes of change, are fundamental to orderly relations in the international community and are by no means irrelevant to the Vietnam conflict. In fact, the dangers inherent in that conflict reinforce the conviction that these norms for the maintenance of at least minimum world public order are the crucial policies in the situation. The principal inquiry for assessment of lawfulness must be appraisal of the activities of both sides in the light of the basic contemporary legal norms that force, pursuant to the right of individual or collective defense or expressly authorized by the centralized peacekeeping machinery of the United Nations, is lawful, and that essentially all other major uses of force in international relations are unlawful. These contemporary norms, also embodied in the United Nations Charter, are binding alike on members and non-members of the United Nations.[45] Meaningful discussion of the lawfulness of United States assistance must relate to these fundamental expectations of the world community as to the lawfulness of the use of force.

Claims by the participants that their actions are lawful defensive actions and those of the opponents unlawful and aggressive must be evaluated by appraisal of the total context. Relevant features include the strategies employed, the arena of the conflict, and particularly the outcomes sought and objectives of the participants. So appraised, United States assistance is lawful and the attack of the D.R.V. is unlawful.

Any reasonably impartial analysis of the context must conclude that a major objective of the D.R.V. use of the military instrument against the R.V.N. is fundamental change of the existing and at least *de facto* situation in Vietnam. The context strongly suggests that the unilateral D.R.V. resort to force is aimed at the

---

45. See Moore & Underwood, *supra* note 6, at 14980, note 248; JESSUP, *supra* note 37, at 167-68.

political and territorial integrity of the R.V.N. Principal D.R.V. objectives, sought through coercion, seem to be settlement of political disputes with the R.V.N., change in the political form of government in the R.V.N. in favor of one similar and closely related to, if not controlled by, the D.R.V., and probably also eventual if not immediate unification of Vietnam under the government of the D.R.V. In the process it seeks United States withdrawal from the R.V.N. The conflict was unmistakably not precipitated by any real threat to the political or territorial integrity of the D.R.V. D.R.V. use of the military instrument against the R.V.N. evidences this in that it does not have as its principal object interdiction of the use of the military instrument against the D.R.V. This use by the D.R.V. of military force as a modality of major change in Vietnam is the central feature of the conflict. It is evidenced by the South and not the North as the principal arena of the fighting, the stated objectives of the parties and their conditions of settlement, and the continuing aggressive, not defensive, strategies in the use of the military instrument by the D.R.V. This D.R.V. attempt at forceful extension of its values is neither defensive nor pursuant to United Nations authorization. Such a resort to coercion as a modality of major change is unlawful.

On the other hand, judged by the same framework, the United States response is not aimed at the territorial and political integrity of the D.R.V. The use of coercion against the D.R.V. is of a limited nature and designed to interdict the D.R.V. attack against the R.V.N. An acceptable outcome would leave the D.R.V. as a viable and continuing entity. In fact, assistance has even been offered for the economic development of the D.R.V. The United States does not seek to change by force the existing state of affairs in Vietnam and Southeast Asia. Its emphasis is on conservation, not extension, of values in its use of military force in that area. Such defensive action is lawful.

Because of the great community interest in restricting coercion, a particularly relevant feature of the total context is the stress placed by the participants on removing the conflict from the battlefield to the negotiating table. The emphasis on settlement of disputes by pacific means is a corollary of the community interest in restricting coercion and is incorporated in Chapter VI of the United Nations Charter. The context of the Vietnam conflict indicates a substantial dichotomy between the positions of the opposing participants with respect to willingness to adopt more rational procedures for conflict resolution. During 1966 the United States, Britain, Canada, India, the R.V.N., 17 non-aligned nations, and Thailand, Malaysia, and the Philippines called for unconditional negotiations or a reconvening of the Geneva or other peace conference on Southeast Asia.[46] These extensive efforts to achieve a peaceful solution pursuant to Article 33 of the Charter through negotiation, the machinery of the Geneva Accords, and the machinery of the United Nations were refused by the D.R.V., the U.S.S.R., and the People's Republic of China.[47] Subsequently, the efforts of Prime Minister Wilson of Great Britain, Prime Minister Indira Gandhi of India, and United Nations Secretary-General U Thant to obtain a reconvening of the Geneva Conference on Vietnam were rebuffed by the U.S.S.R.,[48] and the efforts of Thailand, Malaysia, and the Philippines to invoke an Asian peace conference were rebuffed by Peking and Hanoi.[49] In the face of this largely one-sided refusal to negotiate or substitute peaceful and more rational procedures for settlement of the Vietnam conflict, principal responsibility for the continuation of the conflict must rest with those opposing peaceful procedures and who seem determined to continue reliance on the use of force to achieve their objectives.

46. See Moore & Underwood, *supra* note 6, at 14977-79, note 233; N.Y. Times, Aug. 19, 1966, at 2, col. 7 (city ed.); Aug. 7, 1966, at 10, col. 1; Aug. 4, 1966, at 4, col. 3 (city ed.).

47. *Id.* See also *id.*, July 25, 1966, at 3, col. 5 (city ed.). But U.N. Secretary General U Thant has indicated that in 1964 and early 1965 Hanoi may have had more interest in negotiations.

48. *Id.*, July 31, 1966, at 3, col. 5 (city ed.). British Foreign Secretary George Brown was equally unsuccessful in his efforts to convince the Soviets to convene a peace conference. See the N.Y. Times, Nov. 26, 1966, at 6, col. 4 (city ed.).
   There have recently been some hints that the Soviet attitude on the Vietnam issue is thawing.

49. See N.Y. Times, Aug. 19, 1966, at 2, col. 7 (city ed.); Aug. 11, 1966, at 2, col. 4 (city ed.); Aug. 9, 1966, at 2, col. 4 (city ed.).

New Myths and Old Realities

THE AMBIGUOUS GENEVA SETTLEMENT

The election arguments from the text of the 1954 Geneva Accords are high on the list of aphorisms offering false certainty. Critics of United States assistance point to the language of the Final Declaration with respect to the elections which were to be held in 1956 to indicate that the D.R.V. has been justly aggrieved by R.V.N. non-cooperation on such elections, and by implication that D.R.V. use of force against the R.V.N. is thereby justified. And they assert that the R.V.N. has widely violated the Accords by receiving military assistance from the United States, again with the implication that D.R.V. use of force is thereby justified. Although the use of force by the D.R.V. certainly does not follow, even if the D.R.V. were justly aggrieved on these issues, such assertions mask false certainty and largely ignore the totality of the Geneva settlement and its context in favor of a verbalistic microcosm. Similar difficulties arise in the invocation by all major participants of the Geneva Accords as the basis for settlement. Although such joint invocation would normally lead to expectations of immediate settlement, the positions of the major participants in the conflict are not close. The invocation of the Geneva Accords has masked fundamentally different objectives. The cause of all this obscurity is that the Geneva Accords themselves reflect a highly ambiguous settlement and conceal a number of fundamental problems with which the Conference—perhaps intentionally—did not come to grips. For example, although the Accords adverted briefly to elections to be held in 1956, they did not devote major attention to implementing unification and there is some evidence that at least some of the participants actually intended a semi-permanent partition of Vietnam at least until such time as there might be a rapprochement between the D.R.V. and the state of Vietnam, the predecessor government of the R.V.N.[50]

50. For documentation with respect to the discussion in this section see Moore & Underwood, *The Lawfulness of United States Assistance to the Republic of Viet-Nam*, 112 CONG. REC. 14943, 14972, notes 74 and 75 (daily ed., July 14, 1966). In a recent article in *The Reporter*, Victor Bator makes many of these same points with respect to the ambiguities

Anthony Eden, who was apparently a chief proponent of partition, seems to have had more than merely provisional partition in mind, and President Eisenhower indicated that the settlement implied nothing else but partition. The state of Vietnam protested against the partition in the settlement, and some of the provisions of the settlement, such as those for the transfer of civilians between zones, suggest longer-term partition was adverted to. Although it is likely that there will continue to be a dispute as to the "real" intention of the participants at Geneva, if in fact they shared any common intention, the fact was that the central feature of the settlement was the division of Vietnam between two

---

of the 1954 Geneva settlement. See Bator, *Geneva, 1954: The Broken Mold*, THE REPORTER 15 (June 30, 1966). According to Bator:

> The primary motivation of the Vietminh was to consolidate their rule somewhere, anywhere, in Vietnam. To accomplish this, Ho Chi Minh was willing to make political concessions from his militarily superior position. So it came about that, on May 25, the head of the Vietminh delegation first mentioned partition. It was to be based on a regrouping of forces on either side of a line of demarcation that would give both parties an area with a sufficiently large population to exist independently. . . .

> The contradictions and the equivocations in the documents that emerged from the Geneva Conference gain added emphasis by the procedure by which they were reached. As narrated in memoirs such as those of Anthony Eden, who presided at Geneva, or in the detailed accounts of Bernard B. Fall, Jean Lacouture, and Philippe Devillers, partition—so ambiguously treated in the documents—was the most important subject of bargaining, both in principle and in its geographical application. It was discussed continually, if confidentially, within each delegation, but for a time was carefully ignored when the delegations met.

> When at last partition was openly breached by the Vietminh, the French and British were elated. From that moment the location of the dividing line became the principal hurdle blocking the road to a settlement. Secretary of State Dulles, in order to underscore his insistence that it be drawn on the 17th parallel and to demonstrate western unity on this point, flew from Washington to Paris to meet with Eden and Premier Pierre Mendès-France. There were discussions even about the viability of the two parts. It is hard to believe that all this activity could have been devoted to the location of a temporary military demarcation line, a kind of billeting arrangement that would shortly disappear. The innocent-sounding text of the final agreement must have signified something of greater import.

Id. at 17.

essentially economically viable and at least *de facto* international entities. The election provisions, which obviously would be the key to unification, received only rather airy treatment.

Major difficulties were also papered over with respect to the position of the state of Vietnam, certainly a necessary participant in any future unification.[51] For the state of Vietnam objected and refused to be bound by the agreements prior to Geneva, at Geneva, and after Geneva, a position which was certainly clear to all of the participants at the Conference. Although the state of Vietnam indicated at the Conference that it would not use force to resist the cease-fire, it made it clear that it reserved to itself complete freedom of action. Since the French had to a substantial degree granted independence to the state of Vietnam prior to the signing of the Accords, and had in any event entered into a series of independence agreements with the state of Vietnam which would, under generally accepted principles of international law, take precedence over later inconsistent treaty obligations, there was at least substantial question whether France had capacity to bind the state of Vietnam. Moreover, there is little indication that France intended to bind the state of Vietnam by the Accords, and both the separate presence of the state of Vietnam at the Conference and the statements of the French delegates at the Conference suggest that France neither intended to bind nor felt itself legally capable of binding the state of Vietnam. As a background to all of this, by the time of the Conference the state of Vietnam had been recognized by more than 30 states, was a member of a number of specialized agencies of the United Nations, and for the past two years had been endorsed by the General Assembly of the United Nations as a state qualified for membership. These factors greatly strengthen the consistent position of the R.V.N. that it was not bound by the provisions of the Accords other than to refrain from disturbing the cease-fire by force, and specifically lend credence to its position that it was not bound by the election provisions of the Accords. That the Confer-

51. For documentation with respect to discussion of this point, see Moore & Underwood, *supra* note 50, at 14944-48, 14956-58, 14969-71, notes 22, 23, 24, 33, 34, 36, 37, 41, 44, and 49; 14980-82, notes 251, 252, 254, 261, 262, 267, 270, 274, 275, 276, and 278.

ence tolerated such an independent position with respect to a major participant was a surprising failing of the hard-headed diplomats at the Conference, unless, of course, they adverted to semi-permanent partition as a possible basis for settlement, recognizing the fact that an unambiguous settlement was politically impossible at the time.

In addition to these major ambiguities in the Geneva settlement, the Accords were seriously lacking in provisions for an effectively policed cease-fire, and their military restrictions, which seemed to have a significantly greater impact on the state of Vietnam, were inadequate to ensure meaningful demilitarization or military supervision of both north and south. The principal military restriction in the Accords, other than the core provision making unlawful the use of force by one zone against the other, was a ban on *introduction* of troop reinforcements, additional military personnel, and reinforcements of armaments and munitions. Contrary to popular interpretations, the Accords did not prohibit build-up of indigenous forces, and as such the effectiveness of the Accords was reduced.[52] The Accords also prohibited military alliances. Since it was the state of Vietnam which depended most heavily upon outside assistance for its defense, these provisions of the Accords, while only doubtfully ensuring effective demilitarization of North and South Vietnam, seemed to fall most heavily on the defensive ability of the state of Vietnam, an entity that had expressly refused to accept the Accords except to respect the cease-fire. Moreover, the International Commission for Supervision and Control (the International Control Commission), which was composed of representatives of India, Canada, and Poland, had little real power, no real peacekeeping force, was chronically underfinanced, and was hampered by a requirement of unanimous action for most major decisions. It was also reduced in effectiveness by the consistent and understandable position of the R.V.N. that it was not bound by the agreements, although it would cooperate in maintaining the cease-fire. Under the circumstances, when the participants perceived non-cooperation as in their interest, the I.C.C. could do little but issue reports. Several proposals to strengthen I.C.C. con-

52. See Moore & Underwood, *supra* note 50, at 14970, note 46.

trol over the Cambodian border and the demilitarized zone have been supported by the United States and the R.V.N.

There are in the ambiguous Vietnam context also arguments that the R.V.N. was bound by the Accords,[53] and evidence that the participants expected elections to be held in 1956. Limited military control was fairly effectively achieved by the Commission, at least in the early years. But the point is, though the separation of Vietnam between the D.R.V. and the R.V.N. is the central feature of the present context and the starting point for any settlement in Vietnam, the 1954 settlement in its totality always has been seriously ambiguous and inadequate. The text of the "agreements" concealed continuing serious *disagreements* among the people of Vietnam as well as between and among major East-West Powers. Provisions for implementation avoided the difficulties. The nebulous legal status of the unsigned Final Declaration of the Conference reflected them. Had it been otherwise, there would probably be no Vietnam conflict today. It is not helpful, then, that the D.R.V., while refusing to negotiate, can

---

53. The principal argument seems to be based on Art. 27 of the Agreement on the Cessation of Hostilities, which says that: "The signatories of the present Agreement and their successors in their functions shall be responsible for ensuring the observance and enforcement of the terms and provisions thereof. . . ." It is argued that the R.V.N. succeeded to the obligations of the French Union Forces. But if the R.V.N. is not otherwise bound by the Agreement, there is little reason to suggest that it is bound by Art. 27. In light of the evidence suggesting that France considered the state of Vietnam independent prior to the signing of the Accords, that France did not intend to bind the state of Vietnam and that the state of Vietnam expressly refused to be found by the Agreements, this argument from the text of Art. 27 is not persuasive. There remain among others the questions of whether France had legally granted independence to the state of Vietnam prior to the signing of the Accords and, even if not, whether the independence agreements entered into by France with the state of Vietnam prior to the Accords would take precedence over any later inconsistent agreements entered into by France. Moreover, it is not clear from this provision that the parties adverted to the R.V.N. as a successor "in their functions"; for example, it is also open to the interpretation that they were referring to successive Commanders in Chief of the PAVN and French Union Forces. Nor would this argument solve the question of whether the R.V.N. was bound by the Final Declaration. Attempts to find certainty in the basic outline of the Geneva settlement, whether from the language of Art. 27 or any other, oversimplify the case.

nevertheless righteously invoke immediate implementation of the text of the Accords—as interpreted by the D.R.V., of course, and ignoring D.R.V. encroachments of the text—as a precondition for negotiations.

It should also be pointed out that the United States is not bound by the Geneva Accords of 1954 other than to refrain from disturbing the agreements by force in accordance with pre-existing obligations under the United Nations Charter. Bedell Smith, the United States delegate to the Geneva Conference, made it evident to all concerned that the United States would not be bound by the Agreement on the Cessation of Hostilities or the Final Declaration of the Conference. President Eisenhower, in a statement issued the day of the Final Declaration of the Conference, also affirmed that the United States was not a "party to or bound by the decisions taken by the Conference."[54] Nothing in the United States assistance is inconsistent with its unilateral declaration at Geneva, which pointed out that "it would view any renewal of the aggression in violation of the . . . agreements with grave concern and as seriously threatening international peace and security."

Perhaps most importantly, the legal relevance of the Accords to the present conflict must be analyzed in the context of community norms with respect to the lawfulness of the use of force. Wide publication of I.C.C. reports indicating "violations" of the Accords against both sides and indicating R.V.N. objections to the "agreements" has been popularly interpreted as proof that the United States position is unlawful. These reports, like any others, must be viewed in their total context; that means awareness of the ambiguities and limitations of the Geneva settlement, the broader context of fundamental community norms as to the lawfulness of the use of force, and the role and function of the International Control Commission. The I.C.C., established pursuant to the Agreement on the Cessation of Hostilities, was given the task of supervising application "of the provisions of the agreement."[55] As

---

54. *Background Information Relating to Southeast Asia and Vietnam, Committee on Foreign Relations, United States Senate* (Rev. ed., Comm. Print, June 16, 1965), at 60.
55. Arts. 34 and 36 of the Agreement on the Cessation of Hostilities.

such, it has been principally concerned with certain control tasks assigned to it, and with investigation and report on implementation of the text of the Accords. Because of this emphasis on application "of the provisions of the agreement," the I.C.C. reports are a useful indication of factual breaches of that text by both sides, and of interpretation of the text. But the I.C.C. has not reconciled the fundamental ambiguities in the Geneva settlement and has quite naturally concentrated on textual "violations." Consequently, in the context of the evidence suggesting that the R.V.N. was not bound by the Accords and their continuing refusal to be bound other than to respect the cease-fire, I.C.C. criticism of R.V.N. objections is hardly surprising. Moreover, the I.C.C. is not an international tribunal which has authority, or which has attempted, to evaluate the overall lawfulness of the actions of the participants in the Vietnam conflict. It has been principally concerned with securing implementation of the Accords and to that end has been interested in pointing out "violations" of the text without effectively relating the actions of the parties to asserted justifications or attempting to assess the lawfulness of those claims by reference to fundamental community proscriptions. Even this function has been carried out with restraint and concern lest the Commission jeopardize its usefulness as a neutral body. An example of this approach is the 1962 Special Report of the Commission, which cautiously reported "violations" by the D.R.V. for its use of force against the R.V.N. and then continued to record "violations" by the R.V.N. for its receiving defensive military assistance from the United States. The Polish delegate even dissented from these cautious conclusions, feeling that it emphasized D.R.V. violations too much rather than receipt of assistance by the R.V.N. This dissent and others suggest, perhaps not surprisingly, that not all the members of the I.C.C. can be said to be truly disinterested participants. But as a factual report and an interpretation of the text of the Accords, the 1962 Special Report is authoritative. The D.R.V. *was* using force against the R.V.N., the United States *was* providing defensive assistance to meet that attack, and both actions *were* interpreted by the Commission as "violations" of the text of the Accords. Meaningful assessment of the lawfulness of United States assistance to the R.V.N., however, must relate these actions to the broader community norms with respect to the lawfulness of the use of force. Judged in this total context, the D.R.V. attack on a separate international entity documented in this report was unlawful, and the defensive response of the United States indicated by this report was entirely lawful and justified departure from the text, even if the United States and the R.V.N. were bound by the agreement. Judged by community standards as to the lawfulness of the use of force, there are profound differences between the aggressive "violations" recorded against the D.R.V. and the defensive "violations" recorded against the R.V.N., and these aggressive actions of the D.R.V. justify the responding defensive assistance. There is no question but that such defensive assistance does not justify the aggressive actions of the D.R.V. This application of the fundamental community norms with respect to the use of force in international relations to the facts of the situation in Vietnam is the central task in ascertaining the lawfulness of United States assistance and is one with which the I.C.C. was *not* concerned. That the United States defensive assistance is lawful is also supported in this context by the conventional legal norm that material breach of agreement permits suspension of any corresponding obligations.[56]

An examination of the major ambiguities and limitations of the Geneva settlement reinforces for the Vietnam context the importance of the fundamental community expectation that asserted breach of agreement or political grievances which do not present defense situations do not justify resort to unilateral coercion. The progress of implementation of those Accords must be viewed in the total context of tbe Geneva settlement and the community norms relating to the lawfulness of the use of force. The inherent ambiguities of the Geneva settlement cast doubt on the reasonableness of asserted D.R.V. expectations with respect to short-range unification of Vietnam. The use of force to assert such D.R.V. interpretations is unequivocally unlawful. Any other conclusion sanctions unilateral determination to resort to force as an instrument of major change and, as has been aptly demonstrated in the Vietnam conflict, endangers minimum world public order.

56. See authorities cited in Moore & Underwood, *supra* note 50, at 14959, 14982, notes 289 and 290.

Civil War and "Intervention"—The Sound and the Fury

Popularly, the Vietnam conflict is often referred to as a civil war, and critics of United States assistance argue that by assisting the R.V.N. the United States has unlawfully "intervened" in a civil war. The Lawyers Committee even sees a close analogy to the United States Civil War.[57] Interestingly, critics differ as to whether they view the conflict as a civil war within the R.V.N. or as a civil war between the R.V.N. and the D.R.V. Although they may characterize the Vietnam conflict a civil war in either of these two senses, and sometimes shift back and forth between them, such characterizations mask the real issues at stake, which are the lawfulness of the use of force by the D.R.V. against the R.V.N. and the lawfulness of responding United States assistance. Characterization of the Vietnam conflict as a civil war in either of these senses for the purpose of assessing the lawfulness of the use of force and the lawfulness of responding defensive assistance is misleading. For, although the Vietnam conflict does have some features of a civil war, the context is substantially different for purposes of assessing the lawfulness of the use of force. Features such as an international military demarcation line between the D.R.V. and the R.V.N., substantial international recognition of both entities, prolonged separate development, division between major contending ideological systems of the world, and substantial outside influence and assistance to the rebels in the R.V.N., set the Vietnam conflict apart. In this context, as discussed in section I, force by the D.R.V. against the R.V.N. as a modality of major change is unlawful. The use of force by one such entity against the other is too disruptive of minimum world public order. In these circumstances, it is perfectly lawful for the R.V.N. to receive defensive assistance for the purpose of preserving its territorial and political integrity against unlawful armed attack from the D.R.V.

Similarly, for purposes of assessing the lawfulness of the use of force, it is misleading, or at least obscures the issue, to charac-

---

57. *Memorandum of Law of Lawyers Committee on American Policy Toward Vietnam, reprinted in* 112 CONG. REC. 2552, at 2554 (daily ed. Feb. 9, 1966).

terize the conflict *within* the R.V.N. as a civil war. For whether or not the Vietcong are militarily controlled by Hanoi, and whether or not the major conflict was precipitated by Hanoi, there can be little doubt that substantial military assistance and direction is supplied by Hanoi. Such assistance and direction, which is in violation of the international cease-fire line separating the D.R.V. and the R.V.N., is unlawful. In its totality it unmistakably constitutes an armed attack aimed at the political and territorial integrity of the R.V.N. In these circumstances it is entirely lawful for the R.V.N. to receive defensive assistance for the purpose of preserving its integrity against unlawful armed attack. Invocation of authorities concerned with civil wars and talk of intervention substantially miss the point in the complex context of the Vietnam conflict. Discussion in this context of norms governing the right to assist one or another of the parties in a context characterized by unaided indigenous revolt, while fascinating, is not very helpful. In fact, even in the classic civil war of an essentially indigenous revolt unaided significantly by outside assistance, the prevailing expectation, although controversial, seems to be that the recognized government may receive assistance but the insurgents may not.[58] A principal policy with respect to such norms is

---

58. See, *e.g.*, authorities collected in Moore & Underwood, *supra* note 50, at 14975-76, notes 176 and 179. But see, *e.g.*, Wright, *International Law and Civil Strife*, 1959 PROC. AM. SOC'Y INT'L L. 145, 149.

Professor Sohn has pointed out a number of recent examples of assistance to widely recognized governments in contexts of civil strife:

[S]ince the early days of the United Nations the practice has developed that military assistance to a recognized government is permitted, even if its purpose is to assist in suppressing civil strife. . . . When objections were raised in 1946 to the presence of British troops in Indonesia and Greece, the defense that they were there on invitation was accepted by a majority of the Security Council. . . . When military revolts tried to overthrow the Governments of Kenya, Uganda and Tanganyika in 1964, these Governments asked for British assistance and no objection was raised by anybody to it, though attempts were made later to replace the British troops with African troops. . . . Similarly, when revolts started in Gabon and other French-speaking West African States in 1964, French troops were invited to restore peace.

Letter from Louis B. Sohn, Bemis Professor of International Law, Harvard, to John Norton Moore, April 21, 1966.

the ensuring of self-determination to the peoples of the entity in question. When the insurgents are at least significantly aided by third parties, as in the Vietnam conflict, it is difficult to see how self-determination can be invoked to prohibit offsetting defensive assistance to the recognized government. Not surprisingly, the authorities are essentially unanimous in recognizing the right of assistance to the recognized government to offset unlawful outside assistance to the rebels.[59] The direction and assistance from the D.R.V. is at least substantial enough to create grave doubt that, if offsetting United States assistance were not provided to the recognized government, the resulting outcome would reflect majority sentiment within the R.V.N. And even in the absence of a military nose-count or weapons-count with respect to D.R.V. control and assistance of the insurgency in the R.V.N., the evidence that the D.R.V. has always exercised substantial control of the Communist Party apparatus within the R.V.N. casts serious doubt on assertions that the N.L.F. and Vietcong apparatus are meaningfully representative of indigenous sentiment.[60]

Neither polity in Vietnam is a happy one with respect to ideal operation of the principle of self-determination. Neither party has a government meaningfully responsive to the electorate through democratic processes. These difficulties are shared by many emerging nations, and the context of a major conflict has made it particularly difficult for the R.V.N. to improve. The situation does not convince, however, that the D.R.V.-Vietcong offer the people of the R.V.N. a more meaningful chance for self-determination. Despite the often-quoted dictum of President Eisenhower writing in a different context about a different issue some sixteen years ago,[61] the repeated assertions of most South Vietnamese leaders, including those opposing the present government, indicate that

59. *Id.* Also see I. BROWNLIE, INTERNATIONAL LAW AND THE USE OF FORCE BY STATES 327 (1963).
60. A brief discussion of the policies underlying the norms of non-intervention which appeared at this point in the original version of this Chapter published in the *American Journal of International Law* has been omitted. The discussion is unnecessary to conclusion on the legal issues of the Vietnam conflict and a more recent and complete statement is made in Chapter IV of this volume, "The Control of Foreign Intervention in Internal Conflict."
61. See D. EISENHOWER, MANDATE FOR CHANGE 449 (Signet ed., 1963).

they share no illusion that the N.L.F. stands for their right of self-determination. It is extremely doubtful that a scientific observer could fairly conclude from the evidence today that the majority of the South Vietnamese feel that they are represented by the N.L.F. Even if the recognized government assisted is not the happiest example of operation of the democratic process, if lack of such assistance would result in takeover by an even more undemocratic regime which does not convince that it is representative of indigenous majority sentiment and which holds little hope for meaningful democratic processes, there is little reason to suggest that self-determination prohibits such assistance. If the unhappy fact of a non-democratically elected government, prohibits assistance to prevent minority takeover by the destructive modality of wars of national liberation, many of the underdeveloped areas of the world lie vulnerable. Minimum world public order would be largely illusory. Non-democratically based governments must be encouraged to yield to more democratic and socially sensitive processes, but a requirement that they cannot be assisted against coercive takeover by even more undemocratic regimes is an overkill. Such a requirement would seriously impair minimum world public order while not enhancing genuine self-determination.

In the ambiguous context of the Vietnam conflict, this question of the impact of the probable outcome on genuine self-determination, should defensive military assistance not be provided, is particularly relevant. Criticism of support to the present government must take cognizance of the effect on self-determination of effectuating an alternative which would withdraw such assistance, as well as the potentialities of the major contending systems to implement genuine self-determination in the sense of the widest possible participation in decision-making. Certainly a principal goal of the United States must be the genuine self-determination of the people of the R.V.N., and it is to be hoped that the United States will make every effort to promote alternatives which maximize the freedom of choice of the people of the R.V.N. and encourage truly democratic government. There are some indications that the present government of the R.V.N. is trying to move in this direction. But it is not unreasonable to recognize that today the people of the R.V.N. are entitled to their own self-determination free from D.R.V. or communist coercion. That means the freedom to choose their own form of government and social institutions and to decide for themselves whether they wish unification with the north at some future time. That is the reality in Vietnam and one which the D.R.V. is seeking to alter by force. Such an attempt is unlawful and may properly be opposed by defensive assistance.

Lawfulness and Beyond—Political Initiatives and the Search for Peace

An analysis of the relevant legal norms indicates that providing defensive military assistance to the Republic of Vietnam is a lawful policy alternative. That lawfulness means compliance with existing structures of international law and the United Nations.

The conflict in Vietnam continues because of wide differences between the objectives of the participants and the willingness of the D.R.V. aggressively to pursue its aims by force. Until that willingness is changed or unless the United States withdraws from Vietnam, the conflict is likely to continue. This unhappy prognosis underscores the tremendous importance of the search for a negotiated settlement. The United States efforts to obtain a peaceful solution to the conflict should be continued and intensified. It may be useful in this regard to continue to underscore United States willingness to achieve a peaceful solution by periodic scaledowns or bombing pauses, the continuation of which is announced to be conditioned on some reciprocal reduction of hostilities. Initiation and support of proposals for strengthening I.C.C. effectiveness should be stressed.[62] Any responsibility for failure to adopt such proposals should be assessed and publicized. The search for peace might also be aided by greater emphasis on clarification of long-run United States goals in Vietnam. Such emphasis on goal clarification might be coupled with comprehensive alternative solutions which would be acceptable to the United States and the R.V.N. If specific compromise solutions are placed before the international community by the United States and the R.V.N., world opinion might contribute to

---

62. See generally N.Y. Times, Aug. 23, 1966, at 1, col. 1 (city ed.).

greater pressure on Hanoi to negotiate a settlement. Such clarification should not mean abandonment of United States willingness to hold unconditional negotiations, which should be continually sought and stressed. Such clarification would mean offering as additional bases for negotiation specific long-run solutions to the Vietnam conflict which would be satisfactory to the United States and the R.V.N. without prejudice to future negotiation on alternative plans. Such alternatives should preserve the basic integrity of the R.V.N. as an entity whose peoples are entitled to self-determination. Consistent with that goal, such alternatives should also provide opportunity for elements opposed to the government of the R.V.N. to express their preferences democratically rather than militarily. Much of the uneasiness among members of the world community about United States policies in Vietnam is caused by their concern in the ambiguous Vietnam context with whether the United States actions are conducive to genuine self-determination of the people of the R.V.N. That the United States is acting in the interest of self-determination could be clarified by proposing specific plans for meaningfully supervised elections allowing participation of all factions within the R.V.N. Such plans might be conditioned on cessation of hostilities. They would affirm that the principal goal of the United States in Vietnam, as in the rest of the world, must be human dignity and meaningful self-determination.

There is nothing concrete or uniquely creative about these suggestions. Their purpose is simply to indicate that there may be value in the United States' proposing positive plans for solution to the Vietnam conflict in addition to maintaining its position in favor of unconditional negotiations. Should Hanoi continue to refuse publicly offered reciprocal reduction of hostilities or reject publicly proposed compromise solutions, the world must not mistake which side refuses to adopt rational procedures for conflict resolution. These and other political initiatives are an important technique for discouraging D.R.V. aggression in Vietnam and should continue to be pressed. The political initiatives endorsed here may or may not be practical, but the important point is that political initiatives should play a major role in the United States response. Such initiatives have a substantial capacity for increasing the pressure on Hanoi to seek a non-military solution. If the present D.R.V. determination to achieve its objectives by the use of force continues, such measures are unlikely to achieve a short-term settlement of the Vietnam conflict. But they may aid in clarifying the United States position in Vietnam and increase the pressure on Hanoi to limit its aggression and seek a rational solution. As such, they may hasten the day when the use of force will yield to more rational processes.

January, 1967

CHAPTER VIII

International Law and the
United States Role in Vietnam: A Reply
to Professor Falk*

In an article published in the *Yale Law Journal* Professor Richard Falk raises a number of questions about the lawfulness of the United States role in Vietnam.[1] The importance of some of these questions for the direction of contemporary international law as well as for the appraisal of the United States role in Vietnam calls for continuing dialogue.

In analyzing the United States role in Vietnam, Professor Falk focuses on the problem of the international law of "internal war."[2] He indicates that "the central issue is whether an externally abetted internal war belongs in either of the traditional legal categories of war—'civil' or 'international.' "[3] In answering this question and the subsidiary questions it poses, Falk constructs a framework focused on assistance in the context of civil strife. Analytically, as a tool for clarifying policy choices, he divides vio-

---

* This Chapter is a reply to the arguments made by Professor Richard A. Falk in *International Law and the United States Role in the Viet Nam War*, 75 YALE L.J. 1122 (1966). Professor Falk's response appears in 76 YALE L.J. 1095 (1967).

1. Falk, *International Law and the United States Role in the Viet Nam War*, 75 YALE L.J. 1122 (1966). A condensation of Professor Falk's views carries some risk of distortion. The reader is urged to consult Professor Falk's article before reading this reply. My own views are elaborated and further documented in Moore, *The Lawfulness of Military Assistance to the Republic of Viet-Nam*, 61 AM. J. INT'L L. 1 (1967). Additional background documentation supporting this view may be found in Moore & Underwood, *The Lawfulness of United States Assistance to the Republic of Viet Nam*, 112 CONG. REC. 14,943 (daily ed. July 14, 1966), *reprinted* in 5 DUQUESNE L. REV. 235 (1967). See also Alford, *The Legality of American Military Involvement in Viet Nam: A Broader Perspective*, 75 YALE L.J. 1109 (1966); Partan, *Legal Aspects of the Vietnam Conflict*, 46 B.U.L. REV. 281 (1966); Wright, *Legal Aspects of the Viet-Nam Situation*, 60 AM. J. INT'L L. 750 (1966).

2. Falk, *supra* note 1, at 1122.

3. *Id.*

lent conflict into Type I conflict, involving "the direct and massive use of military force by one political entity across a frontier of another,"[4] Type II conflict, involving "substantial military participation by one or more foreign nations in an internal struggle for control,"[5] and Type III conflict, involving "internal struggle for control of a national society, the outcome of which is virtually independent of external participation."[6] He postulates that while it is appropriate "to use force in self-defense"[7] in Type I conflict, in Type II conflict it is only "appropriate . . . to take off-setting military action confined to the internal arena,"[8] and in Type III conflict "it is inappropriate for a foreign nation to use military power to influence the outcome."[9] Professor Falk then characterizes the Vietnam conflict as Type III,[10] but "if this position entailing non-participation is rejected,"[11] it follows, according to Falk's view, that international law prohibits United States participation in the Vietnam conflict or at least limits the maximum response to Type II counter-intervention within the internal arena of South Vietnam.[12]

Although his critique is both scholarly and creative, the framework proposed by Professor Falk is oversimplified for use in clarifying Vietnam policy choices. His resulting conclusions about the illegality of the United States role in Vietnam are unsound. The Vietnam conflict is highly ambiguous, and it begs the question to analyze it in a framework for "civil strife."[13] Although generalization is a useful tool for decision, a generalization that the Vietnam conflict is either Type II or Type III "civil strife" ignores features of the total context which are crucial in any assessment of long-run community common interest. Vietnam, while evidencing features of "civil strife," also evidences features of the divided-

---

4. *Id.* 1126. 5. *Id.* 6. *Id.* 7. *Id.*
8. *Id.* 9. *Id.* 10. *Id.* 1127. 11. *Id.*
12. *Id.* Professor Falk seems to retreat from the non-participation argument when he later asserts: "International law offers no authoritative guidance as to the use of force *within* South Viet Nam, but the bombing of North Viet Nam appears to be . . . a violation of international law." *Id.* 1155.
13. Professor Falk begins to beg the question in his second sentence when he says: "A war is usefully classified as internal when violence takes place primarily within a single political entity, regardless of foreign support for the contending factions." *Id.* 1122.

nation problem and raises questions of permissible use of force across *de facto* boundaries and cease-fire lines. Analysis of the lawfulness of the United States role must consider this total context in the light of the major community policies at stake.

Real-World Vietnam: An Ambiguous Context

Both sides in the Vietnam debate characteristically select from the highly ambiguous context those features which reinforce their perceptions of the conflict. The "White Papers"[14] issued by the State Department in 1961 and 1965 painted too one-sided a picture of the conflict in not recognizing the extent of indigenous support for the Vietcong within South Vietnam and in proclaiming a homespun view of the failure to implement the election provisions of the Geneva Accords. As a result, the White Paper model of "aggression from the North" has never captured the complex reality of the Vietnam problem. But similarly, critics of Vietnam policy have also engaged in this "model building." In characterizing the conflict as a "civil war" and the United States role as "intervention," they focus on the features of the context pointing to Vietnamese national unity, the ill-fated unity and election provisions in the Accords, and the instability of governments in the south. In building this "civil war-intervention" model, critics characteristically do not focus on the very real ambiguities in the Geneva settlement, the more than sixteen-year territorial, political, and ideological separation of the north and south, the existence of a cease-fire line dividing north and south, and the close relations between Hanoi and the Vietcong. Professor Falk's model essentially reflects the critics' one-sided focus.[15] As a result,

14. U.S. DEP'T OF STATE, A THREAT TO THE PEACE: NORTH VIET-NAM'S EFFORT TO CONQUER SOUTH VIET-NAM (1961); U.S. DEP'T OF STATE, AGGRESSION FROM THE NORTH, THE RECORD OF NORTH VIET-NAM'S CAMPAIGN TO CONQUER SOUTH VIET-NAM (1965) (reprinted in 52 DEP'T STATE BULLETIN 404).

15. Professor Quincy Wright relies on a similar substantially one-sided fact selection in building a "model" of the conflict as civil strife between Hanoi and Saigon. See Wright, *supra* note 1, at 756-59.
    It is somewhat uncertain whether Professor Falk's Type III characterization refers to "civil strife" within the south, "civil strife" between north and south, or both. Although he indicates that he regards "the war in South Vietnam primarily as a Type III conflict," much of the

his first choice characterization of the conflict as "an internal struggle for control of a national society, the outcome of which is virtually independent of external participation [Type III conflict]" is misleading for purposes of evaluating the permissibility of United States assistance. The issues in Vietnam are not nearly so neat and tidy, and no amount of "model building" will make them so. Real-world Vietnam combines some elements of civil strife (both within the south and between north and south) with elements of the cold-war divided nation problem and "aggression from the North," all complicated by an uncertain international settlement. Because of the complexity of this total context, neither the official nor the critical model provides a sufficiently sensitive analytic tool for clarifying policy choices in the conflict. The starting point for selection of important contextual features must be analysis of the principal community values at stake.

A prominent feature of contemporary international law is the prohibition of coercion in international relations as a strategy of major change. The most widely accepted understanding of the requirements of both customary international law and the United Nations Charter is that force pursuant to the right of individual or collective defense or expressly authorized by the centralized peacekeeping machinery of the United Nations is lawful. Essentially all other major uses of force are unlawful.[16] These norms reflect awareness both of the great destructiveness of war and of the necessity for the maintenance of defensive rights in a world divided between competing public order systems and with only limited expectations toward the success of existing centralized peacekeeping machinery. At a lower level of generality, customary international law and the United Nations Charter outlaw major use of military force to redress grievances, however deeply felt, in the absence of major military attack on fundamental

---

evidence on which he relies for this characterization seems to argue more for a north-south characterization. See Falk, *supra* note 1, at 1128-32. See also the North-South arguments, *id.* at 1138 and 1153 and notes 45, 48 and 67 *infra*.

16. See M. MᴄDᴏᴜɢᴀʟ & F. Fᴇʟɪᴄɪᴀɴᴏ, Lᴀᴡ ᴀɴᴅ Mɪɴɪᴍᴜᴍ Wᴏʀʟᴅ Pᴜʙʟɪᴄ Oʀᴅᴇʀ 121-260 (1961). See also McDougal & Lasswell, *The Identification and Appraisal of Diverse Systems of Public Order*, 53 Aᴍ. J. Iɴᴛ'ʟ L. 1 (1959).

values such as political and territorial integrity. In the nuclear age it is usually better that international disputes not be settled than that they be settled by unilateral military strategies. And this is particularly true of disputes between the major contending public order systems, with their almost unlimited potential for escalation and destruction. These community norms also reflect the judgment, evident as well in national law, that when centralized peacekeeping machinery is not effectively available it is necessary to preserve the right of defense to those attacked. In a world in which power plays a large role in international affairs, this right of defense is a major source of control and sanction against aggression.[17] As such, it may be crucial to conflict minimization that this defensive right be maintained.

In light of the critical values of world order at stake, conflict between contending governments of a nation at least *de facto* divided into continuing international entities and paying allegiance to contending public order systems presents a problem of major international concern. "Rational community policy must be directed to the coercive interactions of territorially organized communities of consequential size, whatever the 'lawfulness' of their origin."[18] And this is particularly true of boundaries separating major contending public order systems. The balance of power makes the use of the military instrument across such boundaries particularly hazardous, as both Korea and Vietnam have demonstrated. For the purposes of assessing the lawfulness of coercion across such boundaries and the lawfulness of extending assistance to the entity attacked, these real-world boundaries must be recognized as such. The label "civil strife" must not be allowed to obscure this major problem in conflict minimization. If we believe that long-run community common interest in minimization of coercion is against unilateral coercion across continuing *de facto* international boundaries and cease-fire lines, particularly when such boundaries separate the major cold-war camps, then for purposes of policy clarification about the lawfulness of force, conflict between North and South Vietnam is not "civil strife," regardless

17. See generally H.L.A. HART, THE CONCEPT OF LAW 208-31 (1963); H. MORGENTHAU, POLITICS AMONG NATIONS 293-96 (3d ed. 1966).
18. M. McDOUGAL & F. FELICIANO, *supra* note 16, at 221 n.222.

of other features of the context evidencing similarity with "civil strife." The ambiguous 1954 Geneva settlement certainly differentiates Vietnam from the other divided nations of China, Germany, and Korea, but the continuing and at least *de facto* division of Vietnam has a substantial parallel to the cold-war divided nation problem when analyzed with regard to the vital policies of minimum world public order. It is in the long-run common interest not to permit change of existing and relatively permanent international divisions by unilateral military coercion, however unjust the existence of the condition may seem to the protagonist of change. The Kashmir and Palestine disputes present additional contemporary examples of the importance of this principle.

As applied to Vietnam, there is substantial evidence of the at least *de facto* separateness of north and south, regardless of one's view of the effect of the Geneva settlement. Thus, the State of Vietnam (the predecessor government of South Vietnam) and the Democratic Republic of Vietnam (North Vietnam) were to some extent separate *de facto* states even prior to the Accords of 1954,[19] and subsequent to the Accords their real separateness became much stronger. Prior to the Accords, each government was recognized by a number of states as the government of Vietnam and each carried on separate international activities.[20] Although nations had differing expectations from the Geneva settlement, the major effect of the settlement was to consolidate territorially the existing division of Vietnam between the two rival governments. South Vietnam is now recognized by about 60 nations and North Vietnam by about 24, a recognition pattern closely approxi-

---

19. For discussion on this point see Moore & Underwood, *supra* note 1, 112 Cong. Rec. at 14,944.

20. The State of Vietnam had been recognized by about 30 to 35 states prior to the Geneva settlement. See Documents Relating to the Discussion of Korea and Indo-China at the Geneva Conference (*Misc.* No. 16) Cmd. No. 9186 (1964); 31 Parl. Sessional Papers 109, 133 (1953-54); U.S. Dep't of State, American Foreign Policy—Current Documents 121 n.3 (1958).

   The Democratic Republic of Vietnam had been recognized by the People's Republic of China, the Soviet Union and a number of East European Nations. See B. Murti, Vietnam Divided 171 (1964). See also Royal Institute of International Affairs, Survey of International Affairs 1949-50 429-30 (1953).

mating that of North and South Korea.[21] The substantial expectations of the separateness of North and South Vietnam after the Accords is indicated by the January, 1957, draft resolution of the U.S.S.R., a Co-Chairman of the Geneva Conference, calling for the simultaneous admission to the United Nations of North Vietnam, South Vietnam, North Korea, and South Korea as four separate "states."[22] Both north and south have functioned for over sixteen years since the Accords as separate international entities with governmental institutions of their own operating along different ideological lines. Both have long maintained separate foreign embassies and diplomatic representation, and have administered separate territories and populations. That the contending governments claim sovereignty to all of Vietnam can hardly be decisive for purposes of conflict minimization, as the situation is parallel in this respect to that in Korea, China, and Germany. Under the circumstances, this at least *de facto* separation can not be ignored for meaningful clarification of policy alternatives.

In addition to the continuing real-world division of Vietnam, a factor which exists as a crucial contextual feature regardless of any interpretation of the Geneva settlement, north and south are

21. See U.S. Dep't of State, Legal Status of South Viet-Nam (4/31b-865BT). South Korea has full relations with about 64 nations while North Korea is recognized by about 25. *Id.*
22. See 11 U.N. GAOR Annexes, Agenda Item No. 25, at 5-7 U.N. Doc. A/SPC/L.9 (1957).

   During the debates on this and other draft resolutions calling for the admission of the Republic of Vietnam, the three Soviet delegates said between them:

   [B]oth in Korea and in Viet-Nam two separate States existed, which differed from one another in political and economic structure. . . .

   The fact was that there were two States in Korea and two States in Viet-Nam. . . .

   The realistic approach was to admit that there were two States with conflicting political systems in both Korea and Viet-Nam. In the circumstances, the only possible solution was the simultaneous admission of the four countries constituting Korea and Viet-Nam. . . .

   [T]wo completely separate and independent States had been established in each of those countries, [Korea and Viet Nam] with different political, social and economic systems.

   11 U.N. GAOR Spec. Pol. Comm. 79, 81, 87, 101 (1957).

also divided by a military cease-fire line created by that settlement. In a Special Report in 1962, the International Commission for Supervision and Control in Vietnam found that North Vietnamese military activity across that line was a specific violation of the Accords.[23] Some critics reply by pointing out that the Commission also found that South Vietnam violated the Accords by accepting American defensive aid. But this neutral reporting proves little. The crucial question is whether these indicated breaches should be treated alike for purposes of community policy about maintenance of world public order. The clear answer is no. When put in context of community norms proscribing the use of force for settlement of disputes, the indicated breach of the north is exactly that kind of aggressive coercion proscribed, whereas the indicated breach of the south is permitted defensive response to such coercion. It is not at all anomalous in this context to assert that the norm, material breach of agreement justifies suspension of corresponding obligations, is available as a defense to the south but not the north.[24] For even if the south did breach the election provisions of the Accords, and there are serious questions here as to the legal position of the south with respect to these provisions of the Accords,[25] aggressive military strategies by the north are not a permitted response to such breach. The point is that there is a major difference in character of the indicated breaches north and south which is crucial for community policies of maintenance of minimum order and which is inherent in overriding community norms as to the lawfulness of the use of force. Failure to recognize this distinction is failure to grasp the essential community policies against unilateral coercive change embodied in the United Nations Charter. Rational community policy

23. SPECIAL REPORT TO THE CO-CHAIRMEN OF THE GENEVA CONFERENCE ON INDO-CHINA, CMD. No. 1755 (1962); 39 PARL. SESSIONAL PAPERS 6-7 (1961-62).

24. Professor Falk fails to meet this point. In criticizing the State Department's "breach of agreement" argument he says: "One wonders why this 'international law principle' is not equally available to North Vietnam after Saigon's refusal even to consult about holding elections. Why is Hanoi bound by the reasoning of footnote 10 and Washington entitled to the reasoning of reciprocal breach?" Falk, *supra* note 1, at 1154.

25. For discussion of these questions see Moore, *The Lawfulness of Military Assistance to the Republic of Viet Nam, supra* note 1.

concerned with conflict minimization must be concerned with coercion across such international cease-fire lines. This is true regardless of the merits of the dispute between north and south with respect to the Accords. Even if the underlying agreement created expectations denied by one of the participants, community policies against force as a strategy of change militate against resumption of hostilities. The existence of such an international cease-fire line in Vietnam is another particular feature casting doubt on the utility of characterization of the conflict as an "internal struggle for control of a national society, the outcome of which is virtually independent of external participation."

It is one of the paradoxes of the Vietnam dialogue that both sides rely on the 1954 Geneva settlement. In characterizing the Vietnam conflict as a Type III conflict, Professor Falk relies heavily on a model of the Geneva settlement which he pictures as basically creating expectations of short run unification of Vietnam under the government of Ho Chi Minh, although he admits "the intentions of the participants at Geneva were somewhat ambiguous."[26] The subsequent United States role in assisting the

26. Falk, *supra* note 1, at 1129. This theme runs all through Professor Falk's critique and constitutes one of his major assumptions. By way of some representative statements:

My own judgment, based on the analysis of the Geneva settlement in 1954, is that the war in South Viet Nam represents more an American attempt at "rollback" than a Communist attempt at "expansion." The Geneva Conference looked toward the reunification of the whole of Viet Nam under the leadership of Ho Chi Minh. The introduction into South Viet Nam of an American military presence thus appears as an effort to reverse these expectations and to deny Hanoi the full extent of its victory against the French. *Id.* 1125 n.15.

Hanoi was "entitled" to prevent Saigon from establishing itself as a political entity with independent claims to diplomatic status as a sovereign state. A separation of Viet Nam into two states was not contemplated by the participants at Geneva. *Id.* at 1130 n.31.

[T]he injection of an American political and military presence was, from the perspective of Hanoi, inconsistent with the whole spirit of Geneva. The United States decision to commit itself to maintaining a Western-oriented regime in South Viet Nam upset the expectations regarding the Southeast Asian balance of power. . . . *Id.* 1138.

The strength of Hanoi's claim [to exercise control over the South] arises from . . . the expectations created at Geneva that the elections would confirm that military victory. *Id.* 1138 n.66.

south, according to this model, "contrasts radically" with "the expectations created at Geneva."[27] There are factors in the manifold of events constituting the Geneva settlement that point to such a conclusion. Chief among them are Articles 6 and 7, the "no boundary" and "election" provisions of the Final Declaration. These provisions suggest that at least those participants agreeing to the Final Declaration expected that Vietnam would be united by elections in 1956 and that the division was to be temporary. But the language of the Final Declaration is not the only source for ascertaining the genuine expectations of all the participants and in this case may be unreliable. There are at least equally important factors in the context of the Geneva settlement that cast serious doubt on the legitimacy of placing major reliance on alleged short run expectations of Hanoi with respect to unification of Vietnam. These are factors to which Falk does not advert in constructing his model.

The memoirs of Anthony Eden[28] and the preliminary seven-point program agreed to by the United States and the United Kingdom and apparently supported by French Prime Minister Mendès-France[29] strongly suggest that the real core of the settle-

27. *Id.* 1131.
28. A. EDEN, FULL CIRCLE (1960). Eden writes that prior to the conference "it . . . seemed inevitable that large parts of the country would fall under Communist control, and the best hope of a lasting solution lay in some form of partition." *Id.* 117. And "I felt that the Chinese might yet be constrained to come to an arrangement which would . . . allow a free life to some part of Vietnam. . . ." *Id.* 137. And "I decided to persevere at our next meeting [with Chou En-lai] with my plan for what I called the 'protective pad.' Many countries had an interest in this and, if I could once get the conception established, the position might hold, perhaps for years. . . . It would be best if communism could be . . . halted as far north as possible in Vietnam." *Id.* 138. And Eden writes that after the Conference "The Vietnamese had saved more of their country than had at one time seemed possible. . . . In the months ahead the United States would be playing a greater part in all their [Viet Nam, Cambodia and Laos] destinies." *Id.* 160-61. See also *id.* 97, 101-02, 148-49, 156-57.
29. See *id.* 149, 156-57. Under the terms of this program the United States and the United Kingdom agreed "to respect an armistice agreement on Indo-China which:

   . . .

     2. Preserves at least the southern half of Vietnam, and if possible an enclave in the delta. . . .

ment, at least from a western standpoint, was partition of Vietnam between the two major contending public order systems, a division to some extent shared by the Vietnamese people. In fact, Eden, the individual Chairman of the Conference, was a chief proponent of partition although Eisenhower indicated concern because of the loss *of the north* to "Communist enslavement."[30] Nowhere does Eden indicate that he felt he had failed to set up a permanent barrier between Ho Chi Minh and Malaya, one of his chief concerns.[31] *The Survey of International Affairs 1954,* published by the British Royal Institute of International Affairs, has this account of the Viet Minh position at the Conference:

> On 25 May the Viet Minh Foreign Minister, Mr. Dong, put forward a detailed plan, which was clearly in the nature of a first approximation to the "accepting price" of the insurgents. . . . This plan was, clearly, rather more than a proposal for a regroupment of forces; if put into effect it would in fact provide something like a *de facto* military partition of the country, and one that, with its provision that the two areas chosen should be economically viable, seemed to be envisaged as lasting for some time.[32]

---

3. Does not impose on . . . retained Vietnam any restrictions materially impairing . . . [its] capacity to maintain [a] stable non-Communist regime. . . .

4. Does not contain political provisions which would risk loss of the retained area to Communist control. . . ."

Id. 149. According to Eden, M. Mendès-France supported this program. Eden writes that Mendès-France "described to us his negotiations with the Vietminh on the question of the demarcation line in Vietnam and effectively demonstrated that at no point had his position diverged from the minimum terms which had been defined by the Americans and ourselves." *Id.* 156.

30. "To me these French proposals . . . implied nothing else but partition. We knew, from experience in Korea, that this would probably lead to Communist enslavement of millions in the northern partitioned area." D. EISENHOWER, MANDATE FOR CHANGE 432 (Signet ed. 1963).

31. A. EDEN, FULL CIRCLE 97 (1960).

32. ROYAL INSTITUTE OF INTERNATIONAL AFFAIRS, SURVEY OF INTERNATIONAL AFFAIRS 1954 48 (1957). And see Do VANG LY, AGGRESSIONS BY CHINA 151 (2d ed. 1960).

The actual proposal made by the Vietminh Chief Delegate, Mr. Dong, on May 24 was:

The public record indicates that the South Vietnamese government opposed partition and supported provisional control by the United Nations of all of Vietnam pending free elections.[33] Their refusal to agree to the political provisions of the settlement is consistent with expectations on their part that those provisions would be unworkable from their standpoint and that the agreement would actually result in *de facto* partition. Moreover, France had entered into a series of independence agreements with the State of Vietnam, the predecessor government of South Vietnam, prior to the conclusion of the Indo-China phase of the Geneva Conference[34] and French Foreign Minister Bidault indicated at the Conference that the State of Vietnam was independent and that it was

---

The readjustment is made on the basis of *an exchange of territory*, the following elements to be taken into consideration: area, population, political and economic interests so as to accord each party *zones all of a piece*, relatively widespread and offering facilities for economic activities and administrative control respectively within each zone. The demarcation line between these zones should as much as possible not create communication and transport difficulties within the respective zones.

Ngo Ton Dat, The Geneva Partition of Vietnam and the Question of Reunification During the First Two Years 163 (1963) (unpublished Ph.D. dissertation, Cornell Univ.). The author accompanied the Vietnamese Prime Minister to the Geneva negotiations. He sums up this Vietminh proposal as: "Clearly Mr. Dong's declaration could only mean one thing: the partition of Vietnam." *Id.*

33. See "The News In Review," *United Nations Review* 2 (Vol. 1, July 1954). Moore & Underwood, *supra* note 1, 112 Cong. Rec. at 14981 n.267.

34. See Moore & Underwood, *supra* note 1, 112 Cong. Rec. 14,969-70 nn.22, 23, 33, 36, 41. Like most of the context surrounding the Conference, these agreements were ambiguous and seem not in fact to have effectuated complete independence to the State of Vietnam prior to the conclusion of the Conference. But taken together these agreements did provide some status to the State of Viet Nam as an international entity in its own right. For a restrictive interpretation of the effect of the agreement initialed on June 4, 1954 see Weinstein, Vietnam's Unheld Elections 12-14 (1966) (Data Paper No. 60, Southeast Asia Program, Cornell Univ.).

Ngo Ton Dat seems to conclude that the State of Vietnam was not bound by the Accords since the Commander in Chief of the French Union Forces did not have a sufficient delegation of power from the State of Viet Nam to conclude a "general armistice of vital importance." See Ngo Ton Dat, *supra* note 32, at 303-10.

"fully and solely competent to commit Viet Nam."[35] Both the separate presence of the State of Vietnam and these statements of the French delegate at the Conference suggest that France did not intend to bind the State of Vietnam by the political provisions of the Final Declaration. In the face of this French position at the Conference and the clear refusal of the State of Vietnam to adhere to the political provisions of the agreements,[36] the experienced diplomats at the Conference must have been aware of the possibility that few provisions other than cease-fire and partition would be carried out.[37] In this regard it is significant that even prior to the Conference the State of Vietnam was recognized by about thirty states and had been endorsed by the General Assembly of the United Nations as a state qualified for membership.[38] Professor Falk himself somewhat inconsistently points out that "at the time of the Geneva proceedings, the Saigon regime exerted control over certain areas in the South, and this awkward fact made it unrealistic to suppose that the Geneva terms of settlement would ever be voluntarily carried out."[39]

35. DOCUMENTS RELATING TO THE DISCUSSION OF KOREA AND INDO-CHINA AT THE GENEVA CONFERENCE (Misc. No. 16) CMD. No. 9186 (1954); 31 PARL. SESSIONAL PAPERS 108-09, 132-34 (1953-54).
36. See COUNCIL ON FOREIGN RELATIONS, THE UNITED STATES IN WORLD AFFAIRS 1954 252-53 (1956).
37. According to P. J. Honey of the University of London:
    In signing the agreements they [the Vietnamese Communists] were forced to bow to strong Soviet pressure, a fact that robbed them of much prestige at home, and the only face-saving concession made to them was the unsigned "Declaration of Intention," which prescribed national elections for the reunification of Vietnam, to be held not later than July 1956. The worthlessness of this concession can be seen in a remark made by the Communist North Vietnam (DRV) Prime Minister, Pham Van Dong, to one of my Vietnamese friends immediately after the signing of the agreements. When asked which side he thought would win the elections, Dong replied, "You know as well as I do that there won't be any elections."
    P. HONEY, COMMUNISM IN NORTH VIETNAM: ITS ROLE IN THE SINO-SOVIET DISPUTE 5-6 (1966). See also id. 67. But see Weinstein, supra note 34, at 17-18 n.71.
38. 7 U.N. GAOR Annexes, Agenda Item No. 19, at 10, U.N. Doc. A/2341 & Corr. 1 (1952); 7 U.N. GAOR 410 (1952).
39. Falk, supra note 1, at 1152. He also writes: "In a sense it was naive of Hanoi to accept the Geneva arrangement or to rely upon its implementation." Id.

Some of the terms of the settlement and the fact that the Final Declaration of the Conference which contained the political settlement provisions was unsigned also suggest that the real settlement was partition, or at least that the parties were never really agreed on much but a territorial division and cease-fire. The key to unification would clearly be the election provisions, which were surprisingly vague for so important a question. The only reference to elections in the signed Agreement on the Cessation of Hostilities appears in Article 14(a) and reads in full: "Pending the general elections which will bring about the unification of Vietnam. . . ." The *unsigned* Final Declaration of the Conference adverts to the election problem only in the three sentences of paragraph seven.[40] The first two sentences are unclear and add little beyond a date for elections and the general composition of a supervisory commission, and the third sentence leaves the monumental problems to be solved by future consultations between the "representative authorities of the two zones . . . ," one of which was already publicly declaring that it would refuse to be bound by these provisions. This cavalier treatment of the political settlement must be considered a major weakness of the settlement and suggests that the parties were aware of the possibility of an extended partition in Vietnam. In contrast, the *signed* military cease-fire agreement dealt in great detail with provisions for a continuing cease-fire, and the central feature of the settlement was the division of Vietnam between two essentially economically viable and at least *de facto* international entities. The major real impact of the settlement was to stop the fighting and to reinforce an already existing political division. The provisions for allowing initial transfer of civilians between zones[41] also suggest continuing partition and are difficult to reconcile with genuine expecta-

40. See FURTHER DOCUMENTS RELATING TO THE DISCUSSION OF INDO-CHINA AT THE GENEVA CONFERENCE (Misc. No. 20) CMD. No. 9239 (1954); 31 PARL. SESSIONAL PAPERS 9-11 (1953-54); 161 BRITISH & FOREIGN STATE PAPERS 359-61 1954).

41. See Article 14 (d) of the Agreement on the Cessation of Hostilities in Viet Nam, July 20, 1954, and Article 8 of the Final Declaration of the Geneva Conference, July 21, 1954, in SENATE FOREIGN RELATIONS COMM., 89TH CONG. 1ST SESS., BACKGROUND INFORMATION RELATING TO SOUTHEAST ASIA AND VIETNAM 32, 59 (rev. ed. June 16, 1965).

tions of short-run unification by election. In large part they reflected western concern about loss *of the north* to communism and a desire to enable non-communists in the north to opt for a non-communist system in the south. Victor Bator makes much the same point with respect to the ambiguities of the settlement. According to Bator:

> The contradictions and the equivocations in the documents that emerged from the Geneva Conference gain added emphasis by the procedure by which they were reached. As narrated in memoirs such as those of Anthony Eden, who presided at Geneva, or in the detailed accounts of Bernard B. Fall, Jean Lacouture, and Philippe Devillers, partition—so ambiguously treated in the documents—was the most important subject of bargaining, both in principle and in its geographical application. It was discussed continually, if confidentially within each delegation, but for a time was carefully ignored when the delegations met.
>
> When at last partition was openly breached by the Vietminh, the French and British were elated. From that moment the location of the dividing line became the principal hurdle blocking the road to a settlement. Secretary of State Dulles, in order to underscore his insistence that it be drawn on the 17th parallel and to demonstrate western unity on this point, flew from Washington to Paris to meet with Eden and Premier Pierre Mendès-France. There were discussions even about the viability of the two parts. It is hard to believe that all this activity could have been devoted to the location of a temporary military demarcation line, a kind of billeting arrangement that would shortly disappear. The innocent-sounding text of the final agreement must have signified something of greater import.[42]

42. Bator, *Geneva; 1954: The Broken Mold*, THE REPORTER, JUNE 30, 1966, at 15, 17. Bator also writes:
> The primary motivation of the Vietminh was to consolidate their rule somewhere, anywhere, in Vietnam. To accomplish this, Ho Chi Minh was willing to make political concessions from his militarily superior position. So it came about that, on May 25, the head of the Vietminh delegation first mentioned partition. It was to be based on a regrouping of forces on either side of a line

There is also evidence in the ambiguous context surrounding the Conference which points to the conclusion that Hanoi placed reliance on elections being held in 1956.[43] A review of the negotia-

---

of demarcation that would give both parties an area with a sufficiently large population to exist independently.

Id. at 17. See also B. FALL, VIET-NAM WITNESS 75-76, 123 (1966); DOCUMENTS RELATING TO THE DISCUSSION OF KOREA AND INDO-CHINA AT THE GENEVA CONFERENCE (Misc. No. 16) CMD. No. 9186 (1954) (record of Conference discussions); FURTHER DOCUMENTS RELATING TO THE DISCUSSION OF INDO-CHINA AT THE GENEVA CONFERENCE (Misc. No. 20) CMD. No. 9239 (1954); 31 PARL. SESSIONAL PAPERS (1953-54).

Lacouture candidly points out:

A great deal of confusion surrounds this Geneva settlement. It must be emphasized that the only texts signed at Geneva were the armistice agreements between the French and the Vietminh. No one at all signed the "final declaration" of the conference—both the United States and South Vietnam had reservations about it—and it carried only the force of suggestion. But apart from the North Vietnamese, the French were the only nation that formally guaranteed to carry out the Geneva accords that provided both for partition at the 17th parallel and for elections.

Lacouture, *Vietnam: The Lessons of War, Hearings on S. 2793 Before the Senate Comm. on Foreign Relations*, 89th Cong., 2d Sess., pt. 1, at 655, 656-57 (1966).

Ellen Hammer says of the political settlement provisions of the "Accords":

[a]lthough the Franco-Vietminh war was ended at Geneva in July 1954, a political solution for Vietnam was postponed to some unspecified future date.

The agreements outlined at Geneva . . . contained few if any provisions for their long-term execution. They were a series of desires for the future, drawn up by the conference participants.

E. HAMMER, VIETNAM YESTERDAY AND TODAY 247 (1966).

43. See Weinstein, *supra* note 34. *See also* G. KAHIN & J. LEWIS, THE UNITED STATES IN VIETNAM 43-65 (1967).

These scholars argue that Hanoi placed major reliance on the election provisions and assert a model of the Geneva settlement which de-emphasizes the ambiguities in the political settlement. Interestingly, Kahin and Lewis point out that Dulles indicated in his press statement shortly after the Conference that now the United States could build up "the truly independent states of Cambodia, Laos and southern Vietnam." *Id.* 61. They concluded that SEATO "signalled the American intent to underwrite a separate state in southern Vietnam if, despite the inadmissibility of this under the Geneva Agreements, one could be established." *Id.* 63. The authors, however, fail to draw the inference that the immediate inclusion of "the free territory under the jurisdiction of the State of Vietnam" within the protection of Article IV of

tions at Geneva, however, suggests that the core of the settlement was the partition and cease-fire, and that the major agreement came when both sides accepted partition as the basis for settlement. There was substantially less agreement on the political settlement provisions and at least the British, American and State of Vietnam governments were opposed to these provisions, which they feared would work in practice to jeopardize maintenance of a non-communist south. The State of Vietnam and the United States indicated to the Conference participants that they would not consider themselves bound by these provisions. In light of the major feature of the settlement—a *de facto* division between two contending governments—and the expressed negative attitudes toward the political settlement provisions by other major participants at the Conference, there is serious doubt about the reasonableness of placing great reliance on the election provision.

The totality of evidence suggests that the western nations, particularly the United States and Britain, desired that the settlement would lead to a non-communist south and expected that it had some chance of doing so; that the Vietminh desired that the settlement would lead to unification under northern control and may have expected that takeover by political settlement or military activities would be feasible if the regime in the south proved nonviable; and that the Diem government expected that the agreement would lead to *de facto* partition because the election provisions were unacceptable to them. Fair interpretation of the settlement should take into account not only asserted expectations

---

the SEATO Treaty, strongly indicated Western expectations that the Geneva settlement would lead to a non-communist South Viet Nam. It should be recalled that Britain and France were also parties to SEATO.

Jean Lacouture points out that Mendès-France addressed a letter to the Saigon leaders the day after the Geneva negotiations "assuring them that France would not recognize another trustee of Vietnam's sovereignty" and ending "any chance of political co-operation between Paris and Hanoi." He refers to this letter and the signing of the SEATO Treaty on the day after Geneva as the two shadows quickly darkening the Geneva Agreement. These and subsequent actions of the British, French, Soviet and United States governments support an interpretation that partition was the core of the agreements. See J. LACOUTURE, VIETNAM: BETWEEN TWO TRUCES 11-12 (Vintage ed. 1966).

of the north, but also the contrary expectations of the United States and the State of Vietnam *at the time of the settlement* which were communicated to all participants.

The later Soviet lack of concern toward the non-implementation of the political settlement provisions and the Soviet attempt to admit both North and South Vietnam to the United Nations reinforces the substantial evidence that partition was the core of the settlement.

The point is that there seem to have been only minimal shared expectations on the *political* settlement, and that because of this ambiguity it is particularly unreasonable to assert the "Accords" as a justification for North Vietnamese military activities when *de facto* partition did result.[44]

When viewed in context there is considerable doubt as to the completeness of the model of the Geneva settlement relied on by Professor Falk in characterizing the conflict as Type III. It seems implicit in much of his argument for this characterization that north and south are one international entity.[45] But the total mani-

44. For a detailed treatment of the background of the Conference and the negotiations leading up to the settlement, see Ngo Ton Dat, *supra* note 32.

45. Although Professor Falk's Type III characterization is in his terms a characterization of "the war in South Vietnam," most of the considerations listed by him as leading him to so regard the conflict, such as Ho Chi Minh's asserted expectations from the Geneva settlement, asserted United States neglect of opportunities to negotiate with Hanoi, and the economic strain on Hanoi when relations between the North and South were not normalized, seem implicitly to argue that the conflict is a Type III conflict between the North and South. This suggestion that Falk is in effect substantially arguing that the conflict is civil strife between North and South is reinforced by the notable lack in his stated considerations of any analysis of the degree of independence of the Vietcong.

In the absence of any real analysis of the relationship between Hanoi and the Vietcong, particularly of the important questions of extent of military interaction prior to the first substantial increase in United States forces in late 1961, and prior to the commencement of regular bombing of the North in February, 1965, Falk's characterization of the conflict as Type III within Vietnam is unconvincing. In fact, most of the considerations which he relies on seem to indicate on their face that Hanoi's role is a major one in the total picture. See Falk, *supra* note 1, at 1127-32, 1137-38, 1151-52, 1158. See *infra* notes 48, 67.

fold of events surrounding the settlement suggests that partition was the real core of the settlement. And there can be little doubt that in its total context the political settlement was highly ambiguous. This very ambiguity reinforces the danger to world order inherent in the north's attempting to force its asserted expectations by use of the military instrument.

It is perhaps not unimportant that the continuing division of Vietnam between governments of conflicting ideologies significantly reflects a traumatic split among the Vietnamese people as well as between east and west. The 1954 settlement and continued division have provided an opportunity for the Vietnamese people to choose systems, an opportunity principally taken advantage of by a flood of refugees from north to south.[46] Under the circumstances it is difficult to see the inequity in treating the two divisions as entities whose peoples are entitled to freely express their own preferences in regard to governmental institutions and unification. The conclusion "civil strife" obscures serious inquiry about this question of which territorially organized communities in Vietnam ought to have their own right to self-determination to-

---

46. According to the *Fourth Interim Report* of the International Control Commission, by July 20, 1955, 892,876 had moved from the North to the South and only 4,269 had moved from the South to the North under Article 14 (d). FOURTH INTERIM REPORT OF THE INTERNATIONAL COMMISSION FOR SUPERVISION AND CONTROL IN VIETNAM (Vietnam No. 3) CMD. No. 9654 (1955); 45 PARL. SESSIONAL PAPERS 30, App. IV (1955-56).

These figures seem incomplete but the ratio of civilians going South to those going North probably remained about 10 to 1. This ratio resulted despite what one scholar has termed the "co-ordinated campaign of obstruction instituted by the authorities of the Democratic Republic of Vietnam against persons wishing to move to the south." Dai, *Canada's Role in the International Commission for Supervision and Control in Vietnam*, 4 CAN. YB. INT'L L. 161, 168 (1966).

According to Anthony Eden, "There were some indications of a greater willingness in Vietnam to face partition. There was no love lost between north and south. We felt that the distress at amputation might prove more apparent than real." A. EDEN, FULL CIRCLE 101 (1960).

P. J. Honey writes:

[A]ntagonism of long standing exists between the peoples of North and South Vietnam. The halves were divided for roughly two hundred years between the end of the sixteenth and the end of the eighteenth centuries—the dividing line was remarkably close to the present one—and a state of war existed between them.

P. HONEY, *supra* note 37, at 18.

day. Harrison Salisbury's *New York Times* reports on the relation between the N.L.F. and Hanoi indicate that even North Vietnam concedes, at least publicly, some right to short-run southern self-determination.[47] The seriousness with which the South Vietnamese Constituent Assembly functions is an indication of the substantiality of these expectations within the south. The continuing territorial separation of north and south, compounded by the ideological split among the Vietnamese people, has understandably given rise to significant expectations of individualized self-determination in the north and south. Under these circumstances it is at least as reasonable to regard both north and south as entities whose peoples are now entitled to their own self-determination about political institutions and unification as to view north and south as one entity for these purposes.[48]

47. See N.Y. Times, Jan. 16, 1967, at 1, col. 1.
   Brian Crozier points out that:
   > [T]he circumstances of the Vietnamese drive to the south, the distance between Saigon and Hanoi, and the difficulty of pre-air age communications have all fostered separatist sentiment in the south. For about 200 years, until the close of the eighteenth century, Vietnam was divided into mutually hostile halves roughly coinciding with the present division. This, too, colours the view that the current troubles are just another civil war.

   B. Crozier, Southeast Asia in Turmoil 135 (Pelican rev. ed. 1966).
   At least one Vietnamese observer wrote in 1963: "South Vietnam has a large anti-Communist majority. And if the people of South Vietnam can really cast a free vote, it is a foregone conclusion that the Vietnamese nationals will win." Ngo Ton Dat, *supra* note 32, at 385.

48. Although the evidence on which Professor Falk relies to characterize the conflict as Type III seems to argue implicitly for characterization as Type III between north and south, he somewhat inconsistently places major reliance on characterization as Type III *within* South Vietnam. But the evidence as related at pp. 1070-73 *infra*, simply does not support characterization of the conflict as Type III within South Vietnam. For even if the insurgency in the south was initially an indigenous reaction to the oppressive measures of the Diem government, a proposition on which scholars differ, *compare* D. Pike, Viet Cong 53, 80, 321 (1966) *with* G. Kahin & J. Lewis, *supra* note 43, at 119, *and* B. Fall, Viet Nam Witness 130-32 (1966), the evidence indicates that the Vietcong were receiving assistance from Hanoi prior to the first significant increase in United States forces over pre-insurgency levels. As is evident in the writings of such Vietnam scholars as Crozier, Fall, Lacouture, Pike, Schlesinger and Warner, there is general agreement that by 1961 Hanoi had entered the war and was assisting the Vietcong.

Armed Attack and Defensive Response

Professor Falk argues alternatively that at most Vietnam is a Type II conflict involving "substantial military participation by one or more foreign nations in an internal struggle for control."[49] In this alternative characterization of the conflict he is apparently focusing on the conflict as "civil strife" within the south substantially assisted by northern military participation, rather than as "civil strife" between north and south. If, of course, North and South Vietnam could be treated as one nation for the purpose of characterizing the conflict as "civil strife," it would be inconsistent to contend that the bombing of the north is an impermissible attack on a separate assisting state. Apparently focusing on "civil strife" within the south, then, Falk contends that "the United States could legitimately give military assistance to Saigon, but is obli-

---

See note 67 *infra*. Pike indicates that by conservative estimate about 1,900 NLF cadres infiltrated from the north in the period from 1954 through 1960 and that in 1961, 3,700 more entered the South. But there is also general agreement that prior to 1961 the United States had only a very limited Military Assistance Advisory Group in South Vietnam—probably not more than about 800-900, and that the first substantial increase in United States forces began in late 1961 with the rapid buildup of military advisory personnel, as recommended by the Taylor-Rostow report. Kahin and Lewis indicate that the major increase in United States assistance over pre-insurgency levels took place in early 1962. See G. KAHIN & J. LEWIS, *supra* note 43, at 77-78, 137. Apparently it was also in late 1961 and early 1962 that the United States first began direct military support with the use of helicopter units to ferry Vietnamese troops into combat. The testimony of Secretary of State Dean Rusk before the Senate Foreign Relations Committee that the first United States military casualty in South Vietnam occurred in December, 1961, is indicative of the relatively small military role played by the United States prior to late 1961. THE VIET NAM HEARINGS 263 (Vintage ed. 1966). A juxtaposition in time sequence of assistance rendered by both sides indicates that the United States did not significantly expand its assistance over pre-insurgency levels prior to the critical impetus given the conflict by Hanoi's increasing assistance and direction. The increase in United States forces was a *response* to the quickening pace of the war and the increasing assistance from Hanoi. To characterize the conflict as Type III within the south for the purpose of asserting the illegality of this offsetting United States response at a time when the Vietcong were clearly receiving increasing assistance from Hanoi is meaningless.

49. Falk, *supra* note 1, at 1126, 1127, 1132.

gated to limit the arena of violence to the territory of South Vietnam."[50] He argues that it is impermissible to treat North Vietnamese assistance to the insurgents in the south as an armed attack justifying a defensive response against the north.[51] This analysis disarmingly fails to separate the relevant intellectual task of description of past trends in decision from that of appraisal of alternatives. Although the is and the ought are both component elements of "law," intellectual clarification requires that the scholar differentiate widespread community expectations about law (whether of the is or the ought and whether evidenced by the practices of states or the writings of publicists, etc.) from his own personal policy recommendations. But though Professor Falk argues as policy recommendation that it *ought* to be the law, he cites no authority for his thesis that in what he calls a Type II conflict it *is* appropriate to take offsetting military action only if confined to the internal arena.

In the absence of substantial authority, his conclusion that the bombing of the north *"appears to be* . . . a violation of international law"[52] (emphasis added) is somewhat mysterious, particularly since he elsewhere qualifies this thesis by a footnote reference that this "assertion . . . must be qualified to the extent that the United States decision to bomb North Vietnam is treated as a law-creating precedent. . . ."[53] Candor requires acknowledgment that just as the problem of external assistance to the internal arena is unclear, there are no "authoritative" rules of international law prohibiting the bombing of the north. Moreover, although international law may have great gaps in this area, in the context

50. *Id.* 1132.
51. See *id.* 1136, 1140, 1150-51. This argument is crucial to Professor Falk's thesis. He writes: "South Viet Nam would have had the right to act in self-defense *if an armed attack had occurred,* and the United States would then have had the right to act in collective self-defense." *Id.* 1140.
52. *Id.* 1155.
53. *Id.* 1123 n.5. Although Professor Falk concludes that "international law offers no authoritative guidance as to the use of force *within* South Viet Nam," strangely he does not seem to find even equal uncertainty with respect to his thesis that in Type II conflict it is appropriate to take offsetting military action only if confined to the internal arena. See *id.* 1155.

of Vietnam there is greater reason to believe both as a matter of the is and the ought that the bombing of the north is a permissible defensive response.

There are two principal issues with respect to the legitimacy of defensive response against externally initiated or assisted insurgency. First, the question of whether offsetting assistance within the internal arena is legitimate and, second, whether response against the territory of the assisting entity is legitimate. As Falk's proposed restriction of the armed-attack test indicates, the armed-attack inquiry is principally responsive to the second of these. It may be that assistance may be provided to the government forces in order to offset external military assistance provided to the insurgents even in the absence of an armed attack as long as such assistance is confined to the internal arena. This distinction seems implicit in Falk's conclusion for Type II conflicts. It would mean that the United States could provide offsetting assistance to South Vietnam even in the absence of an armed attack and that the question of whether there has been an armed attack is only relevant with respect to interdictive attacks against the north. But if this is the principal relevance of the armed-attack test to the "internal war" situation then existing authority about armed attack suggests that defensive response against the north is permissible. Professor Kelsen suggests that this is the rule when he says:

> Since the Charter of the United Nations does not define the term "armed attack" used in article 51, the members of the United Nations in exercising their right of individual or collective self-defense may interpret "armed attack" to mean not only an action in which a state uses its own armed force but also a revolutionary movement which takes place in one state but which is initiated or supported by another state.[54]

54. Kelsen, *Collective Security Under International Law*, 49 INT'L LAW STUDIES 88 (1956). Kelsen also points out that "Participation of a state, with its armed forces, in the civil war within another state on the side of the insurgents is certainly international war in the relationship between the two states concerned." H. KELSEN, RECENT TRENDS IN THE LAW OF THE UNITED NATIONS 935 (1951). See also H. KELSEN, THE LAW OF THE UNITED NATIONS 798 (1950).

And Professor Brownlie supports this interpretation that there need not be a "direct invasion" to constitute an armed attack.[55]

For reasons of national interest or strategy inherent in the balance of power, states may choose only rarely to reply against the territory of an entity assisting insurgents, as the Spanish Civil War demonstrated.[56] Moreover, if the assistance to insurgents is not militarily substantial (and that is frequently the case), it may not amount to an armed attack. But there is nothing inherent in the armed-attack test which restricts this right of response to instances of overt invasion. Yet that would be substantially the consequence of Professor Falk's proposal.

The purpose of the armed-attack requirement in Article 51 of the United Nations Charter is to restrict the right to use force in individual or collective defense to very serious situations in which there is no reasonable alternative to the use of force for the protection of major values. By such requirements, contemporary international law expresses the judgment that minor encroachments on sovereignty, political disputes, frontier incidents, the use of non-coercive strategies of interference, and generally minor aggression which does not threaten fundamental values such as political and territorial integrity may not be defended against by major resort to force against another entity. These tests are simply representative of the community interest in restricting intense

55. I. BROWNLIE, INTERNATIONAL LAW AND THE USE OF FORCE BY STATES 373 (1963). Brownlie clearly seems to assume that foreign assistance to insurgents can constitute an "armed attack." *Id.* at 327. He seems to adopt an "agency and control" test for armed attack in the civil strife context. *Id.* at 370-73. Although he adverts to the desirability of confining defensive measures to the territory of the defending state, his discussion does not rule out response against the territory of an assisting state in the face of a major threat. *Id.* at 327, 372-73.

56. See generally N. PADELFORD, INTERNATIONAL LAW AND DIPLOMACY IN THE SPANISH CIVIL STRIFE (1939). *Cf.* A. THOMAS & A. THOMAS, NON-INTERVENTION 225 (1956):

> Such recognition, [German and Italian recognition of the insurgents as the legitimate government] being premature, was an illegal intervention and following it the Spanish war was converted from a civil war to an international war, and it should then have been treated as such. To apply the rules of international law devised to deal with insurgency to an international war is a great misuse of the law.

responding coercion to those situations where fundamental values are seriously threatened by coercion.[57] Such coercive threats to fundamental values can be effectuated as realistically by covert invasion and significant military assistance to insurgents as by armies on the march.

In the Vietnam context the evidence strongly suggests that Hanoi provided significant military leadership and assistance to the Vietcong from about 1959-60, an assistance which has greatly increased since then. Bernard Fall's account of the beginning of the Second Indo-China war in *The Two Viet-Nams*[58] suggests that the insurgency was substantially under the control of the Communist Party apparatus even in the early years and that the National Liberation Front was substantially interrelated with Hanoi. By way of some relevant observations by Fall, certainly a qualified observer:

> A last rationale for the autonomous rise of a resistance movement in South Viet-Nam, advanced notably by the French writer Philippe Devillers, is that "the insurrection existed before the Communists decided to take part, and that they were simply forced to join in" by Diem's oppressive measures. Devillers, however, advances no evidence to the effect that the movement was not taken in hand by Hanoi *later*, precisely because it had a popular character, and thus was useful.[59]

The wholly artificial character of the National Liberation Front, at least during the first year of its operation, is perhaps best shown by the fact that until April 13, 1962, it had not disclosed the names of its alleged leaders. . . .[60]

In order to promote the concept that the Front and the Lao-Dong Party were separate entities, Hanoi informed the world on January 20, 1962, that a "conference of representatives of Marxists-Leninists in South Viet-Nam" had taken place on December 19, 1961, in the course of which it was decided to set up the Viet-Nam People's Revolutionary Party

57. See M. McDougal & F. Feliciano, Law and Minimum World Public Order 259 (1961).
58. B. Fall, The Two Viet-Nams (rev. ed. 1964).
59. *Id.* 358.   60. *Id.* 356.

(Dang Nhan-Dan Cach Mang), which officially came into existence on January 1, 1962. . . .

[L]ike the National Liberation Front itself, the Revolutionary Party failed to announce the names of any of its founding members. According to two circulars emanating from the Lao-Dong authorities and infiltrated into South Viet-Nam, members of the Lao-Dong were notified as early as December 7, 1961 (twelve days before the founding meeting) that the new party was created merely out of tactical necessity but would remain under the over-all control of the Lao-Dong. . . .

In all likelihood, the establishment of a "separate" Communist organization for South Viet-Nam follows the same pattern as the dissolution of the old ICP in the 1940's to give the Laotian and Khmer Communist movements a semblance of national autonomy. . . .[61]

In terms of its political-adminstrative apparatus, the South Vietnamese insurgency operated until December, 1960, as simply an extension of the then-existing Communist underground apparatus. . . .

Inside South Viet-Nam, the Viet-Minh seems to have maintained its old administrative structure of Interzones (lien-khu) V and VI, the former covering Central Viet-Nam south of the 17th parallel, and the latter covering the Nam-Bo (the southern part, i.e., South Viet-Nam proper, or Cochin-china). . . .

On the military side, the two zone commanders are equals *and apparently get their orders directly from Hanoi.* In 1960-62, they were Brigadier General Nguyen Don for Interzone V and a "civilian" guerrilla leader, Nguyen Huu Zuyen, for the Nam-Bo.[62]

Fall speaks of "Regiment 126, reinforced by a special 600-man battalion, infiltrated into South Viet-Nam in May, 1961, and likewise operating in the mountains west of Quang-Ngai . . . ,"[63] and reports that by mid-1963 infiltration may have involved 12,000

61. *Id.* 357-58.   62. *Id.* 355 (emphasis added).
63. *Id.* 353.

men.[64] He also points out that Americans were authorized to "shoot first" only in February, 1963.[65]

United Nations Secretary-General U Thant, although disagreeing with those categorizing the National Liberation Front as a mere "stooge" of Hanoi, nevertheless says that the N.L.F. receives "perhaps very substantial help from the North."[66] And according to Douglas Pike, whom Arthur Schlesinger describes as the most careful student of the Vietcong,[67] Hanoi was involved in

64. *Id.* 330. Fall also writes that:
> Close to 100,000 South Vietnamese of Communist obedience left the southern area for North Viet-Nam, thus providing the latter with native southerners a plenty who were given extensive training for later operations in their home areas; among them were close to 10,000 mountaineers from the Central Plateau area. At the same time, the repatriates going north included the dependents of the hard-core fighters who were ordered to go underground in the south, as well as the raw recruits with whose training and protection the southerners had been burdened until then.

> *Id.* 358-59.

65. *Id.* at 333.

66. N.Y. Times, Jan. 11, 1967, at 4, col. 5.

67. A. SCHLESINGER, THE BITTER HERITAGE 18 (1967). Bernard Fall says of Pike:
> Pike's presence is one of those small illustrations of the good side of the American system. No other book is likely to demolish more completely and more seriously all the convenient myths dished out officially about the National Liberation Front (NLF), for this is the work of an "insider." In his job Pike sees more material than anyone except the Front Leaders themselves. He has read reports from captured Viet Congs, translations of the huge quantities of captured documents . . . and publications from Hanoi or from Front sources abroad.

> Fall, *The View from Vietnam,* THE NEW YORK REVIEW OF BOOKS, Feb. 9, 1967, at 13, col. 2.

> Although not all scholars agree with Douglas Pike's thesis "that the DRV was . . . the godfather of the NLF," see D. PIKE, VIET CONG 321 (1966), most concede that the DRV played a significant role in the development of the Front and that Hanoi provided significant military leadership and assistance from about 1959-60.

> According to Schlesinger:
> The civil insurrection in South Vietnam began to gather force by 1958; it was not until September 1960 that the Communist Party of North Vietnam bestowed its formal blessing and called for the liberation of the south from American imperialism. Ho Chi Minh was now supplying the Viet Cong with training, equip-

the planning and direction of N.L.F. activities from the very beginning of the Front in 1959 and provided from the start what the N.L.F. most needed, organizational knowhow and expertise in insurgency.[68] As Pike puts it, "By 1959 an over-all directional

---

ment, strategic advice and even men—perhaps two thousand a year by 1960.

A. SCHLESINGER, THE BITTER HERITAGE 17 (1967).

Bernard Fall rejects both the Lacouture-Devillers thesis that the insurgency began "simply as an internal response to the repressive nature of the Diem regime" and the "White Paper" thesis that the insurgency was instigated from the north. He adopts a middle position which seems to concede that Hanoi played a significant role. See B. FALL, VIET-NAM WITNESS 130-32 (1966); M. RASKIN & B. FALL, THE VIET-NAM READER 252-61 (Vintage ed. 1965). See also P. HONEY, *supra note* 37, at 25-26, 67-68.

Even Lacouture gives a chronology indicating D.R.V. intervention prior to major United States expansion of forces. He writes: "[I]n 1960 the N.L.F. had been created with the authorization of Hanoi, which thus renounced its non-intervention; in 1961 the United States entered the war." J. LACOUTURE, VIETNAM: BETWEEN TWO TRUCES 61 (Vintage ed. 1966).

Denis Warner's account of the beginning of the second Indo-China conflict indicates that Hanoi played a significant role which preceded the first substantial United States response in late 1961 and early 1962 and that prior to that time Hanoi had "abandoned any pretence that it was not behind the rising tide of violence." D. WARNER, THE LAST CONFUCIAN 162 (Penguin ed. 1964); see also *id.* 160-76.

Brian Crozier's account strongly suggests that although the Viet Minh were a minority when the second conflict broke out at the beginning of 1958, the north was substantially directing the southern guerrillas prior to the end of 1961. He also says: "Indeed the evidence of North Vietnamese direction and control of operations in South Vietnam is overwhelming." B. CROZIER, *supra note* 47, at 137; see also *id.* 96-97, 135-43.

Professor Zasloff wrote in 1961 prior to major buildup of United States advisers in South Vietnam:

Currently the government of South Viet Nam is struggling for survival against well-organized, strongly sustained guerrilla forces —the Viet Cong—inspired and supported by the Communist Vietminh government of the North, which has made no secret of its goal of crushing the southern government and uniting Viet Nam under its hegemony.

Zasloff, *Peasant Protest in South Viet Nam*, in M. KAPLAN, THE REVOLUTION IN WORLD POLITICS 192 (1966).

68. See D. PIKE, VIET CONG 77-84 (1966).

hand was apparent. The struggle became an imported thing."[69] By the end of 1963, there was evidence not only of the presence of two North Vietnamese generals in the south[70] but northern trained cadres were being captured in numbers.[71] When the Vietcong buildup in mid-1964 made increased material support necessary, Hanoi sent anti-aircraft and heavier weapons south.[72] And according to Pike, by the end of 1965 the N.L.F. was taken over by cadres from North Vietnam, even down to the village level, a regularizing process which began in mid-1963.[73] There is evidence that regular units of the Army of North Vietnam were mov-

69. *Id.* 78. Pike also points out:
> [T]he creation of the National Liberation Front, . . . was premeditated, planned, organized at length and in detail, and then pushed and driven into existence and operation. Such an effort had to be the child of the North.

Id. 80.
In differentiating the current Viet Nam conflict from the earlier Viet Minh war, Pike says:
> [T]he later struggle in the South had a distinct imported quality about it that did not characterize either the Viet Minh war or the Communist revolution in China. The alien character was not simply a matter of outside aid or leadership. The struggle was in essence an expansionist drive by the North Vietnamese who asserted, and truly believed, that their goal of reunification was legally and morally justified.

Id. 53.

70. *Id.* 102.

71. *Id.* 323. In what he describes as a conservative estimate, accurate within plus or minus 10%, Pike sets out the following figures on infiltrators:

NLF Cadres from the North, 1954-1965

Year	Number
1954 through 1960	1,900
1961	3,700
1962	5,800
1963	4,000
1964	6,500 (at least a third Northerners)
1965	11,000 (almost all Northerners)
	32,900

Id. 324.

72. *Id.* 321, 325.   73. *Id.* 116.

ing into the south[74] prior to commencement of regular bombing of the north, and subsequent to 1965 it is clear that such regular units were substantially engaged in the south.[75] The seriousness of this military threat is indicated by the Mansfield Report which reported that at the time regular bombing of the north began, South Vietnam was in imminent danger of total collapse.[76] This Vietcong-North Vietnam attack is the kind of serious and sustained attack threatening political and territorial integrity which justifies assistance to the south and an interdictive defensive response against the territory of the north.

As a matter of policy preference, Professor Falk argues that in a Type II conflict offsetting military assistance must be confined to the internal arena as an alternative for limiting violence.[77] This rationale is suspect as a blanket proposition and is especially weak as applied to Vietnam. North Vietnam is not simply a third-party state providing assistance to a completely independent insurgency in "an internal struggle for control" of another state. Falk's implicit characterization of the conflict between north and south as "civil strife" or at least much of the evidence that he relies on to characterize the conflict as Type III[78] suggests the obvious weakness of simply treating North Vietnam as a third party rendering assistance to an independent insurgency. But in making the alternative Type II characterization of the conflict he swings to the other extreme of minimizing the very important relationships between north and south—particularly the significant interrelation between the National Liberation Front and the

---

74. See MANSFIELD, MUSKIE, INOUYO, AIKEN & BOGGS, THE VIETNAM CONFLICT: THE SUBSTANCE AND THE SHADOW—REPORT TO THE SENATE COMMITTEE ON FOREIGN RELATIONS, 112 CONG. REC. 140, 141 (daily ed. Jan. 13, 1966); N.Y. Times, July 31, 1966, at 2, col. 5. See also D. PIKE, VIET CONG 164 (1966).

75. N.Y. Times correspondent Charles Mohr reported in August, 1966, that according to informed sources the latest intelligence estimates indicated that ". . . of the 177 enemy combat battalions in South Vietnam, 81, or 46 per cent, are now North Vietnamese. . . ." N.Y. Times, Aug. 10, 1966, at 1. col. 4, at 5, col. 5.

76. See MANSFIELD et al., supra note 74, at 140.

77. See Falk, *International Law and the United States Role in the Viet Nam War*, 75 YALE L.J. 1122, 1123 (1966).

78. See notes 15 & 45 *supra*.

Communist Party apparatus of North Vietnam. North Vietnam is one half of an at least *de facto* divided nation rendering assistance across an international cease-fire line to an armed insurgency in the other half whose leadership is significantly interrelated with leadership in Hanoi. It is generally believed that a more or less long-run objective of that assistance is to unify Vietnam under the leadership of the Communist Party of Vietnam, largely dominated by the north.[79] North Vietnamese Premier Pham Van Dong's reiterated goals of "freedom and independence" cannot be meaningfully interpreted as applying only to North Vietnam. Given the continuation of the struggle, they can only be interpreted as signifying a wider intention encompassing South Vietnam as well. To assert that the war "should be viewed as primarily between factions contending for control of the southern zone," is to minimize this important relationship and objective of North Vietnam and indeed the whole background of the conflict. Real-world Vietnam will not fit either Falk's Type II or Type III paradigms, and certainly cannot be both at once. Although the assistance from the territorially adjacent north is covert and is supported by a substantial network of indigenous guerrillas, the long-run objectives of the north have significant similarity with those of North Korea in the overt invasion of South Korea. They are not simply those of a third-party assisting state such as the territorially remote assisting participants in the Spanish Civil War. Although, of course, there are many differences, the analogy to the Korean war is for this reason alone closer than Professor Falk's analogy to the Spanish Civil War.[80] In determining permissibility of defensive measures against the territory of an assisting participant the objectives of the participant in rendering assistance

79. According to Harrison Salisbury: "Both the Northern regime and the Liberation Front are committed to reunification and the creation of a single Vietnamese state." N.Y. Times, Jan. 16, 1967, at 1, col. 1, at 10, col. 3. But according to Wilfred Burchett: "Reunification is a long-range project realizable only in the far distant future, which Vietnamese leaders in the North and Liberation Front leaders in the South privately agree may be 10 or 20 years away." Charlottesville Daily Progress, Feb. 10, 1967, at 1, cols. 1-2. See also D. PIKE, VIET CONG 367-71 (1966); A. EDEN, TOWARD PEACE IN INDOCHINA 21-22 (1966); P. HONEY, *supra* note 37, at 168-71.
80. See Falk, *supra* note 77, at 1126.

and its relationship to the insurgency are highly relevant. North Vietnam is not simply assisting in a struggle for "internal control" of the south but is substantially tied up with the military and political leadership of the insurgency in the south and has as a major, although possibly long-term, objective: unification with the south. This is not to argue the extent of the military assistance Hanoi was providing in the early years. The importance of the amount of that early assistance whether small or large has been greatly oversold.[81] But it is to indicate that prior to regular interdictive attacks against the north, Hanoi was so involved in the conflict in terms of its objectives in rendering assistance and its interaction with the Vietcong that it is anomalous to speak of it as just a third-party assisting state.

It should also be pointed out that there is conflicting evidence on the extent to which Hanoi was the moving party in the effective insurgency and that Professor Falk's model, which relies heavily on the controversial Lacouture-Devillers thesis, is one which minimizes Hanoi's role.[82] If a third state substantially initiates an insurgency instead of simply rendering assistance to an on-going insurgency it would seem anomalous to treat it as within Falk's Type II conflict. If the reality is that the *effective military insurgency* in South Vietnam was substantially initiated and is substantially supported and directed by the Communist Party of Vietnam largely controlled from Hanoi, Falk's view applied to Vietnam would simply immunize states invading covertly.

Further, even in a Type II paradigm, to restrict defensive re-

81. I share Schlesinger's judgment that the same is true of the failure to hold the 1956 elections. See A. SCHLESINGER, *supra* note 67, at 15.
82. Douglas Pike's overall thesis seems to assign a substantial role to Hanoi in the creation of the effective military insurgency in the south, see D. PIKE, *supra* note 79, in contrast to Professor Falk's "interpretation of the internal war as primarily a consequence of indigenous forces." Falk, *supra* note 77, at 1129. The Canadian representative to the I.C.C. concluded in a minority statement to the February 13, 1965, Special Report that North Vietnamese activities "aimed at the overthrow of the South Vietnamese administration . . . constitute the root cause of general instability in Vietnam. . . ." SPECIAL REPORT TO THE CO-CHAIRMEN OF THE GENEVA CONFERENCE ON INDO-CHINA, FEBRUARY 13, 1965 (Vietnam No. 1) CMND. No. 2609, at 14-15 (1965). For discussion of this 1965 Special Report which was prompted by the commencement of regular bombing of the north see Dai, *supra* note 46, at 171-72.

sponse to the internal arena may be an undesirable restriction of the right of defense in the absence of a more effective peacekeeping machinery. It would mean, in effect, that a state might have to endure interminable outside intervention with little hope of ending the conflict by appropriate defensive actions. Presumably under this thesis even a widely recognized government could not defend its territory from massive external military assistance to insurgent factions, because if it could it would seem that assisting states participating in collective defense with the state attacked should have the same defensive rights. Although Falk's proposed rule might theoretically minimize international escalation, it might also maximize destruction within the unfortunate internal arena that gets trapped as the battleground, and it might encourage external intervention in general. The Spanish Civil War does show the great internal destructiveness of a territorially restricted conflict in the absence of an effective sanction against intervention. In a world relying heavily on power the right of *effective* defense is a major deterrent to outside intervention in internal conflicts. Providing immunity to the real bases of power of the attackers both fails to provide an effective sanction against third-party assistance and drastically undermines defensive rights. In doing so it closes out an option which may in some situations be the most effective method of conflict resolution at least cost to all participants. In the final analysis that is the real question and one not convincingly answered by Professor Falk's *a priori* "geographic" rule. For a number of reasons, then, there is considerable question whether the proposal to immunize the territories of intervening nations would in the long run reduce conflict or whether it would increase conflict by encouraging intervention and prolongation of conflict. Moreover, as the interdictive response against North Vietnam illustrates, the alternatives in proceeding against an aggressively assisting external power are considerably greater than an either-or, all-or-nothing response. It might be that enlightened community policy would rule impermissible all-out attack against the territorial and political integrity of such an assisting entity, while allowing necessary limited defensive measures against resources closely related to the assistance. This alternative, which is the one being pursued in Vietnam, stops short of ultimate escalation of the conflict while providing some sanction against unlawful military intervention.

There are sound reasons for suggesting, just as there are for doubting, that the limited bombing of the north may be an option leading to termination of conflict in the shortest period of time at least cost to all participants. Without the interdictive attacks against the north there might be less reason for the north ever to stop rendering assistance to the insurgents or to seek a negotiated settlement. The cost of guerrilla attack is by the lopsided arithmetic of such conflict much less than the cost of defense. The interdictive attacks both substantially raise the cost of assistance to the insurgents in the south, and impede assistance reaching the insurgents. They were initiated in close support of the struggle in the south in terms of supply, morale, and settlement factors and do lend support to the defensive effort in these respects. To balance the picture, though, it should be pointed out that as a strategy choice, the effect of the bombing is difficult to assess and it has some serious weaknesses. For example, it is unable to prevent a substantial flow of assistance from reaching the south, it increases the risk of international escalation, it may harden the attitude of the citizenry of the north, and it has a strong negative effect on world opinion. In view of the question marks connected with it, the limited bombing of the north may or may not be the best strategy for pursuing legitimate defense objectives in Vietnam, but it is within the range of reasonable responses, allowing for supportable differences of opinion as to the effectiveness of a particular strategy for conflict termination.

At one point Professor Falk contends that "since the United States has far greater military resources potentially available, our use of insufficient force violates general norms of international law."[83] But surely it does not violate international law to take into account the risk of escalation and of generating a nuclear war if the objective is widened from limited defensive aims. His combined argument, then, seems to be that given some United States response, international law may require a greater military commitment in the south with no hope of proceeding against the

83. See Falk, *supra* note 77, at 1144.

major resources in the north which are facilitating continuation of the struggle. By this observation Falk seems to have put his finger on a major difficulty with his proposal for limiting permissible response to the internal arena in Type II conflict. Since international law does seek conflict minimization by a requirement of effective force, should not such force be applied against military resources whether within or without the internal arena, if a determination is reasonably made that such response is necessary to end the conflict with minimum destructiveness on all sides? This determination must, of course, include assessment of the risk of conflict escalation under each alternative and must be reasonable under all the circumstances, allowing some leeway for reasonable differences of opinion as to the effectiveness of a particular strategy. But Falk's proposed territorial limitation on responding defensive measures cuts down on a series of options which may well lead to conflict resolution with minimum destructiveness for all participants. The determination of what course of action will end the conflict with minimum destructiveness and risk is, of course, the real question and one which in the terribly difficult Vietnam context is not served by the sterile accusation that "our use of insufficient force violates general norms of international law."

In view of Professor Falk's concern with conflict minimization evident in his proposal to limit responding coercion to the internal arena of a Type II conflict, it would also seem important to stress the danger to world order in providing assistance to insurgents across an international cease-fire line in a country at least *de facto* divided between the major contending public order systems. With respect to these activities of the north, however, he merely says "international law neither attempts nor is able to regulate support given exile groups. The activities of Hanoi between 1954 and 1964 conform to patterns of tolerable conflict in contemporary international politics."[84] And he concludes: "North

84. *Id.* 1139.
    This statement is also misleading in failing to advert to Hanoi's activities with respect to Laos during this period. North Vietnamese intervention in Laos has been on a substantial scale, has not been confined to supporting exile groups and has been in flagrant disregard of the

Viet Nam's action does not seem to constitute 'aggression.' "[85] As a description of power processes these statements may be accurate, but as statements of contemporary international law and policies of conflict minimization they are not the most useful picture.

The United Nations has repeatedly condemned the creation or support of civil strife by external elites using internal agents. Thus the General Assembly said in condemning external assistance to the communist guerrillas in Greece:

> The General Assembly . . . condemning the intervention of a state in the internal affairs of another state for the purpose of changing its government by the threat or use of force,
>
> Solemnly reaffirms that whatever the weapons used, any aggression, whether committed openly or by fomenting civil strife in the interest of a foreign power, or otherwise is the gravest of all crimes against peace and security throughout the world.[86]

Geneva Accords of 1962. Yet this intervention in Laos is in close support of Hanoi's activities against South Viet Nam.

John Hughes, staff correspondent of The Christian Science Monitor, writes from Laos that:

> Though Laos is technically neutralized by the Geneva agreement of 1962, it in fact harbors what Premier Souvanna Phouma estimates to be 60,000 North Vietnamese troops, who of course have no right to be on Laotian soil. In part they are stiffening pro-Communist Pathet Lao units, but mainly they are support and garrison troops down the length of the Ho Chi Minh Trail, ensuring the continued passage through Laos to South Vietnam of North Vietnamese infiltrators.

Christian Science Monitor, May 3, 1967, at 1, col. 4. Some scholars indicate that Hanoi's military intervention in South Viet Nam should be placed in a larger temporal and geographical context of Viet Minh aggression against Laos and Cambodia and the drive for an all Indo-China Communist party dominated by Hanoi. See P. HONEY, *supra* note 37, at 168-71; B. CROZIER, *supra* note 47, at 114-33.

There is also evidence that North Viet Nam is providing training and assistance to insurgents operating in Thailand. See Christian Science Monitor, May 12, 1967, at 1, col. 2.

85. Falk, *supra* note 77, at 1159.
86. G.A. Res. 380 (v), 5 U.N. GAOR Supp. 20, at 13, 17, U.N. Doc. A/1775 (1950). See also A. THOMAS & A. THOMAS, NON-INTERVENTION 226-29 (1956).

And the International Law Commission Draft of a Code of Offenses Against the Peace and Security of Mankind condemned:

> The organization, or encouragement of the organization, by the authorities of a state, of armed bands within its territory or any other territory for incursions into the territory of another state; or the toleration of the organization of such armed bands in its own territory, or the toleration of the use by such armed bands of its territory as a base of operation or as a point of departure for incursions into the territory of another state as well as direct participation in or support of such incursions.[87]

And in December, 1966, the General Assembly "condemned all forms of intervention in the domestic affairs of States, and urged all States to refrain from armed intervention, subversion, terrorism, or other indirect forms of intervention for the purpose of changing the existing system of another State or interfering in civil strife in another State."[88] These representative pronouncements reflect the substantial community expectation that inciting or assisting civil strife is not only aggression, but is aggression presenting a particularly grave threat to minimum order in today's world. In postulating that external military assistance is inappropriate to influence the outcome in a Type III conflict, Falk seems to be concurring in this judgment although he later somewhat inconsistently asserts that "international law offers no authoritative guidance as to the use of force *within* South Viet Nam. . . ."[89] The policy of conflict minimization strongly suggests the illegitimacy of military assistance to an insurgency sustained at a high level of coercion across *de facto* boundaries separating major contending public order systems.[90] Should the West Ger-

87. International Law Comm'n, Report, 9 U.N. GAOR, Supp. 9 at 10, 11 U.N. Doc. A/2693 (1954).
88. U.N. Weekly News Summary, Press Release WS/273, at 6 (December 22, 1966). It is peripheral but perhaps useful to point out that the recognition of contending public order systems does not depend on acceptance of dogma about "monolithic communism."
89. Falk, *supra* note 77, at 1155. See also *id.* 1137.
90. The interesting thesis of Robert Ardrey would to some extent seem to reinforce *de facto* control of territory as the important standard for

mans or Nationalist Chinese provide sustained high levels of military assistance to insurgents in East Germany or mainland China, ultimately fielding regular army units, the threat to world order would be obvious. And if the analogies are not on all fours with Vietnam, events in Vietnam prove them relevant if not as obvious with respect to consequences for public order when such assistance is provided. In seeking to effectuate community policies of conflict minimization, it may be more effective to focus attention on the illegality of aggressive coercive strategies across *de facto* international boundaries rather than attempting to further restrict the right of defense against such aggressive strategies.

External Participation in Intra-State Conflict: A Policy Inquiry

Even though Professor Falk's "civil strife" framework does not seem sufficiently sensitive to crucial features of the total Vietnam context to provide a valid analytic base for conclusion about that conflict, his framework is a creative contribution to stimulation of general policy inquiry with respect to external participation in intra-state conflict. Since his own conclusions about Vietnam are based on this framework it may be helpful to attempt further clarification of the major policies applicable to external participation in intra-state conflict. This discussion is intended only to air some doubts about suggested norms for Type III conflict and is not intended to offer a definitive rule if, indeed, any is possible or desirable. In fact, preliminary inquiry suggests that "Type III conflict" may encompass too wide a variety of contexts to generalize meaningfully and that more sensitive contextual clarification may be desirable.

The principal policies relevant to decision about the permissibility of external participation in intra-state conflict seem to be self-determination and maintenance of minimum public order. Self-determination, the right of peoples within an entity to choose

---

purposes of conflict minimization. See generally R. ARDREY, THE TERRITORIAL IMPERATIVE (1966).

Brownlie indicates that "the right of self-defence should be based upon peaceful possession and *de facto* exercise of authority." I. BROWNLIE, INTERNATIONAL LAW AND THE USE OF FORCE BY STATES 382 (1963).

their own institutions and form of government, is a basic community policy reflected in community condemnation of intervention and colonialism. The striking thing about self-determination as a touchstone of permissibility is that realistically it may cut for as well as against outside intervention in an internal arena and it may cut for or against assistance to either insurgents or *de facto* government. In the colonial war in Algeria in 1960, self-determination may have been served by assistance to insurgents, whereas in the Congo in 1961, in Greece in 1948, in Kenya, Uganda, and Tanganyika in 1964, and possibly at the beginning of the Spanish Civil War in 1936, self-determination may have been better served by assistance to the government. A simplistic version of self-determination espoused by Hall[91] and advocated by some, however, identifies self-determination with anything that happens in an entity. According to this view, states should be left alone in all circumstances to work out their own form of government. If aid to the recognized government were legitimate then it would impair the right to revolution, and if aid to the insurgents were legitimate it would violate independence by interfering with the regular organ of the state. This judgment that self-determination requires that neither the recognized government nor insurgents can ever be aided conceals the naive assumption that whatever takes place within the confines of a territorial entity is pursuant to genuine self-determination of peoples and that outside "intervention" is necessarily disruptive of self-determination. Such simplistic deductive notions that territorial entities should be left alone to work out their own self-determination at all costs and by any modalities ignores the twin reality that today ruthless governments in control of the total resources of a society can suppress their peoples and that minorities can through terror, sabotage, and the control of the military establishment capture control of governmental machinery. The Hall view seems to adopt a kind of Darwinian definition of self-determination as survival of the fittest within the national boundaries, even if fittest means most adept in the use of force.

It may be that proscribing unilateral outside assistance to

91. See W. HALL, INTERNATIONAL LAW 287 (6th ed. 1909); W. HALL, INTERNATIONAL LAW 347 (8th ed. 1924).

either faction will in fact result more often in genuine self-determination than allowing such assistance to either side. And the difficulty of appraising objectives of the assisting participants and determining where self-determination really lies may militate for this solution. If these assumptions really underlie a neutral rule of nonintervention in Type III conflicts, then we ought to recognize it as such and reflect both on the accuracy of the assumptions and on whether it is necessary to have this broad a prophylatic rule. Some relevant questions might be: What is the aggregate contemporary experience as to whether self-determination is aided or hindered by assistance to insurgents, by assistance to recognized governments, or by both? In what cases would a broad prophylatic rule cut against self-determination, and might we find recurring features which would signal an exception to the rule in those cases? In light of the great variety of situations presenting the problem, what is the criterion for "civil strife" triggering the rule? What functions do recognized governments serve that might make any such rule as to them more difficult or unworkable? Might legitimacy of aid to either faction be conditioned on holding free elections or on some other indicia of genuine self-determination? In view of the interdependencies among states in a world divided between contending states and blocs, to what extent is a rule focused on self-determination of only one entity realistic or desirable?[92] What are the expectations that nations will observe such rules? Answers to these questions might militate for no rule, a neutral non-intervention rule, or a more narrowly drawn rule aimed, for example, at assistance to insurgents. But without more the present arguments for a neutral non-intervention rule in all Type III conflicts are unpersuasive as a requirement of self-determination.

As seems implicit in the suggested norm for Type II conflict, any rule of non-intervention based on self-determination should be modified where one participant has received external assistance. Although self-determination might still cut either way, the rule is much too suspect to operate as a prophylactic rule against

92. Professor Falk adverts to this question in pointing out that "the outcome of a Type III conflict may affect the relative power of many other countries." Falk, *supra* note 77, at 1126.

external intervention after there has already been intervention on one side.

A second major policy in analyzing the permissibility of external participation in intra-state conflict is the maintenance of minimum public order. A hypothesis for inquiry with respect to public order consequences is that external assistance to insurgent groups and the fomenting of civil strife by external elites is more often seriously disruptive of minimum public order than assistance to recognized governments. Assistance to insurgents often involves high risk of prolonged conflict with entrenched elites as well as high risk of expansion of the conflict through external support for the recognized government. Recognized governments may be incorporated in a world-order bloc that views their overthrow as an unacceptable impairment of bloc power or security, or they may have defensive arrangements with third powers which will be triggered by assistance to insurgents. It is one of the functions of government to preserve stability and maintain internal order, and it is to be expected that ruling elites will resist change sought through force and will call on their established international partners to help them. Recognized governments usually control greater resources than insurgents and frequently control the organized military. These conditions make insurgent attacks employing guerrilla armies and terrorist tactics likely to be prolonged costly struggles. Compare, for example, such diverse situations as Hungary and the Dominican Republic with Algeria and Vietnam. Moreover, fomenting an insurgency, or providing assistance to it in early stages, can be simply a sophisticated form of attack. Such attacks are particularly pernicious in that they are difficult to prove and are frequently couched in rhetoric about self-determination and social reform which may or may not be the principal objectives of the attacker.

As a rule to prevent outside powers from becoming involved with one another, there is little reason to believe that a "neutral" norm would be more effective than a rule prohibiting external assistance to insurgencies only. In fact, in the cold-war context there is good reason to believe that it is particularly unrealistic to ask that military aid be withheld from continuing *de facto* governments. Soviet assistance to the regimes in Hungary and East

Germany, and United States assistance to Greece and South Vietnam, indicate that realistic projections militate against attempting to proscribe assistance to entrenched governments. In contrast, expectations of violence are particularly acute when assistance is rendered to insurgent elements across cold-war boundaries. Determined United States assistance to Hungarian freedom fighters would have involved high risk of acute conflict with Russia. North Vietnamese assistance to insurgents in South Vietnam has fueled a major conflict. And substantial military assistance by Formosa to mainland insurgents would seem to carry an especially grave risk of major war. It is an observable cold-war phenomenon that major powers tend to support regimes threatened by military actions initiated or supported by opposing bloc powers. In light of this practice there is certainly a strong community interest in not attempting coercive change across such boundaries.

In contrast, public order consequences are not as acute in situations of less direct cold-war confrontation. For example, in newly independent African countries intervention by a former colonial power on either side may not provide the same risk of protracted and escalating conflict although the risk of extended conflict is still significant and would usually be greater if intervention were on the side of the insurgents. Where the risk of major conflict is slight, grave and continuing denial of self-determination may outweigh dangers of the use of coercive strategies of change. But where such risk is grave, minimum public order may be the most important consideration.

It may be argued that since both sides may recognize separate elite groups as the lawful representative of the state, if any rule is to be effective in preventing outside powers from confronting each other on separate sides of a civil war, the rule must proscribe assistance to both government and insurgents. But although states can always prematurely recognize one or another group as the legal representative of a state, there is usually no doubt as to which side is the government and which the insurgents despite such opposing recognition. In Greece, Algeria, Spain, the Congo, South Vietnam, Venezuela, Cuba, Colombia, and Thailand, to name a few past and present trouble spots, there can be little doubt which authority was the real-world government. The situation of contending governments without territorial separation and both with approximately equal credentials in terms of past legitimacy, *de facto* governmental control, and international recognition does not seem to be the major "civil strife" problem. Even if this were a problem one criterion for assistance to a government should be that it is the only widely recognized *de facto* or *de jure* government.[93]

A rule of no assistance to either faction also runs into the problem that it is a not uncommon practice to enter into treaty arrangements with a widely recognized government to assist it in maintaining the existing form of government against external attack or internal subversion. This practice reflects the real interdependencies felt among nations. Query whether assistance to a recognized government should be impermissible if pursuant to such a pre-existing treaty of guarantee or assistance, or whether failure to honor such a treaty would itself amount to intervention? A major difference between the insurgents and government is that the government is the internationally authorized agency to receive external assistance. To prohibit such assistance is more difficult than proscribing assistance to insurgents. There are at least two other reasons for this greater difficulty in addition to the problem of pre-existing treaties. First, since the recognized government is the international agency of the state entitled to receive assistance, it is legitimate even under a "neutral" norm to render assistance *prior* to "civil strife." Under this norm, then, a difficult fact determination must be made as to when "the outcome is uncertain"[94] or "civil strife" or "belligerency" or "insurgency" or some such cabalistic point has been reached before assistance becomes impermissible. By that point an assisting state may already feel committed. It is probably unrealistic to assume

93. A related question is to what extent assistance to exile groups such as the Bay of Pigs exiles or the South Vietnamese that had gone north in 1954 is legitimate in situations where assistance to insurgents would be otherwise illegitimate. Although this circumstance may somewhat strengthen claims from the standpoint of self-determination, it is hardly decisive of genuine self-determination and has only peripheral relevance with respect to the policy of minimum public order.

94. See generally Wright, *United States Intervention in the Lebanon*, 53 AM. J. INT'L L. 112, 121-22 (1959).

that assistance will often be stopped after once being legitimately begun, particularly if the facts are at all hazy, as they usually are. Moreover, could levels of assistance provided prior to "civil strife" be continued as, for example, the Military Assistance Advisory Group in Vietnam? Must they be, on the theory that a reduction amounts to intervention on the side of the insurgents? And if some level of assistance is permissible or mandatory, is it realistic to argue that it cannot be increased?

This picture is further complicated with respect to assistance to the government forces in that one of the functions of the government is to maintain order within the community. Although at some point one can philosophically argue that maintenance of order must yield to the right to revolution, until that point is reached external assistance may be consistent with internal autonomy. Because of this function of government within the internal arena, as well as its function as international representative of the state, there is likely to be great difficulty in determining when the level of "civil strife" is such that assistance is violative of internal autonomy. Second, since under Professor Falk's framework assistance to a recognized government becomes legitimate again after significant military assistance has been received by the insurgents, another difficult determination must be made as to when such assistance has been rendered. But because of the difficulty of proving covert assistance to the insurgents, as Vietnam aptly demonstrates, assistance to the recognized government even if legitimately provided in a Type II situation is likely to remain shrouded in controversy and condemned as much as, or more than (because more visible), assistance to the insurgents. Query also whether Professor Falk intends that offsetting assistance to insurgents would be permissible as a Type II conflict after the recognized government has received assistance? This would be the ultimate in "neutral" rules. Under such a rule almost any situation could become open-ended. For since the recognized government is entitled to receive assistance prior to civil strife, external elites assisting both sides will point out that the other side's aid legitimates their own. It would seem then that an effective rule for conflict minimization must at least proscribe counter-intervention (legitimate in Type II conflict) on behalf of insurgents.

Because of the real functions of recognized governments, any attempt to fashion "neutral" rules treating the government and insurgents alike is suspect. There are some reasons for suggesting that a rule preventing assistance to insurgents only might be a more realistic and no less efficacious rule in many contexts than a rule preventing assistance to both factions. Such a rule might also desirably focus attention on the probably greater threat of providing assistance to foment civil strife as compared with assistance to a widely recognized government.

Although scholars are divided on the permissibility of assistance to the two sides in Professor Falk's Type III conflict, the area of disagreement significantly reflects the greater danger to world order of providing assistance to insurgents rather than to a widely recognized government. There are a number of writers who take the position that international law does not prohibit assistance to a recognized government in a Type III conflict, and there are substantial community expectations that such assistance is permitted even if its purpose is to assist in suppressing civil strife.[95] There is, on the other hand, wider agreement that assistance to insurgents is impermissible.[96]

Although exploration of the role of international law in dealing with "civil strife" will not by itself result in valid answers for Vietnam, such exploration is relevant to the Vietnam problem. A preliminary attempt to clarify community policies most relevant to contexts of "civil strife" indicates that the "civil strife" structures relied on to condemn United States policy in Vietnam are

95. See the authorities collected in Moore & Underwood, *The Lawfulness of United States Assistance to the Republic of Viet Nam*, 112 CONG. REC. 14,943, 14,975-76 n.179 (daily ed. July 14, 1966), and the discussion in Moore, *The Lawfulness of Military Assistance to the Republic of Viet-Nam*, 61 AM. J. INT'L L. 1, 28-32 (1967).

96. See the authorities cited in note 95, *supra*.

In the context of Vietnam, whatever assistance to insurgents might otherwise be permissible is clearly prohibited by the express provisions of Articles 19 and 24 of the Agreement on the Cessation of Hostilities. In its 1962 Special Report, the International Control Commission found that "there is sufficient evidence to show beyond reasonable doubt" that North Viet Nam had violated these provisions. SPECIAL REPORT TO THE CO-CHAIRMEN OF THE GENEVA CONFERENCE ON INDO-CHINA (Vietnam No. 1), CMND. NO. 1755 (1962). 31 PARL. SESSIONAL PAPERS 7 (1961-62).

over-simplified—even if Vietnam could be treated as "civil strife." Professor Falk's Type III conflict encompasses a range of different contexts from colonial wars to "wars of national liberation," and it may be preferable that resulting norms be more contextually discriminating. That genuine self-determination requires in situations of "civil strife" that assistance never be provided either insurgents or the government is questionable. With respect to the policy of minimum order, assistance to insurgents seems considerably more dangerous than assistance to a widely recognized government. This difference and realism about cold-war expectations suggest that at least in inter-bloc contexts it may be preferable to have a norm condemning unilateral assistance to insurgents and thereby focusing attention on the greater threat, rather than attempting to prohibit assistance to both widely recognized governments and insurgents. Community expectations more clearly condemning such assistance to insurgents, and problems implicit in the functions of the recognized government, also militate for distinguishing between assistance to insurgents and widely recognized governments. Whatever the ultimate solution, if any in terms of such rules, the assistance of the United States to South Vietnam would seem to be a permissive defensive response to at least offset substantial military assistance provided to the Vietcong. North Vietnamese assistance to the Vietcong, however, exceeds tolerable levels of inter-bloc coercion and is an impermissive strategy of attempted change.

In appraising the role of international law in intra-state conflict, clarification of the process side—the international machinery and procedures to control conflict—is as deserving of attention as normative clarification. Substantial progress toward the rule of law in large measure depends on more effective centralized or regional peacekeeping machinery. Effective regional organizations able to make authoritative fact determinations and to authorize collective action to keep the peace would go far to alleviate the problem of regulating external participation in intra-state conflict. The United Nations Congo and Cyprus operations show that in some contexts (principally characterized by an absence of high order conflict between the major competing ideological systems) the United Nations can be an effective participant in controlling such conflict. It is important that these hopeful precedents be strengthened, and it is tragic that the United Nations has been unable to significantly moderate the Vietnam conflict. Certainly every effort should continue to be made to strengthen its role. But emphasis on the process side, however necessary for achieving more effective control of international coercion, should not obscure fundamental differences in attitudes of major participants regarding existing peacekeeping machinery. Although the United States has formally placed before the Security Council a draft resolution calling for immediate negotiations without preconditions and indicating willingness to achieve the purpose of the resolution by arbitration or mediation,[97] Hanoi and Peking have consistently rejected any role for the United Nations in settling the Vietnam War.[98] Similarly, emphasis on the process side

97. See N.Y. Times, Feb. 1, 1966, at 12, cols. 2-6.
98. Secretary-General U Thant said at a news conference on February 24, 1965:

> The government of North Viet-Nam has all along maintained that the United Nations is not competent to deal with the question of Viet-Nam since, in its view, there is already in existence an international machinery established in 1954 in Geneva. They have all along maintained that position and, as you all know, it is a position also maintained by the Peoples Republic of China. As far as the United Nations is concerned, I think the greatest impediment to the discussion of the question of Viet-Nam in one of the principal organs of the United Nations is the fact that more than two parties directly concerned in the question are not members of this organization. I therefore do not see any immediate prospect of useful discussion in the Security Council. . . .

Press Conference, Feb. 24, 1965, quoted in M. RASKIN & B. FALL, THE VIET-NAM READER 263, at 267 (Vintage ed. 1965).
As stated by Pham Van Dong, the North Vietnamese position is:

> The Government of the Democratic Republic of Vietnam declares that . . . any approach tending to secure a U.N. intervention in the Vietnam situation is also inappropriate because such approaches are basically at variance with the 1954 Geneva Agreements on Vietnam.

RECENT EXCHANGES CONCERNING ATTEMPTS TO PROMOTE A NEGOTIATED SETTLEMENT OF THE CONFLICT IN VIET-NAM (Viet-Nam No. 3) CMND. No. 2756, at 51 (1965). Hanoi reiterated this stand by way of public reply to the March 14th peace proposals of Secretary General U Thant. The public statement of Hanoi asserted:

> [I]t is necessary to underline once again the views of the Gov-

should not downgrade the relevance of the existing normative structure. We have not yet attained an ideal world and in the absence of a more effective peacekeeping process the existing normative structure condemning force as a strategy of major international change and preserving the right of defense against major military attack remains the principal framework for appraisal of the Vietnam War.

The State Department Brief in Context

One of the principal strengths of an approach to foreign relations which inquires of "international law" as opposed to the neo-realist preoccupation with "the national interest"[99] is that a balanced international law approach seems to achieve a real focus on clarification of long-run community interest. The kinds of questions focused on in this legal dialogue—regulation of international use of force and regulation of external participation in internal strife

---

ernment of Hanoi, which has pointed out that the Viet-Nam problem has no concern with the United Nations and the United Nations has absolutely no right to interfere in any way in the Viet-Nam question.
56 DEP'T STATE BULLETIN 618 (1967).
Peking militantly declares:
> The United Nations has never taken a just stand on the Viet Nam question. It has absolutely no say concerning settlement of the South Viet Nam question. . . . U.N. intervention in affairs of Indo-China cannot be tolerated. . . .
> We would like to advise U Thant save yourself the trouble. There is nothing for the United Nations to do in Viet Nam, neither is it qualified to do anything there.
Extract from an article in the Peking Peoples' Daily "Serious Advice for U Thant" contained in RECENT EXCHANGES, supra, 54-55.
It might also be noted that Hanoi refused to submit the Tonkin Gulf incident to Security Council investigation despite a South Viet Nam request and offer to send a delegation to the Security Council to participate in debates on the incident. See Moore & Underwood, *The Lawfulness of United States Assistance to the Republic of Viet Nam*, 112 CONG. REC. 14,943 (daily ed. July 14, 1966), reprinted in DUQUESNE L. REV. 235 (1967), at note 228 and accompanying text.

99. See H. MORGENTHAU, POLITICS AMONG NATIONS 227-33, 275-311 (3d ed. 1966); H. MORGENTHAU, IN DEFENSE OF THE NATIONAL INTEREST (1951); Morgenthau, *To Intervene or Not to Intervene*, 45 FOREIGN AFFAIRS 425 (1967).

—achieve a different focus from *realpolitik* discussions of the same problems and as such add an additional dimension to the policy considerations available to the national decision-maker. In these inquiries policy justification is not principally short-run national interest but common and long-run community interest. Legal discourse can also aid in evaluating legal arguments made by the adversaries and used as the basis of attacks on or justification for national policy, for example North Vietnam's assertion that it has a legal right to use force against South Vietnam. A balanced international law approach, one neither unduly focusing on "legal idealism"[100] nor "naked power"[101] and not legalistically self-limiting, *is* relevant to problems such as Vietnam. Because of this relevance, I share Professor Falk's view that inquiry of international law is an important and helpful inquiry for the national decision-maker and that international law should not be used by either side solely to "bolster or bludgeon foreign policy positions. . . ."[102] Professor Falk's criticism of the State Department brief as "formalistic" and "legalistic" and as responding to irrelevant and trivial points,[103] however, is unfair without further exposition of the context in which it was written. As he points out, the State Department brief was principally written in response to arguments made in the Lawyers' Committee Memorandum[104] which had been widely circulated in the United States and to similar legal arguments which were being made by some members of Congress. Many of the legal arguments made in the Lawyers' Committee Memorandum and in Congress against the United States position, such as the arguments that a member of the United Nations cannot collectively assist in defense of a nonmember and that it is unconstitutional to commit United States armed forces to South Vietnam without a formal congressional

---

100. This is a sound admonition from George Kennan. See generally G. KENNAN, AMERICAN DIPLOMACY 1900-1950 (1951).
101. See *e.g.*, H. MORGENTHAU, *supra* note 99.
102. See Falk, *supra* note 77, at 1155. See also Meeker, *Role of Law in Political Aspects of World Affairs*, 48 DEP'T STATE BULLETIN 83 (1963).
103. Falk, *supra* note 77, at 1139, 1146, 1155.
104. Memorandum of Law of Lawyers' Committee on American Policy Toward Vietnam, *reprinted* in 112 CONG. REC. 2552-59 (daily ed. Feb. 9, 1966).

declaration of war, were legalistic in the extreme. They were also inaccurate, and Falk properly repudiates them.[105] Such arguments had achieved a wide hearing, however, and were given substantial credence by many laymen and even some members of the bar. In fact, the "word magic" of the Article 51 collective defense argument was still a major tenet of arguments against lawfulness made by the Chairman of the Lawyers' Committee in an article in the *American Bar Association Journal* as late as July, 1966.[106] Moreover, a number of outstanding international legal scholars, including Professor Falk, had become associated with the Lawyers' Committee efforts and by their association lent credence to these and other legalistic arguments made in the Memorandum.[107] Because of this widespread credence which the adversary arguments of the Lawyers' Committee achieved, and their use as a basis for criticizing Vietnam policy, they needed reply if there was to be balanced appraisal of the issues. The State Department brief performed that function. And although Professor Falk emphasizes the adversary nature of the State Department brief he does not point out that the Lawyers' Committee Memorandum was at least an equally adversary document.

105. See Falk, *supra* note 77, at 1139-40, 1154.
106. See Standard, *United States Intervention in Vietnam Is Not Legal*, 52 A.B.A.J. 627 (1966).
107. See Letter from the Lawyers' Committee to President Lyndon B. Johnson, Jan. 25, 1966, *reprinted* in 112 CONG. REC. 2551-52 (daily ed. Feb. 9, 1966). Professor Falk is currently Chairman of the Consultative Council of the Lawyers' Committee. The work of the Consultative Council has been somewhat better than the earlier much circulated Lawyers' Committee efforts but is still essentially polemical.

For an example, see The Military Involvement of the United States in Vietnam: A Legal Analysis (1966).

Scholars certainly have a duty to appraise the activities of their own as well as foreign governments. See generally Finman & Macaulay, *Freedom to Dissent: The Vietnam Protests and the Words of Public Officials*, 1966 WIS. L. REV. 632. The point is simply that the wide circulation of the Lawyers' Committee Memorandum, endorsed by leading international law scholars and accompanied by the vocal theories of some Congressmen, created public attitudes about a number of legal points which it was hardly irrelevant or trivial to rebut. The legalistic "declaration of war" and "non-member" arguments were two of the principal arguments against lawfulness held out to the public.

Candor would suggest acknowledgment that both sides in the Vietnam debate have tended to take adversary positions.[108]

It is perhaps inevitable in any on-going national dialogue with the importance of the Vietnam debate that both sides will appeal as adversaries to legal arguments. Perspectives about authority are important in evaluating the wisdom of policies, and both proponents and opponents characteristically invoke legalities. The administration stress on the "obligation" arising from the SEATO treaty[109] and the critics' "non-member" argument are examples of attempts to invoke authority for contending foreign policy positions. When such appeals are made, the importance of perspectives about authority in shaping national policy makes it imperative for legal scholars and advisers to point out essential discrepancies. In doing so they should recognize that they are performing only one task of the scholar or adviser and that, to the extent possible, clarification of community policies prior to decision may be a more important task.

The Vestiges of a Constitutional Attack

Although Professor Falk rejects the early Lawyers' Committee arguments that the President has no constitutional authority to

108. Even the latest Lawyers' Committee efforts can only be fairly described as adversary in nature. See The Military Involvement of the United States in Vietnam: A Legal Analysis, *supra* note 107, and the nearly full-page advertisement "U.S. Intervention in Vietnam is Illegal," N.Y. Times, Jan. 15, 1967, at E 9.

According to a 1965 report of the International Association of Democratic Lawyers, apparently circulated principally in Europe, the Lawyers' Committee Memorandum was "distributed to 250,000 American lawyers." The Return of the I.A.D.L. Delegation from Vietnam, 1965, at 9 (unpublished manuscript). An advertisement of the Lawyers' Committee puts the distribution figure at 173,000 lawyers. THE NEW REPUBLIC, June 24, 1967, at 29. The advertisement also boasts distribution of 23,000 reprints of the N.Y. Times advertisement. *Id.*

109. The real force underlying the "obligation" argument is that United States action with respect to Vietnam have over a period of more than twelve years created substantial and very real expectations on the part of many Vietnamese and other Asians that the United States will assist in the defense of South Vietnam. The SEATO Treaty was one such act both embodying and creating these expectations. SEATO grew out of the defeat of the French in the first Indo-China War, and historically has been intimately associated with the Vietnam problem. See A. EDEN, FULL CIRCLE 148-49, 158-63 (1960).

use American military forces in Vietnam without a declaration of war,[110] he contends that:

> The President has the constitutional authority to commit our armed services to the defense of South Viet Nam without a declaration of war *provided* that such "a commitment" is otherwise in accord with international law. Whether all or part of the United States action violates international law is also a constitutional question. . . . [T]he bombing of North Viet Nam appears to be an unconstitutional use of Presidential authority as well as a violation of international law.[111]

In this watered-down form, Falk's somewhat monistic argument presents no independent grounds for unconstitutionality but depends in the first instance on the establishment of an international violation. And in postulating that international violation is a sufficient condition for constitutional violation the argument is erroneous. The international and constitutional consequences of exercise of the foreign relations power are not identical. The Supreme Court has held that Congress may constitutionally override valid treaties by later inconsistent legislation even though the later enactment would be a violation of international law.[112] These holdings are particularly relevant in light of the congressional authorization for executive use of the armed forces in Vietnam, making such action in fact executive-congressional action.[113]

110. Falk, *supra* note 77, at 1154. Professor Quincy Wright seems to substantially agree with Falk. "The issue seems unimportant in view of the broad Constitutional powers of the President to use armed force without Congressional support or declaration of war." Wright, *Legal Aspects of the Viet-Nam Situation*, 60 AM. J. INT'L L. 750, 768 (1966).
111. Falk, *supra* note 77, at 1155.
112. See Chae Chan Ping v. United States, 130 U.S. 581 (1889); Whitney v. Robertson, 124 U.S. 190 (1888); Dickinson, *The Law of Nations as National Law: "Political Questions,"* 104 U. PA. L. REV. 451, 487-90 (1956). For an illustration from Great Britain, see Mortensen v. Peters, 14 Scots L.T. 227 (1906).
113. For an analysis of the lawfulness of United States assistance to South Vietnam under internal constitutional processes and a review of congressional action authorizing and affirming United States assistance, see Moore & Underwood, *The Lawfulness of United States Assistance to the Republic of Viet Nam*, 112 CONG. REC. 14,943, 14,960-67, 14,983-89 (daily ed. July 14, 1966).

The Executive and Congress substantially exercise the foreign affairs power of the nation, and it is not clear that they are *ever* acting *unconstitutionally* solely because of violation of international norms. And if there is any authority that such action is *necessarily* unconstitutional Professor Falk does not share it with us.

It is one thing to recognize that customary and treaty norms of international law are part of "the law of the land" under Article VI for the purpose of binding the states (which essentially have no independent foreign relations power), and quite another to argue, as Professor Falk must under his thesis, that this article constitutionally restricts the exercise of the foreign relations power of the United States. It may be that in some contexts or when dealing with some types of international norms Congress or the Executive should be so restricted, but Professor Falk offers no constitutional standards as to what those contexts are. Some major problems which would have to be explored before his thesis could be applied to Vietnam, even assuming international violation, are: What is the constitutional effect of the congressional authorization of the use of armed forces in Vietnam by the Southeast Asia Resolution and other congressional actions with respect to Vietnam? How do the "political question" problems affect the impact of this thesis?[114] And in what circumstances is it feasible or desirable to compel judicially changes in foreign policy because of an asserted violation of international law? As it stands, Professor Falk's constitutional argument is even more unpersuasive than the earlier "declaration of war" argument which he rejects.

Conclusion

The persistence of competing models of the Vietnam conflict suggests that the conflict cannot be meaningfully generalized in black and white terms. Real-world Vietnam is unalterably ambiguous, and writers on both sides do not perform a service when they assume a certainty and simplicity that does not exist. Although the conflict is not solely a product of "aggression from the North," the substantial interaction between Hanoi and the Vietcong, the historical background of the conflict, and the objectives of Hanoi in

114. See generally Dickinson, *supra* note 112.

supporting the sustained attack also belie meaningful characterization as civil strife. And Hanoi's unwillingness to negotiate mutual withdrawal from the south in the face of repeated United States declarations of willingness to promulgate a timetable for withdrawal does not support a model which portrays Hanoi as merely concerned with offsetting United States assistance.

If because of Vietnam Americans are asking themselves hard questions about the use of national power and the goals of foreign policy, the North Vietnamese must ask themselves hard questions about the use of force as an instrument of major international change. It is to be hoped that this introspection will yield to a negotiated settlement. Neither side seems to have sufficient usable military and political power to win decisive victory short of a protracted struggle at great human and material cost. Secretary-General U Thant is right both in perception and in emphasis when he terms the Vietnam War basically a political problem that can only be solved by a political settlement. This, however, is a stricture that both sides must be willing to accept, and to date the North Vietnamese have shown but flickers of interest in such a settlement. Despite this hard line from Hanoi, the United States must continue to emphasize a negotiated solution to the conflict and must energetically exploit any interest in negotiated settlement shown by participants in the opposing camp. A negotiated peace is the only alternative to a prolonged and increasingly dangerous conflict.

Emphasis on negotiated settlement should not obscure the fact that the conflict did not merely arise by accident, but that it reflects major differences in objectives of the contending participants and a value structure in Hanoi which exhibits greater willingness to achieve extension of its values by force. North Vietnamese disregard of this basic proscription against unilateral change by force is central to the conflict in Vietnam. At Potsdam, Stalin promised that Korea would be divided only temporarily,[115] but when temporary occupation of the north turned into permanent communization South Korea did not militarily attack across a major cold-war dividing line despite United Nations support for a unified Korea. Such an attack from South Korea, like military

115. S. Morison, The Oxford History of the American People 1065 (1965).

assistance from North Vietnam, could have been expected to trigger major conflict. The parallel, like all foreign affairs analogy, is not exact, but the contrast accurately points up a fundamental departure by North Vietnam and those nations supporting it from the basic principle of the United Nations Charter outlawing war as an instrument of national policy. Acceptance by all nations of that fundamental requirement of minimum public order is a crucial first step toward a world community able to set aside its differences and get on with the real task of applying its immense resources to the alleviation of poverty, ignorance, and disease.

May, 1967

CHAPTER IX

Law and Politics in the Vietnamese War:
A Response to Professor Friedmann

IN a recent issue of the *American Journal of International Law*[1] Professor Wolfgang Friedmann published a critique of my article on the lawfulness of military assistance to South Vietnam which appeared in the January, 1967, issue of the *Journal*.[2] His reply was welcome both because continuing dialogue has proven a helpful method for clarification of the legal issues on Vietnam and because it was particularly gratifying, following our debate at the 1966 Annual Meeting of the Society, to have an opportunity to clarify the issues separating us. Nevertheless, Professor Friedmann's reply was disappointing: disappointing partly because of his misunderstanding of my position but principally because he failed to develop any substantive position on Vietnam.

Before responding to the three points which he makes to support his criticism, it may be helpful to elaborate on the principal reason for disappointment at his reply and to briefly evaluate the assumptions underlying what seems to be his position on the legal issues of the Vietnam conflict.

Despite the fact that Professor Friedmann has debated the subject on a number of occasions, his position is unclear. Apart from short references in articles devoted to other subjects[3] he seems to

1. Friedmann, *Law and Politics in the Vietnamese War: A Comment*, 61, AM. J. INT'L L. 776 (1967).
2. Moore, *The Lawfulness of Military Assistance to the Republic of Viet Nam*, 61 AM. J. INT'L. L. 1 (1967).
   My own views are further elaborated in *International Law and the United States Role in Viet Nam: A Reply*, 76 YALE L.J. 1051 (1967) and *The Role of Law in the Viet Nam Debate*, 41 CONN. B.J. 389 (1967). Additional background documentation supporting this view may be found in Moore & Underwood, *The Lawfulness of United States Assistance to the Republic of Viet Nam*, 112 CONG. REC. 14943 (daily ed., July 14, 1966), *reprinted* in 5 DUQUESNE L. REV. 235 (1967).
3. See Friedmann, *United States Policy and the Crisis of International Law*, 59 AM. J. INT'L L. 857, 865-66 (1965); Friedmann, *Intervention, Civil War and the Role of International Law*, 1965 PROC. AM. SOC'Y INT'L L. 67.

have developed no analysis of his own. His earlier endorsement of the Lawyers' Committee Memorandum[4] would lead one to conclude that he regards military assistance to Vietnam as unlawful, were it not for his repudiation of some (which ones and why he does not clarify) of the conclusions of the Memorandum.[5] His reply does not say whether he regards such assistance as lawful or unlawful, and is stated in such equivocal terms as

the refusal to accept the claim of the United States to be acting in Viet-Nam in defense of international law and the U.N. Charter does not necessarily lead to the conclusion that the United States is an aggressor.[6]

But other than this equivocal statement, and the statement that South Vietnam is today a *de facto* state,[7] one looks in vain for discussion supporting any aspect of the South Vietnamese position or questioning any aspect of the North Vietnamese resort to force —a surprising position for one who condemns as "scholarly indefensible" writers who assertedly fail to advert to both sides.

Although there is some risk of error in defining it, his position seems to be that the conflict within South Vietnam is primarily a "civil war," that therefore the United States is prohibited from rendering assistance to the recognized government, and that the United States intervened "in violation of the Geneva Accords by the establishment of the state of South Viet-Nam and the refusal to contemplate elections."[8]

There are a number of difficulties with this position. In the first place, it assumes as "objective fact" a simplified version of the Geneva settlement, the failure to hold elections, and the evolution

4. See the letter from the Lawyers' Committee on American Policy Toward Vietnam to President Johnson, Jan. 25, 1966, in 112 CONG. REC. 2551 (daily ed., Feb. 9, 1966).

5. Friedmann, *supra* note 1, at 778-79. Professor Friedmann has informed me that his endorsement of the Lawyers' Committee Memorandum was qualified but that his reservations were not published. By way of further clarification of his reservations, however, he indicates only that he does "not agree with some of their [the Lawyers' Committee] statements, *e.g.*, on the U.S. aggression and the *de facto* status of South Vietnam."

6. Friedmann, *supra* note 1, at 779.

7. *Id.* 8. *Id.* at 783.

of the Republic of Vietnam as a state, and places undue emphasis on United States support to South Vietnam after the Accords, without offering any evidence or even adverting to the serious ambiguities and shortcomings of the Geneva settlement.

There is substantial evidence that the Geneva settlement was a power compromise between bitter and powerful protagonists, that it suffered from substantial ambiguity because of an inability of all of the participants to agree, and that it may have created contradictory expectations in the major participants in the negotiations. The central feature of the settlement was the division of Vietnam between two already existing political rivals. This division, coupled with the weakness of the political settlement provisions, suggests that the parties were aware of the possibility of an extended partition. The later Soviet attempt to admit both north and south to the United Nations reinforces the suggestion that partition was the major reality of the settlement.

The settlement in its total context was laudable in effectively halting the immediate fighting, but beyond that, its major outlines were contradictory and ambiguous, its peacekeeping and political settlement provisions were weak, and it is a mistake to idealize it as a starting point for condemnation of the lawfulness of United States assistance.[9] Most importantly, regardless of interpretation of the Geneva settlement, the grievances of the north with respect

9. The evidence is developed in Moore, *International Law and the United States Role in Viet Nam: A Reply*, 76 YALE L.J. 1051 (1967). By way of illustration, Ellen Hammer writes that:

> In contrast to the detailed implementation provided for ending hostilities and for the *de facto* partition of the country (including the right of each Vietnamese to decide whether he wished to live North or South of the seventeenth parallel), the Final Declaration offered no long term perspective for a definitive settlement of the Vietnamese question. The method by which the desirable conditions laid down in Article 7 were to be achieved, was not explained. . . .
>
> Thus, although the Franco-Vietminh war was ended at Geneva in July 1954, a political solution for Vietnam was postponed to some unspecified future date.
>
> The agreements outlined at Geneva . . . contained few if any provisions for their long-term execution. They were a series of desires for the future, drawn up by the conference participants.

E. HAMMER, VIETNAM YESTERDAY AND TODAY 144, 247 (1966).

to implementation of the Accords are of a qualitatively different order from Hanoi's resort to force.

Second, it is highly questionable, in the light of the whole background of the conflict and the relationship and objectives of the north with respect to the fighting, whether "civil war" non-intervention norms provide the most useful structure for analysis of the conflict.

Critical models of the Vietnam conflict which picture it as "civil war" and the White Paper models which picture it as "aggression from the North" oversimplify the reality. Real-world Vietnam combines some elements of civil strife (both within the south and between north and south) with elements of the cold-war divided-nation problem and "aggression from the North"; all complicated by an uncertain international settlement. North Vietnam is one half of an at least *de facto* divided nation rendering assistance across an international cease-fire line to an armed insurgency in the other half whose leadership is significantly interrelated with leadership in Hanoi. It is generally believed that one of the objectives of that assistance is more or less long-run unification of Vietnam under the hegemony of Hanoi, an objective which Hanoi says is justified by the Geneva settlement. This context suggests that the conflict is not most usefully characterized as an internal struggle for control of the South Vietnamese government. Features which make the application of non-intervention norms particularly questionable include the acutely dangerous cold-war divided-nation element, an international cease-fire line separating north and south, the historical interrelation between Hanoi and the Viet-Minh-Vietcong, and the objectives of Hanoi in sustaining the conflict. In these circumstances, assistance from Hanoi is considerably more serious than third-party assistance to insurgents to influence a struggle for internal control.

Community concern about the use of force, particularly the acutely dangerous use of force across *de facto* cold-war boundaries and cease-fire lines, suggests that in this context the Charter proscription outlawing the use of force as a modality of major change is the most crucial norm for appraisal of the war.

But though Professor Friedmann acknowledges that North and South Vietnam are separate *de facto* states, he ignores discussion of the legal consequences flowing from this characterization and the surrounding context and fails to apply the principle of Article 2(4) of the Charter to the relations between the two states. The facts that he stresses, such as the failure to hold the 1956 elections, United States assistance to the south after Geneva, and the range of non-forceful violations recorded by the International Control Commission against both north and south, seem to focus more on considerations suggesting the nineteenth-century concept of "just war" than contemporary Charter proscriptions outlawing the use of force except in defense against armed attack.

Under the Charter the central focus for analysis of the lawfulness of the use of force in Vietnam must be whether one of the international entities that Professor Friedmann acknowledges are separate *de facto* states made an armed attack on the other. The historical process by which north and south became separate states and their non-forceful grievances against each other are no more the *central* issues than focus in the Arab-Israeli conflict on how Israel became a state.

Third, even if it is accepted that the conflict is best characterized as a "civil war" within the south, and that non-intervention norms provide the best normative framework, the most reliable evidence of what has been happening in Vietnam, as set out in the writings of Fall, Lacouture, Schlesinger, Crozier, Warner, Zasloff, Pike, and many others, some of whom are critical of United States policy, indicates that substantial North Vietnamese assistance and direction to the insurgents preceded the first significant United States increase in military assistance over pre-insurgency levels.[10] Although scholars differ about the degree of control exercised by Hanoi, and whether in its initial stages the insurgency within the south was an indigenous reaction to the oppressive measures of the Diem regime, the evidence from all sources strongly supports the conclusion that the north was rendering substantial assistance and direction to the insurgency prior to the first major military response from the United States— which took place in late 1961 as a partial implementation of the Taylor-Rostow Report. Though this crucial chronology has been

10. The evidence is developed in Moore, *supra* note 9.

largely overlooked, an examination of any of the scholarly treatments of the subject indicates that the United States military build-up was a reluctant response to an increasingly deteriorating military posture caused at least in part by increasing assistance and direction from Hanoi.

There is almost unanimous agreement among international-law scholars that assistance provided to a widely recognized government is a lawful response to offset assistance provided to insurgents. Since one of the major policies of the non-intervention norms is to ensure self-determination, a "neutral non-intervention" norm that neither side can be aided in a "civil war" is much too suspect as a general prophylactic rule after insurgents have begun to receive substantial external assistance. So even if non-intervention norms did provide the best normative framework for appraisal of the conflict, the facts of the struggle in Vietnam would still strongly support the conclusion that assistance to South Vietnam is lawful.

Lastly, the "neutral non-intervention" norm which Professor Friedmann relies on is itself controversial.[11] It may be that in some contexts such a rule will better effectuate community goals, but for reasons that this writer has outlined elsewhere,[12] and which are partly developed in reply to Professor Friedmann's third point, there are some reasons for suggesting that a norm allowing assistance only to the widely recognized government may be more realistic in the inter-bloc conflicts such as Vietnam.

Professor Friedmann's own position with respect to the legal issues of the Vietnam conflict is not clear. The position which he seems to adopt is questionable in relying on a "model" which oversimplifies the conflict, in failing to focus on the differences between the use of force and grievances not involving use of force, in relying on a "neutral non-intervention" norm without analysis of impact on applicable community policies, and in failing to apply his own legal assumptions to a widely held view of the facts.

11. See, for example, Farer, *Intervention in Civil Wars: A Modest Proposal*, 67 COLUM. L. REV. 266 (1967).
12. See Moore, *supra* note 9.

Though these assumptions seem to implicitly underlie much of Professor Friedmann's criticism of my article, he offers three specific aspects of the presentation to support his criticism.

He first criticizes:

> . . . the selection of official statements and documents purporting to prove that North Viet-Nam but not South Viet-Nam or the United States had violated international agreements before the United States resorted to direct military action. . . .[13]

There are a number of reasons why this criticism is unpersuasive. First, the documentation referred to was cited as *evidence of fact* that North Vietnam had rendered substantial military assistance and direction to the conflict within the south, and the text makes this clear. It was not offered to prove the conclusion of law "that North Viet-Nam but not South Viet-Nam or the United States had violated international agreements before the United States resorted to direct military action. As *evidence* of this use of the military instrument by the north the article relied on: the findings of the International Control Commission in its 1962 Special Report, a dissenting statement (labeled as such) of the Canadian representative in a February, 1965, I.C.C. Report, a short excerpt from a State Department memorandum, the articles of two highly regarded journalists, Neil Sheehan and Takashi Oka, one a reporter for the *New York Times* and the other a former Far East correspondent for the *Christian Science Monitor,* and the Mansfield Report, which is generally regarded as a reasonably objective treatment. The presentation of this evidence commences with the statement "among other evidence of this 'armed attack,'" and concludes with the statement that:

> Although there is certainly evidence that the conflict in the R.V.N. also has internal support, the totality of evidence— *whether or not the above evidence is accepted in its entirety* —strongly indicates that the campaign to overthrow the recognized government of the R.V.N. by intense coercion receives at least substantial military assistance and direction

13. Friedmann, *supra* note 1, at 779.

from the D.R.V. and suggests that prior to any significant increase in United States assistance, D.R.V. initiative was a critical element in the conflict. . . ."[14]

Second, Professor Friedmann offers no evidence of any kind to contradict any of the factual conclusions, and contents himself with the charge that the sources are one-sided official statements and that "The statements in the State Department's brief of March, 1966, and in other U.S. pronouncements, are taken as objective facts. . . ."[15] But neither the State Department brief of March, 1966, nor the White Papers are mentioned or cited in the article. And although not developed in the article, the writings of Fall, Lacouture, Schlesinger, Warner, Crozier, Pike, and Zasloff, among others, provide evidence that this summary is a minimum statement of North Vietnam's involvement. Since the evidence has been developed in greater detail in a *Yale Law Journal*[16] article, there would be little point in repeating it here.

Last, and most important, Professor Friedmann's criticism suggests that he missed the major thrust of the argument regarding the fundamental limitation on the use of force as an instrument of national policy. For it is not of great significance whether North Vietnam or South Vietnam first violated the Accords. The crucial questions are what kinds of "violations" were indicated, and who resorted to the military instrument as a modality of major change? The implication of Professor Friedmann's statement that the United States first resorted to "direct military action" is unsupported.

Professor Friedmann purports to show bias in fact selection in the choice of "highly selective quotations"[17] from I.C.C. Reports and in the discussion of I.C.C. findings. He states that "The impression given by the quotations [on pages 8 and 9 of his article] is that the Commission allotted all or most of the blame for violations of the Geneva Accords to North Vietnam,"[18] but he fails to reveal that in a note to this quotation on page nine it is said:

14. See Moore, *supra* note 2, 8-11 at 11 (emphasis added).
15. Friedmann, *supra* note 1, at 779.
16. See Moore, *supra* note 9.
17. Friedmann, *supra* note 1, at 780.
18. Friedmann, *supra* note 1, at 779-80.

. . . The Commission also found after recording this armed aggression from the D.R.V. that the R.V.N. had violated Arts. 16, 17 and 19 of the Geneva Agreements by receiving military assistance. . . . It is erroneous to merely "balance" the violations recorded against both sides in this report. The kinds of violations recorded against the two sides are crucially different. . . .[19]

Professor Friedmann does not deal with the point that the kinds of violation are crucially different but instead proceeds to take the writer to task for not including all of the I.C.C. findings of "violations" of the Accords against both sides from 1956 until about 1959. He asserts "the reports of the International Control Commission . . . date from 1956,[20] and even the most superficial study will reveal that until about 1959 the Commission, while acknowledging violations of the demilitarization provisions by both sides, attributed at least equal and more serious violations of the obligations to South Viet-Nam."[21] Professor Friedmann fails to note that my article lists all of the principal grievances of the north against the south which are evident in a complete reading of the I.C.C. Reports.[22] They are failure to consult on the holding of elections in 1956; reprisals against resistance leaders; inadequate cooperation with I.C.C. controls; and entering into a military alliance with and receiving military assistance from the United States.

None of these grievances constitutes justification under Article 51 of the Charter for military attack on the south or for substantial military assistance to insurgents in the south across a cease-fire line. Perhaps the major point of my article is that there is a major difference in kind between these north and south grievances under the settlement. The south, which Professor Friedmann concedes is a *de facto* state separate from the north, did not

19. Moore, *supra* note 2, at 9 note 20.
20. This is inaccurate. The Commission issued in 1954 and 1955 four reports which, among other things, indicate the serious concern of the Commission with northern implementation of Art. 14 (c), the provision allowing persons to choose zones.
21. Friedmann, *supra* note 1, at 780.
22. Moore, *supra* note 2, at 12.

institute a major military attack on the territorial and political integrity of North Vietnam. North Vietnam did use the military instrument against the south, seriously threatening its political and territorial integrity. Even if all North Vietnam's grievances were accepted as legally justified, an attack by North Vietnam against the south is a violation of Article 2(4) of the Charter, and the south and its allies may lawfully defend against it.

At Potsdam Stalin promised that Korea would be divided only temporarily; but when temporary occupation turned into permanent communization, South Korea did not militarily attack across a major cold-war dividing line, despite United Nations support for a unified Korea. Such an attack from South Korea, like military assistance from North Vietnam, could have been expected to trigger major conflict and must be regarded as outlawed by Article 2(4). Such disputes which do not involve major military threats to fundamental values do not justify resort to force. This conclusion reinforces a broad rather than a narrow interpretation of the Charter and substantially strengthens applicability of the prohibition of force as an instrument of national policy.

This is perhaps the single most crucial norm of contemporary international law—that resort may not be had to the use of the military instrument as a modality of major change or as an instrument of national policy for dispute-settlement. Surely Professor Friedmann, who is deeply committed to strengthening international law as an effective force for peace, should recognize the fallacy of trying to justify use of the military instrument by reference to grievances which do not remotely constitute an armed attack. That is what is meant by the reference to North Vietnam's grievances, which do not involve a military threat to its political and territorial integrity, as "political grievances" not justifying resort to the use of force. Since the major issue is the lawfulness of military assistance to South Vietnam, it is the fundamental normative structure restricting the use of force which is most important to this determination. Emphasis on the kinds of non-forceful "violations" indicated by the I.C.C. Reports from 1956 to 1959 is misleading.

A reading of the first ten Interim Reports of the I.C.C. supports Professor Friedmann's statement that the Commission attributed "more serious violations" to South Vietnam, but the statement fails to take into account the overall judgment of the Commission itself expressed in its 11th Interim Report. In this Report the Commission stated:

> The Indian and Canadian Delegations are convinced that there have been many instances of non-co-operation by both Parties which have impeded the work of the Commission and its Teams. These have not in all cases reached the stage of formal citations because of evasions and lack of co-operation on the part of the Party concerned. For this reason the two Delegations agree that, in the experience of the Commission, the number of formal citations in itself is no fair measure of the degree of co-operation received from either party.[23]

Professor Friedmann's discussion also fails to note that the consistent South Vietnamese position was to deny that they were bound by other than the cease-fire provisions of the Accords and that as a result they submitted fewer formal complaints of violation than did the D.R.V.[24] And he fails to note that in 1958 the Commission found Hanoi so "incongenial" for its effective functioning that it transferred its headquarters from Hanoi to Saigon.[25]

Undoubtedly the south did not live up to the text of the Accords in a number of ways. Their record is poor, as a study of the I.C.C. Reports during the Diem period demonstrates. But these

23. Eleventh Interim Report of the International Commission for Supervision and Control in Vietnam (Vietnam No. 1 [1961], Command Paper 1551). Great Britain Parliamentary Sessional Papers XXXIX 25 (1961/62).

24. See the articles from the Indian daily, *The Hindustan Times*, and the New Delhi periodical, *Thought*, discussing the operation and reports of the Commission, collected in Ngo Ton Dat, "The Geneva Partition of Vietnam and the Question of Reunification During the First Two Years," 481-87, Appendix U. (Unpublished Ph.D. dissertation, Cornell University, 1963.) On December 16, 1961, the *Hindustan Times* wrote: "On the whole . . . the non-co-operation of the North seems more ominously purposeful than the non-co-operation of the South." *Id.* at 485.

25. Ngo Ton Dat, *supra* note 24, at 419 n.4. Dat adds that "the members of the Commission were constantly denied freedom of circulation and investigation by the Viet-Minh." *Id.*

"violations," in large part procedural violations for failure to co-operate with I.C.C. controls, should be read in the broader context of the ambiguous Geneva settlement, increasing militarization of the north, an on-going insurgency in the south, and South Vietnam's refusal to be bound by other than the cease-fire provisions. Most important, a complete reading of the Commission Reports from 1954 through the Special Report of 1962[26] indicates that no complaint of the north qualitatively approaches the complaint of the south of armed aggression by the north against the south. The major use of force is the one asserted violation by both sides that is crucially different in kind and much more serious if the issue is the lawfulness of the use of force.

It was the use of force by the north that directly precipitated the dangerous military confrontation, and on this question of which side initiated and sustained the use of force—which was the purpose of relying on the I.C.C. Reports—there was no "fact selection." The Reports indicate a serious use of the military instrument by the north against the south but not vice versa. In short, Professor Friedmann's criticism for not placing equal emphasis on the charges and procedural violations recorded against the south from 1956 to 1959 is neither wholly informed nor responsive to the purpose in emphasis of facts most pertinent to conclusion about the lawfulness of military assistance to the south.

Professor Friedmann also charges that the I.C.C. Reports are cited as "authoritative proof of North Vietnamese aggression,"[27] but when "reference is made to observations of the I.C.C. that diverge from the U.S. viewpoint, its status is deprecated."[28] Since, as has been previously pointed out, the I.C.C. Reports were cited as *evidence of fact* of North Vietnamese use of the military instrument against the south, evidence that is not contradicted elsewhere in the Reports, Professor Friedmann's statement that the

---

26. Citations for all of the Commission reports and a summary of the principal grievances asserted against both sides may be found in Moore & Underwood, *supra* note 2, at note 285 and accompanying text. See also Dai, *Canada's Role in the International Commission for Supervision and Control in Vietnam*, 4 CANADIAN YR. BK. INT'L L. 161 (1966).
27. Friedmann, *supra* note 1, at 780.
28. *Id.*

article relied on it as "authoritative proof of North Vietnamese aggression," *a conclusion of law*, is inaccurate. As in Professor Wright's article, the point is made that the I.C.C. has only limited responsibility.[29] It is not "an international tribunal which either has authority, or which has attempted, to evaluate the overall lawfulness of the actions of the participants in the Viet-Nam conflict."[30] My article indicates, however, that its Report is authoritative, "as a factual report and an interpretation of the text of the Accords," and it explicitly accepts the factual findings of the I.C.C. and its interpretation of the text that "the D.R.V. *was* using force against the R.V.N., the United States *was* providing defensive assistance to meet that attack, and both actions *were* interpreted by the Commission as 'violations' of the text of the Accords."[31] There is nothing inconsistent in using the Reports as evidence of what happened but not as authoritative determinations of the lawfulness of those actions and this same standard is applied to both U.S. and North Vietnamese actions.

Professor Friedmann's second criticism is:

> . . . the differential treatment of the North Vietnamese complaints about the violations of the Geneva Accord provisions for elections to be held in 1956, as "political grievances whether they be legitimate or illegitimate," not justifying "unilateral action," as compared with the practically ignored intervention of the United States immediately after the Geneva Accord in the establishment of a separate and fully recognized state of South Viet-Nam. . . .[32]

Nowhere does Professor Friedmann demonstrate more clearly his failure to deal with the major argument. The "differential treatment" of North Vietnamese actions against South Vietnam and U.S. actions with respect to South Vietnam results from the fact that their actions *are* crucially different. The fundamental question is whether these indicated actions should be treated alike for purposes of community policy about restrictions on the use of

29. Wright, *Legal Aspects of the Viet-Nam Situation*, 60 AM. J. INT'L L. 750 763 (1966).
30. Moore, *supra* note 2, at 27.   31. *Id.*
32. Friedmann, *supra* note 1, at 779.

force. The clear answer is no. North Vietnam's grievance with regard to the failure to hold elections was "political" in the sense that Article 2(4) of the Charter outlaws the use of force except in defense against a major military attack threatening fundamental values. South Vietnam's grievance with respect to North Vietnam's use of the military instrument was not at all "political" in this sense. It constituted a serious threat to the political and territorial integrity of South Vietnam and could lawfully be met with the use of defensive force and military assistance from its allies. Any other result would tie the hands of South Vietnam while allowing North Vietnam to pursue its objectives by force. And if we are talking about appraisal of the lawfulness of the use of force, it is not at all anomalous in this context, as Professor Friedmann contends,[33] to assert that the norm—material breach of agreement justifies suspension of corresponding obligations—is available as a defense to the south but not to the north. The major concern, of course, is the use of force, not material breach of agreement.

It is one of the tasks of the writer to focus on differences which are crucial for the legal determinations being made and to select and develop questions which are most pertinent to decision. Such fact selection is a necessary task of decision, and Professor Friedmann's failure to even note these crucial differences is a fundamental error in his position.

This second criticism also reflects Professor Friedmann's acceptance, without discussion, of a simplified version of the Geneva settlement which pictures the United States as upsetting the expectations created at Geneva. This assumption is also questionable.

The object of Professor Friedmann's third criticism is

> ... the contention that "the requirements of minimum world public order, that is, the avoidance of unilateral coercion as a modality of major change, would in most contexts seem more strongly applicable to insurgent groups than to assistance to the recognized government."[34]

In elaborating this criticism he summarizes my analysis of the non-intervention norms as a "Metternich doctrine of legiti-

33. *Id.* at 780-81.   34. *Id.* at 779.

macy."[35] But, as was emphasized in the article, it is doubtful that "civil war" norms even provide the most useful analytic framework for appraisal of the Vietnam conflict. The substantial assistance provided by the north across a continuing *de facto* boundary separating the major cold-war camps, in violation of the major purpose of the 1954 Agreement on the Cessation of Hostilities, and provided with a more or less long-run objective of territorial and political absorption of the south, involves features which distinguish the Vietnam conflict from a "civil war." Even if the norms regarding intervention in intra-state conflict were applicable to Vietnam, it was pointed out that essentially all scholars are in agreement that assistance provided to a widely recognized government is at least legitimate to offset substantial assistance provided to the insurgents, as is the case in Vietnam. If the north is privileged to use force to aid the insurgency in the south, it is difficult to see why South Vietnam's allies are not privileged to assist her against this use of force.

These principal contentions do not even raise the question of non-intervention in situations of purely intra-state conflict. But Professor Friedmann does not even advert to these principal points. Instead, he proceeds to focus on the policy critique of the intervention norms themselves, characterizing my views as "Professor Moore's legitimacy doctrine."[36] This is a misnomer of my position. As even the passage which Professor Friedmann quotes makes clear, my article questions the traditional approach which lays down a single rule that only the widely recognized government can be aided or a "neutral non-intervention" rule that neither side can be aided. Neither rule is exclusively supported by state practice, and there is reason to suggest that both greatly oversimplify the range of intra-state conflict and, when mechanically applied, may be counter-productive. As a preliminary alternative the article calls for examination of the policies underlying the purpose of restrictions on intervention and their application to more precisely differentiated contexts.

My analysis tentatively identified self-determination and minimum public order as the principal policies applicable (although there may be others which will more clearly emerge in other con-

35. *Id.* at 782.   36. *Id.* at 783.

texts), and concluded that both policies supported defensive assistance to South Vietnam considerably more than they supported North Vietnam's assistance to insurgents in the south. In the analysis of minimum public order as a policy, it was stated that

> The requirements of minimum world public order, that is, the avoidance of unilateral coercion as a modality of major change, would in most contexts seem more strongly applicable to assistance to insurgent groups than to assistance to the recognized government.[37]

It is apparently this statement on which Professor Friedmann relies as indicative of "Professor Moore's legitimacy doctrine." The statement calls attention within the overall policy discussion to the real differences in probable consequences for minimization of coercion when military assistance is provided to insurgents rather than to a widely recognized government. Among other reasons for these differences: widely recognized governments generally control the organized military apparatus making military opposition to them likely to result in prolonged conflict; recognized governments may be incorporated in a world order bloc that views their overthrow as an unacceptable impairment of bloc power or security; recognized governments may have defensive arrangements with third powers which will be triggered by the conflict; and recognized governments as the representative of the state may be receiving continuing military assistance from external powers commenced prior to insurgency. Analysis is incomplete which fails to take account of these and other real differences between the widely recognized government and insurgents which effect the consequences of rendering assistance to the two sides.

And although both the traditional "legitimacy doctrine" and the "neutral non-intervention" norm are questionable as absolutes, both are supported by distinguished contemporary scholars, and there is reason to suggest that, at least in the inter-bloc context, the "aid to widely recognized government only" doctrine has as much reason to support it in real-world application as the "neu-

---

37. Moore, *supra* note 2, at 31. This statement is part of the overall discussion of "Civil War" non-intervention norms, *id.* at 28-32.

tral non-intervention" norm. Considerations which suggest this conclusion are the desirability of focusing on the great threat to peace in providing sustained assistance to insurgents across cold-war boundaries, the difficulty of appraising covert assistance in externally sponsored "wars of national liberation," and realism about constraints felt by opposing bloc powers to support existing friendly regimes, as evidenced by the events in Hungary, East Germany, Malaysia, Korea, Greece, and now Vietnam.

Having elsewhere attempted a more detailed preliminary policy analysis with respect to non-intervention norms,[38] I will merely point out here the importance of continuing analysis of the whole non-intervention area, with respect to both the normative and the process sides of the problem. The most profitable direction for study on the normative side may be careful analysis of goals to be served, greater breakdown of the diverse types of intra-state conflict with more precise recommendation for each major type, and exploration of a range of alternatives to total prohibition of assistance.[39]

Professor Friedmann's three points, which must bear the burden of his criticism, do not show that there is anything "scholarly indefensible"[40] in my analysis, and he fails to show that military assistance to South Vietnam is not a lawful policy alternative.

As a unifying theme, Professor Friedmann criticizes what he says is a dangerous use of international law norms professedly as objective standards but actually as rationalizations of national policy.[41] He further implies that the differences between us with

38. Moore, *supra* note 9. See also my brief recommendation of a framework for inquiry about non-intervention norms in 1967 PROC. AM. SOC'Y INT'L L. 75.

39. Professor Farer's recent suggestion of a prohibition on tactical support is the kind of alternative which breaks new ground and which should be explored. See Farer, *supra* note 11. Though this writer doubts that this alternative, which focuses solely on the modalities of assistance, is realistic for all contexts, for example, the inter-bloc conflict, it may be a useful alternative for some types of intra-state conflict. The important point is that alternatives other than either/or should be explored and that the modalities of assistance, objectives of the participants, arenas of fighting and outcomes (supervised elections, perhaps), are highly relevant.

40. Friedmann, *supra* note 1, at 781.

41. *Id.* at 778.

regard to the legal issues of the Vietnam conflict are not based on the inevitable discrepancies in legal interpretation but rather exist because he takes international law seriously while I merely rationalize government policy.

It is true that blind loyalty to one's country will neither move the world toward a more civilized state of international relations nor serve the national interest. This is true but is also largely non-controversial. This universal agreement makes it tempting to brand scholars who support the lawfulness of a particular national action as seeking only to serve a nationalistic bias. But a coincidence of national policy and the norms of international law does not prove guilt by association. And preoccupation with this theme is a form of tilting at windmills which can result in as serious an impairment of meaningful communication as the labeling and dismissing of dissenters.[42]

The most useful dialogue requires presentation of the conclusions which the author thinks correct and reply to the substantive arguments made by others. And particularly on an emotional and divisive issue such as Vietnam, it is imperative to keep in mind that it is an issue on which reasonable men *do* differ. Professor Friedmann's reply is disappointing in each of these respects.

The general tone of much of Professor Friedmann's critique suggests a jurisprudential ambivalence which may be partly responsible for his concern about rationalization of national policy. Though his discussion of non-intervention norms indicates a jurisprudence sensitive to policy argument, he seems uncomfortable when confronted with more explicit policy analysis. This takes the form of his damning without explanation or illustration my "method of thinking" and my "ambiguous use of terminology."[43] Later he elaborates on this theme:

> Time and again Professor Moore invokes "minimum world public order," a formula made familiar by Professor McDougal's many writings. This goes together with the rejection

---

42. Professor Friedmann reiterates this theme in a debate with Professors A. J. Thomas and A. A. Berle on the Dominican Republic crisis. See THE DOMINICAN REPUBLIC CRISIS 1965: THE NINTH HAMMARSKJÖLD FORUM 112-113 (1967).

43. Friedmann, *supra* note 1, at 779.

of "black letter rules," and contempt for "Alice-in-Wonder-land search for neutral principles." This is ominously reminiscent of the similar formulas used by the Lord Chancellor in Britain during the Suez Canal crisis in order to justify the Franco-British intervention and, almost a decade later, by the Legal Adviser of the State Department in justification of the U.S. intervention in the Dominican Republic. . . . [I]n the absence of third-party determination, "minimum world public order" means, Humpty-Dumpty-like, what the policy-maker wants it to mean, a catch-all phrase to justify whatever action the writer wishes to justify. . . .[44]

No formula or approach, whether policy-oriented or the most pedantic search for "black and white" rules, guarantees "correct" results in analysis of complex issues of international law or the same result when applied by different scholars. All suffer alike from the absence of third-party determination. Yet Professor Friedmann's suspicion of policy analysis suggests both that he believes that a search for "black and white" rules offers greater certainty of "correct" results and that he thinks consciously or unconsciously that policy justification is unnecessary and even dangerous. But there are strong reasons for suggesting that the available range of complementary norms of international law makes a simplistic rule application a more dangerous exercise (dangerous in the sense of ease of manipulation of result) when dealing with complex major issues than the conscious application of norms in the light of their function.

It is a mistake to read the Charter as if it were a municipal traffic ordinance. The Lawyers' Committee Memorandum is a prime example of pseudo-scholarship anchored in this "red and green" approach. Such simplistic approaches are frequently characterized by over-concern for literal meaning such as the now discredited "non-member" argument and by single-factor analysis such as the argument that the Vietnam War is a "civil war" because the Geneva Accords indicated that the military demarcation line was provisional. This kind of preoccupation with a single feature fails to take into account the total manifold of events

44. *Id.* at 783.

which are important for determination about the aggression-defense abstractions of the Charter.

The check on policy argument, like that on any other kind of legal argument, is scholars willing to reply to it: to point out why a particular policy is not applicable, or why there are overriding policy considerations against its application, or to show why an argument represents a personal recommendation and does not reflect existing norms. There is nothing mysterious or subject to greater abuse in such analysis. And in the long run those methods of analysis which seek not only the "identification" of norms but also the appraisal of their application by some kind of widely shared community values provide greater hope for reaching satisfactory decision. Legal scholarship must be concerned not only with rules and principles but also with purpose and values.

Norms of international law provide standards of conduct for the United States and all other national actors. But a purely "legalistic" approach to international law is as deficient as a raw *realpolitik* approach. The former emphasizes rules without consideration of function or context and ignores the problem of control in an imperfect world, and the latter ignores, among other things, the importance of perspectives of authority as an influence on international affairs. The theory of international law exhibited by both of these schools is incomplete.

International law is vital in innumerable ways, not the least of which are to provide norms of conduct for national and international decision-makers, to provide guides to the reasonable expectations of other actors in the international arena, and to clarify, through emphasis on dialogue about community common interest, a different range of policies.

Because of this relevance of international law to problems of contemporary foreign relations Professor Friedmann's seemingly realistic statement that the Vietnam conflict "moves in a legal vacuum"[45] is not the most useful appraisal. The question is not simply whether the decisions taken on both sides leading to the Vietnam conflict were "motivated" by international law, or wheth-

---

45. *Id.* at 785. This statement is difficult to reconcile with Professor Friedmann's earlier endorsement of the "Lawyers' Committee Memorandum," which condemned United States assistance as illegal.

er international law "controls" the conflict, but is also what international law has to say about those decisions today. The structure embodied in the United Nations Charter regarding the lawfulness of the use of force has a great deal to say about them and is essential for balanced appraisal of the conflict.

The Vietnamese War is as ambiguous and difficult a conflict as this century has seen. Politically, the alternatives and the national interest are heatedly, honestly, and sometimes irrationally argued. Debated are interests in credibility of commitments, containment of communism, effects on the domestic order, and the morality of the use of force. Legal dialogue adds a unique dimension to this debate—the focus on the regulation of coercion in international affairs. In this normative structure the Clausewitzian pursuit of war as an instrument of national policy and the "just war" concept have been scrapped. In their place the Charter proscribes all use of the military instrument as a modality of major change in international affairs. If this is a rigidity of international law, it is a rigidity well founded in the danger of a nuclear Dunkirk and the bitter experience of two world wars. The more recent tragedies of Korea, Kashmir, the Sino-Indian border dispute, Vietnam and lately Israel, for the third time in twenty years, are testimony to the vital truth of this principle. Political disputes, black, white, or gray, provide no justification for major resort to force. There *is* a South Vietnam and its neighbors must learn to live in peace with it.

October, 1967

CHAPTER X

Legal Dimensions of the Decision
to Intercede in Cambodia

IN appraising national security decisions, such as the recent decision to send United States combat forces into the North Vietnamese and Vietcong border sanctuaries in Cambodia, it is useful to focus on three interrelated questions. First, is the decision consistent with national and international law? Second, is the decision consistent with the national interest? And third, are there other alternatives which are likely to be more satisfactory in implementing the national interest? Each of these questions represents an important perspective for appraisal. Though the answer to the first question is important for answering the second and third questions, international lawyers should resist the temptation to regard an affirmative answer to the legal question as equivalent to proof that a decision is the best option for national action. Conversely, international lawyers should also avoid the temptation to regard personal doubts about the efficacy of a particular option as equivalent to proof of the illegality of the option. An international-legal perspective is a critical input in national security decisions and should have a major role in defining the national interest and in introducing and delimiting options for national action.[1] Efforts to overuse international law, however, whether by way of support or criticism of national action serve only to obscure the vital role that an international-legal perspective should play.

In focusing on the legal dimensions of the decision to intercede in Cambodia, this chapter will first examine the international law issues in the conflict, will then examine the internal constitutional issues, and finally will focus on the functioning of the national security process in the Cambodian crisis.

---

1. See Falk, *Law, Lawyers, and the Conduct of American Foreign Relations,* 78 YALE L.J. 919 (1969); Moore, *The Control of Foreign Intervention in Internal Conflict,* 9 VA. J. INT'L LAW 205, 310-14 (1969).

I. The International Law Issues

A Brief Background of the Cambodian Conflict

Cambodia emerged from the Geneva Conference of 1954, which ended the first Indo-China War, as a fully autonomous state.[2] Article Twelve of the Final Declaration of the Conference provided that:

> each member of the Geneva Conference undertakes to respect the sovereignty, the independence, the unity and the territorial integrity . . . [of Cambodia, Laos and Vietnam], and to refrain from any interference in their internal affairs.

In addition, Articles Four, Thirteen, and Twenty-one of the Agreement on the Cessation of Hostilities in Cambodia, which was signed by North Vietnam's Vice-Minister of National Defense, made clear that foreign military forces were to be withdrawn from Cambodia.

At the Conference, the Chinese Premier, Chou En-lai, sought an agreement to prevent Cambodia from joining military alliances such as SEATO. Though there was general Conference agreement on the neutralization of Cambodia, the Cambodian delegation successfully held out for an agreement permitting Cambodia to request foreign military assistance in the event its security was threatened.[3] Robert Randle's description of the Geneva negotiations is quite specific on this point.

> Sam Sary [a member of the Cambodian delegation] said he would not sign the agreements because they limited the freedom of the Cambodian government to decide whether or not it would join an alliance; moreover, the agreements limited Cambodia's right to request military assistance from the United States or any other country. Limitations such as these, Sam Sary said, were unacceptable restrictions upon

2. See generally R. RANDLE, "The Settlement for Cambodia" in GENEVA 1954: THE SETTLEMENT OF THE INDOCHINESE WAR 482-503 (1969). The Final Declaration of the Geneva Conference, the Agreement on the Cessation of Hostilities in Cambodia, and the Declarations by the Royal Government of Cambodia are reprinted in R. RANDLE at 569-81, 608.

3. R. RANDLE, *supra* note 2, at 339-41, 486. See also M. FIELD, THE PREVAILING WIND: WITNESS IN INDO-CHINA 169-70 (1965).

Cambodia's newly won independence. The Cambodian minister also expressed concern for the future of his country, which he said might become an object of Communist expansionism, and he wanted to reserve the right to ask the United States to establish bases on Cambodian territory.

The great-power ministers argued with Sam Sary to no avail. The American diplomat assured him the SEATO pact, then being prepared, would give Cambodia some assurance against Communist aggression, but Sam Sary persisted. Mendès-France's midnight deadline passed; and shortly after 2 a.m. the Cambodian minister announced that he had seventeen other demands! Molotov thereupon announced that he would acquiesce in the first demand: Cambodia would be permitted to request foreign military assistance in the event its security was threatened.[4]

This understanding was embodied in a unilateral declaration by the Cambodian delegation at Geneva which stated:

> The Royal Government of Cambodia is resolved never to take part in an aggressive policy and never to permit the territory of Cambodia to be utilized in the service of such a policy.
>
> The Royal Government of Cambodia will not join in any agreement with other States, if this agreement carries for Cambodia the obligation to enter into a military alliance not in conformity with the principles of the Charter of the United Nations, or as long as its security is not threatened, the obligation to establish bases on Cambodian territory for the military forces of foreign Powers.
>
> The Royal Government of Cambodia is resolved to settle its international disputes by peaceful means, in such a manner as not to endanger peace, international security and justice.
>
> During the period which will elapse between the date of the cessation of hostilities in Viet Nam and that of the final settlement of political problems in this country, the Royal Government of Cambodia will not solicit foreign aid in war

4. R. RANDLE, *supra* note 2, at 340.

material, personnel or instructors except for the purpose of the effective defence of the territory.[5]

The second and fourth paragraphs of this declaration were incorporated in Article Seven of the Agreement on the Cessation of Hostilities in Cambodia. The declaration was also adverted to in Article Four of the Final Declaration of the Conference, in which the Conference took note of Cambodia's declaration "not to request foreign aid, whether in war material, in personnel or in instructors, except for the purpose of the effective defence of . . . [its] territory . . . ," and in Article Five of the Final Declaration in which the Conference took note of the Cambodian declaration:

> that . . . [it] will not join in any agreement with other States if . . . [the] agreement includes the obligation to participate in a military alliance not in conformity with the principles of the Charter of the United Nations . . . or, so long as . . . [its] security is not threatened, the obligation to establish bases on Cambodian . . . territory for the military forces of foreign Powers.

In short, the Conference provided that Cambodia was to remain neutral but would have the right to obtain the full range of foreign assistance when necessary for the effective defense of Cambodia. In the absence of such a threat to Cambodian security, foreign military bases were to be prohibited on Cambodian territory even if Cambodia consented to their presence.

Prince Norodom Sihanouk moved rapidly after the Geneva Conference to establish Cambodian neutrality. Though from time to time he was accused by both communist and non-communist states as being pro-western or pro-communist, the "mercurial" Prince seems to have been genuinely preoccupied throughout most of the interim years with preservation of Cambodian neutrality as the best way to preserve Cambodian existence.[6] In May, 1955, Sihanouk did enter into a military aid agreement with the United States, but the defensive nature of the agreement and

5. R. RANDLE, *supra* note 2, at 485.
6. See M. FIELD, *supra* note 3, at 161-251.

the limited quantities of military supplies were unanimously declared by the International Commission for Supervision and Control in Cambodia as "not in excess of . . . [Cambodia's] effective defence requirements."[7] In November, 1957, Cambodia's neutral status was enacted into law by the National Assembly of Cambodia. The neutrality law stipulated that Cambodia was to be "a neutral country." Consistent with the earlier Geneva understanding, it also provided that in case of aggression Cambodia reserved the rights to: "(1) self-defence by arms; (2) call on the United Nations; and (3) call on a friendly country."[8] In its Sixth Interim Report, the International Commission for Supervision and Control in Cambodia took note of this Cambodian law after stating that Cambodia "has continued to fulfil most satisfactorily its responsibility under Articles 7 and 13(c) of the Geneva Agreement."[9]

During the early sixties Sihanouk began to take a progressively harsher line toward the United States, culminating in renunciation of American aid in 1963 and termination of diplomatic relations in 1965. Apparently, from 1965 until the Cambodian crisis, the United States had not provided Cambodia with significant military or economic assistance. In contrast, as the Vietnam War heated up, Vietcong and North Vietnamese military presence and influence in Cambodia grew progressively. By March and April of 1970, the *New York Times* reported estimates ranging from forty to fifty thousand Vietcong and North Vietnamese troops in

7. R. RANDLE, *supra* note 2, at 501. In its Sixth Interim Report the International Commission for Supervision and Control in Cambodia reiterated that: "the imports of war materials by the Royal Government were not in excess of requirements for its effective defence." *Sixth Interim Report of the International Commission for Supervision and Control in Cambodia* (Cambodia No. 1 [1958] Command Paper 526) at 8.

8. See *Sixth Interim Report, supra* note 7, at 9. See also M. FIELD, *supra* note 3, at 232.

9. See *Sixth Interim Report, supra* note 7, at 9. Article 13 (c) of the Agreement on the Cessation of Hostilities in Cambodia provides that the International Supervisory Commission shall:

> Supervise, at ports and airfields and along all the frontiers of Cambodia, the application of the Cambodian declaration concerning the introduction into Cambodia of military personnel and war materials on grounds of foreign assistance.

Cambodia.[10] It seems to be generally accepted that at least during the last several years sizeable Vietcong and North Vietnamese forces have used Cambodian territory for infiltration into South Vietnam, for supply, command, communications, and training functions in support of belligerent activities in South Vietnam, and as staging areas and sanctuaries for repeated attacks on targets in South Vietnam.[11]

Perhaps because he suspected a communist victory in Indo-China, during the last few years Sihanouk seemed increasingly leery of challenging the substantial North Vietnamese and Vietcong forces operating on Cambodian territory. In February, 1970, however, Cambodian forces began engaging North Vietnamese forces, and by March domestic opposition to the sizeable Vietnamese forces in Cambodia led to a Cambodian demand that the North Vietnamese leave Cambodian territory.[12] At the same time,

10. N.Y. Times, March 17, 1970, at 1, col. 8 (city ed.); N.Y. Times, April 4, 1970, at 3, col. 1 (city ed.); N.Y. Times, April 23, 1970, at 4, col. 4 (city ed.). See also the Staff Report, "Cambodia: May 1970" prepared for the Senate Committee on Foreign Relations, 91ST CONG., 2D SESS. 6 (Comm. Print June 7, 1970), *reprinted* in 9 INT'L LEG. MAT. 858, 864 (1970).

11. According to John R. Stevenson, the Legal Adviser of the Department of State:

> In the past 5 years 150,000 enemy troops have been infiltrated into South Viet-Nam through Cambodia. In 1969 alone, 60,000 of their military forces moved in from Cambodia. The trails inside Cambodia are used not only for the infiltration of troops but also for the movement of supplies. A significant quantity of the military supplies that support these forces came through Cambodian ports. . . .
>
> During 1968 and 1969 the Cambodian bases adjacent to the South Vietnamese Provinces of Tay Ninh, Pleiku, and Kontum have served as staging areas for regimental-size Communist forces for at least three series of major engagements—the 1968 Tet offensive, the May 1968 offensive and the post-Tet 1969 offensive.

Stevenson, *United States Military Actions in Cambodia: Questions of International Law*, 62 DEP'T STATE BULLETIN 765, 767 (1970), *reprinted* in 9 INT'L LEG. MAT. 840, 846-47 (1970).

12. See N.Y. Times, March 16, 1970, at 1, col. 5 (city ed.); N.Y. Times, March 17, 1970, at 1, col. 8 (city ed.).

> Cambodia had sent notes to the Vietcong and Hanoi Governments demanding that the troops leave by yesterday, but the deadline passed with no apparent exodus of troops.

Id.

Prince Sihanouk undertook a trip to Moscow and Peking apparently to persuade the Soviets and Chinese to assist in removing the Vietnamese presence.[13] During his absence on March 18, Prime Minister Lon Nol and Deputy Prime Minister Sirik Matak formally deposed Prince Sihanouk as Chief of State. The coup, if it can be accurately called that, was limited. Since the summer of 1969, Lon Nol had been Prime Minister, a position he had also held once before, in 1966-67, and Sirik Matak, a cousin of Sihanouk's, had been First Deputy Prime Minister. Apparently Sihanouk's personal control of power, which according to Jean Lacouture had been eroding since 1966,[14] had been slipping faster during the last year as a result of economic problems, more active political opposition, and the increased presence of North Vietnamese in Cambodia. Perhaps reflecting this reduction in personal power, in the summer of 1969 Sihanouk requested Lon Nol to form a new government to replace that of Pen Nouth, who resigned after a long illness. Lon Nol seems to have accepted only on the condition that he be named Prime Minister and empowered to appoint his own ministers and have them report to him instead of to Sihanouk.[15] Apparently Sihanouk accepted Lon Nol's conditions. Lon Nol was the overwhelming choice of a special session of Congress called by Sihanouk to name a new government, and he took office on August 12, 1969.[16] During the next few months the Lon Nol government took a number of actions over the opposition of Sihanouk, including closing the Phnom Penh Casino and diverting to the government taxes which had previously been paid to Sihanouk personally.[17] Since January 6, when Sihanouk left for France on vacation, Lon Nol and Sirik Matak were in control of the Cambodian government. According to an account by Robert Shaplen, Lon Nol and Sirik Matak sent word to Sihanouk in Paris that he could return as Chief of State "if he

---

13. See N.Y. Times, March 16, 1970, at 11, col. 1 (city ed.). Staff Report, note 10 above, at 1, 9 INT'L LEG. MAT. at 860.
14. Lacouture, *From the Vietnam War To An Indochina War*, 48 FOREIGN AFFAIRS 617, 624-25 (1970).
15. See N.Y. Times, March 19, 1970, at 16, cols. 8-9.
16. See N.Y. Times, March 19, 1970, at 16, col. 9.
17. See N.Y. Times, March 19, 1970, at 16, col. 9; Shaplen, "Letter From Indo-China," *The New Yorker*, May 9, 1970, at 130, 135.

accepted what had already been implied as early as the previous summer and was now made explicit—that he would no longer run things single-handed in his old manner."[18] When Sihanouk refused to receive the emissaries, the coup was formally approved by the Cambodian National Assembly. On March 18, the Assembly unanimously voted to dismiss Sihanouk as Chief of State and named Cheng Heng, the head of the Assembly, as Acting Chief of State.[19] On March 21, Cheng Heng was sworn in as Chief of State.

According to the *New York Times,* there was no evidence of foreknowledge of the Lon Nol takeover among senior United States officials.[20] Robert Shaplen is even more explicit on this point. He writes that "there is no evidence that the Americans participated in the coup or that they were even apprised of it until a few hours before it took place, although they were undoubtedly aware of what might happen and did nothing to try to prevent it."[21] For the most part, the new government did not seem to have serious recognition problems, foreign governments simply assuming that the Lon Nol government was the legitimate successor government of Cambodia. In fact, even Peking, North Vietnam, and North Korea did not formally break diplomatic relations until as late as May 5.[22]

18. Shaplen, *supra* note 17, at 136.
19. See Shaplen, *supra* note 17, at 139. According to the Staff Report prepared for the Senate Committee on Foreign Relations: "On March 18, Sihanouk was removed as Chief of State by unanimous vote of the Cambodian Parliament." Staff Report, *supra* note 10, at 2, 9 INT'L LEG. MAT. at 860.
20. N.Y. Times, May 6, 1970, at 17, col. 6 (city ed.).
21. Shaplen, *supra* note 17, at 139.
22. See N.Y. Times, May 7, 1970, at 1, col. 5. North Vietnam and the Vietcong, however, recalled their diplomats from Phnom Penh on March 25, 1970. See N.Y. Times, March 26, 1970, at 17, col. 1.
   The Staff Report prepared for the Senate Committee on Foreign Relations points out that:
   > On May 5, Sihanouk announced in Peking the formation of a Royal Government of National Union. It was recognized by Communist China the same day and by North Vietnam and the Provisional Revolutionary Government the following day.
   Staff Report, *supra* note 10, at 4, 9 INT'L LEG. MAT. at 862. With respect to this government-in-exile, Robert Shaplen suggests that "Sihanouk is more a captive of Peking today than a spearhead of an independent

The more conservative Lon Nol government continued to seek North Vietnamese and Vietcong withdrawal and intensified the military effort to dislodge them from border sanctuaries. There were also several small-scale cross-border operations conducted by the South Vietnamese forces against the border sanctuaries, some in collaboration with Cambodian forces.[23] The North Vietnamese and Vietcong reacted with military initiatives apparently directed at widening the sanctuaries, restoring supply routes to the Cambodian port of Sihanoukville, and threatening the viability of the new government.[24] Throughout the month of April the daily accounts of the Cambodian fighting indicated a steadily deteriorating military situation.[25] On April 20, Cambodia requested the use of units of ethnic Cambodians from Vietnam which had been associated with American-operated units in South Vietnam.[26] Two days later, Cambodia appealed to the United Nations Security Council for assistance from all countries to help the new government fight "invading Vietcong and North Vietnamese forces."[27] And on April 23, the *New York Times* reported that:

> An atmosphere of heightening national emergency is overtaking Cambodia.
>
> The emergency atmosphere is due to evidence that the Cambodian Army is unable to turn back the Vietnamese

---

government-in-exile. . . ." Shaplen, *supra* note 17, at 135. See also note 51 *infra*.

23. See Staff Report, *supra* note 10, at 1-4, INT'L LEG. MAT. at 859-62.

24. The *New York Times* reported "an acceleration of the Communist invasion" following efforts by the new government "for negotiations on its demand for the withdrawal of Vietnamese Communist troops." N.Y. Times, May 7, 1970, at 16, col. 1 (city ed.).

25. See *e.g.*, N.Y. Times, April 8, 1970, at 1, col. 8 (city ed.); N.Y. Times, April 9, 1970, at 1, col. 4 (city ed.); N.Y. Times, April 10, 1970, at 1, col. 4 (city ed.); N.Y. Times, April 13, 1970, at 1, col. 2 (city ed.); N.Y. Times, April 20, 1970, at 1, col. 8 (city ed.); N.Y. Times, April 21, 1970, at 1, col. 6 (city ed.); N.Y. Times, April 23, 1970, at 1, col. 8 (city ed.); N.Y. Times, April 25, 1970, at 3, col. 4 (city ed.); N.Y. Times, April 27, 1970, at 1, col. 8 (city ed.); N.Y. Times, April 27, 1970, at 5, col. 1 (city ed.).

26. See N.Y. Times, May 4, 1970, at 1, col. 6 (city ed.). Apparently about 2,000 ethnic Cambodians arrived in Phnom Penh on May 1 and 2. *Id.*

27. See N.Y. Times, April 23, 1970, at 4, col. 5 (city ed.).

Communist forces, who at one point are within 15 miles of the capital, and to the lack of response from any nation except Indonesia to Premier Lon Nol's appeal to all nations for arms aid. . . .[28]

Military analysts said the 30,000-man Cambodian Army would be no match for the 40,000 to 50,000 North Vietnamese and Vietcong soldiers in Cambodia, if a determined assault were pressed by the Communist forces.[29]

On April 27, three days before the United States and South Vietnam interceded in Cambodia, the *New York Times* described the situation in Cambodia as "rapidly deteriorating."[30]

This brief background of the events leading up to the April 30 United States and South Vietnamese intercession in Cambodia necessarily omits a number of important events such as repeated United States protests against North Vietnamese and Vietcong use of neutral Cambodian territory, Cambodian protests against sporadic allied incursions into Cambodian territory, Cambodian requests to the International Supervisory Commission for investigation of the activities of belligerents in both camps, the formation by Sihanouk of a Cambodian government in exile, and the killing of substantial numbers of Vietnamese civilians living in Cambodia by the Cambodian Army.[31]

THE RIGHTS AND DUTIES OF CAMBODIA

Cambodian obligations with respect to the war in Vietnam stem from at least four sources. They are the United Nations Charter, the Geneva Accords, the customary international law of non-intervention, and the customary international law of neutrality.

Cambodia is, of course, bound by Article 2(4) of the United Nations Charter which prohibits "the threat or use of force

---

28. N.Y. Times, April 23, 1970, at 1, col. 8 (city ed.).
29. N.Y. Times, April 23, 1970, at 4, col. 4 (city ed.).
30. N.Y. Times, April 27, 1970, at 5, col. 1 (city ed.).
31. See N.Y. Times, April 11, 1970, at 1, col. 4 (city ed.); N.Y. Times, April 14, 1970, at 1, col. 5 (city ed.); N.Y. Times, April 18, 1970, at 1, col. 1 (city ed.); N.Y. Times, April 25, 1970, at 3, col. 1 (city ed.). *But see* N.Y. Times, April 23, 1970, at 5, col. 3 (city ed.), announcing the formation by the Cambodian government of a "Commission responsible for the safety of all foreigners. . . ." *Id.*

against the territorial integrity or political independence of any state. . . ." To the extent that the North Vietnamese use of force against South Vietnam violates Article 2(4) of the Charter,[32] Cambodia would also be prohibited from providing assistance to the North Vietnamese forces.

Second, "as long as its security is not threatened" Cambodia is obliged by Article Seven of the Agreement on the Cessation of Hostilities in Cambodia not to permit the establishment of "bases on Cambodian territory for the military forces of foreign Powers." Moreover, arguably it is bound by Article Twelve of the Final Declaration of the Conference "to refrain from any interference in . . . [the] internal affairs [of Vietnam]."[33] North Vietnamese and Vietcong bases in Cambodia used to prosecute the Vietnam War would seem to violate these provisions of the Geneva Accords, at least to the extent that Cambodia is able to prevent their establishment in Cambodia.

Third, Cambodia is bound by the customary law of non-intervention.[34] The 1965 General Assembly Declaration on Inadmissibility of Intervention is representative of many authoritative pronouncements when it provides:

> [N]o State shall organize, assist, . . . or *tolerate* subversive, terrorist or armed activities directed towards the violent overthrow of the regime of another State. . . . [Emphasis added].[35]

Thus, to the extent that it is politically and militarily feasible, Cambodia is under an obligation to prevent the use of its territory for Vietcong armed attacks directed against the Saigon government.

Finally, Cambodia is bound by the customary international law of neutrality, which according to most commentators survived the

32. For a discussion of the legal issues raised in the Vietnam War and whether the North Vietnamese use of force against South Vietnam violates Article 2 (4) of the Charter see I & II R. FALK (ED.), THE VIETNAM WAR AND INTERNATIONAL LAW (Vol. I, 1968, Vol. II, 1969).
33. *But see* R. RANDLE, *supra* note 2, at 414-15.
34. For a general discussion of the customary law of non-intervention see Moore, *supra* note 1, at 242-46, 315-32.
35. G.A. RES. 2131, 20 U.N. GAOR, Supp. 14, at 11-12, U.N. DOC. A/6014 (1965).

United Nations Charter.[36] Application of the customary law of neutrality would seem particularly appropriate in view of the neutralization of Cambodia by the Geneva Accords, the neutralization of Cambodia by Cambodian internal law, and the repeated declarations of Cambodian and non-Cambodian spokesman recognizing Cambodian neutrality.[37] The duties of a neutral include obligations to prevent belligerents from transporting troops or supplies across neutral territory and to prevent neutral territory from being used for base camps, munitions factories, supply depots, training facilities, communications networks, or staging areas for attack. Belligerent troops seeking asylum must be disarmed and interned for the duration of the conflict.[38] These obligations do not require a neutral to engage in impossible political or military efforts but only to employ "due diligence" or the "means at their disposal" to prevent belligerent violations.[39] Though the Sihanouk government seems sometimes to have cooperated with North Vietnamese and Vietcong forces to the point of violating Cambodian neutrality, the extremely precarious military and political posture of Cambodia should be taken into account in assessing Sihanouk's actions.[40] In any event, at least after

36. See G. SCHWARZENBERGER, A MANUAL OF INTERNATIONAL LAW 218 (5th ed. 1967); J. STONE, LEGAL CONTROLS OF INTERNATIONAL CONFLICT 382 (1959). See also M. GREENSPAN, THE MODERN LAW OF LAND WARFARE 540 (1959); Note, *International Law and Military Operations Against Insurgents in Neutral Territory*, 68 COLUM. L. REV. 1127, 1142-46 (1968).

37. See, *e.g.*, the declaration of the Royal Government of Cambodia of May 29, 1955 in R. RANDLE, *supra* note 2, at 489.

38. See generally on the duties of a neutral state E. CASTRÉN, THE PRESENT LAW OF WAR AND NEUTRALITY 459, 470-88 (1954); L. OPPENHEIM, INTERNATIONAL LAW 687-726 (7th ed. Lauterpacht 1952); M. MC DOUGAL & F. FELICIANO, LAW AND MINIMUM WORLD PUBLIC ORDER 436-69 (1961); G. SCHWARZENBERGER, *supra* note 36, at 219-26.

39. See E. CASTRÉN, *supra* note 38, at 442; M. GREENSPAN, *supra* note 36, at 537-38; III C. HYDE, INTERNATIONAL LAW CHIEFLY AS INTERPRETED AND APPLIED BY THE UNITED STATES 2344 (1945); L. OPPENHEIM, *supra* note 38, at 757-58; J. STONE, *supra* note 36, at 391. Greenspan says: "the practice of the two world wars appears to indicate that a small neutral state is not at fault for failure to offer resistance to the invasion of its territory, where such resistance would be hopeless." M. GREENSPAN, *supra* note 36, at 537.

40. One writer points out:
    [I]t has been suggested by a student of Cambodian foreign policy that Prince Sihanouk believed that the continued inde-

February, 1970, the Cambodian government seemed to be genuinely engaged in attempting to prevent North Vietnamese and Vietcong violations of Cambodian neutrality.

With respect to Cambodian rights to defend its political and territorial integrity, Cambodia would seem to have the option pursuant to both Article 51 of the United Nations Charter and the Geneva Accords to request foreign assistance in defense against an armed attack. The sustained North Vietnamese and Vietcong attacks on Cambodian forces during the months immediately preceding the incursion, and the military occupation of sizeable areas of Cambodian territory from which Cambodian officials were ousted certainly constitute an "armed attack" within the meaning of Article 51 of the Charter, and a "security threat" within the meaning of Article Seven of the Agreement on the Cessation of Hostilities in Cambodia. As such, Cambodia may lawfully request external assistance for its defense.

It should also be pointed out that Cambodia has an obligation under international law to protect ethnic Vietnamese residing in Cambodia. A deliberate governmental policy aimed at killing ethnic Vietnamese civilians residing in Cambodia would violate the Convention on the Prevention and Punishment of the Crime of Genocide, in force since 1951.[41] There is some evidence that the deaths of Vietnamese civilians in Cambodia in April, 1970, may have resulted from a Cambodian governmental policy, if not of commission at least of omission.[42] Subsequent actions by which the Cambodian government has moved more vigorously to protect Vietnamese refugees suggest that the principal impetus to the earlier killings may have been traditional Cambodian-Vietnamese antagonisms inflamed by the North Vietnamese and Viet-

---

pendence of his state depended upon entering into a *modus vivendi* with the Chinese People's Republic and the Democratic Republic of Vietnam. At present, Cambodia is threatened by a Communist inspired insurgency; the consequence probably would have been far worse for the Cambodian government had impartiality been maintained throughout the war in Vietnam.

Note, *supra* note 36, at 1145.

41. 78 U.N.T.S. 277 (1951). See generally McDougal & Arens, *The Genocide Convention and the Constitution*, 3 VAND. L. REV. 683 (1950).

42. See the *New York Times* articles, *supra* note 31.

cong attacks and coupled with a lack of effective control over middle-echelon Cambodian Army officers.[43] In any event, Cambodia has a continuing obligation for the protection of Vietnamese civilians in Cambodia.

THE LAWFULNESS OF NORTH VIETNAMESE AND VIETCONG ACTIVITIES IN CAMBODIA

Whether incident to operations in Vietnam or an internal conflict in Cambodia, North Vietnamese and Vietcong military activities in Cambodia are unlawful.

If North Vietnamese and Vietcong activities are sought to be justified as incident to hostilities in South Vietnam, they violate both the Geneva Accords and the customary international law of neutrality, whether or not North Vietnamese claims of acting in defense in the Vietnam War are accepted. Thus, North Vietnam agreed pursuant to Article Four of the Cambodian Cease-fire Agreement and Article Twelve of the Final Declaration to withdraw her forces from Cambodia and to respect the sovereignty and territorial integrity of Cambodia. And pursuant to the customary law of neutrality, it is unlawful for a belligerent to violate neutral territory by using it for transportation of military forces or supplies, the establishment of staging areas for attack, or the establishment of training, command, communication, or supply facilities.[44] Such violations may amount to aggression against the neutral giving rise to a corresponding right of defense. As McDougal and Feliciano put it:

43. In late April the Cambodian government announced the formation of a "Commission responsible for the safety of all foreigners. . . ." N.Y. Times, April 23, 1970, at 5, col. 3 (city ed.).

44. See generally on the duties of a belligerent toward neutral states E. CAS-TRÉN, *supra* note 38, at 440-42; M. GREENSPAN, *supra* note 36, at 534; C. HYDE, *supra* note 39, at 2336-44; L. OPPENHEIM, *supra* note 38, at 690.
   Since in 1910 France ratified the Hague Convention Respecting the Rights and Duties of Neutral Powers and Persons in Case of War on Land, North Vietnam might be bound as a successor state. See J. SCOTT (ed.), THE REPORTS TO THE HAGUE CONFERENCES OF 1899 AND 1907, 583, 898 (1917). In any event, the general obligations of neutrality stemming from the Hague Conventions seem firmly established as customary international law.

By violating a neutral state, an aggressor-belligerent may compound its offense and commit a new and separate act of aggression. In such situations, the permission of self-defense becomes available to the target neutral and the whole panoply of sanctioning measures contemplated in the United Nations Charter becomes relevant.[45]

Some scholars support a right of a belligerent state to take preventive action to forestall an impending occupation of a neutral state by enemy belligerents.[46] In view of Sihanouk's jealous guarding of Cambodian neutrality, his lack of even formal diplomatic relations with the United States or South Vietnam, and the total lack of factual basis for the claim, any North Vietnamese claim to this effect would seem considerably more far-fetched than the German claim rejected by the Nuremberg tribunal that the German invasion of Norway was justifiable preventive action.[47]

It may also be urged that the law of neutrality has been modified by the Charter to permit belligerents who are acting in defense to violate neutral territory when necessary for effective defense. Even aside from the difficulty in characterizing North Vietnamese activities in South Vietnam and Cambodia as lawful defense, however, any such theory would work dangerously to expand permissible areas of conflict. At least in the absence of an authoritative community determination pursuant to Chapter VII of the Charter, such a theory would add yet another technique of conflict expansion through self-serving claims subject to little factual verification. Community policies for minimization of conflict suggest that it is important to preserve the requirement of prior or immediate threat of belligerent use of neutral territory as at least a minimum prerequisite for lawful belligerent activities in neutral territory. Though the Charter may increase the customary law requirements for lawful belligerent activities on neutral territory, it seems doubtful that it should decrease those re-

---

45. M. MC DOUGAL & F. FELICIANO, *supra* note 38, at 404.

46. See M. GREENSPAN, *supra* note 36, at 539-40; L. OPPENHEIM, *supra* note 38, at 698. But see C. HYDE, *supra* note 39, at 2341.

47. See M. GREENSPAN, *supra* note 36, at 539.

quirements. For these reasons, most scholars seem to have rejected arguments that the Charter has eliminated the law of neutrality applicable to belligerent activities on neutral territory.[48]

If North Vietnamese and Vietcong military activities are sought to be justified as participation in an internal conflict in Cambodia, such activities would violate both the Geneva Accords and the customary international law of non-intervention even if the internal conflict characterization were accepted. Pursuant to Article Twelve of the Final Declaration of the Geneva Conference North Vietnam undertook "to respect . . . the territorial integrity . . . [of Cambodia] and to refrain from any interference in . . . [its] internal affairs." With respect to the customary law of non-intervention, the majority view today seems to support a rule prohibiting external intervention in civil strife absent some prior foreign intervention on behalf of insurgents.[49] This rule is reflected in the 1965 General Assembly Declaration on Inadmissibility of Intervention which provides that: ". . . [N]o State shall . . . assist . . . armed activities directed towards the violent overthrow of the regime of another State, or interfere in civil strife in another State. . . ."[50] Thus, even if the claim were accepted that North Vietnamese and Vietcong forces were assisting the Sihanouk government in exile at its invitation and that that government was the widely recognized government of Cambodia,[51] North Vietnamese

48. See authorities cited note 36 above. One scholar writes:
> The thesis that under the Pact and Charter the neutral state has a duty to assist the victim of aggression is tenable only if there exists a set of standards which members of an international tribunal can apply impartially, regardless of their ideological inclinations to determine which side has in fact struck the first blow.

Note, *supra* note 36, at 1144.
49. See Moore, *supra* note 1, at 316-20, 333-39.
50. G. A. Res. 2131, 20 U.N. GAOR, Supp. 14, at 11-12, U.N. Doc. A/6014 (1965).
51. A claim that the Sihanouk government-in-exile is a widely recognized government would seem far-fetched. According to the *New York Times,* even the Soviet Union issued a statement in which it "seemed . . . to indicate that it recognized the new government [Lon Nol government] as legal—if not to the Soviet Union's liking." N.Y. Times, April 25, 1970, at 4, col. 4 (city ed.). See also note 22 above.

and Vietcong intervention in the internal strife between the Lon Nol and Sihanouk governments would be unlawful absent prior external intervention on behalf of the Lon Nol government. The reality seems to be, however, that the fighting in Cambodia is principally between Cambodians on the one hand and North Vietnamese-Vietcong on the other. Even after a year of fighting, few Cambodians are fighting with the North Vietnamese forces and the situation more closely resembles an external armed attack than intervention in an internal conflict. As such, North Vietnamese and Vietcong military actions against the Lon Nol government are most appropriately characterized as a violation of Article 2(4) of the Charter.

It is also relevant in appraising the North Vietnamese-Vietcong legal position in Cambodia that far from pursuing peaceful settlement pursuant to Article 33 of the Charter or reporting military measures to the Security Council pursuant to Article 51 of the Charter they have consistently denied even the presence of any North Vietnamese or Vietcong forces in Cambodia[52]—surely a monumental credibility gap!

The Lawfulness of United States and South Vietnamese Activities in Cambodia

United States and South Vietnamese activities in Cambodia present two major claims. They are that military activities in Cambodia are lawful defensive measures incident to the defense of South Vietnam and that some such activities are lawful defensive measures incident to the defense of Cambodia. Some South Vietnamese activities in rescuing ethnic Vietnamese residing in Cambodia may, in view of the widespread killing of Vietnamese civilians by Cambodians, also raise a claim of humanitarian intervention.

For at least two years North Vietnamese and Vietcong military units have made major use of Cambodian border areas in sup-

---

52. "Neither the North Vietnamese nor the Vietcong have ever officially acknowledged that they have troops in Cambodia." N.Y. Times, March 17, 1970, at 14, col. 8 (city ed.).

port of their military operations in South Vietnam. According to Robert Shaplen:

> By mid-1969 . . . [Sihanouk] was forced to acknowledge that between forty and fifty thousand Communist troops were spread out over eight or nine Cambodian provinces, about half of the troops in the usually deserted northeastern border areas and the rest farther south, particularly in the mountainous region of the Elephant Range, just northeast of Sihanoukville and across from Vietnam's Mekong Delta.[53]

The military activities of these troops in Cambodia have included transportation of combatants and supplies, construction of command, communication, training, and supply facilities, and use of Cambodian territory for launching attacks on targets within South Vietnam. Such activities have been substantial and continued and are not mere isolated or sporadic occurrences. Prior to the United States and South Vietnamese intercession, the government of Cambodia was unable to effectively prevent these North Vietnamese and Vietcong activities in Cambodia. In fact, it is evident from *New York Times* accounts of Cambodian military efforts that far from effectively limiting use of the sanctuaries, the military situation throughout April was steadily deteriorating for the Cambodian government.[54] By April 20, 1970, the Cambodian army was fighting North Vietnamese within fif-

53. Shaplen, *supra* note 17, at 133-34. Shaplen continues:
   [Sihanouk] . . . then denounced the Communist incursions and showed less hostility toward the Americans; in fact, he even called upon them to maintain "a presence in Southeast Asia" after the end of the Vietnam war. Secretly, he accepted American intelligence obtained in various ways . . . which enabled him to pinpoint Communist troops and installations, and he used this material in making diplomatic complaints to the Vietcong and to Hanoi. . . .
   Id. at 134. In contrast to the forty to fifty thousand experienced North Vietnamese and Vietcong troops in Cambodia, the Cambodian army was inexperienced and poorly equipped and at the beginning of serious clashes with North Vietnamese troops was only about thirty-five thousand. As such, the Cambodians seemed badly outmatched by the attacking forces. See Staff Report, *supra* note 10, at 10, 9 INT'L LEG. MAT. at 866.
54. See the *New York Times* articles, note 25 above.

teen miles of Phnom Penh, the capital of Cambodia.[55] And by the end of that month repeated Cambodian appeals to reconvene the International Supervisory Commission for Cambodia[56] and a Cambodian appeal to the Security Council had gone unanswered, and Peking, Hanoi, and Moscow had rejected an Asian nation initiative for talks on preserving Cambodian neutrality.[57] The possibility of effective Cambodian control of North Vietnamese and Vietcong use of Cambodian territory incident to activities in South Vietnam seemed by the end of April remote.

On April 30, large-scale United States and South Vietnamese military operations were begun in the border regions of Cambodia. The principal purpose of the operations was announced as clearing out the North Vietnamese and Vietcong border sanctuaries.[58] Though according to the Agence France-Presse an initial statement from a Cambodian spokesman was to the effect that "I do not think the Cambodian Government as a neutral government can approve foreign intervention,"[59] the overall position of the Cambodian government seems to have been one of tacit consent tinged with concern lest favoritism of one side lead to loss of neutrality. Later statements of the Lon Nol government have indicated at least non-opposition to the United States and South Vietnamese actions.[60] United States ground combat operations in

55. N.Y. Times, April 21, 1970, at 1, col. 6 (city ed.).
56. See N.Y. Times, March 22, 1970, at 16, col. 4; N.Y. Times, March 24, 1970, at 3, col. 2; N.Y. Times, March 26, 1970, at 17, col. 2; N.Y. Times, April 1, 1970, at 2, col. 4.
57. See N.Y. Times, April 27, 1970, at 3, col. 5 (city ed.) (Peking and Hanoi); N.Y. Times, April 28, 1970, at 1, col. 8 (city ed.) (Moscow).
58. See President Nixon's Address to the Nation. N.Y. Times, May 1, 1970, at 2, col. 1 (city ed.).
59. N.Y. Times, May 1, 1970, at 3, col. 7.
60. On May fifth the Cambodian government issued the following statement:

In his message to the American nation of 30 April, 1970, the President of the United States, Richard Nixon, made public important measures that he has taken to oppose the growing military aggression of North Vietnam on the territory of Laos, Cambodia and South Vietnam. One of these measures concerned aid of the United States of America in the defense of the neutrality of Cambodia, violated by the North Vietnamese.

The Salvation Government notes with satisfaction that the President of the United States of America has taken into account

Cambodia seem for the most part to have been limited to a self-imposed 21-mile depth along the Cambodian border. Ground combat operations even within this region were announced to be subject to an eight-week deadline for withdrawal of American troops from Cambodia. Consistent with the announced deadline,

---

in his decision the legitimate aspirations of the Cambodian people, which desires only to live in peace, in its territorial integrity, in its independence and in its strict neutrality. For that reason, the Government of Cambodia wishes to declare that it respects the sentiments of President Richard Nixon in his message of 30 April, 1970 and expresses its gratitude for them.

It is high time now that other friendly nations understand the extremely grave situation in which Cambodia finds herself and come to the aid of the Cambodian people, victims of armed aggression. The Salvation Government renews on this occasion its appeal for help issued 14 April, 1970, and points out that it will accept all unconditional help from friendly countries in all forms (military, economic and diplomatic).

N.Y. Times, May 5, 1970, at 16, col. 8. The statement of John R. Stevenson, the State Department Legal Adviser, contains a slightly different version of the Cambodian Government May fifth declaration. Perhaps the only difference worth noting is that the State Department version contains the slightly stronger language "appreciates the views" rather than "respects the sentiments" of President Nixon. Stevenson also points out "Later statements have indicated even more clearly the Cambodian Government's approval of our actions." See Stevenson, *supra* note 11, at 766 n.9, 9 INT'L LEG. MAT. at 843-44 n.8.

On May sixth the High Command of the Cambodian Armed Forces released a communique that:

[United States and South Vietnamese forces are] useful not only in fending off dangers for the American and South Vietnamese forces but also to drive these Vietcong and North Vietnamese aggressors from our territory.

They are indispensable because these occupiers have solidly installed their military and subversive organizations in the zones that they, the Vietcong and North Vietnamese, are seeking to widen as far as possible in view of their future actions.

N.Y. Times, May 6, 1970, at 18, col. 2.

Though, in general, Cambodian government statements prior to the May first incursion indicate a request for military supplies rather than foreign troops, there was some ambiguity in the requests. Thus, on April 15, Lon Nol said:

The Salvation Government has the duty to inform the nation that in view of the gravity of the present situation, it finds it necessary to accept all unconditional foreign aid, wherever it may come from, for the salvation of the nation.

N.Y. Times, April 15, 1970, at 1, col. 3.

by July 1 American units had been withdrawn. South Vietnamese operations were more sweeping and apparently were not limited by the same deadline.

The principal legal issue presented by these United States and South Vietnamese military operations in Cambodian border regions is the scope of defensive rights under the Charter against belligerent operations in neutral territory. It is well established in the customary international law of the rights and duties of belligerents toward neutral states that a belligerent power may take action to end serious violations of neutral territory by an opposing belligerent when the neutral power is unable to prevent belligerent use of its territory and when the action is necessary and proportional to lawful defensive objectives.[61] Scholars endorsing

61. One example of this principle in state practice is the German bombardment of Salonika in neutral Greece during World War I after it had been occupied by the Allied Powers. The Greco-German Mixed Arbitral Tribunal held that the occupation of Salonika by the Allies "entitled Germany to take even on Greek soil any acts of war necessary for her defense." See *Coenca Brothers* v. *German State*, in L. GREEN, INTERNATIONAL LAW THROUGH THE CASES, 667, 668 (1951), discussed in MCDOUGAL & FELICIANO, *supra* note 38, at 407 n.49. Other examples are the seizure of the Italian ship the *Anna Maria* in the neutral Tunisian port of Sousse by allied forces during World War II after a series of warlike acts by German and Italian forces on Tunisian territory, and the 1940 British entry into neutral Norwegian territorial waters to liberate British prisoners held on the *Altmark,* a German auxiliary vessel which had entered Norwegian territorial waters to evade capture by the Royal Navy. Professor Waldock concluded after a study of the *Altmark* incident that:

> A breach of the rules of maritime neutrality in favour of one belligerent commonly threatens the security if not the existence of the other belligerent. The breach is thus seldom really capable of being remedied in full by subsequent payment of compensation. Nothing but the immediate cessation of the breach will suffice. Accordingly, where material prejudice to a belligerent's interests will result from its continuance, the principle of self-preservation would appear fully to justify intervention in neutral waters. The disposition in the past of some neutral opinion to condemn any such action out of hand was therefore not consistent with general principles and in any case flowed from a view of the superior merits of neutral status which no longer obtains. *The right of a belligerent to intervene in a proper case to enforce neutrality is now generally recognized. . . .* (Emphasis added.)

Waldock, *The Release of the Altmark's Prisoners,* 24 BRITISH YEARBOOK OF INT'L LAW 216, 235-36 (1947). For a discussion of the *Anna Maria*

this view include, among others, Professors McDougal and Feliciano,[62] Greenspan,[63] Hyde,[64] Castrén,[65] and Lauterpacht.[66] Thus Professors McDougal and Feliciano point out:

[W]here a nonparticipant is unable or unwilling to prevent one belligerent from carrying on hostile activities within neutral territory, or from utilizing such territory as a "base of operations," the opposing belligerent, seriously disadvan-

---

incident see MC DOUGAL & FELICIANO, *supra* note 38, at 407 n.49.

The United States has also entered foreign territory on a number of occasions to suppress continuing raids launched from the foreign territory against the United States. The principal examples are General Jackson's incursion into Spanish West Florida in 1818 to check raids by Spanish Indians into American territory after the failure of the Spanish authorities to check the raids and the incursion by an American military force into Mexico to check cross-border raids by the Mexican bandit Francisco Villa which the Mexican authorities had allowed to continue. See I C. HYDE, INTERNATIONAL LAW CHIEFLY AS INTERPRETED AND APPLIED BY THE UNITED STATES 240-44 (2d rev. ed. 1945).

62. M. MC DOUGAL & F. FELICIANO, *supra* note 38, at 76, 406-07, 568.
63. M. GREENSPAN, *supra* note 36, at 538.
64. C. HYDE, *supra* note 39, at 2237-41.
65. E. CASTRÉN, *supra* note 38, at 442, 462-63.
66. L. OPPENHEIM (Lauterpacht ed.), *supra* note 38, at 695 n. 1, 698. Lauterpacht adopts the view that:

> Normally, diplomatic representations and a claim for compensation are the proper remedy for any disregard of neutral duties of this nature. However, circumstances may arise in which subsequent redress by the neutral must, in *natura rerum*, be wholly inadequate and in which the aggrieved belligerent must, therefore, be held to be justified in resorting to self-help.

Id. at 695 n.1. See also the excellent note, *International Law and Military Operations Against Insurgents in Neutral Territory, supra* note 36. The author takes the position that:

> Defensive measures may be necessary where neutral territory is used as a sanctuary for tactical retreat and a base of operations for repeated raids. This is the basis on which the United States has sought the right to pursue the Viet Cong into Cambodia.

Id. at 1129.

> Defensive actions which infringe the sovereignty of a neutral state should be justifiable under international law . . . if they are necessary to end repeated raids from a neutral sanctuary, or if they are required to protect the safety of troops under actual attack.

Id. at 1138.

taged by neutral failure or weakness, becomes authorized to enter neutral territory and there to take the necessary measures to counter and stop the hostile activities.[67]

Similarly, Greenspan states:

> Should a violation of neutral territory occur through the complaisance of the neutral state, or because of its inability, through weakness or otherwise, to resist such violation, then a belligerent which is prejudiced by the violation is entitled to take measures to redress the situation, including, if necessary, attack on enemy forces in the neutral territory.[68]

Charles Cheney Hyde writes:

> The obligation resting upon the belligerent with respect to the neutral is not of unlimited scope. Circumstances may arise when the belligerent is excused from disregarding the prohibition. If a neutral possesses neither the power nor disposition to check warlike activities within its own domain, the belligerent that in consequence is injured or threatened with immediate injury would appear to be free from the normal obligation to refrain from the commission of hostile acts therein.[69]

And Professor Castrén says:

> A belligerent may not violate the territorial integrity of a neutral State merely because the other belligerent side has done so. Nevertheless, the situation is different if the neutral State has not taken countermeasures, or if the enemy, in spite of the efforts of the neutral State, has succeeded in acquiring a *permanent stronghold* in its territory, in which case the other belligerent side is entitled to drive off the violator from there. A belligerent is further not bound to tolerate the *continual* passage of enemy military transports through neutral territory.[70]

67. M. MC DOUGAL & F. FELICIANO, *supra* note 38, at 568.
68. M. GREENSPAN, *supra* note 36, at 538.
69. C. HYDE, *supra* note 39, at 2337-38.
70. E. CASTRÉN, *supra* note 38, at 462-63.

For the most part, the customary international law of neutrality seems as applicable after the United Nations Charter as before. In fact, the McDougal-Feliciano, Greenspan, and Castrén statements just quoted were all written after the Charter. Though the Charter introduces additional restrictions on the use of force, nothing in the Charter would seem to cut against the strong community policies for isolating and minimizing coercion which are served by the law of neutrality, at least in the absence of a Security Council decision to take measures under Chapter VII of the Charter. The Charter, however, does introduce restrictions on the use of force which, to the extent that they were not already subsumed under customary international law, seem additionally applicable to appraising defense rights against belligerent operations in neutral territory. Adopting a restrictive view of defense rights under the Charter, the Charter requires that the use of force must be a defensive response to an armed attack and must be necessary and proportional to lawful defensive objectives.[71] As applied to defense rights against belligerent operations in neutral territory, this would seem to require that the use of force against belligerent operations in neutral territory should be necessary and proportional to lawful defense objectives. Though consent of the neutral state may be one factor in appraising the exercise of defense rights against belligerent operations in neutral territory, it does not seem required either by the customary international law of neutrality or by the additional Charter requirements, provided other applicable criteria are met.

Necessity and proportionality are shorthand for community policies restricting coercion to situations where there is no reasonable alternative to the use of force for protection of fundamental values and restricting the responding use of force for protection of fundamental values to that reasonably necessary for defense of the threatened values.[72] In the somewhat over-restrictive language of the famous *Caroline* case, there must be shown a

71. Some scholars would urge a less restrictive interpretation not limiting the right of self-defense to that of Article 51. See, *e.g.*, D. BOWETT, SELF-DEFENSE IN INTERNATIONAL LAW 184-93 (1958); M. MC DOUGAL & F. FELICIANO, *supra* note 38, at 233-41 (1961); J. STONE, AGGRESSION AND WORLD ORDER 92-101 (1958).

72. See M. MC DOUGAL & F. FELICIANO, *supra* note 38, at 217-18, 229-44, 259.

"necessity of self defense, instant, overwhelming, leaving no choice of means and no moment for deliberation."[73] And as McDougal and Feliciano indicate, responding coercion must:

> . . . be limited in intensity and magnitude to what is reasonably necessary promptly to secure the permissible objectives of self-defense . . . by compelling the opposing participant to terminate the condition which necessitates responsive coercion.[74]

As applied to the scope of defense rights against belligerent operations in neutral territory, necessity and proportionality would also seem to subsume community policies for isolating conflict by restricting permissible areas of belligerent operations as well as community policies permitting the use of force reasonably necessary for the defense of major values. As such, the level of belligerent activity on neutral territory, the seriousness of the threat posed by that activity for the protection of major values, the level of control of such activity by the neutral state, and the scope of the responding coercion are all important features in assessing the lawfulness of defensive rights against belligerent operations in neutral territory.

The United States and South Vietnamese military operations aimed at the North Vietnamese base complexes in Cambodian border areas seem adequately to have complied with the relevant international law standards. The level of North Vietnamese and Vietcong activity on Cambodian territory was substantial and continuing. Activities in Cambodia included elaborate base camps, repeated use of staging areas for launching large-scale attacks on targets in South Vietnam, and a major logistics and communications network. At the time of the intercession the number of North Vietnamese and Vietcong personnel operating in Cambodia may have been forty thousand or more. In short, the level of belligerent activity in Cambodia was not occasional, low-level, or merely threatened, as was alleged in the German invasion of Norway, but was an existing major adjunct to North Vietnamese belligerent operations within South Vietnam. The

---

73. See M. MC DOUGAL & F. FELICIANO, *supra* note 38, at 217.
74. M. MC DOUGAL & F. FELICIANO, *supra* note 38, at 242.

existence of such large-scale operations in neighboring Cambodian border regions, which in some areas were as close as thirty-five or forty miles from Saigon, posed a continuing threat to the effective defense of South Vietnam. Moreover, even though the security threat had existed for some time, if North Vietnamese and Vietcong forces succeeded in military operations directed against the Cambodian government, as in late April it looked like they might, it could be expected that the security threat to South Vietnam would increase. With respect to the level of control of the neutral state, Cambodian officials had for the most part been driven out of the contested border areas, and by all accounts the government forces were sorely pressed to defend Phnom Penh and the provincial capitals, much less to take effective action against the sanctuaries. In this context, the United States and South Vietnamese response seems of a scope reasonably related to promptly achieve permissible defensive objectives. The coordinated action was aimed at the North Vietnamese and Vietcong base areas and was not a punitive reprisal raid directed at the host state, as has been true of some Israeli raids in reprisal against guerrilla activities emanating from Jordanian and Lebanese territory.[75] At least United States forces placed a self-imposed 21-mile geographical limit on the invasion of Cambodian territory and an 8-week time limit for the withdrawal of combat units. It also seems relevant in appraising the action that Cambodia did not formally protest the presence of United States or South Vietnamese troops as, on April 22, she had protested the presence of North Vietnamese and Vietcong troops. Although there were some Cambodian statements critical of the joint operation, on balance it seems to have received at least the tacit consent of the Cambodian government. This feature of tacit consent is another factor which makes the case stronger than Israeli action against guerrilla complexes in Jordan, Lebanon, and Syria, or French action in the Algerian war against Tunisian frontier areas.

75. See generally Falk, *The Beirut Raid and the International Law of Retaliation*, 63 AM. J. INT'L L. 415 (1969); Blum, *The Beirut Raid and the International Double Standard: A Reply to Professor Richard A. Falk*, 64 AM. J. INT'L L. 73 (1970). See also the exchange of correspondence between Professor Julius Stone and Professor Richard A. Falk, 64 AM. J. INT'L L. 161-63 (1970).

Military operations within Cambodia, as within South Vietnam, must be carried out in a manner that is consistent with the laws of war. In fact, they should be carried out with a sensitivity which goes beyond the present inadequate protection accorded non-combatants and prisoners of war in internal conflicts. Past military operations within Vietnam have demonstrated that this is not always the case, and that the military has a better job to do both in implementing existing regulations and in evaluating their adequacy for internal conflicts.[76]

The level of North Vietnamese attacks on Cambodian military forces and the virtual occupation of large areas of Cambodian territory over Cambodian objection seemed at least by late April to have constituted an armed attack on Cambodia justifying individual and collective defense under Article 51 of the Charter.[77]

76. See generally Moore, *The Control of Foreign Intervention in Internal Conflict*, 9 VA. J. INT'L LAW 205, 309-10 (1969); Rubin, *Legal Aspects of the My Lai Incident*, 49 OREGON L. REV. 260 (1970).

77. It is firmly established that collective as well as individual defense is permitted pursuant to Article 51 of the Charter. See, *e.g.*, H. KELSEN, THE LAW OF THE UNITED NATIONS 791-805 (1950); M. MC DOUGAL & F. FELICIANO, LAW AND MINIMUM WORLD PUBLIC ORDER 244-53 (1961); J. STONE, LEGAL CONTROLS OF INTERNATIONAL CONFLICT 245 (1959). In fact, Article 51 was drafted largely to reassure the Latin American delegates that collective defense pursuant to regional arrangements would not be disturbed. See generally, P. JESSUP, A MODERN LAW OF NATIONS 165 (1948); M. MC DOUGAL & F. FELICIANO, *supra* at 235; R. RUSSELL & J. MUTHER, A HISTORY OF THE UNITED NATIONS CHARTER 688-712 (1958); Kunz, *Judicial and Collective Self-Defense in Article 51 of the Charter of the United Nations*, 41 AM. J. INT'L L. 872 (1947). The right of collective defense is also confirmed by a host of defense agreements representing a diversity of ideological groupings and including NATO, SEATO, the Rio Pact, the Warsaw Pact, and the Arab League.

One of the few scholars disagreeing with this almost universally accepted interpretation of Article 51 has been Professor Derek Bowett. He argues that:

> [T]he situation which the Charter envisages by the term is . . . a situation in which each participating state bases its participation in collective action on its own right of self-defense. It does not, therefore, generally extend the right of self-defense to any state which desires to associate itself in the defense of a state acting in self-defense.

D. BOWETT, SELF-DEFENCE IN INTERNATIONAL LAW 216 (1958). Not only does Professor Bowett's interpretation conflict with the history of Article 51,

To meet this situation, on April 14 Cambodia made an appeal to the United States and other nations for arms and military supplies.[78] On April 20, Cambodia further requested assistance in the form of ethnic Cambodian mercenaries fighting in South Vietnam, and on April 22 Cambodia complained to the Security Council, seeking assistance from all countries in fighting North Vietnamese and Vietcong forces. Subsequent to the joint United States-South Vietnamese intercession in Cambodia on April 30, the Cambodian government negotiated military aid agreements with Thailand[79] and South Vietnam.[80] The agreement with South Vietnam provides that South Vietnamese military forces

> . . . which had come with the agreement of the Cambodian Government to help Cambodian troops to drive out the Vietcong and North Vietnamese forces, will withdraw from Cambodia when their task is completed.[81]

Although prior to the April 30 intercession Cambodia had not requested United States combat troops to assist in meeting the North Vietnamese and Vietcong attack, at least not openly, the worsening military position of the Cambodian forces seemed to have been one motivating factor in the United States action against the border sanctuaries. Thus, in his April 30 address to the nation President Nixon called attention to the North Vietnamese attacks on Cambodian forces and the Cambodian request to the United States and other nations for assistance. The general United States deemphasis of objectives concerning the defense of Cambodia seemed to result primarily from a desire to disturb the neutrality of Cambodia as little as possible by the action and to reemphasize the Nixon doctrine that the United States would pro-

---

the almost universal acceptance of the claim in state practice, and the writings of most international law scholars, but it would seem poor policy as well. See the discussion of the Bowett position in M. MCDOUGAL & F. FELICIANO, *supra* at 247-53.

78. N.Y. Times, April 23, 1970, at 1, col. 8 and 5, col. 3 (city ed.).
79. See N.Y. Times, June 2, 1970, at 1, col. 5 (city ed.); N.Y. Times, June 3, 1970, at 1, col. 5 (city ed.).
80. See N.Y. Times, May 28, 1970, at 1, col. 2 (city ed.).
81. N.Y. Times, May 28, 1970, at 1, col. 2 (city ed.).

vide assistance but not American combat forces for the long-range defense of Cambodia. In a statement on May 5 in which the Lon Nol government at least tacitly accepted the United States action, Lon Nol seemed to take an intermediate view of the objectives of the United States action. The statement referred to the action as "aid . . . in the defense of the neutrality of Cambodia violated by the North Vietnamese." It also said that "the Government of Cambodia wishes to declare that it respects the sentiments of President Nixon in his message of 30 April 1970 and expresses its gratitude for them."[82]

In view of the magnitude of the North Vietnamese and Vietcong attacks on Cambodian forces and the Cambodian acceptance of the April 30 intercession, it would seem that the United States and South Vietnamese military actions in Cambodia could also be characterized as lawful measures of collective defense of Cambodia.

The minimal involvement of native Cambodians on the side of the North Vietnamese forces suggests that a characterization of the Cambodian conflict as "civil strife" is less appropriate than a characterization as "external armed attack." Even if the "civil strife" characterization were accepted, however, assistance to the Lon Nol government to offset the prior massive foreign intervention on behalf of insurgent forces (the Sihanouk government-in-exile?) would, to the extent that the Lon Nol government is the widely recognized government of Cambodia, be lawful.

Because of the killings of ethnic Vietnamese civilians residing in Cambodia, some of the South Vietnamese military operations in Cambodia aimed at evacuating ethnic Vietnamese refugees may have constituted permissible humanitarian intervention. The justification for humanitarian intervention, though, could only extend to operations principally concerned with evacuating refugees rather than those aimed at affecting authority structures in Cambodia. Since South Vietnamese military actions seem to be defensible on broader grounds, there seems little point in focusing on the possible claim of humanitarian intervention other than

82. The full May fifth statement is set out in note 60 *supra*.

to reassert that the killings of ethnic Vietnamese in Cambodia is another example of the need for an unambiguous right of humanitarian intervention.[83]

When the United States and South Vietnam interceded in Cambodia on April 30, 1970, the factual basis seemed to be present for both the exercise of collective defense in defense of Cambodia and the exercise of defensive rights aimed at belligerent activities in a neutral state. Not surprisingly, objectives relating both to the defense of Cambodia and the destruction of North Vietnamese base areas in Cambodia seemed to have influenced the operation. In fact, Cambodian defense and the possibility of intensified belligerent activities directed against South Vietnam are so interrelated that it seems probable that the precarious military position of the Cambodian government was a principal triggering event of the operation. Prior to the events of March, the Sihanouk government had exercised some restraint on North Vietnamese and Vietcong activities in Cambodia. The fall of Sihanouk followed by a North Vietnamese-Vietcong armed attack on the Lon Nol government threatened to lead to unrestrained North Vietnamese and Vietcong belligerent use of Cambodian territory. This existence of a North Vietnamese armed attack on Cambodia as well as North Vietnamese use of Cambodian territory as a base for belligerent operations sets apart the Cambodian case as a much stronger case for action directed against belligerent operations in a third state than prior instances such as the *Caroline* affair between Britain and the United States, French action against the Tunisian frontier village of Sakiet Sidi Youssef during the Algerian war,[84] or even Israeli raids against guerrilla bases in Jordan, Lebanon, and Syria (which should be distinguished from Israeli reprisal raids directed against the Jordanian and Lebanese governments). Other distinctions between the Cambodian case and these or other instances of actions directed against

83. See generally, Lillich, *Forcible Self-Help by States to Protect Human Rights*, 53 IOWA L. REV. 325 (1967); Moore, *supra* note 76, at 261-64.

84. See M. CLARK, ALGERIA IN TURMOIL—THE REBELLION: ITS CAUSES, ITS EFFECTS, ITS FUTURE 363-66 (1960).

belligerent operations in a third state may also be relevant to legal appraisal. Such distinctions include the presence or absence of consent of the host state, the lawfulness of the defensive effort (the anti-colonial context of the Algerian war makes the French effort suspect), the scope and intensity of belligerent activities in the host state, and the proportionality of the coercive response.[85] It is instructive in this regard to compare the Cambodian situation with that of the *Caroline* affair, which spawned the most frequently quoted test of necessity. The *Caroline* affair took place during the Canadian rebellion of 1838. As William Edward Hall describes it in his *Treatise on International Law*:

> A body of insurgents collected to the number of several hundreds in American territory, and after obtaining small arms and twelve guns by force from American arsenals, seized an island at Niagara within the American frontier, from which shots were fired into Canada, and where preparations were made to cross into British territory by means of a steamer called the Caroline. To prevent the crossing from being effected, the Caroline was boarded by an English force while

85. The comparison suggested by Professor Richard A. Falk between the United States and South Vietnamese action against North Vietnamese and Vietcong base areas in Cambodia and a hypothetical Soviet air strike against United States base areas in Japan, South Korea, Thailand, Okinawa, and Guam is only superficially helpful. Among other differences, the governments of Japan, South Korea, Thailand, Okinawa, and Guam have not requested assistance from the Soviet Union and would be unlikely to consent to Soviet air strikes on their territory, the host governments of Japan, South Korea, Thailand, Okinawa, and Guam have not appealed to the United Nations Security Council for assistance in defense against an armed attack from United States forces, there are no treaty obligations prohibiting the United States and its host governments from establishing United States military bases on their territory, the United States utilizes the base areas with the consent of the host governments, and the strategic posture of the geographically remote United States base areas would make a Soviet air strike a far more provocative action than the Cambodian incursion. Perhaps more important, Professor Falk's seemingly neutral comparison disregards the basic Charter distinction between force used in extension of national values and force used in defense against an armed attack. There is no escape from the fundamental obligation to assess the lawfulness of the contending factions by this basic Charter principle.

at her moorings within American waters, and was sent adrift down the falls of Niagara.[86]

British actions in the *Caroline* case were not in support of the defense of the United States against a major external armed attack, did not take place with the tacit consent of the United States government, and were directed against sporadic actions of "several hundreds" of insurgents rather than the long continued belligerent activities of as many as 40,000 combat troops of a foreign nation, all features present in the Cambodian case. Nevertheless, Professor Hall goes on to suggest that even the English response in the *Caroline* case met the "somewhat too emphatic language" of the *Caroline* test of necessity.[87] In assessing the lawfulness of all of these instances of action directed against belligerent activities emanating from the territory of a third state, a detailed examination of necessity and proportionality in context would seem the most reliable guide. The context of the Cambodian case, particularly the dual basis for the exercise of defensive rights in Cambodia, would seem a strong basis for lawfulness.[88]

Measures taken by members in the exercise of defensive rights must, pursuant to Article 51, be "immediately reported to the Security Council. . . ." The Cambodian operation with South Vietnam was reported by the United States to the Security Council

86. W. HALL, A TREATISE ON INTERNATIONAL LAW 246 (2d ed. 1884).
87. *Id.* at 246-47. Professor Hyde also writes that the facts of the *Caroline* case "seem to have satisfied" the *Caroline* test of necessity. See I HYDE, *supra* note 61, at 239-40.
88. For statements critical of the lawfulness of the Cambodian intercession see Edwards, *The Cambodian Invasion Violates International Law*, CONG. REC. E4551 (May 21, 1970); *Brief of New York University Law Students*, CONG. REC. E4443 (May 19, 1970). The emphasis in the N.Y.U. law students brief that North Vietnamese and Vietcong activities did not constitute an "armed attack" within the meaning of Article 51 of the United Nations Charter is wholly unpersuasive. Though fact selection is an inevitable task in appraising complex public order disputes, the mind boggles at fact selection which virtually ignores the continuing North Vietnamese and Vietcong attacks from the Cambodian sanctuaries on United States and South Vietnamese forces and the massive North Vietnamese and Vietcong military attack on Cambodia.

on May 5, 1970.[89] This reporting, at least in substance if not in speed, complies with the Charter requirement.

The Charter does not require that defensive action taken pursuant to Article 51 first be submitted to the Security Council for approval.[90] Nevertheless, for a number of reasons it would have seemed desirable to have raised the North Vietnamese and Vietcong attacks on Cambodia in the Security Council. Perhaps the most important reason is that every time the Security Council is shunted aside and not encouraged to assume responsibility for dealing with a threat to the peace, the erosion of United Nations utility and authority continues. From a *realpolitik* perspective, it seems unlikely that in the cold-war context of the Cambodian situation the Security Council would have been able to take effective action to preserve the neutrality of Cambodia. But the Security Council might have been effectively used as a forum to expose the rather blatant North Vietnamese and Vietcong acitivities in Cambodia, much as it was used during the *Pueblo* crisis. The importance of such appeals to authority, both in terms of international and domestic audiences, should not be underestimated. Possible drawbacks from raising the Cambodian issue in the Security Council, such as the possibility of a challenge to the credentials of the Lon Nol government, the possibility of forcing a more militant Soviet stand, or the possibility of forcing a confrontation on the Indo-China War which would be detrimental to the United Nations are real and may have been taken into account in the decision (or non-decision) not to go to the Security

89. U.N. DOC. S/9781 (May 5, 1970). The text of the letter from the United States Permanent Representative to the President of the Security Council is reprinted in 9 INT'L LEG. MAT. 838 (1970).

90. See D. BOWETT, SELF-DEFENCE IN INTERNATIONAL LAW, 193, 195 (1958); J. BRIERLY, THE LAW OF NATIONS 319-20 (5th ed., 1955); P. JESSUP, A MODERN LAW OF NATIONS 164-65, 202 (1948); H. KELSEN, THE LAW OF THE UNITED NATIONS 800, 804, 804 n.5 (1964); Kelsen, *Collective Security under International Law*, 49 INT'L LEGAL STUDIES 61-62 (1956); M. MCDOUGAL & F. FELICIANO, LAW AND MINIMUM WORLD PUBLIC ORDER 218-19 (1961); J. STONE, LEGAL CONTROLS OF INTERNATIONAL CONFLICT 244 (1954); A. THOMAS & A. THOMAS, NON-INTERVENTION 171 (1956); Kelsen, *Collective Security and Collective Self-Defense under the Charter of the United Nations*, 42 AM. J. INT'L L. 783, 791-95 (1948).

Council. In the context of events in Cambodia during April, 1970, however, it is questionable whether they outweigh the costs involved in not objecting in the Security Council to the stepped up North Vietnamese-Vietcong activities in Cambodia.

It is probably fair to say that the initial understanding of the signatories to the Southeast Asia Collective Defense Treaty was that in the event of a request from the Cambodian government for assistance to meet a North Vietnamese armed attack each signatory would "act to meet the common danger in accordance with its constitutional processes." Article IV Section 1 of the treaty provides:

> Each Party recognizes that aggression by means of armed attack in the treaty area against any of the Parties or against any State or territory which the Parties by unanimous agreement may hereafter designate, would endanger its own peace and safety, and agrees that it will in that event act to meet the common danger in accordance with its constitutional processes. Measures taken under this paragraph shall be immediately reported to the Security Council of the United Nations.[91]

By a protocol to the SEATO treaty concluded the same day, Cambodia was unanimously designated by the parties as a protocol state "for the purposes of Article IV of the Treaty."[92] Cambodia did not sign the SEATO treaty or the protocol, however, and under Sihanouk Cambodia sought to withdraw from SEATO protection as a protocol state.[93] The Sihanouk action and the general political collapse of SEATO make it pointless to consider whether the United States and other signatories were "obligated" under the terms of Article IV of the SEATO treaty to respond to Cambodian requests for assistance. Article IV, Section 3 of the Treaty, however, may contain some lingering relevance for the Cambodian incursion. It provides:

91. Southeast Asia Collective Defense Treaty, Sept. 8, 1954, T.I.A.S. No. 3170 (Feb. 19, 1955).
92. Protocol to the Southeast Asia Collective Defense Treaty, Sept. 8, 1954, T.I.A.S. No. 3170 (Feb. 19, 1955).
93. See N.Y. Times, April 30, 1965, at 2, col. 6.

It is understood that no action on the territory of any State designated by unanimous agreement under paragraph 1 of this Article or on any territory so designated shall be taken except at the invitation or with the consent of the government concerned.

The purpose of Section 3 seemed to be to reassure the protocol states, none of which was a signatory to the SEATO treaty, that action pursuant to Article IV would not be taken against their will. Quite apart from the issue of whether the treaty has any continuing validity, it is unlikely that Section 3 was intended to alter the existing international law of neutral rights and duties by which a belligerent power may take action to end serious violations of neutral territory by an opposing belligerent when the neutral power is unable to prevent belligerent use of its territory —whether or not the neutral consents to the action. Since the action against the sanctuaries was largely based on the international law of neutral rights and duties and did not invoke the collective defense provisions of the SEATO treaty, Section 3 would seem to have only minimal relevance. In any event, the subsequent consent of the Cambodian government largely moots the issue. The broad language of Section 3, however, is an additional reason suggesting that it would have been preferable to secure an unambiguous prior agreement with the Cambodian government consenting to the United States and South Vietnamese actions.

II. The Constitutional Issues

President Nixon's decision to intercede in Cambodia and congressional reactions to it present two principal constitutional issues: the constitutional authority for the presidential decision to intercede in Cambodia, and the constitutional authority for a range of proposed congressional restraints on military operations in Indo-China.[94]

In general, constitutional structure and practice require congressional authorization of major initial commitments to combat abroad and accord Congress the authority to terminate hostilities

---

94. For a discussion of the full range of constitutional issues in the use of the armed forces abroad see Chapters XI and XII.

abroad. On the other hand, the President seems to have some independent authority to initially commit the armed forces to "minor" hostilities abroad. Though the parameters of this independent authority are unclear, constitutional history and policy support a test of "the commitment of regular combat units to sustained hostilities" as the threshold for requiring congressional authorization. The President also has unquestioned authority as Commander in Chief to make command decisions incident to the conduct of a constitutionally authorized conflict, and any congressional authority to limit such command options is subject to a severe burden of constitutional justification. Moreover, though congressional authorization or termination of conflict does not require any particular formality such as a formal declaration of war, congressional action should be based on careful analysis of the context giving rise to authorization or termination and should clearly advert to the scope of the authority granted or the congressional intent to terminate hostilities. With this necessarily simplified overview of the congressional and presidential roles,[95] resolution of the constitutional issues surrounding the Cambodian incursion depends on characterization of those issues in the context of the full range of constitutional issues and a more detailed look at the constitutional authority on each relevant issue.

95. See generally on the merits of the war power controversy Kurland, *The Impotence of Reticence*, 1968 DUKE L.J. 619; Moore, "The Constitution and the Use of the Armed Forces Abroad," (Testimony before the Subcommittee on National Security Policy and Scientific Developments of the House Committee on Foreign Affairs, June 25, 1970); Moore, *The National Executive and the Use of the Armed Forces Abroad*, 21 NAVAL WAR COLLEGE REV. 28 (1969); Reveley, *Presidential War-Making: Constitutional Prerogative or Usurpation?*, 55 VA. L. REV. 1243 (1969); Velvel, *The War in Viet Nam: Unconstitutional, Justiciable and Jurisdictionally Attackable*, 16 KANSAS L. REV. 449 (1968); Francis D. Wormuth, *The Vietnam War: The President v. The Constitution* (An Occasional Paper of the Center for the Study of Democratic Institutions, 1968); Note, *Congress, the President, and the Power to Commit Forces to Combat*, 81 HARV. L. REV. 1771 (1968). See also the memoranda prepared by Yale law students and professors, *Indochina: The Constitutional Crisis*, 116 CONG. REC. (No. 76, May 13, 1970), and *Indochina: The Constitutional Crisis—Part II*, 116 CONG. REC. (No. 82, May 21, 1970); and the proceedings of the Symposium on "The Constitution and the Use of Military Force Abroad" held at the University of Virginia Feb. 28-March 1, 1969, reprinted in 10 VA. J. INT'L L. 32 (1969).

THE CONSTITUTIONAL AUTHORITY FOR THE PRESIDENTIAL DECISION TO INTERCEDE IN CAMBODIA

The Constitution provides that "the President shall be Commander-in-Chief of the Army and Navy of the United States. . . ." Hamilton wrote in *The Federalist* that this provision means that the President has "the supreme command and direction of the military and naval forces. . . ."[96] It seems never to have been questioned that this power includes broad authority to make strategic and tactical decisions incident to the conduct of a constitutionally authorized conflict. Constitutional practice includes a range of presidential command decisions unquestionably taken on presidential authority. Examples include President Roosevelt's decision in World War II to give priority to the Atlantic rather than the Pacific theater, Roosevelt's decisions committing American forces to landings in French North Africa (at the time a neutral government), Italy, and the Pacific Islands, and President Truman's decision to use the atomic bomb against Japan.

The limited nature of the Cambodian action, both geographically and temporally, and its close relation to the Vietnamization effort in support of American withdrawal strongly suggest that the action is most appropriately characterized as a command decision incident to the conduct of the Vietnam War. For the most part, the actions of United States military forces were directed against North Vietnamese and Vietcong sanctuaries in Cambodian border regions rather than in direct support of the Cambodian government. The cautious United States response to Cambodian government requests for assistance during April, 1970, also suggests that the action was aimed largely at what was perceived as an increased threat to the United States position in Vietnam, even though the increased threat was in large measure attributable to fear of the effects of a collapse of the Cambodian government in the face of increased North Vietnamese attacks. The Sihanouk government had exerted some restraint on North Vietnamese and Vietcong belligerent activities in Cambodia, and the Lon Nol government was vigorously but precariously seeking to reassert the neutrality of Cambodia. Had the Cambodian gov-

96. THE FEDERALIST, Number 69, at 463 (Heritage Press 1945).

ernment fallen to one controlled by the North Vietnamese, it seemed likely that belligerent activities in Cambodia in support of the struggle in South Vietnam would increase, perhaps endangering the program of phased United States withdrawal which was a cornerstone of President Nixon's policy. There is substantial basis for saying, then, that even a decision to commit United States forces in direct support of the Lon Nol government would have been under the circumstances a command decision incident to the Vietnam War. In any event, the more limited decision to intercede against the border base areas seems most appropriately characterized as a command decision incident to the conduct of the Vietnam War. As such, there is little doubt that President Nixon was acting within his constitutional authority as Commander in Chief.

Though the Cambodian incursion seems more accurately characterized as a decision concerning the conduct of hostilities incident to the Vietnam War rather than an initial commitment to new hostilities, regardless of the characterization the Southeast Asia Resolution lends substantial support to presidential authority. The Southeast Asia Resolution, which is the principal constitutional authorization for the Vietnam War, provides that:

> [Sec. 1. . . .] Congress approves and supports the determination of the President, as Commander in Chief, to take all necessary measures to repel any armed attack against the forces of the United States and to prevent further aggression. . . .
>
> Sec. 2. . . . the United States is, therefore, prepared, as the President determines, to take all necessary steps, including the use of armed force, to assist any member or protocol state of the Southeast Asia Collective Defense Treaty requesting assistance in defense of its freedom.[97]

In view of the continued use of Cambodian border sanctuaries in support of armed attacks launched against South Vietnamese and United States forces, the President would seem to have con-

97. 78 Stat. 384 (Approved Aug. 10, 1964).

gressional authorization under Section 1 of the Southeast Asia Resolution for limited actions directed against the sanctuaries. Apparently the sanctuaries served as staging areas for the 1968 Tet offensive, the May 1968 offensive, and the post-Tet 1969 offensive, among others, and these continued armed attacks on United States forces would seem to qualify under Section 1 of the resolution. It should be emphasized that the issue is not merely one of anticipated attacks from the sanctuaries or a remote threat of attack, but a continuing pattern of armed attack on United States and South Vietnamese forces substantially aided by the existence of the sanctuaries.

Since Cambodia, like Vietnam, is a protocol state of SEATO, in the event of a request for assistance from Cambodia the language of Section 2 of the resolution would also seem to authorize a presidential decision to take military action necessary to the defense of Cambodia. There is some evidence from its legislative history that the resolution was understood at the time of its passage to include action in defense of Cambodia. Thus, in his address to Congress on August 5, 1964, requesting the Southeast Asia Resolution, President Johnson specifically asked for a resolution broad enough to "assist nations covered by the SEATO treaty."[98] And in an exchange between Senators Cooper and Fulbright on the floor of the Senate during the passage of the resolution it was said:

> *Mr. Cooper*: . . . Does the Senator consider that in enacting this resolution we are satisfying that requirement [the constitutional processes requirement] of Article IV of the Southeast Asia Collective Defense Treaty? In other words, are we now giving the President advance authority to take whatever action he may deem necessary respecting South Vietnam and its defense, *or with respect to the defense of any other country included in the treaty?* [emphasis added].
>
> *Mr. Fulbright*: I think that is correct.

98. President's Message to Congress, August 5, 1964, in BACKGROUND INFORMATION RELATING TO SOUTHEAST ASIA AND VIETNAM, COMMITTEE ON FOREIGN RELATIONS, UNITED STATES SENATE 122, at 124 (Rev. ed. Comm. Print June 16, 1965).

Mr. Cooper: Then, looking ahead, if the President decided that it was necessary to use such force as could lead into war, we will give that authority by this resolution?

Mr. Fulbright: That is the way I would interpret it. If a situation later developed in which we thought the approval should be withdrawn, it could be withdrawn by concurrent resolution.[99]

Moreover, the resolution is entitled the "Southeast Asia Resolution," not the "Vietnam Resolution." As such, Section 2 of the resolution would seem to lend substantial authority to President Nixon's decisions to provide military support requested by the Cambodian government, such as the military equipment or Khmer mercenary forces requested by the Cambodian government in April. And though the action against the sanctuaries was apparently not requested in advance, subsequent Cambodian government approval of the action and further Cambodian requests for assistance raise the possibility that this action may also be brought within the authority of Section 2 of the resolution.

The Southeast Asia Resolution has been criticized as hurriedly rushed through Congress and as predicated on an exaggerated attack on American destroyers in the Gulf of Tonkin.[100] Though the abbreviated debate during the passage of the resolution was a sorry exercise of congressional responsibility, the resolution is nevertheless a valid exercise of the congressional war power.[101] It is also relevant in considering congressional involvement that an amendment introduced by Senator Wayne Morse in March, 1966, to repeal the resolution was tabled in the Senate by a vote of 92 to 5.[102] In fact, according to the *New York Times*, a resolu-

99. 110 CONG. REC. 18409-10 (1964).

100. See *The Gulf of Tonkin, The 1964 Incidents, Hearings before the Senate Committee on Foreign Relations*, 90TH CONG., 2D SESS. (Comm. Print Feb. 20, 1968) and Part II *Supplementary Documents* (Comm. Print Dec. 16, 1968). There seems to be no doubt that the first attack on August 2 occurred.

101. For a review of the congressional debates on the Southeast Asia Resolution and the constitutional issues concerning authority for the Vietnam War see Moore & Underwood, *The Lawfulness of United States Assistance to the Republic of Vietnam*, 112 CONG. REC. 14943, 14960-67, 14983-89 (daily ed. July 14, 1966).

102. 112 CONG. REC. 4226 (daily ed. March 1, 1966).

tion to reaffirm it would have easily passed.[103] Prior to the Cambodian decision, a new effort to repeal the resolution had begun, but at the time of the action the resolution to repeal had cleared only the Senate Foreign Relations Committee.[104]

In summary, quite apart from whatever independent authority the President may have to initially commit the armed forces to combat abroad,[105] the President had constitutional authority for the actions directed against the sanctuaries under his power as Commander in Chief to take command decisions incident to an ongoing conflict and under Section 1 of the Southeast Asia Resolution to repel armed attacks against United States forces. Under Section 2 of the Southeast Asia Resolution, and possibly within his power as Commander in Chief to take command decisions incident to an ongoing conflict, the President also had constitutional authority to provide military assistance at the request of the Cambodian government.

THE CONSTITUTIONAL AUTHORITY FOR CONGRESSIONAL RESTRAINTS ON MILITARY OPERATIONS IN INDOCHINA

The decision to intercede in Cambodia has given rise to or accelerated a number of congressional initiatives intended to confine belligerent operations to Vietnam or to require termination of the American combat presence after a particular date.[106] These

103. N.Y. Times, March 2, 1966, at 1, col. 8 (city ed.).
104. See "Fulbright Panel Votes to Repeal Tonkin Measure," N.Y. Times, April 11, 1970, at 1, col. 5 (city ed.).
105. The President has only limited power to initially commit the armed forces to combat abroad. Nevertheless that power probably includes the power to take at least limited action in defense against attacks made on United States military forces stationed abroad and the power to provide military assistance short of the commitment of regular combat units to sustained hostilities. Though the Cambodian incursion seems more appropriately characterized as a decision relating to the conduct of hostilities rather than initial commitment, even if it were an initial commitment decision the President probably has independent constitutional authority to take limited action to defend United States forces stationed in South Vietnam and to provide low-level military assistance to the Cambodian government. See Moore, *supra* note 94.
106. See, *e.g.*, the resolutions appended to the REPORT ON THE TERMINATION OF THE SOUTHEAST ASIA RESOLUTION, the SENATE FOREIGN RELATIONS COMMITTEE, REP. NO. 91-872 (Comm. Print, May 15, 1970); S. 3964 (introduced by Senators Dole and Javits on Monday, June 15, 1970); H. J. Res.

initiatives raise issues concerning the authority of Congress to terminate hostilities, the form of congressional termination of hostilities, and the authority of Congress to limit presidential command options incident to the conduct of a constitutionally authorized conflict.

The Constitution does not specifically address the issue of congressional authority to terminate hostilities. Moreover, apparently there is no instance in the constitutional history of the United States in which Congress has terminated ongoing hostilities over the objection of the President. Nevertheless, it seems a fair inference from the power to declare war, the power to raise and maintain an Army and a Navy, and the power to authorize appropriations, as well as the absence of any evident constitutional scheme for entrusting the power to terminate hostilities exclusively to the President, that Congress has authority to terminate hostilities abroad. Congress is also the most broadly based and democratically responsive branch, and unless there is a strong functional reason such as secrecy, speed, or decisiveness which would suggest entrusting the power exclusively to the President, which seems not to be the case, Congress probably ought to be able to terminate as well as commence hostilities.[107] The complete absence of instances in which Congress has terminated hostilities against the wishes of the President despite numerous highly unpopular conflicts, however, suggests that the exercise of a congressional policy for termination of hostilities which conflicts with a presidential policy should be adopted only with the greatest reluctance. The President is the chief representative of the nation for negotiation of an end to hostilities, has an almost exclusive responsibility to make command decisions concerning the conduct of hostilities, and in many instances has better information concerning the overall strategic situation than individual mem-

---

1151 (introduced by Representative Findley on March 26, 1970); H. R. 17598 (introduced by Representative Fascell).

107. See the "Legal Memorandum on the Constitutionality of the Amendment to End the War," prepared under the supervision of Professors Abram Chayes and Frank Michelman and introduced in the record of the Hearings before the Subcommittee on National Security Policy and Scientific Developments of the House Committee on Foreign Affairs, June 25, 1970.

bers of Congress. As such, Congress should be particularly cautious in undercutting a presidential policy.

Should Congress choose to terminate hostilities, termination, like authorization, should clearly advert to the context and meaning of the congressional action. Just as the Southeast Asia Resolution has been criticized as being hurried through Congress without adequate debate, so too congressional action seeking to terminate hostilities in Indo-China should be based on adequate debate and should be clearly understood as to meaning and scope. Congressional termination must also allow adequate protection of United States forces during withdrawal from hostilities, as fairly appraised under all the circumstances. Though termination would not seem to require any particular magic formulae, it is unclear whether it must be in the form of a bill vetoable by the President or whether a concurrent resolution of Congress would be sufficient. The language of Section 3 of the Southeast Asia Resolution indicating that the resolution can be terminated "by concurrent resolution of the Congress" suggests that, at least with respect to the Southeast Asia Resolution, a concurrent resolution would be adequate.

The third issue presented by the congressional initiatives surrounding the Cambodian crisis is the authority of Congress to limit presidential command options incident to an ongoing war. The Constitution makes the President Commander in Chief. There is no parallel in the powers entrusted to Congress. Professors Egger and Harris, in their study of *The President and Congress*, conclude that this plan means that:

> . . . the President has the . . . exclusive power . . . of exercising military command in time of peace and in time of war; this command power, moreover, involves as an absolute minimum, upon which the Congress is powerless to encroach, the direction of military forces in combat. . . .[108]

Corwin points out that "Congress has never adopted any legislation that would seriously cramp the style of a President attempting to break the resistance of an enemy or seeking to assure the

___

108. R. EGGER & J. HARRIS, THE PRESIDENT AND CONGRESS 35 (1963). See also II D. WATSON, THE CONSTITUTION 913-17 (1910).

safety of the national forces."[109] In fact, Roland Young reports that during World War II:

> No method was worked out by which Congress as a whole was informed on the developments of the war, and, in the aggregate, members of Congress had no more intimate knowledge of how the war was going than the average reader of a metropolitan newspaper.[110]

In *Ex Parte Milligan*,[111] a famous case arising out of the Civil War, Chief Justice Chase pointed out that congressional authority did not extend to interference with command decisions. According to the Chief Justice, congressional authority:

> ... necessarily extends to all legislation essential to the prosecution of war with vigor and success, except such as interferes with the command of the forces and the conduct of campaigns. That power and duty belong to the President as commander-in-chief.[112]

In addition to the textual grant of power to the President as Commander in Chief and the uninterrupted constitutional practice supporting an exclusively presidential command power, there are strong policy reasons inherent in the nature of Congress and the presidency that support the exclusive nature of the presidential power. Tactical decisions incident to an ongoing conflict are frequently decisions in which speed, secrecy, superior sources of information, and military expertise are at a premium. In general, the presidency seems better suited to such decisions than Congress.[113] To give one example, Roland Young reports that the one

109. E. CORWIN, THE PRESIDENT: OFFICE AND POWERS 1787-1957 259 (1957).
110. R. YOUNG, CONGRESSIONAL POLITICS IN THE SECOND WORLD WAR 145 (1956).
111. 71 U.S. (4 Wall.) 2 (1866).
112. *Id.* at 139. (Opinion of the Chief Justice and Justices Wayne, Swayne, and Miller.) See also Swaim v. United States, 28 Ct. Cl. 173, 221 (1893), *aff'd*, Swaim v. United States, 165 U.S. 553 (1897).
113. Professor Watson points out that the provision making the President Commander in Chief may have resulted from the difficulties Washington experienced with the Continental Congress in the conduct of hostilities during the War for Independence. He writes:
    [D]uring the Revolution Washington experienced great trouble and embarrassment resulting from the failure of Congress to sup-

attempt at a secret session of the Senate during World War II resulted in a garbled version of the session being leaked to the press.[114] More recently, the report on Cambodia prepared by the staff of the Senate Foreign Relations Committee dramatically details the difficulties encountered by an important congressional committee in seeking to inform itself as to the conduct of an ongoing war.[115] Perhaps for these reasons Hamilton wrote, in *The Federalist*: "Of all the cases or concerns of government, the direction of war most peculiarly demands those qualities which distinguish the exercise of power by a single hand."[116]

Applying these constitutional principles to the proposed legislation triggered by the Cambodian action, it would seem that Congress would have authority to terminate United States participation in hostilities in the Indo-China War. Thus measures such as the McGovern-Hatfield Amendment[117] which would prohibit the expenditure of military appropriations anywhere in Indochina after June 30, 1971, would seem to be constitutional if at the time of enactment there were sufficient time allowed for a safe withdrawal of United States forces.[118] The wisdom of setting a deadline for unilateral withdrawal is another matter and one which seems highly dubious in view of the complete absence of historical precedent and the certainty of undercutting the presidential negotiating position.

As to form of termination, the double vote by the Senate to re-

---

port him with firmness and dispatch. There was a want of directness in the management of affairs during that period which was attributable to the absence of centralized authority to command. The members of the Convention knew this and probably thought they could prevent its recurrence by making the President Commander-in-Chief of the Army and Navy.

D. WATSON, *supra* note 108, at 912.

114. R. YOUNG, *supra* note 110, at 145.

115. See the Staff Report, "Cambodia: May 1970" prepared for the *Senate Committee on Foreign Relations*, 91ST CONG., 2D SESS. (Comm. Print June 7, 1970), *reprinted* in 9 INT'L LEG. MAT. 858 (1970).

116. THE FEDERALIST, Number 74, 497 (Heritage Press 1945).

117. An Amendment to the Defense Authorization Bill, H.R. 17123, 91st Cong., 2d Sess. (1970).

118. See generally the "Legal Memorandum on the Constitutionality of the Amendment to End the War," *supra* note 107.

peal the Southeast Asia Resolution[119] is precisely the kind of ambiguous and unclear congressional action which should be avoided. In fact, by a strange quirk of partisan senatorial warfare, it was unclear whether a vote to repeal the Southeast Asia Resolution was a vote to terminate presidential authority or to affirm a constitutional interpretation that the President would have constitutional authority even if the Southeast Asia Resolution had never existed. Neither camp seems to have clearly adverted to whether the vote on repeal of the resolution was directed at revoking authority for future actions in Southeast Asia on the authority of the resolution or whether it was intended to be an exercise of the congressional authority to terminate the Indo-China War as of the date of repeal. In the absence of clear congressional intent to terminate hostilities, the President would certainly be justified in interpreting any repeal to mean only the former. Again, the wisdom of repeal of the principal constitutional authority for a major war while that war continues seems highly suspect. Repeal, of course, would also require action by the House of Representatives.

Perhaps the legislation most directly related to the Cambodian incursion is the Cooper-Church Amendment[120] which passed the Senate by a vote of 58 to 37 on June 30, 1970.[121] The amendment provides that:

> In concert with the declared objectives of the President of the United States . . . no funds authorized or appropriated pursuant to this act or any other law may be expended after July 1, 1970, for the purposes of—
> (1) Retaining United States forces in Cambodia;
> (2) Paying the compensation or allowances of, or otherwise supporting, directly or indirectly, any United States

119. See N.Y. Times, June 25, 1970, at 1, col. 1; N.Y. Times, July 11, 1970, at 7, col. 4. The first vote to repeal was on June 24, 1970, and took the form of an amendment to the Foreign Military Sales Act, H.R. 15628, 91st Cong., 2d Sess. (1970). The second vote to repeal was on July 10, 1970, and took the form of a concurrent resolution, S. Con. Res. 64, S. Rept. 91-872, 91st Cong., 2d Sess. (1970).

120. An Amendment to the Foreign Military Sales Act, H.R. 15628, 91st Cong., 2d Sess. (1970).

121. N.Y. Times, July 1, 1970, at 13, col. 1 (city ed.).

personnel in Cambodia who furnish military instruction to Cambodian forces or engage in any combat activity in support of Cambodian forces;

(3) Entering into or carrying out any contract or agreement to provide military instruction in Cambodia, or to provide persons to engage in any combat activity in support of Cambodian forces; or

(4) Conducting any combat activity in the air above Cambodia in direct support of Cambodian forces.

Nothing contained in this section shall be deemed to impugn the constitutional power of the President as Commander in Chief, including the exercise of that constitutional power which may be necessary to protect the lives of United States armed forces wherever deployed. . . .[122]

The principal constitutional issue in appraising the Cooper-Church Amendment is whether it should be characterized as within the congressional authority to withdraw authorization for assistance to the Cambodian government and termination of such assistance, or whether it encroaches on the presidential authority to take command decisions incident to the Vietnam War. To the extent that the amendment prohibits actions directed against the sanctuaries in direct support of the military effort in Vietnam (the extent to which the amendment would prohibit future actions directed against the sanctuaries is unclear), it would seem to be dealing with command options. On the other hand, if it only seeks to limit the United States involvement in Southeast Asia by proscribing military support of the Cambodian government, a stronger case can be made that it is within the congressional authority to terminate hostilities. Nevertheless, the interrelation between the survival of the Cambodian government and the military effort in Vietnam lends substantial support to the proposition that even direct military assistance in support of the Cambodian government is within the Commander in Chief's power. The ambiguity as to the conduct proscribed by the Cooper-Church Amendment, the difficulty in characterizing the constitutional effect of the amendment, and the uncertainty of the lim-

122. N.Y. Times, July 1, 1970, at 13, cols. 5-6 (city ed.).

its of congressional authority to proscribe presidential command options suggest that the amendment is in a constitutional twilight zone likely to precipitate a clash between Congress and the President, and that resolution of the constitutional issue will depend largely on the actions of each branch rather than any analytically discoverable *a priori* constitutional hypothesis. With respect to form, since congressional termination of hostilities, whether in whole or in part, should, like congressional authorization, be carefully considered and debated on its own merits by both houses of Congress, it seems a poor precedent that the Cooper-Church Amendment took the form of an amendment to the Foreign Military Sales Act which will be linked with the broader bill rather than considered individually by the House as well as the Senate.[123]

THE NEED FOR CONGRESSIONAL-EXECUTIVE COOPERATION ON WAR-PEACE ISSUES

The interdependency of the congressional and executive war powers suggests a need for cooperation rather than conflict. Cooperation requires that the President should candidly inform Congress of developments affecting national security and that congressional leaders should be consulted prior to major military decisions even if they fall within the President's constitutional authority as Commander in Chief. Failure to inform congressional leaders prior to the Cambodian intercession involved a high cost in the authority of the action and in congressional disaffection from presidential initiatives. Cooperation also requires that in its understandable interest in reassuming a greater role in war-peace decisions, Congress should not lose sight of the need to protect legitimate presidential authority. In the wake of the Cambodian action there are a number of general bills in both houses of Congress aimed at reasserting the congressional role.[124]

123. Spokesmen for the Senate have implied that if the House wants the Foreign Military Sales Bill it also will have to accept the Cooper-Church Amendment.

124. See S. 3964 (introduced by Senators Dole and Javits on Monday, June 15, 1970); H.J. Res. 1151 (introduced by Representative Findley on March 26, 1970); and H. R. 17598 (introduced by Representative Fascell).

Most, however, which seek to delimit presidential authority in advance, run the dual risk of unconstitutional encroachment on presidential authority and irrelevance as conditions change. The real need seems to be for more careful consideration of congressional measures authorizing and terminating hostilities and for greater liaison between the President and Congress during the course of major hostilities.[125]

III. International Law and the Functioning of the National Security Process

In the last few years a great deal of attention has been focused on the role actually played by international law in national security decisions.[126] The results are frequently discouraging. It is surprising, then, that so little attention has been devoted to the role that international law ought to play in such decisions and how the national security process might be better structured to more systematically take it into account. In an article in the *Virginia Journal of International Law* I have urged that an international-legal perspective is an important perspective in national security decisions and that the present structure of the process is inadequate for reliably bringing such perspectives to the attention of national decision-makers.[127]

The Cambodian decision dramatically illustrates the continuing high cost of failing to structure an international-legal perspective into the national security process. Though the United States intercession in Cambodia was lawful, the ambiguity surrounding certain features of the operation, for example the consent of the Cambodian government, contributed unnecessarily to domestic and international misunderstanding of the action. There were at

125. For an analysis of legislative initiatives concerning the war powers and recommendations for improved congressional-executive cooperation see J. N. Moore, "Strengthening the Role of Congress in the Use of the Armed Forces Abroad," testimony before the Senate Foreign Relations Committee April 26, 1971.

126. See, *e.g.*, L. SCHEINMAN & D. WILKINSON, INTERNATIONAL LAW AND POLITICAL CRISIS (1968). The American Society of International Law currently has a Panel on the Role of International Law in Government Decision-Making in War-Peace Crises which has a number of thoughtful studies in process.

127. Moore, *supra* note 76, at 310-14.

least two options which were likely to be persuasively presented by someone focused on an international-legal perspective which might have strengthened the United States response. First, North Vietnamese and Vietcong attacks on and from Cambodia might have been vigorously protested by the United States in the Security Council during March or April. The Cambodian complaint to the Security Council on April 22, 1970, would have seemed a particularly opportune occasion to press a complaint in the Security Council. The North Vietnamese belligerent use of neutral Cambodian territory and attacks on the Cambodian government presented about as clear a case of impermissible action as is ever possible in complex world order disputes. To ignore the North Vietnamese actions when there was no longer room for doubt as to their armed attack on Cambodia was to unnecessarily undercut both the United Nations and the United States authority positions. Second, a prior understanding with Cambodia might have been obtained for public release at the time of the operation. In view of the consent requirement of Article IV, Section 3, of the SEATO treaty such an advance agreement would have seemed particularly advisable. Though concern has been expressed that such an agreement might have undercut the neutrality of Cambodia, it should have been possible to word it in such a way that neutrality was supported rather than compromised. Thus, Cambodia might have "recognized the right of the United States and South Vietnam to take defensive action against the unlawful belligerent activities of the North Vietnamese and Vietcong forces on neutral Cambodian territory." The agreement might also have emphasized that under international law it is not a breach of neutrality for a neutral state to use force against unlawful belligerent activities on its territory,[128] that Cambodia had no intention of relinquishing its neutrality, that the action was geographically and temporally limited, and that the action was taken with the consent of the Cambodian government within the meaning of Article IV,

---

128. See M. GREENSPAN, THE MODERN LAW OF LAND WARFARE 536-37, 584 (1959). Similarly, lawful actions by one belligerent directed against violations of neutral territory by another belligerent do not constitute hostilities against the neutral. See L. OPPENHEIM, INTERNATIONAL LAW 685 (7th ed. Lauterpacht 1952).

Section 3, of the SEATO treaty. Though such an advance agreement was not strictly required by international law, it would have materially strengthened both the United States position and the continuing neutrality of Cambodia. As a minor third point, the United States should have immediately reported its action to the Security Council instead of waiting five days. Finally, President Nixon's speech to the Nation on April 30, and other public pronouncements on Cambodia, might have been more focused and carried greater impact had they emphasized the international legal right of a belligerent to take action to end serious continued violations of neutral territory by an opposing belligerent. These suggestions are not put forth as grand new solutions to the tensions which produced the Cambodian crisis but only to illustrate how an international-legal perspective might have been sensitive to a range of issues and options which could have improved the United States response to the situation. Had the proposed Cambodian intercession been illegal, of course, then an international-legal perspective might have been even more important in counseling restraint.[129]

The constitutional debate surrounding the Cambodian situation also illustrates a need to more systematically structure a constitutional-legal perspective into the foreign policy process. The rhetoric of both the Executive and the Congress was frequently overly broad, contributing to a potentially costly confusion. For example, President Nixon failed to make clear that the Southeast Asia Resolution was a principal constitutional basis for the Vietnam War. Partly as a result of this presidential failure to clearly support retention of the resolution, the Senate voted twice to repeal the resolution amid great confusion as to the meaning of the vote. And in its eagerness to reassert a stronger congressional role, Congress sometimes seemed to unrealistically downgrade the independent authority of the President as Commander in Chief, as for example in the resolutions introduced in both houses of Congress seeking to narrowly define in advance the limits of

129. In the sense that non-compliance with international law subjects a state to all of the sanctions of the global community, however imperfect those sanctions may be in particular instances, states do not have a genuine option whether or not to comply with international law.

presidential authority to commit the armed forces to combat abroad.

There is no real remedy to the lack of an international-legal perspective in the national security process other than increasing the awareness of the importance of such a perspective. Institutional changes may help significantly, however, and I am more than ever convinced of the soundness of the earlier recommendation to upgrade the office of Legal Adviser of the Department of State to Under Secretary of State for International Legal Affairs, and to make the new Under Secretary a permanent *ex officio* member of the National Security Council. Perhaps, in addition, the President should add to his staff an Assistant to the President for International Legal Affairs. It might also be helpful for the Senate Foreign Relations Committee and the House Foreign Affairs Committee to add similar positions to their staffs.[130]

Though the decision to intercede in Cambodia was lawful both under international law and the United States Constitution, the functioning of the national security process in the Cambodian crisis indicates a need for greater sensitivity to the legal dimensions of security decisions. Several options which could have been pursued, particularly referral to the United Nations Security Council and advance agreement with the Cambodian government, do not seem to have been adequately considered. Similarly, failure to inform congressional leaders of the pending decision may have unnecessarily weakened the authority of the action. For international lawyers, the principal lesson of the Cambodian crisis may be that they have failed to convince national decision-makers that an international-legal perspective should be heard. If so, soul-searching among international lawyers might better give way to a concerted effort to ensure that others practice what we preach.

August, 1970

130. For an exploration of these and other suggestions for more systematically introducing an international-legal perspective into the national security process see Moore, *supra* note 76, at 310-14, 340-42.

PART FOUR
THE INDO-CHINA WAR
AND THE STRUCTURE
OF THE NATIONAL
SECURITY PROCESS

Introduction

THE proper role of Congress and the President in the commitment of the nation to war has been recurrently controversial since the administration of Jefferson. In the Indo-China debate this controversy has taken on an intensity not equaled since the Mexican war. Characteristically, participants in the debate have tended to take a position either pro-Congress or pro-Executive, much in the fashion of the famous clash between Hamilton, writing as Pacificus, and Madison, writing as Helvidius. Lacking has been any attempt to particularize the range of issues and to relate answers on each to the functional differences between the two branches. Chapters XI and XII are efforts at remedying this lack, drawing on the extraordinary range of constitutional issues raised during the Indo-China war.

The constitutional debate about the Indo-China war has passed through two principal phases. The first swirled around the independent power of the President to commit the armed forces abroad and the constitutional effect of the Southeast Asia Resolution. This phase reached its peak during 1966 and 1967 with the Senate Foreign Relations Committee hearings on Vietnam and on National Commitments. The second phase was triggered by the constitutional issues surrounding the Cambodian incursion and reached a peak in a flurry of legislative activity during the summer of 1970 and the spring of 1971. The issues in this second phase of the debate were much broader, extending to the authority of the President to make command decisions incident to an on-going war and the authority of Congress to terminate hostilities and to limit the President in the conduct of hostilities, as well as the earlier issues. The discussion in Chapter XI focuses on the Executive role and largely corresponds to the issues raised during the first phase of the debate. Chapter XII shifts the emphasis to the congressional role and considers the issues raised by the second phase of the debate. Although not included in Part Four, Chapter X, "Legal Dimensions of the Decision to Intercede in Cambodia," includes an analysis of the specific constitutional issues raised by the presidential initiative in the Cambodian incursion and the range of congressional responses.

The issues in both phases of the constitutional debate about the Indo-China war are of transcendent importance. Their manner of resolution is likely to significantly shape the course of American foreign policy and the distribution of foreign affairs power within the American government. As such, it is particularly important that they receive a full hearing on their own merits rather than being linked with the ups and downs of opinion polls on the war.

Historically, from about the turn of the century, the balance between Congress and the President has shifted dramatically in the direction of increased presidential power. The shift has been influenced by the transition from a stable balance of power to a revolutionary and highly competitive international system, an increasing global interdependence, an explosion in military technology, and the predominance of limited, proxy, covert, and quasi-internal conflict, all of which have favored the more rapid and decisive Executive branch. The high-water mark of this increased Executive power was the commitment by President Truman of a quarter of a million American troops to sustained high-level conflict in the Korean war without explicit congressional approval before or after the action. Although Truman's action was made possible by congressional and United Nations support, it nevertheless set a broad precedent for presidential power. During the next few years, Congress responded to the pressures of the cold-war by passing broad resolutions, the Formosa Resolution in 1955 and the Middle East Resolution in 1957, delegating great discretion to the President to use force in those areas. Thus, the immediate constitutional background at the oubreak of the Indo-China war recognized very broad Executive discretion. It is in this context that one should judge the hastily passed Southeast Asia Resolution which provided the principal constitutional authority for the Indo-China war. The subsequent debate, with the benefit of a broader sweep of history, has indicated a need for more careful congressional exercise of the war power and for a more limited (but still substantial) presidential power. There should be no mistake, however, amid all the confusion as to whether or not a second attack actually occurred in the Gulf of Tonkin: Congress did support and participate in United States involvement in the Indo-China war. This conclusion is compelled by a full reading of the congressional debates on the passage of the Southeast Asia Resolution, by congressional response to special Vietnam appropriation measures, and by overwhelming congressional rejection of early efforts to repeal the Southeast Asia Resolution.[1] But whatever one's view of the specifics of the Indo-China debate the more important issue is the institutional issue as to how Congress and the Executive should be structured for optimum response on war-peace issues. The Indo-China conflict has revealed a mutual uncertainty which is destructive of a cohesive and stable foreign policy. The task for the future is for Congress and the President to work together to develop a balanced and functionally sound framework for mutual cooperation.[2]

Chapter XIII, "The Justiciability of Challenges to the Use of Military Forces Abroad," considers the extent to which courts are capable of handling the international and constitutional issues involved in major war-peace issues. At this writing, no court has held such issues justiciable, and by refusing to grant *certiorari* to review them the Supreme Court has acquiesced in this judgment. During 1970, however, the campaign to obtain Supreme Court consideration received a major boost when the State of Massachusetts passed an act intended to force Supreme Court consideration of the constitutional authorization for the Indo-China war.[3] As a result of the Massachusetts Act, the international and constitutional law issues in the Vietnam war and the justiciability of such issues may come repeatedly before the Court, a possibility which gives special relevance to the legal issues in the Indo-China debate.[4] In general, supporters of the campaign for

---

1. See John N. Moore & James L. Underwood, *The Lawfulness of United States Assistance to the Republic of Viet Nam*, 112 CONG. REC. 14943, 14,960-67, 14,983-89 (daily ed. July 14, 1966).
2. For a discussion of the full range of issues in such a framework and a preliminary effort at functional division of the war powers between Congress and the Executive with respect to each see Chapter XII in this volume and J.N. Moore, "Strengthening the Role of Congress in the Use of the Armed Forces Abroad," testimony before the Senate Foreign Relations Committee on April 26, 1971.
3. [1970] Mass. Acts Ch. 174.
4. On November 9, 1970, the Supreme Court denied a motion by the Commonwealth of Massachusetts for leave to file a bill of complaint against

Supreme Court review have underestimated both the constitutional underpinnings for the Indo-China war and the difficulties in judicial consideration of executive-congressional action authorizing the use of the armed forces abroad. Chapter XIII points up the difficulties in judicial review of such executive-congressional action and suggests—from a functional perspective—the kinds of war-peace issues which might be suitable for review. Careful separation of issues and application of a functional yardstick to each should prove more sensitive than either-or approaches to justiciability.

In addition to the constitutional issues, a second set of issues in the structure of the national security process is the structure of that process for more systematically taking into account the international and constitutional legal aspects of national security issues. The Indo-China conflict has demonstrated repeated instances of congressional and presidential insensitivity to international and constitutional law and some costly instances of insensitive implementation of policies. It might be reassuring to ascribe the difficulties to the unique problem of the Indo-China War. But there seems to be nothing inherent in the war that has caused the problem. Rather, the problem is, at least in part, a continuing institutional problem: the national security process is poorly structured to regularly take account of the international-legal aspects of national security issues. Unlike many

---

the Secretary of Defense brought pursuant to the Massachusetts Act. Mr. Justice Douglas dissented in an opinion in which he urged that Massachusetts had standing and the controversy was justiciable. Justices Harlan and Stewart also dissented indicating that they would set the motion for argument on the questions of standing and justiciability. Massachusetts v. Laird, 400 U.S. 886 (1970). The issues seem likely to again be presented to the Court under the impetus of the Massachusetts Act, the second time pursuant to the appellate rather than the original jurisdiction of the Court.

It would seem that in an appropriate case the Court should hear argument and write a full opinion on standing and justiciability. It is important in considering major national issues that courts fully articulate their reasons for decision. In the Indo-China context, however, the merits of these issues strongly suggest that such an opinion would conclude that the basic international and constitutional issues in the war are non-justiciable or, what may be another way of saying the same thing, are constitutionally entrusted to another branch for decision.

international problems, a variety of useful remedies are readily available, and there would seem to be strong reason and little excuse for not implementing them in the immediate future. Two such changes likely to work significant improvement are creation of an Assistant to the President for International-Legal Affairs and placement of the State Department Legal Adviser on the National Security Council. As a nation we will get more out of international law if we are willing to invest more. These minor shifts in the national security process to more adequately take international law into account seem a small price to pay.

CHAPTER XI

The National Executive
and the Use of the
Armed Forces Abroad*

HISTORICALLY, the controversies about the war power and the treaty power seem to have been the most important constitutional issues in the scope of the President's foreign affairs power. Of these, the treaty power controversy has been in at least a state of temporary quiescence since the heated controversy in 1954 over the Bricker amendment. With the defeat by a narrow margin of the Bricker amendment, which had been aimed at restricting the President's power to make international agreements, this controversy was resolved in favor of a continuing broad view of Executive authority. In contrast, the debate on Vietnam has heated white hot the controversy over the extent of presidential power to use the armed forces abroad, and has generated a concern with presidential power as insistent as any in our century.[1]

Basically, the controversy concerns the authority of the President to order the armed forces into combat abroad and the question of when and how Congress must authorize the use of the armed forces abroad. Although this problem is presented more dramatically today than ever before, it is not new. Much of the

---

* Delivered as an address at the Naval War College on October 11, 1968.

1. See generally on the national executive and the use of the armed forces abroad E. CORWIN, THE PRESIDENT: OFFICE AND POWERS 1787-1957 (4th rev. ed. 1957); F. Wormuth, *The Vietnam War: The President v. The Constitution* (An Occasional Paper of the Center for the Study of Democratic Institutions 1968); Kurland, *The Impotence of Reticence*, 1968 DUKE L.J. 619; Moore & Underwood, *The Lawfulness of United States Assistance to the Republic of Viet Nam*, 112 CONG. REC. 14,943, 14,960-67, 14,983-89 (daily ed. July 14, 1966); Velvel, *The War in Viet Nam: Unconstitutional, Justiciable, and Jurisdictionally Attackable*, 16 KANSAS L. REV. 449 (1968); *U.S. Commitments to Foreign Powers, Hearings Before the Committee on Foreign Relations of the United States Senate*, 90TH CONG., 1ST SESS. (1967); *National Commitments Report*, S. Rep. No. 797, 90TH CONG., 1ST SESS. (1967).

current debate borrows argument from the clashes of Jefferson and Hamilton over the power of the President in the 1801 naval war against the Bashaw of Tripoli and from the rhetoric of President Polk and Representative Abraham Lincoln in the 1846 Mexican war.

The starting point of the debate is the Constitution, which gives Congress the power to declare war and to raise and support armies and which makes the President the Commander in Chief and in practical effect the chief representative of the nation in foreign affairs. It seems reasonably clear from the debates at the Federal Constitutional Convention that most of the framers sought to place the major war power in Congress and to leave the President only the right to repel sudden attacks. The framers sought this restriction on presidential power because of their fear of concentrated power in the President. But the convention debates are not very useful in telling us who has power in situations which may be short of war or in resolving controversy about how Congress might authorize the President to use the Army and Navy. Moreover, the Constitution is a living document, and its meaning is shaped by the experience of successive Congresses and Presidents in filling in its broad outlines and in adapting it to changing circumstances. As Mr. Justice Frankfurter pointed out: "It is an inadmissibly narrow conception of American constitutional law to confine it to the words of the Constitution and to disregard the gloss which life has written upon them."[2] Nowhere is this statement or that of Mr. Justice Holmes that "the life of the law has not been logic: it has been experience"[3] been more apt than in the interpretation of the war power.

In the 180 years since the adoption of the Constitution, our nation has moved from a position of comparative isolation epitomized by Washington's warning to stay clear of entangling alliances to one of intense international involvement evidenced in 1972 by agreements for collective defense with 42 countries. In the same period, the international system has shifted from a balance-of-power system to a loose bipolar system marked by intense

2. Mr. Justice Frankfurter, concurring in *Youngstown Sheet and Tube Co. v. Sawyer*, 343 U.S. 579, 593 at 610 (1952).
3. O. W. HOLMES, THE COMMON LAW 1 (1881).

global competition among competing public order systems and a nuclear balance of terror. And international law has moved from the notion of a just war to the prohibition of all force as a means of major change under the U.N. Charter. The increasing involvement of the United States in world affairs, the shift to an intensely competitive bipolar system, and the limitation of the lawful use of force to defense have greatly strengthened the hand of the Executive in the contest with Congress over the war power. Hamilton and Jefferson fought over whether, in the absence of congressional authorization to use force, a Tripolitanian cruiser must be released after capture by an American naval vessel. Jefferson took the position that in the absence of congressional authorization for U.S. naval forces to go on the offense, the cruiser must be released after being disabled from committing further hostilities. But the contemporary debate is about the power to commit from a quarter- to a half-million troops in major wars such as Korea and Vietnam. As the contrast in subjects debated shows, there has been a gradual increase in presidential power to use the military abroad over this period, an increase which has accelerated during the twentieth century.

Some commentators, such as Professor Wormuth and Senator Fulbright, tell us that the increase in presidential power vis-à-vis Congress has gone too far. They paint a picture of Executive usurpation of authority. But though they have a great deal to show us, the trouble is that the frame they use may be too small. We cannot just look to the language of the Constitution or the experience of 150 years ago for the answer to problems and conditions not wholly anticipated. If we are to display a proper instinct for the jugular instead of an instinct for the capillaries, we must apply the policy of the framers to the diverse problems and conditions of today.

The policy of requiring congressional authority for the major use of force abroad as a check on presidential power remains as valid today, if not more so, as in 1789. But problems of collective defense pursuant to treaty obligations, the need for implementation of sanctions under article 42 of the United Nations Charter, an increasingly global defense interdependence, the wide range of responses to situations of intrastate conflict, and the swiftness of modern attack militate against absolute answers based on that policy.

The nature of our problem is such that we are unlikely to find many of what Mr. Justice Frankfurter termed bright-line distinctions. It will help immeasurably, however, if we first briefly indulge in the luxury of a minimum of clarification about the nature of the major questions we must deal with. Although there are really many more, as a first-stage complexity it is convenient to take four questions. With each we are concerned with authorization to use the armed forces abroad in conflict situations.

First, what may the President do on his own authority without congressional authorization? Second, if congressional authorization is necessary, what form must it take? Must there be a formal declaration of war? Third, what terms of congressional authorization are valid? Can Congress delegate the authority to use troops abroad to the President, and, if so, how broad a delegation is permissible? Last, to what extent can the answers to the first three questions be resolved by the courts? Are they "political questions" or otherwise issues which it is unwise for a court to adjudicate? Failure to separate these questions has carried more than its share of confusion. I will deal with these one at a time and then apply them all to the Vietnam situation.

First, what may the President do on his own authority without congressional authorization?

There is no doubt that the President, acting on his own authority, may order the military to repel sudden attacks on the United States or American forces. The draft proposals of the Constitution initially contained language authorizing Congress to "make war," but at the instance of James Madison the language was changed from "to make war" to "to declare war." The reason given for the change was to leave to the President "the power to repel sudden attack." Beyond that, there is greater controversy. On the one hand, there are those who take a broad view of presidential power such as Craig Mathews who writes:

> Constitutional history has shown that the President can take military action under his independent powers whenever the interests of the United States so require. In the modern

world the scope of America's interest can be determined only by reference to the state of affairs in the international arena as a whole and to the overall purposes of our foreign policy. Any rigid test of protectable interest would leave the nation dangerously unequipped for survival.[4]

Similarly, Under-Secretary Katzenbach, in testifying before the Senate Foreign Relations Committee, said that he doubts that any president has ever acted to the full limits of his presidential authority.[5] There is substantial precedent in history for this broad interpretation of presidential authority. Former Assistant Secretary of State James Grafton Rogers tells us that in the over 100 uses of U.S. forces abroad from 1789 to 1945 the Executive ordered the use on his own authority in at least 80.[6] And a 1951 study for the Committee on Foreign Relations says that: "Since the Constitution was adopted there have been at least 125 incidents in which the President, without congressional authorization, . . . has ordered the armed forces to take action or maintain positions abroad."[7]

Since these studies were completed we could add President Truman's use of a quarter of a million American troops in Korea, President Eisenhower's landing of the marines in Lebanon, President Kennedy's limited use of American forces in the Bay of Pigs invasion and as "advisers" in Vietnam, and President Johnson's landing of troops in the Dominican Republic. All of this certainly represents a substantial gloss which experience has placed on the Constitution.

On the other hand, those who take a narrow view of presidential power, such as Professor Ruhl Bartlett in testimony before

4. Mathews, *The Constitutional Power of the President to Conclude International Agreements,* 64 YALE L.J. 345, 365 (1955).
5. *U.S. Commitments to Foreign Powers, Hearings Before the Senate Committee on Foreign Relations on S. Res. 151,* 90TH CONG., 1ST SESS., 76 (Comm. Print 1967).
6. Rogers, *World Policing and the Constitution* in 11 AMERICA LOOKS AHEAD 78 (World Peace Foundation 1945).
7. Study prepared for the use of the Senate Joint Committee of the Committee on Foreign Relations and the Committee on Armed Services, 82 CONG., 1ST SESS., *Powers of the President to Send the Armed Forces Outside the United States* 2 (Comm. Print Feb. 28, 1951).

the Senate Foreign Relations Committee during the National Commitments hearings in 1967, point out that most of these actions, with the greatest exception being Korea, did not involve sustained hostilities or more than minor casualties.[8] Typically, they involved protection of U.S. citizens abroad, pursuit of pirates, alleged humanitarian intervention, reprisals, or consensual assistance to a recognized government. And protracted and sustained use of troops abroad resulting in substantial casualties has usually been highly controversial; the Korean war and President Polk's initiation of the Mexican war of 1846 being prime examples.

Given this degree of disagreement by sincere and informed scholars, what guideposts are there for delimiting presidential authority in those situations in which the President acts without congressional authorization? Although they can easily be overstated, there are some policy considerations which, in my opinion, suggest a need for substantial presidential authority. First, there is a need for the President to be able to quickly react to sudden armed attacks threatening U.S. defense interests. The sudden attack in Korea and the rapid response of President Truman in initiating a process of troop commitment to Korea is, I believe, a real example of this need. Though subject to abuse, possibly some actions to protect American citizens abroad fall into an analogous category. The joint United States-Belgian rescue operation in the Congo and the first stage of the Dominican operation are examples. There is also sometimes a need for secrecy, decisiveness, and negotiating responsiveness which can best be met by presidential action. In this category I would cite the actions of President Kennedy in the Cuban missile crisis. It seems to me that the wisdom of congressional debate about whether the response to the Soviet emplacement of medium-range ballistic missiles in Cuba should be quarantine, air strikes on the missile sites, invasion of Cuba, or no response at all, which is the debate which went on within the administration, is open to serious doubt. Robert Kennedy tells us in his account of the missile crisis that he doubts as satisfactory an outcome could have been achieved if the debate over alternatives had taken place in the full glare of publicity. And lest we

8. See *U.S. Commitments to Foreign Powers*, note 5 *supra*, at 9-21.

succumb to the myth that the President is always hawkish and Congress is always dovish, we should remember Kennedy's account of the hawkish pressures from leading Congressmen during the missile crisis.

There is also a category of what might be called "ongoing command decisions," which are day-to-day decisions about the operation of existing military assistance programs within the network of U.S. defense interests or about defensive deployment of our armed forces. By their recurrent nature, many of these decisions inevitably will be left, in the first instance at least, to presidential authority. Examples would be the conduct of established military advisory missions, military assistance programs, and intelligence missions necessary for national security. Moreover, I believe that some of the arguments for strictly limiting presidential authority misconceive the nature of presidential power and elevate form over substance. Presidential power, even in the exercise of the Commander in Chief power, is not autonomous and, as Richard Neustadt compellingly argues, is in large measure the power to persuade.[9] It is difficult for a President to pursue sustained military actions without the active support of a substantial segment of Congress and the American people. And although Congress would usually be reluctant to do so, if things got too bad Congress could refuse to appropriate funds or could even institute impeachment proceedings against the President. And short of these measures, the Congress can bring great pressure to bear on the President through the power of critical public hearings, as the Fulbright hearings on Vietnam perhaps more than adequately demonstrate.

Despite these reasons for some presidential authority in the use of troops abroad, it seems neither wise nor necessary to encourage too great an expansion of presidential power. Within the limits of survival in the world we live in, we should require the more broadly based authorization which only Congress can give and should strive to revitalize the role of Congress in the making of foreign policy.

As a dividing line for presidential authority in the use of the

9. See R. NEUSTADT, PRESIDENTIAL POWER (1964).

military abroad, one test might be to require congressional authorization in all cases where regular combat units are committed to sustained hostilities. This test would be likely to include most situations resulting in substantial casualties and substantial commitment of resources. Under this test, the Mexican war, the Korean war, and the Vietnam War would all require congressional authorization. The test has the virtue of responsiveness to precisely those situations historically creating the greatest concern over presidential authority, but like all tests is somewhat frayed at the edges. In conflicts which gradually escalate, the dividing line for requiring congressional authorization might be initial commitment to combat of regular U.S. combat units as such. As to the suddenness of Korea, and conflicts like Korea, I would argue that the President should have the authority to meet the attack as necessary but should immediately seek congressional authorization. In retrospect, the decision not to obtain formal congressional authorization in the Korean war, in which the United States sustained more than 140,000 casualties, seems a poor precedent. And in those situations in which presidential authority is based on the need for secrecy or immediacy of response, the need should be a real one.

To say that the President should have authority to act in some circumstances without congressional authorization is not to advise that he should not consult Congress or key congressional leaders. The President should involve Congress as much as practicable in every case. In fact, failure to pursue congressional involvement meaningfully when it could have been done has been the cause of a great deal of unnecessary presidential grief. As Under-Secretary Katzenbach points out "there can be no question that . . . [the President] acts most effectively when he acts with the support and authority of the Congress."[10]

The second question is: When congressional authorization is necessary, what form should it take? Is a formal declaration of war required?

Much of the popular discussion about the war power seems to assume that a formal declaration of war is the only means of con-

10. *U.S. Commitments to Foreign Powers*, note 5 *supra*, at 76.

stitutionally obtaining congressional authorization for the use of the military. But this is largely a red herring. As a matter of logic, the syntax of the Constitution that "Congress should have power . . . to declare war" does not mean that Congress may not authorize hostilities without a formal declaration of war. And as a matter of intent of the framers, the requirement is congressional control of hostilities, not a particular mode of authorization. This was so clear that within 12 years of the adoption of the Constitution no less an authority than Chief Justice John Marshall recognized in the case of *Talbot v. Seeman*[11] that congressional action not amounting to a formal declaration of war could be a valid congressional authorization of hostilities. The case arose out of the 1789 naval war with France, the first war of a fledgling United States. As a result of French raiding of American shipping, Congress had passed a series of acts suspending commercial relations with France, denouncing the treaties with France, and establishing a Department of the Navy and a Marine Corps. The Court treated these acts as congressional authorization for limited hostilities with France. Practice since then shows that Congress has declared war only five times, despite the much larger number of occasions on which the United States has been at war. There is little reason, then, to believe that a formal declaration of war is the only means of congressional authorization of hostilities. A joint congressional resolution, which must be approved by both houses of Congress, authorizing the President to use the military abroad is certainly, as Under-Secretary Katzenbach puts it, "a functional equivalent of the declaration of war."

There are also numerous policy arguments why the formal declaration of war is undesirable under present circumstances. Arguments made include increased danger of misunderstanding of limited objectives, diplomatic embarrassment in recognition of nonrecognized guerrilla opponents, inhibition of settlement possibilities, the danger of widening the war, and unnecessarily increasing a President's domestic authority. Although each of these arguments has some merit, probably the most compelling reason for not using the formal declaration of war is that there is no reason to do so. As former Secretary of Defense McNamara has

11. (The Amelia) 5 U.S. (1 Cr.) 1, 25 (1801).

pointed out "[T]here has not been a formal declaration of war—anywhere in the world—since World War II."[12]

More serious questions as to form of congressional authorization include to what extent Congress can authorize the President to engage in hostilities by prior approval of an international agreement. And to what extent can congressional acquiescence in appropriation measures constitute congressional authorization to engage in hostilities? One obvious problem with treaty authorization is that although the House of Representatives would participate in a declaration of war, it would not participate in treaty-making. This objection would be alleviated if the international agreement took the form of a congressional-executive agreement sanctioned by a joint resolution. Problems in recognizing appropriation measures as authorization include confronting Congress with a *fait accompli* and ascertaining the scope of congressional intent in a vote to approve an appropriation measure.

The third question is: What terms of congressional authorization are valid? Can Congress delegate the authority to use troops abroad to the President, and if so, how broad a delegation is permissible?

The permissibility of congressional delegation of the war power to the President and exactly what constitutes a delegation have been disputed throughout U.S. history. In 1834, President Jackson sought congressional authorization to undertake reprisals upon French property unless France paid her outstanding debts for damages to American shipping during the Napoleonic wars. There were objections in Congress on the grounds that it would amount to an unconstitutional transfer of Congress' war power to the President, and Jackson did not get his resolution. Similarly, in 1857, President Buchanan sought congressional authorization to use the military at his discretion, if necessary to preserve freedom of communication across the Isthmus of Panama. Despite three requests, Congress refused to grant Buchanan the authority he requested. A principal argument against granting his re-

12. The statement is from an address by former Secretary of Defense Robert S. McNamara to the American Society of Newspaper Editors on May 18, 1966. N.Y. Times, May 19, 1966, at c.11, col. 1 (city ed.), at col. 2.

quest was that to do so would be a surrender to the President of Congress' war power. The objection was again raised by Senators opposed to President Wilson's request for congressional authority to take defensive measures in protection of American shipping. Corwin tells us that Wilson went ahead and armed American merchant vessels despite congressional inaction.

More recent experience has seen Congress take a broader view on the delegation issue. In the 1945 United Nations Participation Act, Congress provided for delegation of authority to the President to engage in hostilities if acting pursuant to an article 43 U.N. collective peace force agreement approved by Congress. Apparently, however, no such agreement has yet been approved by Congress. And in the 1955 Formosa Resolution, the 1957 Middle East Resolution, and the 1964 Tonkin Gulf Resolution, Congress authorized the President to use force to assist certain areas if subjected to armed attack. In the case of the Formosa Resolution, the Middle East Resolution, and the Tonkin Gulf Resolution, all were passed over the objection of at least one Congressman, Senator Wayne Morse, that the resolution amounted to an "unconstitutional pre-declaration of war." In none of these situations does the delegation issue seem to have been considered very adequately, and the practice is probably inconclusive.

Professor Wormuth, arguing largely on the basis of now defunct precedents of domestic delegation law, urges a strict anti-delegation rule.[13] But the domestic delegation analogy concerned with the limits of congressional delegation of legislative power is not only questionable today, but is also of only limited usefulness in the war power context. The President has in his own right both substantial authority to use the military abroad and authority as Commander in Chief, neither of which is present in comparable degree in the domestic delegation cases.

And in view of the great power of the President to pursue a diplomatic course leaving Congress little choice but war, and his great discretion as Commander in Chief after formal congressional authorization is given, it seems somewhat quixotic to take

13. See F. Wormuth, *The Vietnam War: The President v. The Constitution* (An Occasional Paper of the Center for the Study of Democratic Institutions 1968), at 43-53.

a rigid antidelegation stance. Moreover, there are substantial problems in any antidelegation stance as to when Congress is granting authorization with full knowledge of the circumstances. And what is the standard for too broad a delegation? Certainly the test would be unrealistic if simply one of whether discretion is left to the President, as the President probably always has the right as Commander in Chief to refuse to order American troops into combat. And unless Congress speaks to the issue, he certainly has very crucial discretion as to theater of operations, weapons systems employed, and settlement terms, any of which can be as decisive for conflict limitation as the original decision to use force.

It is hard to get away from the fact that the war power is in reality a joint executive-congressional power and that the President is always going to have a substantial discretionary role. The delegation problem is more likely to be resolved by a pattern of practice responding to felt needs than by overly neat *a priori* constitutional hypotheses. If there is to be a delegation test, I would suggest that it be one asking whether there has been meaningful participation by a Congress reasonably informed of the circumstances giving rise to the need for the use of U.S. forces.

The fourth question is: To what extent can the answers to the first three questions be resolved by the courts? Are they "political questions" or otherwise issues which it is unwise for a court to adjudicate?

The tradition of judicial review runs deep in the American system. But it is not every question that is suitable for judicial review. Considerations of lack of manageable standards and interference with another coordinate branch of government are reasons which the Supreme Court has given for declining to decide a question. These considerations frequently arise in the separation-of-powers context and are all present to some degree in judicial determination of the scope of presidential authority to use the armed forces abroad. For example, what could a court do which would not have a major adverse impact on the course of a war if it wanted to declare the war unconstitutional? This dilemma has led one ingenious advocate to argue that the court should give a declaratory judgment in such circumstances. According to him, "a declaratory judgment would give little comfort to the other side in the negotiations since the Executive can always go to the Congress for a declaration of war if the negotiations break down."[14]

If that is the case, one wonders why the need for a declaratory judgment. And in any event, the suggestion shows a most unprofessional naivete in understating the possible impact of such a ruling.

For these and other reasons, in July, 1968, a U.S. District Court in Kansas dismissed a class action instituted against the President, the Secretary of State, and the Secretary of Defense seeking a declaratory judgment that they had acted unconstitutionally in the Vietnamese War.[15] Though the scope of the President's authority to use the armed forces abroad is a constitutional question, it is a question in separation of powers with few manageable standards, often running great risk of serious interference with legitimate defense requirements, and which is probably subject to more lasting solution from the continuing interplay between the checks and powers of Congress and the President. Though I believe that a decision on the merits would uphold the constitutionality of the executive-congressional action in the Vietnam War, the refusal to adjudicate the issue is certainly the wisest course during the continuation of the conflict. There are, after all, other checks in our system than judicial review, the chief among them being the election of a president.

Let me briefly apply these tests to the constitutional issues in the Vietnam conflict. First, the present magnitude of the Vietnam War in terms of troop levels, casualties, and impact on the nation strongly militates for requiring congressional authorization. I would say that the point at which congressional authorization should be required in Vietnam was the initiation in February, 1965, of the regular interdictive air attacks against the north and the first sustained use of regular U.S. combat units in the summer and fall of 1965.

And though I believe that at the current level of hostilities con-

---

14. The context was that of the Vietnam conflict. Velvel, *The War in Viet Nam: Unconstitutional, Justiciable, and Jurisdictionally Attackable*, 16 KANSAS L. REV. 449, 484 (1968).

15. Velvel v. Johnson, 287 F. Supp. 846 (1968).

gressional authorization should be required, given the Korean experience and the breadth of Executive authority acquiesced in by both Congress and the President for the last 50 years, argument to the contrary can certainly be in good faith.

Second, congressional authorization need not and should not take the form of a formal declaration of war. A joint resolution authorizing the use of combat forces in hostilities in Vietnam, such as the Tonkin Gulf Resolution of August, 1964, is preferable and adequate. Preferable since there is no good reason to declare war, since a formal declaration of war might connote an objective of subjugating North Vietnam and thus widening the war, and since avoidance of NLF recognition at too early a stage in the negotiating process or prior to reciprocal concessions may be an important diplomatic goal. And adequate since Congress authorized President Johnson to use the armed forces "to assist any member or protocol state of SEATO requesting assistance in defense," and the President's use of U.S. forces in Vietnam pursuant to this resolution is constitutionally authorized executive-congressional action. Some argue that Congress was not aware of the magnitude of the war which it was authorizing, that the Tonkin Gulf Resolution was hurried through Congress with a sense of urgency precluding adequate consideration, that Congress was poorly informed as to the extent of attacks on American ships, and that therefore the resolution cannot be taken as sufficient congressional authorization. But the language of the resolution is certainly broad enough to include the present hostilities. It is that "Congress approves and supports the determination of the President, as Commander-in-Chief, to take all necessary measures to repel any armed attack against the forces of the United States and to prevent further aggression." And I believe that a fair reading of the congressional debates in their entirety shows that although there was confusion and disagreement about the scope of the authorization, the Congress and the Senate floor leader of the resolution, Senator Fulbright, were aware that Congress was giving the President the authority, within his discretion, to take whatever action he deemed necessary with respect to the defense of South Vietnam. In fact, that is the wording of an exchange on the floor of the Senate between Senators Fulbright and Cooper. The same exchange indicated an understanding that the resolution was intended to ratify the constitutional process requirement of article IV of the SEATO Treaty.[16]

Although consideration of the Tonkin Gulf Resolution was hasty, President Johnson went to Congress because of his awareness of doubts raised during the Korean war as a result of President Truman's failure to request formal congressional authorization. The attacks on American ships in the Gulf of Tonkin were the opportunity but not the object of the resolution.

The Tonkin Gulf Resolution has also been attacked as an invalid delegation of the congressional war power. But even if there is a constitutional requirement as to the breadth of congressional delegation of the war power to the President, a proposition open to considerable doubt, the Congress which passed the Tonkin Gulf Resolution was, I believe, reasonably informed of the circumstances giving rise to the need for the use of U.S. forces. It was aware that there was an ongoing guerrilla war in Vietnam which had been escalating since 1959, that the United States had had over 12,000 advisory troops there since 1962, a figure dra-

16. The relevant exchange was:
> MR. COOPER. . . . Does the Senator consider that in enacting this resolution we are satisfying that requirement [the constitutional processes requirement] of Article IV of the Southeast Asia Collective Defense treaty? In other words, are we now giving the President advance authority to take whatever action he may deem necessary respecting South Vietnam and its defense, or with respect to the defense of any other country included in the treaty?
> MR. FULBRIGHT. I think that is correct.
> MR. COOPER. Then, looking ahead, if the President decided that it was necessary to use such force as could lead into war, we will give that authority by this resolution?
> MR. FULBRIGHT. That is the way I would interpret it. If a situation later developed in which we thought the approval should be withdrawn, it could be withdrawn by concurrent resolution. . . .
> 110 CONG. REC. 18,409-10 (1964).

For a compilation of excerpts from the congressional debates supporting a broad interpretation of presidential authority under the Tonkin Gulf Resolution see Moore & Underwood, *The Lawfulness of United States Assistance to the Republic of Viet Nam*, 112 CONG. REC. 14,943, 14,960-67, 14,983-89 (daily ed. July 14, 1966). For a highly selective compilation of excerpts suggesting a narrower interpretation see Velvel, note 1 *supra*, at 473-77. To resolve the controversy, a reading of the debates in their entirety is suggested.

matically on the increase since then, and that recently the President had ordered retaliatory air strikes on facilities in the north. As such, Congress was validly exercising its war power no matter how desirable or illuminating additional debate might have been.

Although there are, as indicated, difficulties in reading too much into appropriation measures or other indicia of congressional authorization, the subsequent refusal to repeal the Tonkin Gulf Resolution and passage of military appropriation measures also lend some congressional authority to President Johnson's actions. This is particularly true of the $700-million special Vietnam appropriation measure of May, 1965. This measure, requested shortly after President Johnson's major step-up of the U.S. response, was billed as an opportunity for expression of congressional opinion on the buildup.

Lastly, although there are those who argue for judicial review of the constitutionality of the authorization of the use of American forces in Vietnam, the lack of standards, the availability of other checks in the system, and the possibly grave impact on the course of negotiations strongly suggest the lack of wisdom of judicial review of such questions while the war continues. Without passing judgment on all future questions which may arise, the constitutional questions involved in the use of the armed forces in Vietnam should best be left to resolution between Congress and the President and almost certainly will be.

If in grappling with these questions there is a complexity that tends to overwhelm, or if we vacillate from time to time in our thinking as to precisely where the line should be drawn, we can take comfort in Arthur Schlesinger, Jr.'s point that sometimes the genuine intellectual difficulty of a question makes a degree of vacillation and mind changing eminently reasonable.

CHAPTER XII

Congress and the Use of the Armed Forces Abroad*

THE constitutional issues surrounding the use of the armed forces abroad have been a subject of controversy throughout our history. One reason for this continuing controversy is the vagueness and complementarity of the constitutional grants of power to Congress and the President. Another reason is that for the most part the constitutional issues surrounding use of the armed forces abroad have not been suitable for judicial determination.[1] As a result, resolution of the issues has been left largely to the wisdom and restraint of Congress and the President. It is important that both branches continue to exercise that wisdom and restraint.

The starting point in attempting to define the proper scope of congressional and presidential authority is the language of the Constitution. It provides that "Congress shall have Power . . . to declare War," and that the President "shall be Commander-in-Chief." Since no constitutional language is self-interpreting, particularly the broad brush strokes with which the framers set out the war powers, constitutional history, the practice of successive Congresses and Presidents, changed global conditions, and functional distinctions between Congress and the Executive are all relevant to defining constitutional policy.[2] Sound policy also re-

---

* Delivered as testimony before the Subcommittee on National Security Policy and Scientific Developments of the House Committee on Foreign Affairs, June 25, 1970.

1. See Mora v. McNamara, 389 U.S. 934 (1967); Mitchell v. United States, 386 U.S. 972 (1967). See also Moore, *The Justiciability of Challenges to the Use of Military Forces Abroad*, 10 VA. J. INT'L L. 85 (1969).

2. See Reveley, *Presidential War-Making: Constitutional Prerogative or Usurpation?*, 55 VA. L. REV. 1243 (1969).

   Plain meaning is an illusory goal in the interpretation of a document, such as the Constitution, which governs the continuing conduct of an immensely complex process in language notable for its abstraction, complementarity and frequent failure to speak to vital issues. Such a document must receive much of its meaning from sources other than its wording.

   Id. at 1251.

quires an adequate analytic framework which focuses on the range of issues in the use of armed forces abroad. Inadequate focus on the full range of issues may lead to an overgeneralized response which threatens the proper balance between congressional and presidential authority. Since a host of informative studies have provided a useful historical background,[3] this paper will focus on a framework for analysis of the constitutional issues, and on each, will make policy recommendations for clarifying the congressional and Executive roles. The principal issues in defining the congressional and presidential roles seem to include the following:

The Initial Commitment of the Armed Forces to Combat Abroad:

What authority does the President, acting on his own, have to commit the armed forces to combat abroad?

When Congressional authorization is necessary, what form should it take?

What authority does Congress have to limit Presidential authority to commit the armed forces to combat abroad?

The Conduct of Hostilities:

What authority does the President, acting on his own, have to make command decisions incident to the conduct of a constitutionally authorized conflict?

What authority does Congress have to limit command op-

---

3. See generally on the constitutional issues and their historical background: Kurland, *The Impotence of Reticence*, 1968 DUKE L.J. 619; Moore, *The National Executive and the Use of the Armed Forces Abroad*, 21 NAVAL WAR COLLEGE REV. 28 (1969); Reveley, *supra* note 2; Rogers, *World Policing and the Constitution* in 11 AMERICA LOOKS AHEAD (World Peace Foundation 1945); Velvel, *The War in Viet Nam: Unconstitutional, Justiciable and Jurisdictionally Attackable*, 16 KANSAS L. REV. 449 (1968); Francis D. Wormuth, *The Vietnam War: The President v. The Constitution* (An Occasional Paper of the Center for the Study of Democratic Institutions, 1968); Note, *Congress, The President, and the Power to Commit Forces to Combat*, 81 HARV. L. REV. 1771 (1968); Symposium, *The Constitution and the Use of Military Force Abroad*, 10 VA. J. INT'L L. 32 (1970); *Hearings Before the Committee on Foreign Relations of the United States Senate on Senate Resolution 151*, 90TH CONG., 1ST SESS., U.S. COMMITMENTS TO FOREIGN POWERS (Comm. Print 1967).

tions incident to the conduct of a constitutionally authorized conflict?

The Termination of Hostilities:

What authority does the President, acting on his own, have to terminate or negotiate an end to hostilities?

What authority does Congress have to require termination of hostilities?

On each of these issues I will briefly explore the constitutional history and practice and suggest what I believe to be policy-responsive conclusions.

The Initial Commitment of the Armed Forces to Combat Abroad: What authority does the President, acting on his own, have to commit the armed forces to combat abroad? The Constitution provides that "Congress shall have Power . . . to declare War. . . ." It seems evident from Madison's notes on the debates in the Constitutional Convention that the power to commit the nation to war was to be lodged in Congress. Though the question of what constituted "war" for purposes of requiring congressional action was not clarified, it was suggested by Madison that the President was to have authority to repel sudden attacks.[4] In general, constitutional practice in the eighteenth and nineteenth centuries supported only a minor presidential role in the commitment of troops to hostilities abroad. Though there were a large number of exercises of presidential authority, most were relatively minor actions for the protection of nationals, actions directed against pirates, or reprisals for alleged breach of international law. Prevailing conditions, which included the geographical isolation of the United States, a limited military technology, and a European balance of power, were conducive to a United States policy of relative isolation which may have been a contributing factor in the relatively minor presidential role. Practice within the last seventy years, however, has supported a stronger presidential role. Instances of presidential commitment of the armed forces to combat abroad include President McKinley's commitment of several thousand troops to the international army which rescued western nationals during the Boxer rebellion, Pres-

---

4. 5 ELLIOT'S DEBATES 438-39 (1845).

ident Wilson's arming of American merchantmen with instructions to fire on sight after Germany's resumption of unrestricted submarine warfare in 1917, President Franklin Roosevelt's Atlantic war against the Axis prior to the United States entry into World War II, President Truman's commitment of a quarter of a million American men to the Korean war, President Kennedy's commitment of substantial numbers of military advisory personnel to Vietnam, and President Johnson's commitment of marines to the Dominican Republic.[5] Changed global conditions which seem to have contributed to this growth in the presidential role include an increasing global defense interdependence, an explosion in military technology, a shift from a relatively stable to a revolutionary international system, and a growth in internal conflict as a principal source of conflict between competing world order blocs.

In spite of changed global conditions, the expanded presidential role may have gone too far. In particular, the waging of a sustained major war in the Korean conflict without explicit congressional authorization, a war in which the United States sustained more than 140,000 casualties, seems a poor precedent.[6] On the

5. Rogers pointed out in his *World Policing and the Constitution* in 1945:

> A review of our history is a little surprising. Congress has never declared war except as a consequence of the President's acts or recommendation. It has never refused to authorize war when requested by him. Four of our nine serious and extended engagements with force against another nation were conducted without Congress "declaring war" at all. In fact Congress has never in any case "declared war" in a strict sense. It has merely recognized the prior existence of the fact. . . .

Rogers, *supra* note 3 at 45.

6. Though President Truman did not obtain explicit congressional authorization for the Korean war, Congress in fact supported the war. Had Congress actively opposed Truman's action it seems doubtful that the President could have continued the war. Truman may also have had some increased authority as a result of senate consent to ratification of the United Nations Charter followed by United Nations support for the Korean action. In fact, Senator Douglas presented a paper to Congress on the constitutional basis for the President's action in using armed forces to repel the attacks against South Korea in which he concluded that despite the absence of Congressional authorization the President's action was "in thorough harmony with the legislative

other hand, experience does suggest a real need for some independent presidential authority in committing troops to combat abroad. Thus, there may be a need for defense against sudden attacks on American forces abroad, sudden attacks on areas which the United States is committed by treaty to defend, minor commitments such as humanitarian intervention or the protection of nationals, defensive actions such as the Cuban missile crisis requiring secrecy and negotiating responsiveness, and "ongoing command decisions" concerning day-to-day operations of military assistance programs or defensive deployment of American forces. These may all be areas in which the need for decisiveness, speed, secrecy, negotiating responsiveness, or simply the difficulty in informing Congress on a day-to-day basis call for some room for presidential authority.

If the issue of independent presidential authority is not one of absolutes, and neither constitutional language nor practice suggests that it is, the real need is for criteria delimiting the congressional and presidential roles. Elsewhere I have suggested as a test that congressional authorization might be required "in all cases where regular combat units are committed to sustained hostilities."[7] This test would include all of the wars declared by Congress as well as the Korean and Vietnam Wars. A principal virtue of the test is that it focuses on just those conflicts which have required a substantial commitment of American blood and treasure and which have historically been the most controversial. Like all tests it is somewhat frayed at the edges, but in most cases it should be reasonably workable. In conflicts like the Korean war, in which there may be a genuine need for speed, the President would be required to submit his action to congressional scrutiny at the earliest opportunity. And in conflicts which gradually escalate, the dividing line for requiring congressional authorization might be the initial commitment to combat of regular United

---

intent of the framers of the Constitution" and "in line with sound historical precedent." Douglas, *The Constitutional and Legal Basis for the President's Action in using Armed Forces to Repel the Invasion of South Korea*, 96 CONG. REC. 9,647, 9,649 (1950).

7. Moore, *supra* note 3 at 32. See also the more complete discussion of alternatives for drawing this line in Note, *supra* note 3 at 1744-1803.

States combat units as such. The judgment that Congress should oversee the nation's involvement in major hostilities abroad remains as valid today as it was in 1789. Implementation of that policy, however, should not destroy needed presidential flexibility.

The second issue is, when congressional authorization is necessary what form should it take? Though the Constitution speaks of congressional power "to declare War," constitutional scholars are in substantial agreement that congressional authorization does not require a formal declaration of war.[8] The purpose of the constitutional provision is to ensure congressional consideration and authorization of decisions to commit the United States to major hostilities abroad. It would both elevate form over substance and unduly restrict congressional flexibility to require a formal declaration of war as the only modality of congressional authorization. Constitutional practice strongly supports this conclusion. In the early days of the Republic, Congress authorized hostilities in the naval war with France and in the protection of American shipping from attacks by Tripoli and Algiers without formally declaring war. Though there was a later formal declaration of war, the Spanish-American War was initiated by a joint resolution authorizing the President to use force to carry the resolution into effect. And since World War II Congress has repeatedly authorized the President to use force to resist armed attacks against certain areas. Examples include the 1955 Formosa Resolution, the 1957 Middle East Resolution, and the 1964 Southeast Asia Resolution. Such resolutions authorizing limited hostilities or delegating authority to the President are constitutional options open to Congress. In exercising its congressional responsibility, however, Congress should carefully consider the context giving rise to its authorization and should clearly advert to the scope of the authority granted. Thus, as Taylor Reveley has written:

8. See, *e.g.*, Reveley, *supra* note 2 at 1289. See also the *Report of the Senate Committee on Foreign Relations*, 90TH CONG., 1ST SESS., NATIONAL COMMITMENTS 25 (Report No. 797, November 20, 1967). "The committee does not believe that formal declarations of war are the only available means by which Congress can authorize the President to initiate limited or general hostilities." *Ibid.*

A joint resolution, signed by the President, is the most tenable method of authorizing the use of force today. To be meaningful, the resolution should be passed only after Congress is aware of the basic elements of the situation, and has had reasonable time to consider their implications. The resolution should not, as a rule, be a blank check leaving the place, purpose and duration of hostilities to the President's sole discretion. To be realistic, however, the resolution must leave the Executive wide discretion to respond to changing circumstances. If the legislators wish to delegate full responsibility to the President, it appears that such action would be within the constitutional pale so long as Congress delegates with full awareness of the authority granted.[9]

Since the formal declaration of war is itself nothing more than a delegation of authority to the President to use the armed forces abroad in pursuit of a particular objective, the real issue as to form of congressional authorization seems to be one of constitutional policy regarding the process and scope of congressional authorization rather than one of formal declaration of war versus non-formal authorization or delegation of authority versus non-delegation.

Process criteria for effective authorization would seem to include adequate deliberation by Congress, awareness of the context giving rise to the use of force, and awareness of the scope of the authorization. Noncompliance with these criteria both needlessly detracts from the constitutional responsibility of Congress and creates a risk that the resolution will be an unstable basis for presidential reliance when most needed. With respect to the scope of congressional authorization, it would usually seem a minimum requirement that Congress state the objective of the use of force. Additional requirements might include limitations as to area of permissible belligerent activities, kinds of activities authorized, and duration of the authorization. Such additional requirements, however, should not be such as to limit needed flexibility of the President to respond to changed circumstances or to interfere with the President's power to make command decisions inci-

9. Reveley, *supra* note 2 at 1289-90.

dent to successful prosecution of the war. The recommendations of the Senate Foreign Relations Committee concerning congressional authorization of the use of armed forces abroad are useful in this regard. The Committee Report of the National Commitments Hearings recommends:

> ... that, in considering future resolutions involving the use or possible use of the armed forces, Congress—
> (1) debate the proposed resolution at sufficient length to establish a legislative record showing the intent of Congress;
> (2) use the words authorize or empower or such other language as will leave no doubt that Congress alone has the right to authorize the initiation of war and that, in granting the President authority to use the armed forces, Congress is granting him power that he would not otherwise have;
> (3) state in the resolution as explicitly as possible under the circumstances the kind of military action that is being authorized and the place and purpose of its use; and
> (4) put a time limit on the resolution, thereby assuring Congress the opportunity to review its decision and extend or terminate the President's authority to use military force.[10]

The suggestion that Congress should always place a time limit on authorizations may be overly rigid, at least for contexts in which Congress is authorizing the immediate use of force as opposed to authorizing a possible use of force at some future time. And the possible inference that the President does not have any independent authority to use the armed forces in situations short of war would be erroneous. In general, though, the recommendations of the Foreign Relations Committee are a useful starting point concerning the form of congressional authorization.

Third, what authority does Congress have to limit presidential authority to commit the armed forces to combat abroad? At a minimum, that authority includes authority to repel sudden attacks on the United States or United States forces. Both constitutional experience and policy suggest that presidential authority also extends to a range of activities short of war and to responses to situations of genuine emergency in which prior congressional

10. Report, NATIONAL COMMITMENTS, *supra* note 8 at 26.

authorization is not possible. Congress certainly has the authority to limit presidential use of the armed forces abroad in areas which fall within exclusive congressional authority. Using my earlier test, I believe that Congress clearly would have the authority to prohibit presidential commitment of regular combat units to sustained hostilities abroad. In areas which do not fall within exclusive congressional authority, it is unclear whether Congress could limit presidential authority. At least one scholar suggests that such a limitation would be unconstitutional.[11] It may be urged, of course, that Congress could limit presidential authority by virtue of its power "to raise and support Armies," "to provide and maintain a Navy" and to appropriate funds for federal expenditures. As a matter of constitutional policy, however, it is not clear that such powers authorize limitation of the President's independent authority to commit armed forces to combat.

With respect to congressional authority to limit presidential authority, constitutional practice offers little help. There seem to be few instances in which Congress has sought to place prior restraints on Executive action. One such restraint was enacted by Congress as a proviso to the Selective Training and Service Act of 1940. It provided: "Persons inducted into the land forces of the United States under this Act shall not be employed beyond the limits of the Western Hemisphere except in the Territories and possessions of the United States, including the Philippine Islands."[12] The proviso was repealed shortly after the outbreak of World War II. A second restraint was enacted by Congress in 1969 as a section of the Defense Appropriation Act. It provides that: "In line with the expressed intention of the President of the United States, none of the funds appropriated by this Act shall be used to finance the introduction of American ground combat

---

11. Professor Quincy Wright indicates that if the President considers: action essential for the enforcement of acts of Congress and treaties and for the protection of the citizens and territory of the United States, the President is obliged by the Constitution itself to use his power as commander-in-chief to direct the forces abroad, and this duty resting on the Constitution itself cannot be taken away by act of Congress.
 Q. WRIGHT, THE CONTROL OF AMERICAN FOREIGN RELATIONS 307 (1922).
12. Act of September 16, 1940 (54 Stat. 885, 886).

troops into Laos or Thailand."[13] Except for possible interference with the power of the President to make command decisions incident to hostilities in Vietnam, this recent restraint on commitment of ground combat troops to Laos or Thailand seems close to the core area of congressional power.[14] As such, it is not a particularly helpful precedent for more sweeping congressional limitation of presidential authority. In any event, even if Congress has authority to limit all presidential authority to commit troops to combat abroad, the same constitutional policies which suggest some independent presidential authority also suggest that except in extreme cases of presidential abuse Congress should not place prior restraints on presidential authority. Overly specific congressional attempts to mark off congressional and presidential roles in the commitment of armed forces to combat are probably a mistake. Functional reasons inherent in the presidency suggest that it is important to preserve an area of presidential flexibility short of the commitment of regular combat units to sustained hostilities. It does not seem possible to adequately anticipate and delimit each issue on which independent presidential authority to use the armed forces abroad should be preserved. The felt necessities of the time rather than overly neat *a priori* constitutional hypothesis would seem a better guide to congressional action.

The Conduct of Hostilities: What authority does the President, acting on his own, have to make command decisions incident to the conduct of a constitutionally authorized conflict? The Constitution provides that "the President shall be Commander-in-Chief of the Army and Navy of the United States. . . ." Hamilton wrote in *The Federalist* that this provision means that the President has "the supreme command and direction of the military and naval forces. . . ."[15] It seems never to have been questioned that this

13. 83 Stat. 469 (1969).
14. This is true at least to the extent that the Act is aimed prospectively at preventing the commitment of regular United States combat troops to sustained hostilities in defense of the governments of Laos or Thailand. To the extent that it prevents defensive action against North Vietnamese and Vietcong border sanctuaries which become a threat to the conduct of the Vietnam War, however, the Act may be an unconstitutional restraint on the presidential command power.
15. THE FEDERALIST, Number 69 at 463 (Heritage Press 1945).

power includes broad authority to make strategic and tactical decisions incident to the conduct of a constitutionally authorized conflict. Constitutional practice includes a range of presidential command decisions unquestionably taken on presidential authority. Examples include President Roosevelt's decision in World War II to give priority to the Atlantic rather than the Pacific theater, Roosevelt's decisions committing American forces to landings in French North Africa, Italy, and the Pacific Islands, and President Truman's decision to use the atomic bomb against Japan.

In an era of limited war, the President's authority to take command decisions incident to an ongoing conflict should not be absolute. One obvious example is that he should not have authority to bomb Peking incident to the Indo-China War. Such a response runs a high risk of triggering a greatly enlarged war or even World War III. Short of such horribles, however, the President should be accorded substantial latitude in making strategic and tactical decisions incident to a constitutionally authorized conflict. Criteria for permissible presidential command decisions might include consistency with initial objectives in authorizing the use of force, whether the response is confined to actions against forces already committed as active belligerents, and whether the action runs a high risk of major escalation. Though it is always advisable for the President to inform congressional leaders of planned major strategic decisions, there is little doubt that President Nixon was acting within his constitutional authority to take command decisions incident to the Vietnam War when he ordered limited action against North Vietnamese and Vietcong border sanctuaries in Cambodia. Such actions were taken in response to repeated attacks from Cambodian staging areas, were limited to support of the effort in Vietnam, received at least the tacit consent of the government of Cambodia, and were directed against the principal belligerents in the war.[16]

16. In fact, some features of the context bear a striking similarity to President Roosevelt's decision as Commander in Chief to land American forces in French North Africa during World War II. In both cases the incursions took place in an at least nominally neutral state being used by opposing belligerent forces. For a discussion of the legal issues involved in the Cambodian incursion see Chapter X.

Second, what authority does Congress have to limit command options incident to the conduct of a constitutionally authorized conflict? The Constitution makes the President Commander in Chief. There is no parallel in the powers entrusted to Congress. Professors Egger and Harris in their study of *The President and Congress* conclude that this plan means:

> ... the President has the ... exclusive power ... of exercising military command in time of peace and in time of war; this command power, moreover, involves as an absolute minimum, upon which the Congress is powerless to encroach, the direction of military forces in combat. ...[17]

Corwin points out that "Congress has never adopted any legislation that would seriously cramp the style of a President attempting to break the resistance of an enemy or seeking to assure the safety of the national forces."[18] In fact, Roland Young reports that during World War II:

> No method was worked out by which Congress as a whole was informed on the developments of the war, and, in the aggregate, members of Congress had no more intimate knowledge of how the war was going than the average reader of a metropolitan newspaper.[19]

In addition to the textual grant of power to the President as Commander in Chief and the uninterrupted constitutional practice supporting an exclusively presidential command power, there are strong policy reasons inherent in the nature of Congress and the presidency that support the exclusive nature of the presidential power. Tactical decisions incident to an ongoing conflict are frequently decisions on which speed, secrecy, superior sources of information, and military expertise are at a premium. In general the presidency seems better suited to such decisions than Congress. To give one example, Roland Young reports that the one attempt at a secret session of the Senate during World War II resulted in a garbled version of the session being leaked to the

17. R. EGGER & J. HARRIS, THE PRESIDENT AND CONGRESS 35 (1963).
18. E. CORWIN, THE PRESIDENT: OFFICE AND POWERS 1787-1957 259 (1957).
19. R. YOUNG, CONGRESSIONAL POLITICS IN THE SECOND WORLD WAR 145 (1956).

press.[20] Perhaps for these reasons Hamilton writes in *The Federalist*: "Of all the cares or concerns of government, the direction of war most peculiarly demands those qualities which distinguish the exercise of power by a single hand."[21]

Despite the strong case for denying congressional authority to limit presidential command options incident to a constitutionally authorized conflict, it seems unwise to take an absolute position. That the reasons for exclusive presidential authority are strong does not necessarily mean that all congressional decisions limiting command options would be unconstitutional in an era of limited war. One example of a permissible limitation might be a congressional prohibition on the use of internationally prohibited chemical or biological weapons. Though reasons suggesting executive authority are still relevant to such decisions, the profound effects on international relations and the grave risk of escalation and unnecessary suffering suggest a strong congressional competence in such decisions. In any event, the command of the armed forces during a constitutionally authorized conflict is a core area of presidential authority and has apparently never been limited by congressional action. Congressional limitation of such command options would usually be most unwise and would in every case bear a heavy burden of constitutional justification. In this respect, a congressional limitation of the President's authority to order attacks on North Vietnamese and Vietcong border sanctuaries in Cambodia or Laos would seem highly doubtful.[22] That such a limitation of presidential command authority is pur-

20. *Id.* at 145.

21. THE FEDERALIST, Number 74, 497 (Heritage Press 1945).

22. See the letter from Professors Eugene V. Rostow, Ralph K. Winter, Jr., and Robert H. Bork of the Yale Law School to Senator Gordon Allott, May 26, 1970.

> The constitutional validity of congressional action limiting the President's discretion with respect to the attack upon the Cambodian sanctuaries seems highly dubious. Given the use of Cambodia as a sanctuary from which military operations against United States forces have been and are undertaken and the attitude of the present Cambodian government, the President's order to clean out the bases there was a tactical decision and, therefore, within his exclusive powers as Commander-in-Chief.

Id. at 1.

sued indirectly by limitations on appropriations would not seem to significantly alter congressional power. Appropriations measures, as much as any other congressional measures, must conform to the limits of the Constitution.

The Termination of Hostilities: The first issue concerning the termination of hostilities is what authority does the President, acting on his own, have to terminate or negotiate an end to hostilities? Both the power of the President as Commander in Chief and his power as chief representative of the nation in foreign affairs support presidential authority to terminate or negotiate an end to hostilities. At least in the absence of congressional action, the President's authority seems clear. Corwin states that:

> The President has . . . the power of any supreme commander to terminate hostilities by arranging an armistice, a power that has at times blended into and merged with his theoretically distinct power as the sole organ of diplomatic relations to negotiate the final peace.[23]

Examples of presidential exercise of this power include President McKinley's protocol with the Spanish government which foreshadowed the Peace of Paris, President Roosevelt's participation in the succession of conferences which terminated World War II and set post-war policy, and President Eisenhower's negotiation of the agreement on the cessation of hostilities which terminated the Korean war.

The second issue concerning termination is what authority does Congress have to require termination of hostilities? The text of the Constitution offers little guidance on the congressional power to terminate hostilities. Nevertheless, it seems a fair inference from the power to declare war, the power to raise and maintain an army and a navy, and the power to authorize appropriations that Congress has authority to terminate hostilities abroad. Though there is little constitutional practice on the issue, there is at least one incident which suggests this conclusion. In 1919, a resolution was introduced in the Senate to express the opinion of the Senate that American troops, then engaged in an international intervention in the Russian Civil War, should be withdrawn. The

23. See Corwin, *supra* note 18 at 259.

resolution provided: "That in the opinion of the Senate the soldiers of the United States as soon as practicable should be withdrawn from Russia."[24] The resolution was tabled, but only when the Chair cast the deciding vote to break a 33-to-33 tie.[25] The cautious wording of the resolution merely expressing an "opinion of the Senate," and the fact that the resolution did not pass, limit the usefulness of the incident as a precedent for congressional authority. A House version which also did not pass, however, read: "That the President be, and hereby is, instructed to withdraw at once all American troops now on Russian soil."[26] Assuming that Congress has constitutional authority to terminate hostilities, it must not exercise that authority in a manner which would interfere with the power of the President as Commander in Chief to safeguard American armed forces during withdrawal. Similarly, a congressional policy for termination of hostilities which conflicts with a presidential policy should be adopted only with the greatest reluctance. The President has substantial independent authority in foreign affairs and is the chief representative of the nation in negotiating settlement of hostilities. To the extent that Congress adopts a separate policy, it may seriously undercut presidential ability to represent the nation or to achieve a negotiated settlement. Specifically, proposals to require withdrawal of United States troops from Vietnam by a particular date would seem to dangerously undercut the presidential negotiating role. Though such proposals may be constitutional in a formal sense, they should be adopted only if Congress has strong reason to doubt the wisdom of presidential policies.

The constitutional division of powers between Congress and the President, then, suggests a need for cooperation rather than conflict. For his part, the President should be sensitive to the major congressional role in authorizing the initial commitment of combat forces to sustained hostilities abroad. Similarly, the President should be sensitive to the need to consult and inform members of Congress of important decisions, even in areas which may be committed exclusively to presidential authority. It might be use-

24. 57 CONG. REC. 3334 (Feb. 14, 1919).
25. *Id.* at 3342.   26. *Id.* at 4066.

ful in this regard to institute regular meetings between the President and congressional leaders during the course of major conflicts.[27]

For its part, Congress should be sensitive to the predominantly presidential role in the conduct of hostilities and the need to retain some presidential flexibility to commit the armed forces abroad in situations short of commitment of regular combat troops to sustained hostilities. Functional advantages inherent in the presidency strongly support presidential authority in both these areas. Since it does not seem possible to adequately anticipate and delimit each issue on which independent presidential authority to use the armed forces abroad should be preserved, overly specific congressional attempts to mark off the presidential roles are probably a mistake. Finally, even in areas which may be subject to overriding congressional authority, Congress should be extremely reluctant to undercut the ability of the President to represent the nation in foreign affairs or to achieve a negotiated settlement of hostilities.

Congress is understandably concerned with maintaining its proper role with respect to the use of the armed forces abroad. The best way to maintain that role is to make sure that congressional authorization of commitments to sustained hostilities are adequately deliberated, are undertaken with awareness of the context giving rise to the use of force, and clearly indicate the scope of congressional authorization. And in its concern to maintain its proper role Congress should not unduly limit needed presidential flexibility. Overly specific legislation, passed during the heat of the Vietnam debates, runs a risk of seriously limiting that flexibility. History teaches that a division of powers between both Congress and the President is better calculated to lead to wise decisions than exclusive reliance on either branch alone.

27. Roland Young says of the World War II experience:
> A case can be made for the proposition that the failure to inform Congress of major decisions and significant developments in the military-political sphere of action may lead to an erosion of confidence between the President and Congress.

R. YOUNG, *supra* note 19 at 232.

CHAPTER XIII

The Justiciability of
Challenges to the Use of
Military Forces Abroad*

To his colleagues from abroad, the American lawyer seems to
have an extraordinary preoccupation with the judicial process.
Whether because of the major role of the Supreme Court in the
American system, the strength of the common law tradition, or
the dominance of the Langdell-Ames case method of instruction
in American law schools, it is second nature for the American lawyer to turn to the courts for solution of major issues. It is not surprising, then, that the controversy surrounding the Vietnam war
has given rise to a multitude of cases in American courts. These
cases have arisen in a variety of contexts, including prosecution
for refusal to be inducted,[1] prosecution for destroying Selective
Service records or other acts of civil disobedience against the
war,[2] suits by servicemen to prevent their being sent to Vietnam,[3]

---

* This Chapter is a revised version of a paper presented at a Regional
Meeting of the American Society of International Law on "The Constitution and the Use of Military Force Abroad" at the University of Virginia, Feb. 28—March 1, 1969. I am indebted to Professor Peter W. Low
for his helpful suggestions on the earlier paper.

1. See, *e.g.*, Mitchell v. United States, 386 U.S. 972 (1967); Kemp v. United
States, 415 F.2d 1185 (5th Cir. 1969); United States v. Owens, 415 F.2d
1308 (6th Cir. 1969); United States v. Sisson, 294 F. Supp. 511, 515, 520
(D. Mass. 1969), *prob. juris. noted*, 38 U.S.L.W. 3113 (U.S. Oct. 13,
1969); United States v. Gillette, 420 F.2d 298 (2d Cir. 1970).

2. See, *e.g.*, United States v. Rehfield, 416 F.2d 273 (9th Cir. 1969); United
States v. Spock, 416 F.2d 165 (1st Cir. 1969); United States v. Berrigan,
283 F. Supp. 336 (D. Md. 1968), 417 F.2d 1002 (4th Cir. 1969), *appeal
dismissed*, 38 U.S.L.W. (U.S. Feb. 24, 1970).

3. See, *e.g.*, Mora v. McNamara, 389 U.S. 934 (1967). Massachusetts recently
passed an Act requiring the State Attorney General to bring suit to
prevent servicemen from Massachusetts from being required:
> [t]o serve outside the territorial limits of the United States in the
> conduct of armed hostilities not an emergency and not otherwise
> authorized in the powers granted to the President of the United
> States in Article 2, Section 2, of the Constitution of the United

and taxpayer suits seeking injunctions to end American involvement.[4] Though the diversity of the contexts in which these cases arise assures a large number of legal issues, four major claims seem to run through most of these cases. They are claims that American involvement has not been constitutionally authorized; that American participation is in violation of international law; that the method of conducting hostilities violates international law; and that participation in the war will entail personal responsibility under the Nuremberg principles.[5] To date, these claims

---

States designating the President as the Commander-in-Chief, unless such hostilities were initially authorized or subsequently ratified by a congressional declaration of war according to the constitutionally established procedures in Article 1, Section 8, of the Constitution of the United States.

The Act, which was accompanied by much publicity, is intended to force Supreme Court consideration of the justiciability of the constitutional issues in the use of United States troops in the Vietnam War. Though it may achieve its objective of requiring the Court to fully consider the justiciability issue, the implication in the Act that the only congressional authorization of the use of armed forces abroad which is constitutionally permissible is a formal declaration of war, may make the Act unconstitutional. [1970] Mass. Acts Ch. 174.

4. See, *e.g.*, Velvel v. Johnson, 287 F. Supp. 846 (D. Kan. 1968).

5. A fifth claim is that one who is conscientiously opposed to participation in a particular war may not constitutionally be conscripted for combat service in that war. In United States v. Sisson, 297 F. Supp. 902 (D. Mass. 1969), Judge Wyzanski held that the free exercise of religion clause of the First Amendment and the due process clause of the Fifth Amendment constitutionally barred the conscription for combat service in Vietnam of one who was conscientiously opposed to the war. In doing so, Judge Wyzanski drew a distinction between declared and undeclared wars and foreign wars and wars in defense of the homeland.

[T]his Court . . . assumes that a conscientious objector, religious or otherwise, may be conscripted for some kinds of service in peace or in war. This court further assumes that in time of declared war or in defense of the homeland against invasion, all persons may be conscripted even for combat service.

Id. at 908. Anticipating an appeal to the Supreme Court, Judge Wyzanski also based the decision on the conclusion that the distinction in the 1967 Selective Service Act between religious conscientious objectors and those objecting on other grounds violates the free exercise and establishment clauses of the First Amendment. Judge Wyzanski's holding has enormous significance for the constitutional law concerning conscientious objection, but seems to be confined in its impact to the operation of the selective service laws.

have been treated as nonjusticiable "political questions" by every domestic court which has considered them. And the Supreme Court, by refusing to grant *certiorari* to review them, has acquiesced in this judgment, albeit without reasons.[6]

During the past few years several articles have been written taking the courts to task for refusing to meet these issues on the merits.[7] Professor Warren Schwartz articulately presents this point of view when he says:

> In the Vietnam case the personal stakes could not be higher. The litigants are being directed to place their lives in jeopardy and perhaps even take the lives of others in a conflict they assert to be illegal and immoral.[8]

If the judiciary, the organ of government most fundamen-

On appeal by the government, the Supreme Court dismissed the appeal for lack of jurisdiction on narrow procedural grounds. United States v. Sisson, 399 U.S. 267 (1970). For the Solicitor General's Memorandum to the Supreme Court in the *Sisson* case, see 8 INT'L LEG. MAT. 1248 (1969).

The jury nullification issue, argued by William Kunstler during the course of the panel on "The Use of Domestic Courts to Challenge Employment of Military Force Abroad," might be listed as a sixth claim. It arises, however, only in cases presented to a jury and is largely a dispute about the breadth of the judge's charge to the jury. Among other problems, the Kunstler position raises serious questions about location of prescriptive competence in a democratic system and uniformity in the administration of justice. So far he has not persuasively answered either question. See Kunstler, *Jury Nullification in Conscience Cases*, 10 VA. J. INT'L L. 71 (1969).

6. See Mora v. McNamara, 389 U.S. 934 (1967) (in brief opinions Justices Stewart and Douglas dissented from the denial of *certiorari*); Mitchell v. United States, 386 U.S. 972 (1967) (in a brief opinion Mr. Justice Douglas dissented from the denial of *certiorari*).

7. See Schwartz & McCormack, *The Justiciability of Legal Objections to the American Military Effort in Vietnam*, 46 TEXAS L. REV. 1033 (1968); Velvel, *The War in Viet Nam: Unconstitutional, Justiciable and Jurisdictionally Attackable*, 16 KANSAS L. REV. 449 (1968). See also Henkin, *Viet-Nam in the Courts of the United States: "Political Questions,"* 63 AM. J. INT'L L. 284 (1969); Forman, *The Nuremberg Trials and Conscientious Objection to War: Justiciability under United States Municipal Law*, 1969 PROC. AM. SOC'Y INT'L L. 157. The proceedings of the complete panel on "The Nuremberg Trials and Objection to Military Service in Viet-Nam," are also useful. See *id.* at 140-81.

8. Schwartz & McCormack, *supra* note 7, at 1045.

tally committed to the vindication of constitutional principle, decides it cannot play its accustomed role in the Vietnam controversy, our basic institutional alternative to lawlessness is lost.[9]

While agreeing with Professor Schwartz and others who urge that the judiciary should fairly meet the challenge, I believe that they greatly oversimplify the difficulties in judicial decision on the merits of these major claims. First, they have focused largely on the constitutional rather than the international law claims and as a result have failed to adequately consider the full range of problems inherent in judicial decision of the Vietnam issues. Second, even on the constitutional issue, they have not adequately taken into account the reasons for judicial abstention stemming from the separation of powers and the nature of the judicial process. This is not to suggest that the opposite extreme, that there is no role for the judiciary in considering challenges to the use of military forces abroad, is correct, but only that the issues are a great deal more difficult than has yet been admitted by the proponents of either position. Similarly, to suggest that fundamental policies may sometimes favor abstention is not to suggest that courts should stand mute about their reasons for decision. In a democratic society there are strong reasons for judicial candor in decision-making.[10] And like all other judicial decisions, decisions

---

9. *Id.* at 1036. Professor Schwartz overstates the case when he implies that challenges to the use of the armed forces abroad are the "accustomed role" of the judiciary. There is an abundance of sweeping judicial language, which probably overstates the case in the other direction, suggesting no role at all for the judiciary in this area. For example, Mr. Justice Jackson, writing for the Court in *Johnson v. Eisentrager*, 339 U.S. 763 (1950), said:
    Certainly it is not the function of the Judiciary to entertain private litigation—even by a citizen—which challenges the legality, the wisdom, or the propriety of the Commander-in-Chief in sending our armed forces abroad or to any particular region. . . .
    Id. at 789.
10. While the author does not embrace all of the arguments of Professor Herbert Wechsler in his famous "neutral principle" article, Wechsler made an important point worth emphasizing when he stressed the need for candid judicial articulation of reasons for decision. Wechsler, *Toward Neutral Principles of Constitutional Law*, 73 HARV. L. REV. 1, 20-22 (1959).

to abstain from consideration of a claim on the merits should be supported by adequate reasons rather than simply invocation of the "political question" formula or denial of *certiorari*. Such reasons, if rooted in important policies, are every bit as principled as decision on the merits. Thus, to pose the issue of abstention as one of "unspoken *ad hoc* adjustments" versus principled decision-making, as Professor Schwartz has done, is to miss the point.[11] Judge Wyzanski saw the point when, in holding that a defendant in a prosecution for refusal to be inducted could not challenge the legality of the Vietnam War, he wrote:

> It is not an act of abdication when a court says that political questions of this sort are not within its jurisdiction. It is a recognition that the tools with which a court can work, the data which it can fairly appraise, the conclusions which it can reach as a basis for entering judgments, have limits.[12]

There may also be room for Professor Bickel's judgment that the newness of some issues or the difficulty of foreseeing the limits of principle may justify some "expedient muddling through."[13] In fact, the decisions uniformly denying justiciability of challenges to the Vietnam War on what is at best sparse reasoning may be examples of this. Ultimately, however, if abstention is to be justifiable, it must be rooted in policies which command allegiance and which in their generality transcend any particular case. The real question must be what is the strength of any such policies in contexts such as Vietnam?

The Functions of Justiciability

Justiciability in its broadest sense refers to a range of policies for judicial abstention on the merits of a particular claim. These policies are inarticulately embodied in the doctrines of standing, ripeness, adversariness, and political question. Though interrelated, they can most usefully be considered as abstention because of inadequate assurance of full adversary presentation of

11. Schwartz & McCormack, *supra* note 7, at 1053.
12. United States v. Sisson, 294 F. Supp. 511, 515 (D. Mass. 1968).
13. See A. Bickel, The Least Dangerous Branch (1962); Scharpf, *Judicial Review and the Political Question: A Functional Analysis*, 75 Yale L.J. 517, 534 (1966).

the issues, and abstention because of more fundamental and less easily removed considerations stemming from the separation of powers and the limitations of the judicial process.[14]

Because of the great effect a major war has on all of us and the variety of contexts in which challenges to a war can be presented, it is safe to say that these lesser reasons for abstention, embodied in the doctrines of standing, ripeness, and adversariness, will not be present in some if not in most cases seeking to challenge the use of armed forces abroad. In the middle of the heated Vietnam debate arguments for abstention based on the danger of inadequate adversary presentation seem strangely out of place. And if the challenge is presented in a prosecution for refusal to be sent to Vietnam such arguments seem positively grotesque. As such, these lesser reasons for abstention should not bar consideration of the merits in cases in which the litigants have a personal stake in the outcome.[15]

The more fundamental policies for abstention stemming from the separation of powers and the limitations of the judicial process, however, cut across the range of contexts in which challenges to the war are made and raise persistent questions about the wisdom of judicial review of such challenges. These more fundamental policies for abstention are usually invoked by reference to the "political question" doctrine. The "political question" doctrine subsumes two different but interrelated reasons for abstention.[16] The first is simply that the decision of a particular

14. See generally authorities cited note 13 *supra*.
15. This is not to suggest that these lesser reasons for abstention might not serve useful purposes in some contexts. For example, it may be that criminal prosecution for destruction of a draft card or for refusal to be inducted is not the proper place to consider challenges to the use of military forces abroad. Whether they are or not, however, relevance rather than the danger of inadequate adversary presentation would seem the real issue. Thus, the illegality of a particular war would not necessarily taint the entire Selective Service process (or the process of collection of federal revenues), and the illegality of an object of protest would not necessarily be a valid defense to prosecution for draft card burning. See United States v. Eberhardt, 417 F.2d 1009, 1012 (4th Cir. 1969). *But see* Sax, *Civil Disobedience: The Law is Never Blind*, SATURDAY REVIEW, Sept. 28, 1968, at 22.
16. See Henkin, *supra* note 7, at 285-86; Schwartz & McCormack, *supra* note 7, at 1041.

question has been constitutionally entrusted to another branch for decision. Or perhaps a better way to state the same thing is that the court has reviewed the contested action and found that it is within the constitutional competence of the deciding branch, whether Congress, the Executive, or both. If the reasons for the judgment that the issue is constitutionally entrusted to another branch are persuasive, presumably such "abstention" would be noncontroversial. For such a decision is a decision on the merits as much as any constitutional judgment delimiting the separation of powers. The second reason for abstention is somewhat different. It is that even though the contested action may in fact violate constitutional principles, there are prudential reasons why the courts should not examine the constitutional claim.

A short framework for analysis is not the place to debate the merits of the classical theory of judicial review championed by Professor Wechsler and challenged by Professor Bickel and others. Since it bears on this second reason for abstention, however, an outline of the skirmish is a useful starting point. Professor Wechsler has argued that the courts are constitutionally compelled to decide concrete controversies on the merits unless "the Constitution has committed the determination of the issue to another agency of government than the courts."[17] Professor Bickel, on the other hand, argues that courts may constitutionally abstain from decision on the merits for a number of systemic reasons which he refers to as "the passive virtues."[18] The considerable difficulty in reconciling Supreme Court cases with Professor Wechsler's test, and the difficulty in accepting his method of arriving at it by logical derivation from the supremacy clause and the judiciary article suggest that the merits of the prudential reasons given for abstention are a better guide for decision. Thus, the most fruitful starting point for evaluating justiciability claims would seem to be the functional approach suggested by Professor Scharpf.[19] Under his approach the first task is to identify the systemic reasons for judicial abstention. Applying this

17. Wechsler, *supra* note 10, at 9.
18. See A. Bickel, *supra* note 13; Bickel, *Foreword: The Passive Virtues, Supreme Court, 1960 Term*, 75 HARV. L. REV. 40 (1961).
19. See Scharpf, *supra* note 13, at 566-97.

approach, as well as maintaining the separate focus on both types of "political question" decisions, considerations relevant to the decision to abstain on challenges to the use of military forces abroad include:

1. Has the decision been constitutionally entrusted to the discretion of another branch of government?

2. Are there prudential or systemic considerations which suggest that it would be unwise for the judiciary to decide the issue on the merits?

a. Will judicial consideration interfere with political resolution by another branch which has greater control of the problem and greater flexibility in solution?

b. Are there "judicially discoverable and manageable standards for resolving" the issue?

c. Does the court have sufficient access to information and is it suited for the problems of fact appraisal presented?

d. Would judicial consideration interfere with a need for uniformity and consistency in foreign relations?

e. Are there institutional checks in the system other than the courts which are capable of responding more sensitively to the challenge?

These considerations are suggested by analysis of the full range of "political question" cases, most recently the 1962 reapportionment case, *Baker v. Carr*,[20] as well as by the analysis of Professor Scharpf and some speculations of my own.

Though these two major questions subsumed under the "political question" doctrine provide a useful focus for analysis, in fact they seem inextricably related, and the criteria for abstention on the second issue may well influence characterization on the first. Similarly, the answers to both questions are frequently interrelated with the merits of the claims presented. For example, if the answer to the constitutional claim is that military forces may not constitutionally be used abroad without a declaration of war, there would be no problem of judicially manageable standards. On the other hand, if the real constitutional issues are the extent of independent presidential authority to use force abroad and the

20. 369 U.S. 186, 217 (1962). See generally Scharpf, *supra* note 13.

limits of congressional delegation of authority to the President, there may well be a serious standards problem. To take another example: under existing precedents it is certainly clearer that the Congress and the President acting together may constitutionally disregard a valid treaty than that the President acting alone may do so. Characterization on the first issue, then, might possibly turn on the extent to which the contested action is congressional-executive action rather than simply Executive action. Professor Schwartz refers to this feedback as "the dynamic relationship between construction and application of a governing standard."[21] This dynamic interrelation between the merits of the issue presented and the strength of the reasons for abstention suggests that answers in one context ought not be writ large as absolutes. It further suggests that analysis of the abstention question should be preceded by some awareness of the problems inherent in analysis on the merits.

If the reasons given above include most of the policies for judicial abstention, then the application of these policies to specific challenges to the use of armed forces abroad should suggest the wisdom of judicial abstention on each challenge. The four major challenges which seem to recur in a variety of contexts are claims that the use of military forces abroad has not been constitutionally authorized; claims that the use of military forces in a particular war violates international law; claims that the method of conducting hostilities violates international law; and claims that individual participation in a particular war would entail personal responsibility under the Nuremberg principles.[22]

21. Schwartz & McCormack, *supra* note 7, at 1043-44. Judge Wyzanski also noted this interrelation in his opinion in *United States v. Sisson:*
    The court has a procedural, as well as a substantive, problem. It must decide whether the question sought to be raised is in that category of political questions which are not within a court's jurisdiction and, if the issue falls within the court's jurisdiction, whether, as a matter of substance the defendant is right in his contention that the order is repugnant to the Constitution. Again, while those two aspects are technically separate, they are so close as often to overlap.
    United States v. Sisson, 294 F. Supp. 511, 513 (D. Mass. 1968).
22. See the discussion of other possible claims at note 5 *supra*.

Claims that the Use of Military Forces Abroad has not been Constitutionally Authorized

The controversy concerning the war power has raged at least since the clashes of Jefferson and Hamilton over the power of the President in the 1801 naval war against the Bashaw of Tripoli.[23] The three principal issues in the debate are, first, what independent authority does the President have to order the use of military forces abroad? Second, if congressional authorization is necessary, what form must it take? And third, may Congress delegate authority to use the armed forces abroad to the President, and if so, how broad a delegation is permissible?[24] The starting point of the debate is the Constitution, which gives Congress the power to declare war and which makes the President the Commander in Chief. A second major input is the nearly 200 years of constitutional experience in which successive Presidents and Congresses have interpreted these provisions. It is particularly relevant in this regard that during the present century there has been a strong tradition of substantial independent Executive authority to employ the armed forces abroad, highlighted by President Truman's use of a quarter of a million American troops in Korea. The extent to which this practice may have departed from the original constitutional scheme is hotly debated.

Applying the functional criteria previously set out, the first question is whether the decision has been constitutionally en-

23. For discussion on the merits of the war power controversy see Henkin, *Constitutional Issues in Foreign Policy*, 23 J. Int'l Aff. 210, 214-18 (1969); Kurland, *The Impotence of Reticence*, 1968 Duke L.J. 619; Moore, *The National Executive and the Use of the Armed Forces Abroad*, 21 Naval War College Rev. 28 (1969); Reveley, *Presidential War-Making: Constitutional Prerogative or Usurpation?* 55 Va. L. Rev. 1243 (1969); *supra* note 7; F. Wormuth, The Vietnam War: The President v. The Constitution (An Occasional Paper of the Center for the Study of Democratic Institutions 1968); Note, *Congress, The President, and the Power to Commit Forces to Combat*, 81 Harv. L. Rev. 1771 (1969).

24. These issues are posed and discussed in Moore, *supra* note 23, at 30-35. A fourth and perhaps potentially more explosive set of issues is the extent to which Congress may limit or withdraw authority from the President to use the armed forces abroad. See *Fulbright Panel Votes to Repeal Tonkin Measure*, N.Y. Times, April 11, 1970, at 1, col. 5 (city ed.).

trusted to the discretion of another branch of government. Professor Velvel answers this by making a distinction between the decision to use forces abroad which he characterizes as a "political question" and the decision as to which branch has the power to decide to commit forces abroad which he says is justiciable:

> [T]he question is not *whether* the nation is to fight a large war, but which branch of government has the *power to decide* if it is to fight such a war. The author would be the first to agree that *whether* this country is to fight is a political question; but which branch has the *power to decide whether to fight is a judicial question.*[25]

The difficulty with this seemingly attractive position is that the issue of who has the power to decide is not as unitary as Professor Velvel's characterization suggests. If the issue is the independent authority of the President to use force abroad and there has been no congressional participation in that decision, then a strong case can be made that the delineation of Executive authority is as much a judicial function as delineating the authority of Congress by declaring acts of Congress unconstitutional. That practice has been good law since *Marbury v. Madison.*[26] Moreover, the Court's negation of President Truman's asserted power to seize the steel mills in aid of the Korean war effort supports the Court's authority to be the final arbiter on questions of the constitutional authority of the President.[27] If the issue is the form of congressional authorization or the extent of the congressional power to delegate the war power to the President, however, it is not as clear that the Court should assert independent authority. Though such decisions are just as much decisions concerning the constitutional power of Congress, past precedent in the foreign affairs area suggests that the Court has left the form of authorization and the extent of delegation of the war power to the discretion of

---

25. Velvel, *supra* note 7, at 480. Professor Velvel must mean that the decision whether *Congress* or the *President* has the power to decide whether to fight is a judicial question. For if the Court decided that it had the power to decide whether to fight, the decision as to whether this country is to fight could hardly be termed a political question as he posits.
26. 5 U.S. (1 Cranch) 137 (1803).
27. Youngstown Sheet & Tube Co. v. Sawyer, 343 U.S. 579 (1952).

Congress. Thus, in the case of *Talbot v. Seeman*,[28] also authored by Chief Justice John Marshall, the Court did not feel that a formal declaration of war was required for congressional authorization of hostilities. More recently, the *Curtiss-Wright*[29] case established a tradition of broad congressional power to delegate authority to the President in foreign affairs. In fact, even in domestic law where the power of the Executive is not as great, anti-delegation authority is largely defunct. If the constitutional requirement is congressional authorization of the commitment, it is a substantial extension to say that the process by which Congress chooses to provide that authorization and the degree of control which they exercise over it are matters for the courts. In the Vietnam context, however unsatisfactory the Tonkin Gulf Resolution is as a general practice,[30] it does establish congressional involvement and remove the constitutional issue from the category of simply ascertaining the limits of independent Executive authority. Decision on the merits in the Vietnam context, then, is inevitably tied up with the form of authorization and breadth of delegation issues both of which may have been constitutionally entrusted to Congress for decision.

The second question is are there prudential or systemic considerations which suggest that it would be unwise for the judiciary to decide the issue on the merits? Though not necessarily

28. (The Amelia) 5 U.S. (1 Cranch) 1 (1801).
29. United States v. Curtiss-Wright Export Corp., 299 U.S. 304 (1936). One commentator interprets the *Curtiss-Wright* decision as withdrawing "virtually all constitutional limitation upon the scope of congressional delegation of power to the President to act in the area of international relations." Jones, *The President, Congress and Foreign Relations*, 29 CALIF. L. REV. 565, 575 (1941).
30. Though in its historical context the Tonkin Gulf Resolution should be construed as a valid exercise of the congressional power to authorize the use of armed forces abroad, it is a sorry discharge of congressional responsibility. Moreover, the circumstances of its passage and the ambiguity of the congressional debates served to isolate the President and to increase the political cost of the war.

For discussion of the Tonkin Gulf Resolution and excerpts from the congressional debates see Moore & Underwood, *The Lawfulness of United States Assistance to the Republic of Vietnam*, 112 CONG. REC. 14,943, 14,960-67, 14,983-89 (daily ed. July 14, 1966). See also Velvel, *supra* note 7, at 473-77.

conclusive, at least three of the prudential criteria seem relevant to abstention on the constitutional claim.

First, to challenge the constitutionality of the use of troops abroad while those troops are engaged in a major conflict may impair the ability of the President to negotiate a settlement or otherwise disengage without total defeat. Even a declaratory judgment that a war is unconstitutional might strengthen the position of the opponent or cause him to hold out for greater concessions in negotiation, particularly in a war in which domestic public opinion may be an important factor. And if judicial decision sanctions refusal to be inducted for service in the war or has some other more concrete impact, this interference with the settlement process might be dramatic. Certainly it has the potential to be much more serious than presidential inability to take over the steel mills during the Korean war. Since the courts do not have the kind of effective control of the total situation necessary for settlement of the war, they should be particularly sensitive to the impact which their decisions might have on the settlement efforts of other branches which do. Professor Schwartz has suggested as factors mitigating this risk that the government might win on the merits, that constitutional objection might be cured by subsequent congressional action, and that the courts could frame relief to minimize the impact.[31] Though these factors do mitigate the risks they do not take into account the psychological impact of declaring an on-going war unconstitutional or of forcing a direct confrontation between Congress and the President during the course of a war.

Second, the constitutional issues raise major problems as to "judicially discoverable and manageable standards." If, of course, the Court was willing to say that absent a prior formal declaration of war the commitment of troops to combat abroad is unconstitutional, then the standards problem would not seem major. But the argument that a formal declaration of war is constitutionally required is the most extreme constitutional claim put forward.

The real issues seem to be the extent of independent Executive authority and the power of Congress to delegate its authority to the President. Either with or without congressional authorization,

31. See Schwartz & McCormack, *supra* note 7, at 1049-52.

then, there is a serious standards problem. What is the test for independent Executive authority or an invalid delegation? Short of a no-independent-authority position, which seems unrealistic and policy defeating, there is no test as neat as the "one man, one vote" of the reapportionment decisions. The dividing line which I have tentatively suggested for marking off Executive authority, "congressional authorization in all cases where regular combat units are committed to sustained hostilities,"[32] is still much less certain than this "one man, one vote" standard. And what is a serious problem in the absence of congressional authorization is nearly insoluble in a Vietnam-type case where there is congressional involvement, and the issue is the limits of the congressional power to exercise or delegate its authority. What standards comparable to "one man, one vote" are discoverable on that issue? Must a time limitation be used, or an area limitation, or a size of forces or weapons limitation? All of these factors and more may be critical for conflict management. This difficulty suggests the wisdom of entrusting the delegation issue to Congress.

Third, since these constitutional claims are intended to resolve a dispute about the relative role of Congress and the Executive and not to apply some constitutional prohibition limiting total governmental power to act, such as the Bill of Rights, if there are institutional checks other than judicial determination which each branch exercises on the other it is certainly relevant to the abstention decision. Although it would not be totally satisfactory in view of the demands to "support our boys" once a major commitment of troops abroad has been made, Congress could refuse to appropriate funds or to conscript the necessary troops, could censure the President as the House did President Polk for his Mexican war activities,[33] or could even institute impeachment proceedings against the President. And short of these checks, Congress can hold public hearings and mobilize public opinion in a manner which can have a major impact on Executive discretion.[34] This

32. See Moore, *supra* note 23, at 32. See also the more complete discussion of alternatives for drawing this line in Note, *Congress, The President, and the Power to Commit Forces to Combat, supra* note 23, at 1744-1803.
33. Reveley, *supra* note 23, at 1275.
34. The nationally televised Senate Foreign Relations Committee hearings on the Vietnam War are an example.

existence of other institutional checks on the relationship between the political branches suggests that the judiciary should go slow in intervening in the processes of political adjustment between them. The felt necessities of the time and the interplay of the political branches may be a more reliable guide than overly neat *a priori* constitutional hypotheses.

Delay in decision until after the war would substantially ameliorate the first policy for abstention, that adverse decision might interfere with broader settlement. It would not, however, significantly negate the force of the second or third prudential policies for abstention.

Taken together, the answers to these first and second questions concerning abstention suggest that in a situation in which the armed forces abroad are committed pursuant to joint executive-congressional action, the courts should defer to the political interaction between Congress and the President rather than engage in a line-drawing exercise for which there are no adequate constitutional guidelines. In a situation, however, in which the dominant issue is the extent of the independent Executive power to commit troops abroad, although there still may be significant costs from judicial action, it is not as clear that the courts should always abstain from decision. Vindication of the constitutional principle that major use of force ought to be acquiesced in by Congress may support some role for the court in delineating Executive authority if it remains sensitive to the costs and difficulties of judicial involvement.

Claims that the Use of the Armed Forces in a Particular War Violates International Law

Despite occasional sweeping judicial statements to the contrary, it is clear that not every decision affecting foreign relations requires abstention. One need not subscribe to the simplicities of either the monist or dualist theories of the relation between national and international law to recognize that "international law is part of our law."[35] Validly ratified treaties are, pursuant to the supremacy clause, part of the law of the land and in appropriate cases domestic courts may also apply customary international

35. The Paquete Habana, 175 U.S. 677, 700 (1900).

law. Moreover, for a nation vitally interested in strengthening international law, and in a system where there are too few viable international tribunals, it might be particularly useful to set an example by expanding the role of domestic courts in the creation and application of meaningful international standards. Professor Schwartz makes this point well:

> If the international legal system is to prevail over national conceptions with respect to the use of force, perhaps a person should not be compelled to serve in support of a military effort contravening international standards.[36]

Despite strong tugs in this direction, there are persistent questions as to the suitability of domestic courts for such a role, at least in the absence of specific congressional authorization.

Applying the functional criteria for evaluation of abstention, the first question is whether the decision has been constitutionally entrusted to the discretion of another branch of government. Whatever the ought of this question, there is substantial authority for the proposition that decisions concerning foreign relations taken by the Congress or the President within their constitutional authority are valid whether or not in violation of international law. That is, within their constitutional sphere of action the political branches have the authority to violate international law if they so choose. In the *Chinese Exclusion Case*[37] a unanimous Supreme

36. Schwartz & McCormack, *supra* note 7, at 1040. Professor Wallace McClure has also been a strong supporter of the position that one ought not be compelled to serve in a war if that war is illegal under international law.

37. Chae Chan Ping v. United States, 130 U.S. 581 (1889). Just a year earlier, in Whitney v. Robertson, 124 U.S. 190 (1888), Mr. Justice Field said, in writing for a unanimous court:

> By the Constitution a treaty is placed on the same footing, and made of like obligation, with an act of legislation. Both are declared by that instrument to be the supreme law of the land and no superior efficacy is given to either over the other. When the two relate to the same subject, the courts will always endeavor to construe them so as to give effect to both, if that can be done without violating the language of either, but if the two are inconsistent, the one last in date will control the other, provided always the stipulation of the treaty on the subject is self-executing.

Id. at 194.

Arguably the subsequent executive-congressional exercise of the war

Court held that Congress may constitutionally override a valid treaty by later inconsistent enactments even though the non-application of the treaty would be a violation of international law. And of particular relevance to the waging aggressive war claim, Mr. Justice Field said in dictum:

> When once it is established that Congress possesses the power to pass an act, our province ends with its construction, and its application to cases as they are presented for determination. Congress has the power under the Constitution to declare war, and in two instances where the power has been exercised—in the war of 1812 against Great Britain, and in 1846 against Mexico—the propriety and wisdom and justice of its action were vehemently assailed by some of the ablest and best men in the country, but no one doubted the legality of the proceeding, and any imputation by this or any other court of the United States upon the motives of the members of Congress who in either case voted for the declaration, would have been justly the cause of animadversion.[38]

The principle of the *Chinese Exclusion Case* has been widely criticized, and it is true that it evolved in an earlier era when bilateral rather than multilateral treaties were the usual fare.[39] But any other decision would still raise substantial questions as to the source of the Court's constitutional authority to strike down joint actions of the political branches on the basis of international law. Moreover, although in some areas affecting foreign relations there may be a stronger constitutional case for the primacy of treaties or the courts may have primary competence, it is particularly questionable with respect to executive-congressional decisions to commit armed forces abroad.

---

power presents an even stronger case than other kinds of subsequent legislation.

See also Dickinson, *The Law of Nations as National Law; "Political Questions,"* 104 U. PA. L. REV. 451, 487-90 (1956). For an illustration from Great Britain, see Mortensen v. Peters, 14 Scots L.T.R. 227 (1906).

38. Chae Chan Ping v. United States, *supra* note 37, at 603.
39. See the remarks of Professor Louis B. Sohn, 1969 PROC. AM. SOC'Y INT'L L. 180.

The case of *Reid v. Covert*,[40] which established the preeminence of the Constitution over treaty obligations, also supports the authority of the political branches, when they are acting pursuant to their constitutional authority, to take domestically valid action even though in violation of international law. The Constitution makes the President the Commander in Chief and gives to Congress the power to declare war. In light of *Reid*, it is open to question whether these powers may be domestically limited by prior treaty obligations. Judge Northrop summarized these points in *United States v. Berrigan*[41] when he said:

> Whether the actions by the executive and the legislative branches in utilizing our armed forces are in accord with international law is a question which necessarily must be left to the elected representatives of the people and not to the judiciary. This is so even if the government's actions are contrary to valid treaties to which the government is a signatory. . . . The categorization of this defense as a "political question" is not an abdication of responsibility by the judiciary. Rather, it is a recognition that the responsibility is assumed by that level of government which under the Constitution and international law is authorized to commit the nation.[42]

While it is clear from these decisions that Congress and the President acting together have constitutional authority to act even in violation of international law, the issue is not nearly so clear if the President, acting alone, violates a valid treaty approved by the Senate. The answer in that case lies somewhere in the poorly charted limits of Executive and congressional authority in foreign relations issues. In any event, the focus must be on the constitutional authority of the President or Congress to take the action as

40. 354 U.S. 1 (1957). *Reid v. Covert* decided a very different issue involving the Bill of Rights jury trial guarantees. The argument which can be made on the basis of the *Reid* case, however, is that if the Constitution entrusts the war power to Congress and the President, that power cannot be constitutionally limited by agreement with a foreign nation.
41. 283 F. Supp. 336 (D. Md. 1968).
42. *Id.* at 342.

well as on whether the action is in violation of international law. It is to be hoped (and urged) that Congress and the President will be sensitive to the importance of adherence to international law, but under the Constitution it is questionable whether the Court has authority to police the international law violations of the political branches when they are acting within their sphere of constitutional authority.

The second question asks are there prudential or systemic considerations which suggest that it would be unwise for the judiciary to decide the international law issues on the merits. While they should not be taken as absolutes, at least four of the prudential criteria seem relevant to abstention on the international law claim.

First, there is a serious problem in ascertaining manageable standards for decision. Although the General Assembly has appointed a succession of Special Committees on the Question of Defining Aggression, the latest of which is still working on the question, there is still no agreed definition of aggression with which to implement the standards of the United Nations Charter or the Kellogg-Briand Pact.[43] Moreover, as is evidenced by the Vietnam War, since World War II the principal public order issue has become the control of intervention in internal conflict. The UN Charter is only poorly responsive to the problem of intervention, and in the absence of a more adequate Charter framework there has been wide disagreement about the applicable nonintervention norms of customary international law.[44] As a result, if the issue is one of major use of force—and particularly intervention in internal conflict, as it is in the Vietnam War[45]—there is

---

43. See generally Report of the Special Committee on the Question of Defining Aggression, 24 U.N. GAOR, Supp. 20, U.N. Doc. A/7620 (1969); M. McDougal & F. Feliciano, Law and Minimum World Public Order 143-60 (1961).

44. For an account of the Charter inadequacies in dealing with intervention and a review of the competing nonintervention norms see Moore, *The Control of Foreign Intervention in Internal Conflict*, 9 Va. J. Int'l L. 205 (1969).

45. For discussion on the merits of the legal issues in the Vietnam War see I & II r. falk (ed.) The Vietnam War and International Law (Vol. I 1968, Vol. II 1969). Both volumes are sponsored by the "Civil War" Panel of the American Society of International Law.

a severe standards problem. This problem is compounded on international law issues, because unlike the case with respect to domestic law, a United States court cannot promulgate an international standard which will be definitive for any other nation. At most, the domestic formulation will simply be an input into the much broader determination of international law by reference to state practice. The limited power of United States courts to clarify doubtful areas in international law means that domestic court jurisdiction could result in the United States following a restrictive view of international law without other nations feeling reciprocally bound. To some extent this problem is present with all applications by domestic courts of customary international law, and it can easily be overstated as a reason for abstention. Nevertheless, as the issues approach the most sensitive areas of national discretion, a lack of adequate international standards becomes a relevant consideration in deciding whether to exercise competence.

Second, and closely related to the first, judicial formulation of standards for decision in the most sensitive areas of national action may interfere with the ability of the political branches to formulate standards or to obtain international agreement on them. The decision on the desirability and content of a definition of aggression or whether the United States will follow the traditional or newer nonintervention norms are among the most sensitive issues of foreign relations. This problem of interference with the authority of the political branches and of uniformity and consistency in foreign relations is closely tied to the constitutional submission of foreign relations decisions to the political branches. If the political branches have by their actions taken a position in foreign relations, it is not clear that the courts have authority to override that action.

Third, judicial determination by a domestic court during the course of conflict to the effect that a particular war violates international law may interfere with settlement by the political branches which are in the best position to terminate the conflict. Few major international conflicts are so onesided that conformance with international law requires sacrifice of all of the objectives of either of the participants. Yet judicial declaration that a

589

particular conflict is in violation of international law may contribute to the loss of even justifiable defensive objectives. Thus, if relief takes the form of a declaratory judgment it may have adverse psychological consequences on the government's negotiating position. And if it involves more effective sanctions, such as prohibition of induction, it might have a much more serious impact. Moreover, unlike the constitutional claims, the ameliorative devices which depend on subsequent congressional action would be unavailable. Another point relative to the settlement issue is that normally a domestic court has both parties to a dispute before it and may fashion relief fair to both. In adjudicating the legality of a war, however, the adversary is not subject to the jurisdiction of the court.

Fourth, a decision that a particular use of force is a violation of international law may require fact assessments which present particularly difficult problems for domestic courts. The assessment of the lawfulness of the Vietnam war, for example, involves fact determinations about the extent of military involvement of North Vietnam and the interrelation of Hanoi and the Vietcong which a domestic court may be poorly equipped to handle.[46] Under some theories it might also involve questions of the statehood of North and South Vietnam or the validity of recognition of the Saigon government, which even in the nonwar context have been issues on which the courts have deferred to the Executive.[47] Moreover, adequate presentation of the government position might require disclosure of sensitive information compiled by the national intelligence agencies which would be prejudicial to future intelligence operations or settlement efforts.

Delay in decision until termination of hostilities would ameliorate the danger of interference with the settlement process, but the other three prudential considerations for abstention would still be largely operative.

The strength of these prudential considerations for abstention

46. See generally Moore, *Law and Politics in the Vietnamese War: A Response to Professor Friedmann*, 61 AM. J. INT'L L. 1039 (1967).

47. See generally Moore, *The Role of the State Department in Judicial Proceedings*, 31 FORDHAM L. REV. 277 (1962), and authorities collected at 277 n. 8.

can be oversold and will certainly vary with the context. A court might feel in a particularly extreme context that the price of ignoring these prudential considerations is sufficiently offset by other considerations, particularly the importance of vindication of international law. The major issue which would still remain, however, would be the court's constitutional authority to declare the otherwise valid actions of the political branches invalid because in violation of international law. Existing precedents suggest that at least with respect to executive-congressional action such decisions have been constitutionally entrusted to Congress and the President.

CLAIMS THAT THE METHOD OF CONDUCTING HOSTILITIES VIOLATES INTERNATIONAL LAW

Another international law claim, in addition to the claim that the use of the armed forces in a particular war violates international law, is that a particular method of conducting hostilities violates international law, that is, that the use of particular tactics or weapons systems or the treatment of civilians or prisoners of war violates international law. Since the United States is a party to most of the Hague and Geneva Conventions regulating the conduct of hostilities, many of these claims can be expected to have a specific treaty base. Though the awkwardness of demonstrating a "personal stake in the outcome" may make standing a more serious obstacle to claims in this category, one can imagine a number of contexts in which standing probably ought not bar consideration of the issues. For example, if a serviceman sought an injunction against widespread violations of the laws of war in a unit to which he had been assigned, or if a prisoner of war sought protection under applicable treaties, both claimants would seem to have a very real personal stake in the outcome. Assuming the standing hurdle can be overcome, a case can be made for judicial activism in policing violations of the laws of war.

The first question concerning abstention, whether a decision has been constitutionally entrusted to another branch of government, would only be relevant in those contexts in which the Executive is alleged to have ordered a violation of a customary or treaty law obligation. In the absence of such an order, a treaty at least represents an executive-congressional decision and if intended to be self-executing should be applied by the court. Many, if not most, of the violations of the laws of war probably fall into this category of unauthorized deviation from command directives and as such do not present a significant problem in judicially contradicting a constitutionally authorized decision-maker. The recent tragic events at Son My are an example. Even when this first question is relevant, though, or when a clear command directive contradicts a prior treaty obligation, it is still not at all clear that a court should defer to the later Executive decision. Although the Constitution makes the President the Commander in Chief, it does not provide satisfactory guidance for the resolution of a clash between the Commander in Chief power and the treaty power. It is at least a reasonable resolution of such a clash that the treaty power would prevail and that departure from treaty or executive-congressional agreement standards would require Senate or congressional participation. The uncertainties whether a particular treaty is meant to be self-executing and whether the power of the President as Commander in Chief can be limited by treaty may in particular cases somewhat qualify these tentative conclusions.

The second question, whether there are prudential or systemic considerations suggesting that it would be unwise for the judiciary to decide the issue on the merits, similarly turns up only weak reasons for abstention. In most contexts judicial policing of the laws of war would not have the severe impact on the conduct of the war which might accompany judicial consideration of participation claims. Even if the method of conducting hostilities were altered, the war effort could still proceed. In fact, there is good reason to believe that violations of the laws of war are usually counter-productive and that judicial intervention would more often than not better promote national goals. Certainly in view of the large number of applicable treaties to which the United States is a party, in most cases there would be no standards problem in policing violations of the laws of war. Similarly, though fact appraisal may be somewhat more difficult than in the usual domestic case, there do not seem to be any overwhelming obstacles either from the difficulty of fact appraisal or the need for uniformity and consistency in foreign relations. It might be urged, of course, that there are other institutions better suited to the role of policing violations of the laws of war, particularly self-policing by the military. The argument proves too much, however, since the availability of other institutions is never by itself a wholly persuasive reason for abstention. Moreover, despite good faith efforts at self-policing, like all institutions the military has built in limitations which may hinder its own self-policing operations. For example, self-policing in the Vietnam War, though it seems to have been sincerely pursued, got off to a slow start and has certainly been inadequately implemented. In these circumstances a judicial boost to lagging policing efforts might have served both the national and the litigants' interests.

The wide variety of situations in which claims concerning the conduct of hostilities may arise precludes meaningful generalization in advance. Analysis of the functions served by judicial abstention, however, suggests that there are few fundamental obstacles to a more aggressive judicial role in policing violations of the laws of war.

CLAIMS THAT INDIVIDUAL PARTICIPATION IN A PARTICULAR WAR WOULD ENTAIL PERSONAL RESPONSIBILITY UNDER THE NUREMBERG PRINCIPLES

One way in which the international law issues are sought to be presented in a variety of contexts challenging the use of armed forces abroad is by invocation of the Nuremberg principles. If the Nuremberg principles are invoked simply as one source of the international-law obligations not to engage in aggressive war or not to violate the laws of war, such allegations raise the same justiciability problems as claims that the use of the armed forces in a particular war violates international law or claims that the method of conducting hostilities violates international law. If, however, the purpose in invoking the Nuremberg norms is to avoid personal liability, then different considerations are introduced. The 1945 Charter of the Nuremberg Tribunal, since codified by the International Law Commission, ascribes individual responsibility under international law for:

(a) *Crimes against peace*: namely, planning, preparation, initiation or waging of a war of aggression, or a war in violation of international treaties, agreements or assurances. . . .

(b) *War crimes*: namely, violations of the laws or customs of war. . . .

(c) *Crimes against humanity*: namely, murder, extermination, enslavement, deportation, and other inhumane acts committed against any civilian population, before or during the war. . . .[48]

At least acts in the category of "war crimes" are also substantially covered by the Uniform Code of Military Justice.[49] To the extent that an action would entail personal responsibility under the Nuremberg principles, the Uniform Code of Military Justice, or any other valid national or international standard, certainly the criminality of the action should be a valid defense to state compulsion to engage in it. The sense of justice boggles at the thought that a man may be legally compelled to perform an act entailing criminal liability.

The category of actions for which one may be held criminally accountable under the Nuremberg principles is much narrower, however, than is popularly supposed. Though the Nuremberg principles are not absolutely clear, the most widely shared interpretation of them is that no soldier is liable simply because he participates in an aggressive war.[50] To include participation as

---

48. *Agreement for the Prosecution and Punishment of the Major War Criminals of the European Axis*, Aug. 8, 1945, 82 U.N.T.S. 279. See generally G. MUELLER & E. WISE, INTERNATIONAL CRIMINAL LAW 227-90 (1965).

   For more detailed analysis of the justiciability of this third claim concerning allegations that participation in a particular war would be contrary to the Nuremberg principles see Forman, *supra* note 7.

49. See Forman, *supra* note 7, at 161; D'Amato, Gould & Woods, *War Crimes and Vietnam: The "Nuremberg Defense" and the Military Service Resister*, 57 CALIF. L. REV. 1055 (1969).

50. Claims that clearly identified belligerents are "war criminals" simply because combatants in a military apparatus engaged in aggressive war have not been accepted by the world community, including the International Military Tribunal at Nuremberg, and are clearly in contra-

such would have hardly served the humanitarian objectives of Nuremberg, as hundreds of thousands of soldiers would have been subject to criminal liability when their only crime was to misperceive which side was the aggressor. Instead, for liability under the Nuremberg norms there must be personal participation in high-level planning or in the commission of a war crime or crime against humanity such as the killing or torturing of prisoners of war. Benjamin Forman, the Assistant General Counsel for International Affairs of the Department of Defense, summarized this general Nuremberg law in a paper delivered at the 1969 Annual Meeting of the American Society of International Law:

> No Nuremberg norm makes it criminal to be a soldier or, as such, to carry on belligerent activities injurious to others in accordance with the laws and customs of war, even though the war be an aggressive war. The crime against peace can be committed only by those in a position to shape or influence the policy that initiates or continues it. . . .
>
> As to war crimes and crimes against humanity, liability is similarly individual. The individual must himself commit the substantive offense or conspire to do so.[51]

Perhaps the greatest barrier to invocation of the Nuremberg principles as a defense against personal accountability, then, is that there may be no accountability. Certainly the typical soldier will not be participating in high-level planning necessary for liability under the crimes against peace count. Unless a claimant alleges that he will be personally participating in violation of the laws of war or of crimes against humanity, then, invocation of the Nuremberg principles for the purpose of avoiding individual liability seems to be beside the point. And if his allegation is that he will be personally participating in war crimes or crimes against humanity constituting war crimes, it is implicit in Articles 90-92

---

vention to accepted "standards of human rights for contexts of violence." See M. McDougal & F. Feliciano, *supra* note 40 at 528, 531-34, 541-42, 530-61.

51. Forman, *supra* note 7, at 163.

of the Uniform Code of Military Justice[52] that the illegality of the order to participate in such actions is a valid defense to an action for noncompliance. In fact, the refusal of a soldier to participate in such acts which he should reasonably know are unlawful is not only permitted but required by domestic law.[53] Here too, then, depending on the timing and the specifics of the allegations, the invocation of the Nuremberg principles may be largely beside the point. Thus, it is clear that a soldier would have a valid defense to a charge that he refused to carry out an order to kill prisoners of war or unarmed civilians in his custody (but he would not need Nuremberg to prevail). In fact, as a large segment of the American public seems to have unfortunately ignored in the much publicized Green Beret and Son My cases, the carrying out of such an order which the soldier should reasonably know is unlawful is a violation of both international and domestic law. As a result of this duty, it seems doubtful whether general allegations of the possibility of participating in war crimes could be raised as a defense to an order to report for induction.

It would seem that the existing defenses in domestic law and the areas of individual accountability under the Nuremberg principles are reasonably congruent, at least for the typical soldier. In contexts presenting severe pressure to participate in war crimes, however, this congruence may provide insufficient protection for the claimant. Thus, if a soldier is assigned to a force or unit which he alleges engages repeatedly in a practice which violates the laws of war, it seems reasonable to adjudicate this claim on the merits either in an action to block an assignment or obtain a transfer or in an action to obtain injunctive relief against the continuation of the illegal practices. The kinds of severe pressures an individual soldier would be subjected to in such a unit and the risk which he runs in disobeying an order at his peril should his judgment about its illegality be wrong strongly suggest that judi-

52. 10 U.S.C. § § 890-92 (1964). The illegality of an order is explicitly said to be a defense in the discussion of Articles 90-92 in MANUAL FOR COURTS-MARTIAL (1969), Exec. Order No. 11,476,34, Fed. Reg. 10826-30 (1969). See also ARMY FIELD MANUAL FM 27-10, THE LAW OF LAND WARFARE 182-83 (1956); Forman, *supra* note 7, at 164.
53. See United States v. Kinder, 14 C.M.R. 742 (1954).

cial intervention is proper in such a context. The examination of evidence in the *Levy* trial concerning allegations of widespread violations of the laws of war by the Green Berets supports this conclusion. It is also supported by the weakness of reasons for abstention when the claim is violation of the laws of war. To prevail, of course, a claimant must still prove his case.

Lack of accountability rather than any more fundamental "political question" would seem to be the principal bar to broad invocation of the Nuremberg principles on a theory of avoidance of personal liability. Moreover, in the absence of personal accountability or severe pressures to participate in illegal conduct, it is doubtful whether an individual litigant has the necessary "personal stake in the outcome of the controversy" to satisfy the standing test which the Supreme Court enunciated in *Flast v. Cohen*,[54] at least if the purpose of invoking the Nuremberg norms is to avoid personal accountability. And if the purpose of invoking the Nuremberg norms is to challenge the legality of the war itself, that is to avoid participation in an allegedly illegal war even though participation would not lead to personal accountability, then the more fundamental justiciability policies rather than standing would seem to be the principal bar. In most cases, of course, the two reasons for invoking the Nuremberg norms come mixed together. But whether the difficulty is thought of as relevance, standing, or justiciability, in all but a fairly narrow class of cases involving personal responsibility or a risk of severe pres-

54. 392 U.S. 83, 99-101 (1968). Quoting *Baker v. Carr*, the Court sharply distinguished between standing and justiciability:

> The "gist of the question of standing" is whether the party seeking relief has "alleged such a personal stake in the outcome of the controversy as to assure that concrete adverseness which sharpens the presentation of issues upon which the court so largely depends for illumination of difficult constitutional questions." . . . In other words, when standing is placed in issue in a case, the question is whether the person whose standing is challenged is a proper party to request an adjudication of a particular issue and not whether the issue itself is justiciable. Thus, a party may have standing in a particular case, but the federal court may nevertheless decline to pass on the merits of the case because, for example, it presents a political question.

Id at 99-100.

sure to conform to an unlawful practice constituting a war crime, the Nuremberg challenges to the use of military forces abroad will probably be unsuccessful.

THE tradition of judicial review runs deep in the American system. It is not every issue, however, which is constitutionally entrusted to the judiciary or which is suitable for judicial action. To date no court has held a challenge to the commitment of military forces abroad justiciable.[55] The invocation in these cases of the "political question" formula without explanation of its justification or the denial of *certiorari* without reasons is an unsatisfactory judicial response. Particularly when faced with challenges presented by sincere individuals, some of whom are involuntarily serving in a war to which they object, courts have a duty to fully articulate reasons for their decision. Full articulation calls for identification of the functions served by "justiciability" and their application to the major claims challenging the use of the armed forces abroad. Such a functional analysis of the reasons for judicial abstention is likely to please neither the activists nor the strict constructionists. There are important systemic policies suggesting that for the most part the resolution of claims that a particular use of force abroad has not been constitutionally authorized or is in violation of international law should be left to the interplay of political forces. Nevertheless, the newness and range of the challenges to the use of military forces abroad suggest a lack of wisdom in dogmatic assertion that there is no role for judicial action on such challenges, particularly on challenges to initial commitments instituted solely on the authority of the President. Moreover, there may be considerable room for a more active judicial role in policing violations of the laws of war.[56] Whatever the ultimate resolution of these issues, their importance and complexity calls for full articulation of the reasons for decision.

55. *But see* the discussion of *United States v. Sisson, supra* note 5.
56. See D'Amato, Gould & Woods, *supra* note 48.

DOCUMENTARY APPENDICES

Appendix A

Memorandum by the State Department Legal Adviser, Leonard C. Meeker, on the Legal Aspects of the Vietnam Situation (March 4, 1966).*

* Reprinted from 54 dep't state bulletin 474 (1966). Also reprinted in 75 yale l.j. 1085 (1966), and 60 am. j. int'l l. 565 (1966). The State Department Memorandum was submitted to the Senate Foreign Relations Committee on March 8, 1966.

The Legality of United States
Participation in the Defense of Viet-Nam

*I. The United States and South Viet-Nam have the Right
Under International Law to Participate in the Collective
Defense of South Viet-Nam Against Armed Attack*

In response to requests from the Government of South Viet-Nam, the United States has been assisting that country in defending itself against armed attack from the Communist North. This attack has taken the forms of externally supported subversion, clandestine supply of arms, infiltration of armed personnel, and most recently the sending of regular units of the North Vietnamese army into the South.

International law has long recognized the right of individual and collective self-defense against armed attack. South Viet-Nam and the United States are engaging in such collective defense consistently with international law and with United States obligations under the United Nations Charter.

A. SOUTH VIET-NAM IS BEING SUBJECTED TO ARMED ATTACK BY COMMUNIST NORTH VIET-NAM

The Geneva accords of 1954 established a demarcation line between North Viet-Nam and South Viet-Nam.[1] They provided for withdrawals of military forces into the respective zones north and south of this line. The accords prohibited the use of either zone for the resumption of hostilities or to "further an aggressive policy."

During the 5 years following the Geneva conference of 1954, the Hanoi regime developed a covert political-military organization in South Viet-Nam based on Communist cadres it had ordered to stay in the South, contrary to the provisions of the Geneva accords. The activities of this covert organization were directed toward the kidnaping and assassination of civilian officials—acts of terrorism that were perpetrated in increasing numbers.

1. For texts, see *American Foreign Policy, 1950-1955; Basic Documents*, vol. I, Department of State publication 6446, p. 750.

In the 3-year period from 1959 to 1961, the North Viet-Nam regime infiltrated an estimated 10,000 men into the South. It is estimated that 13,000 additional personnel were infiltrated in 1962, and, by the end of 1964, North Viet-Nam may well have moved over 40,000 armed and unarmed guerrillas into South Viet-Nam.

The International Control Commission reported in 1962 the findings of its Legal Committee:

> . . . there is evidence to show that arms, armed and unarmed personnel, munitions and other supplies have been sent from the Zone in the North to the Zone in the South with the objective of supporting, organizing and carrying out hostile activities, including armed attacks directed against the Armed Forces and Administration of the Zone in the South.
>
> . . . there is evidence that the PAVN [People's Army of Viet Nam] has allowed the Zone in the North to be used for inciting, encouraging and supporting hostile activities in the Zone in the South, aimed at the overthrow of the Administration in the South.

Beginning in 1964, the Communists apparently exhausted their reservoir of Southerners who had gone North. Since then the greater number of men infiltrated into the South have been native-born North Vietnamese. Most recently, Hanoi has begun to infiltrate elements of the North Vietnamese army in increasingly larger numbers. Today, there is evidence that nine regiments of regular North Vietnamese forces are fighting in organized units in the South.

In the guerrilla war in Viet-Nam, the external aggression from the North is the critical military element of the insurgency, although it is unacknowledged by North Viet-Nam. In these circumstances, an "armed attack" is not as easily fixed by date and hour as in the case of traditional warfare. However, the infiltration of thousands of armed men clearly constitutes an "armed attack" under any reasonable definition. There may be some question as to the exact date at which North Viet-Nam's aggression grew into an "armed attack," but there can be no doubt that it had occurred before February 1965.

B. International Law Recognizes the Right of Individual and Collective Self-Defense Against Armed Attack

International law has traditionally recognized the right of self-defense against armed attack. This proposition has been asserted by writers on international law through the several centuries in which the modern law of nations has developed. The proposition has been acted on numerous times by governments throughout modern history. Today the principle of self-defense against armed attack is universally recognized and accepted.[2]

The Charter of the United Nations, concluded at the end of World War II, imposed an important limitation on the use of force by United Nations members. Article 2, paragraph 4, provides:

> All Members shall refrain in their international relations from the threat or use of force against the territorial integrity or political independence of any state, or in any other manner inconsistent with the Purposes of the United Nations.

In addition, the charter embodied a system of international peacekeeping through the organs of the United Nations. Article 24 summarizes these structural arrangements in stating that the United Nations members:

> . . . confer on the Security Council primary responsibility for the maintenance of international peace and security, and agree that in carrying out its duties under this responsibility the Security Council acts on their behalf.

However, the charter expressly states in article 51 that the remaining provisions of the charter—including the limitation of article 2, paragraph 4, and the creation of United Nations ma-

2. See, *e.g.*, Jessup, *A Modern Law of Nations*, 163 ff. (1948); Oppenheim, *International Law*, 297 ff. (8th ed., Lauterpacht, 1955). And see, generally, Bowett, *Self-Defense in International Law* (1958). [Footnote in original.]

chinery to keep the peace—in no way diminish the inherent right of self-defense against armed attack. Article 51 provides:

> Nothing in the present Charter shall impair the inherent right of individual or collective self-defense if an armed attack occurs against a Member of the United Nations, until the Security Council has taken the measures necessary to maintain international peace and security. Measures taken by Members in the exercise of this right of self-defense shall be immediately reported to the Security Council and shall not in any way affect the authority and responsibility of the Security Council under the present Charter to take at any time such action as it deems necessary in order to maintain or restore international peace and security.

Thus, article 51 restates and preserves, for member states in the situations covered by the article, a long-recognized principle of international law. The article is a "saving clause" designed to make clear that no other provision in the charter shall be interpreted to impair the inherent right of self-defense referred to in article 51.

Three principal objections have been raised against the availability of the right of individual and collective self-defense in the case of Viet-Nam: (1) that this right applies only in the case of an armed attack on a United Nations member; (2) that it does not apply in the case of South Viet-Nam because the latter is not an independent sovereign state; and (3) that collective self-defense may be undertaken only by a regional organization operating under chapter VIII of the United Nations Charter. These objections will now be considered in turn.

C. THE RIGHT OF INDIVIDUAL AND COLLECTIVE SELF-DEFENSE APPLIES IN THE CASE OF SOUTH VIET-NAM WHETHER OR NOT THAT COUNTRY IS A MEMBER OF THE UNITED NATIONS

1. SOUTH VIET-NAM ENJOYS THE RIGHT OF SELF-DEFENSE

The argument that the right of self-defense is available only to members of the United Nations mistakes the nature of the right of self-defense and the relationship of the United Nations Charter to international law in this respect. As already shown, the right of self-defense against armed attack is an inherent right under international law. The right is not conferred by the charter, and, indeed, article 51 expressly recognizes that the right is inherent.

The charter nowhere contains any provision designed to deprive nonmembers of the right of self-defense against armed attack.[3] Article 2, paragraph 6, does charge the United Nations with responsibility for insuring that nonmember states act in accordance with United Nations "Principles so far as may be necessary for the maintenance of international peace and security." Protection against aggression and self-defense against armed attack are important elements in the whole charter scheme for the maintenance of international peace and security. To deprive nonmembers of their inherent right of self-defense would not accord with the principles of the organization, but would instead be prejudicial to the maintenance of peace. Thus article 2, paragraph 6 —and, indeed, the rest of the charter—should certainly not be construed to nullify or diminish the inherent defensive rights of nonmembers.

2. THE UNITED STATES HAS THE RIGHT TO ASSIST IN THE
DEFENSE OF SOUTH VIET-NAM ALTHOUGH THE LATTER
IS NOT A UNITED NATIONS MEMBER

The cooperation of two or more international entities in the defense of one or both against armed attack is generally referred to as collective self-defense. United States participation in the

3. While nonmembers, such as South Viet-Nam, have not formally undertaken the obligations of the United Nations Charter as their own treaty obligations, it should be recognized that much of the substantive law of the charter has become part of the general law of nations through a very wide acceptance by nations the world over. This is particularly true of the charter provisions bearing on the use of force. Moreover, in the case of South Viet-Nam, the South Vietnamese Government has expressed its ability and willingness to abide by the charter, in applying for United Nations membership. Thus it seems entirely appropriate to appraise the actions of South Viet-Nam in relation to the legal standards set forth in the United Nations Charter. [Footnote in original.]

defense of South Viet-Nam at the latter's request is an example of collective self-defense.

The United States is entitled to exercise the right of individual or collective self-defense against armed attack, as that right exists in international law, subject only to treaty limitations and obligations undertaken by this country.

It has been urged that the United States has no right to participate in the collective defense of South Viet-Nam because article 51 of the United Nations Charter speaks only of the situation "if an armed attack occurs *against a Member of the United Nations.*" This argument is without substance.

In the first place, article 51 does not impose restrictions or cut down the otherwise available rights of United Nations members. By its own terms, the article preserves an inherent right. It is, therefore, necessary to look elsewhere in the charter for any obligation of members restricting their participation in collective defense of an entity that is not a United Nations member.

Article 2, paragraph 4, is the principal provision of the charter imposing limitations on the use of force by members. It states that they:

> . . . shall refrain in their international relations from the threat or use of force against the territorial integrity or political independence of any state, or in any other manner inconsistent with the Purposes of the United Nations.

Action taken in defense against armed attack cannot be characterized as falling within this proscription. The record of the San Francisco conference makes clear that article 2, paragraph 4, was not intended to restrict the right of self-defense against armed attack.[4]

One will search in vain for any other provision in the charter that would preclude United States participation in the collective defense of a nonmember. The fact that article 51 refers only to armed attack "against a Member of the United Nations" implies no intention to preclude members from participating in the defense of nonmembers. Any such result would have seriously detrimental consequences for international peace and security and

4. See 6 UNCIO Documents 459. [Footnote in original.]

would be inconsistent with the purposes of the United Nations as they are set forth in article 1 of the charter.[5] The right of members to participate in the defense of nonmembers is upheld by leading authorities on international law.[6]

D. THE RIGHT OF INDIVIDUAL AND COLLECTIVE SELF-DEFENSE APPLIES WHETHER OR NOT SOUTH VIET-NAM IS REGARDED AS AN INDEPENDENT SOVEREIGN STATE

1. SOUTH VIET-NAM ENJOYS THE RIGHT OF SELF-DEFENSE

It has been asserted that the conflict in Viet-Nam is "civil strife" in which foreign intervention is forbidden. Those who make this assertion have gone so far as to compare Ho Chi Minh's actions in Viet-Nam with the efforts of President Lincoln to preserve the Union during the American Civil War. Any such characterization is an entire fiction disregarding the actual situation in Viet-Nam. The Hanoi regime is anything but the legitimate government of a unified country in which the South is rebelling against lawful national authority.

The Geneva accords of 1954 provided for a division of Viet-Nam into two zones at the 17th parallel. Although this line of demarcation was intended to be temporary, it was established by international agreement, which specifically forbade aggression by one zone against the other.

The Republic of Viet-Nam in the South has been recognized as a separate international entity by approximately 60 governments the world over. It has been admitted as a member of a number of the specialized agencies of the United Nations. The United Na-

5. In particular, the statement of the first purpose:
    To maintain international peace and security, and to that end: to take effective collective measures for the prevention and removal of threats to the peace, and for the suppression of acts of aggression or other breaches of the peace, and to bring about by peaceful means, and in conformity with the principles of justice and international law, adjustment or settlement of international disputes or situations which might lead to a breach of the peace. . . . [Footnote in original.]
6. Bowett, *Self-Defense in International Law*, 193-195 (1958); Goodhart, "The North Atlantic Treaty of 1949," 79 *Recueil Des Cours*, 183, 202-204 (1951, vol. II), quoted in 5 *Whiteman's Digest of International Law*, 1067-1068 (1965); Kelsen, *The Law of the United Nations*, 793 (1950); see Stone, *Aggression and World Order*, 44 (1958). [Footnote in original.]

tions General Assembly in 1957 voted to recommend South Viet-Nam for membership in the organization, and its admission was frustrated only by the veto of the Soviet Union in the Security Council.

In any event there is no warrant for the suggestion that one zone of a temporarily divided state—whether it be Germany, Korea, or Viet-Nam—can be legally overrun by armed forces from the other zone, crossing the internationally recognized line of demarcation between the two. Any such doctrine would subvert the international agreement establishing the line of demarcation, and would pose grave dangers to international peace.

The action of the United Nations in the Korean conflict of 1950 clearly established the principle that there is no greater license for one zone of a temporarily divided state to attack the other zone than there is for one state to attack another state. South Viet-Nam has the same right that South Korea had to defend itself and to organize collective defense against an armed attack from the North. A resolution of the Security Council dated June 25, 1950, noted "with grave concern the armed attack upon the Republic of Korea by forces from North Korea," and determined "that this action constitutes a breach of the peace."

2. THE UNITED STATES IS ENTITLED TO PARTICIPATE IN THE COLLECTIVE DEFENSE OF SOUTH VIET-NAM WHETHER OR NOT THE LATTER IS REGARDED AS AN INDEPENDENT SOVEREIGN STATE

As stated earlier, South Viet-Nam has been recognized as a separate international entity by approximately 60 governments. It has been admitted to membership in a number of the United Nations specialized agencies and has been excluded from the United Nations Organization only by the Soviet veto.

There is nothing in the charter to suggest that United Nations members are precluded from participating in the defense of a recognized international entity against armed attack merely because the entity may lack some of the attributes of an independent sovereign state. Any such result would have a destructive effect on the stability of international engagements such as the Geneva accords of 1954 and on internationally agreed lines of demarcation. Such a result, far from being in accord with the charter and the purposes of the United Nations, would undermine them and would create new dangers to international peace and security.

E. The United Nations Charter Does Not Limit the Right of Self-Defense to Regional Organizations

Some have argued that collective self-defense may be undertaken only by a regional arrangement or agency operating under chapter VIII of the United Nations Charter. Such an assertion ignores the structure of the charter and the practice followed in the more than 20 years since the founding of the United Nations.

The basic proposition that rights of self-defense are not impaired by the charter—as expressly stated in article 51—is not conditioned by any charter provision limiting the application of this proposition to collective defense by a regional arrangement or agency. The structure of the charter reinforces this conclusion. Article 51 appears in chapter VII of the charter, entitled "Action With Respect to Threats to the Peace, Breaches of the Peace, and Acts of Aggression," whereas chapter VIII, entitled "Regional Arrangements," begins with article 52 and embraces the two following articles. The records of the San Francisco conference show that article 51 was deliberately placed in chapter VII rather than chapter VIII, "where it would only have a bearing on the regional system."[7]

Under article 51, the right of self-defense is available against any armed attack, whether or not the country attacked is a member of a regional arrangement and regardless of the source of the attack. Chapter VIII, on the other hand, deals with relations among members of a regional arrangement or agency, and authorizes regional action as appropriate for dealing with "local disputes." This distinction has been recognized ever since the founding of the United Nations in 1945.

For example, the North Atlantic Treaty has operated as a collective security arrangement, designed to take common measures in preparation against the eventuality of an armed attack for which collective defense under article 51 would be required. Sim-

7. 17 UNCIO Documents 288. [Footnote in original.]

ilarly, the Southeast Asia Treaty Organization was designed as a collective defense arrangement under article 51. Secretary of State Dulles emphasized this in his testimony before the Senate Foreign Relations Committee in 1954.

By contrast, article 1 of the Charter of Bogotá (1948), establishing the Organization of American States, expressly declares that the organization is a regional agency within the United Nations. Indeed, chapter VIII of the United Nations Charter was included primarily to take account of the functioning of the inter-American system.

In sum, there is no basis in the United Nations Charter for contending that the right of self-defense against armed attack is limited to collective defense by a regional organization.

F. The United States Has Fulfilled its Obligations to the United Nations

A further argument has been made that the members of the United Nations have conferred on United Nations organs—and, in particular, on the Security Council—exclusive power to act against aggression. Again, the express language of article 51 contradicts that assertion. A victim of armed attack is not required to forego individual or collective defense of its territory until such time as the United Nations organizes collective action and takes appropriate measures. To the contrary, article 51 clearly states that the right of self-defense may be exercised *"until the Security Council has taken the measures necessary to maintain international peace and security."*[8]

As indicated earlier, article 51 is not literally applicable to the Viet-Nam situation since South Viet-Nam is not a member. How-

8. An argument has been made by some that the United States, by joining in the collective defense of South Viet-Nam, has violated the peaceful settlement obligation of article 33 in the charter. This argument overlooks the obvious proposition that a victim of armed aggression is not required to sustain the attack undefended while efforts are made to find a political solution with the aggressor. Article 51 of the charter illustrates this by making perfectly clear that the inherent right of self-defense is impaired by "Nothing in the present Charter," including the provisions of article 33. [Footnote in original.]

ever, reasoning by analogy from article 51 and adopting its provisions as an appropriate guide for the conduct of members in a case like Viet-Nam, one can only conclude that United States actions are fully in accord with this country's obligations as a member of the United Nations.

Article 51 requires that:

> Measures taken by Members in the exercise of this right of self-defense shall be immediately reported to the Security Council and shall not in any way affect the authority and responsibility of the Security Council under the present Charter to take at any time such action as it deems necessary in order to maintain or restore international peace and security.

The United States has reported to the Security Council on measures it has taken in countering the Communist aggression in Viet-Nam. In August 1964 the United States asked the Council to consider the situation created by North Vietnamese attacks on United States destroyers in the Tonkin Gulf.[9] The Council thereafter met to debate the question, but adopted no resolutions. Twice in February 1965 the United States sent additional reports to the Security Council on the conflict in Viet-Nam and on the additional measures taken by the United States in the collective defense of South Viet-Nam.[10] In January 1966 the United States formally submitted the Viet-Nam question to the Security Council for its consideration and introduced a draft resolution calling for discussions looking toward a peaceful settlement on the basis of the Geneva accords.[11]

At no time has the Council taken any action to restore peace and security in Southeast Asia. The Council has not expressed criticism of United States actions. Indeed, since the United States submission of January 1966, members of the Council have been notably reluctant to proceed with any consideration of the Viet-Nam question.

9. For a statement made by U.S. Representative Adlai E. Stevenson in the Security Council on Aug. 5, 1964, see BULLETIN of Aug. 24, 1964, p. 272.
10. For texts, see *ibid.*, Feb. 22, 1965, p. 240, and Mar. 22, 1965, p. 419.
11. For background and text of draft resolution, see *ibid.*, Feb. 14, 1966, p. 231.

The conclusion is clear that the United States has in no way acted to interfere with United Nations consideration of the conflict in Viet-Nam. On the contrary, the United States has requested United Nations consideration, and the Council has not seen fit to act.

G. International Law Does Not Require a Declaration of War as a Condition Precedent to Taking Measures of Self-Defense Against Armed Attack

The existence or absence of a formal declaration of war is not a factor in determining whether an international use of force is lawful as a matter of international law. The United Nations Charter's restrictions focus on the manner and purpose of its use and not on any formalities of announcement.

It should also be noted that a formal declaration of war would not place any obligations on either side in the conflict by which that side would not be bound in any event. The rules of international law concerning the conduct of hostilities in an international armed conflict apply regardless of any declaration of war.

H. Summary

The analysis set forth above shows that South Viet-Nam has the right in present circumstances to defend itself against armed attack from the North and to organize a collective self-defense with the participation of others. In response to requests from South Viet-Nam, the United States has been participating in that defense, both through military action within South Viet-Nam and actions taken directly against the aggressor in North Viet-Nam. This participation by the United States is in conformity with international law and is consistent with our obligations under the Charter of the United Nations.

II. The United States has Undertaken Commitments to Assist South Viet-Nam in Defending Itself Against Communist Aggression from the North

The United States has made commitments and given assurances, in various forms and at different times, to assist in the defense of South Viet-Nam.

A. The United States Gave Undertakings at the End of the Geneva Conference in 1954

At the time of the signing of the Geneva accords in 1954, President Eisenhower warned "that any renewal of Communist aggression would be viewed by us as a matter of grave concern," at the same time giving assurance that the United States would "not use force to disturb the settlement."[12] And the formal declaration made by the United States Government at the conclusion of the Geneva conference stated that the United States "would view any renewal of the aggression in violation of the aforesaid agreements with grave concern and as seriously threatening international peace and security."[13]

B. The United States Undertook an International Obligation To Defend South Viet-Nam in the SEATO Treaty

Later in 1954 the United States negotiated with a number of other countries and signed the Southeast Asia Collective Defense Treaty.[14] The treaty contains in the first paragraph of article IV the following provision:

> Each Party recognizes that aggression by means of armed attack in the treaty area against any of the Parties or against any State or territory which the Parties by unanimous agreement may hereafter designate, would endanger its own peace and safety, and agrees that it will in that event act to meet the common danger in accordance with its constitutional processes. Measures taken under this paragraph shall be immediately reported to the Security Council of the United Nations.

Annexed to the treaty was a protocol stating that:

> The Parties to the Southeast Asia Collective Defense Treaty unanimously designate for the purposes of Article IV

12. For a statement made by President Eisenhower on June 21, 1954, see *ibid.*, Aug. 2, 1954, p. 163.
13. For text, see *ibid.*, p. 162.
14. For text, see *ibid.*, Sept. 20, 1954, p. 393.

of the Treaty the States of Cambodia and Laos and the free territory under the jurisdiction of the State of Vietnam.

Thus, the obligations of article IV, paragraph 1, dealing with the eventuality of armed attack, have from the outset covered the territory of South Viet-Nam. The facts as to the North Vietnamese armed attack against the South have been summarized earlier, in the discussion of the right of self-defense under international law and the Charter of the United Nations. The term "armed attack" has the same meaning in the SEATO treaty as in the United Nations Charter.

Article IV, paragraph 1, places an obligation on each party to the SEATO treaty to "act to meet the common danger in accordance with its constitutional processes" in the event of an armed attack. The treaty does not require a collective determination that an armed attack has occurred in order that the obligation of article IV, paragraph 1, become operative. Nor does the provision require collective decision on actions to be taken to meet the common danger. As Secretary Dulles pointed out when transmitting the treaty to the President, the commitment in article IV, paragraph 1, "leaves to the judgment of each country the type of action to be taken in the event an armed attack occurs."[15]

The treaty was intended to deter armed aggression in Southeast Asia. To that end it created not only a multilateral alliance but also a series of bilateral relationships. The obligations are placed squarely on "each Party" in the event of armed attack in the treaty area—not upon "the Parties," a wording that might have implied a necessity for collective decision. The treaty was intended to give the assurance of United States assistance to any party or protocol state that might suffer a Communist armed attack, regardless of the views or actions of other parties. The fact that the obligations are individual, and may even to some extent differ among the parties to the treaty, is demonstrated by the United States understanding, expressed at the time of signature, that its obligations under article IV, paragraph 1, apply only in the event of *Communist* aggression, whereas the other parties to the treaty were unwilling so to limit their obligations to each other.

15. For text, see *ibid.*, Nov. 29, 1954, p. 820.

Thus, the United States has a commitment under article IV, paragraph 1, in the event of armed attack, independent of the decision or action of other treaty parties. A joint statement issued by Secretary Rusk and Foreign Minister Thanat Khoman of Thailand on March 6, 1962,[16] reflected this understanding:

> The Secretary of State assured the Foreign Minister that in the event of such aggression, the United States intends to give full effect to its obligations under the Treaty to act to meet the common danger in accordance with its constitutional processes. The Secretary of State reaffirmed that this obligation of the United States does not depend upon the prior agreement of all other parties to the Treaty, since this Treaty obligation is individual as well as collective.

Most of the SEATO countries have stated that they agreed with this interpretation. None has registered objection to it.

When the Senate Committee on Foreign Relations reported on the Southeast Asia Collective Defense Treaty, it noted that the treaty area was further defined so that the "Free Territory of Vietnam" was an area "which, if attacked, would fall under the protection of the instrument." In its conclusion the committee stated:

> The committee is not impervious to the risks which this treaty entails. It fully appreciates that acceptance of these additional obligations commits the United States to a course of action over a vast expanse of the Pacific. Yet these risks are consistent with our own highest interests.

The Senate gave its advice and consent to the treaty by a vote of 82 to 1.

C. The United States Has Given Additional Assurances to the Government of South Viet-Nam

The United States has also given a series of additional assurances to the Government of South Viet-Nam. As early as October 1954 President Eisenhower undertook to provide direct assistance to help make South Viet-Nam "capable of resisting attempted

16. For text, see *ibid.*, Mar. 26, 1962, p. 498.

subversion or aggression through military means."[17] On May 11, 1957, President Eisenhower and President Ngo Dinh Diem of the Republic of Viet-Nam issued a joint statement[18] which called attention to "the large build-up of Vietnamese Communist military forces in North Viet-Nam" and stated:

> Noting that the Republic of Viet-Nam is covered by Article IV of the Southeast Asia Collective Defense Treaty, President Eisenhower and President Ngo Dinh Diem agreed that aggression or subversion threatening the political independence of the Republic of Viet-Nam would be considered as endangering peace and stability.

On August 2, 1961, President Kennedy declared that "the United States is determined that the Republic of Viet-Nam shall not be lost to the Communists for lack of any support which the United States Government can render."[19] On December 7 of that year President Diem appealed for additional support. In his reply of December 14, 1961, President Kennedy recalled the United States declaration made at the end of the Geneva conference in 1954, and reaffirmed that the United States was "prepared to help the Republic of Viet-Nam to protect its people and to preserve its independence."[20] This assurance has been reaffirmed many times since.

III. Actions by the United States and South Viet-Nam are Justified Under the Geneva Accords of 1954

A. DESCRIPTION OF THE ACCORDS

The Geneva accords of 1954[21] established the date and hour for a cease-fire in Viet-Nam, drew a "provisional military demarca-

---

17. For text of a message from President Eisenhower to President Ngo Dinh Diem, see *ibid.*, Nov. 15, 1954, p. 735.
18. For text, see *ibid.*, May 27, 1957, p. 851.
19. For text of a joint communique issued by President Kennedy and Vice President Chen Cheng of the Republic of China, see *ibid.*, Aug. 28, 1961, p. 372.
20. For text of an exchange of messages between President Kennedy and President Diem, see *ibid.*, Jan. 1, 1962, p. 13.
21. These accords were composed of a bilateral cease-fire agreement between the "Commander-in-Chief of the People's Army of Viet Nam" and the

tion line" with a demilitarized zone on both sides, and required an exchange of prisoners and the phased regroupment of Viet Minh forces from the south to the north and of French Union forces from the north to the south. The introduction into Viet-Nam of troop reinforcements and new military equipment (except for replacement and repair) was prohibited. The armed forces of each party were required to respect the demilitarized zone and the territory of the other zone. The adherence of either zone to any military alliance, and the use of either zone for the resumption of hostilities or to "further an aggressive policy," were prohibited. The International Control Commission was established, composed of India, Canada and Poland, with India as chairman. The task of the Commission was to supervise the proper execution of the provisions of the cease-fire agreement. General elections that would result in reunification were required to be held in July 1956 under the supervision of the ICC.

B. North Viet-Nam Violated the Accords From the Beginning

From the very beginning, the North Vietnamese violated the 1954 Geneva accords. Communist military forces and supplies were left in the South in violation of the accords. Other Communist guerrillas were moved north for further training and then were infiltrated into the South in violation of the accords.

C. The Introduction of United States Military Personnel and Equipment Was Justified

The accords prohibited the reinforcement of foreign military forces in Viet-Nam and the introduction of new military equipment, but they allowed replacement of existing military personnel and equipment. Prior to late 1961 South Viet-Nam had received

---

"Commander-in-Chief of the French Union forces in Indo-China," together with a Final Declaration of the Conference, to which France adhered. However, it is to be noted that the South Vietnamese Government was not a signatory of the cease-fire agreement and did not adhere to the Final Declaration. South Viet-Nam entered a series of reservations in a statement to the conference. This statement was noted by the conference, but by decision of the conference chairman it was not included or referred to in the Final Declaration. [Footnote in original.]

considerable military equipment and supplies from the United States, and the United States had gradually enlarged its Military Assistance Advisory Group to slightly less than 900 men. These actions were reported to the ICC and were justified as replacements for equipment in Viet-Nam in 1954 and for French training and advisory personnel who had been withdrawn after 1954.

As the Communist aggression intensified during 1961, with increased infiltration and a marked stepping up of Communist terrorism in the South, the United States found it necessary in late 1961 to increase substantially the numbers of our military personnel and the amounts and types of equipment introduced by this country into South Viet-Nam. These increases were justified by the international law principle that a material breach of an agreement by one party entitles the other at least to withhold compliance with an equivalent, corresponding, or related provision until the defaulting party is prepared to honor its obligations.[22]

In accordance with this principle, the systematic violation of the Geneva accords by North Viet-Nam justified South Viet-Nam in suspending compliance with the provision controlling entry of foreign military personnel and military equipment.

22. This principle of law and the circumstances in which it may be invoked are most fully discussed in the Fourth Report on the Law of Treaties by Sir Gerald Fitzmaurice, articles 18, 20 (U.N. doc. A/CN.4/120 (1959)) II Yearbook of the International Law Commission 37 (U.N. doc. A/CN.4/SER.A/1959/Add.1) and in the later report by Sir Humphrey Waldock, article 20 (U.N. doc. A/CN.4/156 and Add. 1-3 (1963)) II Yearbook of the International Law Commission 36 (U.N. doc. A/CN.4/SER.A/1963/Add.1). Among the authorities cited by the fourth report for this proposition are: II Oppenheim, *International Law* 136, 137 (7th ed. Lauterpacht 1955); I Rousseau, *Principes généraux du droit international public* 365 (1944); II Hyde, *International Law* 1660 et seq. (2d ed. 1947); II Guggenheim, *Traité de droit international public* 84, 85 (1935); Spiropoulos, *Traité théorique et pratique de droit international public* 289 (1933); Verdross, *Völkerrecht*, 328 (1950); Hall, *Treatise* 21 (8th ed. Higgins 1924); 3 Accioly, *Tratado de Direito Internacional Publico* 82 (1956-57). See also draft articles 42 and 46 of the Law of Treaties by the International Law Commission, contained in the report on the work of its 15th session (General Assembly, Official Records, 18th Session, Supplement No. 9 (A/5809)). [Footnote in original.]

D. South Viet-Nam Was Justified in Refusing to
Implement the Election Provisions of the
Geneva Accords

The Geneva accords contemplated the reunification of the two parts of Viet-Nam. They contained a provision for general elections to be held in July 1956 in order to obtain a "free expression of the national will." The accords stated that "consultations will be held on this subject between the competent representative authorities of the two zones from 20 July 1955 onwards."

There may be some question whether South Viet-Nam was bound by these election provisions. As indicated earlier, South Viet-Nam did not sign the cease-fire agreement of 1954, nor did it adhere to the Final Declaration of the Geneva conference. The South Vietnamese Government at that time gave notice of its objection in particular to the election provisions of the accords.

However, even on the premise that these provisions were binding on South Viet-Nam, the South Vietnamese Government's failure to engage in consultations in 1955, with a view to holding elections in 1956, involved no breach of obligation. The conditions in North Viet-Nam during that period were such as to make impossible any free and meaningful expression of popular will.

Some of the facts about conditions in the North were admitted even by the Communist leadership in Hanoi. General Giap, currently Defense Minister of North Viet-Nam, in addressing the Tenth Congress of the North Vietnamese Communist Party in October 1956, publicly acknowledged that the Communist leaders were running a police state where executions, terror, and torture were commonplace. A nationwide election in these circumstances would have been a travesty. No one in the North would have dared to vote except as directed. With a substantial majority of the Vietnamese people living north of the 17th parallel, such an election would have meant turning the country over to the Communists without regard to the will of the people. The South Vietnamese Government realized these facts and quite properly took the position that consultations for elections in 1956 as contemplated by the accords would be a useless formality.[23]

23. In any event, if North Viet-Nam considered there had been a breach of obligation by the South, its remedies lay in discussion with Saigon, per-

IV. The President has Full Authority to Commit United States Forces in the Collective Defense of South Viet-Nam

There can be no question in present circumstances of the President's authority to commit United States forces to the defense of South Viet-Nam. The grant of authority to the President in article II of the Constitution extends to the actions of the United States currently undertaken in Viet-Nam. In fact, however, it is unnecessary to determine whether this grant standing alone is sufficient to authorize the actions taken in Viet-Nam. These actions rest not only on the exercise of Presidential powers under article II but on the SEATO treaty—a treaty advised and consented to by the Senate—and on actions of the Congress, particularly the joint resolution of August 10, 1964. When these sources of authority are taken together—article II of the Constitution, the SEATO treaty, and actions by the Congress—there can be no question of the legality under domestic law of United States actions in Viet-Nam.

A. THE PRESIDENT'S POWER UNDER ARTICLE II OF THE CONSTITUTION EXTENDS TO THE ACTIONS CURRENTLY UNDERTAKEN IN VIET-NAM

Under the Constitution, the President, in addition to being Chief Executive, is Commander in Chief of the Army and Navy. He holds the prime responsibility for the conduct of the United States foreign relations. These duties carry very broad powers, including the power to deploy American forces abroad and commit them to military operations when the President deems such action necessary to maintain the security and defense of the United States.

At the Federal Constitutional Convention in 1787, it was originally proposed that Congress have the power "to make war." There were objections that legislative proceedings were too slow for this power to be vested in Congress; it was suggested that the

---

haps in an appeal to the cochairmen of the Geneva conference, or in a reconvening of the conference to consider the situation. Under international law, North Viet-Nam had no right to use force outside its own zone in order to secure its political objectives. [Footnote in original.]

Senate might be a better repository. Madison and Gerry then moved to substitute "to declare war" for "to make war," "leaving to the Executive the power to repel sudden attacks." It was objected that this might make it too easy for the Executive to involve the nation in war, but the motion carried with but one dissenting vote.

In 1787 the world was a far larger place, and the framers probably had in mind attacks upon the United States. In the 20th century, the world has grown much smaller. An attack on a country far from our shores can impinge directly on the nation's security. In the SEATO treaty, for example, it is formally declared that an armed attack against Viet-Nam would endanger the peace and safety of the United States.

Since the Constitution was adopted there have been at least 125 instances in which the President has ordered the armed forces to take action or maintain positions abroad without obtaining prior congressional authorization, starting with the "undeclared war" with France (1798-1800). For example, President Truman ordered 250,000 troops to Korea during the Korean war of the early 1950's. President Eisenhower dispatched 14,000 troops to Lebanon in 1958.

The Constitution leaves to the President the judgment to determine whether the circumstances of a particular armed attack are so urgent and the potential consequences so threatening to the security of the United States that he should act without formally consulting the Congress.

B. THE SOUTHEAST ASIA COLLECTIVE DEFENSE TREATY AUTHORIZES THE PRESIDENT'S ACTIONS

Under article VI of the United States Constitution, "all Treaties made, or which shall be made, under the Authority of the United States, shall be the supreme Law of the Land." Article IV, paragraph 1, of the SEATO treaty establishes as a matter of law that a Communist armed attack against South Viet-Nam endangers the peace and safety of the United States. In this same provision the United States has undertaken a commitment in the SEATO treaty to "act to meet the common danger in accordance with its constitutional processes" in the event of such an attack.

Under our Constitution it is the President who must decide when an armed attack has occurred. He has also the constitutional responsibility for determining what measures of defense are required when the peace and safety of the United States are endangered. If he considers that deployment of U.S. forces to South Viet-Nam is required, and that military measures against the source of Communist aggression in North Viet-Nam are necessary, he is constitutionally empowered to take those measures.

The SEATO treaty specifies that each party will act "in accordance with its constitutional processes."

It has recently been argued that the use of land forces in Asia is not authorized under the treaty because their use to deter armed attack was not contemplated at the time the treaty was considered by the Senate. Secretary Dulles testified at that time that we did not intend to establish (1) a land army in Southeast Asia capable of deterring Communist aggression, or (2) an integrated headquarters and military organization like that of NATO; instead, the United States would rely on "mobile striking power" against the sources of aggression. However, the treaty obligation in article IV, paragraph 1, to meet the common danger in the event of armed aggression, is not limited to particular modes of military action. What constitutes an adequate deterrent or an appropriate response, in terms of military strategy, may change; but the essence of our commitment to act to meet the common danger, as necessary at the time of an armed aggression, remains. In 1954 the forecast of military judgment might have been against the use of substantial United States ground forces in Viet-Nam. But that does not preclude the President from reaching a different military judgment in different circumstances, 12 years later.

C. The Joint Resolution of Congress of August 10, 1964, Authorizes United States Participation in the Collective Defense of South Viet-Nam

As stated earlier, the legality of United States participation in the defense of South Viet-Nam does not rest only on the constitutional power of the President under article II—or indeed on that power taken in conjunction with the SEATO treaty. In addition, the Congress has acted in unmistakable fashion to approve and authorize United States actions in Viet-Nam.

Following the North Vietnamese attacks in the Gulf of Tonkin against United States destroyers, Congress adopted, by a Senate vote of 88-2 and a House vote of 416-0, a joint resolution containing a series of important declarations and provisions of law.[24]

Section 1 resolved that "the Congress approves and supports the determination of the President, as Commander in Chief, to take all necessary measures to repel any armed attack against the forces of the United States and to prevent further aggression." Thus, the Congress gave its sanction to specific actions by the President to repel attacks against United States naval vessels in the Gulf of Tonkin and elsewhere in the western Pacific. Congress further approved the taking of "all necessary measures . . . to prevent further aggression." This authorization extended to those measures the President might consider necessary to ward off further attacks and to prevent further aggression by North Viet-Nam in Southeast Asia.

The joint resolution then went on to provide in section 2:

> The United States regards as vital to its national interest and to world peace the maintenance of international peace and security in southeast Asia. Consonant with the Constitution of the United States and the Charter of the United Nations and in accordance with its obligations under the Southeast Asia Collective Defense Treaty, the United States is, therefore, prepared, as the President determines, to take all necessary steps, including the use of armed force, to assist any member or protocol state of the Southeast Asia Collective Defense Treaty requesting assistance in defense of its freedom.

Section 2 thus constitutes an authorization to the President, in his discretion, to act—using armed force if he determines that is required—to assist South Viet-Nam at its request in defense of its freedom. The identification of South Viet-Nam through the reference to "protocol state" in this section is unmistakable, and the grant of authority "as the President determines" is unequivocal.

24. For text, see BULLETIN of Aug. 24, 1964, p. 268.

It has been suggested that the legislative history of the joint resolution shows an intention to limit United States assistance to South Viet-Nam to aid, advice, and training. This suggestion is based on an amendment offered from the floor by Senator [Gaylord] Nelson which would have added the following to the text:

> The Congress also approves and supports the efforts of the President to bring the problem of peace in Southeast Asia to the Security Council of the United Nations, and the President's declaration that the United States, seeking no extension of the present military conflict, will respond to provocation in a manner that is "limited and fitting." Our continuing policy is to limit our role to the provision of aid, training assistance, and military advice, and it is the sense of Congress that, except when provoked to a greater response, we should continue to attempt to avoid a direct military involvement in the Southeast Asian conflict.[25]

Senator [J. W.] Fulbright, who had reported the joint resolution from the Foreign Relations Committee, spoke on the amendment as follows:

> It states fairly accurately what the President has said would be our policy, and what I stated my understanding was as to our policy; also what other Senators have stated. In other words, it states that our response should be appropriate and limited to the provocation, which the Senator states as "respond to provocation in a manner that is limited and fitting," and so forth. We do not wish any political or military bases there. We are not seeking to gain a colony. We seek to insure the capacity of these people to develop along the lines of their own desires, independent of domination by communism.
>
> The Senator has put into his amendment a statement of policy that is unobjectionable. However, I cannot accept the amendment under the circumstances. I do not believe it is contrary to the joint resolution, but it is an enlargement. I am informed that the House is now voting on this resolution. The

25. 110 *Cong. Rec.* 18459 (Aug. 7, 1964). [Footnote in original.]

House joint resolution is about to be presented to us. I cannot accept the amendment and go to conference with it, and thus take responsibility for delaying matters.

I do not object to it as a statement of policy. I believe it is an accurate reflection of what I believe is the President's policy, judging from his own statements. That does not mean that as a practical matter I can accept the amendment. It would delay matters to do so. It would cause confusion and require a conference, and present us with all the other difficulties that are involved in this kind of legislative action. I regret that I cannot do it, even though I do not at all disagree with the amendment as a general statement of policy.[26]

Senator Nelson's amendment related the degree and kind of U.S. response in Viet-Nam to "provocation" on the other side; the response should be "limited and fitting." The greater the provocation, the stronger are the measures that may be characterized as "limited and fitting." Bombing of North Vietnamese naval bases was a "limited and fitting" response to the attacks on U.S. destroyers in August 1964, and the subsequent actions taken by the United States and South Viet-Nam have been an appropriate response to the increased war of aggression carried on by North Viet-Nam since that date. Moreover, Senator Nelson's proposed amendment did not purport to be a restriction on authority available to the President but merely a statement concerning what should be the continuing policy of the United States.

Congressional realization of the scope of authority being conferred by the joint resolution is shown by the legislative history of the measure as a whole. The following exchange between Senators Cooper and Fulbright is illuminating:

MR. COOPER [John Sherman Cooper]. . . . The Senator will remember that the SEATO Treaty, in article IV, provides that in the event an armed attack is made upon a party to the Southeast Asia Collective Defense Treaty, or upon one of the protocol states such as South Vietnam, the parties to the treaty, one of whom is the United States, would then take such action as might be appropriate, after resorting to their

26. *Ibid.*

constitutional processes. I assume that would mean, in the case of the United States, that Congress would be asked to grant the authority to act.

Does the Senator consider that in enacting this resolution we are satisfying that requirement of article IV of the Southeast Asia Collective Defense Treaty? In other words, are we now giving the President advance authority to take whatever action he may deem necessary respecting South Vietnam and its defense, or with respect to the defense of any other country included in the treaty?

Mr. FULBRIGHT. I think that is correct.

Mr. COOPER. Then, looking ahead, if the President decided that it was necessary to use such force as could lead into war, we will give that authority by this resolution?

Mr. FULBRIGHT. That is the way I would interpret if. If a situation later developed in which we thought the approval should be withdrawn it could be withdrawn by concurrent resolution.[27]

27. 110 *Cong. Rec.* 18409 (Aug. 6, 1964). Senator [Wayne] Morse, who opposed the joint resolution, expressed the following view on August 6, 1964, concerning the scope of the proposed resolution:
    Another Senator thought, in the early part of the debate, that this course would not broaden the power of the President to engage in a land war if he decided that he wanted to apply the resolution in that way.
    That Senator was taking great consolation in the then held belief that, if he voted for the resolution, it would give no authority to the President to send many troops into Asia. I am sure he was quite disappointed to finally learn, because it took a little time to get the matter cleared, that the resolution places no restriction on the President in that respect. If he is still in doubt, let him read the language on page 2, lines 3 to 6, and page 2, lines 11 to 17. The first reads:
    The Congress approves and supports the determination of the President, as Commander in Chief, to take all necessary measures to repel any armed attack against the forces of the United States and to prevent further aggression.
    It does not say he is limited in regard to the sending of ground forces. It does not limit that authority. That is why I have called it a predated declaration of war, in clear violation of article I, section 8, of the Constitution, which vests the power to declare war in the Congress, and not in the President.
    What is proposed is to authorize the President of the United States, without a declaration of war, to commit acts of war. (110 *Cong. Rec.* 18426-7 (Aug. 6, 1964)). [Footnote in original.]

The August 1964 joint resolution continues in force today. Section 2 of the resolution provides that it shall expire "when the President shall determine that the peace and security of the area is reasonably assured by international conditions created by action of the United Nations or otherwise, except that it may be terminated earlier by concurrent resolution of the Congress." The President has made no such determination, nor has Congress terminated the joint resolution.[28]

Instead, Congress in May 1965 approved an appropriation of $700 million to meet the expense of mounting military requirements in Viet-Nam. (Public Law 89-18, 79 Stat. 109.) The President's message asking for this appropriation stated that this was "not a routine appropriation. For each Member of Congress who supports this request is also voting to persist in our efforts to halt Communist aggression in South Vietnam."[29] The appropriation act constitutes a clear congressional endorsement and approval of the actions taken by the President.

On March 1, 1966, the Congress continued to express its support of the President's policy by approving a $4.8 billion supplemental military authorization by votes of 392-4 and 93-2. An amendment that would have limited the President's authority to commit forces to Viet-Nam was rejected in the Senate by a vote of 94-2.

D. No Declaration of War by the Congress Is Required To Authorize United States Participation in the Collective Defense of South Viet-Nam

No declaration of war is needed to authorize Americans actions in Viet-Nam. As shown in the preceding sections, the President has ample authority to order the participation of United States armed forces in the defense of South Viet-Nam.

Over a very long period in our history, practice and precedent have confirmed the constitutional authority to engage United States forces in hostilities without a declaration of war. This his-

28. On March 1, 1966, the Senate voted, 92-5, to table an amendment that would have repealed the joint resolution. [Footnote in original.]
29. For text, see BULLETIN of May 24, 1965, p. 822.

tory extends from the undeclared war with France and the war against the Barbary pirates at the end of the 18th century to the Korean war of 1950-53.

James Madison, one of the leading framers of the Constitution, and Presidents John Adams and Jefferson all construed the Constitution, in their official actions during the early years of the Republic, as authorizing the United States to employ its armed forces abroad in hostilities in the absence of any congressional declaration of war. Their views and actions constitute highly persuasive evidence as to the meaning and effect of the Constitution. History has accepted the interpretation that was placed on the Constitution by the early Presidents and Congresses in regard to the lawfulness of hostilities without a declaration of war. The instances of such action in our history are numerous.

In the Korean conflict, where large-scale hostilities were conducted with an American troop participation of a quarter of a million men, no declaration of war was made by the Congress. The President acted on the basis of his constitutional responsibilities. While the Security Council, under a treaty of this country— the United Nations Charter—recommended assistance to the Republic of Korea against the Communist armed attack, the United States had no treaty commitment at that time obligating us to join in the defense of South Korea. In the case of South Viet-Nam we have the obligation of the SEATO treaty and clear expressions of congressional support. If the President could act in Korea without a declaration of war, *a fortiori* he is empowered to do so now in Viet-Nam.

It may be suggested that a declaration of war is the only available constitutional process by which congressional support can be made effective for the use of United States armed forces in combat abroad. But the Constitution does not insist on a rigid formalism. It gives Congress a choice of ways in which to exercise its powers. In the case of Viet-Nam the Congress has supported the determination of the President by the Senate's approval of the SEATO treaty, the adoption of the joint resolution of August 10, 1964, and the enactment of the necessary authorizations and appropriations.

V. Conclusion

South Viet-Nam is being subjected to armed attack by Communist North Viet-Nam, through the infiltration of armed personnel, military equipment, and regular combat units. International law recognizes the right of individual and collective self-defense against armed attack. South Viet-Nam, and the United States upon the request of South Viet-Nam, are engaged in such collective defense of the South. Their actions are in conformity with international law and with the Charter of the United Nations. The fact that South Viet-Nam has been precluded by Soviet veto from becoming a member of the United Nations and the fact that South Viet-Nam is a zone of a temporarily divided state in no way diminish the right of collective defense of South Viet-Nam.

The United States has commitments to assist South Viet-Nam in defending itself against Communist aggression from the North. The United States gave undertakings to this effect at the conclusion of the Geneva conference in 1954. Later that year the United States undertook an international obligation in the SEATO treaty to defend South Viet-Nam against Communist armed aggression. And during the past decade the United States has given additional assurances to the South Vietnamese Government.

The Geneva accords of 1954 provided for a cease-fire and regroupment of contending forces, a division of Viet-Nam into two zones, and a prohibition on the use of either zone for the resumption of hostilities or to "further an aggressive policy." From the beginning, North Viet-Nam violated the Geneva accords through a systematic effort to gain control of South Viet-Nam by force. In the light of these progressive North Vietnamese violations, the introduction into South Viet-Nam beginning in late 1961 of substantial United States military equipment and personnel, to assist in the defense of the South, was fully justified; substantial breach of an international agreement by one side permits the other side to suspend performance of corresponding obligations under the agreement. South Viet-Nam was justified in refusing to implement the provisions of the Geneva accords calling for reunification

631

through free elections throughout Viet-Nam since the Communist regime in North Viet-Nam created conditions in the North that made free elections entirely impossible.

The President of the United States has full authority to commit United States forces in the collective defense of South Viet-Nam. This authority stems from the constitutional powers of the President. However, it is not necessary to rely on the Constitution alone as the source of the President's authority, since the SEATO treaty—advised and consented to by the Senate and forming part of the law of the land—sets forth a United States commitment to defend South Viet-Nam against armed attack, and since the Congress—in the joint resolution of August 10, 1964, and in authorization and appropriations acts for support of the U.S. military effort in Viet-Nam—has given its approval and support to the President's actions. United States actions in Viet-Nam, taken by the President and approved by the Congress, do not require any declaration of war, as shown by a long line of precedents for the use of United States armed forces abroad in the absence of any congressional declaration of war.

Memorandum by the State Department Assistant Legal Adviser for Far Eastern Affairs, George Aldrich, on the Applicability of the Geneva Convention of 1949 Relative to the Treatment of Prisoners of War to American Military Personnel Held by North Vietnam (July 13, 1966).*

* Reprinted from 10 M. whiteman, digest of int'l. law 231 (1968). Mr. Aldrich is currently a Deputy Legal Adviser.

Entitlement of American Military Personnel Held by North Viet-Nam to Treatment as Prisoners of War Under the Geneva Convention of 1949 Relative to the Treatment of Prisoners of War*

The United States is submitting this memorandum to show that, by its plain language and obvious purpose, the Geneva Convention of 1949 Relative to the Treatment of Prisoners of War grants prisoner of war rights to United States military personnel held in North Viet Nam.

I. *The Convention applies to the armed conflict in which American airmen have been taken prisoner by North Vietnamese forces.*

Article 2 of the Convention declares that it

> . . . shall apply to all cases of declared war or of any other armed conflict which may arise between two or more of the High Contracting Parties, even if the state of war is not recognized by one of them.

The Convention entered into force for the United States on February 2, 1956; North Viet Nam adhered to the Convention on June 28, 1957; and the Republic of Viet Nam adhered on November 14, 1953. Although there have been no declarations of war, the present conflict in Viet Nam is indisputably an "armed conflict" between parties to the Geneva Conventions of 1949. In one aspect of the war American aircraft are operating against military targets in North Viet Nam, and North Vietnamese forces have engaged these aircraft. Under these circumstances, the Convention applies in its entirety to this conflict. As Jacques Freymond,

---

* Memorandum to the International Committee of the Red Cross, prepared by Assistant Legal Adviser for Far Eastern Affairs, George Aldrich, Office of the Legal Adviser, July 13, 1966, MS. Department of State, file POL 27-7 VIET.

Vice President of the International Committee of the Red Cross, wrote Secretary Rusk in his letter of June 11, 1965:

> The hostilities raging at the present time in Viet Nam—both North and South of the 17th parallel—have assumed such proportions recently that there can be no doubt they constitute an armed conflict to which the regulations of humanitarian law as a whole should be applied.
>
> All Parties to the conflict, the Republic of Viet Nam, the Democratic Republic of Viet Nam and the United States of America are bound by the four Geneva Conventions of August 12, 1949, for the protection of the victims of war, having ratified them and having adhered thereto. The National Liberation Front too is bound by the undertakings signed by Viet Nam.

The Committee was fully justified in reminding all parties to the hostilities in Viet Nam of their "obligations pursuant to the Geneva Conventions," including the obligation to treat a combatant taken prisoner "humanely as a prisoner of war."

Pictet points out that Article 2

> . . . deprives belligerents, in advance, of the pretexts they might in theory put foward for evading their obligations. There is no need for a formal declaration of war, or for the recognition of the existence of a state of war, as preliminaries to the application of the Convention. The occurrence of *de facto* hostilities is sufficient.

He adds that even if both parties to an armed conflict denied the existence of a state of war, "it would not appear that they could, by tacit agreement, prevent the Conventions from applying." [Pictet, *Commentary—III Geneva Convention Relative to the Treatment of Prisoners of War* (Geneva, 1960) pp. 22-23.] In this case, the state of war (under international law) is not disputed; it is merely undeclared. Lauterpacht draws the logical conclusion that the whole Prisoner of War Convention applies to an armed conflict even if both parties do not recognize a state of war. [II Oppenheim's *International Law* (Lauterpacht 7th ed., 1952) p. 369, n.6.]

II. *The American military personnel qualify as prisoners of war under the terms of Article 4 of the Convention.*

The American military personnel captured and held by the North Vietnamese are uniformed members of the United States regular armed forces. As such, they qualify as prisoners of war under Article 4A(1) of the Convention as "members of the armed forces of a Party to the conflict."

III. *The American military personnel cannot be denied their protected status as prisoners of war on the grounds of any reservation noted by the North Vietnamese authorities in adhering to the Convention.*

No nation has reserved the right to nullify its obligations under the Convention by a simple declaration that it regards members of the armed forces of an opposing party in an international conflict as war criminals. Article 85 provides that:

> Prisoners of war prosecuted under the laws of the Detaining Power for acts committed prior to capture shall retain, even if convicted, the benefits of the present Convention.

While a number of Communist parties to the Convention, including North Viet Nam, have indicated, by reservations, that they will not comply with Article 85, these reservations (1) apply only to prisoners guilty of war crimes as opposed to recognized acts of warfare and (2) apply only *after* a prisoner has been tried in accordance with all the judicial guarantees which the Convention provides, and only after conviction.

1. The bombing of the carefully controlled and restricted targets in North Viet Nam is a long-accepted measure of warfare. The United States has not knowingly bombed any target protected by international law and the North Vietnamese authorities have refused to allow any impartial neutral body to investigate their charges to the contrary. Finally, the contention of the North Vietnamese that military action by the United States is unjustified as a matter of law is neither correct nor relevant. The Legal Adviser of the Department of State has prepared a memorandum . . . explaining *inter alia* why the military actions being taken against North Viet Nam are consistent with the requirements of

international law. In any event, the Nuremberg judgments plainly rejected any contention that charges of war crimes could be lodged against military personnel on the grounds that their government was not legally justified in engaging in acts of war.

2. Wholly apart from the lack of substance of any charges of war crimes, American military personnel held in North Viet Nam are entitled to the protections which the Convention grants prisoners of war. Every member of the armed forces of a party to an international conflict is entitled to prisoner of war status unless and until he has been convicted of war crimes in accordance with the procedures set forth by the Geneva Convention. Article 85 of the Convention merely extends this protection to the period after conviction. A number of Communist nations have declined to adopt Article 85, but this in no way effects the rights of prisoners prior to conviction and sentence.

The North Vietnamese reservation states:

> In Article 85: The Democratic Republic of Viet-Nam declares that prisoners of war prosecuted and convicted for war crimes or for crimes against humanity, in accordance with the principles laid down by the Nuremberg Court of Justice shall not benefit from the present Convention as specified in Article 85.

It is virtually identical to the reservations of most other Communist countries. Under these reservations persons who have been prosecuted and convicted of war crimes or of crimes against humanity do not benefit from the provisions of the Geneva Convention during the time they are serving their sentences, whereas Article 85 would continue the protection of the Convention until the prisoner was released. As the language of the reservation "prosecuted *and* convicted" plainly states and as the Soviet Union has itself explained, the reservation does not deprive a prisoner of the protections of the Convention until after final conviction. For the text of the Soviet explanation, see Pictet, *Commentary— III Geneva Convention Relative to the Treatment of Prisoners of War*, pp. 423-425 (1960). Pictet concludes that:

> . . . as stated in the reservation itself, prisoners of war accused of war crimes or crimes against humanity will con-

tinue to enjoy the benefits of the Convention until such time as the penalty to which they have been sentenced becomes enforceable, that is to say until all courses of appeal have been exhausted. They will therefore enjoy all the judicial guarantees which the Convention provides during their trial and, in particular, will have the assistance of the Protecting Power. The Convention would once more be applicable to prisoners of war sentenced to confinement as soon as they have served their sentence. This clarification is very useful as the reservation had given rise to some doubt.

IV. *Conclusion*

The Geneva Convention of 1949 Relative to the Treatment of Prisoners of War indisputably applies to the armed conflict in Viet Nam, American military personnel captured in the course of that armed conflict are entitled to be treated as prisoners of war, and mere allegations of criminality cannot justify depriving them of such treatment.

Appendix C

Address by the State Department Legal Adviser, John R. Stevenson, on the International-Legal Aspects of the Cambodian Incursion (May 28, 1970).*

* Reprinted from 62 DEP'T STATE BULLETIN 765 (1970). Also reprinted in 9 INT'L LEG. MAT. 840 (1970). Mr. Stevenson is the current Legal Adviser.

United States Military Actions in Cambodia: Questions of International Law

BY JOHN R. STEVENSON
LEGAL ADVISER[1]

I welcome the opportunity to present the administration's views on the questions of international law arising out of the current South Vietnamese and United States operations in Cambodia.[2]

I do not intend to review in any detail the legal justification of earlier actions by the United States in Viet-Nam. In 1966 the previous administration set forth at some length the legal justifications for our involvement in South Viet-Nam and our bombing of North Viet-Nam.[3]

In general, reliance was placed squarely upon the inherent right of individual and collective self-defense, recognized by article 51 of the U.N. Charter. This legal case involved the showing that North Viet-Nam had raised the level of its subversion and infiltration into South Viet-Nam to that of an "armed attack" in late 1964 when it first sent regular units of its armed forces into South Viet-Nam. The buildup of American forces in South Viet-Nam and the bombing of North Viet-Nam were justified as appropriate measures of collective self-defense against that armed attack.[4]

1. Address made before the Hammarskjöld Forum of the Association of the Bar of the City of New York at New York, N.Y., on May 28 (press release 166 dated May 30).
2. The views of the administration in the military and political issues have been expressed by the President and other officials. See, in particular, President Nixon's address of Apr. 30 (BULLETIN of May 18, 1970, p. 617) and his news conference of May 8 (BULLETIN of May 25, 1970, p. 641). [Author's footnote.]
3. For text of the Department's legal memorandum of Mar. 4, 1966, entitled "The Legality of United States Participation in the Defense of Viet-Nam," which was submitted to the Senate Committee on Foreign Relations on Mar. 8, 1966, see BULLETIN of Mar. 28, 1966, p. 474.
4. They were also justified on that basis in U.S. reports to the United Nations, pursuant to article 51. For texts of U.S. letters dated Feb. 7

The legal case presented by the previous administration was vigorously attacked and defended by various scholars of the international legal community.[5] Many of the differences rested on disputed questions of fact which could not be proved conclusively. This administration, however, has no desire to reargue those issues or the legality of those actions, which are now history. In January 1969, President Nixon inherited a situation in which one-half million American troops were engaged in combat in South Viet-Nam, helping the Republic of Viet-Nam to defend itself against a continuing armed attack by North Viet-Nam. Our efforts have been to extricate ourselves from this situation by negotiated settlement if possible or, if a settlement providing the South Vietnamese people the right of self-determination cannot be negotiated, then through the process of Vietnamization.[6] The current actions in Cambodia should be viewed as part of the President's effort to withdraw United States forces from combat in Southeast Asia.[7]

I appreciate this opportunity to discuss the questions of international law arising out of our actions in Cambodia. It is important for the Government of the United States to explain the legal basis for its actions, not merely to pay proper respect to the law but also because the precedent created by the use of armed forces

and Feb. 27, 1965, to the President of the U.N. Security Council, see BULLETIN of Feb. 22, 1965, p. 240, and Mar. 22, 1965, p. 419. [Author's footnote.]

5. See the collection, in two volumes, *The Vietnam War and International Law*, edited by Richard A. Falk, sponsored by the American Society of International Law (Princeton University Press, 1968 and 1969). [Author's footnote.]

6. The President reviewed our efforts at negotiation and the progress of Vietnamization in his statement of Apr. 20 (BULLETIN of May 11, 1970, p. 601) and stated: ". . . our overriding objective is a political solution that reflects the will of the South Vietnamese people and allows them to determine their future without outside interference." [Author's footnote.]

7. In his address of Apr. 30, announcing the use of force in Cambodia, President Nixon said: "We take this action not for the purpose of expanding the war into Cambodia, but for the purpose of ending the war in Viet-Nam and winning the just peace we all desire. We have made and we will continue to make every possible effort to end this war through negotiation at the conference table rather than through more fighting on the battlefield." [Author's footnote.]

in Cambodia by the United States can be affected significantly by our legal rationale.

I am sure you recall the choice that was made during the Cuban missile crisis in 1962 to base our "quarantine" of Cuba not on self-defense, since no "armed attack" had occurred, but on the special powers of the Organization of American States as a regional organization under chapter VIII of the U.N. Charter.[8]

Within a narrower scope, the arguments we make can affect the applicability of the Cambodian precedent to other situations in the future. I believe the United States has a strong interest in developing rules of international law that limit claimed rights to use armed force and encourage the peaceful resolution of disputes.

One way to have limited the effects of the Cambodian action would have been to obtain the advance, express request of the Government of Cambodia for our military actions on Cambodian territory. This might well have been possible.[9] However, had we

8. See Chayes, "Law and the Quarantine of Cuba," 41 *Foreign Affairs* (1963), p. 550. [Author's footnote.]

9. On May 1 a Cambodian spokesman said that "the Cambodian Government as a neutral government cannot approve foreign intervention." However, on May 5, the Cambodian Government issued the following statement:

"In his message to the American people of April 30, 1970, President Nixon made known the important measures which he had taken to counter the military aggression of North Viet-Nam in Laos, Cambodia, and South Viet-Nam. One of these measures concerns the aid of the U.S. in the defense of the neutrality of Cambodia violated by the North Vietnamese.

"The Government of Salvation notes with satisfaction the President of the United States took into consideration in his decision the legitimate expressions of the Cambodian people, who only desire to live in peace within their territory, independent, and in strict neutrality. For this reason, the Government of Cambodia wishes to announce that it appreciates the views of President Nixon in his message of April 30 and expresses to him its gratitude.

"It is time now that the other friendly nations understand the extremely serious situation in which Cambodia finds itself and come to the assistance of the Cambodian people, who are victims of armed aggression. The Government of Salvation renews on this occasion its appeal for assistance made April 14, noting that it will accept from friendly countries all unconditional and diplomatic, military, and economic assistance."

Later statements have indicated even more clearly the Cambodian Government's approval of our actions. [Author's footnote.]

done so, we would have compromised the neutrality of the Cambodian Government and moved much closer to a situation in which the United States was committing its armed forces to help Cambodia defend itself against the North Vietnamese attack. We did not wish to see Cambodia become a cobelligerent along with South Viet-Nam and the United States. We are convinced that the interests of the United States, the Republic of Viet-Nam, and Cambodia, and indeed the interests of all Asian countries, will best be served by the maintenance of Cambodian neutrality, even though that neutrality may be only partially respected by North Viet-Nam.

As the President has made clear, the purpose of our armed forces in Cambodia is not to help defend the Government of Cambodia, but rather to help defend South Viet-Nam and United States troops in South Viet-Nam from the continuing North Vietnamese armed attack.[10] This limited purpose is consistent with the Nixon doctrine, first set forth by the President at Guam on July 25, 1969,[11] that the nations of the region have the primary responsibility of providing the manpower for their defense.

The North Vietnamese have continued to press their attack against South Viet-Nam since 1964 and have made increasing use of Cambodian territory in the furtherance of that attack. They have used Cambodia as a sanctuary for moving and storing supplies, for training, regroupment, and rest of their troops, and as a center of their command and communications network. I assume that these facts are generally accepted, but it might be useful to give a few examples.

In the past 5 years 150,000 enemy troops have been infiltrated into South Viet-Nam through Cambodia. In 1969 alone, 60,000 of their military forces moved in from Cambodia. The trails inside Cambodia are used not only for the infiltration of troops but also

10. This is to be distinguished from the furnishing of weapons and ammunition to Cambodia pursuant to the Foreign Assistance Act, 75 Stat. 424, 22 U.S.C. § 2161-2410, which is done to improve the ability of Cambodia to defend itself. [Author's footnote.]

11. The President's statements were not for direct quotation. The President later restated the doctrine in his address to the Nation on Viet-Nam on Nov. 3, 1969 (BULLETIN of Nov. 24, 1969, p. 437), and in his foreign policy report to the Congress on Feb. 18 (BULLETIN of Mar. 9, 1970). [Author's footnote.]

for the movement of supplies. A significant quantity of the military supplies that support these forces came through Cambodian ports.

Since 1968 the enemy has been moving supplies through southern Cambodia to its forces in the Mekong Delta. Further, in the spring and summer of 1969, three to four regiments of regular North Vietnamese troops used Cambodian territory to infiltrate into the Mekong Delta. Up to that time, there had been no regular North Vietnamese combat units operating in this area.

As many as 40,000 North Vietnamese and Viet Cong troops were operating out of the Cambodian base areas against South Viet-Nam prior to April 30. As the war in South Viet-Nam intensified, Viet Cong and North Vietnamese troops have resorted more frequently to these sanctuaries and to attacking from them to avoid detection by or combat with United States and South Vietnamese forces.

During 1968 and 1969 the Cambodian bases adjacent to the South Vietnamese Provinces of Tay Ninh, Pleiku, and Kontum have served as staging areas for regimental-size Communist forces for at least three series of major engagements—the 1968 Tet offensive, the May 1968 offensive, and the post-Tet 1969 offensive.

Many of these North Vietnamese actions violate Cambodian neutrality. Flowing from the Fifth Hague Convention of 1907[12] are the generally accepted principles that a neutral may not allow belligerents to move troops or supplies across its territory, to maintain military installations on its territory, or to regroup forces on its territory. A neutral is obligated to take positive action to prevent such abuse of its neutrality either by attempting to expel the belligerent forces or to intern them.

Both the previous Cambodian government under Prince Sihanouk and the present government headed by Lon Nol have made efforts to limit, if not prevent, these violations of Cambodia's rights as a neutral. While the Sihanouk government did not, in our judgment, do all that, under international law, it

12. I Bevans, *Treaties and Other International Agreements of the United States of America, 1776-1949*, p. 654 (Department of State publication 8407 [1968]). [Author's footnote.]

should have done, it unquestionably made some efforts. As a legal matter, it is clear that a neutral must take active measures commensurate with its power to protect its territory from abuse by a belligerent. It is likewise clear that a neutral's "duty of prevention is not absolute, but according to his power."[13] In any event, however, the control and restraint exercised by the previous Cambodian government was progressively eroded by constant North Vietnamese pressure. Prior to the ouster of Prince Sihanouk, regular supply of arms and munitions through the Port of Sihanoukville had become an established fact.

After the change of government on March 18, in which the United States was not involved in any respect, Cambodian police and other officials were driven out of many localities in the border area. When it became apparent to North Viet-Nam that the new Cambodian government was not willing to permit the same wide scope of misuse of its territory by North Vietnamese forces as the previous government, the decision was evidently taken to expel all Cambodian Government presence from the border areas and move militarily against the Cambodian army, with a view to linking up all the sanctuaries and the Port of Sihanoukville. This would have produced a unified and protected sanctuary from the Gulf of Siam along the entire border of South Viet-Nam to Laos, with virtually unrestricted movement and unlimited supply access. The threat posed by such a situation of renewed and increased attacks against United States and Vietnamese troops in South Viet-Nam is obvious. We also knew that enemy forces were instructed to emphasize attacks on U.S. forces and increase U.S. casualties.

That was the rapidly developing situation the President faced at the time of his April 30 decision to make limited military incursions into the sanctuaries in Cambodia, which had been militarily occupied by North Viet-Nam. It was impossible for the Cambodian Government to take action itself to prevent these violations

13. As the Harvard Research in International Law pointed out in its 1939 Draft Convention on Rights and Duties of Neutral States in Naval and Aerial War, "A neutral State is not an insurer of the fulfillment of its neutral duties. It is obligated merely to 'use the means at its disposal' to secure the fulfillment of its duties." 33 *American Journal of International Law* (1939), Suppl., p. 247. [Author's footnote.]

of its neutral rights. Its efforts to do so had led to the expulsion of its forces. In these circumstances, the question arises of what are the rights of those who suffer from these violations of Cambodian neutrality.

It is the view of some scholars that when the traditional diplomatic remedy of a claim for compensation would not adequately compensate a belligerent injured by a neutral's failure to prevent illegal use of its territory by another belligerent, the injured belligerent has the right of self-help to prevent the hostile use of the neutral's territory to its prejudice.[14] Professor Castrén, the distinguished Finnish member of the International Law Commission, has stated that:[15]

> If, however, a neutral State has neither the desire nor the power to interfere and the situation is serious, other belligerents may resort to self-help.

The more conservative view is that a belligerent may take reasonable action against another belligerent violating the neutral's territory only when required to do so in self-defense.[16]

14. According to Greenspan, *The Modern Law of Land Warfare* (1959), p. 538: "Should a violation of neutral territory occur through the complaisance of the neutral state, or because of its inability, through weakness or otherwise, to resist such violation, then a belligerent which is prejudiced by the violation is entitled to take measures to redress the situation, including, if necessary, attack on enemy forces in the neutral territory." [Author's footnote.]

15. Castrén, *The Present Law of War and Neutrality* (Helsinki, 1954), p. 442. See also II Guggenheim, *Traité de Droit International Public* (Geneva, 1954), p. 346. [Author's footnote.]

16. II Oppenheim, *International Law* (7th ed. 1952), p. 698. This is true whether or not the neutral has met its obligations to use the means at its disposal to oppose belligerent use of its territory. Stone, *Legal Controls of International Conflict* (1954), says (p. 401): "One clear principle is that, the right of self-preservation apart, an aggrieved State is clearly not entitled to violate the neutral's territorial integrity, simply because his enemy has done so. Diplomatic representations and claim are the proper course." A Columbia Law Review Note concludes: "Military action within neutral territory may be justified as a measure of self-defense or as an appropriate response to the failure of a neutral state to prevent the use of its territory by belligerent forces. . . . It is suggested . . . that international law should permit and encourage primary reliance on self-defense as a justification." Note, "International Law and Military Op-

The United States Department of the Army Field Manual relating to the Law of Land Warfare states the following rule:[17]

> Should the neutral State be unable, or fail for any reason, to prevent violations of its neutrality by the troops of one belligerent entering or passing through its territory, the other belligerent may be justified in attacking the enemy forces on this territory.

This rule can be traced to, among others, the decision of the Greco-German Mixed Arbitral Tribunal after the First World War, which had to deal with the German bombardment of Salonika in Greece. During the war the Allied forces had occupied Salonika despite Greece's neutrality, and the Germans responded with a bombardment. The tribunal stated that Allied occupation constituted a violation of the neutrality of Greece and that it was immaterial whether the Greek Government protested against that occupation or whether it expressly or tacitly consented to it. The tribunal then concluded that "in either case the occupation of Salonika was, as regards Germany, an illicit act which authorized her to take, even on Greek territory, any acts of war necessary for her defense."[18]

British naval vessels entered then neutral Norway's territorial waters in 1940 to liberate British prisoners on the *Altmark*, a German auxiliary vessel. A thorough analysis of that case by Professor Waldock led him to the conclusion that in some circumstances a breach of neutrality by one belligerent threatens the security of the other belligerent in such a way that nothing but the immediate cessation of the breach will suffice. Professor Waldock added:[19]

---

erations against Insurgents on Neutral Territory," 68 Col. L. Rev. 1127 (1968). See also *Corfu Channel Case,* ICJ Reports 1949, pp. 34-35 and 77. [Author's footnote.]

17. FM 27-10 (July 1956) par. 520, p. 185. Similar provisions were contained in the U.S. Army *Rules of Land Warfare* of 1940 (par. 366) and in the *British Manual of Military Law* (par. 655). See Greenspan, *The Modern Law of Land Warfare* (1959), p. 538, n. 23. [Author's footnote.]

18. Coenca Brothers v. The German State, 1927, translated in Briggs, *The Law of Nations: Cases, Documents and Notes* (1938), pp. 756-58.

19. Waldock, "The Release of the Altmark's Prisoners," 24 *British Year Book of International Law* (1947), p. 216, at 235-36. See also Tucker, *The Law of War and Neutrality at Sea* (Naval War College, International Law Studies, vol. XLX, 1955, p. 262). [Author's footnote.]

Accordingly, where material prejudice to a belligerent's interests will result from its continuance, the principle of self-preservation would appear fully to justify intervention in neutral waters.

As far back as the 18th century, Vattel had this to say:[20]

On the other hand, it is certain that if my neighbour offers a retreat to my enemies, when they have been defeated and are too weak to escape me, *and allows them time to recover and to watch for an opportunity of making a fresh attack upon my territory* . . . (this is) inconsistent with neutrality. . . . he should . . . not allow them to lie in wait to make a fresh attack upon me; *otherwise he warrants me in pursuing them into his territory.* This is what happens when Nations are not in a position to make their territory respected. It soon becomes the seat of the war; armies march, camp, and fight in it, as in a country open to all comers. [Emphasis added by author.]

The United States itself has sometimes in the past found it necessary to take action on neutral territory in order to protect itself against hostile operations. Professor Hyde cites many such instances, of which I would note General Jackson's incursion into Spanish West Florida in 1818 in order to check attacks by Seminole Indians on United States positions in Georgia; the action taken against adventurers occupying Amelia Island in 1817, when Spain was unable to exercise control over it; and the expedition against Francisco Villa in 1916, after his attacks on American territory which Mexico had been unable to prevent.[21]

I have summarized these precedents and the views of scholars and governments principally to show general recognition of the need to provide a lawful and effective remedy to a belligerent harmed by its enemy's violations of a neutral's rights. I would not suggest that those incidents and statements by themselves pro-

---

20. E. de Vattel, *Le Droit des Gens* (1758), translated by Charles Fenwick, vol. 3, bk. III, sec. 133, p. 277 (Carnegie Institution reprint [1916]). [Author's footnote.]

21. I Hyde, *International Law* (2d ed., 1945), pp. 240-44. [Author's footnote.]

vide an adequate basis for analysis of the present state of the law. We all recognize that, whatever the merits of these views prior to 1945, the adoption of the United Nations Charter changed the situation by imposing new and important limitations on the use of armed force.[22] However, they are surely authority for the proposition that, assuming the charter's standards are met, a belligerent may take action on a neutral's territory to prevent violation by another belligerent of the neutral's neutrality which the neutral cannot or will not prevent, provided such action is required in self-defense.

In general, under the charter the use of armed force is prohibited except as authorized by the United Nations or by a regional organization within the scope of its competence under chapter VIII of the charter or, where the Security Council has not acted, in individual or collective self-defense against an armed attack. It is this latter basis on which we rely for our actions against North Vietnamese armed forces and bases in Cambodia.

Since 1965 we and the Republic of Viet-Nam have been engaged in collective measures of self-defense against an armed attack from North Viet-Nam. Increasingly since that time, the territory of Cambodia has been used by North Viet-Nam as a base of military operations to carry out that attack, and it long ago reached a level that would have justified our taking appropriate measures of self-defense on the territory of Cambodia. However, except for scattered instances of returning fire across the border, we refrained until April from taking such action in Cambodia. The right was available to us, but we refrained from exercising it in the hope that Cambodia would be able to impose greater restraints on enemy use of its territory.

However, in late April a new and more dangerous situation developed. It became apparent that North Viet-Nam was proceeding rapidly to remove all remaining restraints on its use of Cambodian territory to continue the armed attacks on South Viet-Nam and our armed forces there.

Prior to undertaking military action, the United States explored to the fullest other means of peaceful settlement.

22. In particular, article 2, par. 4, of the charter. [Author's footnote.]

We awaited the outcome of the Cambodian Government's efforts to negotiate with the North Vietnamese and the Viet Cong agreed limitations on the use by the latter of Cambodian territory —without success.

We have continually tried in the Paris talks to bring about serious negotiation of the issues involved in the war.

Soundings in the Security Council indicated very little interest in taking up the North Vietnamese violations of Cambodian territorial integrity and neutrality.

We welcomed the French proposal looking to the possibility of an international conference—although not publicly, for fear of discouraging Hanoi's participation. The Soviet Union, after initially indicating interest, backed away.

We were particularly pleased with the calling of the Djakarta conference of interested Asian states to deal with the Cambodian problem on a regional basis. The best longrun approach to East Asian security problems lies through cooperative actions such as this. In the short run, however, they cannot be expected to provide an adequate defense against the North Vietnamese military threat.

The United States has imposed severe limits on the activities of U.S. forces. They will remain in Cambodia only a limited time— not beyond June 30; in a limited area—not beyond 21 miles from the border; and with a limited purpose—to capture or destroy North Vietnamese supplies, to destroy base installations, and to disrupt communications. To the maximum extent possible, we have directed our forces at enemy base areas and have tried to avoid civilian population centers. We have limited our area of operations to that part of Cambodia from which Cambodian authority had been eliminated and which was occupied by the North Vietnamese.

The Cambodian Government and the Cambodian people are not the targets of our operations. During the period from 1967 to 1970 the Cambodian Government became increasingly outspoken in its opposition to the North Vietnamese occupation. In fact, Sihanouk's purpose in going to the Soviet Union and China when he was deposed was to solicit their help in persuading the North

Vietnamese to get out of Cambodia. The Lon Nol government has expressed its understanding of our actions.

Our actions in Cambodia are appropriate measures of legitimate collective self-defense, and we have so reported to the United Nations, as required by article 51 of the United Nations Charter.[23]

23. For text of a U.S. letter dated May 5 to the President of the U.N. Security Council, see BULLETIN of May 25, 1970, p. 652.

APPENDIX D

THE 1954 GENEVA AGREEMENTS FOR CAMBODIA, LAOS, AND VIETNAM*

* Reprinted by permission of Her Majesty's Stationery Office from *Further Documents Relating to the Discussion of Indo-China at the Geneva Conference* (Misc. No. 20 [1954]; Cmd. No. 9239), Great Britain Parliamentary Sessional Papers XXXI (1953-54), at 9-42.

Final Declaration of the Geneva Conference on the problem of restoring peace in Indo-China, in which the representatives of Cambodia, the Democratic Republic of Viet Nam, France, Laos, the People's Republic of China, the State of Viet Nam, the Union of Soviet Socialist Republics, the United Kingdom and the United States of America took part

July 21, 1954

1. The Conference takes note of the agreements ending hostilities in Cambodia, Laos and Viet Nam and organising international control and the supervision of the execution of the provisions of these agreements.

2. The Conference expresses satisfaction at the ending of hostilities in Cambodia, Laos and Viet Nam; the Conference expresses its conviction that the execution of the provisions set out in the present declaration and in the agreements on the cessation of hostilities will permit Cambodia, Laos and Viet Nam henceforth to play their part, in full independence and sovereignty, in the peaceful community of nations.

3. The Conference takes note of the declarations made by the Governments of Cambodia and of Laos of their intention to adopt measures permitting all citizens to take their place in the national community, in particular by participating in the next general elections, which, in conformity with the constitution of each of these countries, shall take place in the course of the year 1955, by secret ballot and in conditions of respect for fundamental freedoms.

4. The Conference takes note of the clauses in the agreement on the cessation of hostilities in Viet Nam prohibiting the intro-

duction into Viet Nam of foreign troops and military personnel as well as of all kinds of arms and munitions. The Conference also takes note of the declarations made by the Governments of Cambodia and Laos of their resolution not to request foreign aid, whether in war material, in personnel or in instructors except for the purpose of the effective defence of their territory and, in the case of Laos, to the extent defined by the agreements on the cessation of hostilities in Laos.

5. The Conference takes note of the clauses in the agreement on the cessation of hostilities in Viet Nam to the effect that no military base under the control of a foreign State may be established in the regrouping zones of the two parties, the latter having the obligation to see that the zones allotted to them shall not constitute part of any military alliance and shall not be utilised for the resumption of hostilities or in the service of an aggressive policy. The Conference also takes note of the declarations of the Governments of Cambodia and Laos to the effect that they will not join in any agreement with other States if this agreement includes the obligation to participate in a military alliance not in conformity with the principles of the Charter of the United Nations or, in the case of Laos, with the principles of the agreement on the cessation of hostilities in Laos or, so long as their security is not threatened, the obligation to establish bases on Cambodian or Laotian territory for the military forces of foreign Powers.

6. The Conference recognises that the essential purpose of the agreement relating to Viet Nam is to settle military questions with a view to ending hostilities and that the military demarcation line is provisional and should not in any way be interpreted as constituting a political or territorial boundary. The Conference expresses its conviction that the execution of the provisions set out in the present declaration and in the agreement on the cessation of hostilities creates the necessary basis for the achievement in the near future of a political settlement in Viet Nam.

7. The Conference declares that, so far as Viet Nam is concerned, the settlement of political problems, effected on the basis of respect for the principles of independence, unity and territorial integrity, shall permit the Vietnamese people to enjoy the fundamental freedoms, guaranteed by democratic institutions estab-

lished as a result of free general elections by secret ballot. In order to ensure that sufficient progress in the restoration of peace has been made, and that all the necessary conditions obtain for free expression of the national will, general elections shall be held in July 1956, under the supervision of an international commission composed of representatives of the Member States of the International Supervisory Commission, referred to in the agreement on the cessation of hostilities. Consultations will be held on this subject between the competent representative authorities of the two zones from July 20, 1955, onwards.

8. The provisions of the agreements on the cessation of hostilities intended to ensure the protection of individuals and of property must be most strictly applied and must, in particular, allow everyone in Viet Nam to decide freely in which zone he wishes to live.

9. The competent representative authorities of the Northern and Southern zones of Viet Nam, as well as the authorities of Laos and Cambodia, must not permit any individual or collective reprisals against persons who have collaborated in any way with one of the parties during the war, or against members of such persons' families.

10. The Conference takes note of the declaration of the Government of the French Republic to the effect that it is ready to withdraw its troops from the territory of Cambodia, Laos and Viet Nam, at the request of the Governments concerned and within periods which shall be fixed by agreement between the parties except in the cases where, by agreement between the two parties, a certain number of French troops shall remain at specified points and for a specified time.

11. The Conference takes note of the declaration of the French Government to the effect that for the settlement of all the problems connected with the re-establishment and consolidation of peace in Cambodia, Laos and Viet Nam, the French Government will proceed from the principle of respect for the independence and sovereignty, unity and territorial integrity of Cambodia, Laos and Viet Nam.

12. In their relations with Cambodia, Laos and Viet Nam, each member of the Geneva Conference undertakes to respect the sov-

ereignty, the independence, the unity and the territorial integrity of the above-mentioned States, and to refrain from any interference in their internal affairs.

13. The members of the Conference agree to consult one another on any question which may be referred to them by the International Supervisory Commission, in order to study such measures as may prove necessary to ensure that the agreements on the cessation of hostilities in Cambodia, Laos and Viet Nam are respected.

Agreement on the Cessation of Hostilities in Cambodia

July 20, 1954

CHAPTER I

Principles and Conditions Governing Execution of the Cease-Fire

Article 1

As from twenty-third July, 1954, at 0800 hours (Peking mean time) complete cessation of all hostilities throughout Cambodia shall be ordered and enforced by the Commanders of the Armed Forces of the two parties for all troops and personnel of the land, naval and air forces under their control.

Article 2

In conformity with the principle of a simultaneous cease-fire throughout Indo-China, there shall be a simultaneous cessation of hostilities throughout Cambodia, in all the combat areas and for all the forces of the two parties.

To obviate any mistake or misunderstanding and to ensure that both the ending of hostilities and all other operations arising from cessation of hostilities are in fact simultaneous,

(a) due allowance being made for the time actually required for transmission of the cease-fire order down to the lowest échelons of the combatant forces of both sides, the two parties are agreed that the complete and simultaneous cease-fire throughout the territory of Cambodia shall become effective at 8 hours (local time) on August 7, 1954. It is agreed that Peking mean time shall be taken as local time.

(b) Each side shall comply strictly with the time-table jointly agreed upon between the parties for the execution of all operations connected with the cessation of hostilities.

Article 3

All operations and movements connected with the execution of the cessation of hostilities must be carried out in a safe and orderly fashion.

(a) Within a number of days to be determined by the Commanders of both sides, after the cease-fire has been achieved, each party shall be responsible for removing and neutralising mines, booby traps, explosives and any other dangerous devices placed by it. Should it be impossible to complete removal and neutralisation before departure, the party concerned will mark the spot by placing visible signs. Sites thus cleared of mines and any other obstacles to the free movement of the personnel of the International Commission and the Joint Commission shall be notified to the latter by the local military Commanders.

(b) Any incidents that may arise between the forces of the two sides and may result from mistakes or misunderstandings shall be settled on the spot so as to restrict their scope.

(c) During the days immediately preceding the cease-fire each party undertakes not to engage in any large-scale operation between the time when the Agreement on the cessation of hostilities is signed at Geneva and the time when the cease-fire comes into effect.

CHAPTER II

Procedure for the Withdrawal of the Foreign Armed Forces and Foreign Military Personnel from the Territory of Cambodia

Article 4

1. The withdrawal outside the territory of Cambodia shall apply to—

(*a*) the armed forces and military combatant personnel of the French Union;

(*b*) the combatant formations of all types which have entered the territory of Cambodia from other countries or regions of the peninsula;

(*c*) all the foreign elements (or Cambodians not natives of Cambodia) in the military formations of any kind or holding supervisory functions in all political or military, administrative, economic, financial or social bodies, having worked in liaison with the Viet Nam military units.

2. The withdrawals of the forces and elements referred to in the foregoing paragraphs and their military supplies and materials must be completed within 90 days reckoning from the entry into force of the present Agreement.

3. The two parties shall guarantee that the withdrawals of all the forces will be effected in accordance with the purposes of the Agreement, and that they will not permit any hostile action or take any action likely to create difficulties for such withdrawals. They shall assist one another as far as possible.

4. While the withdrawals are proceeding, the two parties shall not permit any destruction or sabotage of public property or any attack on the life or property of the civilian population. They shall not permit any interference with the local civil administration.

5. The Joint Commission and the International Supervisory Commission shall supervise the execution of measures to ensure the safety of the forces during withdrawal.

6. The Joint Commission in Cambodia shall determine the detailed procedures for the withdrawals of the forces on the basis of the above-mentioned principles.

Chapter III

Other Questions

A.—THE KHMER ARMED FORCES, NATIVES OF CAMBODIA

Article 5

The two parties shall undertake that within thirty days after the cease-fire order has been proclaimed, the Khmer Resistance Forces shall be demobilised on the spot; simultaneously, the troops of the Royal Khmer Army shall abstain from taking any hostile action against the Khmer Resistance Forces.

Article 6

The situation of these nationals shall be decided in the light of the Declaration made by the Delegation of Cambodia at the Geneva Conference, reading as follows:—

"The Royal Government of Cambodia,

In the desire to ensure harmony and agreement among the peoples of the Kingdom,

Declares itself resolved to take the necessary measures to integrate all citizens, without discrimination, into the national community and to guarantee them the enjoyment of the rights and freedoms for which the Constitution of the Kingdom provides;

Affirms that all Cambodian citizens may freely participate as electors or candidates in general elections by secret ballot."

No reprisals shall be taken against the said nationals or their families, each national being entitled to the enjoyment, without any discrimination as compared with other nationals, of all constitutional guarantees concerning the protection of person and property and democratic freedoms.

Applicants therefor may be accepted for service in the Regular Army or local police formations if they satisfy the conditions required for current recruitment of the Army and Police Corps.

The same procedure shall apply to those persons who have returned to civilian life and who may apply for civilian employment on the same terms as other nationals.

B.—Ban on the Introduction of Fresh Troops, Military Personnel, Armaments and Munitions. Military Bases

Article 7

In accordance with the Declaration made by the Delegation of Cambodia at 2400 hours on July 20, 1954 at the Geneva Conference of Foreign Ministers:

"The Royal Government of Cambodia will not join in any agreement with other States if this agreement carries for Cambodia the obligation to enter into a military alliance not in conformity with the principles of the Charter of the United Nations, or, as long as its security is not threatened, the obligation to establish bases on Cambodian territory for the military forces of foreign Powers.

"During the period which will elapse between the date of the cessation of hostilities in Viet Nam and that of the final settlement of political problems in this country, the Royal Government of Cambodia will not solicit foreign aid in war material, personnel or instructors except for the purpose of the effective defence of the territory."

C.—Civilian Internees and Prisoners of War.—Burial

Article 8

The liberation and repatriation of all civilian internees and prisoners of war detained by each of the two parties at the coming into force of the present Agreement shall be carried out under the following conditions:—

(a) All prisoners of war and civilian internees of whatever nationality, captured since the beginning of hostilities in Cambodia during military operations or in any other circumstances of war and in any part of the territory of Cambodia shall be liberated after the entry into force of the present Armistice Agreement.

(b) The term "civilian internees" is understood to mean all persons who, having in any way contributed to the political and armed struggle between the two parties have been arrested for that reason or kept in detention by either party during the period of hostilities.

(*c*) All foreign prisoners of war captured by either party shall be surrendered to the appropriate authorities of the other party, who shall give them all possible assistance in proceeding to the destination of their choice.

Article 9

After the entry into force of the present Agreement, if the place of burial is known and the existence of graves has been established, the Cambodian commander shall, within a specified period, authorise the exhumation and removal of the bodies of deceased military personnel of the other party, including the bodies of prisoners of war or personnel deceased and buried on Cambodian territory.

The Joint Commission shall fix the procedures by which this task is to be carried out and the time limit within which it must be completed.

Chapter IV

Joint Commission and International Commission for Supervision and Control in Cambodia

Article 10

Responsibility for the execution of the Agreement on the cessation of hostilities shall rest with the parties.

Article 11

An International Commission shall be responsible for control and supervision of the application of the provisions of the Agreement on the cessation of hostilities in Cambodia. It shall be composed of representatives of the following States: Canada, India and Poland. It shall be presided over by the representative of India. Its headquarters shall be at Phnom-Penh.

Article 12

The International Commission shall set up fixed and mobile inspection teams, composed of an equal number of officers appointed by each of the above-mentioned States.

The fixed teams shall be located at the following points: Phnom-Penh, Kompong-Cham, Kratié, Svay-Rieng, Kampot. These points of location may be altered at a later date by agreement between the Government of Cambodia and the International Commission.

The zones of action of the mobile teams shall be the regions bordering on the land and sea frontiers of Cambodia. The mobile teams shall have the right to move freely within the limits of their zones of action, and they shall receive from the local civil and military authorities all facilities they may require for the fulfilment of their tasks (provision of personnel, access to documents needed for supervision, summoning of witnesses needed for enquiries, security and freedom of movement of the inspection teams, &c.). They shall have at their disposal such modern means of transport, observation and communication as they may require.

Outside the zones of action defined above, the mobile teams may, with the agreement of the Cambodian Command, move about as required by the tasks assigned to them under the present Agreement.

Article 13

The International Commission shall be responsible for supervising the execution by the parties of the provisions of the present Agreement. For this purpose it shall fulfil the functions of control, observation, inspection and investigation connected with the implementation of the provisions of the Agreement on the cessation of hostilities, and shall in particular:

(a) control the withdrawal of foreign forces in accordance with the provisions of the Agreement on the cessation of hostilities and see that frontiers are respected;

(b) control the release of prisoners of war and civilian internees;

(c) supervise, at ports and airfields and along all the frontiers of Cambodia, the application of the Cambodian declaration concerning the introduction into Cambodia of military personnel and war materials on grounds of foreign assistance.

Article 14

A Joint Commission shall be set up to facilitate the implementation of the clauses relating to the withdrawal of foreign forces.

The Joint Commission may form joint groups the number of which shall be decided by mutual agreement between the parties.

The Joint Commission shall facilitate the implementation of the clauses of the Agreement on the cessation of hostilities relating to the simultaneous and general cease-fire in Cambodia for all regular and irregular armed forces of the two parties.

It shall assist the parties in the implementation of the said clauses; it shall ensure liaison between them for the purpose of preparing and carrying out plans for the implementation of the said clauses; it shall endeavour to settle any disputes between the parties arising out of the implementation of these clauses. The Joint Commission may send joint groups to follow the forces in their movements; such groups shall be disbanded once the withdrawal plans have been carried out.

Article 15

The Joint Commission shall be composed of an equal number of representatives of the Commands of the parties concerned.

Article 16

The International Commission shall, through the medium of the inspection teams mentioned above and as soon as possible, either on its own initiative or at the request of the Joint Commission or of one of the parties, undertake the necessary investigations both documentary and on the ground.

Article 17

The inspection teams shall transmit to the International Commission the results of their supervision, investigations and observations; furthermore, they shall draw up such special reports as they may consider necessary or as may be requested from them by the Commission. In the case of a disagreement within the teams, the findings of each member shall be transmitted to the Commission.

Article 18

If an inspection team is unable to settle an incident or considers that there is a violation or threat of a serious violation, the International Commission shall be informed; the Commission shall examine the reports and findings of the inspection teams and shall inform the parties of the measures to be taken for the settlement of the incident, ending of the violation or removal of the threat of violation.

Article 19

When the Joint Commission is unable to reach agreement on the interpretation of a provision or on the appraisal of a fact, the International Commission shall be informed of the disputed question. Its recommendations shall be sent directly to the parties and shall be notified to the Joint Commission.

Article 20

The recommendations of the International Commission shall be adopted by a majority vote, subject to the provisions of Article 21. If the votes are equally divided, the Chairman's vote shall be decisive.

The International Commission may make recommendations concerning amendments and additions which should be made to the provisions of the Agreement on the cessation of hostilities in Cambodia, in order to ensure more effective execution of the said Agreement. These recommendations shall be adopted unanimously.

Article 21

On questions concerning violations, or threats of violations, which might lead to a resumption of hostilities, and in particular, (*a*) refusal by foreign armed forces to effect the movements provided for in the withdrawal plan,

(*b*) violation or threat of violation of the country's integrity by foreign armed forces,

the decisions of the International Commission must be unanimous.

Article 22

If one of the parties refuses to put a recommendation of the International Commission into effect, the parties concerned or the Commission itself shall inform the members of the Geneva Conference.

If the International Commission does not reach unanimity in the cases provided for in Article 21, it shall transmit a majority report and one or more minority reports to members of the Conference.

The International Commission shall inform the members of the Conference of all cases in which its work is being hindered.

Article 23

The International Commission shall be set up at the time of the cessation of hostilities in Indo-China in order that it may be able to perform the tasks prescribed in Article 13.

Article 24

The International Commission for Supervision and Control in Cambodia shall act in close co-operation with the International Commissions in Viet Nam and Laos.

The Secretaries-General of these three Commissions shall be responsible for co-ordinating their work and for relations between them.

Article 25

The International Commission for Supervision and Control in Cambodia may, after consultation with the International Commissions in Viet Nam and in Laos, and having regard to the development of the situation in Viet Nam and in Laos, progressively reduce its activities. Such a decision must be adopted unanimously.

CHAPTER V

Implementation

Article 26

The Commanders of the forces of the two parties shall ensure that persons under their respective commands who violate any of the provisions of the present Agreement are suitably punished.

Article 27

The present Agreement on the cessation of hostilities shall apply to all the armed forces of either party.

Article 28

The Commanders of the forces of the two parties shall afford full protection and all possible assistance and co-operation to the Joint Commission and to the International Commission and its inspection teams in the performance of their functions.

Article 29

The Joint Commission, composed of an equal number of representatives of the Commands of the two parties, shall assist the parties in the implementation of all the clauses of the Agreement on the cessation of hostilities, ensure liaison between the two parties, draw up plans for the implementation of the Agreement, and endeavour to settle any dispute arising out of the implementation of the said clauses and plans.

Article 30

The costs involved in the operation of the Joint Commission shall be shared equally between the two parties.

Article 31

The signatories of the present Agreement on the cessation of hostilities and their successors in their functions shall be responsible for the observance and enforcement of the terms and provisions thereof. The Commanders of the forces of the two parties shall, within their respective commands, take all steps and make all arrangements necessary to ensure full compliance with all the provisions of the present Agreement by all personnel under their command.

Article 32

The procedures laid down in the present Agreement shall, whenever necessary, be examined by the Commands of the two parties and, if necessary, defined more specifically by the Joint Commission.

Article 33

All the provisions of the present Agreement shall enter into force at 00 hours (Geneva time) on July 23, 1954.

Done at Geneva on July 20, 1954.

For the Commander-in-Chief of the Khmer National Armed Forces:

NHIEK TIOULONG,
General.

For the Commander-in-Chief of the Units of the Khmer Resistance Forces and for the Commander-in-Chief of the Vietnamese Military Units:

TA-QUANG-BUU,
Vice-Minister of National Defence
of the Democratic Republic of Viet Nam.

Agreement on the Cessation of Hostilities in Laos

July 20, 1954

CHAPTER I

Cease-Fire and Evacuation of Foreign Armed Forces
and Foreign Military Personnel

Article 1

The Commanders of the armed forces of the parties in Laos shall order and enforce the complete cessation of all hostilities in Laos by all armed forces under their control, including all units and personnel of the ground, naval and air forces.

Article 2

In accordance with the principle of a simultaneous cease-fire throughout Indo-China the cessation of hostilities shall be simultaneous throughout the territory of Laos in all combat areas and for all forces of the two parties.

In order to prevent any mistake or misunderstanding and to ensure that both the cessation of hostilities and the disengagement and movements of the opposing forces are in fact simultaneous.

(a) Taking into account the time effectively required to transmit the cease-fire order down to the lowest échelons of the combatant forces on both sides, the two parties are agreed that the complete and simultaneous cease-fire throughout the territory of Laos shall become effective at 8 hours (local time) on August 6, 1954. It is agreed that Peking mean time shall be taken as local time.

(b) The Joint Commission for Laos shall draw up a schedule for the other operations resulting from the cessation of hostilities.

Article 3

All operations and movements entailed by the cessation of hostilities and re-groupings must proceed in a safe and orderly fashion.

(a) Within a number of days to be determined on the spot by the Joint Commission in Laos each party shall be responsible for removing and neutralising mines, booby traps, explosives and any other dangerous substance placed by it. In the event of its being impossible to complete the work of removal and neutralisation in time, the party concerned shall mark the spot by placing visible signs there.

(b) As regards the security of troops on the move following the lines of communication in accordance with the schedule previously drawn up by the Joint Armistice Commission in Laos, and the safety of the assembly areas, detailed measures shall be adopted in each case by the Joint Armistice Commission in Laos. In particular, while the forces of one party are withdrawing by a line of communication passing through the territory of the other party (roads or waterways) the forces of the latter party shall provisionally withdraw two kilometres on either side of such line of communication, but in such a manner as to avoid interfering with the movements of the civil population.

Article 4

The withdrawals and transfers of military forces, supplies and equipment shall be effected in accordance with the following principles:

(*a*) The withdrawals and transfers of the military forces, supplies and equipment of the two parties shall be completed within a period of 120 days from the day on which the present Agreement enters into force.

The two parties undertake to communicate their transfer plans to each other, for information, within 25 days of the entry into force of the present Agreement.

(*b*) The withdrawals of the Vietnamese People's Volunteers from Laos to Viet Nam shall be effected by provinces. The position of those volunteers who were settled in Laos before the hostilities shall form the subject of a special convention.

(*c*) The routes for the withdrawal of the forces of the French Union and Vietnamese People's Volunteers in Laos from Laotian territory shall be fixed on the spot by the Joint Commission.

(*d*) The two parties shall guarantee that the withdrawals and transfers of all forces will be effected in accordance with the purposes of this Agreement, and that they will not permit any hostile action or take action of any kind whatever which might hinder such withdrawals or transfers. The parties shall assist each other as far as possible.

(*e*) While the withdrawals and transfers of the forces are proceeding, the two parties shall not permit any destruction or sabotage of any public property or any attack on the life or property of the local civilian population.

(f) The Joint Commission and the International Commission shall supervise the implementation of measures to ensure the safety of the forces during withdrawal and transfer.

(g) The Joint Commission in Laos shall determine the detailed procedures for the withdrawals and transfers of the forces in accordance with the above-mentioned principles.

Article 5

During the days immediately preceding the cease-fire each party undertakes not to engage in any large-scale operation between the time when the Agreement on the cessation of hostilities is signed at Geneva and the time when the cease-fire comes into effect.

CHAPTER II

Prohibition of the Introduction of Fresh Troops, Military Personnel, Armaments and Munitions

Article 6

With effect from the proclamation of the cease-fire the introduction into Laos of any reinforcements of troops or military personnel from outside Laotian territory is prohibited.

Nevertheless, the French High Command may leave a specified number of French military personnel required for the training of the Laotian National Army in the territory of Laos; the strength of such personnel shall not exceed one thousand five hundred (1,500) officers and non-commissioned officers.

Article 7

Upon the entry into force of the present Agreement, the establishment of new military bases is prohibited throughout the territory of Laos.

Article 8

The High Command of the French forces shall maintain in the territory of Laos the personnel required for the maintenance of two French military establishments, the first at Seno and the second in the Mekong valley, either in the province of Vientiane or downstream from Vientiane.

The effectives maintained in these military establishments shall not exceed a total of three thousand five hundred (3,500) men.

Article 9

Upon the entry into force of the present Agreement and in accordance with the declaration made at the Geneva Conference by the Royal Government of Laos on July 20, 1954, the introduction into Laos of armaments, munitions and military equipment of all kinds is prohibited, with the exception of a specified quantity of armaments in categories specified as necessary for the defence of Laos.

Article 10

The new armaments and military personnel permitted to enter Laos in accordance with the terms of Article 9 above shall enter Laos at the following points only: Luang-Prabang, Xieng-Khouang, Vientiane, Seno, Paksé, Savannakhet and Tchépone.

CHAPTER III

Disengagement of the Forces—Assembly Areas— Concentration Areas

Article 11

The disengagement of the armed forces of both sides, including concentration of armed forces, movements to rejoin the provisional assembly areas allotted to one party and provisional withdrawal movements by the other party, shall be completed within a period not exceeding fifteen (15) days after the cease-fire.

Article 12

The Joint Commission in Laos shall fix the site and boundaries:—
of the five (5) provisional assembly areas for the reception of the
Vietnamese People's Volunteer Forces,
of the five (5) provisional assembly areas for the reception of the
French forces in Laos,

of the twelve (12) provisional assembly areas, one to each province, for the reception of the fighting units of "Pathet Lao."

The forces of the Laotian National Army shall remain *in situ* during the entire duration of the operations of disengagement and transfer of foreign forces and fighting units of "Pathet Lao."

Article 13

The foreign forces shall be transferred outside Laotian territory as follows:—

(1) FRENCH FORCES

The French forces shall be moved out of Laos by road (along routes laid down by the Joint Commission in Laos) and also by air and inland waterway;

(2) VIETNAMESE PEOPLE'S VOLUNTEER FORCES

These forces shall be moved out of Laos by land, along routes and in accordance with a schedule to be determined by the Joint Commission in Laos in accordance with the principle of simultaneous withdrawal of foreign forces.

Article 14

Pending a political settlement, the fighting units of "Pathet Lao," concentrated in the provisional assembly areas, shall move into the Provinces of Phongsaly and Sam-Neua, except for any military personnel who wish to be demobilised where they are. They shall be free to move between these two Provinces in a corridor along the frontier between Laos and Viet Nam bounded on the south by the Line Sop Kin, Na Mi, Sop Sang, Muong Son.

Concentration shall be completed within one hundred and twenty (120) days from the date of entry into force of the present Agreement.

Article 15

Each party undertakes to refrain from any reprisals or discrimination against persons or organisations for their activities during the hostilities and also undertakes to guarantee their democratic freedoms.

CHAPTER IV

Prisoners of War and Civilian Internees

Article 16

The liberation and repatriation of all prisoners of war and civilian internees detained by each of the two parties at the coming into force of the present Agreement shall be carried out under the following conditions:—

(*a*) All prisoners of war and civilian internees of Laotian and other nationalities captured since the beginning of hostilities in Laos, during military operations or in any other circumstances of war and in any part of the territory of Laos, shall be liberated within a period of thirty (30) days after the date when the cease-fire comes into effect.

(*b*) The term "civilian internees" is understood to mean all persons who, having in any way contributed to the political and armed strife between the two parties, have been arrested for that reason or kept in detention by either party during the period of hostilities.

(*c*) All foreign prisoners of war captured by either party shall be surrendered to the appropriate authorities of the other party, who shall give them all possible assistance in proceeding to the destination of their choice.

CHAPTER V

Miscellaneous

Article 17

The Commanders of the forces of the two parties shall ensure that persons under their respective commands who violate any of the provisions of the present Agreement are suitably punished.

Article 18

In cases in which the place of burial is known and the existence of graves has been established, the Commander of the forces of each party shall, within a specified period after the entry into force of the present Agreement, permit the graves service of the other party to enter that part of Laotian territory under his military control for the purpose of finding and removing the bodies of deceased military personnel of that party, including the bodies of deceased prisoners of war.

The Joint Commission shall fix the procedures by which this task is carried out and the time limits within which it must be completed. The Commander of the forces of each party shall communicate to the other all information in his possession as to the place of burial of military personnel of the other party.

Article 19

The present Agreement shall apply to all the armed forces of either party. The armed forces of each party shall respect the territory under the military control of the other party, and engage in no hostile act against the other party.

For the purpose of the present article the word "territory" includes territorial waters and air space.

Article 20

The Commanders of the forces of the two parties shall afford full protection and all possible assistance and co-operation to the Joint Commission and its joint groups and to the International Commission and its inspection teams in the performance of the functions and tasks assigned to them by the present Agreement.

Article 21

The costs involved in the operation of the Joint Commission and its joint groups and of the International Commission and its inspection teams shall be shared equally between the two parties.

Article 22

The signatories of the present Agreement and their successors in their functions shall be responsible for the observance and enforcement of the terms and provisions thereof. The Commanders of the forces of the two parties shall, within their respective commands, take all steps and make all arrangements necessary to ensure full compliance with all the provisions of the present Agreement by all military personnel under their command.

Article 23

The procedures laid down in the present Agreement shall, whenever necessary, be examined by the Commanders of the two parties and, if necessary, defined more specifically by the Joint Commission.

CHAPTER VI

Joint Commission and International Commission for Supervision and Control in Laos

Article 24

Responsibility for the execution of the Agreement on the cessation of hostilities shall rest with the parties.

Article 25

An International Commission shall be responsible for control and supervision of the application of the provisions of the Agreement on the cessation of hostilities in Laos. It shall be composed of representatives of the following States: Canada, India and Poland. It shall be presided over by the representative of India. Its headquarters shall be at Vientiane.

Article 26

The International Commission shall set up fixed and mobile inspection teams, composed of an equal number of officers appointed by each of the above-mentioned States.

The fixed teams shall be located at the following points: Paksé, Seno, Tchépone, Vientiane, Xieng-Khouang, Phongsaly, Sophao (province of Sam Neua). These points of location may, at a later date, be altered by agreement between the Government of Laos and the International Commission.

The zones of action of the mobile teams shall be the regions bordering the land frontiers of Laos. Within the limits of their zones of action, they shall have the right to move freely and shall receive from the local civil and military authorities all facilities they may require for the fulfilment of their tasks (provision of personnel, access to documents needed for supervision, summoning of witnesses needed for enquiries, security and freedom of movement of the inspection teams, &c. . . .). They shall have at their disposal such modern means of transport, observation and communication as they may require.

Outside the zones of action defined above, the mobile teams may, with the agreement of the Command of the party concerned, move about as required by the tasks assigned to them by the present Agreement.

Article 27

The International Commission shall be responsible for supervising the execution by the parties of the provisions of the present Agreement. For this purpose it shall fulfil the functions of control, observation, inspection and investigation connected with the implementation of the provisions of the Agreement on the cessation of hostilities, and shall in particular:—

(a) Control the withdrawal of foreign forces in accordance with the provisions of the Agreement on the cessation of hostilities and see that frontiers are respected;

(b) control the release of prisoners of war and civilian internees;

(c) supervise, at ports and airfields and along all the frontiers of Laos, the implementation of the provisions regulating the introduction into Laos of military personnel and war materials;

(d) supervise the implementation of the clauses of the Agreement on the cessation of hostilities relating to rotation of personnel and to supplies for French Union security forces maintained in Laos.

Article 28

A Joint Commission shall be set up to facilitate the implementation of the clauses relating to the withdrawal of foreign forces.

The Joint Commission shall form joint groups, the number of which shall be decided by mutual agreement between the parties.

The Joint Commission shall facilitate the implementation of the clauses of the Agreement on the cessation of hostilities relating to the simultaneous and general cease-fire in Laos for all regular and irregular armed forces of the two parties.

It shall assist the parties in the implementation of the said clauses; it shall ensure liaison between them for the purpose of preparing and carrying out plans for the implementation of the said clauses; it shall endeavour to settle any disputes between the parties arising out of the implementation of these clauses. The joint groups shall follow the forces in their movements and shall be disbanded once the withdrawal plans have been carried out.

Article 29

The Joint Commission and the joint groups shall be composed of an equal number of representatives of the Commands of the parties concerned.

Article 30

The International Commission shall, through the medium of the inspection teams mentioned above, and as soon as possible, either on its own initiative, or at the request of the Joint Commission, or of one of the parties, undertake the necessary investigations both documentary and on the ground.

Article 31

The inspection teams shall transmit to the International Commission the results of their supervision, investigations and observations; furthermore, they shall draw up such special reports as they may consider necessary or as may be requested from them by the Commission. In the case of a disagreement within the teams the findings of each member shall be transmitted to the Commission.

Article 32

If an inspection team is unable to settle an incident or considers that there is a violation or threat of a serious violation, the International Commission shall be informed; the latter shall examine the reports and findings of the inspection teams and shall inform the parties of the measures which should be taken for the settlement of the incident, ending of the violation or removal of the threat of violation.

Article 33

When the Joint Commission is unable to reach agreement on the interpretation of a provision or on the appraisal of a fact, the International Commission shall be informed of the disputed question. Its recommendations shall be sent directly to the parties and shall be notified to the Joint Commission.

Article 34

The recommendations of the International Commissions shall be adopted by majority vote, subject to the provisions of Article 35. If the votes are equally divided, the chairman's vote shall be decisive.

The International Commission may make recommendations concerning amendments and additions which should be made to the provisions of the Agreement on the cessation of hostilities in Laos, in order to ensure more effective execution of the said Agreement. These recommendations shall be adopted unanimously.

Article 35

On questions concerning violations, or threats of violations, which might lead to a resumption of hostilities and, in particular,

    (*a*) refusal by foreign armed forces to effect the movements provided for in the withdrawal plan,

    (*b*) violation or threat of violation of the country's integrity, by foreign armed forces,

the decisions of the International Commission must be unanimous.

Article 36

If one of the parties refuses to put a recommendation of the International Commission into effect, the parties concerned or the Commission itself shall inform the members of the Geneva Conference.

If the International Commission does not reach unanimity in the cases provided for in Article 35, it shall transmit a majority report and one or more minority reports to the members of the Conference.

The International Commission shall inform the members of the Conference of all cases in which its work is being hindered.

Article 37

The International Commission shall be set up at the time of the cessation of hostilities in Indo-China in order that it may be able to fulfil the tasks prescribed in Article 27.

Article 38

The International Commission for Supervision and Control in Laos shall act in close co-operation with the International Commissions in Viet Nam and Cambodia.

The Secretaries-General of these three Commissions shall be responsbile for co-ordinating their work and for relations between them.

Article 39

The International Commission for Supervision and Control in Laos may, after consultation with the International Commissions in Cambodia and Viet Nam, and having regard to the development of the situation in Cambodia and Viet Nam, progressively reduce its activities. Such a decison must be adopted unanimously.

CHAPTER VII

Article 40

All the provisions of the present Agreement, save paragraph (a) of Article 2, shall enter into force at 24 hours (Geneva time) on July 22, 1954.

Article 41

Done at Geneva (Switzerland) on July 20, 1954, at 24 hours in the French language.

For the Commander-in-Chief of the forces of the French Union in Indo-China:

DELTEIL,
Général de Brigade.

For the Commander-in-Chief of the fighting units of "Pathet-Lao" and for the Commander-in-Chief of the People's Army of Viet Nam:

TA-QUANG-BUU,
Vice-Minister of National Defence
of the Democratic Republic of Viet Nam.

Agreement on the Cessation of Hostilities in Viet Nam

July 20, 1954

CHAPTER I

Provisional Military Demarcation Line and
Demilitarised Zone

Article 1

A provisional military demarcation line shall be fixed, on either side of which the forces of the two parties shall be regrouped after their withdrawal, the forces of the People's Army of Viet Nam to the north of the line and the forces of the French Union to the south.

The provisional military demarcation line is fixed as shown on the map attached.

It is also agreed that a demilitarised zone shall be established on either side of the demarcation line, to a width of not more than 5kms. from it, to act as a buffer zone and avoid any incidents which might result in the resumption of hostilities.

Article 2

The period within which the movement of all forces of either party into its regrouping zone on either side of the provisional military demarcation line shall be completed shall not exceed three hundred (300) days from the date of the present Agreement's entry into force.

Article 3

When the provisional military demarcation line coincides with a waterway, the waters of such waterway shall be open to civil navigation by both parties wherever one bank is controlled by one party and the other bank by the other party. The Joint Commission shall establish rules of navigation for the stretch of waterway in question. The merchant shipping and other civilian craft of each party shall have unrestricted access to the land under its military control.

Article 4

The provisional military demarcation line between the two final regrouping zones is extended into the territorial waters by a line perpendicular to the general line of the coast.

All coastal islands north of this boundary shall be evacuated by the armed forces of the French Union, and all islands south of it shall be evacuated by the forces of the People's Army of Viet Nam.

Article 5

To avoid any incidents which might result in the resumption of hostilities, all military forces, supplies and equipment shall be withdrawn from the demilitarised zone within twenty-five (25) days of the present Agreement's entry into force.

Article 6

No person, military or civilian, shall be permitted to cross the provisional military demarcation line unless specifically authorised to do so by the Joint Commission.

Article 7

No person, military or civilian, shall be permitted to enter the demilitarised zone except persons concerned with the conduct of civil administration and relief and persons specifically authorised to enter by the Joint Commission.

Article 8

Civil administration and relief in the demilitarised zone on either side of the provisional military demarcation line shall be the responsibility of the Commanders-in-Chief of the two parties in their respective zones. The number of persons, military or civilian, from each side who are permitted to enter the demilitarised zone for the conduct of civil administration and relief shall be determined by the respective Commanders, but in no case shall the total number authorised by either side exceed at any one time a figure to be determined by the Trung Gia Military Commission or by the Joint Commission. The number of civil police and the arms to be carried by them shall be determined by the Joint Commission. No one else shall carry arms unless specifically authorised to do so by the Joint Commission.

Article 9

Nothing contained in this chapter shall be construed as limiting the complete freedom of movement, into, out of or within the demilitarised zone, of the Joint Commission, its joint groups, the International Commission to be set up as indicated below, its inspection teams and any other persons, supplies or equipment specifically authorised to enter the demilitarised zone by the Joint Commission. Freedom of movement shall be permitted across the territory under the military control of either side over any road or waterway which has to be taken between points within the demilitarised zone when such points are not connected by roads or waterways lying completely within the demilitarised zone.

CHAPTER II

Principles and procedure governing implementation of the present agreement

Article 10

The Commanders of the Forces on each side, on the one side the Commander-in-Chief of the French Union forces in Indo-China and on the other side the Commander-in-Chief of the People's Army of Viet Nam, shall order and enforce the complete cessation of all hostilities in Viet Nam by all armed forces under their control, including all units and personnel of the ground, naval and air forces.

Article 11

In accordance with the principle of a simultaneous cease-fire throughout Indo-China, the cessation of hostilities shall be simultaneous throughout all parts of Viet Nam, in all areas of hostilities and for all the forces of the two parties.

Taking into account the time effectively required to transmit the cease-fire order down to the lowest échelons of the combatant forces on both sides, the two parties are agreed that the cease-fire shall take effect completely and simultaneously for the different sectors of the country as follows:—

Northern Viet Nam at 8:00 a.m. (local time) on July 27, 1954.
Central Viet Nam at 8:00 a.m. (local time) on August 1, 1954.
Southern Viet Nam at 8:00 a.m. (local time) on August 11, 1954.

It is agreed that Peking mean time shall be taken as local time.

From such time as the cease-fire becomes effective in Northern Viet Nam, both parties undertake not to engage in any large-scale offensive action in any part of the Indo-Chinese theatre of operations and not to commit the air forces based on Northern Viet Nam outside that sector. The two parties also undertake to inform each other of their plans for movement from one regrouping zone to another within twenty-five (25) days of the present Agreement's entry into force.

Article 12

All the operations and movements entailed in the cessation of hostilities and regrouping must proceed in a safe and orderly fashion:—

(*a*) Within a certain number of days after the cease-fire Agreement shall have become effective, the number to be determined on the spot by the Trung Gia Military Commission, each party shall be responsible for removing and neutralising mines (including river- and sea-mines), booby traps, explosives and any other dangerous substances placed by it. In the event of its being impossible to complete the work of removal and neutralisation in time, the party concerned shall mark the spot by placing visible signs there. All demolitions, mine fields, wire entanglements and other hazards to the free movement of the personnel of the Joint Commission and its joint groups, known to be present after the withdrawal of the military forces, shall be reported to the Joint Commission by the Commanders of the opposing forces;

(*b*) From the time of the cease-fire until regrouping is completed on either side of the demarcation line:—

(1) The forces of either party shall be provisionally withdrawn from the provisional assembly areas assigned to the other party.

(2) When one party's forces withdraw by a route (road, rail, waterway, sea route) which passes through the territory of the other party (see Article 24), the latter party's forces must provisionally withdraw three kilometres on each side of such route, but in such a manner as to avoid interfering with the movements of the civil population.

Article 13

From the time of the cease-fire until the completion of the movements from one regrouping zone into the other, civil and military transport aircraft shall follow air-corridors between the provisional assembly areas assigned to the French Union forces north of the demarcation line on the one hand and the Laotian frontier and the regrouping zone assigned to the French Union forces on the other hand.

The position of the air-corridors, their width, the safety route for single-engined military aircraft transferred to the south and the search and rescue procedure for aircraft in distress shall be determined on the spot by the Trung Gia Military Commission.

Article 14

Political and administrative measures in the two regrouping zones, on either side of the provisional military demarcation line:—

(*a*) Pending the general elections which will bring about the unification of Viet Nam, the conduct of civil administration in each regrouping zone shall be in the hands of the party whose forces are to be regrouped there in virtue of the present Agreement.

(*b*) Any territory controlled by one party which is transferred to the other party by the regrouping plan shall continue to be administered by the former party until such date as all the troops who are to be transferred have completely left that territory so as to free the zone assigned to the party in question. From then on, such territory shall be regarded as transferred to the other party, who shall assume responsibility for it.

Steps shall be taken to ensure that there is no break in the transfer of responsibilities. For this purpose, adequate notice shall be given by the withdrawing party to the other party, which shall make the necessary arrangements, in particular by sending administrative and police detachments to prepare for the assumption of administrative responsibility. The length of such notice shall be determined by the Trung Gia Military Commission. The transfers shall be effected in successive stages for the various territorial sectors.

The transfer of the civil administration of Hanoi and Haiphong to the authorities of the Democratic Republic of Viet Nam shall be completed within the respective time-limits laid down in Article 15 for military movements.

(*c*) Each party undertakes to refrain from any reprisals or discrimination against persons or organisations on account of their activities during the hostilities and to guarantee their democratic liberties.

(*d*) From the date of entry into force of the present Agreement until the movement of troops is completed, any civilians residing in a district controlled by one party who wish to go and live in the zone assigned to the other party shall be permitted and helped to do so by the authorities in that district.

Article 15

The disengagement of the combatants, and the withdrawals and transfers of military forces, equipment and supplies shall take place in accordance with the following principles:—

(*a*) The withdrawals and transfers of the military forces,

equipment and supplies of the two parties shall be completed within three hundred (300) days, as laid down in Article 2 of the present Agreement;

(*b*) Within either territory successive withdrawals shall be made by sectors, portions of sectors or provinces. Transfers from one regrouping zone to another shall be made in successive monthly instalments proportionate to the number of troops to be transferred;

(*c*) The two parties shall undertake to carry out all troop withdrawals and transfers in accordance with the aims of the present Agreement, shall permit no hostile act and shall take no step whatsoever which might hamper such withdrawals and transfers. They shall assist one another as far as this is possible;

(*d*) The two parties shall permit no destruction or sabotage of any public property and no injury to the life and property of the civil population. They shall permit no interference in local civil administration;

(*e*) The Joint Commission and the International Commission shall ensure that steps are taken to safeguard the forces in the course of withdrawal and transfer;

(*f*) The Trung Gia Military Commission, and later the Joint Commission, shall determine by common agreement the exact procedure for the disengagement of the combatants and for troop withdrawals and transfers, on the basis of the principles mentioned above and within the framework laid down below:—

1. The disengagement of the combatants, including the concentration of the armed forces of all kinds and also each party's movements into the provisional assembly areas assigned to it and the other party's provisional withdrawal from it, shall be completed within a period not exceeding fifteen (15) days after the date when the cease-fire becomes effective.

The general delineation of the provisional assembly areas is set out in the maps annexed to the present Agreement.

In order to avoid any incidents, no troops shall be stationed less than 1,500 metres from the lines delimiting the provisional assembly areas.

During the period until the transfers are concluded, all the coastal islands west of the following lines shall be included in the Haiphong perimeter:

meridian of the southern point of Kebao Island,
northern coast of Ile Rousse (excluding the island), extended as far as the meridian of Campha-Mines,
meridian of Campha-Mines.

2. The withdrawals and transfers shall be effected in the following order and within the following periods (from the date of the entry into force of the present Agreement) :—

Forces of the French Union

Hanoi perimeter	80 days
Haiduong perimeter	100 days
Haiphong perimeter	300 days

Forces of the People's Army of Viet Nam

Ham Tan and Xuyenmoc provisional assembly area	80 days
Central Viet Nam provisional assembly area—first instalment	80 days
Plaine des Joncs provisional assembly area	100 days
Central Viet Nam provisional assembly area—second instalment	100 days
Pointe Camau provisional assembly area	200 days
Central Viet Nam provisional assembly area—last instalment	300 days

CHAPTER III

Ban on the introduction of fresh troops, military personnel, arms and munitions. Military bases

Article 16

With effect from the date of entry into force of the present Agreement, the introduction into Viet Nam of any troop reinforcements and additional military personnel is prohibited.

It is understood, however, that the rotation of units and groups of personnel, the arrival in Viet Nam of individual personnel on a temporary duty basis and the return to Viet Nam of the individual personnel after short periods of leave or temporary duty outside Viet Nam shall be permitted under the conditions laid down below:—

(*a*) Rotation of units (defined in paragraph (*c*) of this Article) and groups of personnel shall not be permitted for French Union troops stationed north of the provisional military demarcation line laid down in Article 1 of the present Agreement during the withdrawal period provided for in Article 2.

However, under the heading of individual personnel not more than fifty (50) men, including officers, shall during any one month be permitted to enter that part of the country north of the provisional military demarcation line on a temporary duty basis or to return there after short periods of leave or temporary duty outside Viet Nam.

(*b*) "Rotation" is defined as the replacement of units or groups of personnel by other units of the same échelon or by personnel who are arriving in Viet Nam territory to do their overseas service there;

(*c*) The units rotated shall never be larger than a battalion—or the corresponding échelon for air and naval forces;

(*d*) Rotation shall be conducted on a man-for-man basis, provided, however, that in any one quarter neither party shall introduce more than fifteen thousand five hundred (15,500) members of its armed forces into Viet Nam under the rotation policy.

(*e*) Rotation units (defined in paragraph (*c*) of this Article) and groups of personnel, and the individual personnel mentioned in this Article, shall enter and leave Viet Nam

only through the entry points enumerated in Article 20
below;

(f) Each party shall notify the Joint Commission and the International Commission at least two days in advance of any
arrivals or departures of units, groups of personnel and
individual personnel in or from Viet Nam. Reports on the
arrivals or departures of units, groups of personnel and
individual personnel in or from Viet Nam shall be submitted daily to the Joint Commission and the International
Commission.

All the above-mentioned notifications and reports shall
indicate the places and dates of arrival or departure and
the number of persons arriving or departing;

(g) The International Commission, through its Inspection
Teams, shall supervise and inspect the rotation of units and
groups of personnel and the arrival and departure of individual personnel as authorised above, at the points of
entry enumerated in Article 20 below.

Article 17

(a) With effect from the date of entry into force of the present
Agreement, the introduction into Viet Nam of any reinforcements
in the form of all types of arms, munitions and other war material, such as combat aircraft, naval craft, pieces of ordnance, jet
engines and jet weapons and armoured vehicles, is prohibited.

(b) It is understood, however, that war material, arms and
munitions which have been destroyed, damaged, worn out or
used up after the cessation of hostilities may be replaced on the
basis of piece-for-piece of the same type and with similar characteristics. Such replacements of war material, arms and ammuni-
tions shall not be permitted for French Union troops stationed
north of the provisional military demarcation line laid down in
Article 1 of the present Agreement, during the withdrawal period
provided for in Article 2.

Naval craft may perform transport operations between the regrouping zones.

(c) The war material, arms and munitions for replacement

693

purposes provided for in paragraph (*b*) of this Article, shall be introduced into Viet Nam only through the points of entry enumerated in Article 20 below. War material, arms and munitions to be replaced shall be shipped from Viet Nam only through the points of entry enumerated in Article 20 below.

(*d*) Apart from the replacements permitted within the limits laid down in paragraph (*b*) of this Article, the introduction of war material, arms and munitions of all types in the form of unassembled parts for subsequent assembly is prohibited.

(*e*) Each party shall notify the Joint Commission and the International Commission at least two days in advance of any arrivals or departures which may take place of war material, arms and munitions of all types.

In order to justify the requests for the introduction into Viet Nam of arms, munitions and other war material (as defined in paragraph (*a*) of this Article) for replacement purposes, a report concerning each incoming shipment shall be submitted to the Joint Commission and the International Commission. Such reports shall indicate the use made of the items so replaced.

(*f*) The International Commission, through its Inspection Teams, shall supervise and inspect the replacements permitted in the circumstances laid down in this Article, at the points of entry enumerated in Article 20 below.

Article 18

With effect from the date of entry into force of the present Agreement, the establishment of new military bases is prohibited throughout Viet Nam territory.

Article 19

With effect from the date of entry into force of the present Agreement, no military base under the control of a foreign State may be established in the re-grouping zone of either party; the two parties shall ensure that the zones assigned to them do not adhere to any military alliance and are not used for the resumption of hostilities or to further an aggressive policy.

Article 20

The points of entry into Viet Nam for rotation personnel and replacements of material are fixed as follows:—

— Zones to the north of the provisional military demarcation line: Laokay, Langson, Tien-Yen, Haiphong, Vinh, Dong-Hoi, Muong-Sen;
— Zones to the south of the provisional military demarcation line: Tourane, Quinhon, Nhatrang, Bangoi, Saigon, Cap St. Jacques, Tanchau.

CHAPTER IV

Prisoners of War and Civilian Internees

Article 21

The liberation and repatriation of all prisoners of war and civilian internees detained by each of the two parties at the coming into force of the present Agreement shall be carried out under the following conditions:—

(a) All prisoners of war and civilian internees of Viet Nam, French and other nationalities captured since the beginning of hostilities in Viet Nam during military operations or in any other circumstances of war and in any part of the territory of Viet Nam shall be liberated within a period of thirty (30) days after the date when the cease-fire becomes effective in each theatre.

(b) The term "civilian internees" is understood to mean all persons who, having in any way contributed to the political and armed struggle between the two parties, have been arrested for that reason and have been kept in detention by either party during the period of hostilities.

(c) All prisoners of war and civilian internees held by either party shall be surrendered to the appropriate authorities of the other party, who shall give them all possible assistance in proceeding to their country of origin, place of habitual residence or the zone of their choice.

CHAPTER V

Miscellaneous

Article 22

The Commanders of the Forces of the two parties shall ensure that persons under their respective commands who violate any of the provisions of the present Agreement are suitably punished.

Article 23

In cases in which the place of burial is known and the existence of graves has been established, the Commander of the Forces of either party shall, within a specific period after the entry into force of the Armistice Agreement, permit the graves service personnel of the other party to enter the part of Viet Nam territory under their military control for the purpose of finding and removing the bodies of deceased military personnel of that party, including the bodies of deceased prisoners of war. The Joint Commission shall determine the procedures and the time limit for the performance of this task. The Commanders of the Forces of the two parties shall communicate to each other all information in their possession as to the place of burial of military personnel of the other party.

Article 24

The present Agreement shall apply to all the armed forces of either party. The armed forces of each party shall respect the demilitarised zone and the territory under the military control of the other party, and shall commit no act and undertake no operation against the other party and shall not engage in blockade of any kind in Viet Nam.

For the purposes of the present Article, the word "territory" includes territorial waters and air space.

Article 25

The Commanders of the Forces of the two parties shall afford full protection and all possible assistance and co-operation to the Joint Commission and its joint groups and to the International

Commission and its inspection teams in the performance of the functions and tasks assigned to them by the present Agreement.

Article 26

The costs involved in the operations of the Joint Commission and joint groups and of the International Commission and its Inspection Teams shall be shared equally between the two parties.

Article 27

The signatories of the present Agreement and their successors in their functions shall be responsible for ensuring the observance and enforcement of the terms and provisions thereof. The Commanders of the Forces of the two parties shall, within their respective commands, take all steps and make all arrangements necessary to ensure full compliance with all the provisions of the present Agreement by all elements and military personnel under their command.

The procedures laid down in the present Agreement shall, whenever necessary, be studied by the Commanders of the two parties and, if necessary, defined more specifically by the Joint Commission.

CHAPTER VI

Joint Commission and International Commission for Supervision and Control in Viet Nam

Article 28

Responsibility for the execution of the agreement on the cessation of hostilities shall rest with the parties.

Article 29

An International Commission shall ensure the control and supervision of this execution.

Article 30

In order to facilitate, under the conditions shown below, the execution of provisions concerning joint actions by the two parties, a Joint Commission shall be set up in Viet Nam.

Article 31

The Joint Commission shall be composed of an equal number of representatives of the Commanders of the two parties.

Article 32

The Presidents of the delegations to the Joint Commission shall hold the rank of General.

The Joint Commission shall set up joint groups, the number of which shall be determined by mutual agreement between the parties. The joint groups shall be composed of an equal number of officers from both parties. Their location on the demarcation line between the re-grouping zones shall be determined by the parties whilst taking into account the powers of the Joint Commission.

Article 33

The Joint Commission shall ensure the execution of the following provisions of the Agreement on the cessation of hostilities:—

(a) A simultaneous and general cease-fire in Viet Nam for all regular and irregular armed forces of the two parties.
(b) A re-groupment of the armed forces of the two parties.
(c) Observance of the demarcation lines between the re-grouping zones and of the demilitarised sectors.

Within the limits of its competence it shall help the parties to execute the said provisions, shall ensure liaison between them for the purpose of preparing and carrying out plans for the application of these provisions, and shall endeavour to solve such disputed questions as may arise between the parties in the course of executing these provisions.

Article 34

An International Commission shall be set up for the control and supervision over the application of the provisions of the agreement on the cessation of hostilities in Viet Nam. It shall be composed of representatives of the following States: Canada, India and Poland.

It shall be presided over by the Representative of India.

Article 35

The International Commission shall set up fixed and mobile inspection teams, composed of an equal number of officers appointed by each of the above-mentioned States. The mixed teams shall be located at the following points: Laokay, Langson, Tien-Yen, Haiphong, Vinh, Dong-Hoi, Muong-Sen, Tourane, Quinhon, Nhatrang, Bangoi, Saigon, Cap St. Jacques, Tranchau. These points of location may, at a later date, be altered at the request of the Joint Commission, or of one of the parties, or of the International Commission itself, by agreement between the International Commission and the command of the party concerned. The zones of action of the mobile teams shall be the regions bordering the land and sea frontiers of Viet Nam, the demarcation lines between the re-grouping zones and the demilitarised zones. Within the limits of these zones they shall have the right to move freely and shall receive from the local civil and military authorities all facilities they may require for the fulfilment of their tasks (provision of personnel, placing at their disposal documents needed for supervision, summoning witnesses necessary for holding enquiries, ensuring the security and freedom of movement of the inspection teams, &c. . . .). They shall have at their disposal such modern means of transport, observation and communication as they may require. Beyond the zones of action as defined above, the mobile teams may, by agreement with the command of the party concerned, carry out other movements within the limits of the tasks given them by the present agreement.

Article 36

The International Commission shall be responsible for supervising the proper execution by the parties of the provisions of the agreement. For this purpose it shall fulfil the tasks of control, observation, inspection and investigation connected with the application of the provisions of the agreement on the cessation of hostilities, and it shall in particular:—

(a) Control the movement of the armed forces of the two parties, effected within the framework of the regroupment plan.

(*b*) Supervise the demarcation lines between the regrouping areas, and also the demilitarised zones.

(*c*) Control the operations of releasing prisoners of war and civilian internees.

(*d*) Supervise at ports and airfields as well as along all frontiers of Viet Nam the execution of the provisions of the agreement on the cessation of hostilities, regulating the introduction into the country of armed forces, military personnel and of all kinds of arms, munitions and war material.

Article 37

The International Commission shall, through the medium of the inspection teams mentioned above, and as soon as possible either on its own initiative, or at the request of the Joint Commission, or of one of the parties, undertake the necessary investigations both documentary and on the ground.

Article 38

The inspection teams shall submit to the International Commission the results of their supervision, their investigation and their observations, furthermore they shall draw up such special reports as they may consider necessary or as may be requested from them by the Commission. In the case of a disagreement within the teams, the conclusions of each member shall be submitted to the Commission.

Article 39

If any one inspection team is unable to settle an incident or considers that there is a violation or a threat of a serious violation, the International Commission shall be informed; the latter shall study the reports and the conclusions of the inspection teams and shall inform the parties of the measures which should be taken for the settlement of the incident, ending of the violation or removal of the threat of violation.

Article 40

When the Joint Commission is unable to reach an agreement on the interpretation to be given to some provision or on the appraisal of a fact, the International Commission shall be informed of the disputed question. Its recommendations shall be sent directly to the parties and shall be notified to the Joint Commission.

Article 41

The recommendations of the International Commission shall be adopted by majority vote, subject to the provisions contained in Article 42. If the votes are divided, the chairman's vote shall be decisive.

The International Commission may formulate recommendations concerning amendments and additions which should be made to the provisions of the agreement on the cessation of hostilities in Viet Nam, in order to ensure a more effective execution of that agreement. These recommendations shall be adopted unanimously.

Article 42

When dealing with questions concerning violations, or threats of violations, which might lead to a resumption of hostilities, namely:—

(a) Refusal by the armed forces of one party to effect the movements provided for in the regroupment plan;

(b) Violation by the armed forces of one of the parties of the regrouping zones, territorial waters, or air space of the other party;

the decisions of the International Commission must be unanimous.

Article 43

If one of the parties refuses to put into effect a recommendation of the International Commission, the parties concerned or the Commission itself shall inform the members of the Geneva Conference.

If the International Commission does not reach unanimity in the cases provided for in Article 42, it shall submit a majority report and one or more minority reports to the members of the Conference.

The International Commission shall inform the members of the Conference in all cases where its activity is being hindered.

Article 44

The International Commission shall be set up at the time of the cessation of hostilities in Indo-China in order that it should be able to fulfil the tasks provided for in Article 36.

Article 45

The International Commission for Supervision and Control in Viet Nam shall act in close co-operation with the International Commissions for Supervision and Control in Cambodia and Laos.

The Secretaries-General of these three Commissions shall be responsible for co-ordinating their work and for relations between them.

Article 46

The International Commission for Supervision and Control in Viet Nam may, after consultation with the International Commissions for Supervision and Control in Cambodia and Laos, and having regard to the development of the situation in Cambodia and Laos, progressively reduce its activities. Such a decision must be adopted unanimously.

Article 47

All the provisions of the present Agreement, save the second sub-paragraph of Article 11, shall enter into force at 2400 hours (Geneva time) on July 22, 1954.

Done in Geneva at 2400 hours on the 20th of July, 1954, in French and in Vietnamese, both texts being equally authentic.

For the Commander-in-Chief of the French Union Forces in Indo-China:

DELTIEL,
Brigadier-General.

For the Commander-in-Chief of the People's Army of Viet Nam:

TA-QUANG-BUU,
Vice-Minister of National Defence
of the Democratic Republic of Viet Nam.

Annex to the Agreement on the Cessation of Hostilities in Viet Nam

I.—*Delineation of the provisional military demarcation line and the demilitarised zone* (Article 1 of the Agreement; reference map: Indo-China 1/100,000)

(*a*) The provisional military demarcation line is fixed as follows, reading from east to west:—

The mouth of the Song Ben Hat (Cua Tung River) and the course of that river (known as the Rao Thanh in the mountains) to the village of Bo Ho Su, then the parallel of Bo Ho Su to the Laos-Viet Nam frontier.

(*b*) The demilitarised zone shall be delimited by Trung Gia Military Commission in accordance with the provisions of Article 1 of the Agreement on the cessation of hostilities in Viet Nam.

II.—*General delineation of the provisional assembly areas* (Article 15 of the Agreement; reference maps: Indo-China 1/4000,000)

(a) North Viet Nam

Delineation of the Boundary of the Provisional Assembly Area of the French Union Forces

1. The perimeter of Hanoi is delimited by the arc of a circle with a radius of 15 kilometres, having as its centre the right bank abutment of Doumer Bridge and running westwards from the Red River to the Rapids Canal in the north-east.

In this particular case no forces of the French Union shall be stationed less than 2 kilometres from this perimeter, on the inside thereof.

2. The perimeter of Haiphong shall be delimited by the Song-Van-Uc as far as Kim Thanh and a line running from the Song-Van-Uc three kilometres north-east of Kim Thanh to cut Road No. 18 two kilometres east of Mao-Khé. Thence a line running three kilometres north of Road 18 to Cho-Troi and a straight line from Cho-Troi to the Mong-Duong ferry.

3. *A corridor contained between*:

In the south, the Red River from Thanh-Tri to Bang-Nho, thence a line joining the latter point to Do-My (south-west of Kesat), Gia-Loc and Tien Kieu;

In the north, a line running along the Rapids Canal at a distance of 1,500 metres to the north of the Canal, passing three kilometres north of Pha-Lai and Seven Pagodas and thence parallel to Road No. 18 to its point of intersection with the perimeter of Haiphong.

Note.—Throughout the period of evacuation of the perimeter of Hanoi, the river forces of the French Union shall enjoy complete freedom of movement on the Song-Van-Uc. And the forces of the People's Army of Viet Nam shall withdraw three kilometres south of the south bank of the Song-Van-Uc.

Boundary between the perimeter of Hanoi and the perimeter of Haiduong

A straight line running from the Rapids Canal three kilometres west of Chi-ne and ending at Do-My (eight kilometres south-west of Kesat).

(b) Central Viet Nam

Delineation of the Boundary of the Provisional Assembly Area of the Forces of the Viet Nam People's Army South of the Col des Nuages Parallel

The perimeter of the Central Viet Nam area shall consist of the administrative boundaries of the provinces of Quang-Ngai and Binh-Dinh as they were defined before the hostilities.

(c) South Viet Nam

Three provisional assembly areas shall be provided for the forces of the People's Army of Viet Nam.

The boundaries of these areas are as follows:—

1. *Xuyen-Moc, Ham-Tan Area*—
   Western boundary: The course of the Song-Ray extended northwards as far as Road No. 1 to a point thereon eight

kilometres east of the intersection of Road No. 1 and Road No. 3.

Northern boundary: Road No. 1 from the above-mentioned intersection to the intersection with Route Communale No. 9 situated 27 kilometres west-south-west of Phanthiet and from that intersection a straight line to Kim Thanh on the coast.

2. *Plaine des Joncs Area*—

Northern boundary: The Viet Nam-Cambodia frontier.

Western boundary: A straight line from Tong-Binh to Binh-Thanh.

Southern boundary: Course of the Fleuve Antérieur (Mekong) to ten kilometres south-east of Cao Lanh. From that point, a straight line as far as Ap-My-Dien, and from Ap-My-Dien a line parallel to and three kilometres east and then south of the Tong Doc-Loc Canal, this line reaches My-Hanh-Dong and thence Hung-Thanh-My.

Eastern boundary: A straight line from Hung-Thanh-My running northwards to the Cambodian frontier south of Doi-Bao-Voi.

3. *Point Camau Area*—

Northern boundary: The Song-Cai-lon from its mouth to its junction with the Rach-Nuoc-Trong, thence the Rach-Nuoc-Trong to the bend five kilometres north-east of Ap-Xeo-La. Thereafter a line to the Ngan-Dua Canal and following that Canal as far as Vinh-Hung. Finally, from Vinh-Hung a north–south line to the sea.

Declaration by the Royal Government of Cambodia

July 21, 1954

(Reference: Article 3 of the Final Declaration)

The Royal Government of Cambodia,

In the desire to ensure harmony and agreement among the peoples of the Kingdom,

Declares itself resolved to take the necessary measures to integrate all citizens, without discrimination, into the national community and to guarantee them the enjoyment of the rights and freedoms for which the Constitution of the Kingdom provides;

Affirms that all Cambodian citizens may freely participate as electors or candidates in general elections by secret ballot.

Declaration by the Royal Government of Laos

July 21, 1954

(Reference: Article 3 of the Final Declaration)

The Royal Government of Laos,

In the desire to ensure harmony and agreement among the peoples of the Kingdom,

Declares itself resolved to take the necessary measures to integrate all citizens, without discrimination, into the national community and to guarantee them the enjoyment of the rights and freedoms for which the Constitution of the Kingdom provides;

Affirms that all Laotian citizens may freely participate as electors or candidates in general elections by secret ballot;

Announces, furthermore, that it will promulgate measures to provide for special representation in the Royal Administration of the provinces of Phang Saly and Sam Neua during the interval between the cessation of hostilities and the general elections of the interests of Laotian nationals who did not support the Royal forces during hostilities.

Declaration by the Royal Government of Cambodia

July 21, 1954

(Reference: Articles 4 and 5 of the Final Declaration)

The Royal Government of Cambodia is resolved never to take part in an aggressive policy and never to permit the territory of Cambodia to be utilised in the service of such a policy.

The Royal Government of Cambodia will not join in any agreement with other States, if this agreement carries for Cambodia the obligation to enter into a military alliance not in conformity with the principles of the Charter of the United Nations, or, as long as its security is not threatened, the obligation to establish bases on Cambodian territory for the military forces of foreign Powers.

The Royal Government of Cambodia is resolved to settle its international disputes by peaceful means, in such a manner as not to endanger peace, international security and justice.

During the period which will elapse between the date of the cessation of hostilities in Viet Nam and that of the final settlement of political problems in this country, the Royal Government of Cambodia will not solicit foreign aid in war material, personnel or instructors except for the purpose of the effective defence of the territory.

Declaration by the Royal Government of Laos

July 21, 1954

(*Reference*: *Articles 4 and 5 of the Final Declaration*)

The Royal Government of Laos is resolved never to pursue a policy of aggression and will never permit the territory of Laos to be used in furtherance of such a policy.

The Royal Government of Laos will never join in any agreement with other States if this agreement includes the obligation for the Royal Government of Laos to participate in a military alliance not in conformity with the principles of the Charter of the United Nations or with the principles of the agreement on the cessation of hostilities or, unless its security is threatened, the obligation to establish bases on Laotian territory for military forces of foreign Powers.

The Royal Government of Laos is resolved to settle its international disputes by peaceful means so that international peace and security and justice are not endangered.

During the period between the cessation of hostilities in Viet Nam and the final settlement of that country's political problems, the Royal Government of Laos will not request foreign aid, whether in war material, in personnel or in instructors, except for the purpose of its effective territorial defence and to the extent defined by the agreement on the cessation of hostilities.

Declaration by the Government of the French Republic

July 21, 1954

(Reference: Article 10 of the Final Declaration)

The Government of the French Republic declares that it is ready to withdraw its troops from the territory of Cambodia, Laos and Viet Nam, at the request of the Governments concerned and within a period which shall be fixed by agreement between the parties, except in the cases where, by agreement between the two parties, a certain number of French troops shall remain at specified points and for a specified time.

Declaration by the Government of the French Republic

July 21, 1954

(Reference: Article 11 of the Final Declaration)

For the settlement of all the problems connected with the re-establishment and consolidation of peace in Cambodia, Laos and Viet Nam, the French Government will proceed from the principle of respect for the independence and sovereignty, the unity and territorial integrity of Cambodia, Laos and Viet Nam.

THE 1962 GENEVA AGREEMENT FOR LAOS*

* [1962] 14 U.S.T. 1104, T.I.A.S. 5410.

Declaration on the Neutrality of Laos

The Governments of the Union of Burma, the Kingdom of Cambodia, Canada, the People's Republic of China, the Democratic Republic of Viet-Nam, the Republic of France, the Republic of India, the Polish People's Republic, the Republic of Viet-Nam, the Kingdom of Thailand, the Union of Soviet Socialist Republics, the United Kingdom of Great Britain and Northern Ireland and the United States of America, whose representatives took part in the International Conference on the Settlement of the Laotian Question, 1961-1962;

Welcoming the presentation of the statement of neutrality by the Royal Government of Laos of July 9, 1962, and taking note of this statement, which is, with the concurrence of the Royal Government of Laos, incorporated in the present Declaration as an integral part thereof, and the text of which is as follows:

The Royal Government of Laos,

Being resolved to follow the path of peace and neutrality in conformity with the interests and aspirations of the Laotian people, as well as the principles of the Joint Communiqué of Zurich dated June 22, 1961, and of the Geneva Agreements of 1954,[1] in order to build a peaceful, neutral, independent, democratic, unified and prosperous Laos,

Solemnly declares that:

(1) It will resolutely apply the five principles of peaceful co-existence in foreign relations, and will develop friendly relations and establish diplomatic relations with all countries, the neighbouring countries first and foremost, on the basis of equality and of respect for the independence and sovereignty of Laos;

(2) It is the will of the Laotian people to protect and ensure respect for the sovereignty, independence, neutrality, unity, and territorial integrity of Laos;

(3) It will not resort to the use or threat of force in any way

1. For texts, see *American Foreign Policy, 1950-1955: Basic Documents,* vol. I, Department of State publication 6446, p. 775.

which might impair the peace of other countries, and will not interfere in the internal affairs of other countries;

(4) It will not enter into any military alliance or into any agreement, whether military or otherwise, which is inconsistent with the neutrality of the Kingdom of Laos; it will not allow the establishment of any foreign military base on Laotian territory, nor allow any country to use Laotian territory for military purposes or for the purposes of interference in the internal affairs of other countries, nor recognise the protection of any alliance or military coalition, including SEATO.[2]

(5) It will not allow any foreign interference in the internal affairs of the Kingdom of Laos in any form whatsoever;

(6) Subject to the provisions of Article 5 of the Protocol, it will require the withdrawal from Laos of all foreign troops and military personnel, and will not allow any foreign troops or military personnel to be introduced into Laos;

(7) It will accept direct and unconditional aid from all countries that wish to help the Kingdom of Laos build up an independent and autonomous national economy on the basis of respect for the sovereignty of Laos;

(8) It will respect the treaties and agreements signed in conformity with the interests of the Laotian people and of the policy of peace and neutrality of the Kingdom, in particular the Geneva Agreements of 1962, and will abrogate all treaties and agreements which are contrary to those principles.

This statement of neutrality by the Royal Government of Laos shall be promulgated constitutionally and shall have the force of law.

The Kingdom of Laos appeals to all the States participating in the International Conference on the Settlement of the Laotian Question, and to all other States, to recognise the sovereignty, independence, neutrality, unity and territorial integrity of Laos, to conform to these principles in all respects, and to refrain from any action inconsistent therewith.

Confirming the principles of respect for the sovereignty, independence, unity and territorial integrity of the Kingdom of Laos

2. Southeast Asia Treaty Organization.

and non-interference in its internal affairs which are embodied in the Geneva Agreements of 1954;

Emphasising the principle of respect for the neutrality of the Kingdom of Laos;

Agreeing that the above-mentioned principles constitute a basis for the peaceful settlement of the Laotian question;

Profoundly convinced that the independence and neutrality of the Kingdom of Laos will assist the peaceful democratic development of the Kingdom of Laos and the achievement of national accord and unity in that country, as well as the strengthening of peace and security in South-East Asia;

1. Solemnly declare, in accordance with the will of the Government and people of the Kingdom of Laos, as expressed in the statement of neutrality by the Royal Government of Laos of July 9, 1962, that they recognise and will respect and observe in every way the sovereignty, independence, neutrality, unity and territorial integrity of the Kingdom of Laos.

2. Undertake, in particular, that

(a) they will not commit or participate in any way in any act which might directly or indirectly impair the sovereignty, independence, neutrality, unity or territorial integrity of the Kingdom of Laos;

(b) they will not resort to the use or threat of force or any other measure which might impair the peace of the Kingdom of Laos;

(c) they will refrain from all direct or indirect interference in the internal affairs of the Kingdom of Laos;

(d) they will not attach conditions of a political nature to any assistance which they may offer or which the Kingdom of Laos may seek;

(e) they will not bring the Kingdom of Laos in any way into any military alliance or any other agreement, whether military or otherwise, which is inconsistent with her neutrality, nor invite or encourage her to enter into any such alliance or to conclude any such agreement;

(f) they will respect the wish of the Kingdom of Laos not to recognise the protection of any alliance or military coalition, including SEATO;

(g) they will not introduce into the Kingdom of Laos foreign troops or military personnel in any form whatsoever, nor will they in any way facilitate or connive at the introduction of any foreign troops or military personnel;

(h) they will not establish nor will they in any way facilitate or connive at the establishment in the Kingdom of Laos of any foreign military base, foreign strong point or other foreign military installation of any kind;

(i) they will not use the territory of the Kingdom of Laos for interference in the internal affairs of other countries;

(j) they will not use the territory of any country, including their own for interference in the internal affairs of the Kingdom of Laos.

3. Appeal to all other States to recognise, respect and observe in every way the sovereignty, independence and neutrality, and also the unity and territorial integrity, of the Kingdom of Laos and to refrain from any action inconsistent with these principles or with other provisions of the present Declaration.

4. Undertake, in the event of a violation or threat of violation of the sovereignty, independence, neutrality, unity or territorial integrity of the Kingdom of Laos, to consult jointly with the Royal Government of Laos and among themselves in order to consider measures which might prove to be necessary to ensure the observance of these principles and the other provisions of the present Declaration.

5. The present Declaration shall enter into force on signature and together with the statement of neutrality by the Royal Government of Laos of July 9, 1962, shall be regarded as constituting an international agreement. The present Declaration shall be deposited in the archives of the Governments of the United Kingdom and the Union of Soviet Socialist Republics, which shall furnish certified copies thereof to the other signatory States and to all the other States of the world.

In witness whereof, the undersigned Plenipotentiaries have signed the present Declaration.

Done in two copies in Geneva this twenty-third day of July one
thousand nine hundred and sixty-two in the English, Chinese,
French, Laotian and Russian languages, each text being equally
authoritative.

For the Union of Burma:
U Thi Han
For the Kingdom of Cambodia:
Nhiek Tioulong

For Canada:
H. C. Green
Chester Ronning
For the People's Republic of China:
Chen Yi
For the Democratic Republic of Viet-Nam:
Ung-Van-Khiem
For the Republic of France:
Jacques Roux
M. Couve De Murville
For the Republic of India:
V. K. Krishna Menon
For the Polish People's Republic:
A. Rapacki
For the Republic of Viet-Nam:
Vu Van Mau
Thanh
For the Kingdom of Thailand:
Direck Jayanâma
For the Union of Soviet Socialist Republics:
A. Gromyko
For the United Kingdom of Great Britain and
Northern Ireland:
Home
Malcolm Macdonald
For the United States of America:
Dean Rusk
W. Averell Harriman

PROTOCOL TO THE DECLARATION ON THE NEUTRALITY OF LAOS

The Governments of the Union of Burma, the Kingdom of Cambodia, Canada, the People's Republic of China, the Democratic Republic of Viet-Nam, the Republic of France, the Republic of India, the Kingdom of Laos, the Polish People's Republic, the Republic of Viet-Nam, the Kingdom of Thailand, the Union of Soviet Socialist Republics, the United Kingdom of Great Britain and Northern Ireland and the United States of America;

Having regard to the Declaration on the Neutrality of Laos of July 23, 1962;

Have agreed as follows:

ARTICLE 1

For the purposes of this Protocol

(a) the term "foreign military personnel" shall include members of foreign military missions, foreign military advisers, experts, instructors, consultants, technicians, observers and any other foreign military persons, including those serving in any armed forces in Laos, and foreign civilians connected with the supply, maintenance, storing and utilization of war materials;

(b) the term "the Commission" shall mean the International Commission for Supervision and Control in Laos set up by virtue of the Geneva Agreements of 1954 and composed of the representatives of Canada, India and Poland, with the representative of India as Chairman;

(c) the term "the Co-Chairmen" shall mean the Co-Chairmen of the International Conference for the Settlement of the Laotian Question, 1961-1962, and their successors in the offices of Her Britannic Majesty's Principal Secretary of State for Foreign Affairs and Minister for Foreign Affairs of the Union of Soviet Socialist Republics respectively;

(d) the term "the members of the Conference" shall mean the Governments of countries which took part in the International Conference for the Settlement of the Laotian Question, 1961-1962.

716

ARTICLE 2

All foreign regular and irregular troops, foreign para-military formations and foreign military personnel shall be withdrawn from Laos in the shortest time possible and in any case the withdrawal shall be completed not later than thirty days after the Commission has notified the Royal Government of Laos that in accordance with Articles 3 and 10 of this Protocol its inspection teams are present at all points of withdrawal from Laos. These points shall be determined by the Royal Government of Laos in accordance with Article 3 within thirty days after the entry into force of this Protocol. The inspection teams shall be present at these points and the Commission shall notify the Royal Government of Laos thereof within fifteen days after the points have been determined.

ARTICLE 3

The withdrawal of foreign regular and irregular troops, foreign para-military formations and foreign military personnel shall take place only along such routes and through such points as shall be determined by the Royal Government of Laos in consultation with the Commission. The Commission shall be notified in advance of the point and time of all such withdrawals.

ARTICLE 4

The introduction of foreign regular and irregular troops, foreign para-military formations and foreign military personnel into Laos is prohibited.

ARTICLE 5

Note is taken that the French and Laotian Governments will conclude as soon as possible an arrangement to transfer the French military installations in Laos to the Royal Government of Laos.

If the Laotian Government considers it necessary, the French Government may as an exception leave in Laos for a limited period of time a precisely limited number of French military instructors for the purpose of training the armed forces of Laos.

The French and Laotian Governments shall inform the members of the Conference, through the Co-Chairmen, of their agreement on the question of the transfer of the French military installations in Laos and of the employment of French military instructors by the Laotian Government.

ARTICLE 6

The introduction into Laos of armaments, munitions and war material generally, except such quantities of conventional armaments as the Royal Government of Laos may consider necessary for the national defence of Laos, is prohibited.

ARTICLE 7

All foreign military persons and civilians captured or interned during the course of hostilities in Laos shall be released within thirty days after the entry into force of this Protocol and handed over by the Royal Government of Laos to the representatives of the Governments of the countries of which they are nationals in order that they may proceed to the destination of their choice.

ARTICLE 8

The Co-Chairmen shall periodically receive reports from the Commission. In addition the Commission shall immediately report to the Co-Chairmen any violations or threats of violations of this Protocol, all significant steps which it takes in pursuance of this Protocol, and also any other important information which may assist the Co-Chairmen in carrying out their functions. The Commission may at any time seek help from the Co-Chairmen in the performance of its duties, and the Co-Chairmen may at any time make recommendations to the Commission exercising general guidance.

The Co-Chairmen shall circulate the reports and any other important information from the Commission to the members of the Conference.

The Co-Chairmen shall exercise supervision over the observance of this Protocol and the Declaration on the Neutrality of Laos.

The Co-Chairmen will keep the members of the Conference constantly informed and when appropriate will consult with them.

ARTICLE 9

The Commission shall, with the concurrence of the Royal Government of Laos, supervise and control the cease-fire in Laos.

The Commission shall exercise these functions in full co-operation with the Royal Government of Laos and within the framework of the Cease-Fire Agreement or cease-fire arrangements made by the three political forces in Laos, or the Royal Government of Laos. It is understood that responsibility for the execution of the cease-fire shall rest with the three parties concerned and with the Royal Government of Laos after its formation.

ARTICLE 10

The Commission shall supervise and control the withdrawal of foreign regular and irregular troops, foreign para-military formations and foreign military personnel. Inspection teams sent by the Commission for these purposes shall be present for the period of the withdrawal at all points of withdrawal from Laos determined by the Royal Government of Laos in consultation with the Commission in accordance with Article 3 of this Protocol.

ARTICLE 11

The Commission shall investigate cases where there are reasonable grounds for considering that a violation of the provisions of Article 4 of this Protocol has occurred.

It is understood that in the exercise of this function the Commission is acting with the concurrence of the Royal Government of Laos. It shall carry out its investigations in full co-operation with the Royal Government of Laos and shall immediately inform the Co-Chairmen of any violations or threats of violations of Article 4, and also of all significant steps which it takes in pursuance of this Article in accordance with Article 8.

ARTICLE 12

The Commission shall assist the Royal Government of Laos in cases where the Royal Government of Laos considers that a violation of Article 6 of this Protocol may have taken place. This assistance will be rendered at the request of the Royal Government of Laos and in full co-operation with it.

ARTICLE 13

The Commission shall exercise its functions under this Protocol in close co-operation with the Royal Government of Laos. It is understood that the Royal Government of Laos at all levels will render the Commission all possible assistance in the performance by the Commission of these functions and also will take all necessary measures to ensure the security of the Commission and its inspection teams during their activities in Laos.

ARTICLE 14

The Commission functions as a single organ of the International Conference for the Settlement of the Laotian Question, 1961-1962. The members of the Commission will work harmoniously and in co-operation with each other with the aim of solving all questions within the terms of reference of the Commission.

Decisions of the Commission on questions relating to violations of Articles 2, 3, 4 and 6 of this Protocol or of the cease-fire referred to in Article 9, conclusions on major questions sent to the Co-Chairmen and all recommendations by the Commission shall be adopted unanimously. On other questions, including procedural questions, and also questions relating to the initiation and carrying out of investigations (Article 15), decisions of the Commission shall be adopted by majority vote.

ARTICLE 15

In the exercise of its specific functions which are laid down in the relevant articles of this Protocol the Commission shall conduct investigations (directly or by sending inspection teams), when there are reasonable grounds for considering that a violation has occurred. These investigations shall be carried out at the request of the Royal Government of Laos or on the initiative of the Commission, which is acting with the concurrence of the Royal Government of Laos.

In the latter case decisions on initiating and carrying out such investigations shall be taken in the Commission by majority vote.

The Commission shall submit agreed reports on investigations in which differences which may emerge between members of the Commission on particular questions may be expressed.

720

The conclusions and recommendations of the Commission resulting from investigations shall be adopted unanimously.

ARTICLE 16

For the exercise of its functions the Commission shall, as necessary, set up inspection teams, on which the three member-States of the Commission shall be equally represented. Each member-State of the Commission shall ensure the presence of its own representatives both on the Commission and on the inspection teams, and shall promptly replace them in the event of their being unable to perform their duties.

It is understood that the dispatch of inspection teams to carry out various specific tasks takes place with the concurrence of the Royal Government of Laos. The points to which the Commission and its inspection teams go for the purposes of investigation and their length of stay at those points shall be determined in relation to the requirements of the particular investigation.

ARTICLE 17

The Commission shall have at its disposal the means of communication and transport required for the performance of its duties. These as a rule will be provided to the Commission by the Royal Government of Laos for payment on mutually acceptable terms, and those which the Royal Government of Laos cannot provide will be acquired by the Commission from other sources. It is understood that the means of communication and transport will be under the administrative control of the Commission.

ARTICLE 18

The costs of the operations of the Commission shall be borne by the members of the Conference in accordance with the provisions of this Article.

(a) The Governments of Canada, India and Poland shall pay the personal salaries and allowances of their nationals who are members of their delegations to the Commission and its subsidiary organs.

(b) The primary responsibility for the provision of accommodation for the Commission and its subsidiary organs shall rest with the Royal Government of Laos, which shall also provide such other local services as may be appropriate. The Commission shall charge to the Fund referred to in sub-paragraph (c) below any local expenses not borne by the Royal Government of Laos.

(c) All other capital or running expenses incurred by the Commission in the exercise of its functions shall be met from a Fund to which all the members of the Conference shall contribute in the following proportions:

The Governments of the People's Republic of China, France, the Union of Soviet Socialist Republics, the United Kingdom and the United States of America shall contribute 17.6 per cent each.

The Governments of Burma, Cambodia, the Democratic Republic of Viet Nam, Laos, the Republic of Viet Nam and Thailand shall contribute 1.5 per cent each.

The Governments of Canada, India and Poland as members of the Commission shall contribute 1 per cent each.

ARTICLE 19

The Co-Chairmen shall at any time, if the Royal Government of Laos so requests, and in any case not later than three years after the entry into force of this Protocol, present a report with appropriate recommendations on the question of the termination of the Commission to the members of the Conference for their consideration. Before making such a report the Co-Chairmen shall hold consultations with the Royal Government of Laos and the Commission.

ARTICLE 20

This Protocol shall enter into force on signature.

It shall be deposited in the archives of the Governments of the United Kingdom and the Union of Soviet Socialist Republics, which shall furnish certified copies thereof to the other signatory States and to all other States of the world.

In witness whereof, the undersigned Plenipotentiaries have signed this Protocol.

Done in two copies in Geneva this twenty-third day of July one thousand and nine hundred and sixty-two in the English, Chinese, French, Laotian and Russian languages, each text being equally authoritative.

For the Union of Burma:
    U Thi Han

For the Kingdom of Cambodia:
    Nhiek Tioulong

For Canada:
    H. C. Green
    Chester Ronning

For the People's Republic
of China:
    Chen Yi

For the Democratic Republic
of Viet-Nam:
    Ung-Van-Khiem

For the Republic of France:
    M. Couve De Murville
    Jacques Roux

For the Republic of India:
    V. K. Krishna Menon

For the Kingdom of Laos:
    Q. Pholsena

For the Polish People's
Republic:
    A. Rapacki

For the Republic of Viet-Nam:
    Vu Van Mau
    Thanh

For the Kingdom of Thailand:
    Direck Jayanâma

For the Union of Soviet
Socialist Republics:
    A. Gromyko

For the United Kingdom of
Great Britain and Northern
Ireland:
    Home
    Malcolm Macdonald

For the United States
of America:
    Dean Rusk
    W. Averell Harriman

Appendix F

The Southeast Asia Collective Defense Treaty and Protocol*

* [1955] 6 U.S.T. 81, T.I.A.S. 3170.

Southeast Asia Collective Defense Treaty and protocol signed at Manila September 8, 1954;

Ratification advised by the Senate of the United States of America February 1, 1955;
Ratified by the President of the United States of America February 4, 1955;
Ratification of the United States of America deposited with the Government of the Republic of the Philippines February 19, 1955;
Proclaimed by the President of the United States of America March 2, 1955;
Entered into force February 19, 1955.

BY THE PRESIDENT OF THE UNITED STATES OF AMERICA

A PROCLAMATION

WHEREAS the Southeast Asia Collective Defense Treaty and a Protocol relating thereto were signed at Manila on September 8, 1954 by the respective Plenipotentiaries of the United States of America, Australia, France, New Zealand, Pakistan, the Republic of the Philippines, the Kingdom of Thailand, and the United Kingdom of Great Britain and Northern Ireland;

WHEREAS the texts of the said Treaty and the said Protocol, in the English language, are word for word as follows:

Southeast Asia Collective Defense Treaty

The Parties to this Treaty,

Recognizing the sovereign equality of all the Parties,

Reiterating their faith in the purposes and principles set forth in the Charter of the United Nations and their desire to live in peace with all peoples and all governments,

Reaffirming that, in accordance with the Charter of the United Nations, they uphold the principle of equal rights and self-determination of peoples, and declaring that they will earnestly strive by every peaceful means to promote self-government and to secure the independence of all countries whose peoples desire it and are able to undertake its responsibilities,

Desiring to strengthen the fabric of peace and freedom and to uphold the principles of democracy, individual liberty and the rule of law, and to promote the economic well-being and development of all peoples in the treaty area,

Intending to declare publicly and formally their sense of unity, so that any potential aggressor will appreciate that the Parties stand together in the area, and

Desiring further to coordinate their efforts for collective defense for the preservation of peace and security,

Therefore agree as follows:

ARTICLE I

The Parties undertake, as set forth in the Charter of the United Nations, to settle any international disputes in which they may be involved by peaceful means in such a manner that international peace and security and justice are not endangered, and to refrain in their international relations from the threat or use of force in any manner inconsistent with the purposes of the United Nations.

ARTICLE II

In order more effectively to achieve the objectives of this Treaty, the Parties, separately and jointly, by means of continuous and effective self-help and mutual aid will maintain and develop their individual and collective capacity to resist armed attack and to prevent and counter subversive activities directed from without against their territorial integrity and political stability.

ARTICLE III

The Parties undertake to strengthen their free institutions and to cooperate with one another in the further development of economic measures, including technical assistance, designed both to promote economic progress and social well-being and to further the individual and collective efforts of governments toward these ends.

Article IV

1. Each Party recognizes that aggression by means of armed attack in the treaty area against any of the Parties or against any State or territory which the Parties by unanimous agreement may hereafter designate, would endanger its own peace and safety, and agrees that it will in that event act to meet the common danger in accordance with its constitutional processes. Measures taken under this paragraph shall be immediately reported to the Security Council of the United Nations.

2. If, in the opinion of any of the Parties, the inviolability or the integrity of the territory or the sovereignty or political independence of any Party in the treaty area or of any other State or territory to which the provisions of paragraph 1 of this Article from time to time apply is threatened in any way other than by armed attack or is affected or threatened by any fact or situation which might endanger the peace of the area, the Parties shall consult immediately in order to agree on the measures which should be taken for the common defense.

3. It is understood that no action on the territory of any State designated by unanimous agreement under paragraph 1 of this Article or on any territory so designated shall be taken except at the invitation or with the consent of the government concerned.

Article V

The Parties hereby establish a Council, on which each of them shall be represented, to consider matters concerning the implementation of this Treaty. The Council shall provide for consultation with regard to military and any other planning as the situation obtaining in the treaty area may from time to time require. The Council shall be so organized as to be able to meet at any time.

Article VI

This Treaty does not affect and shall not be interpreted as affecting in any way the rights and obligations of any of the Parties under the Charter of the United Nations or the responsibility of the United Nations for the maintenance of international peace and security. Each Party declares that none of the international engagements now in force between it and any other of the Parties or any third party is in conflict with the provisions of this Treaty, and undertakes not to enter into any international engagement in conflict with this Treaty.

ARTICLE VII

Any other State in a position to further the objectives of this Treaty and to contribute to the security of the area may, by unanimous agreement of the Parties, be invited to accede to this Treaty. Any State so invited may become a Party to the Treaty by depositing its instrument of accession with the Government of the Republic of the Philippines. The Government of the Republic of the Philippines shall inform each of the Parties of the deposit of each such instrument of accession.

ARTICLE VIII

As used in this Treaty, the "treaty area" is the general area of Southeast Asia, including also the entire territories of the Asian Parties, and the general area of the Southwest Pacific not including the Pacific area north of 21 degrees 30 minutes north latitude. The Parties may, by unanimous agreement, amend this Article to include within the treaty area the territory of any State acceding to this Treaty in accordance with Article VII or otherwise to change the treaty area.

ARTICLE IX

1. This Treaty shall be deposited in the archives of the Government of the Republic of the Philippines. Duly certified copies thereof shall be transmitted by that government to the other signatories.

2. The Treaty shall be ratified and its provisions carried out by the Parties in accordance with their respective constitutional processes. The instruments of ratification shall be deposited as soon as possible with the Government of the Republic of the Philippines, which shall notify all of the other signatories of such deposit.

3. The Treaty shall enter into force between the States which

have ratified it as soon as the instruments of ratification of a majority of the signatories shall have been deposited, and shall come into effect with respect to each other State on the date of the deposit of its instrument of ratification.

ARTICLE X

This Treaty shall remain in force indefinitely, but any Party may cease to be a Party one year after its notice of denunciation has been given to the Government of the Republic of the Philippines, which shall inform the Governments of the other Parties of the deposit of each notice of denunciation.

ARTICLE XI

The English text of this Treaty is binding on the Parties, but when the Parties have agreed to the French text thereof and have so notified the Government of the Republic of the Philippines, the French text shall be equally authentic and binding on the Parties.

UNDERSTANDING OF THE UNITED STATES OF AMERICA

The United States of America in executing the present Treaty does so with the understanding that its recognition of the effect of aggression and armed attack and its agreement with reference thereto in Article IV, paragraph 1, apply only to communist aggression but affirms that in the event of other aggression or armed attack it will consult under the provisions of Article IV, paragraph 2.

In witness whereof, the undersigned Plenipotentiaries have signed this Treaty.

Done at Manila, this eighth day of September, 1954.

FOR AUSTRALIA: FOR NEW ZEALAND:
R. G. CASEY.   CLIFTON WEBB

FOR FRANCE:
G. LA CHAMBRE

FOR PAKISTAN: Signed for transmission to my Government for its consideration and action in accordance with the Constitution of Pakistan.

ZAFRULLA KHAN

FOR THE REPUBLIC OF THE
  PHILIPPINES:
    CARLOS P GARCIA
    FRANCISCO A. DELGADO.
    TOMÁS L. CABILI
    LORENZO M. TAÑADA
    CORNELIO T. VILLAREAL

FOR THE KINGDOM
  OF THAILAND:
    WAN WAITHAYAKON

KROMMUN NARADHIP
  BONGSPRABANDH
FOR THE UNITED KINGDOM
  OF GREAT BRITAIN AND
  NORTHERN IRELAND:
  READING
FOR THE UNITED STATES
  OF AMERICA:
  JOHN FOSTER DULLES
  H. ALEXANDER SMITH
  MICHAEL J. MANSFIELD

I CERTIFY THAT the foregoing is a true copy of the Southeast Asia Collective Defense Treaty concluded and signed in the English language at Manila, on September 8, 1954, the signed original of which is deposited in the archives of the Government of the Republic of the Philippines.

IN TESTIMONY WHEREOF, I, RAUL S. MANGLAPUS, Undersecretary of Foreign Affairs of the Republic of the Philippines, have hereunto set my hand and caused the seal of the Department of Foreign Affairs to be affixed at the City of Manila, this 14th day of October, 1954.

RAUL S. MANGLAPUS

Raul S. Manglapus
Undersecretary of Foreign Affairs

[SEAL]

Protocol to the Southeast Asia Collective Defense Treaty

Designation of States and Territory as to which provisions of Article IV and Article III are to be applicable

---

The Parties to the Southeast Asia Collective Defense Treaty unanimously designate for the purposes of Article IV of the Treaty the States of Cambodia and Laos and the free territory under the jurisdiction of the State of Vietnam.

The Parties further agree that the above mentioned states and territory shall be eligible in respect of the economic measures contemplated by Article III.

This Protocol shall enter into force simultaneously with the coming into force of the Treaty.

IN WITNESS WHEREOF, the undersigned Plenipotentiaries have signed this Protocol to the Southeast Asia Collective Defense Treaty.

Done at Manila, this eighth day of September, 1954.

FOR AUSTRALIA: R. G. CASEY.

FOR FRANCE: G. LA CHAMBRE

FOR NEW ZEALAND: CLIFTON WEBB

FOR PAKISTAN: Signed for transmission to my Government for its consideration and action in accordance with the Constitution of Pakistan.

ZAFRULLA KHAN

FOR THE REPUBLIC OF THE PHILIPPINES:

FRANCISCO A DELGADO.
CARLOS P GARCIA
TOMÁS L. CABILI
LORENZO M. TAÑADA
CORNELIO T. VILLAREAL

FOR THE KINGDOM OF THAILAND:

WAN WAITHAYAKON
KROMMUN NARADHIP BONGSPRABANDH

FOR THE UNITED KINGDOM OF GREAT BRITAIN AND NORTHERN IRELAND: READING

FOR THE UNITED STATES OF AMERICA:

JOHN FOSTER DULLES
H ALEXANDER SMITH
MICHAEL J. MANSFIELD

I CERTIFY THAT the foregoing is a true copy of the Protocol to the Southeast Asia Collective Defense Treaty concluded and signed in the English language at Manila, on September 8, 1954, the signed original of which is deposited in the archives of the Government of the Republic of the Philippines.

IN TESTIMONY WHEREOF, I, RAUL S. MANGLAPUS, Undersecretary of Foreign Affairs of the Republic of the Philippines, have hereunto set my hand and caused the seal of the Department of Foreign Affairs to be affixed at the City of Manila, this 14th day of October, 1954.

RAUL S. MANGLAPUS

Raul S. Manglapus
Undersecretary of Foreign Affairs

[SEAL]

WHEREAS the Senate of the United States of America by their resolution of February 1, 1955, two-thirds of the Senators present concurring therein, did advise and consent to the ratification of the said Treaty and the said Protocol;

WHEREAS the said Treaty and the said Protocol were duly ratified by the President of the United States of America on February 4, 1955, in pursuance of the aforesaid advice and consent of the Senate;

WHEREAS it is provided in Article IX of the said Treaty that the Treaty shall enter into force between the States which have ratified it as soon as the instruments of ratification of a majority of the signatories shall have been deposited, and it is provided in the said Protocol that the Protocol shall enter into force simultaneously with the coming into force of the Treaty;

WHEREAS instruments of ratification of the said Treaty and the said Protocol were deposited with the Government of the Republic of the Philippines on December 2, 1954 by the Kingdom of Thailand, and on February 19, 1955 by the United States of America, Australia, France, New Zealand, Pakistan, the Republic of the Philippines, and the United Kingdom of Great Britain and Northern Ireland;

AND WHEREAS, pursuant to the aforesaid provision of Article IX of the said Treaty and the aforesaid provision of the said Protocol, the Treaty and the Protocol entered into force on February 19, 1955;

Now, THEREFORE, be it known that I, Dwight D. Eisenhower, President of the United States of America, do hereby proclaim and make public the Southeast Asia Collective Defense Treaty and the Protocol relating thereto to the end that the same and every article and clause thereof shall be observed and fulfilled with good faith, on and after February 19, 1955, by the United States of America and by the citizens of the United States of America and all other persons subject to the jurisdiction thereof.

IN TESTIMONY WHEREOF, I have caused the Seal of the United States of America to be hereunto affixed.

Done at the city of Washington this second day of March in the year of our Lord one thousand nine hundred fifty-five [SEAL] and of the Independence of the United States of America the one hundred seventy-ninth.

DWIGHT D EISENHOWER

By the President:

HERBERT HOOVER JR
Acting Secretary of State

APPENDIX G

THE SOUTHEAST ASIA RESOLUTION
(TONKIN GULF RESOLUTION)*

* 78 Stat. 384 (August 10, 1964), repealed by an amendment to the Military Sales Bill (HR 15628) January 12, 1971.

Joint Resolution

To promote the maintenance of international peace and security in southeast Asia.

Whereas naval units of the Communist regime in Vietnam, in violation of the principles of the Charter of the United Nations and of international law, have deliberately and repeatedly attacked United States naval vessels lawfully present in international waters, and have thereby created a serious threat to international peace; and

Whereas these attacks are part of a deliberate and systematic campaign of aggression that the Communist regime in North Vietnam has been waging against its neighbors and the nations joined with them in the collective defense of their freedom; and

Whereas the United States is assisting the peoples of southeast Asia to protect their freedom and has no territorial, military or political ambitions in that area, but desires only that these peoples should be left in peace to work out their own destinies in their own way: Now, therefore, be it

Resolved by the Senate and House of Representatives of the United States of America in Congress assembled, That the Congress approves and supports the determination of the President, as Commander in Chief, to take all necessary measures to repel any armed attack against the forces of the United States and to prevent further aggression.

Sec. 2. The United States regards as vital to its national interest and to world peace the maintenance of international peace and security in southeast Asia. Consonant with the Constitution of the United States and the Charter of the United Nations and in accordance with its obligations under the Southeast Asia Collective Defense Treaty, the United States is, therefore, prepared, as the President determines, to take all necessary steps, including the use of armed force, to assist any member or protocol state of the Southeast Asia Collective Defense Treaty requesting assistance in defense of its freedom.

Sec. 3. This resolution shall expire when the President shall determine that the peace and security of the area is reasonably assured by international conditions created by action of the United Nations or otherwise, except that it may be terminated earlier by concurrent resolution of the Congress.

Approved August 10, 1964.

A SELECTED BIBLIOGRAPHY
OF WRITINGS ON INDO-CHINA
AND THE LEGAL ORDER

This bibliography includes the principal works relevant to legal analysis of the Indo-China War which have been published through the fall of 1971 and a few important works published after that date. The writings are grouped by subject and include selected general writings as well as those focused specifically on the legal aspects of the war. Those which are of particular interest have been briefly annotated to indicate their relevance.

Subject Index to Bibiliography

Bibliography

I. THE ROLE OF LAW IN THE MANAGEMENT OF INTERNATIONAL CONFLICT

Dillard, *Some Aspects of Law and Diplomacy*, 91 HAGUE RECUEIL DES COURS 447 (1957). A classic!

R. FALK, LAW, MORALITY AND WAR IN THE CONTEMPORARY WORLD (1963).

R. FISHER, INTERNATIONAL CONFLICT (1969). See particularly pages 151-77.

H.L.A. HART, THE CONCEPT OF LAW (1963). See pages 208-31.

L. HENKIN, HOW NATIONS BEHAVE (1968). See particularly pages 3-28 and 45-64.

S. HOFFMANN AND K. DEUTSCH (EDS.), THE RELEVANCE OF INTERNATIONAL LAW (1968). The chapters by Stanley Hoffmann, Karl W. Deutsch, Hans Kelsen, John Fried, and Richard A. Falk are particularly relevant. Collectively they represent some of the most sophisticated analysis to date on the role of law in the management of international conflict.

S. HOFFMANN, THE STATE OF WAR (1965). Chapters four and five are some of Hoffmann's most important writings on international law and the international system. Chapter four, "International Systems and International Law," was originally published in K. KNORR & S. VERBA (EDS.), THE INTERNATIONAL SYSTEM (1961). Chapter five, "The Study of International Law and the Theory of International Relations," was originally published in 1963 PROC. AM. SOC'Y INT'L L. 26 (1963).

——, "Introduction" to L. SCHEINMAN AND D. WILKINSON, INTERNATIONAL LAW AND POLITICAL CRISIS xi-xix (1968).

E. ROSTOW, LAW, POWER AND THE PURSUIT OF PEACE (1968).

Q. WRIGHT, THE ROLE OF INTERNATIONAL LAW IN THE ELIMINATION OF WAR (1961).

Acheson, *The Arrogance of International Lawyers*, 2 THE INT'L LAWYER 591 (1968). For a reply to Dean Acheson see *Communications*, 3 THE INT'L LAWYER 435 (1969).

Falk, *Law, Lawyers, and the Conduct of American Foreign Relations*, 78 YALE L.J. 919 (1969). An excellent recent statement.

——, *New Approaches to the Study of International Law*, 61 AM. J. INT'L L. 477 (1967).

Fisher, "Bringing Law to Bear on Governments," in II R. FALK & S. MENDLOVITZ (EDS.), THE STRATEGY OF WORLD ORDER 18-44 (1966).

McDougal, Lasswell, & Reisman, *Theories About International Law: Prologue to a Configurative Jurisprudence*, 8 VA. J. INT'L L. 188 (1968).

——, *The World Constitutive Process of Authoritative Decision*, 19 J. LEGAL ED. 253, 403 (2 pts. 1967).

McDougal, *Law and Power*, 46 AM. J. INT'L L. 102 (1952). A classic!

Oliver, *Reflections on Two Recent Developments Affecting the Function of Law in the International Community*, 30 TEXAS L. REV. 815 (1952).

II. WORLD ORDER PERSPECTIVES

The United Nations Charter and the Use of Force in International Relations

D. BOWETT, SELF-DEFENCE IN INTERNATIONAL LAW (1958).

I. BROWNLIE, INTERNATIONAL LAW AND THE USE OF FORCE BY STATES (1963).

I. CLAUDE, SWORDS INTO PLOW-SHARES (1956).

H. KELSEN, THE LAW OF THE UNITED NATIONS (1964).

M. MC DOUGAL & F. FELICIANO, LAW AND MINIMUM WORLD PUBLIC ORDER (1961). One of the most comprehensive and important works on the Charter and the use of force in international relations.

M. Kaplan & N. Katzenbach, "Resort to Force: War and Neutrality," in THE POLITICAL FOUNDATIONS OF INTERNATIONAL LAW 198-228 (1961), *reprinted* IN II R. FALK & S. MENDLOVITZ, THE STRATEGY OF WORLD ORDER 276 (1966). An excellent brief history of the international law of conflict management.

R. RUSSELL & J. MUTHER, A HISTORY OF THE UNITED NATIONS CHARTER (1958).

J. STONE, AGGRESSION AND WORLD ORDER (1958).

Nussbaum, *Just War—A Legal Concept?*, 42 MICH. L. REV. 453 (1943).

Rusk, *The Control of Force in International Relations*, 1965 PROC. AM. SOC'Y INT'L LAW 25.

Von Elbe, *The Evolution of the Concept of the Just War in International Law*, 33 AM. J. INT'L L. 665 (1939).

The International Law of Non-intervention

R. FALK (ED.), THE INTERNATIONAL LAW OF CIVIL WAR (1970). Case studies on intervention sponsored by the American Society of International Law Panel on the Role of International Law in Civil Wars.

L. MILLER, WORLD ORDER AND LOCAL DISORDER: THE UNITED NATIONS AND INTERNAL CONFLICTS (1967).

J. ROSENAU (ED.), INTERNATIONAL ASPECTS OF CIVIL STRIFE (1964). One of the basic reference works. An outstanding collection of essays.

R. STANGER (ED.), ESSAYS ON INTERVENTION (1964). Another of the basic reference works. An outstanding collection of essays.

Burke, "The Legal Regulation of Minor International Coercion: A Framework of Inquiry," in R. STANGER (ED.), ESSAYS ON INTERVENTION 87 (1967).

Farer, *Harnessing Rogue Elephants: A Short Discourse on Foreign Intervention in Civil Strife*, 82 HARV. L. REV. 511 (1969). An elaboration of an earlier proposal presented in 67 COL. L. REV. 266 (1967).

——, *Intervention in Civil Wars: A Modest Proposal*, 67 COL. L. REV. 266 (1967). One of the most creative proposals for the control of intervention in recent years.

Fisher, "Intervention: Three Problems of Policy and Law," in R. STANGER (ED.), ESSAYS ON INTERVENTION (1964).

Franck & Rodley, *Legitimacy and Legal Rights of Revolutionary Movements with Special Reference to the Peoples' Revolutionary Government of South Viet Nam*, 45 N.Y.U.L. REV. 679 (1970).

Friedmann, *Intervention, Civil War and the Role of International Law*, 1965 PROC. AM. SOC'Y INT'L L. 67 (1965).

R. Higgins, "Internal War and International Law," in III C. BLACK & R. FALK, THE FUTURE OF THE INTERNATIONAL LEGAL ORDER: CONFLICT MANAGEMENT 81 (1970). A particularly useful contextual breakdown of the issues.

Moore, "Intervention: A Monochromatic Term for a Polychromatic Reality," in II R. FALK (ED.), THE VIETNAM WAR AND INTERNATIONAL LAW 1061 (1969). Reprinted as Chapter III of this volume; see above, p. 83.

——, *The Control of Foreign Intervention in Internal Conflict*, 9 VA. J. INT'L L. 205 (1969). Reprinted as Chapter IV of this volume; see above, p. 115.

Rosenau, *Intervention as a Scientific Concept*, 13 THE JOURNAL OF CONFLICT RESOLUTION 149 (1969).

Schacter, *Intervention and the United Nations*, 3 STANFORD J. INT'L STUDIES 5 (1968).

Young, *Interventions and International Systems*, 22 JOURNAL OF INT'L AFFAIRS 177 (1968).

The American Society of International Law Panel on the Role of International Law in Civil Wars is planning a volume of essays tentatively entitled "Law and Civil War in the Modern World" which will contribute to an interdisciplinary analysis of current problems and prospects in intervention theory. The volume will be edited by John Norton Moore and will be published in late 1972 or early 1973.

Intervention and American Foreign Policy

R. BARNET, INTERVENTION AND REVOLUTION: THE UNITED STATES IN THE THIRD WORLD (1968). Reviewed in Chapter V of this volume. See above, p. 287.

Ehrlich, *The Measuring Line of Occasion*, 3 STANFORD JOURNAL INT'L STUDIES 27 (1968).

Falk, *What We Should Learn from Vietnam*, 1 FOREIGN POLICY 95 (1970).

Firmage, *International Law and the Response of the United States to "Internal War,"* 1967 UTAH L. REV. 517.

Hoffmann, "Vietnam and American Foreign Policy," in II R. FALK (ED.), THE VIETNAM WAR AND INTERNATIONAL LAW 1134 (1969).

Morgenthau, *To Intervene or Not to Intervene*, 45 FOREIGN AFFAIRS 425 (1967).

Rogers, *United States Intervention: Doctrine and Practice*, 3 STANFORD JOURNAL INT'L STUDIES 99 (1968). With commentary by Professor Wolfgang Friedmann and David J. Morris.

Yarmolinsky, *United States Military Power and Foreign Policy* (Center for Policy Study, The University of Chicago, 1967).

The Role of Regional Arrangements in the Maintenance of World Order

Inis L. Claude, Jr., *The OAS, the UN, and the United States*, INT'L CONCILIATION, No. 547 (March 1964). Probably the best starting place on the interrelation of the United Nations and regional arrangements for the maintenance of international peace and security.

E. Frey-Wouters, "The Prospects for Regionalism in World Affairs," in I C. BLACK & R. FALK (EDS.), THE FUTURE OF THE INTERNATIONAL LEGAL ORDER 463 (1969).

Halderman, *Regional Enforcement Measures and the United Nations*, 52 GEO. L.J. 1 (1963).

L. B. Miller, *Regional Organization and the Regulation of Internal Conflict*, 19 WORLD POLITICS 582 (1967).

L. H. Miller, "The Prospects for Order Through Regional Security," in I C. BLACK & R. FALK (EDS.), THE FUTURE OF THE INTERNATIONAL LEGAL ORDER 556 (1969).

Moore, "The Role of Regional Arrangements in the Maintenance of World Order," in III C. BLACK & R. FALK (EDS.), THE FUTURE OF THE INTERNATIONAL LEGAL ORDER: CONFLICT MANAGEMENT 122 (1970). Reprinted as Chapter VI of this volume; see above, p. 296.

Slater, *The Limits of Legitimization in International Organizations: The Organization of American States and the Dominican Crisis*, 23 INT'L ORGANIZATION 1 (1969).

III. BACKGROUND AND PERSPECTIVE ON THE INDO-CHINA WAR

There are many scholarly works about the Indo-China involvement, but the reader should be careful to assess the world order perspectives of any work's author before relying on his conclusions. A principal danger in seeking to record historical truth about the Indo-China war is not so much reliance on inaccurate facts as it is unconscious selection and emphasis of facts which support the model of the conflict most favorable to the world view of the writer. Some of the most important of the general works on Vietnam and the Indo-China war are:

V. BATOR, VIET-NAM: A DIPLOMATIC TRAGEDY (1965).

J. BUTTINGER, VIETNAM: A DRAGON EMBATTLED, VOLUME I: FROM COLONIALISM TO THE VIETMINH. VOLUME II: VIETNAM AT WAR (1967). One of the standard reference works.

B. CROZIER, SOUTHEAST ASIA IN TURMOIL (1965).

B. FALL, STREET WITHOUT JOY: FROM THE INDOCHINA WAR TO THE WAR IN VIETNAM (4th rev. ed. 1964). All of Bernard Fall's writings on Vietnam are standard reference works.

——, THE TWO VIET-NAMS: A POLITICAL AND MILITARY HISTORY (5th rev. ed. 1965).

——, VIET-NAM WITNESS (1966).

——, LAST REFLECTIONS ON A WAR (1967).

—— & M. RASKIN (EDS.), THE VIETNAM READER (1965). The best of the general readers on the Vietnam war.

J. FULBRIGHT, THE ARROGANCE OF POWER (1967). A critique of American foreign policy by the Chairman of the Senate Foreign Relations Committee.

M. GETTLEMAN (ED.), VIETNAM (1965). A general reader on the Vietnam war.

D. HALBERSTRAM, THE MAKING OF A QUAGMIRE (1965).

E. HAMMER, VIETNAM: YESTERDAY AND TODAY (1966).

P. HONEY, COMMUNISM IN NORTH VIETNAM (1963).

G. KAHIN & J. LEWIS, THE UNITED STATES IN VIETNAM (1967).

J. LACOUTURE, VIETNAM: BETWEEN TWO TRUCES (1966). Another of the standard reference works.

B.S.N. MURTI, VIETNAM DIVIDED (1964).

D. PIKE, VIET CONG (1966). Although controversial, the most comprehensive study of the Vietcong to date.

R. RANDLE, GENEVA 1954: THE SETTLEMENT OF THE INDOCHINESE WAR (1969). This study by Robert Randle of the events surrounding the settlement of the first Indo-China war is the most comprehensive and balanced study of the Geneva Accords of 1954. An understanding of the ambiguities and complexities of the Geneva settlement is important for appraisal of subsequent claims concerning the "Accords."

A. SCHLESINGER, JR., THE BITTER HERITAGE—VIETNAM AND AMERICAN DEMOCRACY 1941-1966 (1967).

R. SHAPLEN, THE LOST REVOLUTION (1965).

R. THOMPSON, DEFEATING COMMUNIST INSURGENCY: THE LESSONS OF MALAYA AND VIETNAM (1966).

N.Y. TIMES, THE PENTAGON PAPERS (1971). I-IV THE PENTAGON PAPERS: THE DEFENSE DEPARTMENT HISTORY OF UNITED STATES DECISIONMAKING ON VIETNAM (Gravel ed. 1971). This is the most complete version of the Pentagon Papers published to date.

D. WARNER, THE LAST CONFUCIAN—VIETNAM, SOUTHEAST ASIA, AND THE WEST (1964).

Bundy, *The Path to Viet-Nam: A Lesson in Involvement*, 57 DEP'T STATE BULLETIN 275 (Sept. 4, 1967). This piece, prepared for delivery by the Assistant-Secretary of State for East Asian and Pacific Affairs, is one of the best short historical introductions to the United States involvement.

Lacouture, *From the Vietnam War to an Indo-China War*, 48 FOREIGN AFFAIRS 617 (1970).

Mansfield, Muskie, Inouyo, Aiken, & Boggs, *The Vietnam Conflict: The Substance and the Shadow—Report to the Senate Committee on Foreign Relations*, 112 CONG. REC. 140 (daily ed. Jan. 13, 1966).

Staff of Senate Comm. on Foreign Relations, 91ST CONG., 2D SESS., *Background Information Relating to Southeast Asia and Vietnam* (6th rev. ed. Comm. Print 1970). The Senate Foreign Relations Committee background information compilations are one of the best sources for background documentation on major world order issues.

Staff Report Prepared for the Use of The Senate Committee on Foreign Relations, 91st CONG., 2D SESS., *Cambodia: May 1970* (Comm. Print June 7, 1970).

Reports of the International Commission for Supervision and Control in Vietnam and the International Commission for Supervision and Control in Cambodia (Reprinted in the British Parliamentary Sessional Papers).

IV. INTERNATIONAL LAW AND THE INDO-CHINA WAR

General

Andonian, *Law and Vietnam*, 54 A.B.A.J. 457 (1968). A superficial statement arguing that there is no international law in the Vietnam dispute.

Arnold, *The Growth of Awareness: One Nation's Law and the Law Among Nations*, 1 THE INT'L LAWYER 534 (1967). A salty presentation of the view that the United States has international responsibilities and maintaining a free South Vietnam is one of them. Written in the inimitable style of Thurmond Arnold.

Buchan, *Questions About Vietnam*, 30 ENCOUNTER 3 (1968).

Dai, *Canada's Role in the International Commission for Supervision and Control in Vietnam*, 4 CANADIAN YEARBOOK INT'L L. 161 (1966).

Dillard, *Law and Conflict: Some Current Dilemmas*, 24 WASH. & LEE L. REV. 177 (1967).

I-III R. FALK (ED.), THE VIETNAM WAR AND INTERNATIONAL LAW (Vol. I, 1968; Vol. II, 1969; Vol. III, 1972). This three-volume collection of writings on the Indo-China war and the legal order presents a balanced and well chosen selection of articles and documents on the international and constitutional legal issues. The volumes are sponsored by the American Society of International Law Panel on the Role of International Law in Civil Wars and edited by Professor Richard A. Falk. They are an indispensable source for serious scholarship on the legal issues.

Firmage, *Review: The Vietnam War and International Law*, 1970 UTAH L. REV. 171.

Prosterman, *Land Reform in South Vietnam: A Proposal for Turning the Tables on the Viet-cong*, 53 CORNELL L. REV. 26 (1967).

Robertson, *The Debate Among American International Lawyers About the Vietnam War*, 46 TEXAS L. REV. 898 (1968).

Westerman & McHugh, *Reaching for the Rule of Law in South Vietnam*, 53 A.B.A.J. 159 (1967). An analysis of changes needed in the South Vietnamese legal system.

Wright, *Misperception of Aggression in Vietnam*, 21 J. INT'L AFFAIRS 123 (1967).

Comment, *The Legality of the United States' Involvement in Vietnam —A Pragmatic Approach*, 23 U. MIAMI L. REV. 792 (1969).

The Vietnam War

R. HULL & J. NOVOGRAD, LAW AND VIETNAM (1968). One of the best statements in support of the United States legal position. Written by two students at the Yale Law School.

Alford, *The Legality of American Military Involvement in Viet Nam: A Broader Perspective*, 75 YALE L.J. 1109 (1966).

Chaumont, *A Critical Study of American Intervention in Vietnam*, REVUE BELGE DE DROIT INTERNATIONAL, No. 1, 1968, at 5.

Corbett, "The Vietnam Struggle and International Law," in R. FALK (ED.), THE INTERNATIONAL LAW OF CIVIL WAR 348 (1970). A study commissioned by the American Society of International Law Panel on the Role of International Law in Civil Wars. Professor Corbett's study contains a particularly useful description of the international-legal literature published abroad on the Vietnam War.

Deutsch, *Legality of the War in Vietnam*, 7 WASHBURN L.J. 153 (1968).

——, *Legality of the United States Position in Viet Nam*, 52 A.B.A.J. 436 (1966).

Falk, *International Law and the United States Role in the Viet Nam War*, 75 YALE L.J. 1122 (1966). Together with Professor Falk's article in 76 YALE L.J., this article is the most persuasive of those urging that United States participation in the Vietnam War is unlawful. That it failed to persuade is indicated by the reply to Professor Falk, reprinted as Chapter VIII in this volume. See above, p. 403.

——, *International Law and the United States Role in Viet Nam: A Response to Professor Moore*, 76 YALE L.J. 1095 (1967). Professor Falk's response to my earlier reply reprinted in this volume.

——, *Six Legal Dimensions of the United States Involvement in the Viet Nam War*, Research Monograph #34, Princeton University, Center of International Studies (1968).

Friedmann, *Law and Politics in the Vietnamese War: A Comment*, 61 AM. J. INT'L L., 776 (1967). Chapter IX in this volume (see above, p. 458) responds to this article by Professor Friedmann.

Hawkins, "An Approach to Issues of International Law Raised by United States Actions in Vietnam," in I R. FALK (ED.), THE VIETNAM WAR AND INTERNATIONAL LAW 163 (1968). One of the most objective discussions of the disputed factual and legal issues.

Johnson, *Aquinas, Grotius, and the Vietnam War*, QUIS CUSTODIET?, No. 16, 1967, at 60. A brief discussion of the legal issues which fails to clearly focus on the critical distinction between the "just war" theory and the more modern international law of the Charter that force should not be used in international relations as a technique of value extension.

Margolis, *Escalating the Viet Nam Debate: A Reply to Professor Moore*, 42 CONN. B.J. 23 (1968). A reply to my condensed version of earlier articles on the legal issues in the Vietnam War published in 41 CONN. B.J. 389 (1967).

Mayda, "The Vietnam Conflict and International Law," in II R. FALK (ED.), THE VIETNAM WAR AND INTERNATIONAL LAW 260 (1969).

Meeker, *Viet-Nam and the International Law of Self-Defense*, 46 DEP'T STATE BULLETIN 54 (1967). A statement by the Legal Adviser of the United States Department of State.

Moore, *The Lawfulness of Military Assistance to the Republic of Viet-Nam*, 61 AM. J. INT'L L. 1 (1967). Reprinted as Chapter VII herein; see above, p. 358.

——. *International Law and the United States Role in Viet Nam: A Reply*, 76 YALE L.J. 1051 (1967). Reprinted as Chapter VIII herein; above, p. 403.

——, *Law and Politics in the Vietnamese War: A Response to Professor Friedmann*, 61 AM. J. INT'L L. 1039 (1967). Reprinted as Chapter IX herein; above, p. 458.

——, *The Role of Law in the Vietnam Debate*, 41 CONN. B.J. 389 (1967). A condensed version of earlier articles and intended for a non-specialized audience.

—— & J. Underwood, *The Lawfulness of United States Assistance to the Republic of Vietnam*, 112 CONG. REC. 14943 (daily ed., July 14, 1966), reprinted in part in 5 DUQUESNE L. REV. 235 (1967). This is an early memorandum prepared with the assistance of Professor Myres S. McDougal and distributed to Congress by the American Bar Association. The memorandum is essentially a reply to the widely circulated *Lawyers Committee Memorandum.* Though dated, it is still an important source for the history of congressional involvement in the Indo-China conflict and for factual information relevant to the international-legal issues not readily available elsewhere.

Murphy, *Vietnam: A Study of Law and Politics*, 36 FORDHAM L. REV. 453 (1968).

Partan, *Legal Aspects of the Vietnam Conflict*, 46 BOSTON U. L. REV. 281 (1966).

Schick, *Some Reflections on the Legal Controversies Concerning America's Involvement in Vietnam*, 17 INT'L & COMPARATIVE L.Q. 953 (1968).

Standard, *United States Intervention in Vietnam Is Not Legal*, 52 A.B.A.J. 627 (1966). A polemical piece by the Chairman of the anti-war Lawyers Committee on American Policy Toward Vietnam.

Wright, *Legal Aspects of the Viet-Nam Situation*, 60 AM. J. INT'L L. 750 (1966). An important article critical of the United States legal position.

The Legality of United States Participation in the Defense of Viet' Nam, Memorandum of Law, Office of the State Department Legal Adviser, 54 DEP'T STATE BULLETIN 474 (1966), *reprinted* in 75 YALE L.J. 1085 (1966), and 60 AM. J. INT'L L. 565 (1966). The official statement of the United States legal position reprinted as a documentary appendix herein, p. 601.

Memorandum of Law of the Lawyers Committee on American Policy Toward Vietnam, 112 CONG. REC. 2552 (daily ed., Feb. 9, 1966). A highly polemical attack on the United States legal position by a group of lawyers opposed to the war. The memorandum is important principally because of the wide circulation which it received.

VIETNAM AND INTERNATIONAL LAW (Consultative Council of the Lawyers Committee on American Policy Toward Vietnam, 1967). A second and still polemical effort by the Lawyers Committee.

Note, *American Actions in Vietnam: Justifiable in International Law?*, 19 STAN. L. REV. 1307 (1967).

Comment, *The United States in Vietnam: A Case Study in the Law of Intervention*, 50 CALIF. L. REV. 515 (1962). Apparently the first published legal analysis of the war.

The Cambodian Incursion

Barnes, *United States Recognition Policy and Cambodia*, 50 BOSTON U.L. REV. 117 (1970).

Bender, *Self Defense and Cambodia: A Critical Appraisal*, 50 BOSTON U.L. REV. 130 (1970).

Edwards, *The Cambodian Invasion Violates International Law*, CONG. REC. E4551 (May 21, 1970). A short statement critical of the United States Cambodian action.

Falk, *The Cambodian Operation and International Law*, 65 AM. J. INT'L L. 1 (1971). An important statement critical of the United States legal position in the Cambodian incursion. Initially presented at the American Society of International Law forum on "The Cambodian Incursion and International Law: International and Domestic Issues," Washington, D.C., June 16, 1970.

Moore, *Legal Dimensions of the Decision to Intercede in Cambodia*, 65 AM. J. INT'L L. 38 (1971). Initially presented at the American Society of International Law forum on "The Cambodian Incursion and International Law: International and Domestic Issues," Washington, D.C., June 16, 1970. Reprinted as Chapter X in this volume; see above, p. 479.

Rubin, *SEATO and American Legal Obligations Concerning Laos and Cambodia*, 20 INT'L & COMP. L.Q. 500 (1971).

Stevenson, *United States Military Actions in Cambodia: Questions of International Law*, 62 DEP'T STATE BULLETIN 765 (1970). An important statement by the Legal Adviser of the Department of State reprinted as a documentary appendix herein, p. 641.

Brief of New York University Law Students, CONG. REC. E4443 (May 19, 1970). An argumentative brief against the United States legal position in the Cambodian incursion. See also *The War in Southeast Asia: A Legal Position Paper*, 45 N.Y.U.L. REV. 695 (1970).

Hammarskjöld Forum: *Expansion of the Viet Nam War Into Cambodia—The Legal Issues*, 45 N.Y.U.L. REV. 625 (1970). The Proceedings of the May 28, 1970 Hammarskjöld Forum, the first important debate on the legal issues in the Cambodian incursion. The Proceedings include articles by William H. Rehnquist, Robert B. McKay, John R. Stevenson, and Abram Chayes, statements by Wolfgang Friedmann, Richard Gardner, and Louis Henkin, and an Introduction by Andreas F. Lowenfeld. This Special Issue of the *New York University Law Review* also contains a particularly useful bibliography on the Indo-China War.

The United Nations and the Indo-China War

L. BLOOMFIELD, THE U.N. AND VIETNAM (Carnegie Endowment for International Peace, 1968).

Max Gordon, "Vietnam, the United States, and the United Nations," in II R. FALK (ED.), THE VIETNAM WAR AND INTERNATIONAL LAW 321 (1969).

Submission of the Vietnam Conflict to the United Nations, Hearings Before the Senate Committee on Foreign Relations, 90TH CONG., 1ST SESS. (1967).

BIBLIOGRAPHY

The Laws of War and the Applicability of the Geneva Conventions for the Protection of Civilians and Prisoners of War

AMERICAN ENTERPRISE INSTITUTE FOR PUBLIC POLICY RESEARCH, THE PRISONER OF WAR PROBLEM (1970).

R. FALK, G. KOLKO & R. LIFTON, CRIMES OF WAR (1971). A one-sided but rich collection of readings and documents on Nuremberg, war crimes and the Vietnam War.

T. TAYLOR, NUREMBERG AND VIETNAM: AN AMERICAN TRAGEDY (1970). A scholarly and generally informed analysis of United States responsibilities in the Indo-China War written by a professor of law at Columbia who was formerly Chief Counsel for the Prosecution at Nuremberg.

Falk, *Son My: War Crimes and Individual Responsibility*, 1971 U. TOLEDO L. REV.

——, *The American POW's: Pawns in Power Politics*, 35 PROGRESSIVE 13 (March, 1971).

Ferencz, *War Crimes Law and the Vietnam War*, 17 AM. U.L. REV. 403 (1968).

Havens, *Release and Repatriation of Vietnam Prisoners*, 57 A.B.A.J. 41 (1971). A scholarly and informed article by the counsel for The National League of Families, the principal organization of the families of prisoners of war held by North Vietnam.

Levie, *Maltreatment of Prisoners of War in Vietnam*, 48 BOSTON U.L. REV. 323 (1968). An excellent statement by an expert in the law of the Geneva Conventions.

Meyrowitz, "The Law of War in the Vietnamese Conflict," in II R. FALK (ED.), THE VIETNAM WAR AND INTERNATIONAL LAW 516 (1969). This article originally appeared in French as *Le droit de la guerre dans le conflit Vietnamien*, 13 ANNUAIRE FRANÇAIS DE DROIT INTERNATIONAL 143 (1967).

Petrowski, "Law and the Conduct of the Vietnam War," in II R. FALK (ED.), THE VIETNAM WAR AND INTERNATIONAL LAW 439 (1969).

Rubin, *Legal Aspects of the My Lai Incident*, 44 OREGON L. REV. 260 (1970).

Sheehan, *Book Review*, NEW YORK TIMES BOOK REVIEW (March 28, 1971). See also the list of books reviewed on the conduct of military operations in Vietnam.

Shull, *Counterinsurgency and the Geneva Convention*, 3 THE INT'L LAWYER 49 (1968).

Sponsler, *Universality Principle of Jurisdiction and the Threatened Trials of American Airmen*, 15 LOYOLA L. REV. 43 (1968-69).

755

Symposium, WAR CRIMES: TAYLOR, NUREMBERG AND VIETNAM, 80 YALE L.J. 1456 (1971). Contains articles by Noam Chomsky, Marshall Cohen and Richard A. Falk.

Entitlement of American Military Personnel Held by North Viet-Nam to Treatment as Prisoners of War Under the Geneva Convention of 1949 Relative to the Treatment of Prisoners of War, Office of the State Department Legal Adviser (July 13, 1966), *reprinted in* 10 M. WHITEMAN, DIGEST OF INT'L LAW 231 (1968). The official statement of the United States position reprinted as a documentary appendix herein, p. 633.

Comment, *My Lai Massacre: The Need For an International Investigation*, 58 CALIF. L. REV. 703 (1970).

Note, *International Law and Military Operations Against Insurgents In Neutral Territory*, 68 COLUM. L. REV. 1127 (1968).

Note, *The Geneva Convention and the Treatment of Prisoners of War in Vietnam*, 80 HARV. L. REV. 851 (1967).

Note, *The Geneva Convention of 1949: Application in the Vietnamese Conflict*, 5 VA. J. INT'L L. 243 (1965).

"American Prisoners of War in Southeast Asia," *Hearings Before the Subcommittee on National Security Policy and Scientific Developments of the Committee on Foreign Affairs of the House of Representatives*, 91ST CONG., 1ST SESS. (1969).

"American Prisoners of War in Southeast Asia, 1970," *Hearings Before the Subcommittee on National Security Policy and Scientific Developments of the Committee on Foreign Affairs of the House of Representatives*, 91ST CONG., 2D SESS. (Comm. Print 1970).

Settlement Issues

AMERICAN FRIENDS SERVICE COMMITTEE, PEACE IN VIETNAM (1966).

A. EDEN, TOWARD PEACE IN INDO-CHINA (1966).

R. WOITO (ED.), VIETNAM PEACE PROPOSALS (1967).

Bundy, "Address at De Paul University, October 12, 1968," in II R. FALK (ED.), THE VIETNAM WAR AND INTERNATIONAL LAW 964 (1969).

Falk, *A Vietnam Settlement: The View From Hanoi* (Princeton Center of International Studies 1968).

——, *A Political Solution for Vietnam?*, 16 DISSENT 196 (1969).

Hannon, *The International Control Commission Experience and the Role of an Improved International Supervisory Body in the Viet Nam Settlement*, 9 VA. J. INT'L L. 20 (1968).

——, *A Political Settlement for Vietnam: The 1954 Geneva Conference and Its Current Implications*, 8 VA. J. INT'L L. 1 (1967). With a

Preface by John Norton Moore. Since Hannon's study of the Geneva Accords, the more complete study by Robert Randle, *Geneva 1954: The Settlement of the Indochinese War* (1969), has been published, but Hannon's study remains one of the major studies of the Accords.

Holton, *Peace in Vietnam Through Due Process: An Unexplored Path*, 54 A.B.A.J. 45 (1968). This article somewhat unrealistically urges that the Vietnam war should be submitted to the International Court of Justice.

Hull, *Paris Accords*, 56 A.B.A.J. 34 (1970).

Huntington, *The Bases of Accommodation*, 46 FOREIGN AFFAIRS 642 (1968).

Kissinger, *The Viet Nam Negotiations*, 47 FOREIGN AFFAIRS 211 (1969). An important statement by the current Assistant to the President for National Security Affairs.

McAlister, "Revolution in Viet Nam: The Political Dimensions of War and Peace" (Based on testimony before the Senate Foreign Relations Committee), in II R. FALK (ED.), THE VIETNAM WAR AND INTERNATIONAL LAW 837 (1969).

Vietnam: Matters for the Agenda (An Occasional Paper of the Center for the Study of Democratic Institutions, June 1968).

V. The Indo-China War and the Constitution

The Role of Congress and the Executive in the Use of the Armed Forces Abroad

M. PUSEY, THE WAY WE GO TO WAR (1969).

Faulkner, *The War in Vietnam: Is it Constitutional?*, 56 GEORGIA L.J. 1132 (1968).

Henkin, *Constitutional Issues in Foreign Policy*, 23 J. INT'L AFFAIRS 210 (1969).

Katzenbach, *Congress and Foreign Policy*, 3 CORNELL INT'L L.J. 33 (1970).

Kurland, *The Impotence of Reticence*, 1968 DUKE L.J. 619.

Malawer, *The Vietnam War Under the Constitution: Legal Issues Involved in the United States Military Involvement in Vietnam*, 31 U. PITTSBURGH L. REV. 205 (1969).

McKay, *The Constitutional Issues—Opposition Position*, 45 N.Y.U.L. REV. 640 (1970). A statement by the dean of the New York University School of Law at the Hammarskjöld Forum on the Cambodian Incursion, May 28, 1970.

Moore, "Strengthening the Role of Congress in the Use of the Armed Forces Abroad." Testimony before the Senate Foreign Relations Committee, April 26, 1971.

——, "The Constitution and the Use of the Armed Forces Abroad." Testimony before the Subcommittee on National Security Policy and Scientific Developments of the House Committee on Foreign Affairs, June 25, 1970. Reprinted as Chapter XII in this volume. See above, p. 554.

——, *The National Executive and the Use of the Armed Forces Abroad*, 21 NAVAL WAR COLLEGE REV. 28 (1969). Reprinted as Chapter XI herein, above, p. 538.

Ratner, *The Coordinated Warmaking Power—Legislative, Executive, and Judicial Roles*, 44 S. CAL. L. REV. (1971).

Rehnquist, *The Constitutional Issues—Administration Position*, 45 N.Y.U.L. REV. 628 (1970). An able statement by the then Assistant Attorney General at the Hammarskjöld Forum on the Cambodian incursion, May 28, 1970. Subsequently, Mr. Rehnquist was appointed an Associate Justice of the United States Supreme Court.

Reveley, *Presidential War-Making: Constitutional Prerogative or Usurpation?*, 55 VA. L. REV. 1243 (1969). A particularly well-balanced and scholarly statement.

Rogers, *Congress, the President, and the War Powers*, 59 CALIF. L. REV. 1194 (1971). A statement by the Secretary of State delivered as testimony before the Senate Foreign Relations Committee.

Rogers, *The Constitutionality of the Cambodian Incursion*, 65 AM. J. INT'L L. 26 (1971). Initially presented at the American Society of International Law forum on "The Cambodian Incursion and International Law: International and Domestic Issues," Washington, D.C., June 16, 1970.

Rogers, "World Policing and the Constitution" in 11 AMERICA LOOKS AHEAD (World Peace Foundation, 1945).

Rostow et al., *Letter on the Constitutional Authority of the President in Using American Troops in the Cambodian Incursion*, 116 CONG. REC. S8404 (daily ed. June 4, 1970). A letter in support of the constitutionality of the Cambodian incursion co-authored by a former Under-Secretary of State for Political Affairs and Dean of the Yale Law School.

Spong, *Can Balance be Restored in the Constitutional War Powers of the President and Congress?*, 6 U. RICHMOND L. REV. 1 (1971). A statement by a member of the Senate Foreign Relations Committee concerning recent legislative proposals to define the relation between Congress and the President in the exercise of the war powers.

Velvel, *The War in Viet Nam: Unconstitutional, Justiciable and Jurisdictionally Attackable*, 16 KANSAS L. REV. 449 (1968). Essentially a brief against the war, in Professor Velvel's own words "[t]he article is dedicated to the proposition that the Vietnamese war is patently unconstitutional."

Wooters, *The Appropriations Power as a Tool of Congressional Foreign Policy Making*, 50 BOSTON U.L. REV. 34 (1970).

Wormuth, *The Vietnam War: The President v. The Constitution* (An Occasional Paper of the Center for the Study of Democratic Institutions, 1968). Although somewhat one-sided in favor of congressional power, this paper is well done and is a rich source of constitutional practice.

Symposium, *The Constitution and the Use of Military Forces Abroad*, 10 VA. J. INT'L L. 32 (1969). Proceedings of a regional meeting of the American Society of International Law held at the University of Virginia Feb. 28-Mar. 1, 1969. The Symposium includes articles by Murray J. Belman, William M. Kunstler, John Norton Moore, and Quincy Wright, commentary by W. Taylor Reveley, III, Lawrence R. Velvel, Earl V. Brown, and Warren F. Schwartz, and an introduction by Judge Hardy Cross Dillard.

Note, *Congress, The President, and the Power to Commit Forces to Combat*, 81 HARV. L. REV. 1771 (1968). An outstanding analysis of the issues. Written by a student at the Harvard Law School.

Memorandum, *Indochina: The Constitutional Crisis*, 116 CONG. REC. (No. 76, May 13, 1970), and *Indochina: The Constitutional Crisis—Part II*, 116 CONG. REC. (No. 82, May 21, 1970). A somewhat polemical statement on the constitutional issues surrounding the Cambodian incursion submitted to Congress by a number of Yale law students and faculty.

Study prepared for the use of the Senate Joint Committee of the Committee on Foreign Relations and the Committee on Armed Services, 82D CONG., 1ST SESS., *Powers of the President to Send the Armed Forces Outside the United States* 2 (Comm. Print 1951). An important but somewhat outdated reference source on the constitutional practice in the use of the armed forces abroad.

Hearings Before the Committee on Foreign Relations of the United States Senate on Senate Resolution 151, 90TH CONG., 1ST SESS., U.S. COMMITMENTS TO FOREIGN POWERS (Comm. Print 1967). An important source.

National Commitments Report, S. Rep. No. 797, 90TH CONG., 1ST SESS. (1967). An important source.

Background Information on the Use of United States Armed Forces In Foreign Countries, 91ST CONG. 2D SESS., The House Committee on Foreign Affairs (Comm. Print 1970). An important source.

"Congress, The President, and the War Powers," *Hearings Before the Subcommittee on National Security Policy and Scientific Developments of the Committee on Foreign Affairs of the House of Representatives*, 91ST CONG., 2D SESS. (Comm. Print 1970). An important source.

Documents Relating to the War Power of Congress, The President's Authority as Commander-in-Chief and the War in Indochina, Senate Committee on Foreign Relations, 91ST CONG., 2D SESS. (Comm. Print 1970).

The Justiciability of Challenges to the Use of the Armed Forces Abroad

Cohen, *International Illegality as a Basis for Refusal to Participate in Hostilities—A Tentative Proposal and a Preliminary Analysis of American Law*, 9 WM. & MARY L. REV. 682 (1968).

D'Amato, Gould & Woods, *War Crimes and Vietnam: The "Nuremberg Defense" and the Military Service Resister*, 57 CALIF. L. REV. 1055 (1969).

Henkin, *Viet-Nam in the Courts of the United States: "Political Questions,"* 63 AM. J. INT'L L. 284 (1969). A first-rate piece by one of the most knowledgeable scholars in the constitutional law of foreign relations.

Loeb, *The Courts and Vietnam*, 18 AM. U.L. REV. 376 (1969).

Moore, *The Justiciability of Challenges to the Use of Military Forces Abroad*, 10 VA. J. INT'L L. 85 (1969). Reprinted as Chapter XIII in this volume, above, p. 570.

Schwartz & McCormack, *The Justiciability of Legal Objections to the American Military Effort in Vietnam*, 46 TEXAS L. REV. 1033 (1968). A major statement in support of justiciability. See also Professor Schwartz's brief commentary on my criticism of his position in Symposium, *The Constitution and the Use of Military Force Abroad*, 10 VA. J. INT'L L. 32, 114 (1969).

Tigar, *Judicial Power, The "Political Question Doctrine," and Foreign Relations*, 17 U.C.L.A. L. REV. 1135 (1970). A major statement in support of the justiciability of the major war issues.

Velvel, *The War in Viet Nam: Unconstitutional, Justiciable and Jurisdictionally Attackable*, 16 KANSAS L. REV. 449 (1968).

Proceedings of the Panel on "The Nuremberg Trials and Objection to Military Service in Viet-Nam," 1969 PROC. AM. SOC'Y INT'L L. 140-81 (1969). A provocative and informed exchange of views.

Symposium, *The Constitution and the Use of Military Force Abroad*, 10 VA. J. INT'L L. 32 (1969).

The Indo-China War and First Amendment Freedoms

L. VELVEL, UNDECLARED WAR AND CIVIL DISOBEDIENCE: THE AMERICAN SYSTEM IN CRISIS (1970).

Finman & Macaulay, *Freedom to Dissent: The Vietnam Protests and the Words of Public Officials*, 1966 WISC. L. REV. 632.

Gottleib, *Vietnam and Civil Disobedience*, 1967 ANNUAL SURVEY AM. L. 699.

Lynd, *Civil Disobedience in Wartime*, 19 MAINE L. REV. 49 (1967).

O'Brien, *Selective Conscientious Objection and International Law*, 56 GEO. L.J. 1089 (1968).

Sax, *Conscience and Anarchy: The Prosecution of War Resisters*, LVII, 4 YALE REVIEW 481 (Summer 1968).

Index

Churchill, Winston, 300, 312, 316 n.26

Civilians, protection of, 286, 355, 356, 384, 488, 488 n.31, 495, 507-508, 591, 596; crimes against, 594

Civil strife, 55 n.8, 129, 159, 161, 174, 196, 198 n.148, 353, 403, 407, 426 n.55, 446, 447, 448, 494. *See* War, civil; Conflict, internal

Civil war. *See* War, civil

Clark-Sohn plan, 30

Claude, Inis, Jr., 302, 323, 339, 340

Coercion. *See* Force

Cohen, Felix, 265

Cold war, 86, 87, 111, 116, 118, 146, 195-96, 217, 221-25, 240, 241, 269, 290, 296, 303, 304, 306, 308, 311, 312, 313, 315, 330, 331, 341, 346, 349, 443, 444, 448, 511, 534. *See* Blocs, power; East/west conflict

Cold war divided nations, 92-93, 98, 101, 104, 134, 135, 154, 170, 175, 177, 192, 195, 221-25, 275, 405, 406, 407, 408, 437, 439, 440, 444, 456, 472, 474. *See* China; Germany; Korea; Vietnam; War, cold war divided nation conflicts

Cold war divided nation conflicts. *See* War, cold war divided nation conflicts

Collective action, 15, 35, n.48, 36-37, 55 n.8, 99, 100. *See* American States, Organization of; Defense, collective; International organizations; United Nations

Colombia, 151, 266, 323, 325, 444

Colonialism, 90, 159, 162 n.98, 164, 190, 217, 273, 276, 309, 337, 341, 441; anti-colonialism, 147, 152, 162; anti-colonial powers, 264; colonies, 144, 151, 152, 191, 240, 284; colonial powers, 116, 444; community consensus against, 187, 188, 189, 191; decolonization, 116; neo-colonialism, 129. *See* Imperialism; war, anti-colonial

Colonial wars. *See* War, anti-colonial

Colonies. *See* Colonialism

Combat, 259, 259 n.270, 262. *See* Armed forces; Intervention, military and tactical operations; United States armed forces

Command decision. *See* United States President

Commander in Chief. *See* United States President

Communication, 71, 74, 107 n.20, 116. *See* Diplomatic relations

Communists, 18, 24, 25, 26, 63, 86, 94, 116, 143-44, 146, 150-51, 159, 214; ideology, 147; monolithic, 439 n.88; movement, 143; theorists, 162 n.96, *see also* Marxists. *See* Blocs, power; East/west conflict; Khmer; Lao-Dong Party; Union of Soviet Socialist Republics; Vietnam, Communist Party of

Community expectations, 12, 21, 22-23, 24, 25, 26, 37, 38, 40, 46, 51, 58, 69 n.26, 70, 105, 106, 107 n.20, 108, 119, 120, 120 n.8, 123, 124, 152-53, 154, 157, 179, 202, 223 n.186, 225-26, 280, 358, 360, 361, 362, 363 n.9, 365, 367, 385, 395, 406, 419-20, 424, 439, 447, 448, 477. *See* Public opinion

Community policies, 58, 70, 72, 73, 74 n.33, 75, 85, 89, 128, 129, 131, 252, 271, 272-73, 280, 359, 405, 452, 463; colonialism, 187, 188, 189, 191, 441; conflict minimization, 440, 493, 502, 503; decision making, 313, 316-17; established states, 360; force, use of, 366, 367, 382, 382 n.41, 385, 386, 387, 393, 395, 410, 411, 426, 470-71, 502-503; intervention, 90-98, 99-100, 101, 102, 104, 105, 109, 111, 113, 133, 163-73, 176, 184, 185, 202, 210, 226, 228, 229, 230, 255 n.260, 256, 259, 260, 264, 268, 270, 275, 279, 435, 441; minimum human rights, 163, 169-70, 171; minimum public order, 163, 166, 170-71, 223 n.186, 410, 411; modernization, 165-66; non-intervention, 163-73; race discrimination, 216-17; self-determination, 163-69, 171, 192, 397, 441

Community, world. *See* World community

Complementarity, theory of, 66 n.20, 67 n.22, 71

Conferences, international, 361, 567. *See* individual conferences

Conference on Intervention and the Developing States, 123 n.15, 124-25

Conflict

generally: appraisal of 239; detection of, 233, 234 n.210; prevention of, 12

causes of, 23, 238; international law as causing, 22, 26-28, 29 n.38, 40; self-determination, 197, 205, 206, 207-209

International System (*cont.*)

influences on, 143-45; intervention, 143, 147-48, 152-54, 174; revolution, 136-37, 141

international legal system, 27, 251, 585; compared to, domestic, 155; conflict areas within, 19; consensus on, 18; cooperation in, 19; dangers of legal approach, 39-40; description of, 16; effectiveness of, 15; functions of, 16, 155; impact of international law, 17-20; institutionalization of, 14; lack of centralization, 14; national policy makers effecting, 18; nature of, 14-17; process of, 14, 113, 132, 133, 154-63; revolutionary rather than stable, 17-20; weaknesses of, 155

Interpretation of Agreements, 68, 69, 70-76. *See* Agreements, international; Treaties

Intervention

generally, 55 n.8, 66 n.20, 79-81, 82, Chapter III, 83-114, 126, 128, 130, 132, 133, 134, 142-54, 159, 178, 257, 266, 294, 302, 336; analysis of, 89, 98-113, 130-33, 175-225; appraisal of, 227-28, 233, 236, 243, 275, 276, 282, 283, 284, 285, 294; base values, 98, 101, 105-108; claims, 133, 154-63, 173-225, 252, 254, 260, 265, 270, 275-76, 283; community policy on, 90-98, 99-100, 101, 102, 104, 105, 109, 111, 113, 131, 133, 184, 185, 225-26, 228, *see also* Public order, minimum; conditions for, 98, 103-105, 111, 116, 117, 126, 133, 173; consented to, 145; defined, 84, 89-90, 119-26, 127, 128, 129, 151, 192; examples of, 256, 260, 290-91, *see also* individual countries; justifications for, 194, 196, 252, 270; participants, 98-114, 142; periods of, 142; policies of, 440-50; psychological factor, 110; terminology, 119-27, 129, 130, 159; theory of, 117 n.6, 119-27, 129, 132, 173, 192

approaches to, 128, 132; behavioral, 131, 132, 174; policy responsive, 127-31, 132, 173, 179, 252, 253, 265

area of: against third party state, 126-27, 177, 209-12, 257, 258, 278, 281, 423, 425, 426, 433, 434-35; in domestic jurisdiction, 100, 229,

230; in internal conflict, 79, 80, 81, 82, 83, 86, 87, 88, 90-114, Chapter IV, 133, 396, 397, 438, 439, 494-95, 588-89; into neutral state, 508-10, 513, 564

cessation of, 108, 167, 180, 193, 197, 231, 277, 280

control of, 3, 80, 82, 112, Chapter IV, 133, 145, 148-49, 251-54, 259, 260, 261, 263, 265, 274-75, 281, 282-86, 588; detection of, 259, 265; deterrents to, 239, 435; effect of international system on, 99, 110-12; fact finding (reporting) of, 118, 156, 226-27, 233, 238-43, 281, 282; freeze on aid, 193, 196, 197-201, 206, 254, 255 n.260, 277, 280, 446; ineffectiveness of, 133, 225-28, 276, 282-86; international machinery for, 116-17, 118-19, 254, 256, 260, 271, 275-76, 294; policy responsiveness of, 263; recommendations for, 133; review of, 381

effects of, 98, 103, 109-10, 131-32, 152-53, 219; causing civil strife, 438; legal consequences, 84; on bloc security, 103; on future intervention, 152-53, 219; on international system, 99, 110-12, 128, 134, 143, 174, 219; on public order, 440, 443-47, 448

faction, aid to, 177, 203-205, 268-69

form of: collective, 268, 269, 270, 271, 272, 276, 292, 347-48, 567, *see also* United Nations, intervention; competitive, 80, 104, 149-50, 154, 171, 192, 195, 257-58, 277, 474; regional, 257, 308-10, 337-38; unilateral, 80, 95, 268-72, 276, 289, 291, 292, 333, 337, 338, 341, 348, 349, 441-42, 448

government, aid to, 105-108, 117, 158, 162, 171, 173, 176, 179-82, 184, 185, 186, 194, 196-201, 202, 203, 208, 214, 224, 232, 244, 252, 253, 254, 256, 258, 262, 267-82, 309, 375, 397, 441-42, 443, 444, 445, 446, 447, 448, 471, 472, 473, 491, 494, 497 n.60, 543; prior to insurgency, 88, 180, 181, 182, 184, 185, 186, 197, 203, 205, 209, 257, 258, 276-77, 279, 280-81, 422 n.47, 473; to offset aid to insurgents, 262, 277-78, 281, 292, 333, 353, 373-74, 398, 429,

Socialist self-determination, 147, 159, 162, 165, 214. *See also* Brezhnev Doctrine

Social reform, 85, 95, 99, 111, 116, 134, 142, 148

Sohn, Louis B., 378 n.31, 397 n.58

Son My, 353, 592, 596

South Africa, 145, 147, 156, 165, 168, 213, 229, 230, 231, 231 n.203, 240, 242, 283, 292, 337, 340; intervention of, 218

Southeast Asia, 286, 387, 411 n.26

Southeast Asian Treaty Organization (SEATO), 37, 38, 96, 107, 112, 145, 298, 299, 303, 305, 321, 322, 380, 381, 418 n.43, 480, 481, 505 n.77, 552; protocol states, 512, 516, 517; role in Cambodia, 512-13, 528-29; role in Vietnam, 107 n.20, 306, 346, 418 n.43, 453, 551; text of treaty, 727-35

Southeast Asia Resolution, 455, 516-19, 521, 524, 529, 534, 535, 548, 551, 552, 553, 559, 581; effect of, 533; text of, 739-40

Southern Rhodesia, 145, 167. *See* Rhodesia

South Vietnam. *See* Republic of Vietnam

South Vietnam, Central Office for, 370 n.22

South Vietnamese Constituent Assembly, 422

Southwest Africa, 145, 147, 156, 165, 168, 213, 217, 218-19, 229, 230, 231, 231 n.203, 240, 252, 276, 283

Sovereignty, 19, 32, 120, 214, 215, 252, 348 n.80, 367, 409, 418 n.43, 426, 480, 492

Soviet-Finnish war, 88, 106

Soviet Union. *See* Union of Soviet Socialist Republics

Space law agreement, United States-Soviet, 23, 29

Spain, 150, 230, 231, 444, 499 n.61, 567

Spanish-American war, 559

Spanish Civil War, 86, 87 n.7, 88, 117, 195, 256, 262, 264, 309, 426, 433, 435, 441

Spheres of influence, 94, 152, 170, 253-54. *See* Blocs, power

Stalin, Joseph, 266, 266 n.283, 456, 467

Standard, William, 363 n.9, 367, 376, 377, 378 n.31, 380

State conduct, 21, 22, 24-25, 29, 30, 33, 39, 79, 120, 472, 589

State Department, United States, 42 n.55, 249-50, 353, 370-72, 405, 410 n.24, 450-53, 465, 497 n.60; memorandum

of, *see* "White papers." *See* Legal advisers and Secretary of State

State practice. *See* State conduct

Status quo, 80, 103, 165, 252, 253, 276, 287, 291, 355, 364

Stevenson, Adlai E., 326 n.35, 328

Stevenson, John R., 250, 484 n.11, 497 n.60; address by, 643-54

Stewart, Potter, 536 n.4

Stone, Julius, 378 n.31

Strausz-Hupe, Robert, 322 n.31

Strikes, 91-92

Sudan, 92, 167

Suez crisis, 20, 102, 476

Super powers. *See* major powers

Sweden, 243

Switzerland, 379

Syria, 256, 504, 508

Tactical operations rule, 108-109, 474 n.39. *See also* Intervention, standards

Taiwan. *See* China, Republic of

Talbot v. Seeman, 546, 581

Talleyrand, Charles Maurice de, 122-23

Tanganyika, 181, 182, 262, 264, 277, 397 n.58, 441

Tanzania. *See* Tanganyika

Tass, 214; statement on military intervention, 213 n.171

Taylor-Rostow Report, 422 n.48, 462

Technology, 111, 116, 148, 245, 310, 320 n.27; military, 143, 534, 541, 556, 557. *See also* Arms, race

Territorial integrity, 188, 191, 194, 210, 211, 212, 215, 309, 367, 373, 375, 382, 384, 386, 396, 397, 407, 426, 432, 435, 467, 471, 480, 489, 491, 492, 494, 497 n.60, 501

Territories, trust, 188, 190, 191, 230. *See* United Nations Trusteeship Council

Terrorism/terrorists, 211, 221, 267, 261, 383, 384, 441, 443, 439, 489

Tet offensives, 484 n.11, 517. *See* Vietnam War

Thailand, 83, 87, 118, 153, 182, 226, 260, 291, 295, 387, 444, 562, 563 n.14; role in Cambodia, 506

Third Party Congress, 370 n.22

Third World, 18, 116, 144, 147, 150, 152, 277, 287, 288, 289, 292. *See also* Developing nations

Tonkin Gulf incident, 118, 234, 450 n.98, 518, 534, 552. *See* Southeast Asia Resolution